Philippine English

Philippine English is a comprehensive reference work on the history, sociology, and linguistic structure of Philippine English. It offers readers unprecedented access to a synthesis of the last 50 years of research into Philippine English and puts forward a new and better understanding of the phenomenon of the nativization of English in the Philippines and the emergence of Philippine English. This definitive resource covers in great length and depth all that is currently known about the new English.

The chapters offer detailed descriptions of Philippine English at various linguistic levels in addition to examining the psychosociolinguistic factors which shaped the language. Offering discussions of practice, language policy, language education, language teaching, and the relevance of English in various social phenomena in the Philippines, readers will find everything they need to know on theory, methodology, and application in the study of Philippine English.

Ariane Macalinga Borlongan's education and experience across the world have inspired him to passionately work with English speakers in non-Anglo-American contexts. As a sociolinguist, he has analyzed variation, change, and standardization across Englishes. He earned his Ph.D. in Applied Linguistics at age 23 via a competitive accelerated program in De La Salle University (Manila, the Philippines) and is presently Associate Professor of Sociolinguistics at the Tokyo University of Foreign Studies (Japan).

Routledge Studies in World Englishes

Series Editor: Ee Ling Low, National Institute of Education, Nanyang Technological University, Singapore and President of Singapore Association of Applied Linguistics

This **Singapore Association for Applied Linguistics** book series will provide a starting point for those who wish to know more about the aspects of the spread of English in the current globalized world. Each volume can cover the following aspects of the study of World Englishes: issues and theoretical paradigms, feature-based studies (i.e. phonetics and phonology, syntax, lexis) and language in use (e.g. education, media, the law and other related disciplines).

The Shetland Dialect
Peter Sundkvist

English in Southeast Asia and ASEAN
Transformation of Language Habitats
Azirah Hashim and Gerhard Leitner

English in China
Language, Identity and Culture
Emily Tsz Yan Fong

English in East and South Asia
Policy, Features and Language in Use
Edited by Ee Ling Low and Anne Pakir

Nominal Pluralization and Countability in African Varieties of English
Susanne Mohr

Philippine English
Development, Structure, and Sociology of English in the Philippines
Edited by Ariane Macalinga Borlongan

Chinese English
Names, Norms, and Narratives
Zhichang Xu

For a full list of titles in this series, visit www.routledge.com/Routledge-Studies-in-World-Englishes/book-series/RSWE

Philippine English
Development, Structure, and Sociology
of English in the Philippines

**Edited by
Ariane Macalinga Borlongan**

First published 2023
by Routledge
4 Park Square, Milton Park, Abingdon, Oxon OX14 4RN

and by Routledge
605 Third Avenue, New York, NY 10158

Routledge is an imprint of the Taylor & Francis Group, an Informa business

© 2023 selection and editorial matter, Ariane Macalinga Borlongan;
individual chapters, the contributors

The right of Ariane Macalinga Borlongan to be identified as
the author of the editorial material, and of the authors for their
individual chapters, has been asserted in accordance with sections
77 and 78 of the Copyright, Designs and Patents Act 1988.

All rights reserved. No part of this book may be reprinted or
reproduced or utilised in any form or by any electronic, mechanical,
or other means, now known or hereafter invented, including
photocopying and recording, or in any information storage or
retrieval system, without permission in writing from the publishers.

Trademark notice: Product or corporate names may be trademarks
or registered trademarks and are used only for identification and
explanation without intent to infringe.

British Library Cataloguing-in-Publication Data
A catalogue record for this book is available from the British Library

ISBN: 9781138370760 (hbk)
ISBN: 9781032221724 (pbk)
ISBN: 9780429427824 (ebk)

DOI: 10.4324/9780429427824

Typeset in Times New Roman
by codeMantra

Contents

List of figures	ix
List of tables	x
List of contributors	xii
Preface	xv
ARIANE MACALINGA BORLONGAN	
Deconstructing Ma. Lourdes S. Bautista: A Non-Linguistic Perspective	xx
TERESO S. TULLAO, JR.	
Prologue: Philippine English in the 'Concerto' of World Englishes	xxiv
EDGAR W. SCHNEIDER	

PART 1
Introduction — 1

1 Conspectus — 3
ARIANE MACALINGA BORLONGAN

2 History — 9
ARIANE MACALINGA BORLONGAN

3 Resources — 27
DOMINIK HEPS AND MIKHAIL ALIC C. GO

Special Feature: Ma. Lourdes Bautista and Philippine English — 41
ANNE PAKIR

vi *Contents*

PART 2
Linguistic Structure

47

4 Phonology

49

IRWAN SHAH SHAHRUDDIN, RAN AO, AND EE LING LOW

5 Lexicon

73

THOMAS BIERMEIER

6 Grammar

87

SHIRLEY N. DITA, PHILIP RENTILLO, AND ALDRIN P. LEE

7 Discourse

100

MARILU B. RAÑOSA-MADRUNIO

8 Spelling and Punctuation

113

ROBERT FUCHS

PART 3
Sociolinguistic Variation and Change

123

9 Internal Variation

125

ALDRIN P. LEE AND ARIANE MACALINGA BORLONGAN

10 Diachronic Change

135

ARIANE MACALINGA BORLONGAN AND PETER COLLINS

11 Philippine English in Relation to American English

143

EDGAR W. SCHNEIDER

12 Contact with Other Languages

156

MA. ALTHEA T. ENRIQUEZ

13 Hybridization

170

WILKINSON DANIEL WONG GONZALES

PART 4
Linguistic and Literary Canon

185

14 Lexicography

187

DANICA SALAZAR

Contents vii

15 Standard Philippine English 199
ARIANE MACALINGA BORLONGAN

16 Philippine Literature in English 210
ISAGANI R. CRUZ

PART 5
Psychosociolinguistic Dimensions 219

17 Intelligibility 221
SHIRLEY N. DITA AND KRISTINE D. DE LEON

18 Attitudes 231
PHILIP RENTILLO

19 Multilingualism 242
LOY LISING

20 Language Policy 257
RUANNI TUPAS

PART 6
Learning and Teaching 269

21 Acquisition and Learning 271
AIREEN BARRIOS

22 Language Teaching 283
ALEJANDRO S. BERNARDO

23 Language Testing 297
DAVE KENNETH TAYAO CAYADO AND JAMES F. D'ANGELO

24 Teacher Education 305
EDWARD JAY M. QUINTO AND STERLING M. PLATA

PART 7
Contemporary Issues 315

25 Internet 317
LEAH E. GUSTILO AND CHENEE M. DINO

viii *Contents*

26 Migration   327
BEATRIZ P. LORENTE

27 Outsourced Call Centers   340
ERIC FRIGINAL AND RACHELLE FRIGINAL

28 Teaching English as a Foreign Language in the Philippines   353
AIDEN YEH

Special Feature: World Englishes and Social Change   363
AHMAR MAHBOOB AND RUANNI TUPAS

Epilogue: Philippine English: Past, Present, and Future   373
KINGSLEY BOLTON

Index   383

Figures

4.1	Formant Plot for Male Speakers	52
4.2	Formant Plot for Female Speakers	53
4.3	Scatter Plot for /iː/ and /ɪ/ Vowels for Male Speakers	53
4.4	Scatter Plot for /iː/ and /ɪ/ Vowels for Female Speakers	54
4.5	Scatter Plot for /ɛ/ and /æ/ Vowels for Male Speakers	54
4.6	Scatter Plot for /ɛ/ and /æ/ Vowels for Female Speakers	55
4.7	Scatter Plot for /ʌ/ and /ɑː/ Vowels for Male Speakers	55
4.8	Scatter Plot for /ʌ/ and /ɑː/ Vowels for Female Speakers	56
4.9	Scatter Plot for /ɒ/ and /ɔː/ Vowels for Male Speakers	56
4.10	Scatter Plot for /ɒ/ and /ɔː/ Vowels for Female Speakers	57
4.11	Scatter Plot for /ʊ/ and /uː/ Vowels for Male Speakers	57
4.12	Scatter Plot for /ʊ/ and /uː/ Vowels for Female Speakers	58
4.13	Scatter Plot for BATH and TRAP Vowels for Male Speakers	60
4.14	Scatter Plot for BATH and TRAP Vowels for Female Speakers	60
4.15	PVI of PhE, AmE, Malaysian English and SgE	68
8.1	Relative Frequency (%British variants) of All Lexical and Spelling Variants in PhE of the 1960s and 1990s (adapted from Fuchs, 2017)	117
15.1	A Conceptual Model of the Standardization of Philippine English	205
22.1	The Concentric Circles of the Three Levels of Instructional Conceptualization	287
27.1	Comparison of Agents' Average Dimension Scores for Dimension 1: Addressee-Focused, Polite, and Elaborated Speech vs. Involved and Simplified Narrative. Note: Only troubleshoot tasks were available from Central American agents	345
27.2	Politeness and Respect Markers across Agent Groups. Note: Frequency of features reported here is normalized per 1,000 words	347

Tables

4.1	Incidence of Reduced Vowels	50
4.2	Incidence of Variations of the /æ/ Vowel	50
4.3	Monophthongs Measured and Sample Words Selected from the Wolf Passage and Sentence Sets	51
4.5	Substitution of /ð/ with /d/ in the Wolf Passage	62
4.6	Substitution of /θ/ with /t/ in the Wolf Passage	62
4.7	Occurrences of Devoicing in the Wolf Passage	62
4.8	Occurrences of Consonant Cluster Simplification	63
4.9	Aspiration of Voiceless Stops	63
4.10	Average VOT Values of Voiceless and Voiced Stops in PhE	64
4.11	VOT Values of PhE, AmE, Malaysian English and SgE	65
4.12	F3 Values of PhE in Comparison with AmE and BrE	65
4.13	T-Test Results of r-Colored Vowels in PhE and AmE for F3 at Midpoint and 75% Interval (Two-Sample Assuming Unequal Variances, Two-Tailed)	65
4.14	Variations in Lexical Stress in Multi-Syllabic Words, Grouped According to Expected Syllable Stress	66
4.15	PVI for PhE and AmE Speakers	67
4.16	PVI Values of PhE in Comparison with Those of AmE, Malaysian English and SgE	67
4.17	Comparison of *t*-Test Results between PhE and AmE	68
5.1	Frequency of Compound Nouns (Sample of 100 Items)	75
5.2	Frequency of Nouns in -hood	79
5.3	Frequency of Nouns in -ism	79
5.4	Frequency of Adjectives in -ish	81
5.5	Frequency of Adjectives in -y	82
10.1	The Composition of Phil-Brown	138
10.2	1960s vis-à-vis 1990s Comparison of PhE Using Phil-Brown and ICE-PH	138
11.1	Proportions of AmE Choices per Categories, Corpora, and Varieties	148
13.1	Summary of Hybrids Involving Philippine English	180
14.1	Some "Webster Words" in *Webster's* and the *OED*	193

14.2	Recently Added PhE Words to the *OED*	194
21.1	Survey of Child Language Studies from 1986 to Present	273
24.1	Proposed Revisions on the Descriptions of BS Education, Major in English Courses	310
27.1	Composition of a Test Call Center Corpus[a] Analyzed for This Chapter	342
27.2	Addressee-Focused, Polite, and Elaborated Speech vs. Involved and Simplified Narrative in Call Center Interactions (Friginal, 2008, 2009b)	344

Contributors

Ran Ao, Research Fellow, National Institute of Education, Nanyang Technological University, Singapore

Aireen Barrios, Associate Professor, Department of English and Applied Linguistics, De La Salle University, Manila, the Philippines

Alejandro S. Bernardo, Associate Professor, Department of English, University of Santo Tomas, Manila, the Philippines

Thomas Biermeier, Lecturer, Department of English and American Studies, University of Regensburg, Germany

Kingsley Bolton, Professor Emeritus of English Linguistics, Department of English, Stockholm University, Sweden

Ariane Macalinga Borlongan, Associate Professor of Sociolinguistics, Graduate School of Global Studies, Tokyo University of Foreign Studies, Japan

Dave Kenneth Tayao Cayado, Doctoral Student, Department of Linguistics, Queen Mary University of London, the United Kingdom

Peter Collins, Honorary Professor, Department of Linguistics, the University of New South Wales, Sydney, Australia

Isagani R. Cruz, Professor Emeritus and University Fellow, Department of Literature, De La Salle University, Manila, the Philippines

James F. D'Angelo, Professor, School of Global Studies, Chukyo University, Nagoya, Japan

Kristine D. de Leon, Assistant Professor, Faculty of Language Studies, Sohar University, Oman

Chenee M. Dino, Professorial Lecturer, Graduate Studies and Transnational Education Department, Far Eastern University, Manila, the Philippines

Shirley N. Dita, Associate Professor, Department of English and Applied Linguistics, De La Salle University, Manila, the Philippines

Contributors xiii

Ma. Althea T. Enriquez, Associate Professor, Department of Filipino and Philippine Literature, University of the Philippines at Diliman, Quezon City, the Philippines

Eric Friginal, Professor, Department of English and Communication, the Hong Kong Polytechnic University

Rachelle Friginal, Assistant Manager, Correspondents and Banking Relations, Al Ansari Exchange, Dubai, United Arab Emirates

Robert Fuchs, Associate Professor, Department of English Language and Literature, University of Hamburg, Germany

Mikhail Alic C. Go, Lecturer, Center for English as a Lingua Franca, Tamagawa University, Tokyo, Japan

Leah E. Gustilo, Full Professor, Department of English and Applied Linguistics, De La Salle University, Manila, the Philippines

Wilkinson Daniel Wong Gonzales, Doctoral Student, Department of Linguistics, the University of Michigan at Ann Arbor, the United States

Dominik Heps, Master's Student, English Linguistics Department, University of Wurzburg, Germany

Aldrin P. Lee, Associate Professor, Department of Linguistics, University of the Philippines at Diliman, Quezon City, the Philippines

Loy Lising, Senior Lecturer, Department of Linguistics, Macquarie University, Sydney, Australia

Beatriz P. Lorente, Lecturer, Department of English, University of Bern, Switzerland

Ee Ling Low, Professor of Applied Linguistics and Teacher Education, National Institute of Education, Nanyang Technological University, Singapore

Marilu b. Rañosa-Madrunio, Professor, Department of English, University of Santo Tomas, Manila, the Philippines

Ahmar Mahboob, Associate Professor, Department of Linguistics, the University of Sydney, Australia

Anne Pakir, Honorary Fellow, Department of English Language and Literature, National University of Singapore

Sterling M. Plata, Associate Professor, Department of English and Applied Linguistics, De La Salle University, Manila, the Philippines

Edward Jay M. Quinto, Associate Professor, School of Social Sciences and Education, Mapua University, Manila, the Philippines

xiv *Contributors*

Philip Rentillo, Assistant Professor, Department of English and Applied Linguistics, De La Salle University, Manila, the Philippines

Danica Salazar, World English Editor, Oxford English Dictionary, Oxford, the United Kingdom

Edgar W. Schneider, Emeritus Professor of English Linguistics, Department of English and American Studies, University of Regensburg, Germany

Irwan Shah Shahruddin, Doctoral Student, National Institute of Education, Nanyang Technological University, Singapore

Tereso S. Tullao, Jr., Professor Emeritus and University Fellow, School of Economics, De La Salle University, Manila, the Philippines

Ruanni Tupas, Lecturer in Sociolinguistics of Education, Institute of Education, University College London, the United Kingdom

Aiden Yeh, Associate Professor, Department of English, Wenzao Ursuline University of Languages, Kaoshiung, Taiwan

Preface

Half a century ago, in the same year when the Linguistic Society of the Philippines and the *Philippine Journal of Linguistics* were founded, Professor Teodoro Llamzon published his monograph titled *Standard Filipino English*, where he proposed the emergence of a standardized variety of English in the Philippines. The birth of Philippine English (PhE) is usually dated at least 50 years before Professor Llamzon's 1969 publication but it is that publication which we so rightly consider as the beginning of PhE scholarship. It is worth noting that the concept of 'world Englishes' was not yet popular at that time; Professor Braj Kachru first talked about Indian English in a 1965 paper. Hence, we can also say that PhE was one of the earliest documented Englishes, at least within the framework of variationist sociolinguistics.

As my academic work has been mainly on PhE, I consider Professor Llamzon's publication to be very important in linguistics scholarship in the Philippines and so I thought it is but appropriate that its 50th anniversary be commemorated. My initial plan in 2016 was just a modest special issue in a journal. But when I drew up the list of possible contributors, I realized I would need more than an issue to be able to include them all. Certainly, no journal editor would let me do an issue with at least 15 contributions so I approached a few series editors who became interested with my still, at that time, a rather sketchy plan for a volume on PhE.

But it was Professor Ee Ling Low, editor of the Routledge Studies in World Englishes series, who buoyed this project into a grand one that it is now. It was 2017 and I just came from a Visiting Lectureship at the University of Malaya in Kuala Lumpur, Malaysia, which allowed me to meet Ee Ling personally in Singapore. I asked for a meeting and she scheduled it exactly on my 30th birthday, which intruded on my supposedly well-planned affairs on that day. I was already keen on wearing shorts and flip-flops to frolic around the Lion City with friends but I knew it was in bad taste to wear such at the office of the then Chief Planning Officer of the National Institute of Education, Singapore. Therefore, I decided to make a last minute costume change. Imagine my surprise and disillusionment when I entered a Hello Kitty-themed office, with every small detail rendered in flashy, pink-and-white, ribboned felines. If it is any consolation, it assured me that the

xvi *Preface*

meeting would not be a digression from the crazy plans I had for that day. Mindful of our busy schedules, I immediately told Ee Ling what I had in mind and, as each time you talk to a visionary, as with mentor Professor Anne Pakir, any small idea becomes a great plan. She suggested that, instead of just soliciting random articles on PhE, the better idea would be to put up a comprehensive reference work on PhE. And, more importantly, that such a milestone work be dedicated to my mentor, Professor Emeritus Ma. Lourdes Bautista (or 'Dr. Tish' to those who know her more personally). The meeting was indeed a 'Crazy Rich Asian' academia-style.

After the side trip to Singapore, I phoned Dr. Tish herself to let her know of the project and she was thankful beyond words. I then harassed prospective contributors and rushed drafting the official proposal for the Routledge series. I made sure I covered most comprehensively every important aspect and dimension relating to PhE. For my doctoral dissertation, it was my dream to codify PhE by preparing a grammar. As I will elaborate on later, this did not materialize. But then, in the middle of doing this project, I realized, editing this handbook of PhE is somehow a realization of that dream, and an even bigger endeavor. And so I am very happy about this project.

In identifying prospective contributors, I made sure I included as many colleagues, students, and friends of Dr. Tish as possible. I am proud that I have the perfect list of contributors and I could never think of any better roster of contributors to write its chapters. It boasts of the most important names in world Englishes and Philippine linguistics. The 31 contributors come from across four continents of the world. I thank them for their cooperation and patience, for making this dream possible. I specially thank Dr. David Jonathan Bayot for helping me reach out to Professor Isagani Cruz.

I also need to thank the high-profile roster of reviewers, who add prestige to the volume (in alphabetical order): Suresh Canagarajah (The Pennsylvania State University, University Park, the United States), Peter Collins (The University of New South Wales, Sydney, Australia), Daniel Davis (The University of Michigan at Dearborn, the United States), James D'Angelo (Chukyo University, Nagoya, Japan), Raymond Hickey (University of Duisburg and Essen, Germany), Ee Ling Low (National Institute of Education, Singapore), Ahmar Mahboob (The University of Sydney, Australia), Christian Mair (University of Freiburg, Germany), Aya Matsuda (Arizona State University, Tempe, the United States), James McLellan (University of Brunei Darussalam), Robert McKenzie (Northumbria University, Newcastle upon Tyne, the United Kingdom), Vincent Ooi (National University of Singapore), Anne Pakir (National University Singapore), Michael Percillier (University of Mannheim, Germany), Pam Peters (Macquarie University, Sydney, Australia), Stefanie Pillai (The University of Malaya, Kuala Lumpur, Malaysia), Edgar W. Schneider (University of Regensburg, Germany), Peter Siemunds (University of Hamburg, Germany), Peter Tan (National University of Singapore), and Lionel Wee (National University of Singapore).

Preface xvii

Likewise, I also need to thank the other people and institutions involved in the entirety of the project: Of course, my fairy godmother and fellow Japanese strawberry shortcake fan Ee Ling, the series editor, as well as Routledge staff led by Katie Peace, for the help with the publication of the volume. The Tokyo University of Foreign Studies funded many of my trips to Singapore, to Manila, and to many places to persuade people to join me in the project and also to follow up many things about it. Professor Tereso Tullao, Jr., and the Angelo King Institute for Economic and Business Studies sponsored the elaborate tribute dinner for Dr. Tish, on the same occasion the publication of this volume was announced.

But as a Lasallian, I am specially proud that 6 contributions come from La Salle, 14 contributions are from graduates of La Salle, and 6 contributions are from students of Dr. Tish. I am happiest about the contributions of the two youngest Filipino linguists today—both from La Salle—Wilkinson Gonzales and Philip Rentillo, one of my students in the first English major course I taught in this university. Undoubtedly, La Salle is the Philippines' most prominent school for linguistics and the 2019 Quacquarelli Symonds (QS) world university rankings by subject confirm this as it lists La Salle as the lone Philippine university for the subject linguistics. Thanks to the support of Professor Raymund Sison, current dean of the Br. Andrew Gonzalez FSC College of Education, and also the former dean Dr. Voltaire Mistades, for ensuring that linguistics in La Salle is very much alive and well and the vision of Br. Andrew Gonzalez for Lasallian linguistics remains true even up to today.

Of course, above all, this is because of the work and the legacy of Dr. Tish who, together with Br. Andrew, tirelessly labored in the field of linguistics not only for La Salle but also for the Philippines. When I began my undergraduate studies at La Salle, I was already certain that, when I do my doctoral studies, I will not get any other dissertation supervisor except Dr. Tish. I say in my lecture for the Br. Andrew Gonzalez FSC Distinguished Professorial Chair in Linguistics and Language Education awarded to me by the Linguistic Society of the Philippines and De La Salle University in 2019, a choice of a good mentor is an excellent, important career and professional investment. In addition, a good mentor would require you to suffer much to achieve great things. Allow me to share a few recollections from my dissertation writing days to prove this.

When I began my studies in La Salle, I wanted to codify standard PhE for my Ph.D., as I mentioned earlier. Very much ambitious, it was, but Dr. Tish feared that the volume of work necessary was beyond what could be done within the parameters of dissertation writing. We were on a phone call then, and I was discussing with her the grant application for my dissertation. She said that, at least, for the purposes of the application, I should just focus on the verb phrase. But at the end of the phone call, she reminded me, "I think you should start forgetting about 'the grammar of PhE' and just focus on 'the grammar of the PhE verb'". She certainly knows how to send her message without being explicit about it.

xviii *Preface*

I successfully defended the proposal. I knew she had very high hopes for a well-written dissertation. So she said, "Ariane, I am after quality and not punctuality". She regretted saying that. I was enrolled in dissertation writing for two years. She only knew recently that it was because I got addicted to Korean dramas when I was writing my dissertation, *Boys over Flower*, to be specific, that I neglected my counting of the 10,000 verbs in my dataset. But as the centennial of De La Salle University approached, I realized I needed to finish my dissertation sooner than later. I wrote the whole dissertation in one month. I remember I wrote one whole 80-page chapter on a Thursday evening, gave her the draft on Friday morning, and required her to give me back her corrections Saturday when I would in turn give her a new chapter. Poor Dr. Tish obliged. But she was very, very, very meticulous with data analysis, which I very much appreciated. I remember she once commented, "Ariane, your paper is actually very good. It's just that it didn't pass my standards". I eventually defended my dissertation and it got an outstanding distinction from the university and she was very pleased. But I think I tired her so much she decided she will never mentor anyone else after me.

More recently, she is more interested with my personal life. Probably, she trusts I will no longer mess up my career. Two years ago, I posted rather many photos with a specific someone in social media. I am sure that, even if she does not have Facebook and Instagram accounts, rumors reached her. And so I remember during my first meeting with her after those posts proliferated in social media, she asked me after all my career updates, "So Ariane, aside from linguistics, what else do you do?" I knew what answer she would like to hear but I still wanted to whet her appetite. I innocently answered, "Oh, I've been seeing many musicals lately, visiting exhibitions on Baroque and Impressionist paintings, and making pilgrimages to Marian shrines". The sociolinguist who wrote on probing definitely knew how to throw the strategic second question, "No, Ariane, I mean, are you meeting people?" I grinned and I knew that was the very moment to shock her. I gave her the answer she would like to hear and she smiled. Recently though, I think she became more comfortable with the topic. She has been more direct with her questions and, to use a term in Brown and Levinson's 1987 theory on politeness, she now utilizes a bald-on-record strategy. Last time, I visited her right after my birthday, she forthrightly said as we sat down her couch in her home, "Ariane, tell me about your love life".

I will cherish Dr. Tish forever, and I keep her as one of the most important figures in my life. Even though we sometimes have differing opinions most especially with shopping, fashion, and what makes a good life, she will forever be my doktormutter. We share the same devotion to Our Lady, Undoer of Knots, who I frequently visit as a side trip when I see Professor Edgar Schneider in Regensburg, Germany. I promise her that I always remember her in my prayers as I clasp the mantle of the Blessed Virgin.

Even though there is this volume edited in her honor, certainly, it will never be enough for everything that she has done for us, in big and small ways, in linguistics particularly and life generally. At this point, it is compelling to recall the reflection offered by Saint John Baptist de La Salle on the feast of Saint Peter: "To touch the hearts of your students is the greatest miracle you can perform". Dr. Tish not only taught our minds and transformed our lives, she most importantly touched our hearts. We have become who we are because she touched our hearts. We are here because she has performed a great miracle. We are the great miracle she has performed. For that and many other things, we will forever be grateful.

Ariane Macalinga Borlongan
February 11, 2019, the feast of Our Lady of Lourdes
Tokyo, Japan

Deconstructing Ma. Lourdes S. Bautista

A Non-Linguistic Perspective

Tereso S. Tullao, Jr.

Last February 10, 2018, the eve of the feast of Our Lady of Lourdes, I saw Tish with her mother Lourdes Bautista together and an aunt at our parish, the National Shrine of Our Lady of Lourdes in Quezon City, the Philippines. As they approached the church courtyard, the scene which I witnessed of a daughter in her 70s cautiously assisting her mother in her 90s as they enter the shrine is a perfect picture which captures the personality of Ma. Lourdes Bautista as a devoted daughter.

Devotion is probably the most prominent and powerful virtue which radiates in Tish's personality. This commitment can be seen in her faithful observance of the sacraments and rituals of the Roman Catholic Church. More specifically, it is her desire to achieve a deep attachment to Mary which makes Tish a devout Roman Catholic more than being a Catolico cerrado who goes out of her way to defend the Magisterium just like her Syquia cousins. Her name speaks for itself. The first name Maria is not only to differentiate her from her mother but to emphasize that she was dedicated to Mary specifically to her title as the miraculous Lady of Lourdes, whose feast day falls four days prior to Tish's birthday. Beyond her devotion to Mary, her consistency in visiting sick relatives and friends, comforting the bereaved ones, attending funerals, and doing other corporal acts of mercy make Tish a model Christian.

Even before I formally met Tish at De La Salle University in the early 80s, I had been following her illustrious career since the late 50s when I was still in grade school. It was always a welcome treat from my eldest sister to bring home *The Aquinian*, the student publication of UST High School. A picture of a teenager wearing white eye glasses interestingly called my attention. Her name is Ma. Lourdes Bautista. She was the top of her class every year. In her senior year, she was the editor-in-chief of *The Aquinian*. She graduated valedictorian of the Class of 1961.

Years later, I learned that Tish is the eldest among 12 equally brilliant and distinguished siblings. Like a typical Filipino eldest daughter, Tish is a quintessential *ate* in her devotion to her siblings then, and, now, to the entire Bautista clan. She models what excellence, persistence, and sacrifice for her family is as an archetypical eldest sibling. Ate Tish showed her

Deconstructing Ma. Lourdes S. Bautista xxi

younger siblings the way to shine, which predictively produced valedictorians in high school and summa cum laude in college among her siblings just like her.

A few years ago, the Bautista family was honored by the University of Santo Tomas (UST) as a model Thomasian family for their loyalty to the university, and, more so, for the excellence in academics and prominence of its members in their respective fields of profession. The selection committee attributed these accomplishments primarily to their eminent parents. Their father, Felix, was a distinguished newspaperman, known in the trade for integrity, humility, and industry. He is remembered by generations of men and women in journalism whom he nurtured by unselfishly sharing his expertise on the craft. Her mother, Lourdes, is a retired English and theology teacher at UST who made an impact on her students for her maternal care and inspiring lectures. She was for decades a pillar of the university's Campus Ministry. However, this award committee failed to account for the implicit, albeit significant, contributions of Tish to her siblings' achievements. With Tish showing the way, patiently and consistently, it became easier for her siblings to follow her notable footsteps. Her younger siblings were lucky apprentices imitating the best practices of a great master. That devotion to her family was reciprocated when her siblings, nephews, and nieces gave Tish a surprise party on her 70th birthday. Their smiles and excitement mirror the deep appreciation for their model ate.

Although I am an economist, I was privileged to have encountered and interacted with some of the pillars of Philippine linguistics sans Cecilio Lopez. Thanks to Br. Andrew Gonzalez for the delectable lunches which he hosted in his ancestral home in Kamuning in Quezon, the Philippines. In these engaging occasions, I had friendly debates with the indefatigable Bonifacio Sibayan on the intellectualization of Filipino. Together with Br. Andrew, Boni had reservations but secretly encouraged my work on intellectualizing Filipino in economics. On English grammar, it was always a delight to listen to Teodoro Llamzon's perspective for he was not as threatening as Boni with his dry humor and wit. I was introduced to frequency counts by Curtis McFarland. But it was Ma. Lourdes Bautista who introduced me to sociolinguistics and made me feel comfortable with these giants in Philippine linguistics with her positive disposition, encouraging smiles, and eagerness to listen.

I have known Tish for almost four decades. She was a devoted teacher at La Salle for more than 30 years. After finishing her Ph.D. in Linguistics under the Ateneo de Manila University-Philippine Normal College consortium, Tish was convinced by her mentor-idol Br. Andrew to continue her professional career at La Salle.

It was at La Salle that I met Tish as an engaging teacher. Her undergraduate students appreciated her courses on sociolinguistics as she assigned them to inquire on gay language and code-switching among Filipinos, to name a few. In the graduate school where her impact is more distinct,

xxii *Tereso S. Tullao, Jr.*

Tish has mentored generations of linguists all over the country. Aside from sociolinguistics, Tish is also one of the world-renowned scholars on world Englishes for her chronicling the development of Philippine English. Her excellent teaching and research are reflected in the breadth and depth of her publications as well as the quality of her graduate students whom she mentored and are now leaders in their own right in Philippine linguistics. She models without fanfare what a true academic should be and, for this and many other reasons, she was elected to the Society of Fellows at La Salle. Aside from being an excellent lecturer, she published incessantly and became the editor-in-chief of one of the finest journals cited by the Philippine Social Science Council, the *Philippine Journal of Linguistics*. Because no one can dispute Tish's contributions to Philippine linguistics, her former students informally crowned her the 'Mother of Philippine Linguistics'.

Br. Andrew, as a rule, does not encourage excellent teachers and researchers to be administrators. But he made an exception with Tish because she is very good in organizing and has excellent people skills. For her systems mindset, she became dean of the College of Liberal Arts at La Salle, a methodical director of research at the Integrated Research Center, and a meticulous Vice President for Academics. You give Tish any task and she will deliver on time and with quality. Some of her best accomplishments along this line are being editor-in-chief of the *Philippine Journal of Linguistics* for a long period, and one of the editors of the festschrifts honoring her great mentors, Br. Andrew Gonzalez and Teodoro Llamzon.

Tish is a lover of food and has a sweet tooth. Her way of making her office welcoming is a jar of jellies and chocolates which any visitor can partake. This reflects her positive outlook in life and in everyone. She remembers her friends on their birthdays and has something, even simple things, for them in the Christmas season. When it comes to food, ask her friends about her appetite. I know at least four groups of which Tish is a devoted member and loyal attendee especially for dining. She has her friends who are former La Salle administrators, her friends from the Department of English and Applied Linguistics also of La Salle, her high school classmates, and a group of empowered women who are frustrated nuns, to name a few. If there are seven days a week, I guess Tish has a group for each day. It is in these groups where Tish finds fulfillment and appreciation for her kind words, sweet notes, her devotion, and her sincere friendship.

Aside from being the Mother of Philippine Linguistics, I would not be surprised if others will confer her other titles. Imagine, after the name Ma. Lourdes Bautista, you have the following titles: Mother of Philippine Linguistics, Queen of Philippine English, Empress of Corpus Linguistics, Grand Duchess of Code-Switching, Marchioness of English Grammar, Chronicler of Language Policies, Countess of Conversation Analysis, Lady Eyewitness on the Rise and Fall of English for Specific Purposes, Ever Loyal Baroness of Lasallian Spirituality of Education, and the Fearless Diva of the APA Publication Manual. With all these titles, who cares about being a member of royalty. Queen Victoria had only three royal titles as does Queen Elizabeth II. I am sure they would be envious of Tish's hard-earned titles.

For all of her numerous achievements, Tish continues to be a humble person and, more importantly, for me she is a loyal and true friend. Thank you for the friendship, Ate Tish.

Prologue

Philippine English in the 'Concerto' of World Englishes

Edgar W. Schneider

The discipline of world Englishes has grown and matured over the last few decades, and has established itself as a major branch of research and applications in English linguistics. Initially, it was inspired and shaped strongly by Braj Kachru's influential work and concepts, classifying national varieties of English into 'three circles' and, notably, highlighting the independent quality and importance and the 'norm-developing' character of second-language 'Outer Circle' varieties (Kachru, 1985, 1992). Early in the 21st century, Schneider's (2003, 2007) 'Dynamic Model' introduced a diachronic turn by positing an underlying developmental frame and describing and comparing the trajectories of many of these postcolonial Englishes. Both of these most influential models built upon and interacted with other contributions and frameworks which have been proposed and have shaped the field (cf. Buschfeld & Schneider, 2018 for a recent survey), which continues to thrive (cf. Kachru, Kachru, & Nelson, 2006; Kirkpatrick, 2010; Mesthrie & Bhatt, 2008, for recent handbooks and introductions).

Philippine English (PhE) clearly has been one of the most important postcolonial Englishes, and it is a most timely endeavor, and one which highlights the breadth, strength, and substance which the research into this topic has gained, to accumulate research perspectives and to document facts and issues broadly and authoritatively in the present volume, which also serves as a handbook to this new English. PhE shares some properties with other postcolonial Englishes, but, at the same time, it stands out in some respects and shows some distinctive qualities and a combination of properties and settings which make it unique in the overall framework. Hence, in the present prologue, I wish to set the scene by briefly positioning PhE in the 'concerto' of World Englishes, employing a bird's-eye perspective, and focusing upon a selection of its characteristics. In particular, I focus on the following properties, a subjective selection of aspects which I consider distinctive and important: PhE is (a) unique in its historical roots and American orientation; (b) on its way toward endonormativity; (c) a historically late postcolonial variety; (d) a variety which has emerged remarkably quickly and successfully, (e) despite an endolinguistic national language policy, and (f) in the context of substantial language mixing; (g) a variety whose social function oscillates between being integrative and divisive; and (h) one of the few postcolonial Englishes being strongly exported on a global scale.

In stark contrast to practically all other postcolonial Englishes, which are ultimately products of the British Empire and daughter varieties of British English, PhE is unique among them in its origin in and its orientation toward American English (AmE). In fact, on a global scale, it is the only major variety with this character and target—there are a few more linguistic products of American influence and hegemony but these are either significantly smaller and close to invisible internationally (e.g. Guam) or intertwined with slave repatriation and creolization and hence totally different in character (e.g. Liberia). Furthermore, the succession of a few centuries of Spanish dominance and the half-century of a status as an American colony is equally unique—although the Spanish heritage is linguistically quite limited by comparison. Spanish was replaced quickly and effectively but has left a few lexical traces.

Despite its American roots, PhE is clearly on its way toward endonormativity (though the exact degree to which this process has moved forward remains controversial; cf. Borlongan, 2016; Martin, 2014). This process can be compared to other Asian Englishes: "Recent corpus-based studies of PhilE [...] position the variety behind Singapore English (SingE) in endonormative stabilization, and SingE in turn is behind AmE and BrE. Indian and Hong Kong Englishes are behind PhilE" (Borlongan, 2011, p. 196).

PhE is much younger than most other postcolonial Englishes, and certainly than basically all other deeply rooted Asian Englishes. With its roots in the end of the American-Spanish War and the Treaty of Paris of 1898, it is essentially a child of the 20th century, while, for example, Hong Kong and Singapore Englishes date back to the 19th century, Malaysian English originated in the 18th, and Indian English in the 17th century, respectively. Consequently, it seems largely devoid of some of the conservative, British-derived traits that are occasionally associated with other Asian Englishes (e.g. a reputedly 'bookish' character of earlier texts in Indian English). This temporal setting aligns it more with some African, notably East African Englishes, which also originated after 1900—but did not experience the same intense degree of Anglicization.

This, in fact, is another one of the traits which make PhE unique: English spread incredibly quickly and effectively, more so than in any other postcolonial country that I am aware of. The cause of this is language policy, a deliberate decision made by the colonial power, the US: "In a Letter of Instruction to the Philippine Commission issued on April 17, 1900, US President William McKinley declared that English be the medium of instruction at all levels of the public education system in the Philippines" (Bernardo, 2004, p. 17), and an "English-only-policy" (p. 18) was explicitly pursued in the early period. As is well known, in practice, this policy manifested itself in the presence of some 2,000 American teachers, commonly called the Thomasites, who came to the Philippines during the first two decades of the

xxvi   *Edgar W. Schneider*

new colonial status (Gonzalez, 1997), who not only taught English but, more importantly, trained locals to become English teachers (Bautista & Bolton, 2004) and disseminate the language further. Gonzalez (1997) reports remarkable figures on the quick spread of English, "in 1901 [...] practically no one spoke English: by the 1918 census, about 47.3% of those 10 years and above were reported to be able to speak English, and 55.6% to read and write English" (p. 27). He rightly observes that "[t]he rapid spread of English in the Philippines was unprecedented in colonial history" (p. 28). Despite a supposed "deterioration" later on speaker proportions remain high, much higher than in comparable Asian countries (with the exception of Singapore): 64.50% in 1980 (based on census data), between 56% for speaking and 73% for reading skills in 1994 according to a LSP study (p. 30). Currently, the Ethnologue (Simons & Fennig, 2018) reports over 40 million users of English out of a population of more than 104 million, about 40%.

The high proficiency rate in English amongst Filipinos is all the more remarkable given that, after independence, the country adopted a decidedly endolinguistic national language policy, i.e. while English was retained as an official language, Filipino/Pilipino was deliberately established as and developed toward the status of a true national language. Remarkably, such a policy has been rare amongst former colonies. One might think that removing the former colonial language and thus symbol of outside dominance should be desirable, but in most contexts and countries English has been retained and even strengthened further—perhaps because of its ethnic neutrality in addition to its instrumental, economic, and political usefulness. The only closely comparable cases that I am aware of are Tanzania, with KiSwahili successfully implemented as the national language, and Malaysia, which has developed Bahasa Malaysia. In all three countries, the newly established national languages have spread widely and successfully—least of all, perhaps, in the Philippines, due to resistance to Tagalog predominance in some regions but in all of them English has been retained as a strong national or internally used language as well (least so in Tanzania).

As in many other countries, the multilingual settings in which English operates have produced mixed varieties in which English blends with elements of indigenous languages (Schneider, 2016). In the Philippines, the variety in question is called Taglish. Academic friends assure me they use it a lot in relaxed circumstances; Thompson (2003) provided a comprehensive documentation of properties and characteristic usage contexts (cf. Gonzales, 2017). Bautista (2004) suggests that the use of Taglish is also class-stratified, characterizing middle and upper class speakers, since it requires a relatively high proficiency level in English.

Like elsewhere, and perhaps even more pointedly, the social role of English, and consequently, attitudes toward it, is ambivalent (Bolton, 2000). On the one hand, it is a language of opportunity and economic advancement, and for many individuals, the instrumental motivation to achieve advanced proficiency levels which promise better-paid jobs (e.g. in the call-center

Prologue xxvii

industry) is high. On the other hand, the Philippine society is strongly divided along class and wealth lines, and English is viewed as associated with access to higher education and high-income social strata, an elitist class-divider (Martin, 2014; Thomson, 2003). Sibayan and Gonzalez (1996, p. 140) pointedly state that, during the first 35 years, Filipinos found English "a socioeconomic 'equalizer'" while, later, through elite schools and other gate-keeper institutions, it became a "stratifier". It remains to be seen which of these directions will be strengthened in the future.

Interestingly, PhE has also been transported abroad by significant speaker numbers, and the agents in this process are not educated elite members, quite the contrary (Bolton, 2000). Currently, it is estimated that there are about 2.3 million 'Overseas Filipino Workers' (OFWs) (N.B. Gonzalez [2004] estimates a figure of seven million), who labor in the Gulf States, in Hong Kong, Singapore, and elsewhere, often under harsh conditions—males often as construction workers or in other kinds of manual jobs, females predominantly as house helpers. While most of them are poorly educated and hence not fluent speakers of PhE, in many or most jobs, a minimum communicative ability in English is desired or required:

> [T]he prospect of employment abroad at a much higher salary than they can receive in their own country motivates them to learn English in school and [...] beyond schooling to increase their job prospects. Thus they are willing to enroll for special non-degree short-term courses to learn the special language of a trade or occupation and matriculate for courses in Seamen's English, Hotel and Restaurant English, and Nursing English.
>
> (Gonzalez, 2004, p. 13)

To my knowledge, the linguistic ramifications of these migration movements have hardly ever been investigated.

The present volume, which also serves as the handbook of Philippine English, addresses and covers issues related to PhE, the above-mentioned ones, and many more, in a remarkably comprehensive fashion. As befits a major reference work, it looks into and surveys a wide range of relevant topics on PhE: its history and evolution; resources available for its investigation; its main structural properties on the levels of phonology, vocabulary, syntax, semantics, discourse, and spelling; internal variation and change; its relation to AmE; contact and hybridity; lexicographic coverage, codification, and literary applications; issues of language and education policy; strategies of language acquisition, teaching, testing, and teacher training; sociopsychological dimensions including intelligibility, attitudes, and multilingualism; and contemporary settings such as computer-mediated communication, migration, and call center usage. The breadth of coverage of topics is most impressive.

What causes PhE to stand out in the concerto of world Englishes as well is the fact that there are a very large number of dedicated language scholars and there is a most active Linguistic Society of the Philippines, investigating xxviii *Edgar W. Schneider*

and promoting the subject. For decades, a strong line-up of energetic and competent scholars have built and developed the discipline, have made the variety known to the world, and have developed application strategies. This started out with huge names such as Teodoro Llamzon, Andrew Gonzalez, and, above all, Ma. Lourdes Bautista, and the torch has now been passed on to a younger generation of scholars including (in alphabetical order, and the selection is not meant to be exclusive!) Ariane Borlongan, Priscilla Cruz, the late Danilo Dayag, Shirley Dita, Isabel Martin, Ruanni Tupas, and many more. Their voices and tunes are heard internationally. In the concerto of world Englishes, PhE is clearly audible as a strong and clear voice, growing in intensity, and singing a lead tune!

References

Bautista, Maria Lourdes S. (2004). Tagalog-English code switching as a mode of discourse. *Asia Pacific Education Review* 5, 226–233.

Bautista, Maria Lourdes S. (Ed.) (1997). *English is an Asian language: The Philippine context. Proceedings of the conference held in Manila on August 2–3, 1996.* Sydney: Macquarie Library Ltd.

Bautista, Maria Lourdes S., Teodoro A. Llamzon, and Bonifacio P. Sibayan, eds. (2000). *Parangal cang Brother Andrew. Festschrift for Andrew Gonzalez on his sixtieth birthday.* Manila: Linguistic Society of the Philippines.

Bernardo, Allan B.I. (2004). McKinley's questionable bequest: Over 100 years of English in Philippine education. *World Englishes* 23(1), 17–31.

Bolton, Kingsley. (2000). Hong Kong English, Philippine English, and the future of Asian Englishes. In Bautista, Llamzon & Sibayan, (Eds.) (2000), pp. 93–114.

Borlongan, Ariane Macalinga. (2011). Some aspects of the morphosyntax of Philippine English. In M. L. S. Bautista (ed.), *Studies on Philippine English: Exploring the Philippine component of the International Corpus of English* (pp. 187–199). Anvil Publishing, Inc. for De La Salle University.

Borlongan, Ariane Macalinga. (2016). Relocating Philippine English in Schneider's dynamic model. *Asian Englishes* 18(3), 1–10.

Buschfeld, Sarah, and Edgar W. Schneider. (2018). World Englishes: Postcolonial Englishes and beyond. In Ee Ling Low and Anne Pakir (Eds.), *World Englishes. Rethinking Paradigms* (pp. 29–46). London, New York: Routledge.

Gonzalez, Andrew. (1997). The history of English in the Philippines. In M. L. S. Bautista (Ed.), *English is an Asian language: The Philippine context. Proceedings of the conference held in Manila on August 2–3, 1996* (pp. 25–40). Sydney: Macquarie Library Ltd.

Gonzalez, Andrew. (2004). The social dimension of Philippine English. In M.L.S. Bautista, and K. Bolton, (Guest Eds.) *Special Issue on Philippine English: Tensions and Transitions. World Englishes* (23 (1), pp. 7–16).

Kachru, Braj B. (1985). Standards, codification and sociolinguistic realism: The English language in the outer circle. In Randolph Quirk and Henry G. Widdowson, (Eds.) *English in the world: Teaching and learning the language and literatures* (pp. 11–30). Cambridge: Cambridge University Press & The British Council.

Prologue xxix

Kachru, Braj B., (Ed.) (1992). *The other tongue: English across cultures.* 2nd ed. Urbana, Chicago: University of Illinois Press.

Kachru, Braj, Yamuna Kachru and Cecil Nelson, (Eds.) (2006). *The Handbook of World Englishes.* Malden, MA: Blackwell.

Kirkpatrick, Andy (Ed.), (2010). *The Routledge handbook of World Englishes.* London, New York: Routledge

Martin, Isabel Pefianco. (2014). Beyond nativization?: Philippine English in Schneider's dynamic model. In Sarah Buschfeld, Thomas Hoffmann, Magnus Huber, & Alexander Kautzsch (Eds.), *The evolution of Englishes: The Dynamic Model and beyond* (pp. 70–85). Amsterdam: John Benjamins.

Mesthrie, Rajend, and Rakesh Bhatt. (2008). *World Englishes.* Cambridge: Cambridge University Press.

Schneider, Edgar W. (2003). The dynamics of New Englishes: From identity construction to dialect birth. *Language* 79, 233–281.

Schneider, Edgar W. (2007). *Postcolonial English. Varieties around the world.* Cambridge: Cambridge University Press.

Schneider, Edgar W. (2016). Hybrid Englishes: An exploratory survey. *World Englishes* 35, 339–354.

Sibayan, Bonifacio P., and Andrew Gonzalez. (1996). Post-imperial English in the Philippines. In Fishman et al., (Eds.) 1996: 139–172.

Simons, Gary F., and Fennig, Charles D. (Eds.). (2018). *Ethnologue: Languages of the world* (21st ed.). Dallas, TX: SIL International. Accessible from http://www.ethnologue.com

Thompson, Roger M. (2003). *Filipino English and Taglish. Language switching from multiple perspectives.* Amsterdam, Philadelphia, PA: Benjamins.

Part 1

Introduction

1 Conspectus

Ariane Macalinga Borlongan

1.1 English in the Philippines and Philippine English

English is a language of Filipinos. Stating it more emphatically, Filipinos have then and, even more, now come to own English. Prominent Filipino poet Gemino Abad says of English and Filipinos, "English is now ours. We have colonized it!"

English which has emerged in the Philippines is distinctive, fascinating, and remarkable in many ways. First and foremost, Philippine English (PhE) is distinctive because it is one of the very few American-transplanted new Englishes. Most of the English-using societies of the world were a product of British colonization—including the United States itself—and so PhE stands alone among national varieties of English having an American parental lineage. The language was introduced to the Philippines at the close of the 19th century initially by American soldiers and eventually by the highly qualified teachers sent to the islands by the American government. Yet after roughly two decades, they were replaced by the locals; thus, Filipinos learned English from fellow Filipinos. Also, it is fascinating because it is among the youngest Englishes, having been born out of turn-of-20th-century colonization. As such, it is roughly only a 100 years old. But it is remarkable in that English spread very fast in the Philippines. Filipinos learned and acquired the language rapidly and to a high standard, and Filipinos' learning and acquisition of English could be "[o]ne of the most successful linguistic events in the history of mankind" (Gonzalez, 2000, p. 1).

Most recent data suggest that approximately 80% of Filipinos can understand and even speak English (Borlongan, Agoncillo, & Cequeña, 2014), making the Philippines one of the largest English-using societies in the world, and, with a population of over 100 million people, it even surpasses the United Kingdom and many other Inner Circle countries in terms of number of users of English. The present constitution of the Republic of the Philippines cherishes the language as co-official to the national language Filipino, and it is the primary language of the government, education, business, and science and technology in the country.

DOI: 10.4324/9780429427824-2

4   *Ariane Macalinga Borlongan*

1.2 Studies of Philippine English

Documentations on how English was being used in the Philippines and, more specifically, how it was beginning to move away from its exonormative standard American English (AmE) appeared as early as the first decades of its existence (Borlongan, 2018) but scholarship on PhE veritably began when Llamzon called attention to a standardized variety of English which had arisen in the Philippines through his 1969 pioneering work titled *Standard Filipino English*. He proposed the existence of a standardized local variety based on the premise that there are a sizable number of native users of English in the country. At the same time, he argued for the use of standard PhE as the target in teaching English in the Philippines. PhE thus stands out as one of the earliest as well as one of the most extensively documented of all new Englishes (considering that Kachru's first documentation of Indian English was in 1965 and Llamzon's publication came out in 1969).

Since then, PhE, and English in the Philippines, has been one of the most vibrant topics in linguistic research in the Philippines (Dayag & Dita, 2012) and several themes have been in discourses on PhE (Borlongan, 2017), namely, (1) its emergence and existence, (2) its description, (3) its stabilization and codification, and (4) its suitability as a pedagogical model.

When Llamzon (1969) came out with his then bold thesis on standard PhE, he expectedly met criticism. For example, Gonzalez (1972) and Hidalgo (1970) questioned the existence of a standard on the basis of a sizable number of native speakers of English in the Philippines. But Bautista (2000) argues that many Filipinos would be considered native speakers of Englishes with 'new criteria' for being a native speaker (cf. Mann, 1999, 2012; Richards & Tay, 1981, p. 53).

In describing PhE, as with any English, for that matter, one would always ask Gonzalez' famous question: When does an error become a feature of PhE? Bautista (2000) applies D'Souza's (1998) criteria for standardization of new Englishes: (1) widespread use, (2) systematicity and rule-governedness, and (3) use by competent users in formal situations. But Borlongan (2011) finds Hunston's (2002) predilection for what is 'central' and 'typical' rather than categorically defining what is PhE and what is not more useful. And eventually, Borlongan (2019) says that errors turn into features when an error (1) is frequent enough across registers, sociolects, and dialects, (2) has sociological and structural basis for its emergence, and (3) has increased in frequency across time.

It has been claimed that PhE is quite developed in many dimensions—historically, structurally, and sociologically—that, while nativization is certain (Martin, 2014; Schneider, 2003, 2007), endonormative stabilization (Borlongan, 2016) and differentiation (Gonzales, 2017) seem to be under way. Efforts toward its standardization and codification are in progress, beginning with dictionaries (e.g. Bautista & Butler, 2010) and grammars (e.g. Borlongan, 2011). As a consequence, there has been a need to reconsider existing models in teaching and learning English in the Philippines (Bernardo, 2013).

Ultimately, Borlongan (2019) puts forward that linguistic stabilization entails perceptible restructuring at the microsociolinguistic level (i.e. relative variation with reference to other Englishes and stable diachronic change) and standardization at the macrosociolinguistic level (i.e. codification through dictionaries and grammars and shift to local/pluricentric model in language teaching).

1.3 A Definition of Philippine English

The Philippines has thus legitimately claimed its own variety of English, not any less than other national varieties of English. A definition is therefore effectively offered here:

Philippine English is a postcolonial English which has emerged in the Philippines. It was introduced to the country through American colonization; hence, its exonormative standard is American English but it has since then developed its own norms and standard. It is used in many controlling domains, including government, education, science and technology, and commerce, and also in everyday life. It has formal registers and educated dialects but it also has informal registers, primarily code-switching in a Philippine-type language, and sociolects. Some registers and dialects have also been emerging with reference to other sociolinguistic factors, particularly educational attainment, socioeconomic status, ethnolinguistic group, mode of communication, but also more traditional factors like age, gender, genre, and context.

1.4 A Handbook of Philippine English, and a Festschrift for Ma. Lourdes Bautista

At this point, it is therefore quite compelling to come up with *Philippine English: Development, Sociology, and Structure of English in the Philippines*, essentially the handbook of PhE. It is intended to be the definitive guide not only to the linguistics of the new English, but also to the vast research and scholarship devoted to it. Another reason for a volume such as this is that, as scholarship on PhE began in 1969, the publication of this volume is 50 years since then. It is hoped that this volume will remain a relevant and valuable resource on PhE for many years to come. Indeed, the publication of a handbook catapults PhE to a full recognition of a legitimate national variety, which is essential in the progression of the new English further in Schneider's dynamic model (2003, 2007; also Borlongan, 2016; Gonzales, 2017). It must be mentioned that this is the first 'handbook' on a specific variety of English that has emerged from the roots of the language in the British Isles (technically, through the United States, in the case of the Philippines). It therefore provides a framework for all the other Englishes as they attempt to come up with their own handbooks, too.

And on the corpus of work on PhE, Professor Emerita Ma. Lourdes Bautista of De La Salle University (Manila, the Philippines) shines the brightest.

6 Ariane Macalinga Borlongan

She began her career in 1975 by framing a model of the Filipino bilingual competence based on English-Tagalog code-switching. In 1983, she was the first to publish on less educated sub-varieties of PhE. She spearheaded the compilation of the Philippine component of the International Corpus of English (ICE-PH), from which dataset she came up with a grammatical description of standard PhE in 2000, and which she used to compare PhE with other Englishes in 2009 and 2010. She also explored attitudes toward PhE in 2001(a, b). She has edited three volumes (1997, 2008, and 2011) and two journal special issues (in *Asian Englishes* in 2004 and in *World Englishes* in 2004) on PhE. Therefore, it is fitting that the handbook of PhE also be a festschrift for Professor Ma. Lourdes Bautista, to honor her for the work she has done for PhE.

This volume has been structured to comprehensively cover the many facets of the emergence and existence of PhE. The first section gives an overview of PhE (Ariane Borlongan) as well as its history (Ariane Borlongan) and the available resources on the new English (Dominik Heps and Mikhail Alic Go). A special feature of this section is a tribute to Professor Ma. Lourdes Bautista and her influence to PhE scholarship written by Anne Pakir. The second section is a linguistic description of PhE, covering phonology (Irwan Shah Shahruddin, Ran Ao, and Ee Ling Low), lexicon (Thomas Biermeier), grammar (Philip Rentillo, Shirley Dita, and Aldrin Lee), discourse (Marilu Madrunio), and spelling and punctuation (Robert Fuchs). The third section deals with variation and change in PhE, more specifically internal variation (Aldrin Lee and Ariane Borlongan), diachronic change (Ariane Borlongan and Peter Collins), relationship with AmE (Edgar Schneider), contact with other languages (Ma. Althea Enriquez), and hybridization (Wilkinson Daniel Gonzales). The fourth section alludes to the stabilization of PhE as a new English, in particular through linguistic and literary canon such as lexicography (Danica Salazar), standardization (Ariane Borlongan), and literature (Isagani Cruz). The fifth section looks into the psycholinguistic dimensions of PhE, namely, intelligibility (Shirley Dita and Kristine de Leon), attitudes (Philip Rentillo), multilingualism (Loy Lising), and language policy (Ruanni Tupas). The sixth section deals with learning and teaching of English in the Philippines and PhE, and includes chapters on acquisition and learning (Aireen Barrios), language teaching (Alejandro Bernardo), language testing (James D'Angelo), and teacher education (Edward Jay Quinto and Sterling Plata). Lastly, the seventh section discusses various contemporary issues relating to PhE, as in the Internet (Leah Gustilo and Chenee Dino), migration (Beatriz Lorente), outsourced call centers (Eric Friginal and Rachelle Friginal), and the teaching of English as a foreign language in the Philippines (Aiden Yeh). This section also features a chapter on world Englishes and social change by Ahmar Mahboob and Ruanni Tupas. A prologue on PhE in the 'concerto' of world Englishes and an epilogue on PhE past, present, and future has been written by Edgar Schneider and Kingsley Bolton, respectively.

Conspectus 7

In breadth and depth, the volume constitutes as much as can be said on the theory, description, research, pedagogy, and praxis of PhE, truly a definitive guide to the variety of English which has emerged in the Philippines in as much as it is a handbook of PhE and a festschrift in honor of Professor Ma. Lourdes Bautista. But more than proving to be valuable in the scholarship on PhE particularly and world Englishes generally, perhaps the most significant contribution of this volume remains to be that it legitimizes the Filipino ownership of English. Indeed, this volume could proudly say: English is the language of Filipinos.

References

Bautista, Ma. Lourdes S. (2000). *Defining Standard Philippine English: Its status and grammatical features.* Manila, the Philippines: De La Salle University Press, Inc.

Bautista, Ma. Lourdes S., & Butler, Susan. (Eds.). (2010). *Anvil-Macquarie Philippine English dictionary* (Revised ed.). Pasig City, the Philippines: Anvil Publishing, Inc.

Bernardo, Alejandro S. (2013). *Toward an endonormative pedagogic model for teaching English in Philippine higher education institutions* (Unpublished doctoral dissertation). University of Santo Tomas, Manila, the Philippines.

Borlongan, Ariane M. (2011b). Some aspects of the morphosyntax of Philippine English. In M. L. S. Bautista (ed.), *Studies on Philippine English: Exploring the Philippine component of the International Corpus of English* (pp. 187–199). Anvil.

Borlongan, Ariane Macalinga. (2011). *A grammar of the verb in Philippine English* (Unpublished doctoral dissertation). De La Salle University, Manila, the Philippines.

Borlongan, Ariane Macalinga. (2016). Relocating Philippine English in Schneider's dynamic model. *Asian Englishes, 18*(3), 1–10.

Borlongan, Ariane Macalinga. (2017). Contemporary Perspectives on Philippine English. *The Philippine ESL Journal, 17,* 1–9.

Borlongan, Ariane Macalinga. (2018). Early Philippine English: A historical sociolinguistic analysis of *A survey of the educational system of the Philippine Islands* (1925). Paper presented at the special plenary panel on Philippine English at the 23rd Annual Conference of the International Association for World Englishes, Quezon, the Philippines.

Borlongan, Ariane Macalinga. (2019). *Linguistic aspects of endonormative stabilization: The case of Philippine English.* Keynote lecture delivered at the symposium titled *English in contact* hosted by the Faculty of Languages and Cultures, Kyushu University, March 28–29, 2019, Fukuoka, Japan.

Borlongan, Ariane Macalinga, Agoncillo, Roland Niño L., & Cequeña, Maria B. (2014). *The National Filipino Catholic Youth Survey of 2013* (Commissioned research project report). Episcopal Commission on Youth, the Catholic Bishops' Conference of the Philippines and the Catholic Educational Association of the Philippines through De La Salle University, Manila, the Philippines.

D'Souza, Jean. (1998). Review of Arjuna Parakrama's *De-hegemonizing language standards: Learning from (post)colonial Englishes about "English".* Asian Englishes, 1(2), 86–94.

8   *Ariane Macalinga Borlongan*

Dayag, Danilo T., & Dita, Shirley N. (2012). Linguistic research in the Philippines: Trends, prospects and challenges. In Virginia A. Miralao, & Joanne B. Agbisit (Eds.), *Philippine social sciences: Capacities, directions, and challenges* (pp. 110–126). Quezon, the Philippines: Philippine Social Science Council.

Gonzales, Wilkinson Daniel Wong. (2017). Philippine Englishes. *Asian Englishes, 19*(1), 1–17.

Gonzalez, Andrew. (1972). Review of Teodoro A. Llamzon's *Standard Filipino English. Philippine Journal of Language Teaching, 7*(1–2), 93–98.

Gonzalez, Andrew. (2000). Successful language teaching in Southeast Asia: The Philippine experience (1898–1946). *Philippine Journal of Linguistics, 31*(1), 1–9.

Hidalgo, Cesar A. (1970). Review of Teodoro A. Llamzon's *Standard Filipino English. Philippine Journal of Linguistics, 1*(1), 129–132.

Hunston, Susan. (2002). *Corpora in applied linguistics.* Cambridge, the United Kingdom: Cambridge University Press.

Kachru, Braj B. (1965). The *Indianness* in Indian English. *Word, 21*, 391–410.

Llamzon, Teodoro A. (1969). *Standard Filipino English.* Manila, the Philippines: Ateneo University Press.

Mann, Charles C. (1999). We wuz robbed inni': *Towards redefining the 'native speaker'.* Paper presented at the 12th World Congress of the International Association of Applied Linguistics.

Mann, Charles C. (2012). We wuz robbed, inni'?: Towards reconceptualizing the "native speaker". *Journal of English as an International Language, 7*(2), 1–24.

Martin, Isabel P. (2014). Beyond nativization?: Philippine English in Schneider's dynamic model. In S. Buschfeld, T. Hoffmann, M. Huber, & A. Kautszsch (Eds.), *The evolution of Englishes: The dynamic model and beyond* (pp. 70–85). Amsterdam, the Netherlands: John Benjamins Publishing Co.

Richards, Jack C., & Tay, Mary W. J. (1981). Norm and variability in language use and language learning. In Larry E. Smith (Ed.), *English for cross-cultural communication* (pp. 40–56). London, the United Kingdom: Macmillan.

Schneider, Edgar W. (2003). The dynamics of new Englishes: From identity construction to dialect birth. *Language, 79*, 233–281.

Schneider, Edgar W. (2007). *Postcolonial English: Varieties of English around the world.* New York, NY: Cambridge University Press.

2 History

Ariane Macalinga Borlongan

2.1 Aim and Outline

This chapter narrates the history of English in the Philippines and Philippine English (PhE) using Schneider's (2003, 2007) dynamic model of the evolution of Englishes as framework. As such, the historical narrative is organized according to the stages Schneider identified in his model but it is necessary to begin with a brief description of his model as well as the placement of PhE in the model. Also, some notes on the language situation of the Philippines prior to American colonization are given so as to better understand the transplantation of English in the Philippines and, subsequently, the emergence of a local English, PhE.

2.2 Schneider's Dynamic Model of the Evolution of Postcolonial Englishes

Schneider's conception of the development of postcolonial Englishes was first presented in a 2003 article and elaborated in a 2007 book. His model is so influential that its importance in understanding world Englishes today cannot be underestimated. He succinctly presents the model he developed in this fashion:

1 In the process of the English language being uprooted and relocated in colonial and postcolonial history, postcolonial Englishes (PCEs) have emerged by undergoing a fundamentally uniform process which can be described as a progression of five characteristic stages: foundation, exonormative stabilization, nativization, endonormative stabilization, and differentiation.

2 The participant groups of this process experience it in complementary ways, from the perspective of the colonizers [/settlers] (STL strand) or that of the colonized [/indigenous] (IDG strand), with these developmental strands getting more closely intertwined and their linguistic correlates, in an ongoing process of mutual linguistic accommodation, approximating each other in the course of time.

DOI: 10.4324/9780429427824-3

10   *Ariane Macalinga Borlongan*

> 3   The stages and strands of this process are ultimately caused by and signify reconstructions of group identities of all participating communities, with respect to the erstwhile source society of the colonizing group, to one another, and to the land which they jointly inhabit.
>
> [...] In each case, I distinguish the four constitutive parameters mentioned earlier: extralinguistic (sociopolitical) background; identity constructions; sociolinguistic conditions (contact settings and participants' use of specific varieties; norm orientations and attitudes); and typical linguistic consequences (structural changes on the levels of lexis, pronunciation, and grammar).
>
> (Schneider, 2007, pp. 32–33)

Schneider (2003, 2007) places PhE in the nativization phase, and probably approaching endonormative stabilization phase, and he adds, "Signs foreshadowing codification in phase 4 can be detected, though they remain highly restricted" (Schneider, 2007, p. 143). The body of local literature in English is growing and attempts to codify PhE are increasing—including its adoption as the pedagogical model—but, as Schneider said, this remains highly restricted. He ends what he has for the case for PhE by saying:

> The Philippines appears to be an example of a country where the in-built developmental trends of the Dynamic Model get overruled by changing external conditions, thus coming to a halt. [...] The situation is "quite stable at present" (Sibayan and Gonzalez 1996:160), with Filipino established as a national language and English being strong in certain functional domains but showing no signs of proceeding any further.
>
> (Schneider, 2007, p. 143)

Borlongan (2011b/2016) is the first to suggest a relocation of PhE in the dynamic model. He claimed, with the sociopolitical developments in the Philippines and ongoing linguistic codification of the new English, it must be at the dawn of its endonormative stabilization. Martin (2014a) gives cautionary statements on English remaining as a/the language of the elite and, in fact, among the mechanisms in the marginalization in the society. As such, she argues that PhE has not moved beyond nativization. But more recently, Gonzales (2017) points out that, with quite a number of sociolects emerging, PhE has diversified to become 'Philippine Englishes' by this time.

2.3 (Language) Situation of the Philippines Prior to American Colonization

Very little is known of English language use in the Philippines before the Americans came to colonize the country. It is comforting to believe that there really was not much English language use to talk about rather than that no documentation exists of such use. Prior to American colonization, the British Empire did occupy Manila and its neighboring port in Cavite from October 6, 1762, to May 31, 1764. It was a very short period and the areas covered were relatively small that any significant (sociolinguistic) consequence could not be attributed to it. Even toward the last few decades of Spanish colonization of the Philippines, only a handful of individuals—primarily those Filipinos fortunate to be educated in and/or exposed to Europe—knew English, and among them was national hero Jose Rizal who lived in London from May 25, 1888, to March 19, 1899, and studied and improved his English, which was among his three goals while he was living in the city.

The First Philippine Commission headed by Jacob Schurman (president of Cornell University at that time) submitted their first report to then US president William McKinley to describe the situation in the Philippines at the beginning of the 20th century and also to give recommendations as to how the US could proceed with its business in the country. There was no census-like detailing of the population but the commission estimates roughly 8,000,000 people living in the Philippines. Again, there were no details on the languages used but it is highly likely that the so-called tribes could have been based on the languages they used. There were 84 listed tribes in the report and these were the highest in number (numbers only approximates): Visayans (2,601,600, possibly included Cebuano and the rest of the Visayan languages), Tagalogs (1,663,900), Bicols (518,800), Ilocanos (441,700), Pangasinans (365,500), Pampangas (337,900).

As stipulated in the Educational Decree of 1868 of Queen Isabella II of Spain, instruction in schools for the natives was only in elementary primary instruction. It should include a smorgasbord of what is expected of primary instruction but what was in reality only Catholic doctrine taught in the local language. What was supposed to be instruction in Spanish was "purely imaginary" (p. 31). Catholic friars tasked to do so prohibited it and natives who knew very little of Spanish realized it is to their best interest that they simply used only their native language. Only very few of the 'civilized natives' actually attended school, and those who did so learned only a few prayers and a little catechism in the local language. Nonetheless, Spanish was the language of the colonial government and also of the local educated elite or the 'Ilustrados'. It can be speculated that this situation of deprivation of a common language for education and learning by a multilingual people longing for better treatment from their colonial master, among others, made the Philippines "a favorable soil and climate" (Gonzalez, 2008, p. 14) for the transplantation of what would become the country's 'other tongue' (cf. Kachru, 1982).

2.4 Stage 1: Foundation (1898–1901)

2.4.1 Sociopolitical Background: American Colonial Expansion

After the battles with Spanish forces (an offshoot of the Spanish-American War which began in April of 1898 and centered on Cuba) and, eventually, the Filipino forces fighting for the nation's newly gained independence

12   *Ariane Macalinga Borlongan*

dated June 12, 1898, the Americans established a military government in the Philippines on August 14, 1898. On December 10, 1898, Spain and the US signed the Treaty of Paris ending the war between the two nations and, in effect, ceding the Philippines (and Cuba, Guam, and Puerto Rico) from Spain to the US. Benevolent assimilation of the Philippines was proclaimed by President William McKinley on December 21, 1898, and announced in the Philippines on January 4, 1899. Escalante (2007) notes that the US was unprepared for colonization. The Philippines was "America's first colonial guinea pigs overseas" (Martin & the Editorial Board, the Philippine Historical Commission, 1980, p. 22). Escalante continues, the US did not exactly know what to do with the Philippines and could not even figure out early on which executive department would be in charge of the new colony. It only became more certain about colonizing the Philippines when it was already clear to them how a colony in the Far East would greatly benefit the US.

2.4.2 *Identity Constructions: The American Military versus the Newly Independent People*

The soldiers of the warfare against Filipinos and, eventually, people—the military government—consisted of the English-using new residents of the Philippines. The combat troops who subjugated an archipelago of seven million people were 25,000 on average (Linn, 2000). It is clear that they were in the islands only very temporarily and this is implicated by the nature of the new military government—in itself transitionary. While its period of existence was then undefined, its temporariness was already given. Most of the Americans who came to the Philippines were the soldiers recruited for the Spanish-American war. As such, these few Americans were very detached from the Philippines and were there to only fulfill their duties as a soldier-recruit. Meanwhile, the locals savaged by the tumultuous end to centuries-long Spanish colonization were perturbed by the threat of what appeared then to be yet another colonizer endangering their hard-fought, newly found independence.

2.4.3 *Sociolinguistic Conditions: Limited Exposure to English, Local Language*

By 1898, American English (AmE) had just gone through endonormative stabilization and was about to move to differentiation by the time the US colonized the Philippines (Schneider, 2007). And so though the soldiers sent to the Philippines were young recruits from across the newly born superpower, there would be no very distinctive dialects to speak of. This is in stark contrast to the experience of British colonies where dialects which have already been fully formed in the British Isles were the ones to be transplanted in the new colony in such differentiated state.

History 13

Dealings between the two warring sides were done in English, in Spanish, or with the aid of an interpreter. Also, because quite a number of these newly recruited soldiers came from Spanish-using states and a large number of (elite) Filipinos still were using Spanish, the Ibero-Romance language was valuable in communication between Filipinos and Americans.

2.4.4 Linguistic Effects: Small-Scale Koinéization, Use of General American English, Toponymic Borrowing

As was mentioned earlier, Schneider (2007) locates the beginning of differentiation in AmE in 1898; therefore, koinéization was just starting in the US. It is assumed that small-scale koinéization was taking place among the American soldiers coming from the various states who went to the Philippines at that time, and they must have been using the early forms of General AmE. Understandably, they also needed to refer to local flora and fauna as well as cultural items in their local names and, also sometimes, Spanish names as are called even today.

2.5 Stage 2: Exonormative Stabilization (1901–1935)

2.5.1 Sociopolitical Background: Stable Colonial Status, Establishment of English as an Important Language

Schneider (2007) writes about PhE, "Phases 1 and 2 [...] seem to have practically merged and progressed very rapidly" (p. 140). Indeed, the two phases unfolded in such a short time—the first phase only roughly three years, very likely the shortest among the Englishes. But it is possible to point out when the first phase ends and the second begins in the development of PhE: A civil government was inaugurated on July 1, 1901, with William Taft as civil governor and, eventually, governor-general. War between the Philippines and the US officially ended after the Philippine Organic Act (also the Philippine Bill of 1902 or the Cooper Act, after Henry Cooper who authored that act) was approved, ratified, and confirmed by US president McKinley on July 1, 1902.

2.5.2 Identity Constructions: 'American-plus-Filipino' and 'Filipino-plus-American' Identities

The first official census of the American government conducted in 1903 mentions 8,135 in the population as having been born in the US and 6,931,584 in the Philippines. The only foreign-born population to outnumber those born in the US were those born in China at 41,035 and by that time the Spanish-born population was only 3,888. There were not a large number of Americans who came to settle in the Philippines. The very few who did were clearly on a very temporary stay. Even fewer were those who decided life was

14   *Ariane Macalinga Borlongan*

worth living in the Philippines and they were those who found their vocation to be the upliftment of life in the country or those who eventually built their families in the Philippines, primarily by marrying Filipinos. By 1918, census data (Census Office of the Philippine Islands, 1921) indicate that there were 5,774 Americans in the Philippines (below 0.1% of the total population). Filipinos numbered 9,428,291 (91.4%). Spanish increased only slightly, numbering to 3,945 (below 0.1%). Chinese and Japanese outnumbered Americans at 43,802 (0.4%) and 7,808 (below 0.1%), respectively.

The Filipinos were educated in the American system, and they were taught American ideals;

> [b]y the time Taft left the Philippines in 1903, Filipino students were no longer memorizing Catholic dogmas. They were now busy drawing apples, pears, oranges, and snowcaps. In a relatively short time, Filipinos begin to speak English, idolize George Washington, and dream of a white Christmas.
>
> (Escalante, 2007, p. 151)

And a small but important segment of the Philippine population is what was called 'Pencionados', the 204 Filipino students sent by the colonial government to study in the US who later on became a resource for the then Department of Public Instruction and, more importantly, promoters of American culture in the classroom.

2.5.3 Sociolinguistic Conditions: Competition with Spanish, Expanding Contact, American English as Target

Much earlier, William McKinley wrote a letter of instruction dated April 7, 1900, and ordered that English be established as the common medium of communication as "it is especially important to the prosperity of the islands". This would be the first official policy on the use of English in the Philippines. For a time during American colonization, Spanish was an important language of the legislature and the judiciary and it competed with English as an official language. By the time the 1918 census was conducted though, English had overtaken Spanish; among the literate Filipinos aged 10 and above, 896,258 could use English while the number for Spanish was 757,463, a ratio of 1.2:1.

A very important detail in the history of English in the Philippines and, therefore, Philippine English is the Thomasites, the group of around 500 (numbers vary according to sources) teachers of English sent by the US to the Philippines. These pioneering group of teachers were transported to the new colony largely via the United States Army transport ship *Thomas* (hence they were affectionately labeled as such), but some also came through ships of other names. Alberca (1994) claims that, "With respect to education and experience then, the Thomasites were the finest trained body of teachers

America had ever tried to send from its territory" (p. 55). Alberca is also worth quoting in his assessment of the contribution of Thomasites in the transplantation of English in the Philippines:

> Three hundred years of Spanish rule could have resulted in the ascendancy of Spanish, but at the close of the Spanish occupation in 1898, Americans were hard-pressed to find one or two young Filipinos in any village who could speak Spanish with complete confidence. In contrast, the Americans demonstrated what many observers consider *a phenomenal accomplishment*: alter only about three years, they were able to make many Filipinos throughout the country speak and write English with passable proficiency. Much of the credit for the 'remarkable' ascendancy of English in the Philippines has, of course, gone to the Thomasites, the group of mostly young Americans who taught English to both Filipino students and teachers. [emphasis added]
>
> (p. 69)

It was not explicitly instructed that the target in the classroom was AmE but, with the insistence to 'eradicate' the local patterns of use, the 1925 educational survey of the Philippines made it clear that the classroom target was an exonormative one (Borlongan, 2018). All the while, there was also acknowledgment that those local patterns should be and, as a matter of fact, were indeed understandable, as divergent patterns of use already existed across the English-using world at that time. The survey report can be quoted saying:

> It is entirely within the range of possibility, however, to develop a generation of English-speaking people whose English will be not more different from that spoken in wide regions of America than the latter is from the English typical of vast districts of England, Scotland, Ireland, America, Canada, Australia, and the United States. No more important fact inheres in the present situation than the fact that spoken English varies widely over the English-speaking world without really preventing it from functioning as a common means of communication.
>
> (p. 168).

As the Thomasites had come and more Filipinos had been trained to teach, education in English became more widespread and more Filipinos were able to use English. The number of students enrolled in school rose dramatically from almost 160,000 in 1901 to more than 1,100,000 in 1923 (The Board of Educational Survey, 1925). And by 1923, Filipinos could comprehend and speak in English well enough to communicate even with non-Filipinos, distinguish right from wrong when presented a language sample, and spell much better than their American counterparts. Though there was much to be desired with their readings skills and their patterns of use, being affected by the structure of Philippine-type languages.

16   *Ariane Macalinga Borlongan*

2.5.4 Linguistic Effects: Heavy Lexical Borrowing and, Later, Morphological and Syntactic Restructuring

Though Borlongan (2018) says that there is not much evidence for lexical development of early PhE, he assumed that there was quite heavy borrowing in Philippine cultural items as well as local flora and fauna in the early years of the new English. Yet he pointed to a very clear localization of English phonology, something which the Americans clearly understood as unavoidable—and, likewise, rather acceptable, given that phonological variation does exist in the whole English-using world—despite their efforts to instruct Filipinos with American standard phonology. A listing of grammatical deviations from AmE has been made early on. These, among others, are a prelude to the distinctive features PhE would evolve later on in its development, Borlongan notes. The 1925 Board of Educational Survey gives an indication of the emergence of a local English:

> [...] Filipino children, copying the models presented by their teachers, are learning to speak a kind of English which is characterized by the language features of Malay tongues. Of the thousand and more teachers who were observed and tested by the Commission not one speaks of the kind of English spoken in the United States, and naturally, therefore, we found that of the 3,500 children tested not one spoke American-English. Like teacher, like pupil fairly describes the results of oral language instruction.
>
> (p. 154)

2.6 Stage 3: Nativization (1935–1946?)

2.6.1 Sociopolitical Background: Commonwealth of the Philippines

Philippine Senate president Manuel Quezon successfully lobbied at the US Congress for the passing of the Philippine Independence Act (also the Tydings-McDuffie Act, after the senators who authored the Act) in 1934. Enacted on March 24, 1934, it established the process toward Philippine independence after a ten-year transition period. It also allowed for the drafting of the 1935 Constitution and the establishment of the Commonwealth of the Philippines. With the establishment of the Commonwealth of the Philippines, the Insular Government was dissolved. Though the Japanese were able to occupy the Philippines as a result of World War II, the US was able to recover the Philippines. As indicated in the Philippine Independence Act, the US formally recognized Philippine independence on July 4, 1946, with the Treaty of Manila signed between the governments of the two nations.

At this point, it is clear that the Philippines would no longer be a colony of the US, and Schneider (2007) makes a good mother-child analogy: "[T]he

History 17

'mother country' is gradually not felt that much of a 'mother' any longer, the offspring will start going their own ways, politically and linguistically— slowly and hesitantly at first, gaining momentum and confidence as time passes by" (pp. 40–41). Eventually, independence was attained and the colony became a country on its own.

2.6.2 *Identity Constructions: Separation and Semi-Autonomy*

The lone census (Commission of the Census, 1941) taken during the Commonwealth period was in the year 1939 and, at that time, 8,709 (0.1%) of the population were American citizens. The total number of Filipinos went up to 15,833,649 (99.0%) of the whole population. Chinese and Japanese increased their numbers to 117,487 (0.7%) and 29,057 (below 0.2%), respectively. Spanish increased by a small number at 4,627, but still below 0.1% of the total population. Obviously, there was no significant increase in the American population in the Philippines, and, with the looming promised independence and the eventual outbreak of World War II, there would have been no prospect of reversal of this trend.

2.6.3 *Sociolinguistic Conditions: English as the Most Widely Used Language, Development of a National Language*

The number of people who can use English in the Philippines by 1939 was 4,259,565 (26.6%), making English the most widely used language. Tagalog came second at 4,068,565 (25.4%). Spanish could be used by 417,375 (2.61%). An awakening of consciousness of the need for a national language was crystallized by the 1935 constitution which stated that "[t]he National Assembly shall take steps toward the development and adoption of a common national language based on one of the existing native languages. Until otherwise provided by law, English and Spanish shall continue as official languages". The Commonwealth Act Number 184 established the Institute of National Language tasked with studying Philippine languages and identifying a suitable candidate for national language.

2.6.4 *Linguistic Effects: 'Standard Filipino English'*

It is in this parameter at this developmental stage that PhE provides further evidence of the notion that language change is slow and, as is often said, 'does not happen overnight'. Here, structural nativization is noticed only a little later, and is even couched early on in the time period of the succeeding stage: In 1969, Llamzon pointed out that the English used by Filipinos was neither British nor American but was acceptable in educated circles and so he claimed that Filipinos had already restructured the language even to the point of standardization.

18   *Ariane Macalinga Borlongan*

2.7 Stage 4: Endonormative Stabilization (1946?–Present?/1986?)

2.7.1 *Sociopolitical Background: Post-Independence, Self-Dependence*

Schneider (2007) identifies a defining historical event in transitioning to endonormative stabilization, that which he calls 'Event X',

> an incident which makes it perfectly clear to the settlers that there is an inverse mis-relationship between the (high) importance which they used to place on the mother country and the (considerably lower) importance which the (former) colony is given by the homeland.
>
> (p. 49)

Borlongan (2011b, 2016) considers that ratification and implementation of two post-World War II US congressional acts as Event X in the evolution of PhE. The Tydings Rehabilitation Act of 1946 and the Bell Trade Relations Act of 1946, though meant to aid in the post-war rehabilitation of the Philippines, turned out to disadvantage the Philippines and heavily prioritized the Americans in the exploitation of Philippine natural resources as well as in the regulation of Philippine economy and trade. Even Filipino politicians who are known supporters of the US in the person of President Sergio Osmeña and Senator Claro Recto expressed their dismay over these inequitable acts. Borlongan quotes these words from prominent historiographers Agoncillo and Alfonso (1960, p. 497):

> It is obvious that the United States would help her most loyal ally only if the Americans would be granted the same rights as the Filipinos enjoy in the exploitation of the resources of the country. The United States, then, played the role of a man who, having been aided by a friend who lost everything in defense of the former, now brashly demanded that he be given given [sic] the right to live with his friend's wife in exchange for his financial help.

Borlongan (2011b, 2016) also directs attention to what he calls as post-Event X incidents, or incidents which make more apparent the one-sided relationship between the former colonizer and the new nation. Borlongan argues for two such events in recent Philippine history: The Philippine Senate's rejection of the 1947 Military Bases Agreement between the Philippines and the US in 1991 and the recall of a small humanitarian contingent in Iraq in July 2004 in response to the kidnapping of overseas Filipino worker Angelo dela Cruz. To these which Borlongan cited earlier can be added the anti-American remarks blurted by Philippine president Rodrigo Duterte and his shift in foreign policy more favorable to China, which irked and worried the community of nations.

History 19

2.7.2 Identity Constructions: The Birth of Filipino Nationalism

Because the Philippines was an exploitation colony (using Mufwene's [2001] terms), instead of the settlers remaining in the Philippines, most of them left. According to census data (Bureau of Census and Statistics, 1956), only 6,955 American citizens (or around 0.1% of the population) stayed in the Philippines by 1948.

Sentiments of detachment from the former colonizer cascaded down rather swiftly, most especially in comparison with other British postcolonial societies, because, for one, there is nothing similar to the Commonwealth of Nations after the colonial period to foster a rather sprightly, if not strong, association with the former colonizer. Although, the Philippines was left on its own, and, though the US has constantly presented itself as a reliable ally, the US has nonetheless been helpful only in a manner which ensured certain benefits for itself and not much sacrifices for the other.

Though primarily a pretext to sociolinguistic conditions, the clamor for a 'national language' should be seen as an effort toward the crystallization of national consciousness. Efforts toward the formation of a national language took a major turn when it was named 'Filipino' in the 1973 constitution. The implementing 1987 constitution also puts English at par with the national language in terms of being languages of official communication in the Philippines.

A condition which Schneider (2007) indicates as characteristic of the third stage seems to be felt more in the fourth stage: Though the American colonizers have been demographically removed, their presence is replaced by the persistent desire to maintain contact with the former colonial power. The Philippines still often prides itself as being "America's oldest ally in Asia, and one of America's most valued friends in the world", in the words of former US president George W. Bush to the Philippine Congress in 2003.

2.7.3 Sociolinguistic Conditions: Increasing Acceptance of a Local Norm and Literary Creativity

English continued to be the most widely known language; 7,156,420 or 37.2% of the population indicated in the 1948 census that they can use the language to a communicative level, an increase of 10.6% from 1939 figures. Men know English more than women with the ratio of 1.1:1. Tagalog was known to a close number—7,126,913 or 37.1%—and Spanish had waned to 345,111 or 1.8%. The bilingual education policies of 1974 and 1987 have, by and large, been successful in producing generations of Filipinos bilingual in English (cf. Borlongan, 2009; Gonzalez & Sibayan, 1988).

Albeit the residual linguistic conservatism (which is also characteristic of endonoramtive stabilization), it can be confidently stated that PhE is acceptable to Filipinos, and it can even carry their identity as a Filipino (Bautista, 2001a, 2001b; Borlongan, 2009; also Rentillo, this handbook). And while there remains, too, associations of English with the educated and/or the

20 *Ariane Macalinga Borlongan*

elite, there is no questioning that Filipino society has accepted English as a (crucial) part of their lives, and even identities. Indeed, the educated and/or the elite use English in more domains and verbal activities than the rest of the population but that is not to say that English has not deeply penetrated different levels of Filipino society, which has led Filipinos to be able to identify with the language as their own, too. And as early as the 1960s, the acquisition and learning of English among Filipinos have been perceived as an integration to the Philippine society, which shows that Philippine is already perceived as a Philippine language (Santos, 1969).

And an enduring and esteemed tradition of local literature in English is flourishing, and the Philippines has had its share of contributions to literature in English which have also been read not only by Filipinos but also by other English users around the world. Gruenberg in 1985 developed the canon of Philippine literature in English. "If at first our [Filipino] writers wrote *in* English, later they wrought *from* it" [emphasis original] (Abad, 2004, p. 170); as such, even in literary creativity, there has already been the Filipino claim to the ownership of the language.

2.7.4 *Linguistic Effects: Linguistic Independence and Standardization*

Grammatical descriptions of PhE (i.e. Borlongan, 2011a) have been vigorously prepared. Linguistic independence of PhE has been observed as evidenced in divergences from American patterns of use in modal expressions, present progressives, expanded predicates, among others (Borlongan & Collins, this handbook; Collins & Borlongan, 2017). A pedagogical dictionary (Bautista & Butler, 2000, 2010) has been published for a time now and new entries from PhE have been introduced in the *Oxford English Dictionary* (Salazar, 2017, this handbook). And all these efforts are in the hope that standardization of PhE will soon be completed (e.g. Bautista, 2000; Borlongan, 2007; cf. Borlongan, this handbook). In consonance with Llamzon's recommendation that standard PhE be the local model, a template for teaching PhE has finally been made (Bernardo, 2013, 2017, this handbook). Though residual linguistic conservatism exists incessantly yet expectedly, no one would argue against the acceptance and legitimization of PhE. And indeed, the publication of this handbook is an important and critical step toward the codification of PhE.

2.8 Stage 5: Differentiation (1986?–Present?)

2.8.1 *Sociopolitical Background: Intense Nationalism, Internal Political Fragmentation*

From September 21, 1972, to January 17, 1981, then president Ferdinand Marcos placed the entire Philippines under military rule. Marcos' staunch critic Benigno Aquino Jr. was assassinated upon his return to the country on August 21, 1983, after years of exile with his family in the US. Internal political fragmentation peaked at the People Power Revolution of 1986, which unseated Marcos and gave rise to the Corazon Aquino presidency. The revolution is commemorated and remembered with much valor; Aquino herself is often feted as a quasi-prophet, and *Time* magazine's headline on her death in 2009 so fittingly captures the honor given to her—'The Saint of Democracy'. While democracy, or the pale imitation of it, has been regained since then, the nation has been strife with so much political crisis with two more street revolutions put up and several coups d'état staged. Indeed, a sense of nationalism has been achieved but, at the same time, whose brand of nationalism will take the country to a better state remains a question which no answer could be given in the foreseeable future.

2.8.2 Identity Constructions: Social and Cultural Diversity

A blush of social and cultural diversification may be seen when one looks at the Philippine society at present with a trajectory toward countrywide heterogeneity. While the nation has been so proud of its major and minor accomplishments, whether achieved collectively or individually, social differentiation is also beginning to be born. More than ever, there has been much appreciation of the cultural diversity in the country, including the multilingualism which comes along with it (with 183 living languages). Indeed, the Christian north is vastly different from the Muslim south and ways of life grossly vary among tribes in the highlands, communities in the plains, and settlements in the seaside. Various social groupings have been formed whether positively or negatively—there remains rather privileged access to quality education (access to elementary education in school year 2010–2011 at 95.9% and secondary education at 64.3%) and the gap between the rich and the poor is still widening (Gini index estimate for 2015 at 40.1).

2.8.3 Sociolinguistic Conditions: 'Circles of Philippine English'

Martin (2014b) asserts that, in the same way as Kachru (1985) drew his three concentric circles of Englishes, there could be circles within PhE, too. She identifies an inner circle composed of the educated elite promoting and using it, an outer circle using English but not necessarily promoting its use, and an expanding circle needing English but not having the skills to use it very well. And a fourth circle could be added, those belonging to hard-to-reach groups who totally do not know English and whose lives have been disadvantaged because of their lack of knowledge of the language (Lee & Borlongan, this handbook).

2.8.4 Linguistic Effects: Stylistic, Social, and, to a Lesser Extent, Regional Variation

Nation-internal diversifications and distinctions of language use relative to sociolinguistic groupings have been emerging recently (cf. Lee & Borlongan,

22 *Ariane Macalinga Borlongan*

this handbook). This is most apparent in sociolects like conyo English (Borlongan, 2015) at one end and yaya English (Bautista, 1982) at the other end. And then, distinct ethnolinguistic groups have also come up with their own hybridizations (cf. Gonzales, 2016, this handbook). Contrary to an earlier observation made by Gonzalez (1991), there is now evidence to prove that PhE is able to distinguish appropriate styles across registers and genres (cf. Lee & Borlongan, this handbook). Villanueva (2016) though observed that regional variation is less apparent in grammar and lexicon, which somehow validates Llamzon's claim in 1969 that, even though there would have been a number of substratal languages to influence PhE (187 languages, as mentioned earlier), the phonology of Philippine-type languages is fairly similar throughout such that any substratal influence would have been evened out.

2.9 Discussion and Conclusion

This chapter narrated the evolution of PhE using Schneider's (2003, 2007) dynamic model as its tool for historical accounting. The narrative tells of the ongoing development of the new English, and suggests its furthering in the dynamic model. While it has not consummated parameters in the later phases, it seems to be going through nativization and beyond. The Philippines has thus become one of the largest and most important English-using societies with its nativized English which it can cherish as truly its own.

Certainly, the chapter is an elaboration of Schneider's (2003, 2007) model using the Philippine experience to substantiate the theorizing he did. He writes an important note after his treatise of his model: "It goes without saying that, as with all analyses built upon periodizations and correlated parameters, this model describes an ideal constellation, and in reality room must be provided for variation, fuzzy transitions, and overlapping parameter realizations" (Schneider, 2007, p. 31). And also: "Unavoidably, like all far-reaching claims, models, being abstractions, meet with certain difficulties when faced with the messy realities of real-life situations" (p. 310). The history of PhE alludes to many instances when these stages blur, when some characteristic features of certain parameters of one stage have been carried over onto the next. The time-honored formula in historical linguistics that change does not happen overnight is even more crucial in a short history like that of PhE. The first and fifth stages have been particularly very short and thus have put parametric burdens in the stages succeeding them. Very prudently, question marks ('?') used in indicating inclusive years of each stage in the section headings in the narrative have been used to signal not only uncertainty (given that there has been a debate as to which stage to really locate PhE in the model) but also the liquidity of these periodizations.

History 23

Finally, it is important to emphasize, as an end to this historical narrative, that it has not adopted a particular point of view—be it Martin (2014a) on nativization, Borlongan (2011b, 2016) on endonormative stabilization, or Gonzales (2017) on differentiation—as a centerpiece of its discussion (which makes the use of question marks in specifying inclusive years of the stages more relevant). Instead, it has taken every important contribution from each of them to be able to tell a most beautiful story of how English has been of and by the people who once resisted imperialism through it but eventually found freedom in listening, speaking, reading, writing, thinking, and living their ideals through it.

Acknowledgments

Notes on sociopolitical history made in this narrative would be impossible if not for the discussions with Rene Escalante (presently Chairman of the National Historical Commission of the Philippines), who patiently picked up all my long-distance calls to talk about details included in this narrative. His contributions definitely go beyond mere citations of him in text. I also acknowledge two important scholars who wrote on the location of PhE in the dynamic model for their helpful comments: Wilkinson Daniel Gonzales and, of course, Edgar Schneider himself.

References

Abad, Gemino H. (2004). Filipino poetry in English: A native clearing. *World Englishes, 23*, 169–181.

Agoncillo, Teodoro A., & Alfonso, Oscar M. (1960). *A short history of the Filipino people.* Quezon, the Philippines: University of the Philippines.

Alberca, Wilfredo L. (1994). English language teaching in the Philippines during the Early American period: Lessons from the Thomasites. *Philippine Journal of Linguistics, 25*(1), 53–74.

Bautista, Ma. Lourdes S. (1982). *Yaya* English. *Philippine Studies, 30*, 377–394.

Bautista, Ma. Lourdes S. (2000). *Defining Standard Philippine English: Its status and grammatical features.* Manila, the Philippines: De La Salle University Press, Inc.

Bautista, Ma. Lourdes S. (2001a). Attitudes of English language faculty in three leading Philippine universities towards Philippine English. *Asian Englishes, 4*(1), 4–32.

Bautista, Ma. Lourdes S. (2001b). Attitudes of selected Luzon University students and faculty towards Philippine English. In Ma. Lourdes G. Tayao, Teresita P. Ignacio, & Galileo S. Zafra (Eds.), *Rosario E. Maminta in focus: Selected writings in applied linguistics* (pp. 263–273). Quezon, the Philippines: Philippine Association for Language Teaching.

Bautista, Ma. Lourdes S., & Butler, Susan. (Eds.). (2000). *Anvil-Macquarie Philippine English dictionary.* Pasig City, the Philippines: Anvil Publishing, Inc.

24 Ariane Macalinga Borlongan

Bautista, Ma. Lourdes S., & Butler, Susan. (Eds.). (2010). *Anvil-Macquarie Philippine English dictionary* (Revised ed.). Pasig City, the Philippines: Anvil Publishing, Inc.

Bernardo, Alejandro S. (2013). *Toward an endonormative pedagogic model for teaching English in Philippine higher education institutions* (Unpublished doctoral dissertation). University of Santo Tomas, Manila, the Philippines.

Bernardo, Alejandro S. (2017). Philippine English in the ESL classroom: A much closer look. *The Philippine ESL Journal, 19,* 117–144.

The Board of Educational Survey. (1925). *A survey of the educational system of the Philippine Islands.* Manila, the Philippines: Bureau of Printing.

Borlongan, Ariane Macalinga. (2007). Innovations in Standard Philippine English. In Charles C. Mann (Ed.), *Current research on English and applied linguistics: A De La Salle University special issue* (pp. 1–36). Manila, the Philippines: De La Salle University-Manila, College of Education, Department of English and Applied Linguistics.

Borlongan, Ariane Macalinga. (2009). A survey on language use, attitudes, and identity in relation to Philippine English among young generation Filipinos: An initial sample from a private university. *The Philippine ESL Journal, 3,* 74–107.

Borlongan, Ariane Macalinga. (2011a). *A grammar of the verb in Philippine English* (Unpublished doctoral dissertation). De La Salle University, Manila, the Philippines.

Borlongan, Ariane Macalinga. (2011b, November). *Relocating Philippine English in Schneider's dynamic model.* Paper presented at the 17th Annual Conference of the International Association for World Englishes, Melbourne, Australia.

Borlongan, Ariane Macalinga. (2015, October). *Conyo English: Explorations of Philippine English sociolects.* Paper presented at the colloquium titled *Contemporary studies of Philippine English* convened by Danica Salazar at the 21st Annual Conference of the International Association for World Englishes, Istanbul, Turkey.

Borlongan, Ariane Macalinga. (2016). Relocating Philippine English in Schneider's dynamic model. *Asian Englishes, 18*(3), 1–10.

Borlongan, Ariane Macalinga. (2018). Early Philippine English: A historical sociolinguistic analysis of *A survey of the educational system of the Philippine Islands* (1925). Paper presented at the special plenary panel on Philippine English at the 23rd Annual Conference of the International Association for World Englishes, Quezon, the Philippines.

Bureau of Census and Statistics. (1956). *Census of the Philippines: 1948 (Summary of population and agriculture).* Manila, the Philippines: Bureau of Printing.

Census Office of the Philippine Islands (Comp.). (1921). *Census of the Philippine Islands taken under the direction of the Philippine Legislature in the year 1918* (vol. II: Population and mortality). Manila, the Philippines: The Compiler.

Commission of the Census. (1941). *Census of the Philippines: 1939* (vol. II: Summary for the Philippines and general report for the census of population and agriculture). Manila, the Philippines: Bureau of Printing.

Collins, Peter, & Borlongan, Ariane Macalinga. (2017). Has Philippine English attained linguistic independence?: The grammatical evidence. *The Philippine ESL Journal, 19,* 10–24.

Escalante, Rene R. (2007). *The bearer of Pax Americana: The Philippine career of William H. Taft, 1900–1903.* Quezon, the Philippines: New Day Publishers.

History 25

(First) Philippine Commission. (1900). *Report of the Philippine Commission to the President* (vol. I). Washington, DC: Government Printing Office.

Gonzales, Wilkinson Daniel Wong. (2016). Trilingual code-switching using quantitative lenses: An exploratory study on Hokaglish. *Philippine Journal of Linguistics, 47*, 109–131.

Gonzales, Wilkinson Daniel Wong. (2017). Philippine Englishes. *Asian Englishes, 19*(1), 79–95.

Gonzalez, Andrew. (1991). Stylistic shifts in the English of Philippine print media. In Jenny Cheshire (Ed.), *English around the world: Sociolinguistic perspectives* (pp. 333–363). Cambridge, the United Kingdom: Cambridge University Press.

Gonzalez, Andrew. (2008). A favorable soil and climate: A transplanted language and literature. In Ma. Lourdes S. Bautista, & Kingsley Bolton (Eds.), *Philippine English: Linguistic and literary perspectives* (pp. 14–27). Hong Kong SAR, China: Hong Kong University Press.

Gonzalez, A., & Sibayan, B. P. (Eds.). (1988). *Evaluating bilingual education in the Philippines: 1974–1985*. Manila, the Philippines: Linguistic Society of the Philippines.

Gruenberg, Estrellita Valeros. (1985). *The perceived canon of Philippine literature* (Unpublished doctoral dissertation). De La Salle University, Manila, the Philippines.

Kachru, Braj B. (1982). *The other tongue: English across cultures*. Urbana: University of Illinois Press.

Kachru, Braj B. (1985). Standards, codification and sociolinguistic realism: The English language in the outer circle. In Randolph Quirk, & Henry G. Widdowson (Eds.), *English in the world: Teaching and learning the language and literatures* (pp. 11–30). Cambridge, the United Kingdom: Cambridge University Press.

Linn, Brian McAllister. (2000). *The Philippine war: 1899–1902*. Lawrence: University of Kansas Press.

Llamzon, Teodoro A. (1969). *Standard Filipino English*. Quezon, the Philippines: Ateneo University Press.

Martin, D., & the Editorial Board, the Philippine Historical Commission. (1980). *A century of education in the Philippines: 1861–1961*. Manila, the Philippines: Philippine Historical Commission.

Martin, Isabel Pefianco. (2014a). Beyond nativization?: Philippine English in Schneider's dynamic model. In Sarah Buschfeld, Thomas Hoffmann, Magnus Huber, & Alexander Kautzsch (Eds.), *The evolution of Englishes: The dynamic model and beyond* (pp. 70–85). Amsterdam, the Netherlands: John Benjamins.

Martin, Isabel Pefianco. (2014b). Philippine English revisited. *World Englishes, 33*, 50–59.

Mufwene, Salikoko S. (2001). *The ecology of language evolution*. Cambridge, the United Kingdom: Cambridge University Press.

Salazar, Danica. (2017). Philippine English in the *Oxford English Dictionary*: Recent advancements and implications for ESL in the Philippines. *The Philippine ESL Journal, 19*, 45–59.

Santos, Emma H. (1969). *A study of the roles of aptitude, attitudes and motivation in second language acquisition* (Unpublished master's thesis). Philippine Normal College, Manila, the Philippines.

Schneider, Edgar W. (2003). The dynamics of new Englishes: From identity construction to dialect birth. *Language, 79*, 233–281.

26 *Ariane Macalinga Borlongan*

Schneider, Edgar W. (2007). *Postcolonial English: Varieties of English around the world*. New York, NY: Cambridge University Press.

Villanueva, Rey John Castro. (2016). *The features of Philippine English across regions* (Unpublished doctoral dissertation). De La Salle University, Manila, the Philippines.

3 Resources

Dominik Heps and Mikhail Alic C. Go

3.1 Preamble

This chapter lists the available resources on Philippine English (PhE) and English in the Philippines. It identifies the institutions and organizations which spearhead the study of PhE as well as schools, colleges, and universities which teach, whether directly or indirectly, PhE as a course. It also mentions the datasets available (i.e. corpora and atlas) for research on PhE. An important portion of this chapter is devoted to a comprehensive bibliography of PhE and English in the Philippines. The chapter also makes a commentary on the availability and accessibility of these resources to those interested in PhE.

3.2 Institutions and Organizations

The first publication which called attention to the emergence of a local variety of English in the Philippines was written by Professor Teodoro Llamzon in 1969 at the Ateneo de Manila University in Quezon, the Philippines. Even if his proposal for a 'standard PhE' was met with criticism at that time (i.e. Gonzalez, 1972; Hidalgo, 1969), soon enough other Filipino linguists also became interested in the study of PhE. Among the institutions which did the first works on PhE aside from the Ateneo were De La Salle University (Manila, the Philippines), the Philippine Normal University (Manila, the Philippines), and the University of Santo Tomas (UST, Manila, the Philippines). At present, a course on world Englishes, which has a strong emphasis on PhE understandably, is being offered in La Salle and UST. The work of Ma. Lourdes Bautista and her students at La Salle has been particularly well-received in the world Englishes community; hence, La Salle has been strongly associated with PhE. Because Ariane Borlongan, who has also been actively researching on PhE, is based at the Tokyo University of Foreign Studies (Japan), his courses on world Englishes also give significant attention to PhE.

The study and scholarship of PhE grew alongside the development of linguistics as a discipline in the Philippines as the first scholars of PhE were the founders of the Linguistics Society of the Philippines (LSP), i.e. Teodoro Llamzon and Bonifacio Sibayan, and, a few years later, Ma. Lourdes

DOI: 10.4324/9780429427824-4

Bautista and Andrew Gonzalez. Even in recent years, officers of LSP are active scholars of PhE, i.e. Alejandro Bernardo, Shirley Dita, Marilu Madrunio, and Isabel Martin as well as the late Danilo Dayag. The society has hosted many conferences on world Englishes and PhE, including hosting the 15th Annual Conference of the International Association for World Englishes (IAWE) in 2019 in Cebu, the Philippines.

3.3 Reference Works

The first noteworthy reference work on PhE is the entry in the *Electronic World Atlas of Varieties of English* (Borlongan & Lim, 2020). It briefly describes the historical development of English in the Philippines, the status and use of PhE in different domains today, its social stratification among the countries' population, and a list of features which exist or were attested to be absent in the variety.

Furthermore, there are three different dictionaries which provide an overview on the lexicon of PhE. The first-ever dictionary which considers PhE, namely, *A Dictionary of Philippine English* (Cruz & Bautista, 1993), represents an important milestone in the codification process of the variety, albeit limited to 63 pages. The second variety-exclusive dictionary of PhE, the *Anvil-Macquarie Philippine English dictionary* (Bautista & Butler, 2010), clearly shows a progress in the development of the variety and a resulting increased interest in it, as it contains over 16,000 terms. Eventually, the third edition of *The Macquarie Dictionary: Australia's National Dictionary* (Delbridge, 1997) series not only contains examples exclusive to Australian English but also includes examples of Asian English lexicons, such as PhE among others.

3.4 Corpora

Ma. Lourdes Bautista, Danilo Dayag, and Jenifer Loy Lising of the De La Salle University in Manila, Philippines completed the compilation of the Philippine component of the International Corpus of English in 2004. This corpus follows the common design of the other components of the International Corpus of English (ICE) and thereby enhances possible comparisons between Englishes. It consists of 250 written and 250 spoken text samples of PhE. Partial tagging of the component was done by Ariane Borlongan for his dissertation, a grammar of the PhE verb phrase. He is the present Director of the component now based at the Tokyo University of Foreign Studies.

The second corpus of PhE, the Philippine parallel to the Brown Corpus (Phil-Brown), was compiled by Ariane Borlongan initially at De La Salle University and eventually at the Tokyo University of Foreign Studies. Its design and sampling period is very much similar to other Brown corpora, which allows comparisons between varieties, but, more important, diachronic studies on the variety itself. Ariane Borlongan has also begun compiling the Philippine parallel to the Before-Brown Corpus (PBB). The

Resources 29

Before-Brown Corpus is a corpus compiled by Marianne Hundt at the University of Zurich (Switzerland), which represents American and British Englishes of the 1930s. When completed, PBB should be able to tell of the development of PhE in its entire lifetime.

3.5 Bibliography

The following bibliography represents the contemporary body of work on PhE, including books, edited volumes, chapters in volumes, journal articles, and some oft-cited theses and dissertations as well as special issues of journals, all completed until 2019. This list can serve as an overview for scholars interested in the variety.

Reference Works

Bautista, Ma. Lourdes S., & Butler, Susan (2010). *Anvil-Macquarie Philippine English Dictionary*. Anvil Publishing.

Borlongan, Ariane Macalinga, & Lim, Joo Hyuk (2015). Philippine English. In Bernd Kortmann, Kerstin Lunkenheimer, & Katharina Ehret (Eds.), *The Electronic World Atlas of Varieties of English*. http://www.ewave-atlas.org/

Cruz, Isagani R., & Bautista, Ma. Lourdes S. (1993). *A Dictionary of Philippine English*. Anvil Publishing.

Delbridge, Arthur (Ed.) (1997). *The Macquarie Dictionary: Australia's National Dictionary*. The Macquarie Library.

De La Salle University. http://rzblx10.uni-regensburg.de/dbinfo/frontdoor.php?titel_id=9959 *Phil-Brown*

Special Issues

Bautista, Ma. Lourdes S. (2004). The verb in Philippine English: A preliminary analysis of modal *would*. *World Englishes, 23* (1), 113–128.

Bautista, Ma. Lourdes S., & Bolton, Kingsley (2004). Philippine English: Tensions and Transitions. *Special issue of World Englishes, 23*(1).

Bernardo, Alejandro S. (2017). Philippine English in the ESL Classroom: A much closer look. *The Philippine ESL Journal, 19*, 117–143.

Bernardo, Allan B. (2004). McKinley's Questionable Bequest: Over 100 years of English in Philippine Education. *World Englishes, 23* (1), 17–31.

Biermeier, Thomas (2017). Lexical trends in Philippine English revisited. *The Philippine ESL Journal, 19*, 25–44.

Bolton, Kingsley, & Bautista, Ma. Lourdes S. (2004). Philippine English: Tensions and transitions. *World Englishes, 23* (1), 1–5.

Bolton, Kingsley, & Butler, Susan (2004). Dictionaries and the stratification of vocabulary: Towards a new lexicography for Philippine English. *World Englishes, 23* (1), 91–112.

Borlongan, Ariane Macalinga (2017). Contemporary Perspectives on Philippine English. *The Philippine ESL Journal, 19*, 1–9.

Collins, Peter, & Borlongan, Ariane Macalinga (2017). Has Philippine English attained linguistic independence? The Grammatical Evidence. *The Philippine ESL Journal, 19*, 10–24.

30   *Dominik Heps and Mikhail Alic C. Go*

Fuchs, Robert (2017). The Americanisation of Philippine English: Recent diachronic change in spelling and lexis. *The Philippine ESL Journal, 19*, 60–83.

Salazar, D. (2017). Philippine English in the Oxford English Dictionary: Recent advancements and implications for ESL in the Philippines. *The Philippine ESL Journal, 19*, 45–59.

Schneider, Edgar W. (2017). Philippine English on the move: An afterword. *The Philippine ESL Journal, 19*, 145–148.

Shirley, Dita N., & De Leon, Kristine D. (2017). The intelligibility and comprehensibility of Philippine English to EFL speakers. *The Philippine ESL Journal, 19*, 100–116

Tayao, Ma. Lourdes G. (2004). The evolving study of Philippine English phonology. *World Englishes, 23* (1), 77–90.

Books and Monographs

Alberca, Wilfredo L. (1978). *The distinctive features of Philippine English in the mass media* (Unpublished doctoral dissertation). University of Santo Tomas.

Bautista, Ma. Lourdes S. (2000). *Defining standard Philippine English: Its status and grammatical features.* De La Salle University.

Biermeier, Thomas (2008). *Word-formation in New Englishes: A corpus-based analysis.* LIT Verlag.

Borlongan, Ariane Macalinga (2011). *A grammar of the verb in Philippine English.* De La Salle University.

Gonzalez, Andrew B. FSC, & Alberca, Wilfredo L. (1978). *Philippine English of the mass media.* De La Salle University.

Gonzalez, Andrew B. FSC, Jambalos, Thelma V., & Romero, Ma. Corona Salcedo (2003). *Three studies on Philippine English across generations: Towards an integration and some implications.* Linguistic Society of the Philippines.

Hermosa, Eleanor Eme E. (1986). *Filipino English: A study in contextualization* (Unpublished doctoral dissertation). National University of Singapore.

Llamzon, Teodoro A. (1969). *Standard Filipino English.* Ateneo de Manila University.

Martinez, Norma D. (1975). *Standard Filipino English pronunciation.* National Book Store.

Platt, John Talbot, Weber, Heidi, & Ho, Mian Lian (1984). *The New Englishes.* Routledge & Kegan Paul.

Thompson, Roger M. (2003). *Filipino English and Taglish: Language switching from multiple perspectives.* John Benjamins Publishing Company.

Villanueva, Rey John Castro (2016). *The features of Philippine English across regions* (Unpublished doctoral dissertation). De La Salle University.

Edited Volumes

Abad, Gemino, Evasco, Marjorie M., Pantoja-Hidalgo, Cristina, & Jose, F. Sionil (1997). Standards in Philippine English: The writers' forum. In Ma. Lourdes S. Bautista (Ed.), *English is an Asian language: The Philippine context* (pp. 163–176). The Macquarie Library.

Bautista, Ma. Lourdes S. (1997). The lexicon of Philippine English. In Ma. Lourdes S. Bautista (Ed.), *English is an Asian language: The Philippine context* (pp. 49–72). The Macquarie Library.

Resources 31

Bautista, Ma. Lourdes S. (2000). The grammatical features of educated Philippine English. In Ma. Lourdes S. Bautista, Teodoro A. Llamzon, & Bonifacio P. Sibayan (Eds.), *Parangal cang Brother Andrew: Festschrift for Andrew Gonzalez on his sixtieth birthday* (pp. 146–158). Linguistic Society of the Philippines.

Bautista, Ma. Lourdes S. (2008). Investigating the grammatical features of Philippine English. In Ma. Lourdes S. Bautista, & Kingsley Bolton (Eds.), *Philippine English: Linguistic and literary perspectives* (pp. 201–218). Hong Kong University Press.

Bautista, Ma. Lourdes S. (2011). Some notes on 'no in Philippine English. In Ma. Lourdes S. Bautista (Ed.), *Studies on Philippine English: Exploring the Philippine component of the International Corpus of English* (pp. 75–89). Anvil Publishing.

Bolasco, Ma. Karina A., Lacaba, Jose F., Rodriguez, Gloria F., & Yambot, Isagani (1997). Standards in Philippine English: Forum of representatives of newspaper and book publishing. In Ma. Lourdes S. Bautista (Ed.), *English is an Asian language: The Philippine context* (pp. 147–162). The Macquarie Library.

Bolton (Eds.), *Philippine English: Linguistic and literary perspectives* (pp. 67–81). Hong Kong University Press.

Bolton, Kingsley (2000). Hong Kong English, Philippine English, and the future of Asian Englishes. In Ma. Lourdes S. Bautista, Teodoro. A. Llamzon, & Bonifacio P. Sibayan (Eds.), *Parangal cang Brother Andrew: Festschrift for Andrew Gonzalez on his sixtieth birthday* (pp. 93–114). Linguistic Society of the Philippines.

Bolton, Kingsley (2005). Globalization and Asian Englishes: The local and the global in Asian English-language newspapers. In Danilo T. Dayag, & J. Stephen Quakenbush (Eds.), *Linguistics and language education in the Philippines and beyond: A Festschrift in honor of Ma. Lourdes S. Bautista* (pp. 95–124). Linguistic Society of the Philippines.

Bolton, Kingsley, & Butler, Susan (2008). Lexicography and the description of Philippine English vocabulary. In Ma. Lourdes S. Bautista, & Kingsley Bolton (Eds.), *Philippine English: Linguistic and literary perspectives* (pp. 175–200). Hong Kong University Press.

Borlongan, Ariane Macalinga (2011b). Some aspects of the morphosyntax of Philippine English. In Ma. Lourdes S. Bautista (Ed.), *Studies on Philippine English: Exploring the Philippine component of the International Corpus of English* (pp. 187–199). Anvil Publishing.

Coronel, Lilian (2011). Patterns of intensifier usage in Philippine English. In Ma. Lourdes S. Bautista (Ed.), *Studies on Philippine English: Exploring the Philippine component of the International Corpus of English* (pp. 93–116). Anvil Publishing.

Dayag, Danilo T. (2005). Epistemic modality, concessives, and interpersonal meaning in L2 newspaper editorials. In Danilo T. Dayag, & J. Stephen Quakenbush (Eds.), *Linguistics and language education in the Philippines and beyond: A Festschrift in honor of Ma. Lourdes S. Bautista* (pp. 125–149). Linguistic Society of the Philippines.

Dayag, Danilo T. (2008). English-language media in the Philippines: Description and research. In Ma. Lourdes S. Bautista, & Kingsley Bolton (Eds.), *Philippine English: Linguistic and literary perspectives* (pp. 49–66). Hong Kong University Press.

Dita, Shirley. N. (2011). The grammar and semantics of adverbial disjuncts in Philippine English. In Ma. Lourdes S. Bautista (Ed.), *Studies on Philippine English:*

32   Dominik Heps and Mikhail Alic C. Go

Exploring the Philippine component of the International Corpus of English (pp. 33–50). Anvil Publishing.

Gonzalez, Andrew B. FSC (1997a). The history of English in the Philippines. In Ma. Lourdes S. Bautista (Ed.), *English is an Asian language: The Philippine context* (pp. 25–40). The Macquarie Library.

Gonzalez, Andrew B. FSC (2005). Distinctive grammatical features of Philippine literature in English: Influencing or influenced? In Danilo T. Dayag, & J. Stephen Quakenbush (Eds.), *Linguistics and language education in the Philippines and beyond: A Festschrift in honor of Ma. Lourdes S. Bautista* (pp. 15–26). Linguistic Society of the Philippines.

Linguistic Society of the Philippines.

Llamzon, Teodoro A. (1997). The phonology of Philippine English. In Ma. Lourdes S. Bautista (Ed.), *English is an Asian language: The Philippine context* (pp. 41–48). The Macquarie Library.

Llamzon, Teodoro A. (2000). Philippine English revisited. In Ma. Lourdes S. Bautista, Teodoro A. Llamzon, & Bonifacio P. Sibayan (Eds.), *Parangal cang Brother Andrew: Festschrift for Andrew Gonzalez on his sixtieth birthday* (pp. 138–145).

Marquez, Jeena Rani (1999). When *po* disappears: The linguistic construction of politeness in Philippine English. In Ma. Lourdes S. Bautista, & Grace O. Tan (Eds.), *The Filipino bilingual: A multidisciplinary perspective – Festschrift in honor of Emy M. Pascasio* (pp. 44–49). Linguistic Society of the Philippines.

McFarland, Curtis D. (2008). Linguistic diversity and English in the Philippines. In Ma. Lourdes S. Bautista, & Kingsley Bolton (Eds.), *Philippine English: Linguistic and literary perspectives* (pp. 131–156). Hong Kong University Press.

Nelson, Gerald (2005). Expressing future time in Philippine English. In Danilo T. Dayag, & J. Stephen Quakenbush (Eds.), *Linguistics and language education in the Philippines and beyond: A Festschrift in honor of Ma. Lourdes S. Bautista* (pp. 41–60). Linguistic Society of the Philippines.

Peña, Phebe S. (1997). Philippine English in the classroom. In Ma. Lourdes S. Bautista (Ed.), *English is an Asian language: The Philippine context* (pp. 87–102). The Macquarie Library.

Schneider, Edgar W. (2005). The subjunctive in Philippine English. In Danilo T. Dayag, & J. Stephen Quakenbush (Eds.), *Linguistics and language education in the Philippines and beyond: A Festschrift in honor of Ma. Lourdes S. Bautista* (pp. 27–40). Linguistic Society of the Philippines.

Schneider, Edgar W. (2011). The subjunctive in Philippine English – an updated assessment. In Ma. Lourdes S. Bautista (Ed.), *Studies on Philippine English: Exploring the Philippine component of the International Corpus of English* (pp. 159–173). Anvil Publishing.

Tayao, Ma. Lourdes G. (2008). A lectal description of the phonological features of Philippine English. In Ma. Lourdes S. Bautista, & Kingsley Bolton (Eds.), *Philippine English: Linguistic and literary perspectives* (pp. 157–174). Hong Kong University Press.

Tupas, T. Ruanni F. (1999). Coping up with English today. In Ma. Lourdes S. Bautista, & Grace O. Tan (Eds.), *The Filipino bilingual: A multidisciplinary perspective – Festschrift in honor of Emy M. Pascasio* (pp. 127–131). Linguistic Society of the Philippines.

Tupas, T. Ruanni F. (2008). World Englishes or worlds of English? Pitfalls of a post-colonial discourse in Philippine English. In Ma. Lourdes S. Bautista, & Kingsley..

Resources 33

Chapters in Other Edited Volumes

Bautista, Ma. Lourdes S. (1996). Notes on three sub-varieties of Philippine English. In Ma. Lourdes S. Bautista (Ed.), *Readings in Philippine sociolinguistics* (pp. 93–101). De La Salle University Press.

Bautista, Ma. Lourdes S. (2001a). Attitudes of selected Luzon University students and faculty towards Philippine English. In Ma. Lourdes G. Tayao, Teresita P. Ignacio, & Galileo S. Zafra (Eds.), *Rosario E. Maminta in focus: Selected writings in applied linguistics* (pp. 236–273). Philippine Association for Language Teaching.

Bautista, Ma. Lourdes S. (2001b). Introducing the Philippine component of the International Corpus of English. In Edilberta C. Bala (Eds.) *Parangal sa Philippine Normal University: Festschrift for Philippine Normal University on its 100th foundation anniversary* (pp. 341–351). Philippine Normal University.

Bautista, Ma. Lourdes S. (2010). Comparing spoken and written text-types in Singapore English and Philippine English. In David Jonathan Y. Bayot (Ed.), *Inter/Sections: Isagani R. Cruz and friends* (pp. 175–200). Anvil Publishing.

Bautista, Ma. Lourdes S. (2010). Exemplary analyses of the Philippine English corpus. In Loren Billings, & Nelleke Goudswaard (Eds.), *Piakandatu ami Dr. Howard P. McKaughan* (pp. 5–23). Linguistic Society of the Philippines.

Bautista, Ma. Lourdes S., & Gonzalez, Andrew B. (2006). Southeast Asian Englishes. In Braj B. Kachru, Yamuna Kachru, & Cecil L. Nelson (Eds.), *The handbook of World Englishes* (pp. 130–144). Blackwell Publishing.

Bautista, Ma. Lourdes S., & McArthur, Tom. (1992). Philippine English. In T. McArthur (Ed.), *The Oxford companion to the English language* (pp. 765–767). Oxford University Press.

Biermeier, Thomas (2009). Word formation in New Englishes: Properties and trends. In Thomas Hoffman, & Lucia Siebers (Eds.), *World Englishes – Problems, properties and prospects: Selected papers from the 13th IAWE Conference* (pp. 331–349). John Benjamins Publishing Company.

Borlongan, Ariane Macalinga (2007). Innovations in standard Philippine English. In Charles C. Mann (Ed.), *Current research on English and applied linguistics: A De La Salle University special issue* (pp. 1–36). De La Salle University Press.

Borlongan, Ariane Macalinga (2011). The clerical aspects of English language teaching in the Philippines. In Shirley N. Dita (Ed.), *Issues and trends in applied linguistics in the Philippines: A decade in retrospect* (pp. 12–22). Anvil Publishing.

Collins, Peter (2015). Recent diachronic change in the progressive in Philippine English. In Peter Collins (Ed.), *Grammatical change in English world-wide* (pp. 271–296). John Benjamins Publishing Company.

Collins, Peter, Borlongan, Ariane Macalinga, Lim, Joo Hyuk, & Yao, Xinyue (2014). The subjunctive mood in Philippine English: A diachronic study. In Simone E. Pfenninger, Olga Timofeeva, Anne-Christine Gardner, Alpo Honkapohja, Marianne Hundt, & Daniel Schreier (Eds.), *Contact, variation, and change in the history of English* (pp. 259–280). John Benjamins Publishing Company.

Collins, Peter, Yao, Xinyue, & Borlongan, Ariane Macalinga (2014). Relative clauses in Philippine English: A diachronic perspective. In Lieven Vandelanotte, Kristin Davidse, Caroline Gentens, & Ditte Kimps (Eds.), *Recent advances in corpus linguistics: Developing and exploiting corpora* (pp. 125–146). Rodopi.

34 *Dominik Heps and Mikhail Alic C. Go*

Dayag, Danilo T. (2012). Philippine English. In Ee-Ling Low, & Azirah Hashim (Eds.), *English in Southeast Asia: Features, policy and language in use* (pp. 91–100). John Benjamins Publishing Company.

Gonzalez, Andrew B. FSC (1982). English in the Philippine mass media. In John B. Pride (Ed.), *New Englishes* (pp. 211–226). Newbury House Publishers.

Gonzalez, Andrew B. FSC (1983). When does an error become a feature of Philippine English? In Richard B. Noss (Ed.), *Varieties of English in Southeast Asia* (pp. 150–172). SEAMEO Regional Language Centre.

Gonzalez, Andrew B. FSC (1986). Philippine English. In Loreto Todd, & Ian Hancock (Eds.), *International English usage* (pp. 344–346). Croon Helm.

Gonzalez, Andrew B. FSC (1991a). Stylistic shifts in the English of the Philippine print media. In Jenny Cheshire (Ed.), *English around the World: Sociolinguistic perspectives* (pp. 333–363). Cambridge University Press.

Gonzalez, Andrew B. FSC (1991b). The Philippine variety of English and the problem of standardization. In Makhan L. Tickoo (Ed.), *Languages & standards: Issues, attitudes, case studies* (pp. 86–96). SEAMEO Regional Language Centre.

Gonzalez, Andrew B. FSC (1992). Philippine English. In Tom McArthur (Ed.), *The Oxford companion to the English Language* (pp. 765–767). Oxford University Press.

Gonzalez, Andrew B. FSC (1995). The cultural content in English as an international auxiliary language (EIAL): Problems and issues. In Makhan Tickoo (Ed.), *Language and culture in multilingual societies: Viewpoints and visions* (pp. 54–63). SEAMEO Regional Language Centre.

Gonzalez, Andrew B. FSC (1997b). Philippine English: A variety in search of legitimation. In Edgar W. Schneider (Ed.), *Englishes around the world volume 2: Caribbean, Africa, Asia, Australasia. Studies in honour of Manfred Gorlach* (pp. 205–212). John Benjamins Publishing Company.

Gonzalez, Andrew B. FSC (2002). The transplantation of language to a different culture: Possibilities and alternatives. In Corazon D. Villareal, Lily Rose R. Tope, & Patricia May B. Jurilla (Eds.), *Ruptures & departures: Language and culture in Southeast Asia* (pp. 106–111). University of the Philippines Press.

Hundt, Marianne (2009). Global feature – local norms? A case study on the progressive passive. In Thomas Hoffman, & Lucia Siebers (Eds.), *World Englishes – Problems, properties and prospects: Selected papers from the 13th IAWE Conference* (pp. 287–308). John Benjamins Publishing Company.

Martin, Isabel Pefianco (2014). Beyond nativization? Philippine English in Schneider's dynamic model. In S. Buschfeld, T. Hoffmann, M. Huber, & A. Kautzsch (Eds.), *The evolution of Englishes* (pp. 70–85). John Benjamins Publishing Company.

Regala-Flores, Eden (2012). An exploratory study of the phonological features of basilectal Philippine English: A case of some Cebuano speakers. In Shirley N. Dita (Ed.) *Issues and trends in applied linguistics in the Philippines: A decade of retrospect* (pp. 191–198). Anvil Publishing.

Tayao, Ma. Lourdes G. (2004). Philippine English: Phonology. In Edgar W. Schneider, Kate Burridge, Bernd Kortmann, Rajend Mesthrie, & Clive Upton (Eds.), *A handbook of varieties of English: A multimedia reference tool* (pp. 1047–1061). Mouton de Gruyter.

Tayao, Ma. Lourdes G. (2006). A transplant takes root: Philippine English and education. In Shondel J. Nero (Ed.), *Dialects, Englishes, creoles, and education* (pp. 261–282). Lawrence Erlbaum Associates.

Tinio, Maria T. (2013). Nimble tongues: Philippine English and the feminization of labour. In Lionel Wee, Robbie B. H. Goh, & Lisa Lim (Eds.), *The politics of English: South Asia, Southeast Asia and the Asia Pacific* (pp. 205–224). John Benjamins Publishing Company.

Zipp, Lena, & Bernaisch, Tobias (2012). Particle verbs across first and second language varieties of English. In Marianne Hundt, & Ulrike Gut (Eds.) *Mapping unity and diversity world-wide* (pp. 167–196). John Benjamins Publishing Company.

Journal Articles

Astillero, Susan Fresnido (2017). Linguistic Schoolscape: Studying the Place of English and Philippine Languages of Irosin Secondary School. *Asia Pacific Journal of Education, Arts and Sciences, 4* (4), 30–37.

Bautista, Ma. Lourdes S. (1982). Yaya English. *Philippine Studies, 30*, 377–394.

Bautista, Ma. Lourdes S. (1998a). Tagalog-English Code-Switching and the Lexicon of Philippine English. *Asian Englishes, 1* (1), 51–67.

Bautista, Ma. Lourdes S. (1998b). Varieties of English (in General) and Philippine English (in Particular). *Tanglaw Journal, 6* (1), 78–90.

Bautista, Ma. Lourdes S. (2000). Studies of Philippine English in the Philippines. *Philippine Journal of Linguistics, 31* (1), 39–65.

Bautista, Ma. Lourdes S. (2001a). Attitudes of English Language Faculty in Three Leading Philippine Universities towards Philippine English. *Asian Englishes, 4* (1), 4–32.

Bautista, Ma. Lourdes S. (2001b). Studies of Philippine English: Implications for English Language Teaching in the Philippines. *Journal of Southeast Asian Education, 2* (2), 71–295.

Bautista, Ma. Lourdes S. (2004). An Overview of the Philippine Component of the International Corpus of English. *Asian Englishes, 7* (2), 8–27.

Bautista, Ma. Lourdes S., & Rañosa-Madrunio, Marilu B. (2004). Comparing Letters of Complaint in Philippine English and Singaporean English: Reactions Using a Semantic Differential Scale. *Tanglaw, 10* (2), 1–17.

Bernardo, Alejandro S. (2013). English (es) in College English Textbooks in the Philippines. *US-China Foreign Language, 11* (5), 355–380.

Bernardo, Alejandro S., & Rañosa-Madrunio, Marilou (2015). A Framework for Designing a Philippine-English-Based Pedagogic Model for Teaching English Grammar. *Asian Journal of English Language Studies, 3*, 67–98.

Berowa, Annie Mae C. (2017). Expressing Futurity in the Philippine Academic Announcements. *Online Journal of New Horizons in Education, 7* (3), 33–44.

Bolton, Kingsley (2008). English in Asia, Asian Englishes, and the Issue of Proficiency. *English Today, 24* (2), 3–12.

Borlongan, Ariane Macalinga (2008). Tag Questions in Philippine English. *Philippine Journal of Linguistics, 39* (1–2), 109–134.

Borlongan, Ariane Macalinga (2009). A Survey on Language Use, Attitudes, and Identity in Relation to Philippine English among Young Generation Filipinos: An Initial Sample from a Private University. *The Philippine ESL Journal, 3*, 74–107.

Borlongan, Ariane Macalinga (2011). The Preparation and Writing of a Grammar of the Verb in Philippine English. *The Philippine ESL Journal, 7*, 120–123.

36 *Dominik Heps and Mikhail Alic C. Go*

Borlongan, Ariane Macalinga, & Lim, JooHyuk (2011). Tagalog Particles in Philippine English: The Case of Ba, Na, 'No, and Pa. *Philippine Journal of Linguistics, 42*, 58–74.

Borlongan, Ariane Macalinga (2013). Corpus-based Works on the Philippine English Verb System. *Asian English Studies, 15*, 69–90.

Borlongan, Ariane Macalinga (2016). Relocating Philippine English in Schneider's Dynamic Model. *Asian Englishes, 18* (3), 1–10.

Borlongan, Ariane Macalinga (2017). Dissertation Acknowledgements in Philippine English. *Komaba Journal of English Education, 8*, 15–35.

Borlongan, Ariane Macalinga, Collins, Peter, and Yao, Xinyue (2014). Modality in Philippine English: A Diachronic Study. *Journal of English Linguistics, 42* (1), 68–88.

Borlongan, Ariane Macalinga, & Dita, Shirley N. (2015). Taking a Look at Expanded Predicates in Philippine English across Time. *Asian Englishes, 17* (3), 1–8.

Borlongan, Ariane Macalinga, & Gonzales, Wilkinson Daniel W. (2017). Openings of Telephone Conversations in Philippine English. *Asian Journal of English Language Studies, 5*, 1–13.

Casambre, Nelia G. (1986). What Is Filipino English? *Philippine Journal for Language Teaching, 14* (1–4), 34–49.

Castelo, Lutgarda M. (1972). Verb Usage in Educated Filipino English. *International Review of Applied Linguistics in Language Teaching, 10* (2), 153–165.

Castro, Maria Corazon A., & Roh, Teri Rose Dominica G. (2013). The Effect of Language Attitudes on Learner Preferences: A Study on South Koreans' Perceptions of the Philippine English Accent. *ELTWorldOnline.com, 5*, 1–22.

Collins, Peter (2008). The Progressive Aspect in World Englishes: A Corpus-based Study. *Australian Journal of Linguistics, 28* (2), 225–249.

Collins, Peter (2009). Extended Uses of would in some Asian Englishes. *Asian Englishes, 12* (2), 34–47.

Collins, Peter, Borlongan, Ariane Macalinga, & Yao, Xinyue (2014). Modality in Philippine English: A Diachronic Study. *Journal of English Linguistics, 42* (1), 68–88.

Collins, P. (2016). Grammatical Change in the Verb Phrase in Contemporary Philippine English. *An International Journal of Asian Literatures, Cultures and Englishes, 10* (2), 50–76.

David, Aika Carla M. (2018). The Modal Must in Philippine English: A Corpus-Based Analysis. *Journal of English as an International Language, 13* (2.2), 211–218.

Dayag, Danilo T. (1997). Illocutionary Acts in Philippine English Editorials. *Teaching English for Specific Purposes, 10* (1), 109–139.

Dayag, Danilo T. (2004a). Evidentiality in Philippine English and Filipino Newspaper Editorials. *Philippine Journal of Linguistics, 35* (2), 51–66.

Dayag, Danilo T. (2004b). Negotiating Evaluation in Newspaper Editorials in Philippine English. *Asian Englishes, 7* (2), 28–51.

Dayag, Danilo T. (2004c). Editorializing in L2: The Case of Philippine English. *Asia Pacific Education Review, 5* (1), 100–109.

Dela Rosa, John Paul, Lintao, Rachelle, & Dela Cruz, Maria Grace (2015). A Contrastive Rhetoric Analysis of Job Application Letters in Philippine English and American English. *Philippine Journal of Linguistics, 46*, 68–88.

Dimaculangan, Nimfa G. (2018). Another Look into Philippine English: Towards Users' Awareness and Celebration. *International Journal of Advanced Research and Publications, 2* (8), 17–22.

Dimaculangan, Nimfa G., & Gustilo, Leah E. (2017). Lexical Patterns in the Early 21st Century Philippine English Writing. *Advanced Science Letters, 23* (2), 1094–1098.

Dimaculangan, Nimfa G., & Gustilo, Leah E. (2018). A Closer Look at Philippine English Word-Formation Frameworks. *Advanced Science Letters, 24* (11), 8384–8388.

Fuchs, Robert (2017). The Americanization of Philippine English: Recent Diachronic Change in Spelling and Lexis. *The Philippine ESL Journal, 19,* 64–87.

Gaerlan, Maianne Jennifer M. (2008). Discourse Organization of Want Ads in Philippine English and Qatari English Newspapers. *Philippine Journal of Linguistics, 39,* 41–54.

Gonzalez, Andrew B. FSC (1976). Content in English Language Materials in the Philippines: A Case Study of Cultural and Linguistic Emancipation. *Philippine Studies, 24* (4), 443–454.

Gonzalez, Andrew B. FSC (1984). Philippine English across Generations: The Sound System. *DLSU Dialogue, 20* (1), 1–26.

Gonzales, Sydney D. (2002). Politeness in Letters to the Editor in Philippine English, American English, and Singaporean English. *Philippine Journal of Linguistics, 33* (2), 19–37.

Gonzales, Wilkinson Daniel W. (2017). Philippine Englishes. *Asian Englishes, 19* (1), 79–95.

Gonzales, Wilkinson Daniel W., & Dita, Shirley N. (2018). Split Infinitives across World Englishes: A Corpus-Based Investigation. *Asian Englishes, 20* (3), 242–267.

Gustilo, Leah E. (2002). A Contrastive Analysis of American English and Philippine English News Leads. *Philippine Journal of Linguistics, 33* (2), 53–66.

Gustilo, Leah E. (2009). Although If Is More Frequent than Whether…: An Analysis of the Uses of Adverbial Clauses in Philippine English Research Articles. *The Philippine ESL Journal, 4,* 24–44.

Gustilo, Leah E. (2011). Modal Auxiliaries in Philippine English Newspapers: A Corpus-Based Analysis. *The Philippine ESL Journal, 6,* 81–109.

Gustilo, Leah E., & Dimaculangan, Nimfa (2018). Attitudes of Filipino English Teachers Toward 21st Century Philippine English Writing. *Advanced Science Letters, 24* (11), 8349–8352.

Hernandez, Hjalmar Punla (2017). A (Forensic) Stylistic Analysis of Adverbials of Attitude and Emphasis in Supreme Court Decisions in Philippine English. *Indonesian Journal of Applied Linguistics, 7* (2), 455–466.

Hundt, Marianne (2006). The Committee has/have decided…: On Concord Patterns with Collective Nouns in Inner- and Outer-Circle Varieties of English. *Journal of English Linguistics, 34* (3), 206–232.

Imperial, Rowland Anthony (2014). Lexical Variation in Philippine English: The Case of Deontic MUST and HAVE TO. *Philippine Journal of Linguistics, 45* (1), 1–18.

Jin-pei, Zhang (2013). Compliments and Compliment Responses in Philippine English. *GEMA Online Journal of Language Studies, 13* (1), 25–41.

38   *Dominik Heps and Mikhail Alic C. Go*

Jubilado, Rodney C. (2015). Where is the CR? A Description of Philippine English in Hawaii. *The Philippine ESL Journal, 17,* 86–101.

Kwan Laurel, R. (2005). Pinoy English: Language, Imagination and Philippine Literature. *Philippine Studies, 53* (4), 532–562.

Llamzon, Teodoro A. (1986). Life Cycle of New Englishes: Restriction Phase of Filipino English. *English World-Wide, 7* (1), 101–125.

Lesho, Marivic (2017). Philippine English (Metro Manila Acrolect). *Journal of the International Phonetic Association, 48* (3), 357–370.

Mabuan, Romualdo Atibagos (2017). A Constrastive Rhetorical Analysis of Philippine and Sri Lankan English News Commentaries. *Indonesian Journal of Applied Linguistics, 6* (2), 330–340.

Magpale-Jang, Teri An Joy G., & Ferrer, Ramsey S. (2015). She likes to learn/learning English… On Subjectless Nonfinite Clauses as Monotransitive Variants of Verbal Complements in Philippine English. *The Philippine ESL Journal, 14,* 91–104.

Malicsi, Jonathan (2010). Philippine English: A Case of Language Drift. 立命館言語文化研究, *22* (1), 29–58.

Martin, Isabel Pefianco (2014). Philippine English Revisited. *World Englishes, 33* (1), 50–59.

Martin, Isabel Pefianco (2019). Philippine English in Retrospect and Prospect. *World Englishes, 38* (1–2), 134–143.

McKaughan, Howard (1993). Toward a Standard Philippine English. *Philippine Journal of Linguistics, 24* (2), 41–55.

Mercado, Felixberto M. (2008). Cognitive Structuring of Research Articles in Philippine English. *Philippine Journal of Linguistics, 39,* 15–40.

Morales, Miren M. (2013). Examining the Usage of Actually and in Fact in Philippine English through a Corpus-Based Analysis. *The Philippine ESL Journal, 10,* 88–124.

Nelson, Gerald (2005). The Core and Periphery of World Englishes: A Corpus-Based Exploration. *World Englishes, 25* (1), 115–129.

Pankratz, Kelly (2004). Philippine English vs. the TOEFL: Examining the Validity of Structure and Written Expression Questions. *Asian Englishes, 7* (2), 74–102.

Pariña, Jose Cristina M., & Cruz, Selwyn (2015). An Investigation of the Complexity of Verb Phrases in the ICE of Four Asian Countries. *Malaysian Journal of Languages and Linguistics (MJLL), 4* (1), 43–54.

Pillai, Stefanie, Manueli, Maria Kristina, & Dumanig, Francisco P. (2010). Monophthong Vowels in Malaysian and Philippine English: An Exploratory Study. *Philippine Journal of Linguistics, 41,* 80–93.

Pulido, Dennis Herrera (2011). A Systemic Functional Analysis of Philippine English Newspaper Editorials. *Tesol Journal, 4* (1), 52–63.

Rañosa-Madrunio, Marilu B. (2004a). The Discourse Organization of Letters of Complaint to Editors in Philippine English and Singapore English. *Philippine Journal of Linguistics, 35* (2), 67–98.

Rañosa-Madrunio, Marilu B. (2004b). The Linguistic Features of Complaint Letters to Editors in Philippine English and Singapore English. *Asian Englishes, 7* (2), 52–73.

Regala-Flores, Eden (2014). Phonological Features of Basilectal Philippine English: An Exploratory Study. *International Journal of English and Literature, 5* (6), 128–140.

Samida, Deepak K., & Takahashi, Junichi (2013). World Englishes (3): Malaysian and Philippine English. 北海道文教大学論集, *14*, 71–78.

Schneider, Edgar W. (2008). How to trace Structural Nativization: Particle Verbs in World Englishes. *World Englishes, 23* (2), 227–249.

Schneider, Edgar W. (2016). Hybrid Englishes: An Exploratory Survey. *World Englishes, 35*, 339–354.

Szmrecsanyi, Benedikt, & Kortmann, Bernd. (2009). The Morphosyntax of Varieties of English Worldwide: A Quantitative Perspective. *Lingua, 119* (11), 1643–1663.

Tarrayo, Veronico N. (2011). Metatext in Results-and-Discussion Sections of ESL/EFL Research: A Contrastive Analysis of Philippine English, Taiwanese English, and Iranian English. *Journal on English Language Teaching, 1* (3), 39–52.

Torres, Joel Mayo, & Alieto, Ericson Olario (2019). Acceptability of Philippine English Grammatical and Lexical Items among Pre-service Teachers. *The Asian EFL Journal, 21* (2.3), 158–181.

Tupas, T. Ruanni F. (2004). The Politics of Philippine English: Neocolonialism, Global Politics, and the Problem of Postcolonialism. *World Englishes, 23* (1), 47–58.

Yao, Xinyue, & Collins, Peter (2018). Exploring Grammatical Colloquialisation in Non-native English: A Case Study of Philippine English. *English Language & Linguistics, 22* (3), 457–482.

Yumul-Florendo, Maria Rosario (2012). Initial Study of Emerging Features of Academic Philippine English among Freshmen in the University of the Philippines Baguio. *Educational Research, 3* (7), 566–571.

3.6 Conclusion

Over 50 years ago Llamzon (1969) took the first step in establishing the term PhE. Various scholars have followed, showing interest in studying and conducting research on the variety, and all this even led to a foreign scholar (Tay, 1991) claiming that PhE is one of the most widely explored South East Asian varieties of English. The present body of research shows works belonging to several linguistic fields and addressing common areas of interest within the 'world Englishes paradigm', such as descriptions of variety-exclusive features, attitudinal studies, and corpus research among others. Nevertheless, there are still issues which are underresearched; e.g. the influence of different substratal languages on PhE or more fine-grained analyses of the social dimension. But as the variety itself continues to develop and provide new ground for future research, upcoming scholars will surely follow in the footsteps of previous scholars – especially the contributors of this work – to take on these new challenges.

References

Bautista, Ma. Lourdes S., & Butler, Susan (2010). *Anvil-Macquarie Philippine English Dictionary*. Anvil Publishing.

Borlongan, Ariane Macalinga, & Lim, Joo Hyuk (2020). Philippine English. In Bernd Kortmann, Kerstin Lunkenheimer, & Katharina Ehret (Eds.), *The Electronic World Atlas of Varieties of English*. http://www.ewave-atlas.org/

40 *Dominik Heps and Mikhail Alic C. Go*

Cruz, Isagani R., & Bautista, Ma. Lourdes S. (1993). *A Dictionary of Philippine English*. Anvil Publishing.

Delbridge, Arthur (Ed.) (1997). *The Macquarie Dictionary: Australia's National Dictionary*. The Macquarie Library.

Gonzalez, Andrew. (1972). Review of Teodoro A. Llamzon's *Standard Filipino English*. *Philippine Journal of Language Teaching, 7*(1–2), 93–98.

Hidalgo, Cesar A. (1970). Review of Teodoro A. Llamzon's *Standard Filipino English*. *Philippine Journal of Linguistics, 1*(1), 129–132.

Llamzon, Teodoro A. (1969). *Standard Filipino English*. Ateneo de Manila University.

Philippine Component of the International Corpus of English. (2004). De La Salle University. http://rzblx10.uni-regensburg.de/dbinfo/frontdoor.php?titel_id=9959 *Phil-Brown*

Tay, Mary W. J. (1991). Southeast Asia and Hong Kong. In Jenny Cheshire (Ed.), *English Around the World: Sociolinguistic Perspectives* (pp. 319–332). Cambridge University Press.

Special Feature

Ma. Lourdes Bautista and Philippine English[1]

Anne Pakir

It is such a great privilege to write this tribute to Professor Ma. Lourdes Bautista, whom we all affectionately refer to as 'Tish'. Fittingly, this tribute to Tish and her influence on scholarship on Philippine English (PhE) is part of this volume titled *Philippine English: Development, Structure and Sociology of English in the Philippines*, edited by Ariane Borlongan and published by Routledge in their series on world Englishes. It is a second festschrift for Tish, the first one being published more than a decade ago, to which I will refer again later.

I am excited to add more than a few words in honor of Tish, although a lot has already been said. We all recognize Tish as an outstanding scholar of linguistics, of Philippine linguistics, sociolinguistics, world Englishes, and, above all, as a teacher in the English language landscape of the Philippines. An established visionary, she is the role model for several generations of linguists and language educators in the Philippines, having trained and nurtured most of them into worldwide scholars and outstanding teachers themselves, including Ariane Borlongan, Danilo Dayag, Shirley Dita, and Marilu Madrunio. This volume acknowledges the invaluable contributions made by Tish as a teacher, a scholar, and a humanist above all. It will add immensely to the earlier mentioned work, *Linguistics and Language Education in the Philippines and Beyond: A Festschrift in Honour of Ma. Lourdes S. Bautista*, published by the Linguistic Society of the Philippines in 2005. I wished the earlier festschrift had reached a far wider audience outside of the Philippines as it was a fitting tribute to Tish, "a very productive academic, who not only published widely but also taught, mentored, and inspired her students to pursue careers in linguistics and continue her legacy of research excellence" (see Casilda Luzares' 2006 book review of the 2005 festschrift edited by Danilo Dayag and J. Stephen Quakenbush). Tish, in my estimate, along with other great Filipino scholars in the field of linguistics and language education, including the late Br. Andrew Gonzalez, has contributed to the success of several scholars, linguists, teachers, and professionals in English language studies. And the younger ones have shone in the light of Inner Circle scholars like Kingsley Bolton and Andy Kirkpatrick who have been instrumental in Southeast Asia to raise the profile of Outer Circle

DOI: 10.4324/9780429427824-5

42   Anne Pakir

researchers and teachers. We have seen the rise in Asia, especially in the Philippines (the earlier mentioned scholars) and Singapore (to name just a few, Ee Ling Low, Lisa Lim, and Lionel Wee), of generations of scholars who will raise the international research benchmark even higher.

The scholars who contributed to this volume honor the indubitable Queen Mother of Philippine English, Tish, who has appeared on the international stage with renowned luminaries in the field, like Braj Kachru, Larry Smith, Edgar Schneider, Cecil Nelson, Ayo Bamgbose, Nobuyuki Honna, and Edwin Thumboo, to name just a few. Owing to the extent and influence of Tish's research and publications, she has secured a well-deserved place not only in Philippine linguistics but also in the widening field of world Englishes. On a personal and professional level, I have always appreciated Tish and her sterling work.

I first came to know Tish as a fellow researcher in sociolinguistics and world Englishes. We were language and linguistic travelers for our respective countries: The Philippines and Singapore. We were Asian voices and Asian scholars, at an exciting time when the field of world Englishes was just developing. Very much taken up by emerging paradigms which were coming onto the scene (especially Braj Kachru's) in the late 1980s and 1990s, and culminating in English being proclaimed the global language (led by David Crystal and David Graddol), Tish's work, like mine, was influenced by these newer paradigms which recognized a shift of gravity in scholarship to the making of Englishes (rather than the making of English).

Englishes was not a recognized word, even when I was on a sabbatical at Cornell University in the early 1990s when the librarian there could not help me locate a copy of the journal *world Englishes* at my request. He informed me that there was no such word as *Englishes*! Tish and I have journeyed much together especially during the Kachruvian era. In the 1980s, Sidney Greenbaum, a close colleague of the Kachrus, envisaged a huge project of compiling language data on the educated Englishes around the world, the International Corpus of English (ICE). I was on that project for the Singapore component (ICE-SIN); Tish was in charge of the project for the Philippine component (ICE-PHI). I was pleased to see that, among her many chapters, articles, monographs, and books and (totaling at least 180 publications, and the most important works on PhE listed below), there were two significant articles in 2004 and 2010, based on the ICE corpora. In 2010, in the exemplary analysis of the ICE-PHI, Tish contrasted it against ICE-SIN. After much painstaking analysis, she concluded that the now well-identified standard PhE and Standard Singapore English differed possibly not only because of the different inputs, in the case of the Philippines from Tagalog and other Philippine languages, and in the case of Singapore possibly Chinese and other ethnic mother tongues used in Singapore but also because of the unique developmental trajectory each variety has gone on. Tish's quality of work and high standards reflected her quick and immense ability to recognize gaps in research and to delve deeply into what observers of the emerging Philippine variety of English glibly noticed or noted. The impact of her work, the influence of her ideas, the scope and depth of her scholarship, and the international reach of her scholarly audience are Tish's legacy to the world.

The international community of scholars is always seeking original voices emanating from the countries in the Outer and Expanding Circles. And today, in 2019, there are many more in the Philippines, not least because of the mentorship and leadership of Ma. Lourdes Bautista. She has made new Filipino scholars, whose new voices on linguistics, language education, English language teaching, and particularly world Englishes, and other emerging paradigms like English as a lingua franca, must be heard and will be heard. So Ariane, Isabel (Martin), Marilu, and Shirley, and other young scholars, and younger scholars in the Philippines, please take on the mantle and honor Tish even further.

In conclusion, I cannot think of anyone more deserving than my dear Tish of a second festschrift in her honor. She is indeed the Queen Mother of Philippine English!

Note

1 This chapter is based on a tribute speech given at the dinner honoring Professor Ma. Lourdes Bautista and announcing the future publication of this volume, organized by the Linguistic Society of the Philippines (LSP) to celebrate its 50th anniversary on March 19, 2019, at De La Salle University, Manila, the Philippines.

Selected Works of Ma. Lourdes Bautista

Bautista, M.L.S. (1980). *The Filipino Bilingual's Linguistic Competence: A Model Based on an Analysis of Tagalog-English Code-Switching.* Pacific Linguistics Series C-No. 59. Department of Linguistics, Research School of Pacific Studies, The Australian National University.

Bautista, M.L.S. (1982). *Yaya* English. *Philippine Studies, 30,* 377–394.

Bautista, M.L.S., Ed. (1996). *Readings in Philippine Sociolinguistics, Second Edition* (p. 342). Manila: De La Salle University Press.

Bautista, M.L.S. (1996). Notes on three sub-varieties of Philippine English. In M.L.S. Bautista (Ed.), *Readings in Philippine Sociolinguistics, Second Edition* (pp. 93–101). Manila: De La Salle University Press.

Bautista, M.L.S., Ed. (1997). *English Is an Asian Language: The Philippine Context. Proceedings of the Conference held in Manila, August 2–3, 1996.* Australia: The Macquarie Library Pty. Ltd.

Bautista, M.L.S. (1997). The lexicon of Philippine English. In M.L.S. Bautista (Ed.), *English Is an Asian Language: The Philippine Context* – Proceedings of the Conference held in Manila on August 2–3, 1996 (pp. 49–72). Australia: The Macquarie Library Pty. Ltd.

Bautista, M.L.S. (2000). *Defining Standard Philippine English: Its Status and Grammatical Features.* Manila: De La Salle University Press.

44   *Anne Pakir*

Bautista, M.L.S., Llamzon, T.A. and Sibayan, B.P., Eds. (2000). *Parangal cang Brother Andrew: Festschrift for Andrew Gonzalez on His Sixtieth Birthday*. Manila: Linguistic Society of the Philippines.

Bautista, M.L.S. (2000). The grammatical features of educated Philippine English. In M.L.S. Bautista, T.A. Llamzon and B.P. Sibayan (Eds.), *Parangal Cang Brother Andrew: Festschrift for Andrew Gonzalez on His Sixtieth Birthday* (pp. 146–158). Manila: Linguistic Society of the Philippines.

Bautista, M.L.S. (2000). Studies of Philippine English in the Philippines. *Philippine Journal of Linguistics, 31* (1), 39–65.

Bautista, M.L.S. (2001). Attitudes of selected Luzon university students and faculty towards Philippine English. In M.L.G. Tayao et al. (Eds.), *Rosario E. Maminta in Focus: Selected Writings in Applied Linguistics* (pp. 236–273). Quezon City: Philippine Association for Language Teaching.

Bautista, M.L.S. (Spring 2001). Attitudes of English language faculty in three leading Philippine universities towards Philippine English. *Asian Englishes, 4* (1), 4–32.

Bautista, M.L.S. (December 2001). Studies of Philippine English: Implications for English language teaching in the Philippines. *Journal of Southeast Asian Education, 2* (2), 271–293. (Special Issue on Language Education: Regional Issues in the 21st Century, guest edited by Goh Chi Lan and Christopher S. Ward.)

Bautista, M.L.S. (2003). The New Englishes and the teaching of grammar. In J.E. James (Ed.), *Grammar in the Language Classroom: Changing Approaches and Practices* (pp. 62–90). Anthology Series 43. Singapore: SEAMEO Regional Language Centre.

Bautista, M.L.S. and Bolton, K., Guest Eds. (February 2004). Special Issue on Philippine English: Tensions and Transitions. *world Englishes, 23* (1).

Bolton, K. and Bautista, M.L.S. (February 2004). Foreword – Philippine English: Tensions and transitions. *world Englishes, 23* (1), 1–5. (Special Issue on Philippine English: Tensions and Transitions, guest edited by Ma. Lourdes S. Bautista and Kingsley Bolton.)

Bautista, M.L.S. (February 2004). The verb in Philippine English: A preliminary analysis of modal *would. world Englishes, 23* (1), 113–128. (Special Issue on Philippine English: Tensions and Transitions, guest edited by Ma. Lourdes S. Bautista and Kingsley Bolton.)

Bautista, M.L.S. (February 2004). Researching English in the Philippines: Bibliographical resources. *world Englishes, 23* (1), 199–210. (Special Issue on Philippine English: Tensions and Transitions, guest edited by Ma. Lourdes S. Bautista and Kingsley Bolton.)

Bautista, M.L.S., Lising, L.V., and Dayag, D.T. (April 2004). *ICE-Philippines Lexical Corpus – CD-ROM*. London: International Corpus of English.

Bautista, M.L.S. (2004). Tagalog-English code switching as a mode of discourse. *Asia-Pacific Education Review, 5* (2), 226–233. Education Research Institute, Seoul National University.

Bautista, M.L.S. (Winter 2004). Guest Editor's Introduction to Special Articles on Philippine English. *Asian Englishes, 7* (2), 4–7. ALC Press, Tokyo, Japan.

Bautista, M.L.S. (Winter 2004). An overview of the Philippine component of the International Corpus of English. *Asian Englishes, 7* (2), 8–27. ALC Press, Tokyo, Japan.

Bautista, M.L.S. and Gonzalez, A. (2006). Southeast Asian Englishes. In B.B. Kachru, Y. Kachru and C.L. Nelson (Eds.), *Handbook on world Englishes* (pp. 130–144). Malden, MA; Oxford, the United Kingdom; Carlton, Australia: Blackwell Publishing.

Bautista, M.L.S. and Bolton, K., Eds. (2008). *Philippine English: Linguistic and Literary Perspectives.* Hong Kong SAR, China: Hong Kong University Press. (Reprinted by Anvil Publishing Inc. in the Quezon, the Philippines in 2009)

Bautista, M.L.S. (2011). Some notes on '*no* in Philippine English. In M.L.S. Bautista (Ed.), *Studies of Philippine English: Exploring the Philippine Component of the International Corpus of English* (pp. 75–90). Manila: Anvil Publishing, Inc. for De La Salle University.

Bautista, M.L.S. (2011). A bibliography of Philippine English. In M.L.S. Bautista (Ed.), *Studies of Philippine English: Exploring the Philippine Component of the International Corpus of English* (pp. 251–259). Manila: Anvil Publishing, Inc. for De La Salle University.

Bautista, M.L.S., Ed. (2011). *Studies of Philippine English: Exploring the Philippine Component of the International Corpus of English.* Manila: Anvil Publishing, Inc. for De La Salle University. Manila: Anvil Publishing, Inc. for De La Salle University.

Bautista, M.L.S. (2019). Professor Braj Kachru: A personal appreciation. *world Englishes, 38* (1–2), 323–324.

Bernardino, E. S. (Ed.), *The Maria Lourdes S. Bautista Reader.* Manila: De La Salle University Press.

Part 2
Linguistic Structure

4 Phonology

*Irwan Shah Shahruddin, Ran Ao,
and Ee Ling Low*

4.1 Introduction

The main aim of this chapter is to provide perceptual and acoustic analyses of English speech data produced by educated Filipinos to describe current phonetic features of Philippine English (PhE) and to validate previous descriptions of the phonology of this variety of English with respect to vowels, consonants, lexical stress and rhythm. This chapter also seeks to contribute to the ongoing discussion on PhE in Schneider's dynamic model (2003, 2007).

4.2 Vowels

This section presents the results of perceptual and acoustic analyses of vowels in PhE.

4.2.1 Perceptual Analyses of Vowels

The speech data analyzed for this chapter were obtained with permission from the National Institute of Education Spoken Corpus of English in Asia (NIESCEA) corpus (Low, 2015). The data comprise audio recordings of ten PhE speakers, i.e. five female (F1 to F5) and five male speakers (M1 to M5). The speakers consist of undergraduate and postgraduate students, aged between 18 and 35. The speech data include the informants' reading of the Wolf Passage (Deterding, 2006a) and specially designed sentence sets (Low, 1998). Several vowel features were identified from the NIESCEA data.

4.2.1.1 Lack of Reduced Vowels

One salient feature of PhE vowels is that reduced vowels of unstressed syllables are realized as full vowels among mesolectal and basilectal speakers (Llamzon, 1997; Tayao, 2008b), due to lack of reduction of unstressed vowels (Dayag, 2012; Gonzalez, 1984; Llamzon, 1997). For instance, the word

DOI: 10.4324/9780429427824-7

50　*Irwan Shah Shahruddin et al.*

Table 4.1 Incidence of Reduced Vowels

	Full	Reduced	Total Instances
Content words	10	60	70
Function words (*of, that*)	1	19	20
Function word (*as, to, to*)	20	10	30

correct is realized as /kɒˈrekt/. In order to determine whether unstressed vowels were reduced to a schwa, we selected from the Wolf Passage seven content words including *concern, convinced, escaped, away, chicken, forest* and *threaten*, and four monosyllabic function words including *of, to (twice), as* and *that* for perceptual analysis. The results are displayed in Table 4.1.

The occurrence of full vowels in function words *of* and *that* is low as expected. For the function words *as* and *to*, however, the incidence of full vowels is greater, showing the existence of full or unreduced vowels among educated speakers of PhE. In another Outer Circle variety, Singapore English (SgE), full vowels overwhelmingly occur more than reduced vowels across both content and function words (Deterding, 2005, 2010; Heng & Deterding, 2005). Despite such differences, communication among these Englishes is not hindered but "may in some circumstances actually enhance intelligibility" (Deterding, 2010, p. 371).

4.2.1.2 Free Variation of /æ/ Vowel

To investigate the variations of the /æ/ vowel, nine words were investigated from the Wolf Passage, namely, *plan, have, ran, had, afternoon, after, actually, exactly* and *began*. The results are shown in Table 4.2.

Besides the one incidence of the use of /a/ for *began*, the /æ/ vowel was consistently used for all the other words observed, similar to recent findings in Lesho (2017) and Pillai, Manueli and Dumanig (2010). This shows that free variation of /æ/ may not be uttered as prevalently in PhE.

4.2.1.3 Realization of BATH Vowel

For purposes of clarity, the Standard Lexical Sets developed by Wells (1982) is used alongside the International Phonetic Association (IPA) symbols in the present study for the description of PhE vowels. Following Wells (1982),

Table 4.2 Incidence of Variations of the /æ/ Vowel

	/æ/	/a/ or /ɛ/	Total Instances
Words containing /æ/ vowel	89	1	90

Phonology 51

the BATH vowel may be realized as different vowels in different Englishes. In general, it is realized as /ɑː/ in British English (BrE) but as /æ/ in American English (AmE). As the BATH vowel is used to measure the /ɑː/ vowel in the Wolf Passage, a perceptual analysis of the words *afternoon* and *after* shows that the /æ/ vowel was consistently used by all speakers in this study, which implies that the BATH vowel is pronounced by the PhE speakers in the way similar to the TRAP vowel. An acoustic analysis presented in the next section will validate this perceptual analysis.

4.2.1.4 Realization of LOT and THOUGHT Vowels
as Similar Vowels

Variation occurs for the LOT and THOUGHT vowels. While Wells (1982) neatly assigns the LOT and THOUGHT vowels /ɒ, ɔː/ in BrE and /ɑ, ɔ/ in AmE, recent studies have observed that they are realized as similar vowels (e.g. Heggarty, Maguire, & McMahon, 2013; Labov, Ash, & Boberg, 2006). The perceptual observation among the PhE informants is that some realizations of the LOT vowels are similar to those of the THOUGHT vowels, i.e. with /ɔ/ occurring in THOUGHT vowels, despite some variations, which was also observed in Lesho (2017) for the *bot* vowels.

4.2.2 Acoustic Analyses of Vowels

To validate the perceptual observations in the preceding sections, acoustic analyses were conducted using *Praat* (version 6.0.39) (Boersma & Weenik, 2018). Table 4.3 shows the monophthongs measured and the sample words selected for acoustic measurement.

F1 and F2 values were used to represent vowel quality (Hayward, 2000; Kent & Read, 1992; Ladefoged & Johnson, 2015) and were transformed into the Bark scale using the formula developed by Zwicker and Terhardt

Table 4.3 Monophthongs Measured and Sample Words Selected from the Wolf Passage and Sentence Sets

Keyword (Wells, 1982)	IPA	Words Containing the Vowels
FLEECE	iː	sheep, even (two samples), feast
KIT	ɪ	little, fist, this, chicken, did, convinced
DRESS	ɛ	shepherd, next, get, pleasure, successful
TRAP	æ	plan, exactly, actually, began, had
STRUT	ʌ	company, fun, cousins, much, duck, come
BATH	ɑː	after, afternoon, asked, pass
LOT	ɒ	flocks, hot, not, shot, bother
THOUGHT	ɔː	thought, flaw, flawless, caught
FOOT	ʊ	foot, good, looking
GOOSE	uː	afternoon, soon, two, zoo
NURSE	ɜː	heard, concern, third

52   Irwan Shah Shahruddin et al.

(1980, see Deterding, 2003 for details), with the acoustic dimensions represented in graphical form (Ladefoged, 2001). Due to physical differences between the vocal tracts of male and female speakers, the informants were divided into two groups based on gender (i.e. male versus female) for acoustic analyses.

Figures 4.1 and 4.2 show the formant plots for male and female speakers, while Figures 4.3–4.12 show the scatter plots of vowel pairs as well as the BATH–TRAP vowels for male and female speakers.

4.2.2.1 Comparing Vowel Pairs

/iː/–/ɪ/ VOWEL PAIR

Figures 4.3 and 4.4 show the /iː/–/ɪ/ vowel pair for male and female speakers. For both male and female speakers, the partial merger between /iː/ and /ɪ/ vowels suggests that the quality of the /ɪ/ vowels is partially closer to that of the /iː/ vowel.

A two-sample *t*-test (assuming unequal variances, two-tailed) is conducted for F1 and F2 for all vowel pairs. For the /iː/–/ɪ/ vowel pair, the *t*-test results (F1: $t = 2.01$, $p < 0.005$, df = 48; F2: $t=2.01$, $p < 0.005$, df = 48) show a difference in quality in F1 and F2 between the vowel pair.

The *t*-test results for female speakers (F1: $t=2.01$, $p<0.005$, df=48; F2: $t=2.01$, $p<0.005$, df=48) show a difference for both F1 and F2 values for the

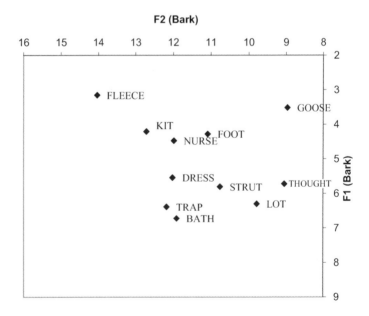

Figure 4.1 Formant Plot for Male Speakers.

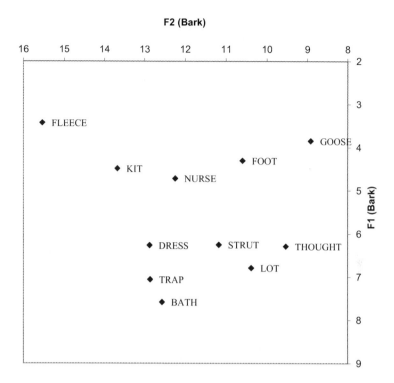

Figure 4.2 Formant Plot for Female Speakers.

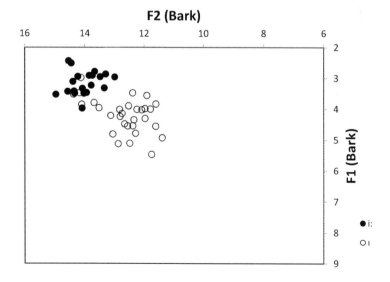

Figure 4.3 Scatter Plot for /iː/ and /ɪ/ Vowels for Male Speakers.

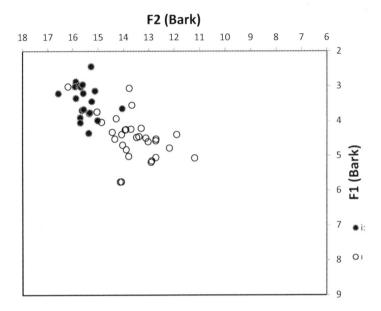

Figure 4.4 Scatter Plot for /iː/ and /ɪ/ Vowels for Female Speakers.

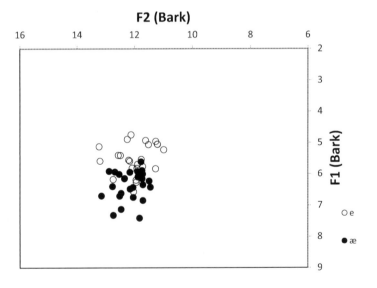

Figure 4.5 Scatter Plot for /ɛ/ and /æ/ Vowels for Male Speakers.

Phonology 55

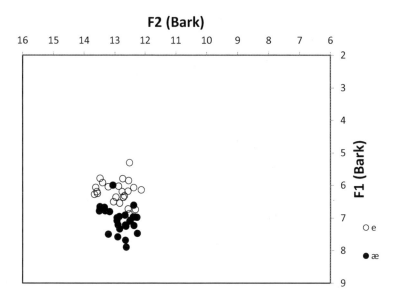

Figure 4.6 Scatter Plot for /ɛ/ and /æ/ Vowels for Female Speakers.

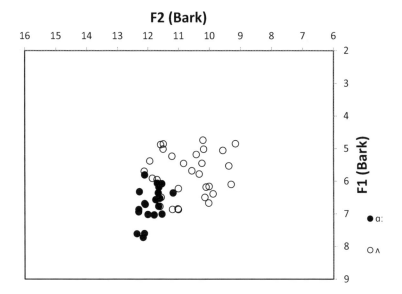

Figure 4.7 Scatter Plot for /ʌ/ and /ɑː/ Vowels for Male Speakers.

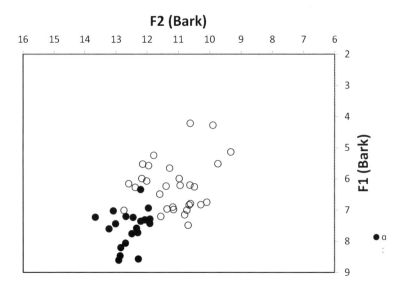

Figure 4.8 Scatter Plot for /ʌ/ and /ɑː/ Vowels for Female Speakers.

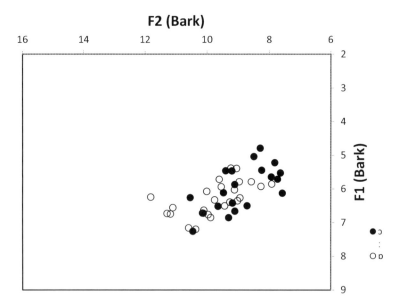

Figure 4.9 Scatter Plot for /ɒ/ and /ɔː/ Vowels for Male Speakers.

Phonology 57

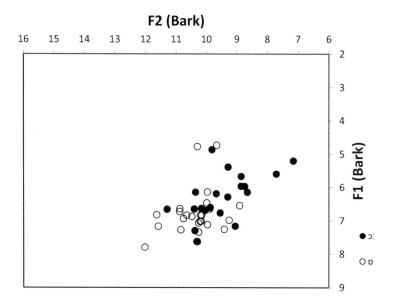

Figure 4.10 Scatter Plot for /ʊ/ and /ɔː/ Vowels for Female Speakers.

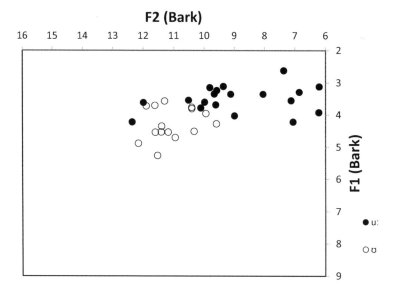

Figure 4.11 Scatter Plot for /ʊ/ and /uː/ Vowels for Male Speakers.

58 *Irwan Shah Shahruddin et al.*

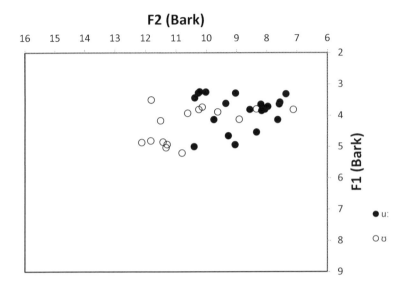

Figure 4.12 Scatter Plot for /ʊ/ and /uː/ Vowels for Female Speakers.

/iː/-/ɪ/ vowel pair for female speakers. The mean duration of the /ɪ/ vowel is 77.6 ms, while the mean duration for the /iː/ vowel is 96.1 ms, which shows a longer duration for the /iː/ vowel as compared to the /ɪ/ vowel.

/ɛ/–/æ/ VOWEL PAIR

Figures 4.5 and 4.6 display the plots for the /ɛ/–/æ/ vowel pair for male and female speakers. The conflation between the two vowels shows a general lack of contrast between them.

The *t*-test results for male speakers show a difference between the vowel pair in terms of only F1 but not F2 (F1: $t = 2.01$, $p < 0.005$, df = 48; F2: $t = 2.01$, $p > 0.05$, df = 46). This is similar to the *t*-test results of the female speakers (F1: $t = 2.01$, $p < 0.005$, df = 48; F2: $t = 2.01$, $p > 0.05$, df = 46). The mean duration for the /ɛ/ vowel is 88.4 ms and for the /æ/ vowel 116.0 ms.

/ʌ/–/ɑː/ VOWEL PAIR

For the /ʌ/–/ɑː/ vowel pair (see Figures 4.7 and 4.8), the partial overlap suggests a more open /ʌ/ vowel. However, in general, both vowels have clear distinct spaces, with the /ɑː/ vowel lower and more front than /ʌ/. The more front /ɑː/ (BATH) vowel reflects the earlier perceptual observation that it is realized closer to the /æ/ vowel.

Phonology 59

The *t*-test result for male speakers (F1: *t*=2.01, *p*<0.005, df=46; F2: *t*=2.01, *p*<0.005, df=44) shows that both vowels are different in F1 and F2. The female speakers display a similar difference (F1: *t*=2.01, *p*<0.005, df=46; F2: *t*=2.01, *p*<0.005, df=48). The mean duration is 77.3 ms for the /ʌ/ vowel and 129.1 ms for the /ɑ:/ vowel, which shows a longer duration for the /ɑ:/ vowel.

/ɒ/–/ɔ:/ VOWEL PAIR

Figures 4.9 and 4.10 show the scatter plots for the /ɒ/–/ɔ:/ vowel pair for both male and female speakers, respectively. The plots show conflation between the two vowels for both male and female speakers.

The plots corroborate the perceptual observation made in the previous section, i.e. the lack of distinction between the LOT and THOUGHT vowels. For both groups of speakers, the /ɒ/ and /ɔ:/ vowels may appear both as rounded and as unrounded based on the position of F2 (refer to Ladefoged, 1971, for a discussion on degree of backness and lip rounding). The *t*-test shows differences in F2 but no difference in F1 for male speakers (F1: *t* = 2.03, *p* = 0.094, df = 35; F2: *t* = 2.02, *p* = 0.0056, df = 43) and a marginal difference in F1 for female speakers (F1: *t* = 2.02, *p* = 0.02, df = 41; F2: *t* = 2.02, *p* < 0.005, df = 38). The mean duration is 119.7 ms for the /ɒ/ vowel and 133.8 ms for the /ɔ:/ vowel, which shows a longer duration for the /ɔ:/ vowel.

/ʊ/–/U:/ VOWEL PAIR

Figures 4.11 and 4.12 show the /ʊ/–/u:/ vowel pair for male and female PhE speakers. For the male speakers, the /u:/ vowel appears more dispersed in terms of F2, while the /ʊ/ vowel appears more central. For the female speakers, the F1 dispersion exists for both vowels.

The *t*-test results for male speakers show a significant difference for both F1 and F2 (F1: *t* = 2.06, *p* < 0.005, df = 25; F2: *t* = 2.05, *p* < 0.005, df = 29. The female speakers show a similar difference (F1: *t* = 2.05, *p* = 0.027, df = 29; F2: *t* = 2.07, *p* < 0.005, df = 22). The mean duration is 68.4 ms for the /ʊ/ vowel and 130.2 ms for the /u:/ vowel, and this shows a longer duration for the /u:/ vowel.

BATH AND TRAP VOWELS

Perceptual observation and scatter plots for the BATH–TRAP vowels suggest that the quality of the BATH vowel is similar to that of the TRAP vowel. This is discernible in the scatter plots of BATH and TRAP vowels in Figures 4.13 and 4.14 for male and female speakers. The conflation between both vowels for male and female speakers suggests similarity in the quality of the two vowels.

To summarize, a consolidated table of the vowel inventory of PhE is shown in Table 4.4.

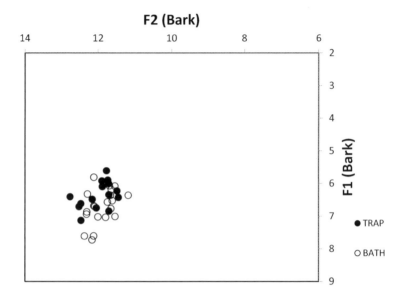

Figure 4.13 Scatter Plot for BATH and TRAP Vowels for Male Speakers.

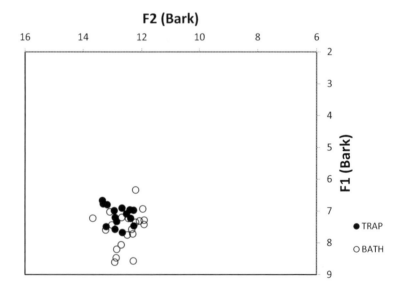

Figure 4.14 Scatter Plot for BATH and TRAP Vowels for Female Speakers.

Table 4.4 Summary of Vowel Inventory of PhE

IPA	Llamzon (1969, 1997)	Tayao (2008a)	Llamzon (1997), Tayao (2008a, 2012)		Regala-Flores (2014)	Dayag (2012)	Lesho (2017)	Present Study
	Acrolect	Acrolect	Mesolect	Basilect	Basilect		Acrolect	
i:	i:	i	i (or ɪ)		I	I	i	i:
ɪ	ɪ	ɪ		i	ɪ		ɪ	ɪ/i:
e	e/ɛ	e	e/ɛ		e/ɛ	ɛ	ɛ	ɛ
æ	æ	a/æ/ɛ	ɑ		A		æ	æ/e
ʌ	ə	ʌ/ə	ʌ	a/ɑ	ʌ	a	ʌ	ʌ
ɑ:	a:	a	ɑ		A		-	æ[a]
ɒ	o/ɔ	o	o		O	ɔ	ɑ	ɒ/ɑ
ɔ:	ɔ:			u	ɔ		ɔ	ɔ:/ɒ
ʊ	ʊ	ʊ	u (or ʊ)		ʊ	u	ʊ	ʊ/u:
u:	u:	u:			U		u:	u:/ʊ
ɜ:	-	-	-	ɑ	-		ɝ	ɝ

a The /ɑ:/ vowel used in this study is based on the BATH vowel in Wells' (1982) lexical set.

4.3 Consonants

This section presents the results of perceptual and acoustic analyses of consonants in PhE.

4.3.1 Perceptual Analyses of Consonants

Based on the perceptual analyses, five salient consonantal features were identified for PhE.

4.3.1.1 Substitution of Dental Fricatives with Alveolar Stops

A perceptual observation was conducted on dental fricatives to determine whether substitution occurs. To determine whether the voiced dental fricative /ð/ is replaced with alveolar stop /d/, some words with /ð/ were selected from the Wolf Passage. These include *there*, *this*, *the*(13), *they*(2), *that*(2), *than*, *them*, *their* and *bother*. Table 4.5 shows that the dental fricative /ð/ is frequently substituted with /d/, though the substitution occurs only at the word-initial position.

Next, words from the Wolf Passage containing /θ/, namely, *thought*, *threaten* and *third* and *with* were selected and perceptually analyzed. The results (see Table 4.6) show that /θ/ is sometimes substituted with /t/ at the word-initial position and with /d/ at the word-final position.

62 Irwan Shah Shahruddin et al.

Table 4.5 Substitution of /ð/ with /d/ in the Wolf Passage

	D	d	Total Instances
/ð/ in the word-initial position (*there, this, the, they, that, than, them, their*)	142	78	220
/ð/ in the word-medial position (*bother*)	10	0	10

Table 4.6 Substitution of /θ/ with /t/ in the Wolf Passage

	θ	t	D	Total Instances
/θ/ in the word-initial position (*thought, threaten* and *third*)	27	3	0	30
/θ/ in the word-final position (*with*)	2	0	8	10

4.3.1.2 Devoicing of /z/ and /ʒ/

A perceptual observation was conducted for words where /z, ʒ/ were potentially devoiced to /s, ʃ/, namely, *raising, cousins, cousins, villagers, pleasure* and *usual* (see Table 4.7). Devoicing of /z/ seems to occur more frequently when it occurs at word-medial and word-final positions whereas devoicing of /ʒ/ appears to occur (at word-medial position) less frequently.

4.3.1.3 Consonant Cluster Simplification

Words containing consonant clusters in the final position were observed, namely, *flocks, fields, homes, fist, feast, forest*(2), *convinced, rushed* and *escaped* (see results in Table 4.8).

As shown in Table 4.8, cluster simplification occurs when the cluster ends with a stop. This feature occurs in many Englishes, such as SgE (Deterding, 2007; Gut, 2005), Malaysian English (MalE) (Baskaran, 2008) and even Inner Circle varieties such as AmE (Guy, 1980; Wells, 1982) and BrE (Fabricius, 2002).

Table 4.7 Occurrences of Devoicing in the Wolf Passage

	Z	s	ʒ	ʃ	Total Instances
/z/ at the word-medial position (*raising, cousins*)	6	14			20
/z/ at the word-final position (*cousins, villagers*)	1	19			20
/ʒ/ at the word-medial position (*pleasure, usual*)			13	7	20

Phonology 63

Table 4.8 Occurrences of Consonant Cluster Simplification

	All Consonants Present	Elision of Final Consonant	Total Instances
Words ending with fricative (*flocks, fields, homes*)	30	0	30
Words ending with plosive (*fist, feast, forest*(2), *convinced, rushed, escaped*)	42	28	70

Table 4.9 Aspiration of Voiceless Stops

	Aspirated	Lack of Aspiration	Total Instances
Words beginning with stop /p/ (*passed, poor, post*)	20	10	30
Words beginning with stop /t/ (*time, told, two*)	24	6	30
Words beginning with stop /k/ (*come, company, cousins*)	18	12	30

4.3.1.4 *Aspirated Voiceless Stops*

Words beginning with stops in CV order were observed, namely, *passed, poor, post, time, told, two, come, company* and *cousins*. The results are shown in Table 4.9.

While a majority of voiceless stops are aspirated, lack of aspiration was also found. This feature is also observed in SgE, where reduced aspiration occurs at times with various speakers (Deterding & Kirkpatrick, 2006). An acoustic investigation was conducted to validate the aspiration of stops in PhE, which is presented in Section 3.2.

4.3.1.5 *Rhoticity*

To determine the rhoticity of PhE, six words containing non-prevocalic /r/ were selected from the Wolf Passage, namely, *before, course, unfortunately, heard, third* and *concern*. It was found that *r*-coloring exists in all samples observed. An acoustic investigation was conducted to validate this. The results will be presented in the next section in comparison with other Englishes.

4.3.2 *Acoustic Analyses of Consonants*

The acoustic analyses of consonants were based on the Wolf Passage and sentence sets. Two key consonantal aspects were acoustically measured, i.e. Voice Onset Time (VOT) (Ladefoged & Johnson, 2015) and F3 of *r*-colored

64 *Irwan Shah Shahruddin et al.*

vowels (Hayward, 2000; Ladefoged, 2003; Ladefoged & Johnson, 2015) in order to investigate aspiration and rhoticity, respectively.

4.3.2.1 Voice Onset Time

Table 4.10 shows the mean VOT values acoustically obtained from the stops in the word-initial position. These values are compared with those of AmE from Ao (2015). It can be seen from the table that the VOT values of PhE are generally lower than those of AmE. A *t*-test (paired two-sample for means, two-tailed) shows a significant difference between the VOT of PhE and that of AmE ($t = 2.11$, $p < 0.005$, df = 17).

In order to examine whether PhE is similar to or different from other Englishes in Southeast Asia in terms of VOT, Table 4.11 shows the VOT values of PhE in comparison with those of MalE and SgE.

While the /p/ stop is more aspirated in PhE as compared to MalE and SgE, the /t/ and /k/ stops are less aspirated than SgE. Therefore, even though the earlier perceptual observation of stops was that PhE is generally aspirated, the PhE VOT values are all lower than those of AmE (except for the VOT of /g/ in *good*), and closer to those of MalE and SgE, both of which are generally described as unaspirated. The *t*-test (paired, two-sample for means) indicates no significant differences with MalE ($t = 2.57$, $p > 0.05$, df = 5) and SgE ($t = 2.57$, $p > 0.05$, df = 5).

Table 4.10 Average VOT Values of Voiceless and Voiced Stops in PhE

Stop	Word	PhE	AmE (Ao, 2015)
/p/	passed	40.95	62.82
	Poor	43.85	75.22
	Post	48.67	72.87
/t/	Time	39.02	58.65
	Told	32.72	55.08
	Two	49.53	81.61
/k/	Come	46.17	63.18
	company	38.68	64.75
	cousins	28.72	68.40
Average		40.92	66.95
/b/	before	9.65	26.40
	Being	10.20	16.78
	bother	7.52	18.85
/d/	Dark	10.93	17.77
	Diet	12.04	17.86
	Duck	8.85	16.39
/g/	Gave	20.87	22.11
	Get	16.22	21.00
	good	22.65	19.80
Average		13.22	19.66

Phonology 65

Table 4.11 VOT Values of PhE, AmE, Malaysian English and SgE

Stop	Philippine English	Malaysian English (Tan, 2011)	Singapore English (Tan, 2011)
/p/	44.49	36.50	39.04
/t/	40.43	36.92	42.51
/k/	37.86	46.99	48.54
/b/	9.12	15.71	14.93
/d/	10.61	16.14	15.24
/g/	19.91	36.87	30.43

4.3.2.2 Rhoticity

Rhoticity was investigated acoustically by measuring words with non-prevocalic /r/, namely, *bars, dark, Mars, before, course, unfortunately, concern, heard* and *third*. These *r*-colored vowels were segmented and the F3 values were taken at both midpoint (50%) and 75% interval to account for the temporal variation of the acoustic reflex of /r/ (Ao, 2015). Table 4.12 shows the F3 values of PhE in comparison with those of AmE and BrE, two reference Englishes known to be rhotic and non-rhotic, respectively.

The values of F3 for PhE are closer to those of AmE than to those of BrE, indicating the existence of rhoticity. *T*-tests were conducted for the F3 values at both midpoint and 75% intervals and are shown in Table 4.13. The

Table 4.12 F3 Values of PhE in Comparison with AmE and BrE

		PhE	AmE (Ao, 2015)	BrE (Ao, 2015)
		F3 (Hz)	F3 (Hz)	F3 (Hz)
At midpoint (50%)	ɑːr	2,075.66	1,967.80	2,718.30
	ɔːr	2,103.13	2,162.04	2,730.78
	ɜːr	2,154.65	2,057.57	2,815.17
At 75% interval	ɑːr	1,946.73	1,960.67	2,708.33
	ɔːr	1,964.76	2,006.70	2,790.64
	ɜːr	2,154.65	2,180.67	2,821.67

Table 4.13 T-Test Results of r-Colored Vowels in PhE and AmE for F3 at Midpoint and 75% Interval (Two-Sample Assuming Unequal Variances, Two-Tailed)

	50%			75%		
	t	df	Statistically significant (p < 0.05)?	t	df	Statistically significant (p < 0.05)?
PhE vs AmE	4.30	2	No	4.30	2	No
PhE vs BrE	4.30	2	Yes	4.30	2	Yes

66   *Irwan Shah Shahruddin et al.*

statistical results show significant differences only between PhE and BrE in terms of F3, indicating that PhE is a rhotic and is different from BrE, a non-rhotic variety.

4.4 Suprasegmental Features

Two salient aspects of suprasegmental features in PhE, namely, lexical (word) stress and rhythm, were investigated in the present study, the results of which are presented in this section.

4.4.1 Lexical Stress

One way of differentiating stress is the prominence of a stressed syllable compared to an unstressed syllable, resulting in a louder sound with a higher pitch (Ladefoged, 2001). In this study, lexical stress is determined by the accent placement of F0 (i.e. pitch) that is used as a main determiner of the stressed syllable on each word. Table 4.14 shows the position of stressed syllables that determines lexical stress of the tokens as uttered by the informants.

While many words in PhE have lexical stress placed in positions similar to those of Inner Circle Englishes, words like *shepherd, cousins, later, chicken* and *bother* occasionally have lexical stress placed on the second syllable. For the word *concern*, however, almost half of the speakers place the stress on the first syllable, which may be attributable to the lack of reduced vowels. For the words *afternoon* and *overcoming*, while stress is expected on the third syllable, there is more variation in stress placement among PhE speakers.

Table 4.14 Variations in Lexical Stress in Multi-Syllabic Words, Grouped According to Expected Syllable Stress

Word	First Syllable	Second Syllable	Third Syllable
First Syllable			
forest, mountain, village, safety, pleasure, villagers	60	0	NA
shepherd, cousins, later, chicken, bother	44	6	NA
company	8	0	2
Second Syllable			
exactly, unfortunately	0	10	0
before	1	9	NA
successful, convinced	4	16	0
concern	4	6	NA
Third Syllable			
afternoon	3	4	3
overcoming	3	2	5

4.4.2 Rhythmic Patterning

Scholars generally agree that PhE is rhythmically syllable-timed (e.g. Bautista, 2001; Dayag, 2012; Gonzalez, 1985; Tayao, 2008a), due to the lack of reduced vowels. The lack of vowel reduction gives each syllable an "equal value" (Gonzalez, 1985, p. 45).

The acoustic measurement of rhythmic patternings in this study was based on the sentence sets used in Low (1998). The sentence sets consist of ten sentences which are further divided into two subsets of five sentences, with one subset containing mainly full vowels (FV), and the other full and reduced vowels (F/RV). In the present study, the rhythmic patternings were measured and calculated using the Pairwise Variability Index (PVI) developed in Low, Grabe and Nolan (2000), with modifications made to the PVI as recommended in Deterding (2006a). The results of the PVI for PhE speakers as compared to those of AmE (Ao, 2015) are shown in Table 4.15.

While the average value of FV of PhE is lower than that of AmE, the average value of F/RV of PhE is higher. This indicates that PhE has less durational variation in the sentences containing mainly FV but more variation in sentences with both full and reduced vowels (F/RV), as compared to AmE. Further comparisons of PVI are made with two neighboring Englishes, i.e. SgE and MalE (Tan, 2011) (see Table 4.16).

As shown in Table 4.16, the PVI values of PhE are higher than those of SgE and MalE, indicating that PhE is more stress-based than these two

Table 4.15 PVI for PhE and AmE Speakers

	PhE		*AmE (Ao, 2015)*	
	FV	*F/RV*	*FV*	*F/RV*
Sentence Set 1	41.57	52.87	41.16	49.54
Sentence Set 2	48.39	79.43	67.23	61.56
Sentence Set 3	33.83	72.83	37.59	57.51
Sentence Set 4	51.19	82.45	66.75	75.90
Sentence Set 5	39.03	79.51	47.87	72.23
Average	42.80	73.42	52.12	63.35

Table 4.16 PVI Values of PhE in Comparison with Those of AmE, Malaysian English and SgE

	Full Vowels	*Full & Reduced Vowels*
PhE	42.80	73.42
AmE (Ao, 2015)	52.12	63.35
MalE (Tan, 2011)	36.18	44.19
SgE (Tan, 2011)	39.83	51.73

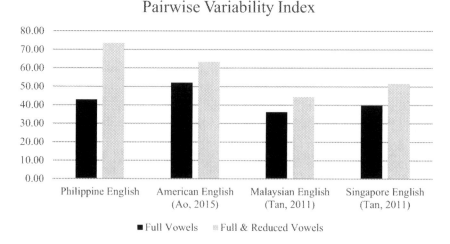

Figure 4.15 PVI of PhE, AmE, Malaysian English and SgE.

Table 4.17 Comparison of *t*-Test Results between PhE and AmE

	Full Vowels			Full and Reduced Vowels		
PhE vs AmE	*t*	*df*	Statistically significant ($p < 0.05$)?	*t*	*df*	Statistically significant ($p < 0.05$)?
	2.45	6	No	2.31	8	No

Englishes. The chart in Figure 4.15 illustrates the contrast between the PVI values of PhE, AmE, MalE and SgE.

The *t*-test (two-sample assuming unequal variances, two-tailed) between FV and F/RV sentences produced by PhE speakers shows a significant difference between the two sets ($t = 2.45$, df = 6, $p < 0.005$). Additionally, the *t*-tests (two-sample assuming unequal variances, two-tailed) between PhE and AmE based on both FV and F/RV sets show that these Englishes are not statistically different (see Table 4.17).

4.5 Discussion and Conclusion

This study has provided a brief description of the features of PhE with respect to vowels, consonants, lexical stress and rhythmic patternings based on perceptual and acoustic analyses of speech data produced by educated PhE speakers. Results from the analyses of vowels reveal some features of PhE, such as conflation of vowel pairs, e.g. LOT–THOUGHT, and wide

Phonology 69

variances in vowel pairs, e.g. FOOT–GOOSE. In addition, it is found that the BATH vowel is realized in PhE in the similar way as in AmE. In terms of consonants, acoustic evidence shows that the non-prevocalic /r/ is pronounced in PhE in a similar way as in AmE, suggesting that PhE, like AmE, is a rhotic variety. While the perceptual analysis of stops shows that PhE is aspirated, the acoustic analyses of VOT show that the VOT values of PhE are lower than AmE but comparable to MalE and SgE. Perceptual analyses also reveal substitution of fricatives with stops, devoicing of sibilants and consonant cluster simplification.

With regard to lexical stress placement, the word *concern* was found to be pronounced with the stress placed on the first syllable by a high number of PhE speakers. Words with three syllables are found to have variations in stress placement, which corroborates the claim by Tayao (2008a). With respect to rhythm, the PVI of PhE is similar to that of AmE, a stress-based variety, and different from those of two other Southeast Asian Englishes, namely, SgE and MalE.

This chapter has validated some phonological features of PhE from previous work and at the same time uncovered some features that have not been described before. In terms of PhE phonology, while Schneider (2003, 2007) in his dynamic model places PhE in Phase 3, i.e. nativization, some scholars (e.g. Borlongan, 2016) argue that PhE has already reached Phase 4, i.e. endonormative stabilization. Based on this study, although the PhE speakers display certain phonological features congruent to that of its reference variety, i.e. AmE, features of a local norm exist. Having said that, this study has only focused on acrolectal PhE speakers. Studies of a wider range of speakers are required to provide sufficient evidence to show whether PhE has reached Phase 4 in terms of phonology. Future studies may include mesolectal and basilectal PhE speakers for a fuller description of PhE. For example, future studies could focus on the basilectal speech to reveal "linguistic practices of genuinely marginalized voices in Philippine society" (Tupas, 2004, p. 54) and, based on this group of speakers, to ascertain whether PhE has reached Phase 4 in terms of phonology according to Schneider's dynamic model.

References

Ao, R. (2015). *An acoustic investigation of segmentals and rhythm in Yunnan English.* (Unpublished doctoral dissertation), National Institute of Education, Singapore.

Baskaran, L. (2008). Malaysian English: Phonology. In R. Mesthrie (Ed.), *Africa, South and Southeast Asia* (pp. 278–291). Berlin: Walter de Gruyter.

Bautista, M. L. S. (2001). Studies of Philippine English: Implications for English Language teaching in the Philippines. *Journal of Southeast Asian Education, 2*(2), 271–295.

Boersma, P., & Weenik, P. (2018). Praat: Doing phonetics by computer (Version 6.0.39) [Software]. Retrieved from http://fon.hum.uva.nl/praat/

70 *Irwan Shah Shahruddin et al.*

Borlongan, A. M. (2016). Relocating Philippine English in Scheider's dynamic model. *Asian Englishes*, 232–241. doi:10.1080/13488678.2016.1223067

Dayag, D. T. (2012). Philippine English. In E. L. Low & A. Hashim (Eds.), *English in Southeast Asia* (pp. 91–100). Amsterdam: John Benjamins Publishing Co.

Deterding, D. (2003). An instrumental study of the monophthong vowels of Singapore English. *English World-Wide, 24*(1), 1–16.

Deterding, D. (2005). Emergent patterns in the vowels of Singapore English. *English World-Wide, 26*(2), 179–198. Retrieved from http://videoweb.nie.edu.sg/phonetic/courses/aae103-web/eww-seng-stat.pdf

Deterding, D. (2006a). The North Wind versus a Wolf: Short texts for the description and measurement of English pronunciation. *Journal of the International Phonetic Association, 36*(2), 188–196.

Deterding, D. (2007). *Singapore English*. Edinburgh: Edinburgh University Press Ltd.

Deterding, D. (2010). Norms for pronunciation in Southeast Asia. *World Englishes, 29*(3), 364–377.

Deterding, D., & Kirkpatrick, A. (2006). Emerging South-East Asian Englishes and intelligibility. *World Englishes, 35*(3), 391–409.

Fabricius, A. (2002). Ongoing change in modern RP: Evidence for the disappearing stigma of t-glotalling. *English World-Wide, 23*(1), 115–136.

Gonzalez, A. (1984). Philippine English across generations: The sound system. *DSLU Dialogue, 20*(1), 1–26.

Gonzalez, A. (1985). *Studies on Philippine English. Occasional papers No. 39*. Singapore: SEAMEO Regional Language Centre.

Gut, U. (2005). The realization of final plosives in Singapore English: Phonological rules and ethnic differences. In D. Deterding, A. Brown, & E. L. Low (Eds.), *English in Singapore: Phonetic research on a Corpus* (pp. 14–25). Singapore: McGraw Hill.

Guy, G. R. (1980). Variation in the group and the individual: The case of final stop deletion. In W. Labov (Ed.), *Locating language in time and space* (pp. 1–36). New York: Academic Press.

Hayward, K. (2000). *Experimental phonetics*. Essex: Pearson Education Ltd.

Heggarty, P., Maguire, W., & McMahon, A. (2013). *Accents of English from around the world*. Retrieved from http://www.lel.ed.ac.uk/research/gsound/Eng/Database/Phonetics/Englishes/Home/HomeMainFrameHolder.htm

Heng, M. G., & Deterding, D. (2005). Reduced vowels in conversational Singapore English. In D. Deterding, A. Brown, & E. L. Low (Eds.), *English in Singapore: Phonetic research on a corpus* (pp. 54–63). Singapore: McGraw-Hill.

Kent, R. D., & Read, C. (1992). *The acoustic analysis of speech*. San Diego: Singular Publishing Group, Inc.

Labov, W., Ash, S., & Boberg, C. (2006). *The atlas of North American English*. New York: Mouton de Gruyter.

Ladefoged, P. (1971). *Preliminaries to linguistic phonetics*. Chicago: University of Chicago Press.

Ladefoged, P. (2001). *A course in phonetics* (4th ed.). Boston: Heinle & Heinle.

Ladefoged, P. (2003). *Phonetic data analysis: An introduction to fieldwork and instrumental techniques*. Malden: Blackwell Publishing.

Ladefoged, P., & Johnson, K. (2015). *A course in phonetics* (7th ed.). Stamford: Cengage Learning.

Lesho, M. (2017). Philippine English (Metro Manila acrolect). *Journal of the International Phonetic Association, 48*(3), 1–14.

Llamzon, T. A. (1969). *Standard Filipino English*. Manila: Ateneo de Manila University.

Llamzon, T. A. (1997). The phonology of Philippine English. In M. L. S. Bautista (Ed.), *English is an Asian Language: The Philippine context: Proceedings of the conference held in Manila on August 2–3, 1996* (pp. 41–48). NSW: The Macquarie Library Pty Ltd.

Low, E. L. (1998). *Prosodic prominence in Singapore English*. (Unpublished doctoral dissertation), University of Cambridge, Cambridge.

Low, E. L. (2015). *The NIE Spoken Corpus in Asia (NIESCEA)*. Singapore: National Institute of Education.

Low, E. L., Grabe, E., & Nolan, F. (2000). Quantitative characterizations of speech rhythm: Syllable-timing in Singapore English. *Language and Speech, 43*, 377–401.

Pillai, S., Manueli, M. K. S., & Dumanig, F. P. (2010). Monophthong vowels in Malaysian and Philippine English: An exploratory study. *Philippine Journal of Linguistics, 41*, 84–98.

Regala-Flores, E. (2014). Phonological features of basilectal Philippine English: An exploratory study. *International Journal of English and Literature, 5*(6), 128–140.

Schneider, E. W. (2003). The dynamics of new Englishes: From identity construction to dialect rebirth. *Language, 79*(2), 233–281.

Schneider, E. W. (2007). *Postcolonial English: Varieties around the world*. Cambridge: Cambridge University Press.

Tan, R. S. K. (2011). *An acoustic investigation of the segmentals and suprasegmentals of Malaysian English*. (Unpublished doctoral dissertation), National Institute of Education, Nanyang Technological University, Singapore.

Tayao, M. L. G. (2008a). A lectal description of the phonological features of Philippine English. In M. L. S. Bautista & K. Bolton (Eds.), *Philippine English: Linguistic and literary perspectives* (pp. 157–174). Hong Kong: Hong Kong University Press.

Tayao, M. L. G. (2008b). Philippine English: Phonology. In R. Mesthrie (Ed.), *Varieties of English: Africa, South and Southeast Asia* (Vol. 4, pp. 293–306). Berlin: Mouton de Gruyter.

Tupas, R. (2004). The politics of Philippine English: Neocolonialism, global politics, and the problem of postcolonialism. *World Englishes, 23*(1), 47–58.

Wells, J. C. (1982). *Accents of English (3 vol.)*. Cambridge: Cambridge University Press.

Zwicker, E., & Terhardt, E. (1980). Analytical expressions for critical-band rate and critical bandwidth as a function of frequency. *Journal of the Acoustical Society of America, 68*, 1523–1525.

Appendix A

The Wolf Passage (Deterding, 2006a)

There was once a poor shepherd boy who used to watch his flocks in the fields next to a dark forest near the foot of a mountain. One hot afternoon, he thought up a good plan to get some company for himself and also have a little fun. Raising his fist in the air, he ran down to the village shouting

72 *Irwan Shah Shahruddin et al.*

"Wolf, Wolf." As soon as they heard him, the villagers all rushed from their homes, full of concern for his safety, and two of his cousins even stayed with him for a short while. This gave the boy so much pleasure that a few days later he tried exactly the same trick again, and once more he was success-ful. However, not long after, a wolf that had just escaped from the zoo was looking for a change from its usual diet of chicken and duck. So, overcoming its fear of being shot, it actually did come out from the forest and began to threaten the sheep. Racing down to the village, the boy of course cried out even louder than before. Unfortunately, as all the villagers were convinced that he was trying to fool them a third time, they told him, "Go away and don't bother us again." And so the wolf had a feast.

Appendix B

Additional Sentence Sets (Low, 1998)

1 Mary asked her to pass a book to me.
2 I went to the shop to buy Mars Bars but they'd totally run out of Mars Bars.
3 He could not find a flaw.
4 Her complexion is flawless.

Appendix C

Specially Designed Sentence Sets (Low, 1998)

1 a John came back through France last Sunday.
   b John was sick of Fred and Sandy.

2 a Don seemed quite cross with John last week.
   b Don was across at Jonathan's.

3 a Paul drives past huge towns by highway.
   b Paula passed her trial of courage.

4 a Jane gets four by post each Thursday.
   b Jane has four to last the winter.

5 a Grace works through huge mounds each Friday.
   b Grace was tired of Matthew Freeman.

5 Lexicon

Thomas Biermeier

5.1 Introduction

In this chapter, special attention will be paid to the lexical properties of Philippine English (PhE). It will be interesting to see whether the demographic trend as well as the continuous spread of English globally will have long-lasting linguistic implications and affect the status of English in the Philippines. To be more precise, can the lexicon of PhE benefit from a rising number of speakers and writers; in other words, can this variety reach endonormative stabilization in Schneider's (2007) dynamic model? According to that model, the variety in question has successfully overcome the stage of nativization by developing its own linguistic forms. Endonormative stabilization (stage 4 in the model) is characterized by codification and a high degree of homogeneity.

This chapter will give an overview of the major categories of word-formation in PhE from the more frequent to the more infrequent types of word-formations. This will be achieved by using the Philippine component of the International Corpus of English (ICE-PHI). On the basis of a systematic comparison with the corpora of Great Britain (ICE-GB), Canada (ICE-CAN), Singapore (ICE-SIN), Hong Kong (ICE-HK) and India (ICE-IND), lexical properties and trends, as well as the current status of PhE word-formation, will be determined and assessed. While British English (BrE) and Canadian English (CanE), as first language or Inner Circle Englishes, serve as a kind of measuring stick, it will be instructive to see how Asian Englishes line up beside each other. In addition, the Corpus of Global Web-Based English (GloWbE) was used, which consists of 1.9 billion words and contains material from web pages and blogs from 20 different Englishes (Davies & Fuchs, 2015).

For the last 20 years, the vocabulary written and spoken in the Philippines has repeatedly attracted the attention of scholars (Bautista, 1997, 2000, 2008; Gonzalez, 1997; Schneider, 2004; Bolton & Butler, 2008; Biermeier, 2010, 2011, 2017). All of them have agreed that the lexicon of PhE is distinctive and continually expanded through lexical innovations. These new coinages are then ideally recorded by standard dictionaries such as the *Oxford English Dictionary* (*OED*) (cf. Salazar, 2014, 2017), provided the new

DOI: 10.4324/9780429427824-8

74　*Thomas Biermeier*

formations are broadly institutionalized, i.e. they are used over a longer time span—ten years to be recorded by the *OED*—and in various text types, both in writing and in speech.

Bautista (1997), who drew her data from the Macquarie Asian corpus, investigated a broad range of lexemes that did not appear in the Macquarie headword list of Australian English and subsequently asked native speakers to provide a definition of an Asian English word that should then be included in an Asian English dictionary. She provides a list of PhE words that have come into existence through normal expansion, coinage and borrowing. Under coinage, she subsumes analogical constructions, clippings, abbreviations, total innovations, English compounds and hybrid forms. In her observations, Bautista points out that PhE speakers make use of standard English word-formation techniques, while it is surprising that there are new formations that "are not words in recognized Englishes" (p. 69). She also states that some items are used differently in PhE, although she does not always refer to word-formations only (e.g. *bath, sleep, prep school*). She concludes that coinages and borrowings "may not cause as much inter-variety misunderstanding and miscommunication as the use of ordinary words that are used differently in different varieties of English" (69).

Despite some efforts and a favorable attitude to codify PhE vocabulary, an official dictionary that contains not only archaic words but also contemporary formations has never been compiled, although the Macquarie Asian corpus would have been a "good starting place for a Philippine English dictionary" (Bautista, 1997, p. 49). This is partly due to the still dominant influence of American English (AmE) in the Philippines (cf. Bolton & Butler, 2008; Crystal, 2003).

As a consequence, the gap between the rather archaic vocabulary as shown in many standard works on PhE and contemporary usage of English in the Philippines is immense. Examples such as *economic plunder, ambush interviews* or *topnotchers* are recorded only in the *OED*, but not in a dictionary of PhE or any other Asian English dictionary. The high token figures of these examples in the mega-corpus GloWbE (*ambush interviews* 20 out of 23 tokens, *topnotcher* 67 out of 67 tokens) are ample evidence of their exclusiveness to PhE.

As in other new Englishes, too, many of the distinctively PhE lexemes date back to the first contact and early development phase between the English-speaking settlers and the indigenous population. Yap (1970), for example, studied two versions of *Webster's* dictionary (1961, 1968) and compiled a list of words that mainly related to flora and fauna. However, only few words in the list could be considered characteristic of present-day PhE, as it appears in the media, for instance (cf. Bolton & Butler, 2008). Thus, it cannot be denied that the English used today "has a creative and vibrant word stock that directly reflects the hybridity of life in Philippine society" (p. 190).

Biermeier (2008, 2011, 2017) has repeatedly studied lexical trends in PhE. By surveying a wide range of word-formation processes, he came to the conclusion that writers and speakers of English in the Philippines use the standard word-formation techniques frequently and widely. Besides, his studies have revealed numerous new coinages which could not be identified by any of the standard dictionaries, such as the *OED*, the *Oxford Dictionary of English* (*ODE*), *Merriam-Webster's*, or by any of the standard computer corpora, such as the British National Corpus (BNC) or the Corpus of Contemporary American English (COCA). In fact, he places PhE alongside other Asian varieties, most notably English in India, Singapore and Hong Kong. Biermeier admits that L1 Englishes, which serve as a kind of benchmark, are still more productive, but he is rather optimistic that PhE might make up ground in the years to come because the potential of creating new words is enormous in his view. While his previous data were taken from the International Corpus of English (ICE), Biermeier (2017) focuses on the mega-corpus GloWbE in his most recent publication. Many of his findings on frequency and productivity from his previous articles on PhE are confirmed by the findings obtained from GloWbE. Crucially, the latter enables researchers to draw data from a much bigger corpus. However, there is no distinction of written and spoken texts. The closest category to spoken English is blogs, which can, however, not be considered spontaneous spoken conversation.

Dimaculangan and Gustilo (2017) clearly show that PhE is not deteriorating but proceeding to endonormative stabilization. They base their conclusions on investigations of texts drawn from a corpus sampled during 2005–2015. Even though the remarkable number of new lexical items they found can be considered products of rule-governed creativity, they clearly attest to the richness of PhE vocabulary.

5.2 Compounding

First and foremost, compounding is generally known to be rather productive. After affixation, compounds are the most common and transparent way of enriching a variety's lexis. According to Bauer (1983), compound nouns are by far the most frequent type. Within this category, the subtype of endocentric nouns, whose semantic head is inside the compound, appears most frequently (Table 5.1).

Table 5.1 Frequency of Compound Nouns (Sample of 100 Items)

	GB	CAN	IND	SIN	PHI	HK
Written	26	29	21	28	32	30
Spoken	33	19	20	17	24	17
Sum	51	38	33	36	43	37
Tokens	126	146	84	125	120	127

Token frequencies normalized to one million words, rounded to nearest integer (Meyer, 2002).

76 *Thomas Biermeier*

In PhE, compound nouns are used frequently, although there is some disparity between written and spoken English, which indicates that compound nouns seem to be preferred by writers rather than by speakers. They appear in letters, essays, academic and non-academic writing, press news reports, novels and stories. Other Asian varieties also show a preponderance of compound nouns in writing. In Ll, the pattern is usually reversed in favor of spoken English.

In terms of new or variety-specific coinages, a number of examples are attested in PhE: *comfort room* (PHI, w/s: 'toilet'), *junk fast foods* (PHI, s: 'very unhealthy fast food'), *junk list* (PHI, w: 'list containing names of people to be dumped'). The latter might be a nonce-formation as there is no occurrence in GloWbE.

In compounding, a rather prolific group consists of coordinative compounds ('conductor-composer'), with Hong Kong English (HKE) generating a notable number of new coinages: *choreographer-dancers* (HK), *missionary-translator* (HK), *friend-philosopher* (IND), *driver-bodyguard* (PHI).

As regards lexical variability in compounding, different lexicalization techniques are used in different varieties for the same semantic concept: *petrol station* in BrE and HKE, *petrol pump* in Indian English (IndE), *petrol kiosk* in Singapore English (SgE), *gasoline station* in PhE. The compound *gas station*, which is the preferred variant in AmE, occurs in CanE to a great extent. In SgE, one even encounters the term *fill-ups*, while the variant *filling station* is recorded in HKE. Besides, in the Philippines the following compounds are attested: *petrol station, gas station, gasoline station, petrol pump, filling station*.

A remarkable pattern can be detected in synthetic compounds, in which individual constituents trigger off a number of formations. PhE in particular comes up with a relatively high number of new formations and thus exhibits a high degree of productivity. In fact, PHI has produced a remarkable range of combinations with 'holder' being the head that is modified by different nouns: *flower holders, passport holders, degree holders, needlepoint holder, record holder, PhD holders, agreement holder, chalk holder*.

The formation *healthchecker* is not used in the sense of a person 'who looks after somebody's health', but in a business context referring to a person 'who evaluates the risks and issues of a project'. The rather creative agent noun *home-wrecker* is certainly informal and describes 'someone who destroys other relationships'. No doubt the lexeme *holduppers* is used in a derogatory sense: 'female [bank] tellers victimized by *holduppers* and pickpockets' (W2A-004). The latter occurs only four times in GloWbE (general website and blog), three of which tokens are attested in PhE (e.g. Americans use *mugger*, Filipinos use *holdupper*.) Interestingly, the Malaysian component of GloWbE refers to precautionary measures one should take "when you go to Phils", especially to Manila. Without doubt, this synthetic compound is variety-specific to PhE.

Next, combining forms in initial position are more common in written English. An in-depth analysis of selected elements of this category

Lexicon   77

(*cyber-* 'connected with electronic communication', *hyper-* 'in excess', *ultra-* 'extremely') shows that IndE, PhE and HKE produce a wide range of formations. Interesting examples in PhE are *cyber-age* (PHI, w), *cyber-bayan* (PHI, w), *cybermail* (PHI, w), *ultrabasic* (PHI, w), *ultra-male* (PHI, w).

Combinations with *cum* and multiple word combinations, which both attest to the varieties' lexical creativity, are frequently used in PhE as well as in the other Asian Englishes. Notable examples are *nation-cum-race* (PHI, w), *a well of affection cum friendship* (PHI, w), *non-formal livelihood cum literacy education programs* (PHI, s), *a rice thresher cum dryer* (PHI, w), *a must-do-by Dec. 31 letter* (PHI, w).

The notion of emphasizing a good relationship is expressed by the rather popular formative—*mate*: An investigation in GloWbE has shown that lexemes such as *batchmate* ('a friend from the same class at school'), *seatmate* and *churchmate* display much higher frequencies in PhE than in any other variety. Moreover, there are formations that have not been recorded so far: *growmate, prayermate, sparmate, province-mate, MTP-mate*. It remains to be seen whether they become established in the lexicon of PhE.

5.3 Hybridization and Indigenous Vocabulary

Owing to the colonial history of the Philippines, the influence of Spanish loan words on Philippine vocabulary is certainly considerable (cf. Schneider, 2007). A *merienda* (s) is a snack that is eaten either in mid-morning or in mid-afternoon. The meaning of 'farewell party' is expressed by the compound *despedida party* (s), even though the word 'party' creates a pleonastic effect.

The lexemes *nipa* and *carabao* are early borrowings denoting 'kind of palm' and 'water buffalo' (cf. Schneider, 2007). In PhE, there are these attestations: *nipa hut* (s), *carabao program* (w), *carabao cultivar* (w), *Carabao Center* (w), *carabao grass* (w), *Carabao race* (w). *Carabao* is extremely frequent in GloWbE-PHI. As regards other Englishes, this lexeme is only attested in Tanzanian English, although the title of the source is *Philippine Folk Tales*.

More famous is the blend *jeepney* denoting 'a small bus'. Consequently, there are a number of compounds consisting of *jeepney*: *jeepney strikes* (w), *jeepney drivers* (w: 2). In contrast to other Englishes, this lexeme is used with exceeding frequency in GloWbE-PHI (1,002 tokens). In the same vein, an interesting lexeme giving rise to hybrid compounds is *barangay*, which stands for 'the smallest political unit': *barangay permit* (w), *barangay officials* (w) and *barangay election* (w). The evidence for the lexeme *cyber* in GloWbE is overwhelming as it offers a wide range of different types and tokens, e.g. *to cyber stalk, cyber-stalking, cyber stalker; cyber libel; cyber Monday*.

Also, the exclamation *sayang* ('expressing sympathy') is derived from local languages (cf. Schneider, 2007). The only example collected in ICE-PHI is used as an adjective and can therefore be regarded as conversion: 'But at

78 *Thomas Biermeier*

least you get a double degree unlike me who gave up Accounting which is very very *sayang*'. PhE generates the adjective *Imeldific* named after the former president's wife, Imelda Marcos: 'The banks are not afraid for they believe in the *Imeldific* … rule … that those who have the gold make the rules' (W2E-010). According to Bautista (1997), it means "anything exaggeratedly ostentatious or in bad taste", referring to clothing, architecture, décor and the like. Here, *Imeldific* has a slightly different meaning. *Marcosian laws* (w) are the laws passed under the presidency of Ferdinand Marcos and many times the term carries a disparaging meaning.

Formations with the prefix *co-* appear to be highly productive in the Philippines. Notable examples of this type from PHI are *co-sufferer* (s), *co-teacher* (s: 5), *(to) co-host* (s: 2), *co-chairman* (s), *co-chair* (w, s), *co-star* (s: 2), *co-conspirator* (s: 2), *co-anchor* (s), *co-convener* (s: 2), *co-advisers* (s). It is interesting to observe that formations with *co-* are also popular in CanE, where we find a remarkable number of coinages in CAN. This parallel between PHI and CAN substantiates the hypothesis that PhE is strongly influenced by Northern American English.

Finally, the lexical item *presidentiable(s)* (s: 6) can be considered typical of PhE. It refers to a person 'who is aspiring to be president' or is perceived to be capable of being president. In GloWbE, it almost exclusively occurs in PhE (17 tokens: 9 general websites, 8 blogs). The same can be said of the term *senatoriable* (PHI, s). In GloWbE, this lexeme denoting a person who is capable of being senator appears only in PhE (3 blogs, 1 general website).

Relating to the semantic field of politics, too, the term *reelectionist* is attested only in the Philippines: 'The latest to make the charge was reelectionist Senator Freddie Webb…' (W2E-007). It denotes a person who runs for election again. Although Bautista (1997: 59) cites this term, there is no evidence of this formation in the standard references.

5.4 Suffixation

5.4.1 *Nominal Suffixes* -ship *and* -hood

The nominal suffixes *-ship* and *-hood* are both frequent and productive (Lieber, 2004). Similar in meaning, both form nouns which denote a state or condition. The suffix *-hood* is rather restricted in its occurrence, while the suffix *-ship* appears more frequently, especially in written English. Similar to the suffix *-ism*, *-ship* often has a political connotation (*hero-ship* PHI, w) (Table 5.2).

There is no clear distribution between written and spoken English for the morpheme *-hood*. Whereas SIN yields a relatively equal type distribution for written and spoken English, PHI clearly favors written texts. PhE displays a wide range of different formations, e.g. *tigerhood* (PHI, w), *womanhood* (PHI, w), *selfhood* (PHI, w), *boyhood* (PHI, w). In terms of token frequencies, *-hood* is most frequently employed in PHI (136), too. An examination of all formations in *-hood* as regards productivity across Englishes has yielded two

Lexicon 79

Table 5.2 Frequency of Nouns in -hood

	GB	CAN	IND	SIN	PHI	HK
Written	5	11	10	12	18	5
Spoken	12	9	13	11	8	5
Sum	12	15	16	16	19	6
Tokens	60	83	60	78	136	77

Token frequencies normalized to one million words, rounded to nearest integer.

unlisted nouns: *graduatehood* (SIN, s), *twentyhood* (PHI, w). In GloWbE, there is one new coinage in PhE (blogs): *abjecthood* ("We expect Marisol to collapse, but except for one traumatic instant of abjecthood, she holds up.").

5.4.2 Nominal Suffix -ism

In fact, scholars have repeatedly attributed a high degree of productivity to the suffix *-ism* (Bauer & Huddleston, 2002; Baumgardner, 1998; Schmid, 2005, 2011) (Table 5.3).

PhE writers and speakers use an exceptionally wide range of formations in *-ism*. Semantically speaking, nouns in *-ism* nearly always have a political, social or religious meaning: *one-worldism* (GB, w), *pan-Canadianism* (CAN, w), *Casteism* (IND), *Jainism* (IND), *anti-Congressism* (IND), *Sufism* (IND), *Ziaism* (IND), *Confucianism* (SIN), *kiasuism* (SIN), *moneytheism* (SIN), *Cartesianism* (PHI), *clientism* (PHI), *xenocentrism* (PHI), *cooperativism* (PHI), *Caesaro Popism* (PHI).

As can be seen from the examples above, Asian Englishes produce a great number of new coinages which are expressive of political and social processes taking place in a particular regional setting. In IndE, formations in *-ism* often convey a religious meaning. With regard to PhE, the unlisted formation *xenocentrism* (PHI, W1A-007) refers to the colonization of Chinese regions. By using the term *clientism* (PHI, W2B-012), the writer expresses his disapproval; he talks about returning to 'democratic politics after a dictatorship without going back to the familiar ways of patronage and clientism'. The same can be said about *clientelism*, which is regarded as a synonym by the *ODE*. Both nouns can be considered relatively recent since they appear only in GloWbE, and here mainly in L1 countries. Further examples from

Table 5.3 Frequency of Nouns in -ism

	GB	CAN	IND	SIN	PHI	HK
Written	87	103	86	63	94	91
Spoken	56	52	70	48	70	44
Sum	114	128	122	88	123	111
Tokens	497	478	619	357	557	420

Token frequencies normalized to one million words, rounded to nearest integer.

80   *Thomas Biermeier*

GloWbE are *turncoatism* ('the unprincipled party-switching of political parties for expediency'), *shopoholism* ('compulsive shopping' blogs), *deskism* ('elegant outward appearance of junior clerks' general website) and *Bounty Hunterism*. The latter refers to a game and the title of the source is 'Adventure Quest Worlds Walkthrough' (general website).

A closer look at the register tags reveals that the unlisted formations appear in informational writing as well as in personal writing. In terms of spoken English, the newly coined words come up in a broader range of categories: direct conversations, broadcast discussions, parliamentary debates, unprepared speeches and non-broadcast talks.

5.4.3 Nominal Suffix -ness

The nominal suffix *-ness*, which denotes a certain quality, is perhaps the most productive suffix in English. This suffix can be attached virtually to any adjective, which accounts for a high number of new coinages.

There are three new coinages in PHI: *Filipino-ness* (PHI, w), *nationness* (PHI, w: 2), *all-at-once-ness* (PHI, w: 2). The latter appears in this text in ICE-PHI:

> Thirdly, the Asian mind resorts to intuition, if logic is no longer able to solve a life problem. From the very fact that it thinks in cyclic *all-at-once-ness*, it must resort to means other than the usual mental processes applicable to the piecemeal and fragmentary. [...] The concept of *all-at-once-ness* which is the hallmark of the mind of Asia is annoying to the Western mind which cannot shake off its structural mode of thinking...
> (W2A-009 academic writing)

A closer look at the results obtained from GloWbE confirms the assumption that the nominal suffix *-ness* is rather creative in PhE: *paranoidness* ('blogs'), *otakuness* ('blogs': "passionate fandom"), *on-your-toes-ness* ('general website': "constant attention during potty training"), *oc-ness* ('general website': "obsessive compulsiveness"). It can be assumed that the person who created the new formation was not aware of the constraints of the written norm and coined the new word spontaneously.

5.4.4 Nominal Suffix -ee

The nominal suffix *-ee* is generally attached to verb bases (Bauer, 1993). According to Plag (2003), this suffix "derives nouns denoting sentient entities that are involved in an event as non-volitional participants" (p. 88), which means that *nominee* is 'someone who is nominated'. Bauer and Huddleston (2002) concentrate on 'the passive use of a past participle' and point out that this suffix is particularly productive in AmE, "though relatively few words in *-ee* become established" (p. 1697).

Lexicon 81

Many new -*ee* nouns evidenced in ICE appear in legal and work contexts. Presumably starting out from BrE or AmE, nouns in -*ee* have succeeded in becoming an important part of noun suffixation in Asian Englishes, too. In addition, a thoroughly carried out search for corpus evidence has yielded a number of lexemes which have not been recorded as yet. Most conspicuously, two of them stem from PhE:

- *Integrees* (PHI, s): The meaning suggested by the text is 'rebels/separatists who have been integrated into the police force' ('broadcast news'). In GloWbE-PHI (blog), we find one attestation of this lexeme: 'preference shall be given to qualified reserve officers in the active service and integrees'.
- *Orientees* (PHI, s): The information provided in the text passage ('business transactions') refers to a group of people who are orientated to a particular direction, in this case 'into the Lasallian community' (the De La Salle University community).

In PhE, nominalizations in -*ee* seem to be highly popular with both writers and speakers. Except for the examples above, a search in GloWbE-PHI revealed one other new coinage: *conveniencee* ('people whose affection or attention is taken for granted by a conveniencer, e.g. friends by friends, parents by children or students by mentors'). Filipinos seem to command a wide range of -*ee*-formations. This result can be accounted for by the historical ties between the United States and the Philippines since we stated above that the -*ee* suffix is more strongly linked to AmE.

5.4.5 Adjectival Suffixes -ish and -y

Finally, the adjectival suffixes -*y* and -*ish* represent a very creative and productive way of making new adjectives in English (Tables 5.4 and 5.5).

With regard to formations in -*ish*, it is especially SgE data that can be taken as evidence of their writers' and speakers' advanced level of language competence by offering an extremely wide range of types (Foley, 2001). Only BrE provides an even wider type range. This result proves the popular assumption that SgE will eventually turn into an L1 variety. PhE, on the other

Table 5.4 Frequency of Adjectives in -ish

	GB	CAN	IND	SIN	PHI	HK
Written	20	21	19 ·	24	16	20
Spoken	34	13	16	22	15	10
Sum	46	32	32	42	24	24
Tokens	74	48	41	79	49	65

Token frequencies normalized to one million words, rounded to nearest integer.

82   *Thomas Biermeier*

Table 5.5 Frequency of Adjectives in -y

	GB	CAN	IND	SIN	PHI	HK
Written	101	116	82	87	94	98
Spoken	112	129	50	73	63	65
Sum	162	185	104	123	120	122
Tokens	606	760	355	575	457	602

Token frequencies normalized to one million words, rounded to nearest integer.

hand, offers two new coinages: *lay-mannish* (PHI, s) and *politickish* (PHI, s). The latter appears in 'direct conversation' in which the speaker does not want to talk about anything that has to do with politics. It must be noted that both examples are derived from spoken English, emphasizing the notion that new words are often coined by speakers who do not have the full lexicon at hand and make words rather spontaneously.

However, in GloWbE-PHI a few new coinages are attested: *pondish state/ lawn, talkish, customer service-ish questions, cliffhangerish ending*. While the former two stem from general websites, the latter two occur in blogs, which are generally considered more informal.

On the other hand, CanE displays the widest range of adjectives in -*y*. Parallel to BrE, most formations come up in spoken English, which can be considered a distinctive trend of L1 varieties since the pattern in the Asian varieties under review is reversed. However, PhE writers seem to be familiar with this type of word-formation. In fact, they use it to a great extent, which can be seen in the high type result for written English. The only new formation obtained from GloWbE-PHI is *revengy*, which appears in a blog and refers to a female character in a movie.

5.5 Conversion

Conversion appears to be a rather popular technique of word-formation with Asian English writers and speakers. This is especially true of PhE, where conversions are used frequently and widely. Stylistically speaking, conversion is more frequent in written texts, except for CanE where we find slightly more types in spoken English. Once again, PhE displays the highest result in spoken English, thus demonstrating its speakers' lexical flexibility, even though the discrepancies between written and spoken English are by far not striking. As conversion is generally more closely associated with AmE (cf. Mencken, 1963), the conspicuous result in PhE may be accounted for by its normative orientation as well as by the colonial legacy left by the United States. This is especially indicated and confirmed by the high number of conversions identified in CanE, which is generally considered close to AmE (Crystal, 2003).

A search for conspicuous lexemes in the corpora produced very interesting results, thus providing substantial evidence that writers and speakers in

Asian Englishes are familiar with the concept of conversion. Spoken English accounts for a number of these striking coinages, thus demonstrating that new formations start out in speech when people rather spontaneously create a word by necessity. Remarkable examples from PhE are *to demo, to premier, traffic* ("it is very traffic and I have a customer to meet up").

5.6 Clippings

In PhE, writers and speakers use different types of clippings: back-clipping (*disco, demo*), mid-clipping (*flu, fridge*), fore-clipping (*phone, plane*). Needless to say that writers and speakers have been following basic patterns of clipping displayed by L1 countries, but have also been developing their own characteristic forms. In doing so, they intend to create snappy or catchy words, often coined in a particular situation, which are easy to bear in mind. Besides, speakers who use clipped forms are somewhat determined to dissociate themselves from other groups or from an outside world.

With regard to style, clippings usually have an informal or colloquial character (cf. Greenbaum, 1996). PhE writers and speakers seem to be well-accustomed to clippings as can be seen from a number of interesting examples. The short form of *documents*, for instance, is *docs*. Further examples worth highlighting are *condo, deli, mag, exaj, slow-mo, demo, Amboy, kinder, promo, aircon, sem* (cf. Bautista, 1997). All these shortenings can be identified in ICE or GloWbE.

5.7 Concluding Remarks

First, the different methods of using and making words in English are both institutionalized and productive in PhE. All word-formation categories under study are used to a considerable extent and, more importantly, nearly all of them display a high degree of productivity (except for conversion and clippings), which is documented by the remarkable number of new coinages found in ICE and GloWbE.

Second, as regards the extent of use, PhE follows closely behind L1 varieties. Some categories are used most frequently or second most frequently: compound nouns, nouns in *-ism*, nouns in *-ee*, nouns in *-hood*. In a number of instances, PhE offers an even wider range of lexical choices than BrE or CanE, which was entirely unexpected and undeniably argues for the advanced level of English in the Philippines. Moreover, PhE shares interesting features with CanE. Both seem to favor conversions, agent nouns and formations preceded by the morpheme *co-*, which attests to the influence of Northern American English on PhE.

Third, new coinages always attest to the degree of productivity of a given variety. Compared with the L1 varieties, we can especially observe a considerable number of new formations in the L2 varieties under study, above all in the Philippines. As regards PhE, the following categories have turned out

84 *Thomas Biermeier*

to be rather fruitful: nominal and neoclassical compounds, nouns in *-ness*, nouns in *-ship/-hood* and nouns in *-ee*. Thus, apart from the numerous lexical contributions through loan words (hybridization), the processes of compounding and suffixation especially contribute to the expansion of the vocabulary in PhE. In the same vein, synthetic compounds appear to be very productive, with the formative *-holder* triggering off a number of new combinations. On top of that, many new coinages are drawn from spoken English, thus underlining the common assumption that new words are created by speakers who do not always feel the constraints of written norms and therefore coin new words more liberally.

Fourth, PhE does not seem to be overly productive when it comes to using relatively recent categories of word-formation; this can be noticed when studying adjectives in *-ish* or *-y*, for example. However, the suffix *-ish* is increasingly used with compounds and nouns of more than one syllable.

Fifth, the findings point to an interesting conclusion. Contrary to what has been maintained about PhE being in a state of decline (Martin, 2014), the vocabulary and word-formation of this variety show a great potential for continuous lexical expansion and linguistic progress. As has been shown, writers and speakers exhibit an advanced level of lexical competence and use the categories of English word-formation both frequently and creatively. Perhaps it can be said that English in the Philippines is about to overcome the phase of nativization and, proceeding to endonormative orientation, will be able to attain the status of a distinctly stabilized variety in the years to come (cf. Borlongan, 2016; Borlongan & Collins, 2017).

References

Bauer, Laurie. (1983). *English Word-Formation*. Cambridge, UK: Cambridge University Press.

Bauer, Laurie. (1993). More *-ee* words. *American Speech*, 68, 222–4.

Bauer, Laurie, & Huddleston, Rodney. (2002). Lexical word-formation. In Rodney Huddleston & Geoffrey K. Pullum (Eds.), *The Cambridge Grammar of the English Language* (pp. 1621–721). Cambridge, UK: Cambridge University Press.

Baumgardner, Robert J. (1998). Word-formation in Pakistani English. *English World-Wide*, 19, 205–46.

Bautista, Ma. Lourdes S. (1997). The lexicon of Philippine English. In Ma. Lourdes S. Bautista (Ed.), *English Is an Asian Language: The Philippine Context. Proceedings of the Conference Held in Manila on August 2–3, 1996* (pp. 49–72). Sydney, Australia: Macquarie Library Ltd.

Bautista, Ma. Lourdes S. (2000). *Defining Standard Philippine English: Its Status and Grammatical Features*. Manila, the Philippines: De La Salle University Press.

Bautista, Ma. Lourdes S. (2008). Investigating the grammatical features of Philippine English. In Ma. Lourdes S. Bautista & Kingsley Bolton (Eds.), *Philippine English: Linguistic and Literary Perspectives* (pp. 201–18). Hong Kong SAR, China: Hong Kong University Press.

Biermeier, Thomas. (2008). *Word-Formation in New Englishes*. Berlin/Münster, Germany: LIT.

Lexicon 85

Biermeier, Thomas. (2010). Lexical trends in Asian Englishes as documented by the International Corpus of English. *Philippine Journal of Linguistics, Proceedings of the IAWE Conference in Cebu*, 41, 13–32.

Biermeier, Thomas. (2011). Lexical trends in Philippine English. In Ma. Lourdes S. Bautista (Ed.), *Studies of Philippine English: Exploring the Philippine Component of the International Corpus of English* (pp. 223–47). Manila, the Philippines: De La Salle University Centennial Book Series.

Biermeier, Thomas. (2017). Lexical trends in Philippine English revisited. *Philippine ESL Journal*, 19, 25–44.

Borlongan, Ariane Macalinga. (2016). Relocating Philippine English in Schneider's dynamic model. *Asian Englishes*, 18(3), 1–10.

Borlongan, Ariane, & Collins, Peter. (2017). Has Philippine English attained linguistic independence? The Grammatical evidence. *Philippine ESL Journal*, 19, 10–24.

Bolton, Kingsley, & Butler, Susan. (2008). Lexicography and the description of Philippine English vocabulary. In Ma. Lourdes S. Bautista & Kingsley Bolton (Eds.), *Philippine English: Linguistic and Literary Perspectives* (pp. 175–200). Hong Kong SAR, China: Hong Kong University Press.

Corpus of Global Web-Based English (GloWbE). http://corpus.byu.edu/glowbe/

Crystal, David. (2003). *The Cambridge Encyclopedia of the English Language*. 2nd ed. Cambridge, UK: Cambridge University Press.

Davies, Mark, & Fuchs, Robert. (2015). Expanding horizons in the study of World Englishes with the 1.9 billion word Global Web-based English Corpus (GloWbE). *English World-Wide*, 36, 1–28.

Dimaculangan, Nimfa, & Gustilo, Leah. (2017). Lexical patterns in the early 21st century Philippine English writing. *Advanced Science Letters*, 23, 1094–8. ASL Publishers.

Foley, Joseph. (2001). Is English a first or second language in Singapore? In Vincent B.Y. Ooi (Ed.), *Evolving Identities: The English Language in Singapore and Malaysia* (pp. 12–32). Singapore: Times Academic Press.

Gonzalez, Andrew. (1997). The history of English in the Philippines. In Ma. Lourdes S. Bautista (Ed.), *English Is an Asian Language: The Philippine Context. Proceedings of the Conference Held in Manila on August 2–3, 1996* (pp. 25–48). Sydney, Australia: Macquarie Library Ltd.

Greenbaum, Sidney (Ed.). (1996). *Comparing English Worldwide: The International Corpus of English*. Oxford, UK: Clarendon.

Lieber, Rochelle. (2004). *Morphology and Lexical Semantics*. Cambridge, UK: Cambridge University Press.

Martin, Isabel P. (2014). Beyond nativisation? Philippine English in Schneider's dynamic model. In Sarah Buschfeld, Thomas Hoffmann, Magnus Huber & Alexander Kautzsch (Eds.), *The Evolution of Englishes: The Dynamic Model and Beyond* (pp. 70–85). Amsterdam, the Netherlands: John Benjamins.

Mencken, Henry L. (1963). *The American Language*. New York: Knopf. Repr.

Meyer, Charles F. (2002). *English Corpus Linguistics: An Introduction*. Cambridge, UK: Cambridge University Press.

Most Populous Countries in the World (2022). https//www.worldometers.info/population/most-populous-countries

Plag, Ingo. (2003). *Word-formation in English*. Cambridge, UK: Cambridge University Press.

86 *Thomas Biermeier*

Salazar, Danica. (2014). Towards improved coverage of Southeast Asian Englishes in the Oxford English Dictionary. Lexicography ASIALEX, 1, 95–108.

Salazar, Danica. (2017). Philippine English in the *Oxford English Dictionary*: Recent advancements and implications for ESL in the Philippines. *Philippine ESL Journal*, 19, 45–59.

Schmid, Hans-Jörg. (2005). *Englische Morphologie und Wortbildung. Eine Einführung.* Berlin: Erich Schmidt Verlag.

Schmid, Hans-Jörg. (2011). *English Morphology and Word-Formation. An Introduction.* 2nd ed. Berlin, Germany: Erich Schmidt Verlag.

Schneider, Edgar W. (2004). How to trace structural nativization: particle verbs in world Englishes. *World Englishes*, 23, 227–49.

Schneider, Edgar W. (2007). *Postcolonial English: Varieties around the World.* Cambridge, UK: Cambridge University Press.

Webster's New International Dictionary of the English Language. (1961).

Webster's Third New International Dictionary of the English Language. (1968).

Yap, Fe A. (1970). *Pilipino Loan Words in English.* Manila: Surian Ng Wikang Pambansa. Athala November 1970.

6 Grammar

Shirley N. Dita, Philip Rentillo, and Aldrin P. Lee

6.1 Aim of This Chapter

If there is a Philippine English (PhE), is there a distinctive PhE grammar? Since the turn of the century, much of research on the grammar of PhE has shifted from broad descriptions of limited spoken and written data to more quantitative approaches using voluminous corpora. These advancements were made possible with the completion of the Philippine component of the International Corpus of English (ICE-PHI). Covering publications from 2000 to 2011, Lim and Borlongan (2012) have identified around 40 papers which analyzed PhE in terms of grammar alone Meanwhile, for the years 2000 to 2013, Borlongan (2013) have listed 18 works focusing only on the verb in PhE. True to the claim by Tay (1991), PhE has a thorough scholarship and possibly remains one of the most comprehensive among postcolonial Englishes.

Decades of theoretical and methodological developments have prompted greater scholarly vigilance on the current grammatical identity of PhE and its evolution. These are all part of the larger question on what PhE truly is as a variety with reference to Schneider's (2003, 2007) dynamic model for the evolution of Englishes. As it was originally described to be undergoing nativization (phase 3 in the dynamic model), Borlongan (2016) argues that PhE has now reached the next phase. This endonormative stabilization, he claims, is evidenced by signs of phonological and grammatical stabilization and an independent national linguistic tradition.

To provide a general description on the current grammatical features of PhE, this chapter discusses the most recent studies that have explored the area over the past 20 years. Included herein are findings on verbs in terms of their morphosyntax, tense and aspect, voice, and modality. This is followed by noun phrases, adjectives and adverbs, prepositions, particles, tag questions, negation, subject-verb concord, and relativizers.

DOI: 10.4324/9780429427824-9

6.2 Verbs

6.2.1 Morphology

Morphosyntactic structure of verbs in PhE is overwhelmingly regular in morphology (Borlongan, 2011b), a pattern akin to that in American English (AmE). Past tense and past perfect tenses usually take the -d/-ed forms instead of the -t form.

1 Most of the others **were burned** or sustained eye injuries from firecrackers. <ICE-PHI:W2C-019#29:2:A>
2 "I think I **burned** my back," he repeated, turning his head to her. <ICE-PHI:W2F-020#124:1:A>
3 This was done in nineteen fifty-one when the United States nor the Philippines **dreamed** of the Spratlys […] <ICE-PHI:S2A-068#76:1:A>
4 […] Rizal remembers the time when as a freshman medical student at the University of Santo Tomas he **dreamed** that he was taking an exam… <ICE-PHI:W2B-013#60:2>
5 I hope to God that the Philippine government **has learned** from the past […] <ICE-PHI:S2B-030#45:1:A>
6 She also **learned** that Louie Ocampo, Tony Tolentino and Robin Rivera, the producer of Eraserheads, were alumni of this prestigious school. <ICE-PHI:W2D-019#105:2>

A common use of the irregular participial form *burnt* is as a modifier.

7 From Ninoy's **burnt**-out candle and thousands like it in cells throughout the garrison state we gathered the melted wax… <ICE-PHI: S2B-027#16:1:A>
8 Right now you just can see the **burnt** remi remains or remnants of the effigies… <ICE-PHI:S2A-004#104:1:F>

There are also lexicalized exceptions such as preference for the irregular participial form *proven* instead of *proved*.

9 Definitely we have **proven** that we are one nation we are able to rise up and we are able to host something of this magnitude… <ICE-PHI: S2A-016#24>
10 Unfortunately, research has **proven** that cooking, processing, irradiating, microwaving and other preservation techniques… <ICE-PHI: W2B-037#110:2>

6.2.2 Tense and Aspect

Among the most notable studies on PhE tense and aspect are those by Gonzalez (1985) and Bautista (2000a) who provided broad descriptions of the

Grammar 89

tense-aspect system based on internal features. These were followed nearly a decade later by cross-variety comparisons (Collins, 2008; Hundt, 2009) on specific and diverse range of constructions. Borlongan (2011a, in press) in his grammar provides a thorough internal analysis of the morphosyntax and semantics of the PhE verb phrase.

Based on the semantic typology of verbs listed by Quirk et al. (1985), the simple present forms are used (in order of frequency) as reference to present states or conditions followed by references to futurity, present habits, instantaneous events, historical present, and, marginally, fictional narratives.

Instantaneous events are dynamic verbs which occur during the very moment of linguistic production as in current real-world events. Given their contextual purpose, they are not found in 11 out of 17 written genres of ICE-PHI. Rather, they are more common in spoken demonstrations, commentaries, and broadcast news. Examples (11) and (12), which are from TV commentators for a basketball match and the 1991 Southeast Asian Games, demonstrate this:

11 Sison throws to Villanueva but nice anticipation by Mangulabnan gives it to Tagupa. <ICE-PHI:S2A-009#117:1:A>
12 The SEA Games flag uh taking its panel of blue for the final march here at the Rizal Memorial Stadium. <ICE-PHI:S2A-016#52:1:A>

The historical present are past events mentioned in the present tense for a more vivid narration or to report a claim such as the use of *say* in (13).

13 Uh in that speech she outlined her thirty-five promises and uh out of the thirty-five there are some groups that say twenty-two promises were uh delivered by the President and her administration her cabinet. <ICE-PHI:S2A-005#16:1:A>

Lastly, fictional narratives from the term itself refer to narration of actions or report of a claim but in a fictional context. These are more commonly found in written texts particularly of literary and academic genres such as in (14).

14 a. Perseus is son of the supreme god Zeus and being so, the god intervenes in Perseus' struggles. <ICE-PHI:W1A-017#83:5>

On the other hand, simple past forms are used as reference to [1] past events followed by [2] past attitudes, [3] past states or conditions, [4] past habits, and marginally [5] indirect thoughts and [6] hypothetical past. Indirect thoughts and the hypothetical past are found in subordinate clauses. The former express assumptions or recall based on the senses as shown in (15).

15 She thought that she felt dizzy and then she asked us did did you feel that <ICE-PHI:S1A-007#6:1:B>

90   *Shirley N. Dita et al.*

The latter express conjectured or aspired events or actions typically contained within an *if*-phrase such as (16) and (17).

16   And then that night I told my parents Dad what if I <u>answered</u> Angelo already. <ICE-PHI:S1A-083#94:1:A>
17   If you <u>were</u> a pickpocket and you <u>got</u> you <u>got</u> caught and you <u>got</u> convicted then you would be given hanging as the sentence. <ICE-PHI: S2A-050#58:1:A>

This general preference for simpler, succinct structures can be assumed to explain for the higher preference for perfectives and progressives. The perfective aspect is found to be used mainly for five temporal interpretations, in order of frequency: [1] state leading to time of orientation, [2] time zone leading to time of orientation, [3] recent event, [4] result of an action leading to time of orientation, and [5] habit leading to time of orientation.

On the one hand, Collins (2008) found that progressives are thrice more likely to be used in spoken over written forms. In terms of genre they are mostly found (in descending order) in conversations, fiction, news, and academic prose. Across forms, present and past progressives (e.g. *is* + *-ing*; *was* + *-ing*) are significantly more common among others.

18   You know my father <u>was asking</u> "what did you learn," and then I told him the Chinese word for "how much." <ICE-PHI:S1A-008#59:1:B>
19   Yeah they <u>are using</u> Filipino for uh *Sibika at Kultura.* <ICE-PHI: S1B-045#26:2:B>
20   In fact uh we <u>were monitoring</u> Pinatubo. <ICE-PHI:S1B-022#76:1:B>
21   Uh *kasi* this happened to me last term and I thought it was when I <u>was wearing</u> headbands... <ICE-PHI:S1B-073#16:1:B>
22   It <u>was moving</u> westward at eleven kilometers per hour in the direction of eastern Luzon. <ICE-PHI:S2B-020#41:1:A>
23   By the way the tenth PCA Open Tennis Championship <u>is being</u> brought to you by San Miguel Beer Super Dry, Milo... <ICE-PHI:S2A-014#17:1:A>

Perfect progressives (e.g. *has been* + *-ing*) are relatively much less common possibly due to their morphological complexity and formal tone. Parallel to what Borlongan (2011a) observed as higher preference for present over past forms, in the one million-word ICE-PHI only 25 past perfect progressives can be identified while the remaining 161 are present perfect progressives.

24   A Filipino dealer <u>has been locating</u> paintings abroad by advertising in newspapers and art publications... <ICE-PHI:W2B-005#59:1>
25   But I think our government <u>has been doing</u> their job, not really excellently, but in a fine way and they may <u>have been doing</u> their job fairly and justly. <ICE-PHI:W1A-011#67:1>

Grammar 91

26 Uh we <u>had been preparing</u> for this uh since we had uh heard from uh Director Punongbayan about the possibility of eruption you know. <ICE-PHI:S1B-022#105:1:D>
27 That's one of the reasons why the Cebuanos <u>have been clamoring</u> for a Cebuano President *'no* so that we can have a Malacañang here in Cebu. <ICE-PHI:S2A-001#2:1:A>

Suárez-Gómez and Seoane (2012) meanwhile found high preference for the non-past form (e.g. *get*) to express present perfectives.

In terms of futurity, PhE uses *will* significantly more than *shall* notably in conversations (Nelson, 2005). The latter is only present in formal, public, and non-interactive contexts particularly legal texts compared to, say, British English which still appears in various spoken and written contexts.

6.2.3 Voice

Specific to PhE *get*-passives is the likelihood to be used in spoken form as pseudo-passive constructions. In terms of semantics, they are used more for adversarial contexts and less for benefactive meaning.

28 …some people don't feel comfortable with that uh with that term they <u>get confused</u> they <u>get threatened.</u> <ICE-PHI:S1B-003#88:1:A>
29 But *eh* but I don't think it's healthy that they <u>get involved.</u> <ICE-PHI: S1A-042#40:1:A>
30 We don't we <u>don't get paid</u> with this right? <ICE-PHI:S1A-026#53:1:A>
31 The pressure up there is so great you could <u>get sucked out</u> of the toilet bowl, you know. <ICE-PHI:W2F-017#110:1>
32 Well she just <u>got sick</u> the other day. <ICE-PHI:S1A-019#13:1:A>

These patterns are much more frequent than in British English (BrE), and evidence of a strong AmE influence (Alonsagay & Nolasco, 2010) as attested in comparisons of American and British corpora (Leech et al., 2009; Mair, 2006).

Meanwhile Hundt's (2006) analysis of PhE progressive passives (e.g. *is being* + participle) found most frequent use in general prose (despite no statistical difference in general frequencies between written and spoken). Consistent with other findings on tense majority are in present.

33 Transonic planting—wherein the Bt endotoxin gene from *Bacillus thuringiensis* <u>is being transferred</u> to corn, *pechay* and Chinese cabbage—<u>is</u> now <u>being done.</u> <ICE-PHI:W2B-038#59:2>
34 Liquidity problems of rural banks on a massive scale <u>is being experienced</u> for the first time. <ICE-PHI:W2B-017#69:1>

92   *Shirley N. Dita et al.*

6.2.3.1 *Modality*

Schneider (2004) was the first to explore modality in PhE with the hypothesis that certain types and uses of particle verbs predominate within specific contexts. He then focused on subjunctive modals, which were found to be more common in ordinary spoken form, and, similar to its AmE parent, were more commonly used in mandative functions (Schneider, 2005, 2011) especially when juxtaposed with verbs that express request, namely *ask*, *demand*, and *recommend*. Peters (2009) meanwhile found that there is a high frequency of mandative subjunctives in spoken contexts.

Bautista (2008) meanwhile investigated the use of *assure* and found high use of a modal without an indirect object in PhE. This seems to be a unique feature based on the premise that the context could already be deduced and thus would deem the information redundant.

Collins (2009b) found that PhE has the highest average frequency of quasi-modal use in both written and spoken forms among the Inner (IC) and Outer Circle (OC) varieties in his corpora analysis.[1] Among the identified structures *have to* and *be going to* are the most preferred and significantly more common compared to other OC varieties, which is a tendency mirroring that of AmE, which in turn has the highest frequency among all IC varieties.

35   But we're just going to prepare the the tomato basil and the and the and the onion soup right. <ICE-PHI:S1A-014#2>

6.2.3.2 **Noun Phrase**

Bautista (2008) as part of her large-scale analysis of PhE grammar covered three types of noun phrase constructions including *one of the*, *majority*, and *such* with high consideration for the collocation of succeeding articles to determine their grammatical nature. She found that Asian varieties involved in her study with PhE included were likelier to have *one of the* + singular noun constructions than BrE, which almost always adheres to the standard use of attaching the phrase to a succeeding plural or collective noun. She deduces that the semantic notion of *one* in preceding phrases could have a greater effect to such grammatical choice among the users of OC Englishes. Meanwhile PhE yielded the highest occurrence of *majority* constructions without a preceding article. This was followed by Singapore English (SgE) and Hong Kong English (HKE), respectively, while it was absent in the entire BrE dataset. This was the same case for the use of *such* with a noun where anaphora may have less influence over the use of articles among the Asian varieties, which Bautista deduces to be a sign of rule simplification. This was pronounced in both PhE and HKE.

In a later study, Bautista (2010b) investigated the case marking of *wh*-pronouns and indefinite compound pronouns *-body* and *-one* of PhE (and SgE) using then-incomplete ICE datasets in comparison with Schneider's (2000) data on Indian English (InE), BrE, and AmE through the Kholapur,

Grammar 93

LOB, and Brown corpora, correspondingly. For *wh*-pronouns she found that mostly in informal contexts there is a greater tendency for PhE to use *who* in objective case in place of *whom*. It was also noted that antecedent animacy was a factor in the use of *whose*. Meanwhile for indefinite compound pronouns the *-one* form yielded higher frequency versus the *-body* form. However, when looking at text type, there was greater frequency of the *-body* form among all said pronouns in the spoken data suggesting that the other carries a more formal tone.

Borlongan (2011b) looked into the use of *s*-genitives through a combination of different corpora datasets. He found that PhE similar to 1960s BrE is "conservative" due to a relatively high occurrence of the said genitive form.

6.2.3.3 *Adjectives and Adverbs*

Similar to other varieties, PhE also has greater preference for inflectional comparatives (i.e. *-er*), while the periphrastic form (*more* + adjective, e.g. *more rich*) and double comparatives (*more* + inflected adjective, e.g. *more richer*) remain marginal (Borlongan, 2011).

36 He broke the tradition of informing his people about the marriage, and became <u>more calm</u> in facing a dilemma (that of a challenge posed by his rival). <W1A-015#47>
37 What's even <u>more sad</u> about it is that Bea... <S1A-081#58>
38 Yes no Bicol is much <u>more farther</u>. <S1A-028#193>

Dita (2011), on the other hand, analyzed the internal use and structure of adverbial disjuncts in PhE by applying a framework based on Quirk et al.'s (1985) and Greenbaum and Nelson's (1996) definitions. Using ICE data, she found that there is a significantly greater occurrence of single-word *-ly* types in spoken texts, which are dominated respectively by *actually, basically*, and *hopefully*. The next in the top 5 with narrower gap in spoken and written usage are *apparently* and *obviously*. Spoken PhE is also strikingly abounding in clausal disjuncts such as *I think, I guess, I believe,* and *I suppose*. These are followed by phrasal disjuncts this time in both spoken and written forms through *in fact, at least*, and *as a matter of fact*. These patterns all in all confirm earlier pre-corpora impressions on the Philippine variety to be strongly academic, formal, and generally spoken as how it is written "based on Victorian models" (Gonzalez, 2005, p. 439). Despite this there are few patterns that suggest deviation such as predominant use as discourse fillers more than the usual evaluative or commentary marker, and departure from restrictions on cooccurrences such as two successive *-ly* disjuncts in one clause (e.g. *No everything [actually] has been [basically] mapped out...*), and juxtapositions such as a combination of a pragmatic marker, a discourse filler, and an adverbial (e.g. *[So] [I guess], [hopefully] I'll, someone would come along, sooner or later hopefully.*).

94 *Shirley N. Dita et al.*

6.2.3.4 Prepositions

Bautista (2008) as part of her chapter on the grammatical features of PhE explores prepositions. Two notable features were found: prevalence of *result to* and arbitrary verb + preposition combinations. She explains that Filipinos' idiosyncratic use of prepositions comes from their difficulty with acquiring and/or learning English prepositions due to Philippine languages, the common L1, having less complex prepositional systems.

Dayag (2016) later on saw great preference for both stranding and pied-piping in spoken forms over written despite the latter being more associated with written, formal contexts. An example would be in (39) below.

39 You know to whom this (touching his heart) belongs. <ICE-PHI: W2F-005#93:1>

6.2.3.5 Particles

Although non-inherently part of English, enclitic particles (also called adverbial particles) as widely used in spoken English among Filipinos was hypothesized to be prevalent in PhE. Such a small yet important word class is distinct relative to English and is found in Tagalog and other Philippine languages grammatically functioning either as adverbs or as emphatic markers. Bautista (2011) conducted a preliminary analysis using ICE on the particle *'no*, its full form as *ano*, on its uses and found much of it within spoken texts. This was later expanded by Lim and Borlongan (2011) who included *ba*, *na*, and *pa*, all of which were found overwhelmingly present in spoken data.

40 If ano uhm it has something to do with intention. <ICE-PHI:S1A-056#270:1:A>
41 Uh so it is really... a very small world ano. <ICE-PHI:S1B-071#65:1:A>
42 This is what we call a generalization 'no. <ICE-PHI:S2A-044#179:1:A>
43 But otherwise the function of the uvula is to close the nasal cavity so that you have a clear oral passage 'no. <ICE-PHI:S1B-017#75:1:A>
44 What sort of people ba do you have to deal with? <ICE-PHI:S1A-006#54:1:A>
45 ...this indicate a direction na eventually you really want to widen the scope of uh of Filipino as a medium of instruction... <ICE-PHI:S1B-045#22:2:A>
46 So and if they have kids of their own pa then that would be really really complicated. <ICE-PHI:S1A-006#174:1:A>

All said particles are used in English just as how they originally function and occur, and thus similarly cover various contextualized functions. For instance, *ba* incites or emphasizes yes-no questions, or emphasizes *wh*-questions. *'no* is used to emphasize or enhance a proposition, to facilitate or sustain conversation, or to request or confirm information. The particle

Grammar 95

na is used as a temporal marker of approximate futurity, of completed state or action, as an imperative marker of urgency and of changed plan, and as a negation collocate of changed plan. *pa* can be a temporal marker of distant futurity, of imperfective state, or of recent perfective action. As an emphatic marker it expresses perfective or imperfective action. As a collocate, it appears beside a *wh*-question or a negation of imperfective action or state.

6.2.3.6 Tag Questions

Borlongan (2008) as of date is the only one to provide a comprehensive analysis of the use of tag questions in PhE. Comparing the Philippine component of ICE with Wong's (2007) data on HKE from ICE, and Tottie and Hoffman's (2006) data on BrE from the British National Corpus (BNC), and AmE from the Longman Spoken American Corpus (LSAC), he found that while both OC Englishes have significantly fewer occurrences than their IC parents, PhE is the least likely to use them. The data could suggest internal norms in PhE as this feature is most commonly used to express emphasis on a proposition without expected response (attitudinal), and to verify information (confirmatory) compared to the other varieties which prefer them for confirmatory and facilitating purposes. In general, however, PhE tag question constructions lean toward the positive-negative polarity the same way as those in AmE and BrE.

6.2.3.7 Negation

To date only one study has so far given a detailed focus on negation patterns in PhE. Bautista (2010a), as part of her chapter on corpus-based analysis, looked into *have*-negation patterns. *Have* + indefinite noun phrase constructions in PhE were found to feature more *do not have a/any* forms as compared to AmE, which prefers *have no* constructions. On the one hand, in terms of definite noun phrases, both OC varieties converge with AmE with their preference for *do not have the* form over the more common BrE form of *have not got the*. In general the *do not have* construction was found to be most typical in spoken private dialog texts, while the *have no* construction in written informational texts.

6.2.3.8 Subject-Verb Concord

Bautista (2000b) reveals that deviations on subject-verb concord were the most frequent. While these instances are indeed errors and cannot be considered part of standard PhE, some deviations can be qualified as localized patterns. Some of these are:

1 Collective nouns and notional concord interfering with grammatical concord
2 Special nouns that have variable number agreement rules

96 *Shirley N. Dita et al.*

3 Intervening prepositional phrases
4 Inverted sentences
5 Predicate nominatives

Hundt (2006) however found that there were no significant differences between PhE and other varieties in terms of subject-verb concord involving collective nouns. Collins (2011) later looked into *there*-constructions and found that PhE patterns are likewise close to AmE in terms of usage patterns of singular agreement with plural noun phrases, tense, 's-contraction, absence of overt noun phrase plural marking, extensions, and sandwiched elements between verb and subject.

6.2.3.9 *Relativizers*

Suárez-Gómez (2018) provides an account of the use of relativizers in spontaneous spoken PhE in comparison with other varieties. In light of the claims that this PhE concurrently maintains both linguistic conservatism and endonormative innovation as a result of contact, the study first aimed to verify if PhE adapted the general distinction between *who* and *that* as seen in other varieties. Findings reveal that the former is used for human antecedents, while the latter for non-human. *Who* is also dominantly used for human antecedents syntactically functioning as the subject, while zero relativizer is preferred for those in object function. On the other hand, *that* is most frequently used regardless of syntactic function, but *which* comes in for antecedents functioning as subjects. It is assumed that the frequency of subject relative clauses is attributed to the influence of significant contact with Tagalog.

Bautista (2008) early on investigated the use of *wherein* in PhE. As a very notable feature, it was found that the relativizer was used significantly. The semantic function of the PhE *wherein* is also quite distinct. It veers away from the canonical use where it rather approximates the Tagalog ligature *na*, and is predominant in informal spoken texts.

6.3 Conclusion

At the beginning of this chapter it was asked: Is there is a distinct PhE grammar? The answer is yes and no. All the observed patterns across its features do suggest that there are some internal norms that are characteristic of this new English. These are evident when looking at a wide range of features in the PhE dataset in comparison with other Englishes, most particularly with its parent AmE. While these are already signs of endonormative stabilization, there remains gravitation toward exonormative norms (Collins & Borlongan, 2017).

Research on PhE grammar has indeed come a long way. The advent of corpus-based, quantitative methods has given more systematic and measurable

Grammar 97

ways to look at the development of English and its varieties around the world. This warrants the need to further explore and understand the grammatical identity of PhE, and where it stands in comparison with other established and emerging Englishes. Through the emergence of corpus-based linguistics, which offer richer datasets than ever before, the possibility of more complex analytical methods (e.g. diachrony), and the involvement of less-explored grammatical features (e.g. complex prepositions), the developmental trajectory of PhE through its grammar could be observed in more detail.

Note

1 Nine (9) varieties were analyzed using the ICE corpora: Australian, New Zealand, British, and American representing the Inner Circle; Philippine, Singapore, Hong Kong, Indian, and Kenyan for the Outer Circle.

References

Alonsagay, Ingrid, & Nolasco, Josephine. (2010). Adversativity and the *get*-passive in Philippine and British English: A corpus-based contrastive study. *Philippine Journal of Linguistics, 41*, 1–13.

Bautista, Ma. Lourdes S. (2000a). *Defining Standard Philippine English: Its status and grammatical features.* De La Salle University Press.

Bautista, Maria Lourdes S. (2000b). Studies of Philippine English in the Philippines. *Philippine Journal of Linguistics, 31*(1), 39–65.

Bautista, Maria Lourdes S. (2008). Investigating the grammatical features of Philippine English. In Maria Lourdes S. Bautista, & Kingsley Bolton (eds.), *Philippine English: Linguistic and literary perspectives* (pp. 201–218). Hong Kong University Press.

Bautista, Maria Lourdes S. (2010a). Comparing spoken and written text-types in Singapore English and Philippine English. In David Jonathan Y. Bayot (Ed.), *Inter/sections: Isagani Cruz and friends* (pp. 175–200). Anvil.

Bautista, Maria Lourdes S. (2010b). Exemplary analyses of the Philippine English corpus. In Loren Billings, & Nelleke Goudswaard (Eds.), *Piakandatu ami Dr. Howard P. McKaughan* (pp. 5–23). Linguistic Society of the Philippines.

Bautista, Maria Lourdes S. (2011). Some notes on *'no* in Philippine English. In Maria Lourdes S. Bautista (Ed.), *Studies on Philippine English: Exploring the Philippine component of the International Corpus of English* (pp. 75–89). Anvil.

Borlongan, Ariane M. (2008). Tag questions in Philippine English. *Philippine Journal of Linguistics, 39*, 109–134.

Borlongan, Ariane M. (2011a). *A grammar of the verb of Philippine English* (Unpublished doctoral dissertation). De La Salle University.

Borlongan, Ariane M. (2011b). Some aspects of the morphosyntax of Philippine English. In Maria Lourdes S. Bautista (ed.), *Studies on Philippine English: Exploring the Philippine component of the International Corpus of English* (pp. 187–199). Anvil.

Borlongan, Ariane M. (2013). Corpus-based works on the Philippine English verb system. *Asian English Studies, 13*, 69–90.

98   *Shirley N. Dita et al.*

Borlongan, Ariane M. (2016). Relocating Philippine English in Schneider's dynamic model. *Asian Englishes, 18*(3), 232–241. https://doi.org/10.1080/13488678.2016.1223067

Collins, Peter. (2008). The progressive aspect in World Englishes: A corpus-based study. *Australian Journal of Linguistics, 28*(2), 225–249. https://doi.org/10.1080/07268600802308782

Collins, Peter. (2009b). Modals and quasi-modals in World Englishes. *World Englishes, 28*(3), 281–292. https://doi.org/10.1111/j.1467-971X.2009.01593.x

Collins, Peter. (2011). Variable agreement in existential-*there* construction in Philippine English. In Maria Lourdes S. Bautista (Ed.), *Studies on Philippine English: Exploring the Philippine component of the International Corpus of English* (pp. 175–186). Anvil.

Collins, Peter, & Borlongan, Ariane M. (2017). Has Philippine English attained linguistic independence? The grammatical evidence. *Philippine ESL Journal, 19*, 10–24.

Dayag, Danilo T. (2016). Preposition stranding and pied-piping in Philippine English: a corpus-based study. In Gerhard Leitner, Azirah Hashim, & Hans-George Wolf (Eds.), *Communicating with Asia: The future of English as a global language* (pp. 102–119). Cambridge University Press. https://doi.org/10.1017/CBO9781107477186.008

Dita, Shirley. (2011). The semantics and grammar of disjuncts in Philippine English. In Maria Lourdes S. Bautista (Ed.), *Studies on Philippine English: Exploring the Philippine component of the International Corpus of English* (pp. 33–50). De La Salle University.

Gonzalez, Andrew. (1985). *Studies on Philippine English*. SEAMEO Regional Language Centre.

Gonzalez, Andrew. (2005). Philippine English. In T. McArthur (Ed.), *Concise Oxford companion to the English language* (pp. 438–440). Oxford University Press.

Greenbaum, Sidney, & Nelson, Gerald. (1996). Positions of adverbial clauses in British English. *World Englishes, 15*(1), 69–81. https://doi.org/10.1111/j.1467-971X.1996.tb00093.x

Hundt, Marianne. (2006). The committee has/have decided… On concord patterns with collective nouns in Inner- and Outer-Circle varieties of English. *Journal of English Linguistics, 34*(3), 206–232. https://doi.org/10.1177/0075424206293056

Hundt, Marianne. (2009). Global feature – Local norms? A case study on the progressive passive. In Thomas Hoffman, & Lucia Siebers (Eds.), *World Englishes – Problems, properties and prospects* (pp. 287–308). John Benjamins.

Leech, Geoffrey, Hundt, Marianne, Mair, Christian, & Smith, Nicholas. (2009). *Change in contemporary English: A grammatical study.* Cambridge University Press.

Lim, Joo Hyuk, & Borlongan, Ariane M. (2011). Tagalog particles in Philippine English: The cases of *ba, na, 'no,* and *pa. Philippine Journal of Linguistics, 42*, 58–74.

Lim, Joo Hyuk, & Borlongan, Ariane M. (2012). Corpus-based grammatical studies of Philippine English and language assessment: Issues and perspectives. *The Assessment Handbook, 8*, 51–62.

Mair, Christian. (2006). *Twentieth-century English: History, variation and standardisation.* Cambridge University Press.

Nelson, Gerald. (2005). Expressing future time in Philippine English. In Danilo T. Dayag, & J. Stephen Quakenbush (Eds.), *Linguistics and language education*

Grammar 99

in the Philippines and beyond: A festschrift in honor of Ma. Lourdes S. Bautista (pp. 41–59). Linguistic Society of the Philippines.

Peters, Pam. (2009). The mandative subjunctive in spoken English. In Pam Peters, Peter Collins, & Adam Smith (Eds.), *Comparative studies in Australian and New Zealand English: Grammar and beyond* (pp. 125–137). John Benjamins.

Quirk, Randolph, Greenbaum, Sidney, Leech, Geoffrey, & Svartvik, Jan. (1985). *A comprehensive grammar of the English language*. Longman.

Schneider, Edgar W. (2000). Corpus linguistics in the Asian context: Exemplary analyses of the Kolhapur corpus of Asian English. In Maria Lourdes S. Bautista, Teodoro A. Llamzon, & Bonifacio P. Sibayan (Eds.), *Parangal cang Brother Andrew: Festschrift for Andrew Gonzalez on his sixtieth birthday* (pp. 115–137). Linguistic Society of the Philippines.

Schneider, Edgar W. (2003). The dynamics of new Englishes: From identity construction to dialect birth. *Language, 79,* 233–281. http://dx.doi.org/10.1353/lan.2003.0136

Schneider, Edgar W. (2004). How to trace structural nativization: Particle verbs in World Englishes. *World Englishes, 23*(2), 227–249. https://doi.org/10.1111/j.0883-2919.2004.00348.x

Schneider, Edgar W. (2005). The subjunctive in Philippine English. In Danilo T. Dayag, & J. Stephen Quakenbush (Eds.), *Linguistics and language education in the Philippines and beyond: A festschrift in honor of Ma. Lourdes S. Bautista* (pp. 27–40). Linguistic Society of the Philippines.

Schneider, Edgar W. (2007). *Postcolonial English: Varieties of English around the world*. Cambridge University Press.

Schneider, Edgar W. (2011). The subjunctive in Philippine English: An updated assessment. In Maria Lourdes S. Bautista (Ed.), *Studies on Philippine English: Exploring the Philippine component of the International Corpus of English* (pp. 159–173). Anvil.

Suárez-Gómez, Cristina. (2018). A sociolinguistic study of relativizers in spoken Philippines English. In Elena Seoane, Carlos Acuña-Fariña, & Ignacio Palacios-Martínez (Eds.), *Subordination in English: Synchronic and diachronic perspectives* (pp. 285–308). De Gruyter.

Suárez-Gómez, Cristina, & Seoane, Elena. (2012). They have published a new cultural policy that just came out: Competing forms in spoken and written new Englishes. In Gisle Andersen, & Kristin Bech (Eds.), *English corpus linguistics: Variation in time, space and genre (Selected papers from ICAME 32)* (pp. 163–182). Rodopi.

Tay, Mary W. J. (1991). Southeast Asia and Hong Kong. In Jenny Cheshire (Ed.), *English around the world: Sociolinguistic perspectives* (pp. 319–332). Cambridge, the United Kingdom: Cambridge University Press.

Tottie, Gunnel, & Hoffmann, Sebastian. (2006). Tag questions in British and American English. *Journal of English Linguistics, 34*(4), 283–311. https://doi.org/10.1177%2F0075424206294369

Wong, May L.-Y. (2007). Tag questions in Hong Kong English: A corpus-based study. *Asian Englishes, 10*(1), 44–61. https://doi.org/10.1080/13488678.2007.10801199

7 Discourse

Marilu B. Rañosa-Madrunio

7.1 Introduction

Discourse studies as compared to other areas of research have probably received the least attention in the study of Philippine English (PhE) (cf. Bautista & Gonzalez, 2006). However, this does not necessarily mean that it is unexplored. Previous research such as that done by Dayag (2004a, 2004b) primarily focused on rhetorical patterns in printed texts (e.g. editorials, press articles, academic articles). Others, like the ones conducted by Gustilo (2002) and Rañosa-Madrunio (2004a, 2004b), dealt with linguistic features that characterize Englishes which highlight their shared as well as contrasting features.

The aim of this chapter is to summarize various research works, and, in case some are found lacking or deemed inadequate in terms of pattern or features, to provide a description of discourse structures in PhE. Thus, an important task of this chapter is also to present the direction for the description and analysis of discourse features and organizational patterns found in PhE texts.

With the onset of PhE in the 1980s, speakers/users of this variety have increasingly taken interest in analyzing the features that characterize PhE. The research topics have covered short and long texts/discourse in Inner Circle, Outer Circle, and Expanding Circle Englishes. Several studies have also done a comparison and contrast of these varieties. In addition, this chapter discusses studies conducted on PhE with emphasis on the discourse features and structures, and then proceeds with comparing PhE with other varieties from Kachru's (1985) Three Concentric Circles. The discussion includes the following: (1) PhE discourse and the discourse of other Englishes, (2) PhE discourse and Filipino/Tagalog discourse, (3) summary of the studies reviewed, and (4) conclusion and future directions. With this structure, the readers may note features that characterize PhE and, later on, assess its similarities and differences with the other Englishes, noting their shared and unshared features.

7.2 Philippine English in the Mass Media

A number of interesting and compelling studies focused mainly on PhE which started in the 1980s. After Llamzon's (1969) classic study on Standard

DOI: 10.4324/9780429427824-10

Discourse 101

PhE, Gonzalez (1985) examined PhE of the mass media, particularly the structural features of spoken PhE, the structural features of written PhE, careful (reading) and casual styles of spoken PhE of the mass media, formal and informal styles of written PhE, and the stylistic underdifferentiation and insecurity in written PhE. According to Gonzalez, PhE of the mass media for casual and formal styles seems to be similar in features, and is 'textbookish' due to the manner of acquisition in school. Whereas written PhE observes a 'composition style', spoken PhE is closer to 'textbook English'. Gonzalez further claims that the composition style in the Philippines is formal, elegant, and in the tradition of essay writing popular before the World War II era. As a rhetorical style, it is being used as a model in Philippine classrooms. Educated Filipinos, who are bilingual or multilingual, generally make use of this writing style because it makes them comfortable as a result of their exposure to the said variety in school. It should be noted, though, that Filipinos have other languages in their repertoire and do not depend solely on English when using different styles in discourse. English, then, is reserved for occasions that call for consultative, formal, and frozen styles based on Joo's (1962) classification on solidarity between interlocutors. Interestingly, Filipinos speak as they write and the differences between spoken and written English do not seem to be extensive. The Filipinos' English then is monostylistic because of the patterns of second language acquisition in the Philippine school setting and the restricted use of English in the domains of the classroom, business, and international contacts.

7.3 Written Discourse

There are numerous studies done on PhE that focus on linguistic and discourse features with written texts as data. The study of Dayag (2004a) is a pioneering work in this area as he discussed the structure of newspaper editorial discourse in PhE in terms of their macrostructure and lexical-grammatical features. Applying Toulmin's (1958, 1964) claim-data-warrant framework to 35 editorials from five newspapers, Dayag's study revealed that more than half of the total number of propositions in the editorials make a claim/assertion, pass judgment, express a view or opinion, or take a stand. He also found that attitudinal adjectives and adverbs, modal auxiliaries, rhetorical questions, conditional and adversative clauses, and verbs in reporting speech were the lexico-grammatical features attributed to the macro-propositions. As such, it can be inferred that mapping function onto form is achieved in this case. This, the author claims, has implications for second language pedagogy.

Dayag (2004b) furthered his study by exploring the phenomenon of evaluation in the discourse of newspaper editorials in PhE in terms of global structure, linguistic features, and semantic relations, the corpus of which was taken from three leading PhE newspapers. He noted that in relation to global structure, Philippine newspaper editorials observe the

102   Marilu B. Rañosa-Madrunio

lead-follow-valuate structure with the tendency to combine background material with evaluative statements as early as the first statement. On the matter of lexico-grammatical markers of evaluation, adjectives, adverbials, modal verbs, negativity markers, and rhetorical questions were the common linguistic aids made available to writers. With regard to semantic relations, the evaluation consisted of concessive relations, expectancy relations, and hypothetical-real patterns.

It is to be noted that in both studies of Dayag (2004a, 2004b) newspaper editorials in PhE have been characterized in terms of their structure and linguistic features. In the first study of Dayag (2004a), the focus was on the description of the macrostructure as well as the discourse microstructure of PhE newspaper editorials in terms of lexico-grammatical features, while the focus on the second study (Dayag, 2004b) was on the phenomenon of evaluation in terms of global structure, linguistic features, and semantic relations. While the studies yielded numerous characteristics of PhE newspaper editorials, the studies were more focused toward drawing implications for second language teaching and not about comparing them with editorials in other Englishes. Since the newspaper editorial is a writing genre not often used for classroom purposes, Dayag (2004b) underscores the need for explicit instruction of global structure of evaluation in argumentative texts, in this case, newspaper editorials which are a convenient source of authentic materials in the teaching of argumentative writing to tertiary-level students. He likewise emphasized that this particular genre reflects national norms of persuasion.

Motivated by Dayag's (2004a, 2004b) studies on PhE editorials, Pulido (2011) embarked on an investigation of the inherent generic structure potential of PhE editorials using Ansary and Babaii's (2005) systemic functional framework based on the concept of obligatory and optional elements of structure developed by Halliday and Hasan (1989). With the 30 collected editorials containing the different rhetorical structures from the online versions of two leading PhE broadsheets downloaded from their websites, Pulido's study found that PhE editorials have a macrostructure and editorials have obligatory (run-on headline, addressing an issue, argumentation, and articulation of a position) and optional (providing background information and closure of argumentation) elements.

Borlongan (2017a) branched out into an investigation of PhE by attempting to examine acknowledgments in doctoral dissertations. Forty dissertations were investigated (20 from the arts and 20 from the sciences), identifying the moves and applying the frameworks of Hyland (2003) and Hyland and Tse (2004). The findings showed that dissertation acknowledgments written in PhE are 'nativized' in relation to the use of an address system which is endemic to Filipino and PhE, the introduction of the step thanking God, which is a step that is the most variable in placement, and the loss of several steps found in the frameworks of Hyland and Hyland and Tse. More importantly, however, is the acceptance of responsibility. Borlongan claims that this finding may be a further evidence of the alleged endonormative stabilization of PhE. As it is, this way of addressing has become part of standard PhE, and is no longer considered as informal in dissertation writing particularly in the acknowledgment section. Borlongan avers that this aspect of PhE may have been the offshoot of the pressure of culture.

Finally, Balgos (2017) conducted a study on the signals of concession in Philippine and American supreme court decisions, specifically focusing on argumentation in jurisprudence. With landmark cases on family relations serving as corpus, these were analyzed by describing how concession is articulated in decisions that debunk the lower court's ruling. It further examined the concessive preferences of supreme court judges. Findings have implications on lawyers practicing foreign and legal affairs as well as Filipino students of legal English. It was found that pseudo-dyadic concessive schema was heavily employed in American and Philippine supreme court decisions possibly in the courts' attempt to guarantee review of lower court claims before pronouncing verdict in every case. She notices that American supreme court decisions utilize more varied concessive disjuncts than Philippine supreme court decisions.

7.4 Spoken Discourse

Zhang (2013) veers away from the usual corpus of written texts as he analyzes spoken texts in the form of compliments. While he noted that numerous studies have been undertaken on many Englishes using everyday conversations, only few studies were done on PhE. Using the Discourse Completion Test (DCT) to elicit data on giving and receiving compliments from at least 30 college students enrolled in a Philippine university, he noted that PhE speakers have the tendency to employ explicit compliments and a bound semantic formula most frequently. Moreover, the compliments in PhE are formulaic at both the syntactic and lexical levels as other Englishes. At the syntactic and lexical level, the pattern *NP is/looks (really) ADJ* (e.g. Your dress is really great) is most frequently used to imply that the participants in the study are quite familiar with the appropriate syntactic structures used in compliments based on Manes and Wolfson's (1981) framework. This finding is similar to the finding for AmE speakers. A significant difference, however, is the fact that AmE speakers tend to express compliments using the syntactic pattern *I (really) like/love NP* in contrast to PhE speakers who favor the ADJ NP or ADJ pattern. Finally, Filipinos generally have the tendency to accept compliments rather than reject them whenever they receive such compliments.

Another recent study which is of equal importance is that of Borlongan and Gonzales (2017), which dealt with a corpus-based description of telephone conversation openings in PhE included in the Philippine component of the International Corpus of English. Using transcripts of telephone calls with at least ten samples, findings revealed that the four core opening

104   *Marilu B. Rañosa-Madrunio*

sequences identified by Schegloff (1972, 1979, 1986) appear to be established tentatively. These are the summons-answer sequence, the identification-recognition sequence, the exchange of greeting tokens, and the how-are-you sequence. These samples were further analyzed for the purpose of looking into those that follow and deviate from Schegloff's four core opening sequences in AmE telephone conversations.

7.5 Reflections of Culture in Philippine English Discourse

It should be noted that a majority of the investigations focused on written texts, perhaps due to the diverse contexts which users of English are in. These studies have shared features found in common text types and genres. These are usually focused on academic texts such as essays and scholarly articles and journalistic texts such as complaint letters, opinions, editorials, and the like.

A comparison of the features of these Englishes became the subject of an scholarly investigation which was grounded on the premise that an interplay of language and culture can be identified as language and writing are both cultural phenomena. Earlier attempts at comparing Englishes centered mainly on student writing. The research efforts were meant to show differences in the thinking patterns of the writers (Connor, 1996; Kaplan, 1966). But as more scholars were attracted to this line of inquiry, other text types became the focus of their attention. The first of these studies can be traced back to 2002, when an issue of the *Philippine Journal of Linguistics* (*PJL*) was devoted to a comparison of PhE with select Englishes such as AmE, Singapore English (SgE), and Filipino.

A study by Genuino (2002) emphasized the interaction between language and culture by analyzing the cohesive devices employed by writers in the Philippines, Singapore, and the US as well as the norms of the written discourse in these countries. Using selected articles taken from views/comments/analysis/opinion sections of three leading broadsheets in the Philippines, Singapore, and the US, the rhetorical patterns were found to be anchored on adversative relations, with these cohesive devices found in different positions in the discourse. Cultural features found to be common in all speech communities highlight the writers being analytical rather than accumulative, and individualist rather than collectivist.

Gonzales' (2002) study investigated politeness markers and strategies in the letters to the editor in three broadsheets from three cultures (the Philippines, Singapore, and the US), applying Brown and Levinson's (1987) framework. Employing the 'discourse bloc' as a method in analyzing the data and as a unit of analysis, findings revealed that all three cultures have one major feature, and that is, reference to the issue from the news articles earlier discussed. Politeness markers in the form of modal auxiliaries such as *should, would,* and *must* have been found to be prevalent among all three cultures and are used as positive or negative politeness strategies. On the matter of

Discourse 105

cultural influences, an interesting finding is that the writers employ strategies to conform to the writing norm and to observe appropriateness instead of allowing conventions to rule them. While the letters revealed a high frequency of face-threatening acts (FTAs), the letters strike a balance through the use of numerous politeness strategies. Whereas Singaporean writers use a standard form of reference, American writers use direct opposition to other writers' opinion while Filipino writers use politeness markers.

Rañosa-Madrunio (2004a) also conducted a study, this time focusing on linguistic features of complaint letters to editors written in PhE and SgE. The linguistic properties examined included (1) grammatical and lexical features such as personal reference pronouns, modal verbs, attitudinal and evaluative adjectives, (2) syntactic features in particular the passives, and (3) speech act verbs such as illocutionary force indicating devices (IFIDs), affect indicating phrases (AIPs), as well as recurring phrases. An interesting finding in the study was the use of certain lexical-syntactic features which served as softening devices for the realization of politeness strategies, which corroborated the claim of Mahboob and Hartford (2001) that the use of passives, impersonals, and complex sentences contributes to the overall politeness level affecting much of the directness. Moreover, the IFIDs and AIPs either strengthen or weaken the intensity of the illocutionary points, thus allowing for the possibility of grading directness and indirectness levels of an illocutionary point or verb in a cline.

Seeing that this investigation revealed very few differences between the PhE and SgE samples, Bautista and Rañosa-Madrunio (2004) conducted another study which determined whether Filipino readers of PhE and SgE complaint letters would detect any differences between the two sets using the semantic differential scale. The said semantic differential scale made the respondents look into the attitude of the raters toward the letters and writers through their assessment of the texts using evaluative descriptors. Interestingly, the 30 respondents did not perceive any difference between the two datasets, thus validating the earlier findings.

Brylko's (2002) research, which replicated the study of Castro in 1997, examined legal texts in relation to the cognitive structure of Philippine criminal cases. However, instead of focusing only on one particular speech community, Brylko's paper compared the underlying cognitive structure of 30 appeal cases in PhE and AmE. Using Bhatia's (1983) model of cognitive structuring in legislative writing, Philippine and American supreme court decisions were found to share similar underlying cognitive structures, having certain obligatory moves that characterize legal cases as a genre. However, differences were identified in relation to moves within three obligatory parts of the criminal appeal case: (1) history of the case, (2) the appeal proper, and (3) the decision on the appeal. While the sequence of these parts is established, the moves within each differ and are realized in various ways.

With the same corpus concentrating on PhE and AmE, Gustilo's (2002) paper analyzed news leads in six leading newspapers in both countries, noting

106 *Marilu B. Rañosa-Madrunio*

that no significant differences could be found in the number of words used between the two Englishes even in terms of summary lead with *who, what*, and *when* as the most frequently used elements and *who* as the heavily used starting element. These recurring similar patterns were attributed by Gustilo to the tendency of Filipino writers to adhere to the expectations of international journalism, perhaps as a form of influence in the Philippine educational system.

Rañosa-Madrunio's (2004b) study on complaint letters to editors analyzed comprehensively the discourse organization of two Outer Circle Englishes: PhE and SgE. Using Mahboob and Hartford's model (2001) and through textual analysis of the discourse features of the 80 samples (40 Philippine letters and 40 Singapore letters), she found out that both samples employed the same number of moves (introduction, praise, attention-getter, background, complaint, appeal to the editor, request for redress, suggestion, and justification for suggestion). Conclusion, which was not part of Mahboob and Hartford's model, was found to be present and considered to be the seventh and last move. With regard to the length of letters, a significant difference was found between the two samples. The Singapore letters were found to be curt and simple while Philippine letters were generally verbose and lengthy. The study, however, recognizes the fact that there are organizational constraints imposed on the newspapers which publish these complaint letters to editors but there is also the possibility that editors in Singapore are more inclined to edit the complaint letters for purposes of brevity, in order to give space for other news items. It is to be noted that the Singapore broadsheet examined was more dense and therefore allotted more spaces for complaint letters than the Philippine broadsheets.

Presenting a more holistic picture of Asian Englishes, Dayag's (2009) monograph is a comprehensive study on the discourse of written argumentation in Asian Englishes focusing on the metadiscourse in newspaper editorials in Asian Englishes from the perspective of contrastive rhetoric. Divided into five chapters, the monograph addressed the preferred global structures of newspaper editorials in Asian Englishes and their interpersonal and textual metadiscourse strategies in newspaper editorials in Asian Englishes. The study employed a total of 360 English-language editorials (30 from each of two leading broadsheets in each of the six Asian countries) published in the Philippines, Singapore, India, Japan, China, and South Korea which represented English-as-a-second-language (ESL) and English-as-a-foreign-language (EFL) contexts. One important finding yielded by the study is that there are significant differences among the Asian Englishes in terms of global structures of newspaper editorials. For instance, newspaper editorials in SgE and PhE follow a predictable organizational pattern (claim-counterclaim pattern) while Indian English appears to be less predictable, leaning more closely to the claim-counterclaim structure, instead of the problem-solution framework. With respect to the Expanding Circle Asian Englishes, Korean English has the tendency to adopt the problem-solution pattern. Furthermore, whereas Japanese English tends to adopt the claim-counterclaim pattern, Chinese English appears to be partial to a pattern consisting of a series of claims. The monograph, which is the first of its kind in the Philippines, aimed to contribute to the growing body of knowledge in the discourse of written argumentation in world Englishes.

7.6 Philippine English Discourse in Comparison with Filipino Discourse

Another important axis of comparison is PhE discourse and Filipino discourse. Veering away from the usual Englishes which were examined, Dayag's (2004c) study on evidentiality in PhE compared PhE with the country's national language Filipino. He compared PhE and Filipino newspaper editorials aimed at describing the sources of information or data (evidentials) found in PhE and Filipino newspapers as well as identify the strategies employed by these editorials in arranging the sources of information vis-à-vis the discourse structure of the texts. Using at least three leading English-medium newspapers and three major Filipino tabloids in the Philippines, the study revealed that there were more similarities than differences shared by the two. Similarities were identified on the aspect of frequent use of more non-visual type of direct evidence than the visual type. On the matter of indirect evidentials, there was a widespread use of inferentials in newspaper editorials in both languages. A difference, however, was identified in the use of mediated evidence (quotatives) as seen in the reported speeches pervasively employed in PhE editorials than in the Filipino morning tabloids. To illustrate this, while quotatives ranked first in the list of mediated evidentials in editorials in both languages, reported speech is used more extensively in PhE editorials than in their Filipino counterpart. Moreover, direct quotation is not fully exploited by Filipino editorials, in contrast to the PhE texts.

Rojo-Laurilla (2002) did a contrastive rhetoric analysis of Philippine advice columns written in English and Filipino by way of investigating self-presentation and self-disclosure as reflected in Filipino magazines and broadsheets written in English and Filipino. After a careful examination of the health advice columns with 20 samples from two Filipino magazines and another 20 from English magazines, Rojo-Laurilla noted that, for the Filipino samples, advice seekers revealed their ages and profession as part of their self-presentation, perhaps to provide the advice-giver more insights about the problem. On the contrary, there were fewer revelations in the English samples, perhaps because age was not deemed necessary by the advice seekers in framing the problem and in the offering of the solution. With respect to self-disclosure, a greater amount has been found in the body of the letter since this is where the collaboration of the problem takes place. Whereas elaboration comes in the form of partial remedies in the Filipino letters to solve the problem, elaboration in the English letters is treated as an expansion of details that seeks to further describe the problem, whether or not a solution has been provided.

108   *Marilu B. Rañosa-Madrunio*

7.7 Summary

With the studies reviewed and summarized, it can be noted that there is a plethora of features that are endemic to PhE both in spoken and in written discourse. Moreover, the studies conducted on PhE alone prove that, indeed, written PhE observes a 'composition style' while spoken PhE is close to 'textbook English' as claimed by Gonzalez (1985). This claim is corroborated by Bautista (2000) in her monograph on standard PhE.

After examining the various investigations done on PhE texts, more researchers are motivated to explore various areas in this variety. This is because PhE is now widely used in different contexts as proven by studies on compliments as part of everyday conversations. The proliferation of the call center industry in the country likewise advanced the study of PhE as well as the pervasive use of social media, which paved the way for the study of identity construction in online intercultural news media. The corpus-based methodology is now in the forefront of PhE scholarship. Finally, in the area of newspaper genre, editorials have become attractive to researchers as this genre makes use of this variety realistically. This is not to forget that discourse in academic writing has and will always be a preferred source of data in analyzing PhE discourse.

Some of the studies previously conducted had the objective of looking into the thinking patterns of writers. A favorite text type investigated in the past was the student essay or other academic papers, as well as newspaper discourse in various sub-genres.

In comparing the Englishes used in different text types with shared or unshared features, one may find the need to raise awareness among language teachers and learners that much has to be understood in terms of writing styles, structures, and moves. These linguistic and discourse features make one variety distinct from the other and are reflective of the culture of the writer. It is to be understood that writers of different discourse communities conform to the writing norms which they are exposed to, and which they employ for communal purposes. For some of the written Englishes analyzed, very few differences can be identified. This may be attributed to the fact that writers from different cultures conform to the set of standards which are often observed by the writing communities in different countries.

7.8 Conclusion and Future Directions

More than 30 years ago, most research in this area of English studies focused on a single variety amid the other Englishes belonging to Kachru's (1985) Concentric Circles of world Englishes that included the Inner, Outer, and Expanding Circles. It is fascinating to note that similarities and differences do exist between and among these Englishes in many aspects as reflected in select genres which usually come from printed texts in the media and academic essays. Studies on PhE alone were often overtaken by studies

Discourse 109

on contrastive rhetoric. Thus, it is essential to trace how the direction has changed dramatically from the time studies on PhE discourse were first conducted in the 1980s.

Needless to say, after work on PhE description started, what caught the attention of scholars at that time was the growing comparison of the PhE variety with other Englishes. One will note that it is only after getting acquainted with the features of one variety that a researcher can be more confident in comparing it with another. In other words, the study of one variety of English will likely undergo more meaningful advancement when it is compared with other Englishes. This means advancing world Englishes to the level of contrastive rhetoric. Equally interesting is the fact that scholars who investigated PhE did it side by side with getting acquainted with their own variety alongside Englishes from the Inner, Outer, and Expanding Circles.

While PhE advances as a field or area in applied linguistics, it is important to note that the said variety may also be compared with other Philippine languages considering that the Philippines is one of the most linguistically and culturally diverse countries in Southeast Asia, with the multitude of major and minor languages used by Filipinos. It would then be interesting to note the linguistic and discourse features found in PhE and compare them with those found in other Philippine languages. As it is, there are only a few studies which compare PhE texts with texts in Filipino, and more so with texts in other Philippine languages.

PhE has, indeed, come a long way. Following Schneider's dynamic model (2003, 2007), it appears that PhE has progressed further and did not get stuck with the nativization phase. Borlongan (2016) counter-argued Schneider's (2003, 2007) claim that PhE is at the stage of nativization (or stage 3) and that it has become fossilized because of restrictions by language policies that push for the use of Filipino, which is the country's national language. Borlongan asserts that PhE is already at the dawn of endonormative stabilization (or stage 4), claiming that the Philippines has formulated its English language policies without any external control and that PhE has already homogenized, paving the way for its possible codification through reference grammars and dictionaries despite residual linguistic conservatism. By the very fact that language scholars continuously make a dent in this area through varying research on different areas of study such as PhE in call centers, PhE as the language of instruction, PhE as used in instructional materials, PhE dictionary, PhE and the regional varieties, among others, prove that this new variety is now being recognized in the different facets of society. Given enough time to develop through the following decades, this variety may soon have its own reference grammar and grammar books published that set up standard guidelines for the use of its grammar. This may not take too long as Filipino writers of English who write Philippine literatures have increased in number over the years with their literary writings receiving recognition not only from local but also from international awarding bodies.

110 *Marilu B. Rañosa-Madrunio*

Finally, with the changing times and the evolving language and communicative situations encountered in daily interactions by different interlocutors, there may be a need to examine possible updates in terms of texts and genres used as texts for analysis. This observation is based on the current trend of interdisciplinarity, multidisciplinarity, and transdisciplinarity of programs and/or courses that translate to research in the field. For instance, with the interface of language and the law, interesting genres may be considered such as courtroom genres with emphasis on opening and closing statements or even suicide notes as a non-academic genre.

In the area of computer-mediated communication, online news galleries which include storytelling practices accompanied by news images may be examined along with investigating verbal and non-verbal communication in technical texts and the interaction of the different codes and symbols. Likewise, text messages as used by language users in a digital environment and how they differ in terms of their lexical and multimodal features is another interesting area to explore, in addition to e-commerce genres in the form of news and blogs.

On the matter of technical texts, studies on laboratory reports are beginning to be noticed for purposes of developing literacy practices and genre awareness among student-writers. Moreover, they have become increasingly important as well for writers of patent summaries who use techniques such as the balanced or unbalanced distribution of content across the different sections of a patent, proposals, reports, critiques, and creative outputs with the use of multidimensional approaches. They have also become useful for purposes of author summary vis-à-vis the abstract that would show the differences between the two text types and even manuscript reviews and how and why they were evaluated as needing major revision or even rejected by reviewers, among others.

In the area of business writing, it might be interesting to study the contents and features of resignation letters as well as instruction manuals for household appliances in terms of their macro and micro structures. In view of the small amount of data currently available on these subjects, there may be a need to pay increased attention on these when analyzing English varieties. Without doubt, all these genres will have an impact on the teaching and learning of the Englishes as they are considered as legitimate sources of research in World/Asian Englishes and PhE discourse that consider the background of the writers whose views or perspectives may have been shaped cognitively by the cultural as well as the linguistic backgrounds of the writers.

References

Ansary, Hasan & Babaii, Esmat. (2005). The generic integrity of newspaper editorials: A systemic functional perspective. *Asian EFL Journal 6* (3), 1–28.
Balgos, Anne Richie G. (2017). Argumentation in legal discourse: A contrastive analysis of concession in Philippine and American Supreme Court decisions. *Asian Journal of English Language Studies 5*, 71–89.

Discourse 111

Bautista, Ma. Lourdes S. (2000). *Defining standard Philippine English: Its status and grammatical features* (Monograph). Manila: De La Salle University Press.

Bautista, Ma. Lourdes S. & Gonzalez, Andrew B. (2006). Southeast Asian Englishes. In B. B. Kachru, Y. Kachru, & C. L. Nelson (Eds.), *The handbook of World Englishes* (pp. 130–144). Blackwell Publishing.

Bautista, Ma. Lourdes S. & Rañosa-Madrunio, Marilu B. (2004). Comparing letters of complaint in Philippine English and Singapore English: Reactions using a semantic differential scale. *Tanglaw,* 1–17.

Bhatia, Vijay. (1983). Simplification v. easification: The case of legal texts. *Applied Linguistics 4* (1), 42–54.

Borlongan, Ariane M. (2016). Relocating Philippine English in Schneider's Dynamic Model. *Asian Englishes 18,* 232–241.

Borlongan, Ariane M. (2017a). Dissertation acknowledgements in Philippine English. *Komaba Journal of English Education 8,* 15–35.

Borlongan, Ariane M. (2017b). Openings of telephone conversations in Philippine English. *Asian Journal of English Language Studies 5,* 1–13.

Brown, Penelope & Levinson, Stephen. (1987). *Politeness: Some universals in language usage.* Cambridge: Cambridge University Press.

Brylko, Arina. (2002). Cognitive structuring of criminal appeal cases in Philippine English and American English. *Philippine Journal of Linguistics 33* (2), 39–51.

Castro, Carolyn. (1997). Cognitive structuring of Philippine criminal appeal cases: An aid to the learner of English for academic legal purposes (EALP). *Teaching English for Specific Purposes 10,* 85–107.

Connor, Ulla. (1996). *Contrastive rhetoric: Cross-cultural aspects of second language writing.* Cambridge: Cambridge University Press.

Dayag, Danilo T. (2004a). Editorializing in L2: The case of Philippine English. *Asia Pacific Education Review 5* (1), 100–109.

Dayag, Danilo T. (2004b). Negotiating evaluation in newspaper editorials in Philippine English. *Asian Englishes 7* (2), 28–51.

Dayag, Danilo T. (2004c). Evidentiality in Philippine English and Filipino newspaper editorials. *Philippine Journal of Linguistics 35* (2), 51–66.

Dayag, Danilo T. (2009). *Metadiscourse, argumentation, and Asian Englishes: A contrastive rhetoric approach.* (Monograph). Manila: University of Santo Tomas.

Genuino, Cecilia. F. (2002). Cohesion: A revelation of cultural practices. *Philippine Journal of Linguistics 33* (2), 1–18.

Gonzales, Sydney D. (2002). Politeness in letters to the editor in Philippine English, American English, and Singaporean English. *Philippine Journal of Linguistics 33* (2), 19–37.

Gonzalez, Andrew B. (1985). *Studies in Philippine English.* (Occasional Papers No. 39.) Singapore: SEAMEO Regional Language Center.

Gustilo, Leah E. (2002). A contrastive analysis of American English and Philippine English news leads. *Philippine Journal of Linguistics 33* (2), 53–66.

Halliday, Michael & Hasan, Ruqaiya. (1989). *Language, context, and text: Aspects of language in a social-semantic perspective.* Oxford: Oxford University Press.

Hyland, Ken. (2003). Dissertation acknowledgements: The anatomy of a Cinderella genre: *Written Communication 20,* 242–268.

Hyland, Ken & Tse, Polly. (2004). "I would like to thank my supervisor": Acknowledgements in graduate dissertations. *International Journal of Applied Linguistics 14,* 259–275.

112   *Marilu B. Rañosa-Madrunio*

Kachru, Braj. (1985). Standards, codification and sociolinguistic realism: English language in the outer circle. In R. Quirk and H. Widowson (Eds.), *English in the world: Teaching and learning the language and literatures* (pp. 11–36). Cambridge: Cambridge University Press.Kaplan, Robert. (1966). Cultural thought patterns in intercultural education. *Language Learning 16*, 1–20.

Llamzon, Teodoro A. (1969). *Standard Filipino English.* Quezon City, Philippines: Ateneo de Manila University Press.

Mahboob, Ahmar & Hartford, Beverly S. (2001). *In search of models: Patterns of complaints in South Asian English.* Hawaii: ELE Roundtable, 1–36.

Manes, Joan &Wolfson, Nessa. (1981). The compliment formula. In F. Coulmas (Ed.). *Conversational routine: Explorations in standardized communication situations and prepatterned speech* (pp. 116–132). Hague: Mouton Publishers.

Pulido, Dennis H. (2011). A systemic functional analysis of Philippine newspaper editorials. *TESOL Journal 4* (1), 52–63.

Rañosa-Madrunio, Marilu B. (2004a). The linguistic features of complaint letters to editors in Philippine English and Singapore English. *Asian Englishes 7* (2), 52–73.

Rañosa-Madrunio, Marilu B. (2004b). The discourse organization of letters of complaint in Philippine English and Singapore English. *Philippine Journal of Linguistics 35* (2), 67–97.

Rojo-Laurilla, Mildred A. (2002). The 'presentation of self' and 'self-disclosure': A contrastive rhetorical analysis of Philippine advice columns in English and Filipino. *Philippine Journal of Linguistics 33* (2), 67–82.

Schegloff, E. A. (1972). Sequencing in conversational opening. In J. Gumpertz (Ed.), *Directions in sociolinguistics* (pp. 346–380). New York: Holt, Reinhart and Winston.

Schegloff, E. A. (1979). Identification and recognition in telephone openings. In G. Psathas (Ed.), *Everyday language: studies in ethnomethodology* (pp. 23–78). New York: Irvington Publication.

Schegloff, E. A. (1986). The routine as achievement. *Human Studies, 9*, 111–152.

Schneider, E. W. (2003). The dynamics of new Englishes: From identity construction to dialect birth. *Language 79*, 233–281.

Schneider, E. W. (2007). *Postcolonial English: Varieties of English around the world.* New York, NY: Cambridge University Press.

Toulmin, S. E. (1958). *The uses of argument.* Cambridge University Press, Cambridge.

Toulmin, S. E. (1964). *The uses of argument* (1st ed.). Cambridge University Press, Cambridge.

Zhang, Jin-Pei. (2013). Compliments and compliment responses in Philippine English. *GEMA Online ^{TM} Journal of Language Studies 13* (1), 25–41.

8 Spelling and Punctuation

Robert Fuchs

8.1 Introduction

Variation in spelling, and, to a lesser degree, punctuation, is of interest to the public and occasionally discussed by non-linguists. For example, the Corpus of Web-Based Global English (GloWBE), a 1.9-billion-word corpus of internet-based English from 20 countries around the world (Davies & Fuchs, 2015), comprises 139 mentions of *American (English) spelling* (3 of which are in the Philippine section) and 77 occurrences of *British (English) spelling*. An analysis of the most frequent collocates of *spelling* in the corpus reveals a strong prescriptive association, with *correct spelling* being among the top three left-hand collocations and *spelling mistakes* and *spelling errors* among the top four right-hand collocations both in the corpus as a whole and in the Philippine section.

Despite the aforementioned public concern with spelling, this topic has sometimes found itself on the sidelines of research on world Englishes. The study of syntax and lexis typically attracts more attention, perhaps because it reveals variation both at the spoken and at the written level. Moreover, linguistic variation in general, and differences between Englishes in particular, is usually more pronounced at the spoken level than at the written level—the former being, overall, comparatively more informal, and the latter more formal.

The spelling standards used in Englishes around the world can be broadly classified along an orientation toward British or American norms. Exceptional, local spellings exist of course, such as *indigenes* for *indigenous* in Nigerian and Ghanaian English: GloWbE includes 884 occurrences of *indigenes*, of which 537 are to be found in the Nigerian and Ghanaian part of the corpus. Compared to the number of mentions of the spelling *indigenous*, this works out as 25.9% *indigenes* in the Nigerian and 13.8% in the Ghanaian part of the corpus, and 1.9% across the whole corpus.

However, cases such as this are few and far between. More generally, even where spelling conventions are held to be locally meaningful, as indicated, for example, by the phrase *Philippine (English) spelling*, they may ultimately

DOI: 10.4324/9780429427824-11

114 *Robert Fuchs*

be defined by reference to an external norm. A case in point are the guidelines set by the editor of the present handbook, specifying that

> [...] Philippine English conventions be followed for spelling, vocabulary, and punctuation [...]. Since the Philippines generally follows American conventions, please refer to American spelling, vocabulary, and punctuation when writing your contribution to the handbook.

This example suggests that Philippine English (PhE) spelling and punctuation largely follows the rules of American English (AmE), i.e. an external norm. However, as the discussion below will show, some British spellings still occur occasionally in present-day PhE and were used with a somewhat higher frequency in earlier PhE. Distinct Philippine spelling variants, i.e. ones that are not used in Englishes such as AmE or British English (BrE), have not so far been documented in the literature. Consequently, variation in spelling and punctuation in PhE can be broken down as a preference for American or British spelling.

8.2 American and British Spelling

Although the terms 'American spelling' and 'British spelling' are seemingly self-explanatory, they merit brief discussion. In the most simple case, we would consider a spelling/punctuation variant A (such as -*ize* as in *fantasize*) to be American if it occurs more frequently than the spelling variant B (such as -*ise* in *fantasise*) in AmE, while at the same time variant B (-*ise*) is more frequent than variant A (-*ize*) in BrE. Variant B (-*ise*) is, consequently, considered British. Beyond this simple case, a somewhat more complicated situation arises when variant A occurs very frequently, and perhaps even in the majority of cases, in both BrE and AmE, but variant B is substantially more frequent in one variety than in the other. This is indeed the case for (-*ise*/-*ize*), as -*ize* is the clearly dominant form in AmE, whereas both -*ise* und -*ize* are used in BrE (where -*ize* has been used historically as the so-called Oxford spelling). The same is true for the derived nominalizations -*isation*/-*ization*. In such a situation, it is still useful to call -*ize* the American variant and -*ise* the British variant because -*ise* is hardly ever used in AmE.

8.3 Empirical Evidence on Spelling and Punctuation in Philippine English

Substantial empirical evidence on variation in spelling and punctuation in PhE comes from two studies, the first, that of Gonçalves, Loureiro-Porto, Ramasco and Sánchez in 2018, taking a broad comparative view with several national varieties of English being considered and based on large amounts of data (social media and Google Books), and the second, that of Fuchs in

Spelling and Punctuation 115

2017, taking a closer look at particular spelling and punctuation variants in PhE both from a synchronic and from a diachronic perspective.

The analysis of Gonçalves et al. (2018) is based on more than 30 million English-language messages on the social media platform Twitter and found that English tweets from the Philippines were on average the third-most American in spelling and lexis out of all 30 countries investigated, after US and Mexican tweets. The finding that AmE contains many American spellings might appear to be somewhat circular, but is in fact useful in that it provides a yardstick against which to measure other Englishes. Moreover, as will be discussed shortly, AmE itself has changed in the Americanness of its spelling.

However, prior to focusing on diachronic developments, it will be interesting consider the three countries with the strongest tendency toward British spelling, which were Ireland, the United Kingdom and New Zealand. The analysis of Gonçalves et al. (2018) relied on 66 word pairs involving spelling alternations, e.g. *skillfull/skillful, flavor/flavor, pyjamas/pajamas* and *armour/armor.* This list involved only items with "a significantly higher frequency in either of the two varieties" (p. 4) based on a prior comparison of the British National Corpus and the Corpus of Contemporary American English. Thus, it excludes items which exhibit a regional preference but no clear-cut difference between AmE and BrE such as verbs (and nouns derived from them) ending in *-ise/-ize,* where both variants are used in British but almost exclusively the latter in AmE.

Adding a diachronic dimension, the same study of Gonçalves et al. (2018) also analyzed the use of British and American spelling in printed books with the Google Books Corpus of Davies (2011). This corpus can be searched separately for books published in the United States and the United Kingdom (but not other countries, such as the Philippines) over the last 200 years. The results reveal a clear diachronic trend away from British and toward American spelling norms. In the United States, this trend started in the 1820s, whereas in the United Kingdom, a major shift was noticeable only by the 1990s. More generally, the identification of diachronic trends in spelling in AmE and BrE suggests that spelling is not a uniform practice—even AmE usage may contain some British spellings and vice versa. Moreover, depending on the frequency of specific forms, the Americanness or Britishness of spelling practices in a particular variety can be described as a continuum.

Similar results, albeit based on a much smaller dataset, were presented by Fuchs (2017) for PhE. This analysis was based on sections of the Philippine component of the International Corpus of English (ICE-PHI; Bautista, Lising, & Dayag, 2004), which consists of data from the 1990s. Overall, the study found a great preponderance of American spelling variants, with no or very few British variants found for seven out of ten spelling alternations. One alternation for which a substantial number of British variants was found is the *-ll-/-l-* alternation, with more than 40% British variants (e.g. *fulfill/fulfil*; in the following, the British variant is always given first). Another is

116   *Robert Fuchs*

-oguel-og, for which exclusively British variants were found (e.g. *demagogue/demagog*). Overall, however, American spelling dominates. British spelling accounted for only 4.9% of all occurrences.

Apart from punctuation, Fuchs' (2017) study also investigated variation in punctuation. More particularly, the analysis focused on whether abbreviated titles (such as *Mrs, Mr, Dr*) were followed by a period, such as in *Mrs.* and *Mr.* (the American norm), or not (the British norm) and found that all occurrences in the dataset followed the American norm.

He demonstrated that 1990s PhE overall followed American spelling and punctuation conventions. The results revealed by Gonçalves et al. (2018) and Fuchs might at first glance be considered to conform to the expected pattern in as far as PhE has in its history been under American, not British influence, unlike many other territories and countries that today widely use English as a second language and in institutional contexts. However, the analysis also revealed that in almost 5% of all cases, British spelling was used, i.e. on average every 20th linguistic item that could potentially show British spelling did indeed do so. Compared to the widely held conviction, referred to in the introduction, that PhE largely relies on American norms, this result is unexpected. Once this, initially surprising, result has been accepted, it leads to a further question, namely, from where this British influence originates. Given the diachronic results from Gonçalves et al. (2018), indicating that in both AmE and BrE British spelling has historically decreased in frequency, PhE might be expected to have undergone a similar diachronic change. During the foundation phase of PhE, the AmE input transported across the Pacific was the kind of AmE used at the time, which, as Gonçalves et al. (2018) showed, still had a greater proportion of British spellings than in the present day.

8.4 Empirical Evidence on Diachronic Change

In order to resolve the question of whether PhE went through a diachronic shift from some, even limited, reliance on British spelling toward almost complete observance of American spelling, Fuchs (2017) investigated diachronic change in spelling and punctuation over a 30-year period from the 1960s to the 1990s. This study was based on data from the Phil-Brown corpus, a corpus designed to match the 1960s Brown Corpus of AmE and Lancaster-Oslo-Bergen (LOB) Corpus of BrE. Because register variation potentially influences which spelling and punctuation variants authors choose, the study took care to select matching registers from Phil-Brown and ICE-PHI (fiction, press and learned writing).

Just as in the 1990s data, American forms accounted for the vast majority in the 1960s corpus (Fuchs, 2017). However, the overall proportion of British spelling variants was significantly higher in the 1960s (8.1%) than in the 1990s (4.9%), i.e. a reduction by two-fifths. Moreover, while, as pointed out, there was not a single case of abbreviated titles following the British pattern

Spelling and Punctuation 117

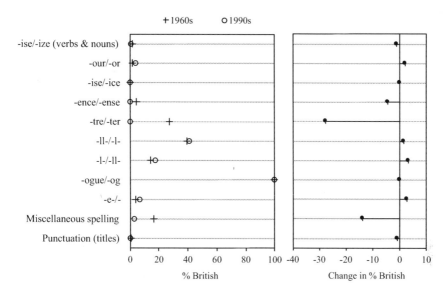

Figure 8.1 Relative Frequency (%British variants) of All Lexical and Spelling Variants in PhE of the 1960s and 1990s (adapted from Fuchs, 2017).
Note: This chart was created using a template provided by Sönning (2016).

in the 1990s corpus, in the 1960s corpus 1.0% of all cases did so. A closer look at specific spelling variants reveals that there is a great deal of variation across different types of spelling variation, as can be seen in Figure 8.1:

One the one hand, there are those that rarely or never occur with British spelling. This is the case for nouns ending in *-ise/-ice* and *-ence/-ense*, where the former is always spelled according to the American convention (across a total of 47 occurrences in the two corpora) and the latter occurs with British spelling in 3.4% of all cases (or 3 vs. 66) in the 1960s data and exclusively with American spelling in the 1990s (20 instances). Example 1 below illustrates the British variant.

1   The president should be commended for viewing this case in its right perspective and for taking action which some people may consider too severe for the **offence** committed. Phil-Brown B2 (emphasis added here and in the following examples).

Further alternations that occur almost exclusively with British spelling at both time points are verbs and nouns ending in *-ise/-ize* and *-isation/-ization* (1.6% and 0.6% British variants in the 1960s and 1990s, respectively) and nouns in *-our/-or* (with a rise in frequency from 1.8% to 4.0%, but very few tokens). Example 2 illustrates the British variant *-ise* and example 3 the British variant *-our*. A further alternation is used slightly more often with

118　*Robert Fuchs*

British spelling. This case of variation in spelling involves epenthetic *-e-* in BrE, which is elided in American spelling. Example 4 shows the American variant.

2　Everybody knows Lakas has never **advertised** leading a virtuous life as a qualification for party membership. ICE-PHI W2E-032#31:2

3　Predatory feeding **behaviour** in many zooplanktonic species of both freshwater and marine habitats is a complex system which requires a more detailed study to elucidate its intricacies. ICE-PHI: W2A-025#10:1.

4　After at least 6 months in storage (**aging**), they were dehulled by a Satake TH-35A dehuller, milled by a McGill miller No. 2, and then stored at −20 C. ICE-PHI:W2A-039#35:1

Three further spelling alternations have maintained a similar proportion of British spellings at moderate to high levels, i.e. from lowest to highest proportion of British spellings:

- *-ll-/-l-* (double *ll* in British, single *l* in American spelling, e.g. *fulfill*, *enroll*), with the British variant accounting for 14.3% (1960s) and 17.4% (1990s); example 5 illustrates the British variant.
- *-l-/-ll-*: single *l* in British, double *ll/[ll]* in American spelling, e.g. *traveling*, *counceling*, with the British variant accounting for 39.7% (1960s) and 41.0% (1990s); example 6 illustrates the American variant.
- *-ogue/-og*: This pair occurred exclusively with British spelling at both time points and is illustrated in example 7.

5　For her, America began to wear a more kindly face, and she thought that America might **fulfill** her dreams after all. ICE-PHI:W2F-019#59:1

6　Gonzalez uses this motif as frame for narration of his experiences as a Filipino writer in English, literally and figuratively **travelling** in foreign lands, seeking his way home. ICE-PHI:W2A-006#8:1

7　Cy Endfield, who also directs, is adept at filling the large Technirama screen with colour and motion and the story has the ring of truth in spite of occasionally inaffective [sic] **dialogue**. Phil-Brown C23

Finally, the spelling alternation *-tre/-ter* has seen a substantial decrease in the proportion of British variants (from 27.7% to 0%, see example 8 for an American variant), as have miscellaneous spellings, such as *grey/gray*, *per cent/percent* and *cosy/cozy* (from 16.4% to 2.7%, see example 9 for an American variant):

8　It had representatives of the world press holding their sides as they watched from their underwater **theater** vantage point 16 feet below the surface. Phil-Brown C15

9   For instance that it may have operational funds the members put into the union fixed deposit earning 8 **percent** annum which normally can not be withdrawn as long as the depositor is a member. Phil-Brown A13

The overall pattern of diachronic development becomes clear from the right-hand panel of Figure 8.1, where no spelling variant shows a substantial increase in British spelling whereas two show a substantial shift toward more consistent American spelling and many a moderate shift, from already very high levels of American spelling. The overall decrease in the use of British spelling variants from a low level to almost negligible over a period of 30 years can be explained with reference to a trend also revealed by Gonçalves et al. (2018), who showed that BrE and AmE have likewise seen change in the use of British vs. American spelling, with a decrease of the former and a consequent increase in the latter in both Englishes (while maintaining an overall difference). Thus, the scenario alluded to above, with the AmE input arriving in the Philippines with American occupation involving a certain proportion of British spelling variants, is compatible with the available evidence. Over time, this small proportion of British forms has seen a further decrease in a large-scale trend, often referred to as Americanization, affecting many Englishes around the world (with empirical evidence coming from Fuchs, 2016; Hian & Gupta, 1992; Tan, 2016; Yao & Collins, 2012). At the same time, PhE has also undergone Americanization in other respects, such as specific syntactic variables (Alonsagay & Nolasco, 2010; Borlongan & Lim, 2012; Collins, 2016; Collins et al., 2014a; 2014b; 2014c; Schneider, 2011).

8.5 Conclusion

This chapter discussed the currently available empirical evidence on spelling and punctuation in PhE, including recent diachronic change. While PhE overwhelmingly follows AmE in spelling and punctuation, a diachronic perspective shows that, in recent decades, the existing, small but noticeable proportion of cases following British spelling and punctuation norms has become even smaller. This trend is paralleled by, on the one hand, shifts toward more consistent American spelling in Englishes, and, on the other hand, shifts toward more consistently American syntax in some cases in PhE.

The currently available evidence leaves much room for future research. A greater diachronic depth, going beyond the currently available period from the 1960s to the 1990s, and involving larger amounts of data, would put research on spelling and punctuation and diachronic change in this area on a firmer empirical footing, just as it would benefit research on other aspects of PhE.

From a broader perspective, the apparent shift toward more consistent adherence to AmE spelling and punctuation also begs the question of norm orientation. As with other postcolonial Englishes, the development of PhE

120   *Robert Fuchs*

has been discussed within the framework of Schneider's (2003, 2007) dynamic model. PhE has been mooted to have reached stage 4 out of 5, i.e. endonormative development (Borlongan, 2016), which is defined as an increasing reliance on local norms. While spelling and punctuation may not be the prime area where local norms come to the fore, the lack of evidence revealing any form of locally distinctive patterns of spelling at least does not support the view that PhE has entered the endonormative stabilization phase at first glance.

However, although this chapter uses the terms 'British' and 'American' to refer to specific spelling variants, which is grounded in a sense of relative differences in frequency in these varieties, it might not necessarily be the case that users of PhE perceive these variants as British or American. It is conceivable that at least some of these spelling variants are perceived as the default orthographic realization. If a particular writer has any awareness of spelling alternations, they might regard the locally more frequent form as the default and the less frequent from as exceptional. In that sense, perceptions and views of spelling alternations might play a role in a potentially increasing endonormativity. Given that no data on the perception of variation in spelling in PhE is available, and indeed there might be a lack of such research in other varieties too, this approach might be a fruitful avenue for future research.

References

Alonsagay, I., & Nolasco, J. (2010). Adversativity and the GET-passive in Philippine and British English: A corpus-based contrastive study. *Philippine Journal of Linguistics, 41*, 1–13.

Bautista, M. L. S., Lising, J. L., & Dayag, D. T. (2004). *The Philippine component of the International Corpus of English (ICE-PHI)*. Department of English and Applied Linguistics, De La Salle University-Manila.

Borlongan, A. M., & Lim, J. (2012). Philippine English in Comparison with American English: A Corpus-Based Grammatical Study. Paper presented at The 18th Annual Conference of the International Association for World Englishes themed *World Englishes: Contexts, Challenges and Opportunities*, December 6–9, 2012, Hong Kong & Guangzhou, China.

Borlongan, A. M. (2016). Relocating Philippine English in Schneider's dynamic model. *Asian Englishes, 18*(3), 232–241.

Collins, P. (2016). Grammatical change in the verb phrase in contemporary Philippine English. *Asiatic, 10*(2), 50–67.

Collins, P., Borlongan, A. M., Lim, J. H., & Yao, X. (2014a). The subjunctive mood in Philippine English: A diachronic analysis. In S. E. Pfenninger, O. Timofeeva, A.-C. Gardner, A. Honkapohja, M. Hundt, & D. Schreier (Eds.), *Contact, variation, and change in the history of English* (pp. 259–280). Amsterdam: Benjamins.

Collins, P., Borlongan, A. M., & Yao, X. (2014b). Modality in Philippine English: A diachronic study. *Journal of English Linguistics, 42*, 68–88.

Collins, P., Yao, X., & Borlongan, A. M. (2014c). Relative clauses in Philippine English: A diachronic perspective. In L. Vandelanotte, K. Davidse, C. Gentens, & D. Kimps (Eds.), *Recent advances in corpus linguistics: Developing and exploiting corpora* (pp. 125–146). Amsterdam: Rodopi.

Davies, M. (2011). Google Books Corpus. *Based on Google Books n-grams.* Available online at http://googlebooks.byu.edu.

Davies, M., & Fuchs, R. (2015). Expanding Horizons in the Study of World Englishes with the 1.9 Billion Word Global Web-Based English Corpus (GloWbE). *English World-Wide, 36*(1), 1–28.

Fuchs, R. (2016). The frequency of the present perfect in varieties of English around the World. In V. Werner, E. Seoane, & C. Suárez-Gómez (Eds.), *Re-Assessing the present perfect* (pp. 223–258). Berlin: de Gruyter.

Fuchs, R. (2017). The Americanisation of Philippine English. Recent diachronic change in spelling and lexis. *Philippine ESL Journal, 19*(1), 60–83.

Gonçalves, B., Loureiro-Porto, L., Ramasco, J. J., Sánchez, D. (2018) Mapping the Americanization of English in space and time. *PLoS One, 13*(5), e0197741. https://doi.org/10.1371/journal.pone.0197741

Hian, T. C., & Gupta, A. F. (1992). Post-vocalic /r/ in Singapore English. *York Papers in Linguistics, 16*, 139–152.

Schneider, E. W. (2003). The dynamics of new Englishes: From identity construction to dialect birth. *Language, 79*, 233–281.

Schneider, E. W. (2007). *Postcolonial English: Varieties of English around the world.* New York: Cambridge University Press.

Schneider, E. W. (2011). The subjunctive in Philippine English: An updated assessment. In M. L. S. Bautista (Ed.), *Studies of Philippine English: Exploring the Philippine component of the International Corpus of English* (pp. 159–173). Manila: Anvil.

Sönning, L. (2016). The dot plot: A graphical tool for data analysis and presentation. In H. Christ, D. Klenovsak, L. Sönning, & V. Werner (Eds.), *A blend of MaLT. Selected contributions from the methods and linguistic theories symposium 2015* (pp. 101–129). Bamberg: University of Bamberg Press.

Tan, Y.-Y. (2016). The Americanization of the phonology of Asian Englishes: evidence from Singapore. In G. Leitner, A. Hashim, & H.-G. Wolf (Eds.), *Communicating with Asia. The future of English as a global language* (pp. 120–134). Cambridge: Cambridge University Press.

Yao, X., & Collins, P. (2012). The present perfect in World Englishes. *World Englishes, 31*(3), 386–403.

Part 3

Sociolinguistic Variation and Change

9 Internal Variation

Aldrin P. Lee and Ariane Macalinga Borlongan

9.1 Introduction

The fifth and final phase in the evolution of postcolonial Englishes is, according to Schneider (2003, 2007), characterized by differentiation both sociolinguistically and linguistically which ultimately results in internal variation. This internal linguistic heterogeneity, while highly characteristic of and, in fact, a parametric requirement to reach the end in the phases of Schneider's evolutionary model, is not exclusive to the fifth and final phase. Schneider (2007) himself notes that variation exists even in earlier phases. However, he makes this clarification:

> Irrespective of whatever variation may have existed before, however, phase 5 marks the onset of a vigorous phase of new or increased, internal sociolinguistic diversification. To some extent, this may simply be regarded as a function of the time that has elapsed: Trudgill has also observed that in colonial varieties "degree of uniformity [is] in inverse proportion to historical depth" (1986:145), and it is known that regional differences tend to increase as time goes by. It is likely that differentiation in this sense primarily concerns regional rather than social variation, given that in most societies some social variation is likely to have persisted but in a newly settled area there was no basis there for regional speech distinctions to emerge up to that point.
>
> (p. 54)

Internal variation may surface in many dimensions: First and foremost, language varies with reference to register and genre. And then, geography also influences language use. Social and ethnolinguistic groups also form their unique patterns of language use. Since Philippine English (PhE) has been recently thought of as progressing beyond nativization and onto endornormative stabilization (Borlongan, 2016) and even differentiation (Gonzales, 2017a), it is instructive to describe variation which exists within the new English in question and to weigh in how much of such has taken place to be able to call attention to further evidence of progress in its evolution.

DOI: 10.4324/9780429427824-13

126 *Aldrin P. Lee and Ariane Macalinga Borlongan*

Such is the aim of this chapter: It describes internal variation within PhE; in particular, it looks at stylistic, regional, and sociolectal variation which has been documented in previous studies of PhE. It ends with an assessment of internal variation in PhE, most especially in relation to the evolutionary status of the new English.

While diachronic variation may arguably be an essential part of the present discussion, since research on diachronic change in PhE is vibrant and has, in fact, pioneered such kind of work on the Englishes, an entirely separate chapter is devoted to it in this handbook though this chapter makes mention of one diachronic study, i.e. Yao and Collins (2017), which is crucial in the discussion of stylistic variation. Another important constellation of work which has been decidedly left out in this chapter is that of Alberca (1978), Gonzalez and Alberca (1978), and Gonzalez (1982, 1985). They focus on PhE in the mass media, which could easily be a sociolectal variation, but was not included in this chapter simply because the aim of these works was to describe educated and ultimately standard PhE and they supposed that the mass media would be a best representative for this high variety of PhE. Findings of these studies on the mass media are summarized in the relevant chapters on linguistic structure in this handbook.

9.2 Stylistic Variation

It was Gonzalez (1982, 1983, 1985) who was notorious for and tenacious in his claim that PhE is monostylistic. But it was in a 1991 paper where he specifically investigated on stylistic shifts in PhE. He found that shifts from casual style to formal style is the most frequent in PhE, and Filipinos are better in holding formal style—even formulaic style—than casual style. He suspected that Filipinos are more comfortable in formal style because this is the style they had most training in. Thus, the relative formality he attributed to PhE is, he surmised, a result of linguistic insecurity, which, in turn, is a product of the educational system being the primary means of learning and venue of exposure to English in the Philippines.

Many years later, two foreign scholars have commented on stylistic variation in PhE: The expression of futurity was the focus of Nelson's analysis of the new English in comparison with other Englishes in 2005. *Will* was found to be the most common future expression in PhE as well as British English (BrE), Singapore English (SgE), and Indian English (IndE). But his most striking observation is that *shall* is stylistically marked in PhE. Though the frequency of the modal in PhE is comparable with that in BrE, the distribution across text categories is more even in the latter. Meanwhile, PhE almost exclusively uses *shall* in formal, public, non-interactive contexts, and most especially in legalistic contexts. And if ever it comes up in informal conversations, it is often with a high degree of self-consciousness. This pattern of modal use is in consonance with its parent American English (AmE). In

Internal Variation   127

explaining this phenomenon, Nelson invokes Gonzalez's (1991) claim that Filipinos' tendency to observe rules taught in basic education textbook on grammar is primarily a result of English in the Philippines being a product of education and, furthermore, that this over-observance of rules is a manifestation of linguistic insecurity.

Hundt in 2005 looked into concord patterns after collective nouns in PhE and SinE, and compared them with their parents AmE and BrE respectively. She found that the two Outer Circle Englishes do not diverge significantly from their parents. She was also in disbelief of an emergence of a new epicenter from the southern hemisphere, with the frequencies of Australian English and New Zealand English (NZE) clearly not being influential for PhE and SgE. And then, she tells that PhE and SgE are both stylistically homogenous, the former much more so. In her conclusion, she gave a note very important to theorizing on Englishes:

> [A] greater internal stylistic homogeneity in some outer-circle varieties could be interpreted as an indication of a persistent exonormative, inner-circle model. If people speak more or less as they write, the abstract, underlying model toward which they aim is that of written Standard English. Why spoken outer-circle varieties of English, especially during the earlier stages of the development toward "new Englishes," should be oriented toward the written norm is most likely a result of the important role of the educational sector with (1) its emphasis of written production, (2) overt notions of "correctness," and (3) a largely imported (written) norm as its yardstick for comparison.
>
> (p. 223)

As such, she said that SinE is indeed more developmentally advanced that PhE.

The interest of Bautista (2010) was in the comparison of speech and writing in PhE and SinE, testing the two Englishes' (non-)adherence to their parent Englishes as well as their stylistic hetero/homogeneity. PhE and SgE follow the generally global preference for the mandative subjunctive over modal alternative, a trend which even BrE is giving in to under AmE pressure. As for modals of obligation, preference for HAVE *to* over *should* and *must* is prevalent in PhE and SinE in the same way as BrE and NZE though HAVE *got to* does not occur much in PhE and SinE but does so in BrE and NZE. In the negation of the lexical *have*, she said that Asian Englishes (the two in question plus IndE) seem to form a group of their own in terms of preferences. In terms of stylistic differentiation between speech and writing, indeed, there is difference in the PhE and SinE speech and writing; however, both Englishes follow the same trends of differentiation in their speech and writing. While mandative subjunctives generally appear to be even in distribution in PhE and SinE speech and writing, HAVE *to* is the preferred modal in speech in the two Englishes while *should* is the preferred modal in their writing. Also, DO *not have* is preferred in PhE and SinE private dialogues while HAVE *no* is preferred in their informational texts.

A detailed description of the PhE verb phrase has been provided by Borlongan (2011) in his corpus-based grammar of the grammatical category in question. His was a most fine-grained analysis of the verb phrase in English, making use of the 32 text categories of the Philippine component of the International Corpus of English. Overall, in all the categories under the verb phrase, he identified many instances when text category is an important variable in determining patterns of use of the PhE verb.

Suárez-Gómez (2018) juxtaposed her analysis of relativizers in spoken PhE with the findings of Collins, Yao, and Borlongan (2014) on written PhE (only of the 1990s, since Collins, Yao, and Borlongan's study is a diachronic study which also includes 1960s data). The frequency of occurrence which Suárez-Gómez found for spoken register is *who* > *that* > *zero* > *which* and this is comparatively different from what Collins, Yao, and Borlongan found for written PhE, i.e. *that* > *which* > *who* > *whose* > *whom*. Suárez-Gómez concluded that PhE has reached the point of endonormative stabilization, and this is manifested in terms of not only stylistic differentiation but also distinct preferences with references to AmE and other Englishes as well.

While ongoing colloquialization of English (in general) is primarily an interest of diachronic studies (cf. Leech, Hundt, Mair, & Smith, 2009), any commentary on colloquialization would always have ramifications for stylistic hetero/homogeneity. The work of Yao and Collins (2017) was on colloquiality, "a combination of the degree of preference for linguistic features more typical of speech, and the degree of dispreference for linguistic features more typical of writing" (p. 5). And so, in two opposing ends, there would be colloquial features and also those which they called as 'anti-colloquial' features. They revealed that PhE registers are not simply following patterns of use in AmE and that it is wrong to say that PhE writers are insensitive to stylistic differences as was earlier thought (cf. Gonzalez, 1991).

9.3 Regional Variation

Only one study exists which attempted to determine possible emergence of regional varieties of PhE and that is the dissertation of Villanueva in 2016. He specifically looked at lexical and grammatical variation and, though he indeed found some variation occurring in the use of prepositions, articles, tenses, and lexical bundles, he admits the differences were not significant enough to point to a rise in regional varieties in the new English.

Llamzon, in making a claim for the standardization of PhE in 1969, argued that such a standard exists and an evidence for it is the homogenization of English across the Philippines, therefore, with no regional distinctions whatsoever. He admitted that speakers of English from across the Philippines might be beset with different pronunciation struggles but would have achieved homogenized, standardized English when a certain level of proficiency has been achieved. In a 1997 paper, he identified phonological peculiarities of basilectal English spoken by Cebuano and Ilocano/Pangasinense speakers. Gonzalez in 1985 was not yet too comfortable though with the idea that PhE is homogenized and that a Tagalog user of English would still speak English differently from a Cebuano user of English so he argues that a homogenized, standardized PhE is still an emerging one, not one which had been arrived at at that time. McKaughan (1993) seconded Llamzon's (1969) claim of a more even phonology rather than a more differentiated one with reference to substratal languages, that, even if there would have been differences in the phonology of Philippine-type languages, their differences could be masked by their overwhelming similarity that it can be confidently said that PhE is homogenized and, therefore, already standardized.

9.4 Sociolectal Variation

Works on PhE phonology (Regala-Flores, 2014; Lesho, 2017; Llamzon, 1997; Tayao, 2004, 2008a, 2008b) have often distinguished features across the lectal continuum. At the acrolectal end, expectedly, the exonormative norms are very closely approximated. At the other end, basilectal speakers tend to substitute phonemes /f/ and /v/ with /p/ and /b/, trill /r/ (which is a retroflex in acrolectal PhE and GAmE), have a reduced vowel inventory depending on one's first language, variable stress placement in multisyllabic words, syllable-timed instead of stress-timed rhythm, among others.

The most oft-cited works on the English of the less educated in the Philippines are the paper of Bautista on yaya English (*yaya* means 'nurse maids') in 1982 and her notes on idiosyncratic varieties of PhE in 1996 (summaries of unpublished papers on the idiosyncratic varieties of PhE, which included two graduate school term papers on the English spoken by bargirls [Aquino & Cruz, 1981; Cotejar, 1983] and a master's thesis on the English spoken by young women studying in an exclusive private college or colegiala English [*colegiala* means 'female college student'] [Perez, 1993]). Yaya English has gross deviations in tense and tense sequence, subject-verb agreement, pronoun-antecedent congruence, use and placement of adverbials, use of articles, verb-preposition collocations aside from its preponderant insertion of Tagalog particles in utterances. Bargirl English resembles yaya English but it also shows the influence of non-standard AmE as manifested by substitution of /n/ for /ŋ/ aside from the usual deviations in vowels and consonants, copula deletions, double negations, idiomatic (and non-Filipino) flavor of utterances. Colegiala English, meanwhile, is distinguished by its frequent use of Tagalog function words, use of Tagalog content words in English, use of Tagalog exclamatives in an English sentence or turn of speaking, and paralinguistic features of giggling and screaming.

Borlongan (2015) explored conyo English, unfortunately derived from the Spanish *coño* for 'cunt'. Garvida (2012) said that the vulgar Spanish word is

130   *Aldrin P. Lee and Ariane Macalinga Borlongan*

sometimes used as an interjection and Filipinos during the Spanish colonial period thus associated the word to refer to Spanish. Borlongan defined the sociolect as

> a type of English-Tagalog code-switching usually associated with people belonging to the upper socioeconomic strata of the Philippine society. It is usually characterized as having more frequent, less smooth switching than the typical English-Tagalog code- switching, and commonly stereotyped as being exaggeratedly playful.

The phonological features of acrolectal PhE seem to be transferred to the Tagalog switches, most notably the typically rolled /r/ rendered like a glide. Meanwhile, Tagalog patterns for intonation and stress are prevalent. Like colegiala English as earlier described, there is also a preponderance of the construction *make* + Tagalog verb as an alternative for low-frequency verbs (e.g. *We're gonna **make takas** in the middle of the lecture.* 'We're gonna sneak out in the middle of the lecture'). Emphasis may also be done through reduplication (e.g. *It's **super-super** pretty talaga.* 'It's really very pretty'.). And English words may also be laid out in Tagalog word order though these are usually shorter sentences (e.g. *Better the Google Map.* 'Google Maps is better [than the new Maps app of Apple]'). Conyo English actually closely resembles colegiala English because they are generally from the same demography though users of conyo English also include non-students—even the elderly rich would use conyo English.

And then, Gonzales (2016, 2017b, this handbook) also talked about the small but important ethnolinguistic group of Chinese Filipinos and their trilingual code-switching—Hokkien-Tagalog-English 'Hokaglish' code-switching as well as Philippine Hybrid Hokkien, which has a Hokkien-lexifier but incorporates English and Tagalog lexicon and structure. These trilingual language mixings are usually done by Chinese Filipinos to embellish themselves with their unique ethnolinguistic identity and to set them apart from other Filipinos, and also other Chinese.

9.5 Discussion

The hallmark of sociolinguistic theorizing is the ascertaining that variation is structured, otherwise what Weinreirch, Labov, and Herzog (1968) refer to as 'orderly heterogeneity'. This chapter endeavored to determine the systematicity of variation in PhE, most especially stylistic, regional, and sociolectal variation. In itself, PhE is a variant of world Englishes, and how PhE discriminates within is a phenomenon worthy of attention. While exonormative influence (including the Americanization of English[es]) and ongoing diachronic change do impress upon PhE on the latter's patterning, the various sociolinguistic predictors and factors of variation should be well-understood, too, to be able to give a better picture of the emergence of

English in the Philippines. Alluding to Weinreich, Labov, and Herzog, the question to ask then is, 'What is the structure of variation in PhE, if indeed it is internally heterogenous?' There is compelling evidence to believe that variation within PhE does exist. The studies cited, among others, would tell of variation with reference to register, geography, and social groups as well as many others expected of any language variety. In terms of register, initially, PhE was thought to be unable to make stylistic distinctions (Gonzalez, 1991), there is now substantial corpus-based evidence to suggest that the new English is able to make such distinctions not only in the broad speech-writing division but even in finer text categorization. Variation between regions is also discernible but less evident than register and style. Between and among social and ethnolinguistic groups in the Philippines, variation could also be evinced, which even prompted Gonzales (2017a) to believe that PhE has already reached the fifth and final phase in the Schneiderian evolutionary model (2003, 2007).

Martin (2014) though lamented on this variational fragmentation, most especially with reference to education and socioeconomic status, of the Philippine society. She argues that it is symptomatic of the elusiveness, inaccessibility, and irrelevance of (Ph)E to a large part of the population. And hence she was able to further draw three more circles—in true Kachruvian fashion (1985)—within PhE, in itself an outer circle in the Kachru's concentric circles model of the spread of English, i.e. the inner circle (the educated elite using and promoting it), the outer circle (the people accepting PhE as a legitimate new English but doing nothing about/for it), and the expanding circle (those unable to use English of whatever variety but needing it to move upward in the society). And a fourth circle could still be added to what Martin initially conceived—the marginal circle. This circle includes what is called in sociology as 'hard-to-reach groups'. It is those totally not having any access to English, which bars them from life chances in a society where English is the primary language of the controlling domains. It may also be those not needing English for upward mobility in their own social circle, e.g. indigenous minorities living in (semi-)isolation. This circle may well thought to be a group not within the first three circles but it may also be important to account for their presence in talking about the spread and penetration of English in the Philippine society. Admittedly, (Ph)E remains to be a stratifying agent in the Philippine society but, undeniably, this resulting social stratification is likewise an agent to internal variation. Furthermore, it is unescapable that a language or a language variety, for that matter, may be(come) a stratifying agent in the society, with or without any established or perceived standard for this language (variety).

Having affirmatively answered the question on whether PhE varies internally, it is likewise important to point out how this variation is structured and the picture which emerges is this: As education and socioeconomic status are important factors in the acquisition, learning, and, subsequently, use of PhE (cf. Gonzalez, 2004), these have been the primary agents of

132 *Aldrin P. Lee and Ariane Macalinga Borlongan*

variation and likewise stratification. Yet they could certainly not overrule factors such as register and genre, geographical origins, social and ethnolinguistic groupings as well as context and situation co-interlocutors. To make this picture clear, it would be helpful to imagine these cases in point: One must have grown up in an English-using environment (but not necessarily English-only) and must be (well-)educated, often a product of good socioeconomic standing, for him/her to be able to have a wider repertoire in his/her English language skills. Thus, she/he would be able to easily switch between styles, regional accents and forms, and social and/or group-specific norms; she/he would know that she/he needs to use formal, educated English when delivering a business report in front of top-level executives of his/her company and very informal, casual mixing of English and a Philippine-type language when talking to his/her friends after work. On the other extreme end, there is one who did not grow up in a situation where she/he could be given more exposure in using English and has not been competitively educated. Consequently, his/her English language skills leave room for improvement, as further exposure to English is faint, and the promise of a good employment is less favorable. Often with difficulty, she/he attempts to profess a workable command of English, most especially when pressed to do so at work. She/he is unimpressed with his/her proficiency and so avoids its use when possible. These two hypothetical cases are mere generalizations of what could be a probable case in the myriad of complex sociolinguistic possibilities in the English-using Philippine society. And what these discourses ultimately manifest is that PhE also varies internally and to a considerable extent to signify maturity and progress further from nativization and toward endonormative stabilization and even differentiation.

References

Alberca, Wilfredo L. (1978). *The distinctive features of Philippine English in the mass media* (Unpublished doctoral dissertation). University of Santo Tomas, Manila, the Philippines.

Bautista, Ma. Lourdes S. (1982). *Yaya* English. *Philippine Studies, 30*, 377–394.

Bautista, Ma. Lourdes S. (1996). Addendum: Notes on three sub-varieties of Philippine English. In Ma. Lourdes S. Bautista (Ed.), *Readings in Philippine sociolinguistics* (2nd ed., pp. 93–101). Manila, the Philippines: De La Salle University Press, Inc.

Bautista, Ma. Lourdes S. (2010). Comparing spoken and written text-types in Singapore English and Philippine English. In David Jonathan Y. Bayot (Ed.), *Inter/sections: Isagani R. Cruz and friends* (pp. 175–200). Manila, the Philippines: De La Salle University Academic Publications Office & Anvil Publishing, Inc.

Borlongan, Ariane Macalinga. (2011). *A grammar of the verb in Philippine English* (Unpublished doctoral dissertation). De La Salle University, Manila, the Philippines.

Borlongan, Ariane Macalinga. (2015, October). Conyo English: Explorations of Philippine English sociolects. Paper presented at the colloquium titled *Contemporary studies of Philippine English* convened by Danica Salazar at the 21st Annual Conference of the International Association for World Englishes, Istanbul, Turkey.

Borlongan, Ariane Macalinga. (2016). Relocating Philippine English in Schneider's dynamic model. *Asian Englishes*, *18*(3), 1–10.

Collins, Peter, Yao, Xinyue & Borlongan, Ariane Macalinga. (2014). Relative clauses in Philippine English: A diachronic perspective. In Lieven Vandelanotte, Kristin Davidse, Caroline Gentens, & Ditte Kimps (Eds.), *Recent advances in corpus linguistics: Developing and exploiting corpora* (pp. 125–146). New York, NY: Rodopi.

Garvida, Mignette Marcos. (2012). "Conyo talk": The affirmation of hybrid identity and power in contemporary Philippine discourse. *Lingue e Linguaggi*, *8*, 23–24.

Gonzales, Wilkinson Daniel Wong. (2016). Trilingual code-switching using quantitative lenses: An exploratory study on Hokaglish. *Philippine Journal of Linguistics*, *47*, 109–131.

Gonzales, Wilkinson Daniel Wong. (2017a). Philippine Englishes. *Asian Englishes*, *19*(1), 79–95.

Gonzales, Wilkinson Daniel Wong. (2017b). Language contact in the Philippines: The history and ecology from a Chinese Filipino perspective. *Language Ecology*, *1*(2), 185–212.

Gonzalez, Andrew. (1982). English in the Philippine mass media. In John B. Pride (Ed.), *New Englishes* (pp. 211–226). Rowley, MA: Newbury House Publishers, Inc.

Gonzalez, Andrew. (1983). On English in Philippine literature in English. *Solidarity*, *3*(96), 29–42.

Gonzalez, Andrew. (1985). *Studies on Philippine English*. Singapore: SEAMEO Regional Language Centre.

Gonzalez, Andrew. (1991). Stylistic shifts in the English of Philippine print media. In Jenny Cheshire (Ed.), *English around the world: Sociolinguistic perspectives* (pp. 333–363). Cambridge, the United Kingdom: Cambridge University Press.

Gonzalez, Andrew. (2004). The social dimensions of Philippine English. *World Englishes*, *23*, 7–16.

Gonzalez, Andrew, & Alberca, Wilfredo. (1978). *Philippine English of the mass media* (Preliminary ed.). Manila, the Philippines: De La Salle University, Research Council.

Hundt, Marianne. (2005). *The committee has/have decided...*: On concord patterns with collective nouns in inner- and outer-circle varieties of English. *Journal of English Linguistics*, *34*(3), 206–232.

Kachru, Braj B. (1985). Standards, codification and sociolinguistic realism: The English language in the outer circle. In Randolph Quirk & Henry G. Widdowson (Eds.), *English in the world: Teaching and learning the language and literatures* (pp. 11–30). Cambridge, the United Kingdom: Cambridge University Press.

Lesho, Marivic. (2017). Philippine English (Metro Manila acrolect). *Journal of the International Phonetic Association*, *47*, 1–14.

Leech, Geoffrey, Hundt, Marianne, Mair, Christian, & Smith, Nicholas. (2009). *Change in contemporary English: A grammatical study*. Cambridge, the United Kingdom: Cambridge University Press.

Llamzon, Teodoro A. (1969). *Standard Filipino English*. Quezon, the Philippines: Ateneo University Press.

Llamzon, Teodoro A. (1997). The phonology of Philippine English. In Maria Lourdes S. Bautista (Ed.), *English is an Asian language: The Philippine context (Proceedings of the conference held in Manila on August 2–3, 1996)* (pp. 41–48). North Ryde, Australia: The Macquarie Library Pty Ltd.

134 *Aldrin P. Lee and Ariane Macalinga Borlongan*

Martin, Isabel Pefianco. (2014). Philippine English revisited. *World Englishes, 33,* 50–59.

McKaughan, Howard P. (1993). Toward a standard Philippine English. *Philippine Journal of Linguistics, 24*(2), 41–55.

Nelson, Gerald. (2005). Expressing future time in Philippine English. In Danilo T. Dayag & J. Stephen Quakenbush (Eds.), *Linguistics and language education in the Philippines and beyond: A festschrift in honor of Ma. Lourdes S. Bautista* (pp. 41–59). Manila, the Philippines: Linguistic Society of the Philippines.

Perez, Imelda Q. (1993). *A description of the English spoken by college students of Assumption College San Lorenzo, Makati: A pilot study* (Unpublished master's thesis). De La Salle University-Manila, the Philippines.

Regala-Flores, Eden. (2014). Phonological features of basilectal Philippine English: An exploratory study. *International Journal of English and Literature, 5*(6), 128–140.

Schneider, Edgar W. (2003). The dynamics of new Englishes: From identity construction to dialect birth. *Language, 79,* 233–281.

Schneider, Edgar W. (2007). *Postcolonial English: Varieties of English around the world.* Cambridge, the United Kingdom: Cambridge University Press.

Suárez-Gómez, Cristina. (2018). A sociolinguistic study of relativizers in spoken Philippines English. In Elena Seoane, Carlos Acuña-Fariña, & Ignacio Palacios-Martínez (Eds.), *Subordination in English: Synchronic and diachronic perspectives* (pp. 283–306). Berlin, Germany & Boston, MA: De Gruyter Mouton.

Tayao, Ma. Lourdes G. (2004). The evolving study of Philippine English phonology. *World Englishes, 23,* 77–90.

Tayao, Ma. Lourdes G. (2008a). A lectal description of the phonological features of Philippine English. In Ma. Lourdes S. Bautista & Kingsley Bolton (Eds.), *Philippine English: Linguistic and literary perspectives* (pp. 157–174). Hong Kong SAR, China: Hong Kong University Press.

Tayao, Ma. Lourdes G. (2008b). Philippine English: Phonology. In Rajend Mesthrie (Ed.), *Varieties of English (vol. 4): Africa, South and Southeast Asia* (pp. 292–306). Berlin, Germany & New York: Mouton de Gruyter.

Trudgill, Peter. (1986). *Dialects in contact.* Oxford, the United Kingdom, & New York: Blackwell.

Villanueva, Rey John Castro. (2016). *The features of Philippine English across regions* (Unpublished doctoral dissertation). De La Salle University, Manila, the Philippines.

Weinreich, Uriel, Labov, William, & Herzog, Marvin I. (1968). Empirical foundations for the theory of language change. In Winfred P. Lehmann & Yakov Malkiel (Eds.), *Directions for historical linguistics* (pp. 97–195). Austin, TX: University of Texas Press.

Yao, Xinyue, & Collins, Peter. (2017). Exploring grammatical colloquialisation in a non-native English: A case study of Philippine English. *English Language & Linguistics, 21,* 1–26.

10 Diachronic Change

*Ariane Macalinga Borlongan
and Peter Collins*

10.1 Introduction

This chapter is concerned with short-term diachronic change in Philippine English (PhE). Until quite recently corpus-based diachronic research in English had been largely restricted to the two 'reference Englishes', British English (BrE) and American English (AmE) (e.g. Hundt & Mair, 1999, Leech, Hundt, Mair, & Smith, 2009, Mair & Hundt, 1995). Its extension to world Englishes is relatively new, the catalyst being a growing awareness of a gap in the research paradigm. In 2014 Nöel, Van der Auwera and Van Rooy edited a special issue of the *Journal of English Linguistics* (vol. 42/1) titled *Diachronic Approaches to Modality in World Englishes*, in which they passionately urged linguists to address the need for short-term historical studies in world Englishes research, and for the capture of data suitable for conducting such research. This special issue heralded the beginning of a new era in which linguists have applied themselves to advancing knowledge of the evolution of world Englishes using real-time historical data where possible, in favor of the more familiar method of using synchronic corpora such as the International Corpus of English for apparent-time studies. Collins explicitly acknowledges his debt to Nöel et al. for providing the inspiration for his 2015 volume, *Grammatical Change in English World-Wide*, containing studies of grammatical change in a wide selection of Inner and Outer Circle Englishes.

Synchronic corpus-based studies of PhE date from 2000, the publication year of Bautista's book on the grammar of standard PhE in which she used preliminary 1990s data from the Philippine component of the International Corpus of English (ICE-PH). A number of synchronic studies based on ICE-PH subsequently appeared (cf. Bautista, 2011), but the first published recognition of the need to look before (and beyond) PhE of the 1990s in order to better understand the historical development of PhE did not appear until 2011. Borlongan, in the concluding sentence in his 2011 paper on morphosyntactic variation in PhE, wrote, "Ultimately, only time will tell – through a diachronic corpus comparison and corpus-based description of PhilE – how PhilE will develop as a distinct variety in the world of Englishes"

DOI: 10.4324/9780429427824-14

136   *Ariane Macalinga Borlongan and Peter Collins*

(p. 197). Later that year, Borlongan undertook the compilation of a Philippine parallel to the American Brown corpus (Phil-Brown), as described in Section 10.2.

The sole diachronic study of PhE prior to 2014 is Gonzalez, Jambalos, and Romero's (2003), an apparent-time investigation of the phonology, lexicon, grammar, and discourse of Filipinos from different periods in the English language teaching history of the Philippines. An important contribution of this paper is its identification of 'perduring features' of PhE, or "recurring 'mistakes' of pronunciation and grammar, not attained by any generation" (p. 109) which could be considered as "empirically established features of Philippine English (at least one variety of it)" (p. 109). The first corpus-based real-time diachronic study of PhE was that of Collins, Borlongan, and Yao (2014). This study and those that followed – mostly based on data extracted from Phil-Brown – are surveyed in Section 10.4. In addition to surveying these studies, the chapter details the genesis of Phil-Brown and of an even more recent Philippine parallel to the American Before-Brown corpus (PBB). Ultimately, the new corpora and the research which they facilitate promise to yield fresh insights into the development of PhE, particularly its progress in Schneider's (2003, 2007) dynamic model of the evolution of Englishes, in particular, its progress onto endonormative stabilization, as Borlongan (2016) argued.

10.2 The Philippine Parallel to the Brown Corpus

Phil-Brown was intended to closely resemble the Brown University Standard Corpus of Present-Day American English (Brown) compiled by Henry Kučera and W. Nelson Francis in the 1960s at the Brown University (Providence, the United States). As such, as a member of what is often referred to nowadays as the 'Brown family of corpora', it takes its place alongside both the 'core members' representing AmE and BrE, and also 'extended family members' representing Australian English (AusE), Indian English (IndE), and New Zealand English (NZE).

The four core members of the Brown family are the Brown corpus, the Lancaster-Oslo/Bergen Corpus (LOB), the Freiburg Brown Corpus (Frown), and the Freiburg Lancaster-Oslo/Bergen Corpus (F-LOB). The Brown contains over one million words (500 samples of roughly 2,000 words each) of running text of edited English prose printed in the United States during the calendar year 1961, and distributed across 15 text categories – 9 informative and 6 imaginative. LOB was prepared, as a British parallel to Brown, in the 1970s, while Frown and F-LOB – whose sampling years are respectively 1991 and 1992 – were compiled in the 1990s.

Further matching corpora, incorporating minor adjustments to the original generic design which respond to local differences, have been compiled in countries other than the United Kingdom and the United States: During the early 1980s, the Kolhapur Corpus of Indian English, with 1978

Diachronic Change 137

set as its sampling year (symbolically thirty years after Indian Independence). In the early 1990s, the Australian Corpus of English (ACE), with 1986 selected as the sampling year (symbolically a quarter-century later than 1961). Not long after the ACE project began, linguists at Victoria University in New Zealand began work on the Wellington Corpus of Written New Zealand English (WCWNZE), selecting 1986 as the sampling year in order to enable direct comparisons to be made between the Australian and New Zealand data.

Drawing his inspiration from the growing body of studies based on the Brown family corpora, Ariane Borlongan initiated sampling for his Phil-Brown corpus in May 2011, assisted by undergraduate students in his course on *Language Research* at De La Salle University in Manila. The criteria for inclusion of material in the corpus were two-fold: (1) Texts must be published in the Philippines; and (2) the author must have a Filipino-sounding name, as this is the only way to verify the nationality of the author (unless she/he was a prominent person in Philippine society). As the intention was to parallel the American Brown corpus, the same textual categories found in the latter were adopted. However, it quickly became apparent from the mining of texts at De La Salle University Library and the National Library of the Philippines that it would not be possible to adhere precisely to the specifications of the American original. Specifically, the deviations were as follows:

- The sampling years were expanded from 1961 to 1956–1966, a decision necessitated by a paucity of Philippine texts in the single sampling year for Brown.
- Instead of separate categories for the broad academic disciplines in the learned texts of Brown, these categories were conflated because there were not many texts in the natural sciences and in science and technology (those locally published being written by foreigners), with most being in the humanities and social sciences.

For the most part, it was not too difficult to obtain materials with appropriate content, but the physical condition of the materials posed considerable problems. Some of the items in the National Library of the Philippines have not been well-archived and the pages have become brittle, which necessitated very careful handling. The composition of Phil-Brown thus far is presented in Table 10.1:

The availability of ICE-PH, which represents both spoken and written PhE in the 1990s and which has a number of written text-category parallels with Phil-Brown, has been exploited in a number of diachronic studies (which typically further exploit the same 1960s vs 1990s parallels using available American and British Brown family corpora). Table 10.2 taken from Collins, Borlongan, and Yao (2014), which details their textual selections from Phil-Brown and ICE-PH, exemplifies this:

138 *Ariane Macalinga Borlongan and Peter Collins*

Table 10.1 The Composition of Phil-Brown

	Category	Content	Approximate Number of Words	
			Target	Current
Press	A	Press Reportage	88,000	28,000
	B	Press Editorials	54,000	30,000
	C	Press Reviews	34,000	59,000
General	D	Religion	34,000	130,000
Prose	E	Skills, Trades, and Hobbies	72,000	0
	F	Popular Lore	96,000	0
	G	Belles Lettres, Biographies, and the like	150,000	60,000
	H	Miscellaneous	60,000	118,000
Learned	J	Learned	160,000	83,000
Fiction	K	General Fiction	58,000	91,000
	L	Mystery and Detective Fiction	48,000	0
	M	Science Fiction	12,000	0
	N	Adventure and Western	58,000	61,000
	P	Romance and Love Story	58,000	14,000
	R	Humor	18,000	0

Table 10.2 1960s vis-à-vis 1990s Comparison of PhE Using Phil-Brown and ICE-PH

	Phil-Brown		ICE-PH	
	Category/Content	Approximate Number of Words	Category/ Content	Approximate Number of Words
Press	A/Press Reportage B/Press Editorials C/Press Reviews	118,000	W2C/Press News Reports W2E/Press Editorials	68,000
Learned	J/Learned	83,000	W2A/Printed Information: Learned	88,000
Fiction	K/General Fiction N/Adventure and Western P/Romance and Love Story	167,000	W2F/Creative Writing	48,000

10.3 The Philippine Parallel to the Before-Brown Corpus

In recent years, further additions to the Brown family have extended its chronological coverage: The Before-LOB Corpus (B-LOB) and the B-Brown corpus (B-Brown), both of which have 1931 as their target sampling year;

and the British English 2006 Corpus (BE06) and the American English 2006 Corpus (AE06), both with 2006 as their target sampling year. Even more recently Collins and Yao compiled a Brown family diachronic corpus of AusE sampled at four time point targets: 1931, 1961, 1991, and 2006 (AusBrown) (cf. Collins & Yao, in press).

Motivated by these extensions to the nuclear Brown family, Borlongan undertook the compilation of his Philippine Before-Brown corpus in 2016. A major challenge at the outset was to locate materials which had survived World War II, as Manila experienced a level of destruction that was second only to the annihilation suffered by Warsaw during the war. The Heritage Library housed in the larger Miguel de Benavides Library of the University of Santo Tomas (Manila, the Philippines) proved indispensable in this endeavor. The Spanish-founded pontifical university has neatly archived works from before the war, though not in sufficient numbers to make possible a direct comparison with Phil-Brown and ICE-PH. Some text types were yet to be produced in the early days of PhE, i.e. ca. 1920s (cf. Borlongan on history and development in this volume). Therefore, in compiling PBB, Borlongan decided that it should comprise only the three text categories used in the pioneering work on grammatical change in English conducted by Leech et al. (2009): Academic, journalistic, and fictional writing. He furthermore determined that each category would have approximately 350,000 words, which would provide a total of roughly one million words for the whole corpus. At present, it is only the fictional texts which have been collected, a task that has confirmed how confronting are the difficulties involved in assembling early texts. When it is complete, PBB will enable direct cross-varietal comparisons to be made between written 1930s PhE, and written 1930s AmE, BrE, and AusE.

10.4 Findings of Diachronic Studies of Philippine English

In a series of studies, Collins, Borlongan, Yao, and others have documented grammatical changes in PhE using Phil-Brown and ICE-PH. The findings of these studies indicate that while, in the case of some grammatical features, there is evidence of a continuing attachment to American patterns, in the case of others, there is a divergence from these, which is suggestive of a progression toward linguistic autonomy in PhE grammar. Areas in which there is alignment with American usage include the strong support for relativizer *that* (Collins, Yao, & Borlongan, 2014), a continuing preference for the subjunctive over *should*-periphrasis in mandative constructions (Collins, Borlongan, Lim, & Yao, 2014), strongly increasing frequencies for the quasi-modals (Collins, Borlongan & Yao, 2014), and increasing frequencies of the progressive aspect (Collins, 2015). By contrast, changes in the grammar of PhE which diverge from American usage include a failure to follow the strongly increasing predilection of Americans for present progressives (Collins, 2015), a disinclination to follow the declining American trend in

140 *Ariane Macalinga Borlongan and Peter Collins*

modal frequencies (Collins, Borlongan, & Yao, 2014), a reluctance to embrace the colonial parent's appetite for expanded predicates (Borlongan & Dita, 2015), and spelling and pronunciation practices which diverge from those in American usage (Fuchs, 2017, and this volume).

Two very recent papers yield a similar mix of results for PhE grammar, some suggestive of independence and others of American-based dependence. The first of these, Yao and Collins (2017), is a multivariate investigation of colloquialization (the shift of writing from a more formal, literary style to a more conversational, speech-like style) in PhE. The general finding of this study, which is in keeping with impressionistic observations made in previous research, is that PhE is less colloquial than AmE. The second paper, Collins's (2016) study of changes in the verb phrase in contemporary PhE, extends the familiar three-decade temporal window beyond the 1990s to 2012, adducing data from the 43,248,407-word Philippine component of the Corpus of Web-based Global English (GloWbE) to supplement that from Phil-Brown and ICE-PH. Collins's contention, that the verb phrase developments he observes reflect a mixture of ongoing endonormativization and American-oriented exonormativity, is in keeping with that of previous studies.

10.5 Conclusion

Like diachronic change itself, research on diachronic change in PhE remains a "work in progress". The two Brown family corpora of PhE which have been described are yet to be completed. Promisingly, findings from the incomplete Phil-Brown have already pushed scholarship on PhE beyond its previous limits. Meanwhile, PBB, when finalized, will help develop a more comprehensive account of the lifespan of PhE, and in turn provide insights into the evolution of new Englishes in general.

Diachronic studies completed thus far provide some details into how PhE has evolved since the 1960s. They provide a tentative answer to the vexing question raised by Collins and Borlongan (2017), 'Has Philippine English attained linguistic independence?' The grammatical evidence, at least, suggests that PhE has moved beyond the third phase in Schneider's (2003, 2007) evolutionary model but has not yet completed the fourth phase, as Borlongan (2016) argued. As linguists continue to explore Collins and Borlongan's question, they are urged to be mindful of the likelihood that, as PhE moves inexorably toward linguistic independence (via divergences from its parent language, and innovations) it may still demonstrate American patterns simply because these are inherent traits, rather than representing vestiges of colonial dependency. To borrow Borlongan's (2011, p. 196) metaphor:

> PhilE does follow AmE, undeniably a child of its parent. But like a typical child of any parent, it has a life of its own, too. One sees traits inherited from the parent ('nature') but, likewise, it manifests traits resulting from developmental and contextual dynamics ('nurture').

References

Bautista, Ma. Lourdes S. (2000). *Defining Standard Philippine English: Its status and grammatical features.* Manila, the Philippines: De La Salle University Press, Inc.

Bautista, Ma. Lourdes S. (Ed.), (2011). *Studies of Philippine English: Exploring the Philippine component of the International Corpus of English.* Manila, the Philippines: Anvil Publishing, Inc.

Borlongan, Ariane Macalinga. (2011). Some aspects of the morphosyntax of Philippine English. In Ma. Lourdes S. Bautista (Ed.), *Studies of Philippine English: Exploring the Philippine component of the International Corpus of English* (pp. 187–200). Manila, the Philippines: Anvil Publishing, Inc.

Borlongan, Ariane Macalinga. (2016). Relocating Philippine English in Schneider's dynamic model. *Asian Englishes, 18*(3), 1–10.

Borlongan, Ariane Macalinga, & Dita, Shirley N. (2015). Taking a look at expanded predicates in Philippine English across time. *Asian Englishes, 17*(3), 1–8.

Collins, Peter. (2015). Recent diachronic change in the progressive in Philippine English. In Peter Collins (Ed.), *Grammatical change in English world-wide* (pp. 271–296). Amsterdam, the Netherlands & Philadelphia, PI: John Benjamins Publishing Co.

Collins, Peter. (2016). Grammatical change in the verb phrase in contemporary Philippine English. *IIUM Journal of English Language & Literature, 10*(2), 50–67.

Collins, Peter, & Borlongan, Ariane Macalinga. (2017). Has Philippine English attained linguistic independence? The grammatical evidence. *The Philippine ESL Journal, 19*, 10–24.

Collins, Peter, Borlongan, Ariane Macalinga, & Yao, Xinyue. (2014). Modality in Philippine English: A diachronic study. *Journal of English Linguistics, 42*(1), 68–88.

Collins, Peter, Borlongan, Ariane Macalinga, Lim, JooHyuk, & Yao, Xinyue. (2014). The subjunctive mood in Philippine English: A diachronic study. In Simone E. Pfenninger, Olga Timofeeva, Anne-Christine Gardner, Alpo Honkapohja, Marianne Hundt, & Daniel Schreier (Eds.), *Contact, variation, and change in the history of English* (pp. 259–280). Amsterdam, the Netherlands: John Benjamins.

Collins, Peter, & Yao, Xinyue. (in press). AusBrown: A new diachronic corpus of Australian English. *ICAME Journal.*

Collins, Peter, Yao, Xinyue, & Borlongan, Ariane Macalinga. (2014). Relative clauses in Philippine English: A diachronic perspective. In Lieven Vandelanotte, Kristin Davidse, Caroline Gentens, & Ditte Kimps (Eds.), *Recent advances in corpus linguistics: Developing and exploiting corpora* (pp. 125–146). New York, the United States: Rodopi.

Fuchs, Robert. (2017). The Americanisation of Philippine English. Recent diachronic change in spelling and lexis. *Philippine ESL Journal, 19*(1), 60–83.

Gonzalez, Andrew, Jambalos, Thelma V., & Romero, Ma. Corona S. (2003). *Three studies on Philippine English across generations: Towards an integration and some implications.* Manila, the Philippines: Linguistic Society of the Philippines.

Hundt, Marianne, & Mair, Christian. (1999). "Agile" and "Uptight" Genres: The Corpus-based Approach to Language Change in Progress. *International Journal of Corpus Linguistics, 4*(2), 221–242.

142 *Ariane Macalinga Borlongan and Peter Collins*

Leech, Geoffrey, Hundt, Marianne, Mair, Christian, & Smith, Nicholas. (2009). *Change in contemporary English: A grammatical study.* Cambridge, the United Kingdom: Cambridge University Press.

Schneider, Edgar W. (2003). The dynamics of new Englishes: From identity construction to dialect birth. *Language, 79,* 233–281.

Schneider, Edgar W. (2007). *Postcolonial English: Varieties of English around the world.* Cambridge, the United Kingdom: Cambridge University Press.

Yao, Xinyue, & Collins, Peter. (2017). Exploring grammatical colloquialisation in a non-native English: A case study of Philippine English. *English Language & Linguistics, 21,* 1–26.

11 Philippine English in Relation to American English

Edgar W. Schneider

11.1 Introduction

As is well known, Philippine English (PhE) stands out from Outer Circle Postcolonial Englishes in having resulted from American, not British, colonialism. While almost all other World Englishes in the Outer Circle are products of a former status as colonies in the British Empire, the Philippines was an American colony between 1898 and 1946, and was anglicized remarkably quickly and efficiently. The country is not quite but almost unique in that respect – other territories derived from American colonial activity are either much smaller (like Guam or the Marshall Islands) or quite different in character and not really English-speaking (like Liberia). Consequently, concepts of linguistic norms and teaching are oriented toward American English (AmE) rather than British English (BrE).

The present paper inquires into the exact nature of the relationship between PhE and AmE. In the first part I survey earlier scholarship and statements on the putatively AmE character of PhE. Subsequently, I conduct a clearly designed empirical investigation of this issue on its own, based on electronic corpora, including the Philippine component of the International Corpus of English (ICE) compiled under the leadership of Prof. Maria "Tish" Bautista. Earlier research by John Algeo (2006) and others has shown differences between the two major varieties of BrE and AmE to be a matter of degree and quantitative tendencies rather than an absolute one – which is what we have to expect here as well.

11.2 The Relationship between PhE and AmE: Earlier Views

As is well known (and frequently referred to in this Handbook), the American orientation of PhE was caused by roughly a half-century (1898–1946) as a colony of the US and by deliberate efforts on the side of the US to anglicize the Philippines, which resulted in remarkably quick increases in speaker numbers of English (Gonzalez, 1997:27–30). In practice, this was achieved by a large number of American teachers sent there (about 2,000 over the first two decades; Gonzalez, 1997:27), the so-called Thomasites. Most

DOI: 10.4324/9780429427824-15

144 *Edgar W. Schneider*

importantly, they had a multiplying effect, being not only or not primarily teachers but rather teacher-trainers (Bautista & Bolton, 2004:3), with the majority of teachers in schools being Filipinos (Gonzalez, 1997). And they had a persistent impact: many Thomasites stayed and married locally, and many "religious organizations ... were managed by American missionaries" (Gonzalez, 2005:16). The effect has remained through the school system being orientated toward AmE (Gonzalez, 2005) and continuing cultural contacts, political dependence, military ties, and family bonds – "almost every Filipino has relatives and family in the United States" (Gonzalez, 1997:39; Sibayan & Gonzales, 1996:148). Martin (2004) labels Filipinos "cultural clones of Americans" (129), with the American literary canon also dominating the school system (cf. Martin, 2014:76).

Hence, PhE, especially in higher education, is exonormatively oriented toward "a 'standard of standards',... Standard American English" (Bautista, 2000b:17), and this variety is also the yardstick against which Bautista (2000a) identifies features of PhE as "deviations" (147). On the other hand, this seems to be more of a default assumption and orientation, accepted somewhat naturally but without much passion or vigorous pursuit. In contrast, as early as in 1969 Llamzon posited "Standard Filipino English" as "a dialectal variety of English, just like American or British English" (1969:84), explicitly contrasting many syntactic examples with AmE (1969:50–78) and arguing against AmE as the target (86–91). Three decades later he notes that "Filipinos are willing to copy American English [only] up to a point" (Llamzon, 1997:43), in formal style; and in a similar vein, Tayao notes that "Filipinos rarely conform to the norms of American English in all settings" (2004:80) and points out phonemic differences.

Legal texts on education and language policy mention "English" as a co-official language (next to Filipino, e.g. in the 1987 Constitution) and as a possible medium of instruction in some subjects, but make no mention of AmE (or of any other variety) as an explicit norm or target (Garcia, 1997). Quite a number of scholarly publications or collections also refer to "English" or "Standard English" but do not mention AmE as a norm – for example, many contributions in Bautista (ed. 1997), which discuss norms and the issue of indigenous orientation but not AmE (similarly the papers in Bautista et al., eds., 2000, Bautista, ed. 2004, Bautista & Bolton, eds. 2004 or Gonzalez, 2004, Bolton & Bautista, 2004).

The question of a possible "independence" of PhE has reached momentum recently with Borlongan's (2016) claim that PhE has reached phase 4, endonormative stabilization, in Schneider's (2007) Dynamic Model, unlike Schneider himself who posits it in late phase 3, nativization (2007:141–143). Borlongan's suggestion is backed by historical data and the claim "that a localized variety is accepted by Filipinos" (2016:236), also as "an emerging local norm" (232). Martin (2014) concedes that the acceptance of a local norm may apply to "middle to upper-income members of Philippine society" (80), but basically disagrees, arguing that due to the association of English with

Philippine English and American English 145

an educated class which prefers AmE PhE is not yet an identity carrier, impeded by an "ambivalent attitude to the variety" (80). On the other hand, W. Gonzales (2017), pointing out distinctive sub-varieties, suggests a reconceptualization as "Philippine Englishes", "at the dawn of stage 5 (differentiation)" (79; cf. 93).

There are comparatively few explicit empirical comparisons of PhE and AmE. Schneider (2005) investigates subjunctive use and finds PhE "a close kin of American English", with "quite remarkable" similarities of frequencies and "fairly subtle detail" (2005:37, 2011:169). Bautista (2011) reports several case studies and finds some strong similarities, concerning, in addition to Schneider's (2011) work on the subjunctive, existential *there* agreement (Collins, 2011:184) and regularization of verb morphology (Borlongan, 2011). Borlongan and Lim (2012), an unpublished conference presentation, compare changes in PhE as opposed to "its parent AmE" and find fewer modals, a higher rate of increase of quasi-modals, very similar figures for *have* negation, a slightly smaller decrease of *whom* and higher decrease of *of which* but smaller decrease of *whose*, and an even higher rate of *-body* forms (like *somebody*) than *-one* (*someone*) forms. Fuchs (2017) compares Borlongan's Phil-Brown corpus (with 1960s data) with the written component of ICE-Phil (from the 1990s) for a few lexical pairs but mainly spelling differences. He finds "remnants of British influence" (60) in the early phase, declining by the 1990s, with American patterns strengthened or "followed completely" (74). He hypothesizes that this "putative early influence of BrE" (64) may be due to its higher prestige at the time of foundation, in the early 20th century.

Borlongan (2011) summarizes the issue quite convincingly through a parent-child analogy, suggesting that PhE resembles AmE much like a child resembles its parents (see below, Section 11.4). Interestingly enough, similar to what Hundt (1998) found for New Zealand English in relation to BrE, he argues that in some respects PhE "is more American than AmE" (192). This, and the broader issue in general, remains to be tested in the next session.

11.3 Structural Similarities: PhE Compared to AmE and Other Varieties

To empirically investigate the question of the putatively American character of PhE, also on a comparative basis, a selected set of corpora, both smaller and very large ones, has been screened for frequencies of British vs. American choices. The research setup has been systematically designed, considering varieties, corpora, and linguistic issues to be compared.

As to varieties, for a comprehensive assessment of the issue it makes sense to look at not only AmE and PhE themselves but a slightly broader range of varieties that may be taken to display varying degrees of American impact. Thus, the comparison comprises BrE, Indian English (IndE, as a prototypically British-derived variety), Singapore English (SgE, as a daughter variety of BrE strongly influenced by AmE), PhE, and AmE.

146 *Edgar W. Schneider*

The discipline of Corpus Linguistics (Lindqvist, 2009) provides useful tools for such a comparison, viz. identically compiled large-scale electronic text collections representing different World Englishes. A standard resource, widely used for comparative studies, are the components of ICE. The setup is described by Greenbaum (1996). By now, close to 20 such corpora have been compiled by independent national teams, all observing the same corpus design with respect to the size and number of texts per genres and text types included. ICE corpora comprise one million words, 60% of which represent transcribed speech, and thus offer a good coverage of variety-specific speech habits. This has been found to be sufficient for mid- to high-frequency phenomena, notably grammatical patterns. In addition, Mark Davies of Brigham Young University has been producing incredibly huge corpora, culled directly from the internet (see www.english-corpora.org). For comparing World Englishes, the primary choice is the GloWbE corpus (of Global Web-based English), with 1.9 billion words from 20 countries, compiled in 2012/13 (Davies & Fuchs, 2015). This corpus is impressively huge but less balanced and thus stylistically representative than ICE, consisting predominantly of texts drawn from online newspapers and blogs. In the present study frequencies in ICE and in GloWbE will be compared. ICE corpora are available for BrE, IndE, SgE, and PhE. For the US, only the written component of ICE has been published; regrettably, a corresponding speech sample has never been produced. What is available, and was meant to be integrated into the spoken part of ICE-US, is the Santa Barbara Corpus of Spoken American English, consisting of transcripts of 60 conversations with an overall token word count of 322,102 (rather than the 600,000 words of speech from a wider range of speech settings in ICE). For the present study both of these components have been joined, yielding a representation of AmE that is slightly smaller and slightly less versatile in the spoken component compared to the real ICE corpora, but it can be taken to be a sufficiently close match.

Apart from pronunciation (which of course is not represented in text corpora) differences between varieties exist on the levels of lexis, spelling, and grammar, and will be investigated. There are quite a number of studies that have systematically compared AmE and BrE (notably Algeo, 2006; Mair, 2006; Mittmann, 2004; Leech et al., 2009; Rohdenburg & Schlüter, 2009). What they all show is that there are hardly ever any clear-cut qualitative differences between both varieties (so that form A comes up in one variety and form B in the other one only). Differences are typically strong tendencies and preferences: both forms A and B occur on both sides of the Atlantic but at substantially disproportional and consistent frequency rates, so that overall the sum total and interplay of such preferences identify any given variety in quite a stable fashion. Evidently, this is what is also to be expected in the comparison of World Englishes – differences are a matter of degree, not of yes-no distributions. So, to assess the degree of similarity between PhE, AmE, and the other varieties chosen pairs of American versus British

Philippine English and American English 147

choices (or rather, preferences) have been selected from the above-mentioned sources and a few more (Strevens, 1971; Crystal, 1995; Biber et al., 1999; Tottie, 2002), and their respective frequencies in the varieties (and corpora) selected have been determined. Verbs and nouns have been lemmatized (i.e. all inflectional variants have been considered). As far as was practically possible homographs and unwanted polysemic uses were excluded, and in a few cases this resulted in the exclusion of potential pairs of choices (e.g. past participle *got*/*gotten*, where corpus searches return mostly the invariable past tense form *got* which cannot be excluded mechanically, or *darling*/*honey*, where it turned out practically impossible to disambiguate the food from the term of endearment amongst the large number of occurrences in GloWbE).

Lexical and grammatical variability has been subcategorized according to relevant parameters which have been suggested to vary between the two main varieties. In the interest of saving space only sum values per subcategory will be reported in detail: Table 11.1 identifies these subcategories and the proportions of putatively AmE choices (out of the sum total of AmE + BrE options) per variety. The individual forms studied will be listed in the text; for convenience, AmE forms are always formally marked by being underlined. Individual forms investigated will be discussed selectively, especially when their distribution turns out to be particularly interesting, i.e. different from the overall category pattern. As in Table 11.1, percentages given in the text always identify the proportion of AmE choices. Overall, token frequencies *n* (important for an assessment of the validity of proportions quoted) will be offered in the text for each subcategory and corpus to identify the magnitudes of the data sets. In general, they range between a few dozen (e.g. with compounding or V-N-collocations) to a few hundred (e.g. for single words or phraseology) per variety in ICE (overall *n* =14,339) but are huge in GloWbE (overall *n* = 3,114,637), in the thousands or tens of thousands for all tokens in each subcategory and in hundreds or thousands for each form investigated (with very few exceptions, e.g. for some suffixed compounds; but there are always at least a few dozen tokens for each BrE+AmE pair).

A few general points can be made on the distributions observed before looking into specific categories and selected forms. First, as is to be expected, we observe varying relative proportions all across the board, a matter of more or less rather than absolute distinctions: a substantial number of AmE forms occur in BrE corpora as well, and vice versa. Second, while in ICE the distributions are more spread out and employ the entire quantitative range (e.g. for spelling from 5.3% in BrE to 97.7% in AmE), practically all GloWbE distributions show less of a spread and a stronger neutralizing tendency toward the mean with relatively higher low values in BrE and lower peak values in PhE and AmE (e.g. 20.7–86.5% for spelling). This may be caused by the more balanced and thus stylistically more differentiated character of ICE, or it may just reflect the impact of some homogenizing high-frequency distributions in GloWbE: When, for example, for "Syntax – concord" AmE

Table 11.1 Proportions of AmE Choices per Categories, Corpora, and Varieties

Category	ICE					GloWbE				
	BrE	*IndE*	*SgE*	*PhE*	*AmE*	*BrE*	*IndE*	*SgE*	*PhE*	*AmE*
Spelling	5.3%	15.0%	8.5%	92.4%	97.7%	20.7%	48.3%	48.0%	84.5%	86.5%
Lexis (single)	14.2%	32.6%	21.2%	75.4%	72.5%	24.5%	45.5%	41.7%	59.0%	72.5%
Lexis (compounding)	19.2%	72.7%	38.2%	78.4%	85.4%	21.6%	44.9%	41.2%	61.6%	80.8%
Lexis (endings)	31.8%	41.8%	46.5%	79.1%	89.1%	45.2%	55.7%	55.2%	73.0%	76.9%
Lexis (suffixes in compounds)	25.0%	14.3%	25.0%	50%	50%	34.0%	41.0%	56.0%	56.4%	72.6%
Preposition choice	8.5%	57.8%	55.1%	91.0%	77.0%	33.6%	61.4%	62.2%	73.4%	72.2%
Verb morphology	50.0%	12.4%	25.5%	95.1%	97.1%	65.5%	54.3%	59.1%	89.4%	92.1%
Syntax – concord	78.1%	95.2%	92.9%	98.62%	92.6%	78.9%	91.0%	89.1%	88.4%	89.2%
Syntax – constituent sequence	13.1%	5.7%	16.8%	9.1%	18.6%	12.9%	8.9%	12.1%	11.4%	16.8%
Syntax – contraction	24.4%	66.0%	54.2%	55.3%	58.0%	49.4%	61.4%	57.2%	58.9%	56.3%
Syntax – article usage	30.8%	92.1%	65.7%	91.9%	97.1%	60.2%	79.9%	82.3%	88.8%	90.7%
Syntax – V-N-collocations	14.6%	21.7%	65.2%	94.3%	88.2%	59.4%	70.0%	80.3%	83.3%	86.5%
Phraseology	26.8%	63.4%	54.0%	84.4%	87.6%	55.1%	72.9%	69.9%	74.5%	74.7%
Sum total	22.0%	42.4%	40.1%	77.1%	80.1%	37.1%	53.7%	52.9%	70.7%	73.0%

Philippine English and American English   149

choices predominate in all varieties and for "Syntax – constituent sequence" they are quite rare everywhere this leads to a centralizing leveling effect. Third, with very few and very minor exceptions basically the distributions are as is to be expected: the proportion of AmE forms is consistently lowest in BrE and highest in AmE. Fourth, IndE and SgE figure persistently in between BrE and AmE, often also numerically near the middle; also, the values for both lie mostly close to each other, with no consistent difference in degree of similarity of either variety to AmE. And finally, PhE is mostly situated very close to AmE, in the majority of categories showing just a slightly lower proportion of AmE forms (and in a few instances, e.g. for single words or preposition choices, an even higher one).

The tension between the obligation to document the forms investigated and space constraints forces me to present results somewhat selectively, with a focus on overall categories and, within these, distributions which are interesting for specific reasons. In principle, very many form and category frequencies observe what I call the "prototypical" distribution, observable also roughly in the sum total values: presence of AmE forms but low frequencies (broadly, 5–20% in ICE, 20–40% in GloWbE) in BrE; intermediate values (around 40–50%) for IndE and SgE; high figures in AmE (80–98% in ICE, 70–90% in GloWbE), and PhE mostly close to, often slightly below, the AmE proportions. I assume such a distribution as the default case in my discussion below and will point to noteworthy deviations from it.

For spelling (n = 2,770[ICE]/822,565[GloWbE]), the following pairs (BrE/AmE) were analyzed: *colour/color, honour/honor, humour/humor, neighbour/neighbor, traveller/traveler, cancelled/canceled, waggon/wagon, theatre/theater, centre/center, plough/plow, catalogue/catalog, dialogue/dialog, licence/license, defence/defense, tyre/tire, standardise/standardize,* and *realise/realize.* Spelling comes up as a clear-cut divider: AmE conventions predominate very strongly in AmE, with PhE very close, and score relatively low in BrE, with IndE and SgE siding unusually strongly with BrE. Supposedly BrE *waggon* is extremely rare everywhere. In GloWbE, AmE *license, tire,* and *realize* take a slightly higher share; otherwise most distributions are roughly prototypical.

Lexis has been approached from several perspectives. The simplest and most obvious manifestation of lexical variability are single words (n = 1,481 [ICE]/339,317[GloWbE]), most of them widely known to vary – the usual suspects, as it were: *tap/faucet, motorway/expressway* or *freeway, solicitor/attorney, lorry/truck, holiday/vacation, windscreen/windshield, postman/mailman, pavement/sidewalk, bookshop/bookstore, rubbish/garbage, hoarding/billboard, railway/railroad, aeroplane/airplane, nappies/diapers, lift/elevator, torch/flashlight,* and *trousers/pants.* The overall distribution is roughly prototypical, with relatively high frequencies of some BrE words in PhE and AmE (e.g. *tap, holiday, postman, luggage, torch*). *Motorway* predominates in BrE but is very rare elsewhere, including IndE and SgE. AmE words which are fairly or very common also in BrE include *attorney, truck, baggage,*

150   *Edgar W. Schneider*

billboard, *airplane*, and *pants*. Forms associated with AmE but found even more frequently in PhE include *vacation*, *garbage*, *billboard*, and *diapers*. Conversely, PhE sides with BrE in the preference of *luggage* over *baggage* (which is extremely rare) and *railway* over *railroad*.

Some putative differences involve compound lexical items (*n* = 149 [ICE]/69,132[GloWbE]). Of these, I tested *ticket collector/conductor, zebra crossing/crosswalk, plaster/band aid, mobile phone/cell phone, notice board/bulletin board, car park/parking lot, expiry date/expiration date, petrol station/gas station, number plate/license plate, sparking plug/spark plug, estate agent/realtor, hall of residence/dormitory, post code/zip code, goods train/freight train, sailing boat/sail boat,* and *dialing tone/dial tone*. The overall pattern is roughly prototypical (with fairly many AmE forms in IndE). Forms postulated to represent BrE but found relatively rarely even there include *ticket collector, notice board, sparking plug, hall of residence, goods train,* and *dialling tone*. Conversely, AmE *band aid* is relatively rare and *realtor* and *sail boat* are only slightly above average in PhE and AmE. Interestingly, PhE shows slightly more uses of *mobile phone* than *cell phone* in GloWbE but it slightly exceeds AmE in the predominance of *conductor, license plate, dormitory,* and *sail boat*.

According to Tottie (2002:149) and Algeo (2006:78), some BrE words, unlike their American correspondents, often take an ending involving *-s* (*n* = 2,681 [ICE]/483,065[GloWbE]). I looked into *maths/math, towards/toward, amongst/among, baker's/bakery,* and *grocer's/grocery*. The hypothesis is confirmed for BrE *maths*; *towards* is strong everywhere and slightly less common than *toward* only in AmE; in all other instances the BrE variants are rare.

In a similar vein, several BrE compound lexemes are supposed to distinguish themselves from AmE ones also by an *-s* suffix (Algeo, 2006:92–94; *n* = 25 [ICE]/4.046[GloWbE]). Cases in point investigated include *drugs policy/drug policy, accounts department/account department, arrivals hall/arrival hall, books section/book section, brains trust/brain trust, on second thoughts/on second thought,* and *traffic lights/traffic light*. Some of these forms are relatively uncommon, but the broadly prototypical overall distribution essentially confirms the claim.

Preposition choices (*n* = 512[ICE]/104.761[GloWbE]) are known to vary. I considered *fill in/out, at/in school, in/under the circumstances, named after/for, different to/than, at/on the weekend(s),* and *as from/of*. In general, frequencies conform to the prototypical pattern, yet in both corpora PhE has higher frequencies of AmE forms than AmE itself. In particular, this applies to *in school* and *under the circumstances*.

In verb morphology, BrE seems to prefer irregular forms, unlike AmE, viz. *burnt/dwelt/learnt/smelt/dreamt/knelt* as against *burned/dwelled/learned/smelled/dreamed/kneeled*. The data (*n* = 582[ICE]/108.181[GloWbE]) show that the regular forms indeed predominate strongly in AmE and (slightly less so, with just about 2% less in both corpora) PhE, and they take half of the time or more even in BrE (while IndE and SgE show conservative behavior, higher proportions of irregular forms than BrE itself).

Philippine English and American English   151

In collective concord structures, AmE is reported to prefer grammatical concord, i.e. singular verb forms, over the plural conceptualizations associated with BrE (Hundt, 2006). I tested all cooccurrences of the subjects *team/military/council/government/company/family/committee* with primary auxiliaries that show concord, i.e. *are/have* versus *is/has* (*n* = 665 [ICE]/125.599[GloWbE]). It turns out that singular concord strongly predominates everywhere, about 90% or more of the time. Notional (plural) concord is moderately common, with slightly over 20%, in BrE only.

BrE is supposed to prefer the placement of simple adverbs after but AmE before auxiliaries, e.g. *can already* but *already can* (Tottie, 2002:171; Algeo, 2006:149). I determined the frequencies of all immediate sequences of *can/will/would/has* with *seldom/never/often/certainly/probably/already* (*n* = 861 [ICE]/264.969[GloWbE]). The result is the opposite of the one in the previous category: The BrE choice predominates strongly throughout; in both corpora the "AmE" V-Adv sequence is stronger in the AmE data than elsewhere but does not exceed 16–18%. In both corpora PhE shows even fewer "AmE" sequences than BrE.

BrE is supposed to prefer one-word contractions of some auxiliaries (Algeo, 2006:19–20): *haven't/don't have, needn't/don't need to* (*n* = 1.721 [ICE]/226.954[GloWbE]). *Haven't* is indeed the (slightly) predominant choice in BrE; otherwise in all other varieties the pattern with *don't* predominates – moderately so with *have*, very strongly with *need*.

Article usage (*n* = 183[ICE]/43.382[GloWbE]) is assumed to vary in some set phrases in both directions (Algeo, 2006:43–46): *in (the) hospital, at (the) university* but *all the afternoon/morning, all the year, all over the town* all without the article in AmE. However, except for *in hospital* (which is extremely common in BrE) the AmE choices are consistently preferred, with highest frequencies in AmE and PhE trailing closely behind.

Alternate choices characterize verb-noun-collocations in light verb constructions or "expanded predicates" (Algeo, 2006:270–278, Leech et al., 2009, ch. 8; *n* = 200[ICE]/38.637[GloWbE]): *do/take a course, have/take a bath, have/take a look, have/take a rest, have a sleep/take a nap, have/go for a swim, have/give it a try, have/take a walk, hitch a lift/ride, sit/take an exam,* and *hire/rent a car.* In ICE, token numbers are low except for *have/take a look* which shows an almost prototypical distribution, except for the fact that PhE (at 95%) shows "American" *take* more frequently than AmE (78%). In GloWbE, AmE choices predominate almost everywhere, with a roughly prototypical internal frequency relationship across varieties. PhE frequencies are slightly behind those of AmE, but PhE, unlike AmE, shows *hitch a ride* and *take an exam* used in all instances, without exception.

Finally, there are alternative preferences in phraseological choices with a roughly identical meaning: *a bit of/something of, don't let's/let's not, come to that/for that matter, at(for) the moment/right now, before time/ahead of time, go and get(see)/go get(see), now and again/once in a while, ages ago/long time ago, in the end/finally, mind you/the question is, what's the matter/what's going*

152 *Edgar W. Schneider*

on, and *can't remember(understand)/don't remember(understand).* The overall distribution (*n* = 2.509[ICE]/484.029[GloWbE]) is roughly prototypical, which broadly confirms the variety differentiation claims. Individual forms may behave differently, though: BrE forms which are rare throughout include *don't let's, come to that, ages ago,* and *in the end.* Conversely, AmE *something of* occurs relatively rarely. In most cases PhE frequencies are slightly lower than those of AmE, but a few AmE forms occur even more frequently in PhE, viz. *once in a while* and *finally.* For *something of, let's not, for that matter,* and *long time ago* frequency proportions in both varieties are almost identical.

11.4 Conclusion

So – what, then, is the verdict on the relationship between PhE and AmE?

Statements in the literature by Philippine and other scholars confirm that both are very close, though of course not identical. AmE was the input variety to PhE; it continues to be the target of orientation in teaching contexts, and it is supported by ongoing contact and exposure. However, many Philippine scholars have insisted on the independent, essentially Filipino character of PhE, both in general and with respect to specific features. How far the variety has proceeded toward endonormativity remains slightly controversial, but there seems to be a consensus on the fact that it has been moving in that direction. Given the sociohistorical background and present-day relationships, its orientation toward AmE appears to be a default assumption, but not one that is defended vigorously or with a great deal of prominence; in many contexts reference is made to just "English" as the object of discussion, without further specification.

The linguistic analysis has shown a very high degree of similarity between PhE and AmE. In the majority of cases the frequency of putatively "AmE" forms in PhE is just slightly lower than in AmE itself. There are a small number of distributions in which PhE is quite different, similar to BrE; there are also a small number of instances where the proportion of AmE forms in PhE even exceeds their frequency in AmE. By comparison, IndE and SgE behave quite differently, typically with a tally somewhere between BrE and AmE frequencies.

In sum, Borlongan's (2011) analogy captures the relationship nicely and convincingly:

> PhE does follow AmE, undeniably a child of its parent. But like a typical child of any parent, it has a life of its own, too. One sees traits inherited from the parent ("nature"), but, likewise, it manifests traits resulting from development and contextual dynamics ("nurture").
>
> (196)

There is no doubt that sociopolitical changes and the inherent dynamics in any language will increase the distinctive identity of PhE even more in the future.

References

Algeo, John. (2006). *British or American English? A handbook of word and grammar patterns.* Cambridge: Cambridge University Press.

Bautista, Maria Lourdes S. (Ed.) (1997). *English is an Asian language: The Philippine context. Proceedings of the conference held in Manila on August 2–3, 1996.* Sydney: Macquarie Library Ltd.

Bautista, Maria Lourdes S. (2000a). The grammatical features of educated Philippine English. In Bautista, Llamzon & Sibayan (Eds.) (2000), pp. 146–158.

Bautista, Maria Lourdes S. (2000b). *Defining Standard Philippine English: Its status and grammatical features.* Manila: De La Salle University Press, Inc.

Bautista, Maria Lourdes S. (Ed.) (2004). Special articles on Philippine English. *Asian Englishes, 7*(2), 8–26.

Bautista, Maria Lourdes S. (Ed.) (2011). *Studies of Philippine English. Exploring the Philippine component of the International Corpus of English.* Manila: Anvil Publishing, Inc. for De La Salle University.

Bautista, Ma. Lourdes S., & Bolton, Kingsley (Eds.) (2004). Special issue on Philippine English. *World Englishes, 23*(1), 1–224.

Bautista, Maria Lourdes S., Llamzon, Teodoro A., & Sibayan, Bonifacio P. (Eds.) (2000). *Parangal cang Brother Andrew. Festschrift for Andrew Gonzalez on his sixtieth birthday.* Manila: Linguistic Society of the Philippines.

Biber, Douglas, Johansson, Stig, Leech, Geoffrey, Conrad, Susan, & Finegan, Edward (1999). *Longman grammar of spoken and written English.* Harlow, Essex: Longman.

Bolton, Kingsley, & Bautista, Ma. Lourdes S. (2004). Philippine English: Tensions and transitions. *World Englishes, 23*(1), 1–5.

Borlongan, Ariane Macalinga. (2011). Some aspects of the morphosyntax of Philippine English. In Bautista (Ed.) (2011), pp. 187–199. *Studies of Philippine English. Exploring the Philippine component of the International Corpus of English.* Manila: Anvil Publishing, Inc. for De La Salle University.

Borlongan, Ariane Macalinga. (2016). Relocating Philippine English in Schneider's dynamic model. *Asian Englishes, 18*(3), 1–10.

Borlongan, Ariane Macalinga, & Lim, JooHyuk. (2012). Philippine English in Comparison with American English: A Corpus-Based Grammatical Study. Paper presented at The 18th Annual Conference of the International Association for World Englishes, Hong Kong & Guangzhou, China.

Collins, Peter. (2011). Variable agreement in the existential-there construction in Philippine English. In Bautista (Ed.) (2011), pp. 175–186.

Crystal, David. (1995). *The Cambridge encyclopedia of the English language.* Cambridge: Cambridge University Press.

Davies, Mark, & Fuchs, Robert. (2015). Expanding horizons in the study of World Englishes with the 1.9 billion word Global Web-based English Corpus (GloWbE). *English World-Wide, 36*(1), 1–28.

Dayag, Danilo T., & Quakenbush, J. Stephen (Eds.) (2005). *Linguistics and language education in the Philippines and beyond. A festschrift in honor of Ma. Lourdes S. Bautista.* Manila: Linguistic Society of the Philippines.

Fishman, Joshua A., Conrad, Andrew W., & Rubal-Lopez, Alma (Eds.) (1996). *Post-imperial English: Status change in former British and American colonies 1940–1990.* Berlin, New York: Mouton de Gruyter.

154 *Edgar W. Schneider*

Fuchs, Robert. (2017). The Americanisation of Philippine English: Recent diachronic change in spelling and lexis. *The Philippine ESL Journal, 19*, 60–83.

Garcia, Ester A. (1997). The language policy in education. In Maria Lourdes S. Bautista (Ed.) (1997). *English is an Asian language: The Philippine context. Proceedings of the conference held in Manila on August 2–3, 1996 (pp. 73–86).* Sydney: Macquarie Library Ltd.

Gonzales, Wilkinson Daniel Wong. (2017). Philippine Englishes. *Asian Englishes, 19*, 79–95.

Gonzalez, Andrew. (1997). The history of English in the Philippines. In Bautista (Ed.) (1997), pp. 25–40. *English is an Asian language: The Philippine context. Proceedings of the conference held in Manila on August 2–3, 1996.* Sydney: Macquarie Library Ltd.

Gonzalez, Andrew. (2004). The social dimension of Philippine English. *World Englishes, 23*(1), 7–16.

Gonzalez, Andrew. (2005). Distinctive grammatical features of Philippine literature in English: Influencing or influenced? In Dayag, Danilo T., & Quakenbush, J. Stephen (Eds.) (2005), pp. 15–26. *Linguistics and language education in the Philippines and beyond. A festschrift in honor of Ma. Lourdes S. Bautista.* Manila: Linguistic Society of the Philippines.

Greenbaum, Sidney (Ed.) (1996). *Comparing English worldwide. The International Corpus of English.* Oxford: Clarendon.

Hundt, Marianne. (1998). *New Zealand English grammar: Fact or fiction? A corpus-based study in morphosyntactic variation.* Amsterdam, Philadelphia, PA: Benjamins.

Hundt, Marianne. (2006). The committee has/have decided … On concord patterns with collective nouns in Inner- and Outer-Circle varieties of English. *Journal of English Linguistics, 34*(3), 206–232.

Leech, Geoffrey, Hundt, Marianne, Mair, Christian, & Smith, Nicholas. (2009). *Change in contemporary English. A grammatical study.* Cambridge: Cambridge University Press.

Lindqvist, Hans. (2009). *Corpus linguistics and the description of English.* Edinburgh: Edinburgh University Press.

Llamzon, Teodoro A. (1969). *Standard Filipino English.* Manila: Ateneo University Press.

Llamzon, Teodoro A. (1997). The phonology of Philippine English. In Bautista (Ed.) (1997), pp. 41–48.

Mair, Christian. (2006). *Twentieth century English. History, variation, standardization.* Cambridge: Cambridge University Press.

Martin, Isabel Pefianco. (2004). Longfellow's legacy: education and the shaping of Philippine writing. *World Englishes, 23*(1), 129–139.

Martin, Isabel Pefianco. (2014). Beyond nativization?: Philippine English in Schneider's dynamic model. In Sarah Buschfeld, Thomas Hoffmann, Magnus Huber, & Alexander Kautzsch (Eds.), *The evolution of Englishes: The Dynamic Model and beyond* (pp. 70–85). Amsterdam: John Benjamins.

Mittmann, Brigitta. (2004). *Mehrwort-Cluster in der englischen Alltagskonversation. Unterschiede zwischen britischem und amerikanischem gesprochenem Englisch als Indikatoren für den präfabrizierten Charakter der Sprache.* Tübingen: Narr.

Philippine English and American English 155

Rohdenburg, Günter, & Schlüter, Julia. (2009). *One language, two grammars? Differences between British and American English.* Cambridge: Cambridge University Press.

Schneider, Edgar W. (2005). The subjunctive in Philippine English. In Danilo T. Dayag & J. Stephen Quakenbush (Eds.), *Linguistics and language education in the Philippines and beyond. A festschrift in honor of Ma. Lourdes S. Bautista* (pp. 27–40). Manila: Linguistic Society of the Philippines.

Schneider, Edgar W. (2007). *Postcolonial English. Varieties around the world.* Cambridge: Cambridge University Press.

Schneider, Edgar W. (2011). The subjunctive in Philippine English: An updated assessment. In Bautista (Ed.) (2011), pp. 159–173.

Schneider, Edgar W., Burridge, Kate, Kortmann, Bernd, Mesthrie, Rajend, & Upton, Clive (Eds.) (2004). *A handbook of varieties of English.* Vol. 1: *Phonology.* Berlin, New York: Mouton de Gruyter.

Sibayan, Bonifacio P., & Gonzales, Andrew. (1996). Post-imperial English in the Philippines. In Fishman et al. (Eds.) (1996), pp. 139–172.

Strevens, Peter. (1971). *British and American English.* London: Collier-Macmillan.

Tayao, Ma. Lourdes G. (2004). Philippine English: Phonology. In Schneider, Edgar W., Burridge, Kate, Kortmann, Bernd, Mesthrie, Rajend, & Upton, Clive (Eds.) (2004), pp. 1047–1059. *A handbook of varieties of English.* Vol. 1: *Phonology.* Berlin, New York: Mouton de Gruyter.

Tottie, Gunnel. (2002). *An introduction to American English.* Malden, MA, Oxford: Blackwell.

12 Contact with Other Languages

Ma. Althea T. Enriquez

12.1 Introduction

Language contact is an important external cause of language change. This dynamic phenomenon assumes the interaction of the people who speak the languages in contact and, consequently, factors such as prestige, power relations, speaker's attitude and other non-linguistic factors are brought to the forefront. Thomason and Kaufman (1988) observe that it is the social context and not the structure of the languages involved that determines the direction and degree of contact-induced interference. In this chapter, two related but different linguistic outcomes are put into focus. Aside from the particular variety of English that Filipinos speak known as Philippine English (PhE), there is the practice of these bilingual Filipinos to sometimes switch between a local language (e.g. Tagalog) and English in certain situations. The latter is popularly known as 'Taglish' and this term will be used here to refer to this specific case of code-switching.

While the other chapters examine the results of such situations through the lens of Second Language Acquisition (SLA), bilingual/multilingualism, English as a World Language (EWL), hybridization and such, in this chapter, the primary theoretical principles utilized come from the perspective of Contact Linguistics. The observable linguistic features in PhE will be shown to be rooted and accounted for by the existing social factors in their development. Put simply, the development of PhE (and consequently, Taglish) will be situated and explained through the types of language contact situations.

12.2 The Types of Contact Situation

Situations and results of language contact are numerous and varied but can be classified into three broad categories: Language Creation, Language Shift and Language Maintenance. These categories are adopted from Winford (2003) who modified and simplified them from Thomason and Kaufman (1988). These situations are outlined very simply but in reality, there are many cases which cannot readily and clearly be assigned to one particular

DOI: 10.4324/9780429427824-16

category. The contact situations which can be found in resultant varieties of the New Englishes,[1] for example, are by no means exactly the same although they are similar in terms of how the language is originally acquired and in the characteristics of its subsequent development. Therefore, prototypical examples can be and are used to illustrate the distinctive features and factors involved in the contact environment characterizing each category.

12.3 Language Creation

Language creation is considered the most "extreme" result in a contact situation, resulting in new languages, i.e. pidgins, creoles and mixed languages. Thomason (1997) observes that cases which have been ascribed with these labels form a very heterogeneous group of languages with different circumstances of creation and structural characteristics. While it can be argued that certain structural features are characteristic of pidgins and/or creoles, she also argues that "they are ultimately diachronic, not synchronic... and the mixed status of all contact languages is the obvious product of their histories" (1997: 73).

12.3.1 The Approaches to Language Creation

There are three broad theoretical approaches to language creation which can be referred to simply as the substratist, superstratist or universalist approach. The Substrate approach basically looks to the influence of dominant substrate or L1 languages in the product of a language contact setting. Thomason and Kaufman (1988) view the importance of the substrate languages in the development of creoles. The grammar of an abrupt creole is argued to be primarily developed from a reanalysis or reinterpretation of the lexifier language since the speakers may not have ready access to the target language (TL) grammar. The TL structures are therefore supplemented by structures from the substrate language.

The Superstratist approach takes the opposite point of view and sees the created language as a restructuring of the lexifier or superstrate language in the contact situation. Mufwene (2001) shows the development of a creole to be primarily determined by a competition-and-selection model where the learner makes a system out of features selected from utterances of different individuals with whom he/she interacted. The general view of this approach is that the newly created languages did not innovate much from out of nothing or from Universal Grammar-based creations, nor accept substrate supplementation unless it had some model, however limited or partial, in the lexifier language.

Lastly, the Universalist approach can be well exemplified by Bickerton's Language Bioprogram Hypothesis (LBH). Bickerton (1999) explains that the LBH evolved out of the observation by earlier researchers of striking similarities in the syntax and semantics of creole languages when no obvious

158   *Ma. Althea T. Enriquez*

reasons for such similarities existed. Contrary to all previous theories, "the distinctive pattern of creole features was not inherited from preexisting languages but rather represented the surfacing, in an unusually direct form, of an innate program for the creation of language that formed part of our species' biological endowment" (Bickerton, 1999: 196). The assumption is that there exists a set of default distinctions that a child exposed to a pidgin would revert to and make maximal use of in the face of limited distinctions.

12.3.2 New Englishes as Varieties vs. Creations

It should be noted that in the case of New English varieties, acquisition was, at least initially in most cases, through school, and, therefore, there was available access to the 'standard' variety of the language since the beginning while this was not the case with pidgins and creoles. This does not mean, however, that similar linguistic accommodation happened in these contact situations because indeed, in these new environments, there are cases where varied accompanying linguistic results have emerged.

Gupta (1992; cited in Winford, 2003), for example, has referred to the formation of Singapore English (SgE) as a case of creolization and Platt (1975) has referred to *Singlish* or the spoken colloquial variety of English in Singapore as a "creoloid" even though the circumstances of its development are parallel with other second language varieties, specifically the New Englishes. The history of the development of Irish English is similar to other cases of creoles and yet it is seen to be much more faithful to its superstrate English. However, these cases seem to be non-prototypical and are exceptions rather than the norm for the "groups" that they generally belong to. Thus, it would seem that it is the social circumstances rather than the linguistic results which differentiate these cases. While new language creations (e.g. creoles) and new language varieties (e.g. indigenized, second language variety, etc.) seem to share some common characteristics, especially in their early stages of their development, there are still fundamental features that set them apart.

Kachru (1991; cited in Mufwene, 1997) considers all these new varieties as indigenized or nativized since they have all been appropriated by their speakers as part of the local linguistic repertoire. Mufwene (1997) comments that the usefulness of maintaining this terminological distinction serves more to point out the different outcomes of the same language restructuring formula. The processes of language creation in the case of creoles and language learning in SLA situations especially in their early stages can be considered similar due to the 'supplementation' of (TL) structures with that of the L1, which is a common strategy in (early) SLA. Some of the L1 features do get retained in the speech of the shifting or learning group even after the shift. However, in the case of creole formation, the speakers generally never have full access to the TL while there is full access to TL models in SLA mainly through formal instruction. Consequently, the newly

Contact with Other Languages 159

formed creole is significantly different from the TL while the acquired second language is nearly identical, if not a perfect copy, of the TL. The terms 'creolization' and 'decreolization' are commonly applied to these situations respectively especially in the context of contact linguistics although scholars such as Thomason and Kaufman (1988) have argued that there is no need to appeal to the notion of 'decreolization' if available access to the TL has always been present in the contact situation.

12.3.3 *Taglish Explored as a New Creation*

While PhE is referred to as the 'indigenized' variety of English, it has been studied vis-à-vis *Taglish* which is a widespread phenomenon of code-switching between Tagalog/Filipino[2] and English especially in the urban capital among Filipino bilinguals. It has led some scholars to believe that Taglish is the beginning to the creation of a new language. Sibayan (1994), for example, talks about Taglish as the fifth major language shift that the country has undergone in its history: from Arabic during the pre-colonization period, to Spanish during the time of the Spanish colonization, to English at the time of American occupation, to Pilipino, or later called Filipino in the 1950s, and finally to Taglish which is done even by teachers in the classroom. Because of the prevalent use of code-switching in all levels of communication and even in some formal domains, Marasigan (1982) explored the possibility of Taglish being considered a pidgin or creole and has concluded that while it is not yet so, it could be considered at most a 'creoloid'. Rafael's (1995) seminal essay considers Taglish a form of speech not necessarily Tagalog, English or Spanish but a lingua franca that manages to create an illusion of the Filipino masses being able to consume and participate in the restructuring or transposing of English in Tagalog as propagated through the mass media and in popular culture by speakers who are not part of them (the masses). He described all varied cases of this language mixing but still in the end, he argues that it is the elite who are aware and can reorder the linguistic elements in their speech. Viewing Taglish as a lingua franca, he has observed that Taglish eludes official codification.

A language variety can be codified, in the sense of having a grammar or a dictionary, but Taglish, in the formal sense, is a sociolinguistic phenomenon, a manifestation of bilingual performance and not a language variety. Therefore, it cannot be codified but can be described by its structural aspects which are usually expressed in terms of linguistic constraints based on the various interspersions of the languages involved.

12.4 Language Shift

The shift from the group's native language or L1 to the TL, either partially or completely, may be accompanied by varying degrees of influence from the group's L1. Winford (2003) discusses two broad categories in which this may

160 *Ma. Althea T. Enriquez*

happen. The first category involves cases of immigrant or minority groups that shift to the language of a dominant group, but some features of their L1 are carried over into the TL. An example is the significant influence from French on English when speakers of Norman French shifted to English in the Middle English period. The second category involves situations where a TL is introduced into new communities by colonizers or invaders. The speech community then adopts the foreign language either as a replacement for its original native language or as a second language that serves other functions of communication.

Cases of indigenized varieties of English are common examples in this category where former colonies have adapted their own versions of the TL. The principles in Universalist and Substratist creation approaches closely resemble the principles involved in SLA with strategies such as simplification and regularization of forms being universally employed in language learning. Transference of features from the L1 and/or analogy of L2 patterns with L1 patterns are also reminiscent of substratum explanations in language creation.

Thomason and Kaufman (1988) define substratum influence as a result of the "imperfect group learning during a process of language shift" in which the "errors" committed spread to the TL. Mufwene (2001) observes that interference at the individual level is the first stage in the establishment of substrate influence in the language of the group. Since an individual's interlanguage innovations contribute to a language's 'feature pool', the features that are replicated and adopted by other individuals may eventually become established as part of the group's linguistic system. Systematic retentions from the L1 are absorbed into the TL and become emergent features of that particular variety. This accommodation with the new speakers as well as adapting innovations from the new environment led to the formation of an 'indigenized' variety of the original TL.

12.4.1 The Case of New English Varieties

New Englishes share some common characteristics as laid out in Platt, Weber and Ho (1984). Kandiah (1998) notes that the most salient factor in differentiating the Older Englishes from the other varieties is that there is a sizeable population of the original English speakers who settled in the new environment. Essentially, there is continuity in the use and progression of the language, and an unchallenged dominance of its use in the new environment. New English varieties, however, are found in former colonies where there were more new users of the language who had to acquire the language initially through formal education before, consequently, adapting it for themselves and their speech forms ultimately served as the models for subsequent generations of learners.

Language shifts in these situations were usually partial shifts since a local language was typically retained while English was used in certain domains;

Contact with Other Languages 161

complete shifts, however, occurred in certain levels of society. It is usually the small elite population who shift partially or completely to the new language; the Filipino educated elite, for example, shifted from Spanish to English after American colonization (Thompson, 2003). While the TL is typically Standard BrE (AmE in the Philippines), in reality, it is the variety spoken by the elite, educators and the mass media which are copied by the local English-speaking population. The features of this particular variety spread and gain acceptance causing these features to crystallize with constant use and reinforcement especially if the diffusers are considered good models of English language use (Malicsi, 2010).

12.4.2 Features of Contact-Induced Influence on PhE

Bautista's (2000b) comprehensive article summarized and reviewed the different studies done on PhE. Three major strands of research were identified focusing on: (1) the status of PhE as a standard variety of English, (2) the description of its linguistic features and (3) evaluating the intelligibility and acceptability of PhE. The majority of the linguistic type of studies were concerned with what particular features were mastered from Standard AmE (SAE) and the systematic errors or deviations which could ultimately mean emergent features in PhE.

Bautista's (2000a) other study in the same year was the first to use the Philippine component of the International Corpus of English (ICE-PH). She used the subset of the written texts data to find the answer to the question "when does an error become a feature of Philippine English?" which was the title of Gonzalez's 1983 article. Her criteria for determining if a deviant feature can be considered 'widespread' is if it occurs in 1/10th of the total number of texts used in the data.

Drawing mostly from the observations of Bautista and Gonzalez (2006), Enriquez (2012) re-examined and sought to account for these features using the principles of contact linguistics. Comparing the ICE-PH data with the BrE and SgE corpora,[3] the findings are summarized below (2012: 243–246):

1   The function of the PhE Perfect marker and *already* correspond to the Tagalog enclitic adverb *na*. The PhE Perfect occurs with a definite time in the past and focuses on the present relevance of the situation. *Already* has a double function: marking the "now"-ness of the situation, and differentiating event and stative predicates, resulting in a perfective and inchoative reading respectively.

2   The Progressive has extended its use and occurs with stative situations in PhE when it should have otherwise been blocked. This is an influence of the substrate which has only one type of Imperfective. Other varieties of English have also exhibited extended (but not necessarily more frequent) use of the Progressive. Among Older English varieties, it has also extended its use not just to mark aspect but to other non-aspectual

usage as well, one of which is to express futurity (see Collins, 2008), which is also a common usage with the progressive form in PhE.

3 *Would*, as with other past forms of modals, conveys tentativeness in events that are perceived to be expectations or predictions. In settings of formality, *would* is also used to express weaker assertion regardless of the speaker's role in the situation. Since there are no markers of politeness in English but there are in Tagalog, the past forms are utilized to convey the necessary effect of politeness. This tendency to use *would* in situations of less certainty and less assertion is also found in other varieties of English such as Brunei English and SgE (Bautista, 2004), and as pragmatically specialized usage to express polite preambles and imperatives in BrE (Coates, 1983).

4 The low usage of both root and epistemic *must* supports the preference to avoid sounding assertive and to displace authority in PhE. In root meaning, *must* is vastly outnumbered by *have to* in usage. *Have to* is used in lieu of a past-modal counterpart for *must* while *have got to* is not found in the data since the pseudo-modal is very close to the meaning of strong assertion as with *must*. In epistemic meaning, the more tentative *should* is used more than *must*.

5 The relatively simpler prepositional marking in the substrate contributes to more frequent deviations in general preposition usage indicating place and time rather than verb + preposition combinations which are learned as a whole in AmE.

These features are present not only in PhE but also in the other mentioned varieties of English as well. In (3) and (4), non-linguistic features, such as social factors, are shown to also play a role in influencing a language's restructuring. In the following, the grammatical features seem to be favored more or unique to PhE:

6 There is a tendency to overuse the *of*-construction in postmodification even with personal nouns when normally the genitive construction should have been used. This is argued to be modeled on the periphrastic Tagalog construction, indicating various relations associated with possession, association or connection.

7 There is substrate influence on adverb placement exhibited by the unusual positioning of adverbs like *already* and *also*, whose counterparts are enclitic adverbs in Tagalog and thus placed after the first element of a sentence. Tagalog verb constructions are realized as a single, inflected form so adverbs are placed after the whole verb form while in SAE adverbs are typically placed before the verb and after a *be* verb or an auxiliary.

8 There is popular use of *wherein* while its appearance in other varieties was almost non-existent. The form *wherein* is preferred by its perceived correspondence to *where* and the Tagalog *saan* 'where' which is used in the local language as part of the relative adverb (Bautista, 2009).

9 The adverbial expression 'as in' appeared more in the PhE data and acquired a new usage as an emphatic expression rather than just to indicate exemplification.

12.5 Language Maintenance

In language maintenance, the language for the most part remains relatively intact in its various subsystems. Changes brought to it involve varying degrees of influence from an external language with which it is in contact, with borrowing as the most common cause. There are many factors that could affect the degree of borrowing but the intensity and the duration of contact between the recipient (borrowing) language and the lexifier language is usually a factor.

A general tendency that determines the direction of borrowing has to do with the power relations or prestige assigned to the languages involved. The perceived prestigious language is the source for borrowing, specifically lexical borrowing. Lexical borrowing is typically done by a substrate group (having the recipient language) from a superstrate group (having the source or model language) while it is the opposite for structural borrowing or substratum transfer, that is, the superstrate language is influenced by the substratum (Thomason & Kaufman, 1988).

Language maintenance situations also involve relatively stable bilingual speech communities where the languages spoken are used in the community and in some cases have specific functions and domains in which they operate. When the choice is regarding which language (or variety) is dependent on the situation or domain of use, it is referred to as a case of diglossia with the languages or varieties typically employed in mutually exclusive functions. In cases where no such restrictions exist and there can be free alternation, it is usual to see this alternation between languages within the same stretch of speech in some situations. This phenomenon is known as code-switching and is typical of stable bilingual communities which more or less put a positive value on the languages involved in the switching (Myers-Scotton, 1993).

12.5.1 Borrowings and Nonce-Switches in PhE

Haugen (1950, 1972) defines borrowing as the "the attempted reproduction in one language of patterns previously found in another" (1972: 81) and categorizes borrowings according to degrees of morphemic and phonemic substitution and importation. If the borrowing result is similar enough to the model and accepted by a native speaker as his/her own, it is said to be *imported* into the recipient language as long as it is an innovation in that language. If the result is an inadequate reproduction of the model, then it can be said that a similar pattern from the recipient language had been *substituted* for it.

164   *Ma. Althea T. Enriquez*

While English words have made their way to Filipino,[4] the local lexicon has also entered PhE. These are typically content words that have cultural or functional usage and are unique to the speech environment rather than being borrowed for reasons of prestige. Bautista (1996) gave a provisional list of PhE lexical items that was to be included in an Asian English dictionary to be published by *Macquarie Dictionary*. This was a subclassification of PhE words according to how lexicons in languages develop, namely, through processes of (a) normal expansion, (b) preservation of items which have been lost or become infrequent in other varieties, (c) coinage and (d) borrowing (1996: 50). Clearly, all but the latter would be English in form. Bautista classifies the borrowings in PhE (not all of which necessarily come from Tagalog) according to semantic fields such as flora and fauna, national identity/culture and expressions.

From a linguistic perspective, there is no basis to determine which language is more 'prestigious' than the other in a borrowing situation, so evidently reasons that are socially motivated determine the direction of borrowing. Aside from the social factor of prestige, "need" is also one of the often cited reasons for borrowing (Winford, 2003). There is a need to name or express local concepts and concrete items, things that are new or unique to the culture and so do not have a counterpart in the lexifier language or in the other communities that use the language. These are considered examples of what Myers-Scotton (1993) refer to as "cultural borrowed forms". Cultural borrowed forms are considered different from the usual type of loanwords since aside from the need to 'fill gaps' in the language, the frequency of use, a criterion used in establishing borrowings, would be irrelevant considering that the initiation of their use must happen when the need to signify the referent happens.

Myers-Scotton (1993) also notes that one of the earliest issues concerning code-switching was the status of single-lexeme items: whether they were to be considered as code-switching forms or cases of borrowings. For some, instances of singly occurring foreign material in a base language, especially when it has base morpheme markers, were considered borrowed forms. Others who accept that some single-lexeme forms might be considered as code-switching material used assimilation in the language as a criterion to distinguish between borrowings and switches. Cultural borrowed forms are exempt from this issue and are integrated into the language as can be seen in PhE by how they are pluralized with the plural marker -*s* such as *titas, titos, barkadas, barongs*, etc., in the ICE-PH data (Enriquez, 2012).

Contrasting with cultural borrowed forms, there are occurrences of borrowings which do not satisfy any lexical need at all. Words like *mahal, pangit* and *lakas,* for example, are found in the ICE-PH data. These are lexical items which are quite common vocabulary items and clearly do not fulfill a lexical need. They also do not meet the criterion of frequency of use to be established as full-fledged borrowings nor can reasons for 'prestige' necessitating its usage be applied.

Contact with Other Languages   165

These examples are considered cases of 'nonce borrowings' (from Poplack, Sankoff & Miller, 1988), which are influenced by other factors than the usual reasons for prototypical borrowings. Studying the borrowing patterns of French/English bilingual speakers in an area of Ottawa, it was shown that the rate of borrowing is dependent on the norms of community behavior rather than on lexical need. In that sense, nonce borrowing can be said to be similar to code-switching in that it is motivated by accommodation of the speakers to the social situation. Studies have also shown that there is a preference for morphologically less complex items to be borrowed than the more complex ones and this is the reason why nouns tend to be borrowed more than verbs for example (Winford, 2003). However, certain borrowings in PhE seem to have been motivated by the fact that from a morphological perspective, Tagalog is structurally more complex than English and it resorted to strategies of simplification to facilitate the nonce borrowing of adjectives and verbs which were more numerous than nouns (Enriquez, 2012). Examples in her study found patterns of 'got + adjective/stative verb': 'got *ligaw*' and the construction 'make + V/N': 'made *kulit* about it', the latter being popularly recognized as characteristic of *kolehiyala* English.

12.5.2 Taglish in Stable Bilingualism

The term 'code-switching' can encompass a variety of situations. Here, it is considered to be closely associated with other by-products of language contact with 'borrowing' on the one hand and 'language mixing/interference' on the other. Code-switching situations are characterized by the ability and practice of bilinguals who are able to freely use the languages they command in various ways. Gonzalez and Bautista (1986) have argued that instead of a sociolectal scale, the subvarieties of PhE can be described better in terms of 'edulects' or an edulectal scale, i.e. from 'idiosyncratic' on one end to 'educated' on the other. However, Gonzalez (1984) stresses that the code-switching practice of skilled Filipino bilinguals is different from the interlanguage of those still in the process of acquiring English, i.e. those employed by the 'idiosyncratic' PhE speakers in quite limited functions. Therefore, Taglish here is defined as the term referring to English and Tagalog language mixture in the form of code-switching which is a widespread phenomenon of speaking for English-educated bilinguals who have access to the two codes involved.

In Auer's (1995; cited in Winford, 2003) four patterns of code-switching, only Pattern IV (intra- and inter-clausal switching) is characterized based on structural features and is considered as 'code-mixing' by some scholars. Bautista (1980) presented a unified set of rules that accounted for Tagalog-English code-switching and constructed a model of the Filipino bilingual's linguistic competence based on a structural analysis of recorded spoken data. Sobolewski (1982), using printed material, identified syntactic constraints, focusing on constraints involving pronouns in sentences and

166 *Ma. Althea T. Enriquez*

those involving main verbs, auxiliary verbs, negators and direct object complements. Other studies on Taglish have found an asymmetrical pattern in that when the base language is in Tagalog, insertion is the primary form of mixing but when English is the base, Tagalog elements are limited mostly to conjunctions, tags, formulaic expressions and function words (Bautista, 1991; Cuadra, 1999; Thompson, 2003).

The two major approaches to code-switching – alternation and embedding as represented by Poplack's (1980) and Myers-Scotton's (1993) frameworks respectively – have both something to contribute to the understanding of code-switching. They are seen to be complementary, rather than being limited to only view Taglish from a single approach as is evident when presented with a regular mixture such as the one below in which one approach cannot completely account for the momentary 'switches' and inter-clausal switching in a supposedly Tagalog base but morphologically dominant English utterance:

"Okay *nagbabalik po tayo dito napaka*-heated *nitong* discussion *natin* about whether you voted for your conscience or not". [S1B-036, ICE-PH]
"Okay, we are back here (on our program). Our discussion about whether you voted for your conscience or not is very heated".

This example exemplifies the level of interspersion of Tagalog and English elements in Taglish. This switching between Tagalog and English is a prominent feature in everyday Filipino communication, especially in the capital region and is evidence of a relatively stable bilingual community precisely because both codes are maintained.

12.6 Summary

Language contact provides a unified view in accounting for the circumstance of a language (English) being used alongside a local language (Tagalog/Filipino) in a particular contact environment. It was shown that it promotes the influencing of one language on the other either linguistically, reflected through contact-induced interference, or socially, resulting in code-switching/mixing and other by-products in between.

Notes

1 The discussion on the classification of New vs. Older Englishes or Inner vs. Outer vs. Expanding Circles of English is tackled in other chapters. The terms New and Older Englishes are used here.
2 It should be clarified that while references are made here seemingly alternating between Tagalog and Filipino, the two concepts are not to be considered identical. Tagalog is one of the major vernaculars in the country and Filipino is the national language based on the widespread lingua franca.

Contact with Other Languages 167

3 Among the ICE data, BrE and SgE were selected to represent an Older English and a New English variety, respectively, for comparison purposes.
4 The discussion here will be on borrowed words from Tagalog/Filipino to PhE since the topic of interest is PhE. Though in typical discussions of language maintenance, the topic of discussion is centered on the local (recipient) language and its borrowings from a lexifier language.

Bibliography

Bautista, Maria Lourdes. (1980). The Filipino bilingual's competence: a model based on an analysis of Tagalog-English code-switching. *Pacific Linguistics*, series C (59).

Bautista, Maria Lourdes. (1991). Code-switching studies in the Philippines. *The International Journal of the Sociology of Language* 88, 19–32.

Bautista, Maria Lourdes. (1996). The lexicon of Philippine English. *English is an Asian language: the Philippine context*. Proceedings of the Conference held in Manila, 2–3 August 1996.

Bautista, Maria Lourdes. (2000a). *Defining standard Philippine English: its status and grammatical features*. Manila, Philippines: De La Salle University Press, Inc.

Bautista, Maria Lourdes. (2000b). Studies of Philippine English in the Philippines. *Philippine Journal of Linguistics,* 32(1), 39–65.

Bautista, Maria Lourdes. (2004). The verb in Philippine English: a preliminary analysis of modal *would*. *World Englishes,* 21(1), 113–128.

Bautista, Maria Lourdes. (2009). Investigating the grammatical features of Philippine English. In Kingsley Bolton and Maria Lourdes S. Bautista (Eds.), *Philippine English: linguistic and literary perspectives.* Hong Kong: Hong Kong University Press.

Bautista, Maria Lourdes and Andrew Gonzalez. (2006). Southeast Asian Englishes. In Braj Krachu, Yamuna Kachru and Cecil Nelson (Eds.), *The handbook of World Englishes* (pp. 130–141). Oxford: Blackwell.

Bickerton, Derek. (1999). Creole languages, the language bioprogram hypothesis, and language acquisition. *Handbook of child language acquisition.* Cambridge, MA: Academic Press Inc.

Coates, Jennifer. (1983). *The semantics of modal auxiliaries.* London & Canberra: Croom Helm.

Collins, Peter. (2008). The progressive aspect in World Englishes: a corpus-based study. *Australian Journal of Linguistics,* 28(2), 225–251.

Cuadra, Christopher. (1999). A description of code-switching patterns among Filipino students in Sendai, Japan. *Philippine Journal of Linguistics,* 29(1&2), 49–67.

Dayag, Danilo. (2002). Code-switching in Philippine print ads: a syntactico-pragmatic description. *Philippine Journal of Linguistics,* 33(1), 33–51.

Enriquez, Ma. Althea. (2012). *Philippine English and Taglish from a language contact perspective.* PhD dissertation, National University of Singapore.

Gonzalez, Andrew FSC. (1983). When does an error become a feature of Philippine English? In Richard B. Noss (Ed.), *Varieties of English in Southeast Asia,* Anthology series 11. Singapore: SEAMO Regional Language Centre.

168   Ma. Althea T. Enriquez

Gonzalez, Andrew FSC. (1984). Evaluating the Philippine bilingual education policy. In A. B. FSC Gonzales (Ed.), *PANAGANI: language planning, implementation and evaluation. Essays in honor of Bonifacio P. Sibayan on his sixty-seventh birthday* (pp. 46–65). Manila: Linguistic Society of the Philippines.

Gonzalez, Andrew and Ma. Lourdes Bautista. (1986). *Language surveys in the Philippines (1966–1984)*. Manila: De La Salle University Press.

Haugen, Einar. (1950). The analysis of linguistic borrowing. *Language,* 26(2), 210–231.

Haugen, Einar. (1972). The analysis of linguistic borrowing. In A. S. Dil (Ed.), *The ecology of language: essays by Einar Haugen* (pp. 306–324). Stanford: Stanford University Press.

Kandiah, Thiru. (1998). Why new Englishes? In Jonathan A. Foley et al. (Eds.), *English in new cultural contexts: reflections from Singapore.* Singapore Institute of Management/Oxford University Press.

Malicsi, Jonathan. (2010). Philippine English: a case of language drift. *Ritsumeikan Studies in Language and Culture,* 22(1), 29–58.

Marasigan, Elizabeth. (1982). *Code-switching and code-mixing in bilingual societies.* Singapore: SEAMO Regional Language Centre.

Mufwene, Salikoko. (1997). Jargons, pidgins, creoles and koines: what are they? In Arthur Spears and Donald Winford (Eds.), *Pidgins and Creoles: structures and status.* Amsterdam and Philadelphia: John Benjamins.

Mufwene, Salikoko. (2001). *The ecology of language evolution.* Cambridge: Cambridge University Press.

Myers-Scotton, Carol. (1993). *Duelling languages: grammatical structure in code-switching.* Oxford: Clarendon Press.

Platt, John. (1975). The Singapore English speech continuum and its basilect 'Singlish' as a 'creoloid'. *Anthropological Linguistics,* 17(7), 363–374.

Platt, John, Heidi Weber and Ho Mian Lian. (1984). *The new Englishes.* London; Boston, MA: Routledge and Kegan Paul.

Poplack, Shana. (1979/1980). Sometimes I'll start a sentence in Spanish y termino en Español: toward a typology of code-switching. *Linguistics,* 18, 581–618.

Rafael, Vicente. (1995). Taglish, or the Phantom Power of the Lingua Franca. *Public Culture,* 8(1), 101–126.

Poplack, Shana, Sankoff, David, & Miller, Chris. (1988). The social correlates and linguistic processes of lexical borrowing and assimilation. *Linguistics,* 26(1), 47–104.

Sibayan, Bonifacio. (1994). The role and status of English vis-à-vis Filipino and other languages in the Philippines. In Thiru Kandiah and John Kwan-Terry (Eds.), *English and language planning: a Southeast Asian contribution.* Singapore: Times Academic Press for Centre for Advanced Studies, National University of Singapore.

Sobolewski, Frank Andrew. (1982). Some syntactic constraints in Tagalog-English language mixing. *Philippine Journal of Linguistics,* 13(2), 35–62.

Thomason, Sarah Grey. (1997). A typology of contact languages. In Arthur Spears and Donald Winford (Eds.), *Pidgins and creoles: structures and status.* Amsterdam and Philadelphia, PA: John Benjamins.

Thomason, Sarah Grey and Terrence Kaufman. (1988). *Language contact, creolization, and genetic linguistics.* Berkeley and Los Angeles: University of California Press.

Thompson, Roger M. (2003). *Filipino English and Taglish: language switching from multiple perspectives.* Amsterdam and Philadelphia, PA: John Benjamins Publishing Company.

Winford, Donald. (2003). *An introduction to contact linguistics.* Malden, MA: Blackwell Publishers.

13 Hybridization

Wilkinson Daniel Wong Gonzales

13.1 Introduction

Linguistic hybridization has always been present in society; it undoubtedly plays a role in the development of most natural languages and varieties. While such is the case, the general awareness of such processes and products – the hybrids – in the field of linguistics (particularly in the study of world Englishes) is relatively recent (Onysko, 2016; Schneider, 2016). There is increasing attention given toward them, but much remains to be investigated particularly in English-using societies where multilingualism is not the exception, but the norm. One such example is the Philippines, where historically indigenous and non-indigenous languages coexist and interact with each other, resulting in various linguistic hybrids.

In this chapter, I investigate hybrids related to Philippine English (PhE) using a bottom-up approach. I survey related works and analyze linguistic data with the goal of broadening the traditional PhE field by including studies of language contact, language documentation, and diaspora sociohistory to PhE research. Another goal of this chapter is to propel studies of PhE beyond the homogenizing paradigm, fulfilling the goal of the field of world Englishes, that is, to study the varied uses of English in various contexts around the world (Smith, 1981).

Hybridization in this chapter refers to a process where distinct and disparate systems create a new system or process – the hybrid – that may have features from varying levels (i.e. phonological, morphological, syntactic, etc.) and multiple source languages (Sanchez-Stockhammer, 2012). In this survey, I refer to three notions of language contact that are relevant in the process of linguistic hybridization. The first, borrowing, is characterized by the process of grafting lexicon onto the recipient language with phonological adaptation (Grosjean, 2010). Although scholars have referred to borrowing of non-lexical items (Thomason, 2001; Thomason & Kaufman, 1988), here these are referred to as instances of substrate influence; I distinguish it from borrowing. The second type involves code-switching, defined here as a situation where a speaker completely shifts to another language for a word, phrase, or clause (Grosjean, 2010). While there is phonological adaptation

DOI: 10.4324/9780429427824-17

Hybridization 171

in borrowing, code-switched words (as defined in this chapter) retain the phonological features of the base. The third process involves "substratum influence" (Thomason, 2001, p. 75) or (system) transfer. Unlike borrowing and code-switching, both of which are analyzed at the lexical level in this chapter, the substratum influence hybridization process referred to here is analyzed at non-lexical levels of language (e.g. syntactic, morphological).

To facilitate the discussion, this chapter surveys three groups of PhE-related varieties based on the three mechanisms above: (1) hybrids with borrowing, (2) hybrids involving code-switching, and (3) substrate-influenced hybridized Englishes. Note that varieties in a certain group need not be mutually exclusive from other groups.

13.2 Hybrid Varieties of English and Other Philippine Languages

13.2.1 Hybrids with Borrowing

The first group of hybrids are *hybrids with borrowing* (hence group-1). One thing hybrids of this group have in common is the salience of lexicon from two or more sources. Lexical items are borrowed from the source(s) into the (original) recipient language.

13.2.1.1 Conyo English/Englog

Conyo English (also known as Englog 'English-Tagalog') is an English sociolect that has Tagalog and Filipino (§ 13.2.1.2) borrowings. The variety indexes privilege, 'elite-ness', and has negative connotations due to the claimed contrived nature of mixing in the variety. It is also viewed as "less smooth" switching (Borlongan, 2015) compared to Tagalog-Filipino-English code-switching (§ 13.2.2.1). While this is partially warranted due to the 'playful' nature of the variety, some syntactic aspects of Conyo English suggests that the variety is more conventionalized than previously characterized. The *make* + Tagalog V construction is a salient attribute of Conyo English. In (1), the Tagalog lexical word *sakay* 'ride' was borrowed into the English clause. A preliminary observation for Tagalog verbal borrowings in Conyo English like this is that they tend to be preceded by *make*. This pattern does not seem to hold for English verbs. Reduplication is also another feature (2); it also seems to be restricted to Tagalog/Filipino lexicon. In this case, there is both borrowing (e.g. *kanto* 'sidewalk') and transfer (e.g. reduplication of *tusok* 'skewer') from Tagalog. If the word reduplicated is English, the utterance does not seem to reflect Conyo English anymore.

1 it was their first time to make ***sakay*** [ride] *sa* jeepney[1]
   "It was their first time to ride the jeepney".

(Garvida, 2012, p. 28)

172   *Wilkinson Daniel Wong Gonzales*

2   <u>they are like making</u> ***tusok*** [skewer] <u>some calamares along the</u> ***kanto***
    [sidewalk]
    "They are like skewering some squid along the sidewalk".

    (Garvida, 2012, p. 28)

13.2.1.2 Filipino

Designed to be the unifying language of the Philippines, Filipino[2] is a language that is primarily based on Tagalog and enriched by other languages like English, Spanish, Hokkien, among many others. This variety has an expanded phonemic inventory from Tagalog that includes phonemes like [f], which is used by other non-Tagalog languages like English. Another feature of this variety is the conventionalized borrowing of historically non-indigenous lexicon. For instance, in (3), the word *parti* derives from the English word *party*. Other English-derived words include *biskwit* 'biscuit', *bolpen* 'ballpen', and *kompyuter* 'computer'. Filipino also has conventionalized Hokkien borrowings like *siomai* 'Chinese dumpling' (4), *bihon* 'rice vermicelli', *ate* 'sister') (Chan-Yap, 1980).

3   *Gusto   ko   ng   pumunta   sa   **parti**,   pero   siya, ayaw.*
    Want   1SG   LNK   go   LOC   party   but   3SG no
    "I want to go to the party but he doesn't want to".

    (Schachter & Otanes, 1972)

4   *salamat   sa   **siomai**   haha   <u>mbtc & god bless</u>
    Thanks   for   dumpling   haha   mbtc & god bless
    "Thank you for the shumai. Haha. Mbtc (?) and god bless!"

    (from Twitter, https://twitter.com/reemfatoum/status/1069963797811654656)

13.2.1.3 Lánnang-uè

Lánnang-uè[3] 'Our People speech' or Philippine Hybrid Hokkien is an oral code with Hokkien, Tagalog/Filipino, English, and Mandarin elements, which has characteristics consistent with descriptions of mixed languages. It is perceived as a broken variety of Hokkien and is generally used by the Lannangs[4] – a group of Philippine-based individuals who have Southern Chinese (majority Hokkien) heritage, specifically a group that primarily comprises late 19th- to early 20th-century Southern Chinese immigrants to the Philippines and their descendants (Gonzales, 2017b).

The lexicon of Lánnang-uè is dominated by Hokkien (220-word Swadesh list, 49% of the lexicon is exclusively sourced from Hokkien). Unlike Philippine Hokkien, it incorporates Tagalog and English features beyond the phonetic level. One role of English in Lánnang-uè is that of a lexical contributor

Hybridization   173

(37% of the basic lexicon can be expressed using the English variant). Preliminary work on Lánnang-uè shows that English is also involved in language transfer processes, such as the transfer of some functional morphemes such as conjunctions (e.g. *so* in 5) and borrowing of noun phrases, such as *manager*, *grade*, and *per semester* (5 and 6) from English to Lánnang-uè.

5 So per semester   *kê*   *khuà*   *o*   *hî*   *ge*   grade?
   So per semester   all   look   PRT   DEM   CLF   grade
   "So, all of the grades were looked at per semester?"

   (Gonzales's Lánnang-uè data)

6 Actually, *tsî*   *ge*   manager   *u*   ***diprensiya***   *la*.
   Actually, DEM   CLF   manager   have   disorder   PRT
   "Actually this manager has a disorder".

   (Gonzales's Lánnang-uè data)

At the suprasegmental level, English-sourced Lánnang-uè words have tone. For instance, in the Lánnang-uè word /ε^{51}ɹej^{51}sɛɹs^{55}/ 'erasers' (pronounced [$\varepsilon^{33\cdot}$ɹej$^{33}\cdot$ sɛɹs^{55}]), all syllables in the word have either falling or high tone. Tone is conditioned by syllable structure (consonant-vowel-consonant [CVC] syllables, high tone; non-CVC syllables, falling tone). This feature is also observed in all other English-sourced words in Lánnang-uè. Along with the borrowings and transfers, the tonal system seems to be conventionalized in the Lánnang-uè-speaking community.

13.2.2 Hybrids Involving Code-Switching

Hybrids involving code-switching are the second group (hence, group-2) of linguistic hybrids. These are similar to group-1 hybrids in that both have lexicon that have multiple sources. What distinguishes this group is that its users shift from one language to another through code-switching, which does not involve processes of phonological adaptation unlike borrowing.

13.2.2.1 Tagalog-Filipino-English Code-Switching

Tagalog-Filipino-English 'Taglish' code-switching in this chapter primarily refers to code-switching among Tagalog, Filipino, and English in the clausal (7) and phrasal level (8). Since word-level 'code-switching' in Tagalog is typically phonologically adapted, word-level 'code-switching' is not treated as code-switching but as a borrowing. This borrowing is part of Filipino (§ 13.2.1.2).

Tagalog-Filipino-English code-switching is primarily used by Filipinos in the metropolitan Manila area, although its use is also salient in other Philippine regions. Apart from its prevalence in Philippine society,

174　*Wilkinson Daniel Wong Gonzales*

Tagalog-Filipino-English code-switching has often been highlighted in (socio)linguistic literature for its functions in Philippine society, as well as its structure (Bautista, 2004; Lesada, 2017; Sobolewski, 1980). Example (7) starts with the English clause *I hope* followed by Filipino relative clause. Example (8), on the other hand, begins with Filipino, followed by Tagalog, and ends with the English phrase *one of his baskets*. The words *teen star* and *bike* in (7) and (8) are phonologically adapted and may be interpreted as borrowings from English.

7　**I hope**　*na*　　*magkaroon*　*sana*　　*ng*　　*pelikula*　*ang*
　　I hope　that　　have　　　　hopefully　of　　move　　NOM

　　<u>fave</u>　　<u>teen star</u>　*ko*　　*-ng*　　*si*　　*Arnold Gamboa.*
　　favorite　teen star　2SG　　that　　NOM　Arnold Gamboa

"I hope that my favorite teenage star Arnold Gamboa will have a film".

(Sobolewksi, 1980)

8　*may*　　*d<um>aan*　　*na*　　*bata*　　*na*　　*may*　　<u>*bike,*</u>
　　have　　<PFV>cross　LNK　　kid　　that　　have　　bike,

　　na-　　*nakaw*　　*yung*　　**one of his baskets.**
　　PFV　　steal　　DEM　　one of his baskets.

"There was a boy with a bike who crossed; one of his baskets was stolen".

(Lesada, 2017, p. 81)

13.2.2.2 *Hokkien-Lánnang-uè-Tagalog-Filipino-English Code-Switching*

Hokkien-Lánnang-uè-Tagalog-Filipino-English 'Hokaglish' code-switching is a phenomenon that involves the inter-phrasal or inter-clausal switching among Hokkien, Lánnang-uè, Tagalog, Filipino, and English. Exclusively used by the Lannang community, particularly those residing in the metropolitan Manila area, this phenomenon has predominantly Hokkien and Lánnang-uè clauses (Gonzales, 2016). Like Taglish, it also has an established community of users. The only difference between this and Tagalog-English-Filipino code-switching is the addition of (Philippine) Hokkien and Lánnang-uè in the switching phenomenon. Example (9) begins with a Tagalog clause, followed by Lánnang-uè, then (Philippine) Hokkien. This is succeeded by English and Filipino.

9　*hindi*　　*niya*　　*b<in>ayad,*
　　NEG　　3SG　　<PFV>pay

　　î　　*tsiageh*　　*diapdì*　　*u*　　*siá*　　*cheke*　　*hó*
　　3SG　January　twenty two　have　write　cheque　PRT

î	laktsap kuí	tshieng	huan	ì	kô	ó
3SG	sixty around	thousand	return	3SG	PRT	PRT

<u>It's</u>	<u>because</u>
It's	because

nag-	*bigay*	*siya*	*ng*	<u>clearance.</u>
PFV	give	3SG	PRT	clearance

"She/he didn't pay. he wrote a check on January returning him/her 60,000. It is because she/he gave him/her clearance".

(Gonzales's Hokaglish code-switching data)

13.2.2.3 A Taishanese Variety Spoken in the Philippines

Taishanese is a dialect of Cantonese historically used in Taishan, located in southern Guangdong. Preliminary observations show that the lexicon of the variety of Taishanese used in the Philippines has been influenced by English, through code-switching with English. For instance, (10) and (11) show that Taishanese Lannang speakers can switch from Taishanese to English. The consultant noted that Cantonese Lannangs mix however they want with whatever language, suggesting that the variety has non-conventionalized code-switching.

10	*Nieng*	*goi*	***fanyekyon***	*hui*	***ngitpun.***
	DEM	CLF	translator	go	Japan

"The translator is going to Japan".

(Gonzales's Taishanese elicitation data)

11	*Nieng*	*goi*	<u>***translator***</u>	*hui*	<u>***Japan.***</u>
	DEM	CLF	translator	go	Japan

"The translator is going to Japan".

(Gonzales's Taishanese elicitation data)

13.2.2.4 Cebuano-English Code-Switching

Cebuano is a language used in the central and southern Philippine regions. Like many other Philippine languages, it came into contact with English around the American occupation period in the 1900s. One outcome of Cebuano-English contact is Cebuano-English code-switching, a phenomenon that has been associated with the upper class and the well-educated (Abastillas, 2015). In (12), the utterance starts with an English utterance, followed by a Cebuano phrase, then another Cebuano phrase headed by English conditional *if*. The English utterance at the beginning of the sentence can be translated to Cebuano freely (13), based on a native speaker consultant.

176 *Wilkinson Daniel Wong Gonzales*

12 **_yeah_** **_sure_** *mas* *nindot* _if_ *di* *sabutan*
    yeah sure more nice if NEG understand
    "Yeah, sure. It'd be nicer if you didn't know".

(Abastillas, 2015, Twitter data)

13 **_O_** **_sige_** *mas* *nindot* *kung* *di* *sabutan*
    yeah sure more nice if NEG understand
    "Yeah, sure. It'd be nicer if you didn't know".

(Cebuano, translation by native speaker, 2018)

13.2.2.5 Contemporary Chabacano Varieties

Commonly identified as one of the few Spanish-lexified creoles in the world, Chabacano is a creole language group (e.g. Zamboanga Chabacano, Cavite Chabacano, and Ternate Chabacano) that is primarily spoken and used in the Philippines. The Chabacano group, like all other Philippine languages and varieties, has also been influenced by peripheral linguistic varieties such as Tagalog, Filipino, and English (Lesho, 2013). In the case of English, this influence primarily manifests in Chabacano in the lexical level through code-switching.[5] Cavite Chabacano data (Lesho, 2013), for example, show that the code-switched words are used interchangeably. So, while Cavite Chabacano speakers use English *accent* to refer to 'accent', they also frequently use Chabacano/Spanish *intonacion* and Filipino/Spanish *tono* to refer to the same thing (14) (Lesho, 2013). From this, Lesho notes from her ethnographic observations that English code-switching in Cavite Chabacano has most likely not conventionalized (Lesho, personal communication). She notes that pinpointing the default language of expression is difficult due to this lack of convention.

14 Tiene medio **class** el **accent.**
    Have APPX class DEF accent
    "Their accent sort of has class".

(Lesho, 2013, Cavite Chabacano)

13.2.3 Substrate-Influenced Hybridized Englishes

The last group of hybrids – *substrate-influenced hybridized Englishes* (group-3) – is distinct from the previous two groups. Hybrids in the third group have mixing in non-lexical levels (e.g. phonological, morphological, and syntactic) that is primarily motivated by the interaction between English and other languages in the language ecology of hybrid user, particularly the substrate influence of these other languages on English. Hybrids from this group in general have a lexicon that is dominantly English, resembling

Hybridization   177

standardized English varieties such as standard American English or standard British English. For this reason, hybridized Englishes may not be immediately recognized as products of linguistic hybridization.

13.2.3.1 *Philippine Korean Learner English*

Philippine Korean Learner English (PKLE) is a hybridized English that has recently emerged in the Philippines – a popular English as a Second Language (ESL) learning destination for young Koreans beginning in the 1990s (Gonzales, 2017a; Imperial, 2016; Kim, 2015; Miralao, 2007). Its use is salient in Korean students particularly in the cities of Manila, Baguio, Cebu, Iloilo who have interacted frequently with Filipino peers and were more involved in their formal English learning.

PKLE distinguishes itself from other (Korean Learner) Englishes by having substrate influences from PhE (most likely Manila English) and Korean. It has phonetic features of the PhE stop system "across segmental and subsegmental levels" as well as stops that assimilate toward Korean production norms (Imperial, 2016, p. 145). Beyond Imperial's (2016) analyses, a closer investigation of PKLE data also shows potential syntactic substrate influence from Korean and PhE as well. Copula deletion, illustrated with a ∅ in (15), appears to be a salient feature of PKLE. A potential account for this might be related to the Korean word order. In Korean, the verbs and copulas are mostly found at the end of the clause since Korean is SOV (16). As they produce the English clause like in (15), Korean learners in the Philippines might be subconsciously delaying the verb/copula until the end of the clause, like in Korean, but upon reaching the end of the clause realize that the delay is not typical of English. By the time they realize this, they are unable to return and correct the 'error' without repeating the clause. This is also a common 'error'/feature in other non-Philippine Korean learners of English (Ji-seung Kim, personal communication) and might explain why Korean learners in the Philippines drop their copula in English, demonstrating Korean substrate influence on English.

On the other hand, in the same utterance, the use of intensifier *really* at the beginning of the clause cannot be traced back to Korean but to PhE (17) and, perhaps, Tagalog (i.e. clause-initial *talaga* 'really'), where similar clause-initial 'really' intensifier constructions are permitted. Although this warrants more investigation, what are demonstrated here collectively show that PKLE is a substrate-influenced hybridized English.

15 Because if somebody ∅ very good at speaking English, **really** I can understand.
   "Because if somebody is very good at speaking English, I can really understand".

   (Imperial, 2016)

178 *Wilkinson Daniel Wong Gonzales*

16 만약 누군가 영어를 매우 잘 한다 면...
   manyag nugunga yeongeoleul maeu jal- handa -myeon...
   if somebody English very well- do -if
   "Because if somebody is very good at speaking English..."

   (Korean, native speaker translation of the first clause of 15)

17 **Really** I mean they they wear this they wore this very short skirt

   (Manila English, ICE-PHI:S1A-080#240:1:A)

13.2.3.2 Manila Lannang English

Manila Lannang English (MLE) (known in previous work as Manila Chinese English) is an English variety of the Manila Lannangs. It is a hybridized English that has Hokkien and Tagalog influence on its English (morpho) syntax (Gonzales, 2017a; Gonzales & Hiramoto 2020). Used specifically in, but not limited to, academia, computer-mediated, and formal settings (e.g. meetings, religious), MLE is characterized by its non-lexical Hokkien and Tagalog/Filipino-sourced features.

For instance, 'standard' English typically places the adverb *only* at the pre-verbal position. In MLE, however, *only* has the tendency to be in the clause-final position (18), similar to *ni* 'only' in Hokkien and *lang* 'only' in Tagalog/Filipino, which both have clause finality. Similarly, MLE also has the plain *than*-comparative marker (19), which can be argued to be due to influence from Hokkien *pi* (comparative) (Gonzales & Hiramoto, 2020). The *pi* comparative does not need to be in proximity with another comparative marker like *kha* (comparative) for the sentence to be grammatical, but such is not the case in Tagalog/Filipino, where you need both comparative markings (i.e. *mas...kaysa* 'more...than'). This suggests that, among the primary source languages, Hokkien is the sole substrate influence on the MLE plain *than*-comparative feature (Gonzales & Hiramoto, 2020). As a Hokkien and Tagalog-influenced English, MLE can belong to the third group of hybrids.

18 Because only limited persons per day **only**.
   "Because they only allow limited persons per day".

   (Gonzales' MLE data)

19 I like Dr. Uayan's suggestion of a laptop or Terabyte as the ultimate chiong guan[6] **than** a TV.
   "I like Dr. Uayan's suggestion of a laptop or a Terabyte hard drive as the first prize rather than (instead of) a TV".

   (Gonzales' MLE data)

Hybridization 179

13.2.3.3 Other Non-Manila Ethno-Geographic Englishes

Apart from Manila English, other ethno-geographic Englishes have also been observed in regions where Cebuano and Hiligaynon are used (Villanueva, 2016). For simplicity, this chapter refers to them as Cebuano English and Hiligaynon English. In these Englishes, the regional language(s) can influence the English used by the speakers. For instance, the formulaic phrase *a lot of* to refer to 'many' in 'standard' English is reduced to *a lot* in Cebuano English (20), potentially because Cebuano does not have this formulaic phrase and realizes this phrase as one phonological word *daghan(g)* 'many' (21). The reduction of three phonological words to two could be attributed to Cebuano influence. Also, 'standardized English' has a more comprehensive prepositional system (e.g. the use of *in*, *on*, etc.), but in Hiligaynon and Tagalog, for example, there is usually only one preposition/locative marker, *sa*. In Hiligaynon English (22), 'incorrect' uses of prepositions such as *in* instead of *with* in English can be observed. This can be due to the lack of a similar system in Hiligaynon.

20 There are **a lot** reasons.
    "There are many reasons".

(Cebuano English, EWCSE-2, Villanueva, 2016)

21 daghang   mga   rason
    many   PLU   reason
    "many reasons"

(Cebuano, Philippine Star – Banat, https://www.philstar.com/banat/balita, November 22, 2014)

22 Similarly, it is claimed that if teachers are happy **in** their job they become productive and effective. (Hiligaynon English)

(Hiligaynon English, TDWHSE-1, Villanueva, 2016)

13.3 Summary and Conclusion

After briefly defining hybridization and situating it in the Philippine (English) context, this chapter surveyed 11 linguistic varieties and code-switching phenomena in the Philippines that can belong to one of the three hybrid groups – (1) hybrids with borrowing, (2) hybrids involving code-switching, and (3) substrate-influenced hybridized Englishes (Table 13.1). This preliminary grouping of hybrids should not be considered a rigid classification because the groups are not meant to be exclusive and the varieties in these groups can change over time. For instance, MLE can be part of group-2 and group-3 if its users code-switch to Hokkien or another language in a specific

180 *Wilkinson Daniel Wong Gonzales*

Table 13.1 Summary of Hybrids Involving Philippine English

#	Group	Varieties and/or Phenomena
1	Hybrids with borrowing	• Conyo English/Englog • Filipino • Lánnang-uè (Philippine Hybrid Hokkien)
2	Hybrids involving code-switching	• Tagalog-Filipino-English code-switching/Taglish • Hokkien-Lánnang-uè-Tagalog-Filipino-English code-switching/Hokaglish • Taishanese variety spoken in the Philippines • Cebuano-English code-switching • Contemporary Chabacano varieties
3	Substrate-influenced hybridized Englishes	• PKLE • MLE • Non-Manila ethno-geographic Englishes (Cebuano English, Hiligaynon English, etc.)

context, like in example (19). Also, the Taishanese variety (§ 13.2.2.3) in the second group might become a group-1 hybrid if its speakers phonologically adapt the code-switched words over time or if sociohistorical factors favor the variety in the future.

Overall, a brief analysis of these Philippine hybrid varieties collectively demonstrates three things. First, it shows that linguistic hybridization is very much present in multicultural and multilingual Philippines. As shown in the survey, hybrids exist in profusion. I have also demonstrated that hybridization in these varieties is realized in different forms and levels ranging from the phonological to the syntactic. Second, my analysis highlights the significant and dynamic role (Philippine) English plays in Philippine hybrid varieties. The preceding sections demonstrate how PhE can contribute to other Philippine languages, varieties, and phenomena through borrowing or code-switching of certain (Philippine) English lexicon. The section on hybridized Englishes (§ 13.2.3) also shows that PhE can also play the role of a malleable language susceptible to substratum influence. Third, this preliminary survey supports the idea that PhE is not a homogenous variety of English (Gonzales, 2017a). The existence of multiple ethno-regional variants of PhE (group-3 hybrids) is not surprising given that English was initially brought to "every province" (p. 179) in the Philippines by the Thomasites during the American occupation period (Bolton & Butler, 2008) and interacted with the languages used in each of those provinces.

As demonstrated, a bottom-up exploration of hybrids can give us a clearer and more accurate picture of the status and development of PhE; it is also crucial for its growth as a field. It would be interesting to look at more varieties and phenomena where PhE assumes different roles in language change and creation: either it was the one being influenced or it was the one contributing the feature. This chapter, however, should be taken as what it is – a simple overview. For reasons of space, we are unable to expound on the individual varieties that for obvious reasons need further elaboration. What one can glean from this chapter, hopefully, is that it is simply inadequate to confine research on PhE *within* the bounds of PhE. While research on and within the general PhE framework is important, there is need to conduct more research *beyond* this 'monolithic' framework by focusing on other languages, varieties, and code-switching phenomena – hybrids – where (Philippine) English does not assume a static role. It is hoped that this chapter would raise an awareness of the gap and current issues hounding PhE, motivating scholars to redress these in previous work and contemplate on how research in PhE should be conducted in the years to come.

Notes

1 In this and the following examples, words sourced from Tagalog, Filipino (in some examples), and Cebuano are italicized while the English ones are underlined. In plain text are words and morphemes of Sinitic origin, i.e. Hokkien, Taishanese, or Mandarin. Other non-Sinitic words (e.g. Korean, Spanish) are also in plain text. Emphasis is expressed in bold face.
2 While a linguistic distinction between Filipino and Tagalog is made, Filipinos use the terms Filipino and Tagalog interchangeably.
3 The term Lánnang-uè is also used to refer to the 'pure' and 'unmixed' variety of Hokkien in the Philippines. For this chapter, I use Lánnang-uè to refer to the mixed code.
4 A lot of Lannangs also refer to themselves as Philippine Chinese, Filipino-Chinese, Chinese Filipinos. For more discussion, read Gonzales (2021).
5 I say code-switching and not borrowing from English because it could be the case that these are Chabacano switches to Filipino English-borrowed words. At the same time, I am not discounting the possibility that the English words could be borrowings from English itself. At this point, there is more evidence of it being code-switching because borrowings are usually more conventionalized but in the case of contemporary Chabacano, the switches are not conventionalized.
6 Since this is from a written source, it is hard to determine whether it has phonologically adapted. This may or may not be a borrowing from Hokkien.

References

Abastillas, Glenn. (2015). *Divergence in Cebuano and English code-switching practices in Cebuano speech communities in the Central Philippines* (Unpublished M.A. Thesis). Georgetown University.

Bautista, Maria Lourdes S. (2004). Tagalog-English code switching as a mode of discourse. *Asia Pacific Education Review, 5*(2), 226–233.

Bolton, Kingsley & Susan Butler. (2008). Lexicography and the description of Philippine English vocabulary. In Ma. Lourdes S. Bautista & Kingsley Bolton (eds.), *Philippine English: Linguistics and literary perspectives*, 175–200. Hong Kong: Hong Kong University Press.

182 *Wilkinson Daniel Wong Gonzales*

Borlongan, Ariane Macalinga. (2015). Conyo English: Explorations of Philippine English sociolects. In D. Salazar (Chair), *Contemporary studies of Philippine English.* Symposium convened at the 21st Conference of the International Association for World Englishes, Istanbul, Turkey.

Chan-Yap, Gloria. (1980). *Hokkien Chinese borrowings in Tagalog.* Canberra: Australian National University.

Garvida, Mignette Marcos. (2012). "Conyo Talk": The affirmation of hybrid identity and power in contemporary Philippine discourse. *Lingue e Linguaggi, 8,* 23–34.

Gonzales, Wilkinson Daniel Wong. (2016). Trilingual code-switching using quantitative lenses: An exploratory study on Hokaglish. *Philippine Journal of Linguistics, 47,* 109–131.

Gonzales, Wilkinson Daniel Wong. (2017a). Philippine Englishes. *Asian Englishes, 19*(1), 79–95.

Gonzales, Wilkinson Daniel Wong. (2017b). Language contact in the Philippines: The history and ecology from a Chinese Filipino perspective. *Language Ecology, 1*(2), 185–212.

Gonzales, Wilkinson Daniel Wong. (2021). Filipino, Chinese, neither, or both? The Lannang identity and its relationship with language. *Language & Communication, 77,* 5–16.

Grosjean, François. (2010). *Bilingual.* Cambridge, MA: Harvard University Press.

Imperial, Rowland Anthony. (2016). *Speech production and sociolinguistic perception in a 'non-native' second language context: A sociophonetic study of Korean learners of English in the Philippines* (Unpublished M.A. Thesis). National University of Singapore.

Kim, Dong-Yeon. (2015). Korea-Philippine relations: From blood-tied alliance to strategic partnership. In Lee Choong Lyol, Hong Seok-Joon, & Youn Dae-yeong (eds.), *ASEAN-Korean relations: Twenty-five years of partnership and friendship,* 674–723. Nulmin: Seoul.

Lesada, Joseph D. (2017). *Taglish in Metro Manila: An analysis of Tagalog-English code-switching* (Unpublished Honors Thesis). University of Michigan.

Lesho, Marivic. (2013). *The sociophonetics and phonology of the Cavite Chabacano vowel system* (Unpublished Ph.D. dissertation). The Ohio State University.

Miralao, Virginia A. (ed.). (2007). Understanding the Korean diaspora in the Philippines. In Virginia A. Miralao and Lorna P. Makil (eds.), *Exploring transnational communities in the Philippines,* 24–39. Quezon City: Philippine Migration Research Network and Philippine Social Science Council.

Onysko, Alexander. (2016). Modeling world Englishes from the perspective of language contact. *World Englishes, 35*(2), 196–220.

Sanchez-Stockhammer, Christina. (2012). Hybridization in language. In Philipp Wolfgang Stockhammer (eds.), *Conceptualizing cultural hybridization: A transdisciplinary approach,* 133–157. Berlin: Springer.

Schachter, Paul & Fe T. Otanes. (1972). *Tagalog reference grammar.* Berkeley: University of California Press.

Schneider, Edgar. (2016). Hybrid Englishes: An exploratory survey. *World Englishes, 35*(3), 339–354.

Smith, Larry E. (1981). *English for cross-cultural communication.* London: Macmillan.

Sobolewski, Frank Andrew. (1980). *Some syntactic constraints in Tagalog-English language mixing* (Unpublished Master's Thesis). University of Hawaii.

Thomason, Sarah Grey. (2001). *Language contact: An introduction.* Washington, DC: Georgetown University Press.

Thomason, Sarah Grey & Kaufman, Terrence. (1988). *Language contact, creolization, and genetic linguistics.* Berkeley: University of California Press.

Villanueva, Rey John Castro. (2016). *The features of Philippine English across regions* (Unpublished doctoral dissertation). De La Salle University, Manila, the Philippines.

Appendix. Glosses

1 First person
2 Second person
3 Third person

APPX   Approximator
CLF   Classifier
DEF   Definite
DEM   Demonstrative
LNK   Linker
LOC   Location marker/locative
NEG   Negation marker
NOM   Nominative marker
PLU   Plural marker/pluralizer
PFV   Perfective marker
PRT   Particle
SG   Singular

Part 4

Linguistic and Literary Canon

14 Lexicography

Danica Salazar

14.1 Introduction

Most language users view the dictionary as the indisputable authority on usage, a representation in print or digital form of what is deemed to be the 'standard'. Its role as the prime arbiter of linguistic propriety and acceptability makes the compilation of a dictionary an essential step toward the legitimization of a language variety (Seargeant, 2011), as has been demonstrated throughout history by national dictionary projects that helped define a distinct identity for Englishes used in places like the United States, Canada, Australia and New Zealand.

In the case of Philippine English (PhE), the documentation of the idiosyncratic lexicon of this variety has been part of the research agenda from its beginnings in the late 1960s and early 1970s, judging from the many dictionaries, word lists and lexical studies that have been published in the Philippines since then, as well as the number of Philippine words that have been included in major dictionaries by internationally renowned names such as *Merriam Webster's* and *Oxford*. This chapter offers a chronological survey of these lexicographical undertakings, whose creation has been complicated by challenges specific to the codification of any postcolonial, second-language variety such as that of the Philippines, and whose outcome and reception have been conditioned by the country's current sociolinguistic situation and its unique lexicographical tradition that dates back centuries into its colonial past.

14.2 Dictionaries in the Philippines

While on the island of Cebu in 1521 as part of the crew accompanying Ferdinand Magellan in his circumnavigation of the globe, the Italian scholar and explorer Antonio Pigafetta carried a journal about with him in which he assiduously noted down words in the language of the island's local people. Antonio Pigafetta's (1975/1524–1525) brief list of Italian words with their Visayan equivalents made it into his chronicle of Magellan's famous voyage and is now considered to be the first attempt at documenting the Cebuano language, or any Philippine language.

DOI: 10.4324/9780429427824-19

188   *Danica Salazar*

It was a few decades later when lexicography as a scholarly endeavor began in the Philippines, motivated in large part by its Spanish colonizers' evangelizing mission in the archipelago. As early as the late 1500s and early 1600s, Spanish friars started to compile vocabularies of the languages spoken by the peoples they wished to Christianize, and given the lack of written sources, the work of these missionary lexicographers had to rely on their own empirical observation of language use as well as the help of the native speakers they came in contact with. What resulted were bilingual dictionaries of Spanish with Philippine languages such as Tagalog, Visayan, Ilocano, Hiligaynon and Kapampangan. Scores of dictionaries, phrasebooks, wordlists and grammars followed in the 18th and 19th centuries, covering an even wider range of languages, including Gaddang, Ivatan, Ibanag, Manobo, Tausug and Tagbanwa (Hidalgo, 1977, 1979).

These early bilingual dictionaries broadly adhered to the models set by Spanish lexicographers like Antonio de Nebrija, as well as similar dictionaries of Amerindian languages previously published in New Spain, while also introducing innovations that responded to the specific needs of their target audience. These are eminently practical works aimed at other missionaries who were to use them for language learning, and their makers strove to include not only lexical content, but also advice on grammar and pronunciation, and phraseological units such as compounds, proverbs, sentences, metaphors and riddles. In seeking to provide as much information as they could about the new world whose languages they were documenting, Spanish missionaries created distinctive features that point to a uniquely Philippine lexicographic tradition, and contributed significantly to the preservation of native Philippine languages (Fernández Rodríguez, 2014).[1]

With the end of the Spanish regime and the beginning of American rule at the dawn of the 20th century, the pioneering lexicographical work of Spanish friars over three centuries was continued to a degree by American anthropological linguists, whose research led to the publication of lexical and grammatical sketches of languages not before covered by the Spanish, and to some progress in the scientific and comparative study of Philippine languages (Blake, 1922).

It is clear that the history of Philippine lexicography is closely tied to the country's colonial history. Hidalgo, writing in 1979, suggested that as an effect of hundreds of years under imperialistic rule, Philippine dictionaries up to that point were chiefly bilingual with Spanish and English, and monolingual dictionaries were non-existent. Indeed, it was not until 1989 that a major monolingual dictionary of a Philippine language saw publication, and this was for Filipino, the Tagalog-based national language.

The official decision to adopt Tagalog as the basis of the Philippine national language was made much earlier, in 1937, and it was a controversial choice that displeased the country's non-Tagalog-speaking ethnic groups. The need to standardize and promote the newly created lingua franca thus provided the impetus for producing an authoritative monolingual dictionary, but the outbreak of the Second World War, the declaration of Philippine independence in 1945, various other political upheavals and severe budget constraints delayed the appearance of such a dictionary by several decades.

Finally, in 1989, the Linangan ng Wika sa Pilipinas (Institute of Philippine Languages), the most authoritative institution on the Filipino language, published the *Diksyunaryo ng Wikang Filipino*. Although celebrated by some as a "milestone in national language development" (Newell, 1991, p. 49), this dictionary was also widely criticized for not including entries for eight new letters (C, F, J, Ñ, Q, V, X, Z) that had long since been added to the originally 20-letter Filipino alphabet to accommodate sounds from other Philippine languages, and from foreign borrowings into Filipino (Lee, 2010). Nine years later, in 1998, the Komisyon ng Wikang Filipino (Commission on the Filipino Language), the institution that evolved from the Linangan, published a new, revised edition of the 1989 *Diksyunaryo*, this time with the eight additional letters duly represented.

The supposed failure of the two editions of the *Diksyunaryo ng Wikang Filipino* to accurately represent Filipino vocabulary prompted the compilation of the *UP Diksiyonaryong Filipino* (*UPDF*), published by the University of the Philippines' Sentro ng Wikang Filipino (Filipino Language Centre) in 2001, with a revised second edition following in 2010. Although certainly a more comprehensive dictionary than its predecessors, the *UPDF* has not been entirely immune to criticism, most of which is leveled at its often circular definitions (Guillermo, Cajote, & Logronio, 2015) and seemingly unprincipled selection of words from various Philippine languages (Lee, 2010).

Although some remarkable advancements and significant milestones have been achieved in the development of Philippine lexicography, there are still several issues that linguists and lexicographers need to address in order to produce reliable monolingual and bilingual dictionaries for Philippine languages that can aid in their study and preservation and meet the requirements of their users.

Foremost among these issues is the lack of a unified theoretical approach that takes into account the semantic structure of Philippine languages (Hidalgo, 1979). Perhaps due to its origins as a Spanish colonial project, Philippine lexicography has usually followed Western models, but practices that work for Indo-European languages are not always guaranteed to do the same for Austronesian languages. It is therefore imperative to find a system of entry organization and data presentation that is specifically adapted to the intrinsic features of the lexicon of Philippine languages, such as the extensive use of affixation in the encoding of meaning.

Scholars such as Lee (2010) have also drawn attention to the dependence of Filipino dictionaries on secondary sources and older works in the generation of lexical content, which often leads to unsystematic, unbalanced word selection and imprecise definitions. To avoid these pitfalls, Philippine lexicography needs to fully embrace modern research methods based on the compilation and analysis of digital language corpora, which provide

190　*Danica Salazar*

authentic examples of language use on which more accurate definitions can be based, as well as frequency data with which to more objectively judge which words deserve inclusion in the dictionary. This is not always easy to implement, however, especially in the case of languages with a predominantly oral rather than written literary tradition.

The challenges facing Philippine lexicography also go beyond the linguistic and into the political. Linguistic issues are always difficult to separate from political ones, but even more so in the Philippines, where regional division, ethnic prejudice and a persistent colonial mentality often result in inconsistent linguistic policies and language attitudes that favor some languages over others. Bolton and Butler (2008) also note that dictionaries made in the Philippines, even those that aspire to national status such as the monolingual dictionaries of Filipino, lack the power and prestige usually accorded to similar dictionaries in other countries—if asked what the most authoritative dictionary of their native language is, speakers of Philippine languages will likely not have a ready answer the way speakers of languages such as English do.

14.3 Philippine English Dictionaries

Interest in documenting Philippine contributions to English vocabulary can be traced back to the very beginning of American occupation, when early American colonists began to borrow native terms and coin neologisms to describe their new environment, and then list and gloss them in their published works. Bolton and Butler (2008) mention the 1906 memoir of William B. Freer, *The Philippine Experiences of an American Teacher*, which provides a glossary of some 187 Philippine lexical items used throughout the book. These authors found that more than a 100 of these words are still present in the language, when they checked a corpus of Philippine texts over a 100 years after the memoir's original publication.

When PhE began to be an object of linguistic study by the end of the 1960s, the identification of its characteristic lexical features became one of the main research concerns, resulting in some groundbreaking studies on the PhE lexicon (e.g., Bautista, 1986, 1997, 1998; Casambre, 1986; Dar, 1973; Ponio, 1974; also cf. Borlongan, 2007 for a later study of lexical innovations in PhE). However, all this lexical investigation has resulted in few monolingual dictionaries of PhE. In 1984, Tabor published the *Filipino English Mini-Dictionary*, which is commercially unavailable and difficult to find even in libraries, and in 1995, Cruz and Bautista released *A Dictionary of Philippine English*, an illustrated word inventory that took a more humorous approach to presenting the lexicon.[2]

What can be considered the most systematic and coherent attempt so far to produce a lexical reference for contemporary PhE is the *Anvil-Macquarie Dictionary of Philippine English for High School*, edited by Bautista and Butler and first published in 2000, with a revised edition released in 2010. As is evident from its title, this dictionary is targeted at Filipino high school

Lexicography 191

students, and features a controlled vocabulary in a list of headwords comprising 16,000 words, along with an informal defining style supported by thousands of example sentences and just as many notes on usage, grammatical problems and easily confused words. While its word selection is similar to other English school dictionaries, what sets it apart is its inclusion of hundreds of words and usages that are typical of PhE. As the editors explain in their preface to the revised edition (Bautista & Butler, 2010):

> The [*Anvil-Macquarie Dictionary*] recognizes [...] that at one end of the spectrum [PhE] merges with English as it is used for international purposes, while at the other it is expressive of local conditions and local choices in language. So in this dictionary you will find the *anahaw,* a palm widespread in the Philippines, and *kalamansi,* the local variety of lemon, and *bananacue,* the roasted banana on a stick. You will find *solon* and *barangay, adobo* and *lechon,* all items which matter a great deal in the Philippines but which are not included in any other comparable dictionary.

The dictionary clearly labels the PhE items within its pages, in order for its users to recognize when their local vocabulary departs from the international standard. These vocabulary items are mostly borrowings from Philippine languages and Spanish, but they also include distinctive Philippine uses of standard English words, which are also easily identifiable from the accompanying labeling or annotations. In the following entries, for instance, the intransitive use of the verb *afford* and the adjectival use of the noun and verb *traffic,* common only in PhE, are marked by italicized labels:

> **afford** *v.* 1. If you can **afford** something, you've got enough money to pay for it: *We can't afford to go to that expensive restaurant.* 2. *Philippine English* If you can **afford**, you have the means for a particular purpose: *I didn't have the blinds changed because I couldn't afford.*

> **traffic** *n.* 1. the coming and going of people or vehicles along a road, waterway, railway line, etc. 2. the people or vehicles that travel along such a route. 3. the business, trade, or dealings carried out between countries or people, sometimes illegally; *traffic in drugs. v.* 4. someone who **traffics** in drugs, arms or stolen goods, buys and sells them illegally: *Police suspect he's been trafficking in drugs. adj.* 5. *Philippine English Informal* heavily congested with **traffic**. *So sorry I'm late, it was really traffic again.*

In the entry for the noun *tricycle,* the definition explicitly states where the concept of such a vehicle differs in the Philippines than in the rest of the English-speaking world:

> **tricycle** *n.* 1. a cycle with three wheels, usually two at the back. 2. (in the Philippines) a motorcycle with a small, one-wheeled car attached to the side, used for transport in housing areas or on side streets.

192   *Danica Salazar*

In the entry for the verb *bring,* a usage note explains how Filipino speakers of English tend to interchange this verb with the verb *take*:

bring *v.* 1. If you **bring** something or someone when you come to a place, you carry it with you or get them to come with you: *Can I bring my friend to your party? | Those black clouds will bring rain.* 2. If something **brings** someone or something to a place or a condition, it causes them to be in that place or state: *The drought brought suffering to everyone.* 3. *Philippine English* To **bring** someone somewhere is to accompany them there: *Let me bring you to the airport.*

NOTE In Philippine English, 'bring' is sometimes used where speakers of other Englishes would use 'take', as in Philippine English *Let me bring you to the airport* instead of *Let me take you to the airport.*

Some usage notes even contain surprisingly pithy social observations:

delicadeza *n. Philippine English* a sense of decency and knowing how to behave with dignity.

NOTE This is considered an important value that present-day Filipinos are thought to have lost. It is used mainly with reference to corrupt politicians who, after being found out, still don't resign from their position.

NOTE This word is borrowed into English from Spanish.

The PhE content in the *Anvil-Macquarie Dictionary* is largely based on the Philippine newspaper, fiction and nonfiction texts in Macquarie's Asiacorp corpus, with some verification from native speakers. Apart from its corpus-based research methodology, this dictionary is also notable for being a collaborative venture between an internationally recognized Australian dictionary publisher and a highly respected scholar of PhE who is also a native speaker of the variety. It is therefore a good illustration of how a lexicographical project can benefit from combining the expertise of an established dictionary company with the knowledge of local experts.

The *Anvil-Macquarie Dictionary* has been well received by the academic community, but it has so far been unable to gain mainstream popularity. Until today, the local market for English dictionaries continues to be dominated by international titles, some of which will be examined in the next section.

14.4 Philippine English in General Dictionaries of English

The limited availability of locally produced English dictionaries leaves Filipinos with little choice but to rely on general dictionaries from the United States and the United Kingdom. But how is their own native variety of English represented in these works, if at all?

The first study to attempt to answer this question was carried out by Yap— in *Pilipino loan words in English* (1970), she lists words of Philippine origin that appear in two of the latest and most prestigious dictionaries of the time:

Lexicography   193

Webster's New International Dictionary of the English Language (1961) and *Webster's Third New International Dictionary of the English Language* (1968). The author then groups these words into the semantic categories "flora and fauna", "household and cultural items" and "names of cultural minorities".

In their 2008 review of the state of PhE lexicography, Bolton and Butler examine Yap's list, and remark on the mainly botanical, zoological and anthropological nature of the majority of words on it, which they termed "Webster words". These authors went further by searching for the words on Yap's list with the then-current online edition of *Webster's Third Unabridged* (2002), and discovered that the Philippines was still chiefly represented in this dictionary by the same archaic, colonial-era words identified by Yap more than 30 years earlier.

In the same 2008 article, Bolton and Butler also consulted the online Third Edition of the *Oxford English Dictionary (OED)*. The *OED* is a historical dictionary with a much more comprehensive coverage of words throughout the entire 1,000-year history of English, and is widely regarded as the definitive record of the language. However, Bolton and Butler (2008) also found the same prevalence of Webster words and an even more limited coverage of Philippine lexical items in the *OED* than the *Webster's* dictionaries. Table 14.1 gives examples of Webster words that Yap found in *Webster's* in 1970, and that Bolton and Butler found in *Webster's* and the *OED* in 2008.

It therefore seems that current mainstream English dictionaries present only a petrified colonial version of the PhE lexicon—one that consists largely of borrowings from native languages that refer to plants and animals, terms for ethnic origin and cultural artifacts. There appears to be limited coverage in these works of the kind of words that reflects the way that English is actually being used in the Philippines.

However, there have lately been some encouraging signs of change. In the case of the third and latest edition of the *OED,* available exclusively and updated quarterly online, there is now much more scope for broader and more varied coverage of World Englishes than in earlier editions. While previously, *OED* editors had to depend on Anglo-American texts for any evidence of words from the Philippines, today the Internet gives them instantaneous

Table 14.1 Some "Webster Words" in *Webster's* and the *OED*

Plants and Animals	Ethnic Groups	Others
Abaca	Bajau	bolo (a type of knife)
buntal	Ifugao	jusi (a type of fabric)
cadang-cadang	Illano/Illanun	vinta (a type of boat)
cogon	Ilocano	
dita	Manobo	
narra	Maranao	
tamarau	Pangasinan	
	Tagalog	

194 *Danica Salazar*

access to locally written newspapers, journals and books that provide more representative examples of PhE usage. The dictionary's editors are now also able to rely on contributions from members of the public, and specialist advice from consultants based in the Philippines. Various forms of social media such as Twitter and Facebook have also opened new avenues of research into slang and informal words and phrases that form part of the everyday vocabulary of today's average PhE speaker.

These new research resources and methods have made it possible for the *OED* to undertake targeted projects for World Englishes, adding particularly large batches of new entries for several varieties, including PhE. In its June 2015 update, the *OED* published 40 new words and senses from PhE, the largest single batch of items from this variety to be added by the dictionary (Salazar, 2017). This was followed by the addition of dozens more Philippine entries in subsequent quarterly updates (see Table 14.2 for a list of Philippine words and senses that have been added to the *OED* from June 2015 up to the time of writing). These inclusions were positively received by the Filipino public and attracted considerable attention in the local media (Quismundo, 2015). A notable example is the addition of the word *kilig* to the dictionary in March 2016, whose wide coverage in the Philippine press

Table 14.2 Recently Added PhE Words to the *OED*

2015		2016	2018
advanced, adj. (fast, as of a watch or clock)	high blood, adj. kikay, n. kikay kit, n.	aggrupation, n. Aling, n. arnis, n.	accomplish, v. (to fill out a form) bagoong, n.
bahala na, n.	KKB, n.	ate, n.	bihon, n.
balikbayan, n.	kuya, n.	balut, n.	bold, adj. (erotic,
balikbayan box, n.	mabuhay, int.	bayanihan, n.	risqué)
baon, n.	mani-pedi, n.	kare-kare, n.	bongga, adj.
barangay, n.	pan de sal, n.	kilig, n. and adj.	carinderia, n.
barkada, n.	pasalubong, n.	leche flan, n.	cartolina, n.
barong, n.	presidentiable, n.	lechon, n.	dirty ice cream, n.
barong tagalog, n.	pulutan, n.	lola, n.	ensaimada, n.
baro't saya, n.	salvage, v. (to	lolo, n.	holdupper, n.
buko, n.	summarily	Mang, n.	palay, n.
buko juice, n.	execute a	pancit, n.	panciteria, n.
carnap, n.	suspected	puto, n.	querida, n.
carnapper, n.	criminal)	tabo, n.	rotonda, n. (a traffic
comfort room, n.	sari-sari store, n.	teleserye, n.	circle)
despedida, n.	sinigang, n.	tita, n.	sisig, n.
dirty kitchen, n.	suki, n.	tito, n.	sorbetes, n.
estafa, n.	utang na loob, n.	yaya, n.	trapo, n.
gimmick, n. (a night out with friends)			turon, n.
go down, v.			viand, n. (a dish of
halo-halo, n.			meat or fish that accompanies rice in a Filipino meal)

(Sabillo, 2016) led to the word becoming one of the dictionary's most consulted entries that year.

Other major dictionary publishers are also turning their attention to PhE. Words from the Philippines entered the *Macmillan Dictionary* for the first time in January 2017, when over 30 new entries from the variety were added to the dictionary. Macmillan also encouraged experts on the variety to help its editors improve its coverage of the PhE lexicon by submitting word suggestions to the Open Dictionary, the online platform through which *Macmillan* users can directly add new words not yet covered by the dictionary (Rundell, 2017).

14.5 Toward an Ideal Dictionary of Philippine English

The general belief in the dictionary as the ultimate authority on language use makes it one of the most potent and effective means of conferring legitimacy to an emerging language variety such as PhE. However, the lexicographical codification of such a variety can be fraught with difficulty, since the conceptual and theoretical challenges inherent to the dictionary-making process are made even more complex by the cultural, ideological and political issues that come with any attempt to document a variety considered to be outside the standard (Salazar, 2015), or whose status and development as an independent world English variety is still being debated (Borlongan, 2016; Gonzales, 2017; Martin, 2014).

The first hurdle in the creation of a PhE dictionary is to overcome the ideological bias against non-standard varieties, and the perceived superiority of British and American English across the English-speaking world. Before any dictionary project involving PhE can commence, the various stakeholders in the process—publishers, public and private funding bodies, language planners, teachers, dictionary users—must be persuaded that PhE has its own separate norms, and that its idiosyncratic vocabulary is a feature that needs to be documented instead of ignored or eradicated (Dolezal, 2006).

Compilers of a PhE dictionary must also be able to clearly delineate the scope of their work, and establish well-defined selection criteria. English in the Philippines is in a diglossic situation typical of postcolonial nations, in which an official, formal, high-prestige variety of English co-exists with a colloquial, informal, low-prestige counterpart (Ooi, 2001). Most language policy makers and dictionary users expect to find words from the high variety in a reference book, since they more closely follow the norms of standard British and American English. The low variety, in contrast, shows more nativized usages that a lexicographer will want to codify, but which a dictionary user may dismiss as 'bad English'. A successful dictionary of PhE must therefore strike a balance between providing an inventory of words that authentically represents the way English is employed by its Filipino speakers, and satisfying the needs and expectations of these very speakers (Dolezal, 2006; Ooi, 2001).

Finally, makers of a PhE dictionary must contend with the relatively limited availability of textual evidence for lexical research. This is due to the fact that

196 *Danica Salazar*

PhE has a much shorter publishing history than British and American English, and also to the reality that many local publications still adhere to the American standard, meaning that PhE words present in speech and informal writing are edited out of published texts. In this regard, alternative resources offered by new technologies can fill the gap—from ever-larger digital language corpora of world Englishes that are becoming available, to online media such as blogs, wikis and social networks that contain much less mediated writing, to online crowdsourcing platforms that allow lexicographers to reach out to language users to ask for lexical information (Salazar, 2014).

Finding reliable sources of primary evidence on which to base lexicographical work will help the ideal PhE dictionary avoid a recurring tendency throughout the history of Philippine lexicography—from the Spanish friars' bilingual dictionaries of Philippine languages, to the *UPDF* monolingual dictionary of Filipino (Lee, 2010), to the coverage of PhE in *Webster's* and the *OED*—a tendency toward an unbalanced word selection that privileges the exotic over the typical. Only the quantitative and qualitative analyses of primary evidence can result in a dictionary that is not just a mere listing of loanwords referring to native plants, animals and cultural artifacts, but one that encompasses all forms of lexical innovation beyond simple borrowing, and contains words and meanings from a broad range of semantic fields that represent both historical and contemporary lexis (Salazar, 2015).

It is only by addressing these issues that comprehensive and balanced lexicographical documentation of the PhE lexicon can be achieved—whether through local dictionary projects or through the inclusion of PhE words in globally renowned dictionaries. By codifying PhE vocabulary, the traditional ideology of the dictionary as the highest linguistic authority can be used to change the way that PhE is regarded, serving as the ultimate recognition of PhE's own separate lexical conventions, as set by the choices made by a distinct Philippine language community.

Notes

1　For a comprehensive list of Philippine language dictionaries and vocabularies, see Hendrickson and Newell (1991).
2　Several dictionaries on specific semantic fields within the PhE lexicon are presented as humor books but are also of considerable lexicographical interest. See, for example, Center for People Empowerment in Governance (2010) and Lacaba (2010).

References

Bautista, Ma. Lourdes S. (1986). English-Pilipino contact: A case study of reciprocal borrowing. In Wolfgang Viereck and Wolf-Dietrich Bald (Eds.), *English in contact with other languages: Studies in honor of Broder Carstensen on the occasion of his 60th birthday,* (pp. 491–510). Budapest: Akademiai Kiado.

Bautista, Ma. Lourdes S. (1997). The lexicon of Philippine English. In Maria Lourdes S. Bautista (Ed.), *English is an Asian language: The Philippine context,* (pp. 49–72). Sydney: The Macquarie Library.

Lexicography 197

Bautista, Ma. Lourdes S. (1998). Tagalog-English code-switching and the lexicon of Philippine English. *Asian Englishes, 1*(1), 51–67.

Bautista, Ma. Lourdes S., & Butler, Susan (2010). *Anvil-Macquarie dictionary of Philippine English for high school,* revised edn. Pasig City: Anvil Publishing.

Blake, Frank R. (1922). The part played by the publications of the United States government in the development of Philippine linguistic studies. *Journal of the American Oriental Society, 42,* 147–170.

Bolton, Kingsley, & Butler, Susan. (2008). Lexicography and the description of Philippine English vocabulary. In Maria Lourdes S. Bautista & Kingsley Bolton (Eds.), *Philippine English: Linguistic and literary perspectives,* (pp. 175–200). Hong Kong SAR, China: Hong Kong University Press.

Borlongan, Ariane M. (2007). Innovations in standard Philippine English. In Charles C. Mann (Ed.), *Current research on English and applied linguistics: A De La Salle University special issue,* (pp. 1–36). Manila: De La Salle University, College of Education, Department of English and Applied Linguistics..

Borlongan, Ariane M. (2016). Relocating Philippine English in Schneider's dynamic model. *Asian Englishes, 18*(3), 232–241.

Casambre, Nelia G. (1986). What is Filipino English? *Philippine Journal for Language Teaching, 14*(1–4), 34–49.

Center for People Empowerment in Governance. (2010). *Corruptionary: A dictionary of Filipino corruption words.* Pasig City: Anvil Publishing.

Cruz, Isagani R., & Bautista, Ma. Lourdes S. (1995). *A dictionary of Philippine English.* Pasig City: Anvil Publishing.

Dar, Rodrigo A. (1973). *A study on the nature of Filipinisms.* Unpublished MA thesis, Ateneo de Manila University, Quezon City.

Diksyunaryo ng Wikang Filipino. (1989). Manila: Linangan ng Wika sa Pilipinas.

Diksyunaryo ng Wikang Filipino, centennial edn. (1998). Manila: Komisyon ng Wikang Filipino.

Dolezal, Fredric. (2006). World Englishes and lexicography. In Braj Kachru, Yamuna Kachru & Cecil Nelson (Eds.), *The handbook of World Englishes,* (pp. 694–708). Oxford: Blackwell.

Fernández Rodríguez, Rebeca. (2014). Lexicography in the Philippines (1600–1800). *Historiographia Linguistica, 41*(1), 1–32.

Freer, William B. (1906). *The Philippine experiences of an American teacher: A narrative of work and travel in the Philippine Islands.* New York: Scribner.

Gonzales, Wilkinson D. W. (2017). Philippine Englishes. *Asian Englishes, 19*(1), 79–95.

Guillermo, Ramon G., Cajote, Rhandley D., & Logronio, Aristeo. (2015). *UP Diksiyonaryong Filipino*: Sinonismong walang hangganan. *Daluyan: Journal ng Wikang Filipino, 2,* 54–71.

Hendrickson, Gail R., & Newell, Leonard E. (1991). *A bibliography of Philippine language dictionaries and vocabularies.* Manila: Linguistic Society of the Philippines.

Hidalgo, Cesar A. (1977). *Philippine lexicography from 1521 to present.* Quezon City: University of the Philippines.

Hidalgo, Cesar A. (1979). Towards a model for writing Philippine dictionaries. *Asian Studies, 17,* 37–64.

Lacaba, Jose F. (2010). *Showbiz lengua: Chika & chismax about chuvachuchu.* Pasig City: Anvil Publishing.

198 *Danica Salazar*

Lee, Aldrin P. (2010). The Filipino monolingual dictionaries and the development of Filipino lexicography. *Philippine Social Sciences Review, 62*(2), 369–401.

Macmillan Dictionary. http://www.macmillandictionary.com.

Martin, Isabel P. (2014). Philippine English revisited. *World Englishes, 33*(1), 50–59.

Newell, Leonard E. (1991). Philippine lexicography: The state of the art. *International Journal of the Sociology of Language, 88*, 45–57.

Ooi, Vincent (2001). Globalising Singaporean-Malaysian English in an inclusive learner's dictionary. In Bruce Moore (Ed.), *Who's centric now? The present state of post-colonial Englishes* (pp. 95–121). Oxford: Oxford University Press.

Oxford English Dictionary, 3rd edn. (2000—). http://www.oed.com.

Pigafetta, Antonio. (1975). Report on the first voyage around the world. In Raleigh A. Skelton (Ed. & Trans.), *Magellan's voyage: A narrative account of the first navigation*. London: The Folio Society. (Original work published 1524–25)

Ponio, Nordian E. (1974). *Determining the sensitivity of educated Filipino and American English speakers to Filipinisms found in leading newspapers.* Unpublished doctoral dissertation, University of Santo Tomas, Manila.

Quismundo, Tarra. (2015, June 26). 40 Filipino-coined words now in Oxford dictionary. *Philippine Daily Inquirer.* Retrieved August 1, 2018 from the Philippine Daily Inquirer website: http://globalnation.inquirer.net/125245/40-filipino-coined-words-now-in-oxford-dictionary.

Rundell, Michael. (2017). New year, new words: Macmillan Dictionary's latest update. Retrieved August 1, 2018 from the Macmillan Dictionary blog: http://www.macmillandictionaryblog.com/new-year-new-words-macmillan-dictionarys-latest-update.

Sabillo, Kristine A. (2016, April 15). 'Kilig,' 'teleserye' included in Oxford English Dictionary. *Philippine Daily Inquirer.* Retrieved August 1, 2018 from the Philippine Daily Inquirer website: http://globalnation.inquirer.net/138631/kilig-included-in-oxford-english-dictionary.

Salazar, Danica. (2014). Towards improved coverage of Southeast Asian Englishes in the *Oxford English Dictionary. Lexicography: Journal of ASIALEX, 1*, 95–108.

Salazar, Danica. (2015). The vocabulary of non-dominant varieties of English in the *Oxford English Dictionary.* In Rudolf Muhr & Dawn Marley (Eds.), *Pluricentric languages: New perspectives in theory and description*, (pp. 73–88). Oxford: Peter Lang.

Salazar, Danica. (2017). Philippine English in the *Oxford English Dictionary*: Recent advancements and implications for ESL in the Philippines. *Philippine ESL Journal, 19*, 45–59.

Seargeant, Philip. (2011). Lexicography as a philosophy of language. *Language Sciences, 33*, 1–10.

Tabor, Myrna G.A. (1984). Filipino English mini-dictionary. In Lawrence Johnson (Ed.), *Mini-dictionaries of Southeast Asian Englishes*, (pp. 65–84). Singapore: SEAMEO Regional Language Centre.

UP Diksiyonaryong Filipino, revised edn. (2010). Quezon City: Sentro ng Wikang Filipino.

Webster's New International Dictionary of the English Language. (1961). Springfield, MA: Merriam-Webster.

Webster's Third New International Dictionary of the English Language. (1968). Springfield, MA.: Merriam-Webster.

Yap, Fe A. (1970). *Pilipino loan words in English.* Manila: Surian ng Wikang Pambansa.

15 Standard Philippine English

Ariane Macalinga Borlongan

15.1 Aim and Outline

The focus of this chapter is on the standardization of Philippine English (PhE) and the various aspects and dimensions of the unfolding of this process. First, it surveys the descriptive works done on PhE which are pivotal to the eventual standardization of the new English. Second, it discusses the issues surrounding the emergence and evolution of a standardized variety of PhE. Third, it reports the status of the ongoing codification of Standard Philippine English (SPhE). Fourth, it discusses prospects for an endonormative model for language teaching in the Philippines. As a conclusion, it provides a conceptual model of the multi-faceted process of standardization of English in the Philippines.

15.2 Linguistic Sketches and Descriptions

In the early years of English in the Philippines, the language would have been learned as a foreign language. Naturally, Filipino learners used English with much first language influence. Americans noticed this and so, in a 1925 nationwide educational survey, it was commented, "Filipino children, copying the models presented by their teachers, are learning to speak a kind of English which is characterized by the language features of Malay tongues" (p. 154). Further to this comment, the survey report also lists phonological features primarily and also lexical, grammatical, and discourse commentaries on the side relating to Filipino learners' use of English. Clearly, such an exercise is within the tradition of the so-called error and contrastive analysis in applied linguistics (cf. Corder, 1967; Lado, 1957).

The first one to call attention to the emergence of a local English in the Philippines was Llamzon in 1969. Upon his return after studying in the United States, he noticed how Filipinos' use of English was different from that of Americans and even the British yet he did not consider it poorly learned English. In fact, he claimed that English in the Philippines had already reached the point of standardization at that time; hence, he called the emerging local English 'Standard Filipino English'. He listed a few

DOI: 10.4324/9780429427824-20

200 *Ariane Macalinga Borlongan*

Filipinisms, "English expressions which are neither American nor British, which are acceptable and used in Filipino educated circles, and are similar to expression patterns in Tagalog" (p. 46), and sketched the phonology of SPhE.

Though Llamzon's 1969 publication was first received with criticism (i.e. Gonzalez, 1972; Hidalgo, 1970), scholarship on PhE flourished, and, as early as the 1990s, a foreign scholar even remarked that the Philippines has the most extensively studied local variety in Southeast Asia. The first systematic study of PhE was that of Gonzalez in 1985. He was interested in mass media because he believed that it is the place to look for models for a standardized local variety. In his 1991 analysis of Philippine print media, one of his well-known characterizations of PhE came about—that the new English is stylistically homogenous, though this claim has later on been disputed (e.g. Yao & Collins, 2017). Bautista began her descriptive studies of PhE in 1982, outlining the features of the English spoken by Filipino nursemaids, thus focusing on the other end of the lectal continuum, if, as Gonzalez said, mass media is the model for SPhE. She also did the first systematic description of the lexicon of PhE in 1997. However, her single most important work is the compilation of the Philippine component of the International Corpus of English (ICE-PH). The corpus project was compiled together with Loy Lising and Danilo Dayag at De La Salle University (Manila, the Philippines) and is now being directed by Ariane Borlongan at the Tokyo University of Foreign Studies (Japan). The availability of PhE has produced more systematic descriptions of the new English, a sample of these are in Bautista (2011). Tayao (2008) meanwhile wrote a description of PhE phonology.

And then, there is the apparent-time study of Gonzalez, Jambalos, and Romero (2003), who investigated on the perduring features of Philippine English, "recurring 'mistakes' of pronunciation and grammar, not attained by any generation" (p. 109) and could be considered "empirically established features of Philippine English" (p. 109). Ariane Borlongan has also been compiling corpora of PhE of the 1930s and the 1960s (i.e. the Philippine parallels to the Brown and Before-Brown corpora [Phil-Brown and PBB, respectively]). Analyzed alongside ICE-PH which represents PhE of the 1990s, his corpora should allow for a study of PhE in its entire lifetime, and, as such, a new generation of studies of PhE has been born, one which follows the methodology Leech, Hundt, Mair, and Smith (2009) call "short-term diachronic comparable corpus linguistics" (cf. Borlongan & Collins, this handbook).

15.3 Question on the Existence of a Standardized Variety

Llamzon's claim that there is a standardized variety of English in the Philippines had already emerged in 1969 (i.e. "there is a standard variety of English which has arisen in the Philippines [and it] stands or falls on the premise that there is a sizable number of native and near-native speakers of

English in the country" [p. 84]) was "truly radical at that time". He identified the users of this standardized variety he claimed to exist through experiments, described their use of it (focusing on phonology), and ascertained the acceptability of their use of English, which led him to recommend the teaching of the local standard instead of an exonormative one. Gonzalez (1972) and Hidalgo (1970) question primarily his claims of an emerging local variety—standardized, at that—and its 'native speakers' sizable enough.

At present, there is no question about the existence of PhE—and all the other new Englishes, for that matter. Kachru (1992) has made a strong case for the legitimacy of new Englishes; the emerging paradigm has thus claimed ownership for anyone who uses the language and has in effect asserted a pluricentric orientation for the language's standards. Filipino poet Gemino Abad declares, "English is ours. We have colonized it too" (p. 170). Hickey (2012) alludes to 'standards' of English, and explains:

> It may be thought that there is a contradiction here. Part of the popular conception of standard English is that it is a single form of language. But this view refers only to written language and even there it is not wholly true. Across the English-speaking world there is variation in spelling, grammar and vocabulary in those forms of language which would be regarded by their users as standard. When it comes to the spoken word the variation among publicly used varieties of English is considerable, from country to country or often from region to region. A pluralistic conception of standard English is thus likely to be closer to linguistic reality in the societies across the world which use English.
>
> (p. 1)

In 1993, McKaughan pointed toward a goal—'toward a standard Philippine English', as conveyed by the title of his paper. And he explained his title:

> [...] I have chosen 'toward' for a specific reason. This preposition is a directional indicator. The movement involved in the context is toward a goal, but that movement has not yet arrived at the goal. In this case, the goal in view is the idea of a standard Philippine English.
>
> (p. 41)

Recently though, Borlongan (2016) argues that PhE has already reached the point of stabilization. Not only in terms of linguistic structure and description but also the sociopolitical history it is in as well as sociolinguistic identities and attitudes it carries, PhE has attained maturity to be able to rightfully have its own national standard.

And it can now also be confidently said that there are a sizable number of native speakers of PhE with the new definitions of who the native speaker is, i.e. "[some]one who learns English in childhood and continues to use it as his dominant language and has reached a certain level of fluency in terms of

202 *Ariane Macalinga Borlongan*

grammatical well-formedness, speech-act rules, functional elaboration, and code diversity" (Richards & Tay, 1981, p. 53) and

> someone, who was born and/or nurtured (to adolescence and/or be-yond) in that language (possibly, in addition to other languages, in a multilingual context) in a relevant speech community/group, who can successfully use it for his/her daily sociocommunicational needs (and therefore thought processes), and who possesses the (minimal) oral-aural skills (in the language).
>
> (Mann, 2012, pp. 15–16)

In a 2013 nationwide survey, roughly 90% of Filipinos identify themselves as being able to use English at a communicable level (cf. Borlongan, Agoncillo, & Cequeña, 2014), and, with a population of more than a hundred million as of 2018, it is certain that there would be a sizable number of native speakers of PhE, following the quoted definitions of what a native speaker is.

Based on the foregoing discussion, discourses on the standardization of PhE have dwelled on its ideological or sociolinguistic bases so much more than its codification and implementation. In fact, methodologically speak-ing, the descriptive-linguistic aspects of its standardization have not been much of a question to be pondered on but simply rather a long-overdue un-dertaking. That said, SPhE thus exists, and with a sizable number of users.

15.4 Efforts toward Codification

Codification in Haugen's (1966) model of language development involves defining and identifying patterns and norms and making them available to the general public through publication of dictionaries and grammars. Schneider (2003, 2007) notes that dictionaries come first before grammars because grammatical patterns and norms take many years to stabilize, and Mair (2002) also notes that changes in grammar also take longer to be no-ticed than in lexicon. The first attempt for dictionary is Cruz and Bautista's (1995) *A Dictionary of Philippine English*. It was a concise dictionary and was simply an extended listing of putatively PhE lexical items. A more seri-ous endeavor was a regional project spearheaded by Susan Butler, publisher of the *Macquarie Dictionary*, the globally received authoritative work on Australian English. The objective was to produce an Asian English diction-ary which would be based on a corpus of press and literary texts from the region. The dictionary has not been produced and the corpus is sadly gone now after being lost when the computer containing it crashed. There is the *Anvil-Macquarie Dictionary of Philippine English for High School* published by Bautista and Butler in 2000 and in 2010 in its second edition. While it was more extensive than that of Cruz and Bautista, it still leaves much to be desired for a fully fledged national dictionary. It is, for all intents and pur-poses, a pedagogical dictionary as its title suggests. But the inclusion of PhE items in recent updates of the *Oxford English Dictionary* (cf. Salazar, 2017, this handbook) has been a source of national pride among Filipinos, and has clearly contributed to a more positive attitude toward the local English.

A grammar of the verb in PhE was prepared by Borlongan in 2011. It was based on an analysis of a subset of the ICE-PH, and it may possibly be the first comprehensive grammatical description of a new English in that it presents painstaking details regarding the morphology, syntax, and semantics of verbal categories across 32 text types. A few years later, Morales (2015) did the same for adjunct adverbials. Borlongan and Lim (2013) make available an outline of the grammar of PhE and it may be juxtaposed with the other 80 or so Englishes documented in the Electronic World Atlas of Varieties of English (eWAVE) of Kortmann and Lunkenheimer (2015).

Two empirical studies attempted to define the lexical and grammatical features of SPhE, that of Borlongan (2007) and Bautista (2000), respectively. But Hickey (2012) quips no layperson would actually consult these empirical papers in linguistics for notions of what the standard is. That aside, since it was fundamental to these two studies that they determine which usages could become a feature of SPhE, it is compelling at this point to discuss in more detail the question famously asked by Gonzalez in 1983 as a title of his paper, 'When does an error become a feature of PhE?', a question which propelled later feature-based studies of PhE, a question which, in fact, has also been asked for all Englishes. He tried to answer his own question by saying that an error must have historical precedence and possess communicative efficiency for it to be considered a feature. He gave a more definite answer in a 1985 paper: Frequency of use among the educated elite makes an error acceptable, and, in this, mass media would be truly influential (hence, his analyses of English in Philippine mass media, as has been mentioned earlier). Bautista and Borlongan, in their studies of SPhE found it more realistic, when confronted with actual data, to invoke D'Souza's (1997) criteria for standardization of features of new Englishes. D'Souza says that a usage must be widespread, systematic, and rule-governed, and must be used by educated users in formal situations for it to be considered part of the standard. Meanwhile, in preparing his grammar, Borlongan (2011) conjectured that it is more prudent to be able to distinguish which usages are 'central' and 'typical' (cf. Hunston, 2002) in describing PhE.

Codification of standards may be overt and covert (Hickey, 2012). Overt codification entails the publication of dictionaries and grammars and dissemination of these among the laypeople, primarily through education. Covert codification is the implicit knowledge of users—and also its non-users and those who aspire to be its users—of what counts as part of the standard without having to write these norms. Earlier, it was believed that there is no standard for PhE pronunciation (Bautista, 2000; McKaughan, 1993) yet contemporary speakers of PhE unconsciously associate specific pronunciation as standard, and they could possibly tell that someone's pronunciation is non-standard or even 'substandard'. SPhE pronunciation is

204   *Ariane Macalinga Borlongan*

understandably acrolectal—devoid of any substratal influence. Hegemonic it may sound but, because of the wield of political power of the nation's capital and the influence of the mass media, the perceived standard pronunciation is usually Manila-centric, though this has also been the case for British English (BrE) and London and many other national standards as well. Therefore, it can be said that, insofar as SPhE is concerned, overt codification through grammars and dictionaries is ongoing and there is sufficient academic resource available to be able to define what counts as SPhE lexicon and grammar but SPhE pronunciation remains overtly codified and left to educated speakers' judgment of inclusion in the pool of SPhE speakers.

15.5 Endonormative Model for Language Teaching

In his 1969 landmark publication, Llamzon had already proposed that SPhE be the target in language teaching in the Philippines. However, in 1981, a group of language specialists represented the Philippines at the Southeast Asian Ministers of Education Organization (SEAMEO) Regional Language Centre's seminar titled *Varieties of English and Their Implications for Language Teaching in Southeast Asia* and they decided during the seminar's Philippine workshop that, until SPhE has been codified, General American English would continue to be the target in English language teaching in the Philippines. But as was just described, the description and codification of SPhE, by and large, has been sufficient enough to inform pedagogy and thus, 40 years since that consensus, it might be necessary to revisit the question as to which target variety is appropriate in English language teaching in the Philippines.

Bernardo (2013, 2017, this handbook) has diligently developed a pedagogical model which targets PhE for language teaching. He observes that, while English language teaching in the Philippines does not incorporate the ideologies of the world Englishes paradigm (cf. Kachru, 1992), features of PhE proliferate in the language use of teachers and students as well as their teaching and learning materials. Hence, the acquisition of PhE is inevitable. Thus, he presents a world Englishes and PhE-inspired pedagogy for language classrooms, expounding on the theoretical, methodological, and technical dimensions of such a pedagogy. Focal to such a pedagogy, still according to him, is a five-stage PhE-aware teaching procedure which involves (1) noticing features of PhE, (2) comparing them with those of American English and/or BrE, (3) commenting that these are not errors but variations and innovations, (4) encouraging the use of local English, and (5) getting familiar with features of other Englishes as well.

An important juncture in the move toward an endonormative model in language teaching in particular and standardization of PhE in general is recalibrating tests, whether teacher-made or standardized, and aligning them with SPhE. It seems, this requires more work than codification as it entails not only psychometric, particularly in the case of standardized tests, but also bureaucratic procedures to be carried out by various stakeholders.

Standard Philippine English 205

Admittedly, while efforts toward a more endonormative orientation in English language teaching in the Philippines have significantly progressed recently, much remains to be desired, more specifically in institutionalizing a local model, i.e. an instructive policy from the Philippine Department of Education and Commission on Higher Education indicating that PhE is the target in language teaching.

15.6 Discussion: A Conceptual Model of the Standardization of Philippine English

In 1969, Llamzon defined SPhE as "the type of English which educated Filipinos speak, and which is acceptable in educated Filipino circles" (p. 15). Given the developments in the study of PhE, it might be timely to further his definition, and so SPhE is the national standard of the Philippines. It is primarily used in the government, the academe, and the press as well as in other formal situations in the country. Its norms, including its description, therefore are based on English language use in these situations. The use of English in these contexts, like its norms and description, is to a large extent a by-product of the positive judgment accorded to it, which leads particular usages to be included in the so-called standard. Ideally, pronunciation should not carry any regional accent but, because of the prominence of the nation's capital, prestige may be associated with Manila accent.

It might be appropriate to give an integration of the discourses on the standardization of PhE by presenting this conceptual model (Figure 15.1)

The process begins with anecdotal observations being made during the early years of English in the Philippines. These observations are primarily notes on what new learners of English in the country are not able to master

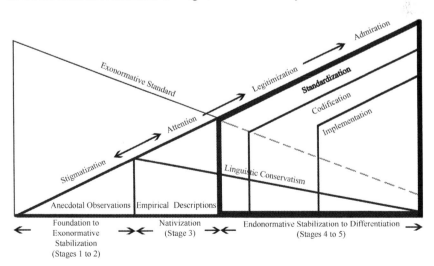

Figure 15.1 A Conceptual Model of the Standardization of Philippine English.

206   *Ariane Macalinga Borlongan*

very well despite the relatively efficacious language instruction they receive, and are within, as mentioned earlier, the contrastive and/or error analysis approach (cf. Corder, 1967; Lado, 1957). Needless to say, at this point in time, the exonormative standard General AmE is accorded a very high status in society. In fact, there is no competition for it at all, except that there is growing awareness that Filipino learners are not able to reach this standard both in controlled and in actual language use. Expectedly, attitudes toward these learners' language use, particularly as perceived by their American teachers, are of stigmatization, though, occasionally as a side note, there is also acknowledgment that their language use might be just the same as those pre-existing, naturally occurring variations across the English-using world (cf. Borlongan, 2018).

When nativization begins, Filipinos, and also Americans and other nationalities as well, come to realize that a localized English is emerging. Attention is no longer given to errors in learning English but to the so-called 'PhE'. Yet there is still intuitive objection to this new English, obviously a manifestation of linguistic conservatism. Indeed, this localized English has drawn attention from scholars and non-scholars alike but, due to linguistic conservatism, it is possible that there may still be a relapse of stigmatization toward it, and this is signaled by the double-headed arrow between stigmatization and attention. That there is an emerging local English triggers awareness that an exonormative standard may be unrealistic and, hence, its prestige continues to decline as depicted by its downward slope.

The significant turning point is the dawn of endonormative stabilization, which begins the actual process of standardization of PhE. It is defined in the model by a bold font and thick border, appropriately so, because it is the centerpiece of the model after all. As the (standardizing/standardized) local is legitimized (primarily through education), the exonormative standard is sent to the background—and hence it is represented by broken lines once actual standardization steps in—and its prestige sees a continuous decline. The exonormative standard in broken lines conspicuously intersects the quadrilaterals for standardization and codification (subsumed in the former) to convey not the indirect correlation between the regard for the exonormative standard and the emergence of an endonormative one made more apparent by its codification. Residual linguistic conservatism also follows the same trajectory. As codification is an element of endonormative stabilization (cf. Borlongan, 2016, this handbook; Schneider, 2003, 2007), dictionaries and grammars are prepared (Bautista & Butler, 2000, 2010; Borlongan, 2011) and PhE lexical items even get to enter dictionaries of global readership (Salazar, 2017, this handbook). The implementation of an endonormative standard is realized primarily when it becomes the target in language teaching (cf. Bernardo, 2013, 2017, this handbook) and results in admiration of (standardized) PhE, even if the exonormative standard remains useful if only for its marginal role as a primary basis for international comparison. Vestiges of Haugen's (1966) classic model on language development thus appear in the model presented here, and rightly so, because it extends the model of Haugen to a new language variety. Linguistic conservatism would have vanished, or, at least, reduced to a point of very low consciousness in the society at large and so it is almost invisible.

The model does not intend to overlook the fact that standardization is a perpetually ongoing process, that it is never a neat, linear progression. But these irregularities should not be so glaring as to make the model totally faulty; as with any proposed (conceptual) model, the primary intention is to represent generalizable tendencies rather than capture every detail in an indiscriminate fashion.

At present, PhE can be located in the middle of codification but there is enough reason to believe that it will reach the end of the process as this chapter has so visualized.

References

Bautista, Maria Lourdes S. (1982). *Yaya* English. *Philippine Studies, 30*, 377–394.

Bautista, Maria Lourdes S. (1997). The lexicon of Philippine English. In Maria Lourdes S. Bautista (Ed.), *English is an Asian language: The Philippine context (Proceedings of the conference held in Manila on August 2–3, 1996)* (pp. 49–72). North Ryde, Australia: The Macquarie Library Pty Ltd.

Bautista, Maria Lourdes S. (2000). *Defining Standard Philippine English: Its status and grammatical features.* Manila, the Philippines: De La Salle University Press, Inc.

Bautista, Maria Lourdes S. (Ed.), (2011). *Studies of Philippine English: Exploring the Philippine component of the International Corpus of English.* Mandaluyong, the Philippines: Anvil Publishing, Inc.

Bautista, Maria Lourdes S., & Butler, Susan. (Eds.). (2000). *Anvil-Macquarie Philippine English dictionary.* Pasig, the Philippines: Anvil Publishing, Inc.

Bautista, Maria Lourdes S., & Butler, Susan. (Eds.). (2010). *Anvil-Macquarie Philippine English dictionary* (Revised ed.). Pasig, the Philippines: Anvil Publishing, Inc.

Bernardo, Alejandro S. (2013). *Toward an endonormative pedagogic model for teaching English in Philippine higher education institutions* (Unpublished doctoral dissertation). University of Santo Tomas, Manila, the Philippines.

Bernardo, Alejandro S. (2017). Philippine English in the ESL classroom: A much closer look. *The Philippine ESL Journal, 19*, 117–144.

The Board of Educational Survey. (1925). *A survey of the educational system of the Philippine Islands.* Manila, the Philippines: Bureau of Printing.

Borlongan, Ariane Macalinga. (2007). Innovations in Standard Philippine English. In Charles C. Mann (Ed.), *Current research on English and applied linguistics: A De La Salle University special issue* (pp. 1–36). Manila, the Philippines: De La Salle University-Manila, College of Education, Department of English and Applied Linguistics.

Borlongan, Ariane Macalinga. (2011). *A grammar of the verb in Philippine English* (Unpublished doctoral dissertation). De La Salle University, Manila, the Philippines.

208 *Ariane Macalinga Borlongan*

Borlongan, Ariane Macalinga. (2016). Relocating Philippine English in Schneider's dynamic model. *Asian Englishes, 18*(3), 1–10.

Borlongan, Ariane Macalinga. (2018). Early Philippine English: A historical sociolinguistic analysis of *A survey of the educational system of the Philippine Islands* (1925). Paper presented at the special plenary panel on Philippine English at the 23rd Annual Conference of the International Association for World Englishes, Quezon, the Philippines.

Borlongan, Ariane Macalinga, & Lim, JooHyuk. (2013). Philippine English. In Bernd Kortmann & Kerstin Lunkenheimer (Eds.), *The electronic world atlas of varieties of English*. Leipzig, Germany: Max Planck Institute for Evolutionary Anthropology. Available from the Electronic World Atlas of Varieties of English website: http://www.ewave-atlas.org/

Corder, S. P. (1967). The significance of learner's errors. *International Review of Applied Linguistics in Language Teaching, V*, 161–170.

Cruz, Isagani R., & Bautista, Ma. Lourdes S. (1995). *A dictionary of Philippine English*. Pasig, the Philippines: Anvil Publishing, Inc.

D'Souza, Jean. (1998). Review of Arjuna Parakrama's *De-hegemonizing language standards: Learning from (post)colonial Englishes about "English"*. *Asian Englishes, 1*(2), 86–94.

Gonzalez, Andrew. (1972). Review of Teodoro A. Llamzon's *Standard Filipino English*. *Philippine Journal of Language Teaching, 7*(1–2), 93–98.

Gonzalez, Andrew. (1985). *Studies on Philippine English*. Singapore: SEAMEO Regional Language Centre.

Gonzalez, Andrew. (1991). Stylistic shifts in the English of Philippine print media. In Jenny Cheshire (Ed.), *English around the world: Sociolinguistic perspectives* (pp. 333–363). Cambridge, the United Kingdom: Cambridge University Press.

Gonzalez, Andrew, Jambalos, Thelma V., & Romero, Ma. Corona S. (2003). *Three studies on Philippine English across generations: Towards an integration and some implications*. Manila, the Philippines: Linguistic Society of the Philippines.

Haugen, Einar. (1966). Dialect, language, nation. *American Anthropologist, 68*, 922–935.

Hickey, Raymond. (2012). Standard English and standards of English. In Raymond Hickey (Ed.), *Standards of English: Codified varieties around the world* (pp. 1–33). Cambridge, the United Kingdom: Cambridge University Press.

Hidalgo, Cesar A. (1970). Review of Teodoro A. Llamzon's *Standard Filipino English*. *Philippine Journal of Linguistics, 1*(1), 129–132.

Hunston, Susan. (2002). *Corpora in applied linguistics*. Cambridge, the United Kingdom: Cambridge University Press.

Kachru, Braj B. (1992). World Englishes: Approaches, issues and resources. *Language Teaching, 25*, 1–14.

Kortmann, Bernd, & Lunkenheimer, Kerstin. (2015). (Eds.), *The electronic world atlas of varieties of English*. Leipzig, Germany: Max Planck Institute for Evolutionary Anthropology. Available from the Electronic World Atlas of Varieties of English website: http://www.ewave-atlas.org/

Lado, Robert. (1957). *Linguistics across cultures: Applied linguistics for teachers*. Ann Arbor: University of Michigan Press.

Leech, Geoffrey, Marianne Hundt, Christian Mair, & Nicholas Smith. (2009). *Change in contemporary English: A grammatical study*. Cambridge, the United Kingdom: Cambridge University Press.

Llamzon, Teodoro A. (1969). *Standard Filipino English*. Quezon, the Philippines: Ateneo University Press.

Mair, Christian. (2002). *Twentieth-century English: History, variation and standardization*. Cambridge, the United Kingdom: Cambridge University Press.

Mann, Charles C. (2012). We wuz robbed, inni'?: Towards reconceptualizing the "native speaker". *Journal of English as an International Language, 7*(2), 1–24.

McKaughan, Howard P. (1993). Toward a Standard Philippine English. *Philippine Journal of Linguistics, 24*(2), 41–55.

Morales, Miren M. (2015). *A grammar of adjunct adverbials in Philippine English* (Unpublished doctoral dissertation). De La Salle University, Manila, the Philippines.

Richards, Jack C., & Tay, Mary W. J. (1981). Norm and variability in language use and language learning. In Larry E. Smith (Ed.), *English for cross-cultural communication* (pp. 40–56). London, the United Kingdom: Macmillan.

Salazar, Danica. (2017). Philippine English in the *Oxford English Dictionary*: Recent advancements and implications for ESL in the Philippines. *The Philippine ESL Journal, 19*, 45–59.

Schneider, Edgar W. (2003). The dynamics of new Englishes: From identity construction to dialect birth. *Language, 79*, 233–281.

Schneider, Edgar W. (2007). *Postcolonial English: Varieties of English around the world*. Cambridge, the United Kingdom: Cambridge University Press.

SEAMEO Regional Language Centre. (1981). *Report of the regional seminar on varieties of English and their implications for language teaching in Southeast Asia*. Singapore: The Author.

Tayao, Ma. Lourdes G. (2008). A lectal description of the phonological features of Philippine English. In Ma. Lourdes S. Bautista & Kingsley Bolton (Eds.), *Philippine English: Linguistic and literary perspectives* (pp. 157–174). Hong Kong SAR, China: Hong Kong University Press.

Yao, Xinyue, & Collins, Peter. (2017). Exploring grammatical colloquialisation in a non-native English: A case study of Philippine English. *English Language & Linguistics, 21*, 1–26.

16 Philippine Literature in English[1]

Isagani R. Cruz

If there is anything that Philippine writers in English love doing more than writing about Philippine literature in English, it is talking about it. On 25 February 1940, during the First Filipino Writers' Conference on Modern Literary Objectives, there were heated debates about English as a literary language. Some of the arguments raised during those debates were collected in *Literature under the Commonwealth* (1940), edited by Manuel E. Arguilla et al., and are still available in the 1973 reprint by Alberto S. Florentino. Twenty-four years later, in March 1964, the same arguments were raised by another generation of Philippine writers at a panel discussion on "Philippine Literature in the Next Decade: A Forward Look." Three of the papers at that panel were published in 1964, again by Florentino, as *Literature and Society: A Symposium on the Relation of Literature to Society* (1964). After more than half a century, this chapter once again rehashes the same old tired arguments and to get excited about the future, if any, of Philippine literature in English.

In 1940 writers in English were concerned about the known views of Manuel L. Quezon, which the charismatic president reaffirmed in his speech during the conference itself, about the relationship of English to Tagalog. "It is completely in your hands," he told the writers,

> whether Filipino literature in English will endure or not, and I want to ask you to do all you can to preserve it forever in the Philippines. I want you to know that I am going to do away, if not immediately, with the use of English as the medium of instruction in the primary schools.

That repudiation of English extended, as far as Quezon was concerned, only to the question of the medium of instruction. He quickly added that "We must have some other language in the Philippines besides Tagalog." Master political manipulator that he was, Quezon placated the writers immediately by insisting that "We have to write in English or in Spanish so that the world may take notice of the advances we are making in the arts, in letters, and in science" (Arguilla 11).

DOI: 10.4324/9780429427824-21

Philippine Literature in English   211

Salvador P. Lopez was one of those listening to Quezon. Writing in his Commonwealth Literary Contest award-winning *Literature and Society* (1940), Lopez described the president as having "so adequately grasped the false and illogical implications of the sentimental argument often advanced in favor of Tagalog that there is hardly any warrant for expatiating any further upon this point" (239). In effect, Lopez thought that it would have been possible to continue writing in English even if schoolchildren learned their 3Rs in Tagalog. In fact, if the war had not stopped Quezon from implementing his language policy, the removal of English as a medium of instruction in the primary grades would have inevitably resulted in the loss of a language as a literary medium as well, as the writers in the 1960s eventually argued.

The 1940 event is usually viewed in light of the famous exchange between Arturo B. Rotor, whose conference paper "Our Literary Heritage" became the manifesto of the powerful Philippine Writers League, and Alfredo E. Litiatco, whose post-conference series articles in the *Graphic*, entitled "Dictatorship in Literature," provoked the 16 June 1940 clarificatory resolution of the League, which stated, among other things, that "In an atmosphere of cultural freedom, no one can presume to dictate what subject matter an artist should deal with or how he should handle it" (Arguilla 65). The key document of the entire controversy, however, is Carlos P. Romulo's quiet "Will Filipino Literature in English Endure?" Romulo later repudiated the ideas in this document in a famous speech at the 1962 writers' conference, a speech that James F. Donelan S.J. described as "one of the turning points in the history of Filipino literature" (Florentino 45). By 1962, Romulo (and Donelan) had lost hope that Filipinos could produce great literature in English, but in 1940, Romulo still had, like most writers of his generation, enormous confidence in the Filipinos' ability to write in English.

The young Romulo diffidently declared, "I personally don't believe that English will ever be completely displaced by the national language." Even in 1940, however, he already suspected that the mere presence of the English language in the country did not guarantee its continued existence as a literary language: "There will always be a place for English in the Philippines, but to say this is not also to say that Filipino literature in English will survive." Although on the side of English, Romulo then was realistic enough to realize that "the question of endurance is more than a matter of government policy" (about the medium of instruction in primary schools):

Another question which Filipino writers in English must face is this: Does Filipino literature in English have in itself qualities of endurance, and do Filipino writers have the capacity to put these into their work?

212   *Isagani R. Cruz*

For apart from the fortunes of the English language in the Philippines, we must consider the question of whether Filipino literature in English has already developed, during the brief period of its existence, qualities that will enable it to endure.

(Arguilla 13–16)

Romulo answered *yes* to both his questions, but that was 1940. When he became president of the University of the Philippines in the 1960s, he championed Tagalog over English and never hesitated to say so. It was not just nationalism. He was convinced, by 1962, that the high regard he had for Filipino writing in English in 1940 was misplaced.

The generally anti-English atmosphere of the 1960s may partly explain the pessimistic tone of the 1962 revival of the 1940 debates. Gregorio Brillantes, Wilfrido Nolledo, and Jose V. Ayala of the new generation took turns lamenting the lack of writers in English. Indeed, by that time, many of the great names of the 1940s seemed to have had their best works behind them. Nick Joaquin was in the 1964 symposium, but was not as pessimistic. To Joaquin, "there are many young writers in English, and they are doing something to the English language: it is no longer simple English; not the English of America or England, but *their* English" (quoted in Bernad 794).

That is how Miguel A. Bernad S.J., writing in *Brown Heritage* (1967), reported the symposium, though Bernad himself hedged his bets, preferring to simply outline the "ideal conditions for the untrammeled development of a healthy Philippine literature in English" in his "The Future of Philippine Literature." These conditions, to Bernad, were writers "who can write in English"

That is to say, who are at home in the idiom—not only in its grammar or vocabulary, but also in its peculiar genius and its nuances: for every language has a peculiar genius which is distinctive to its patterns of thought, and no writer can become great in any language unless he makes these patterns of thought his own;

a reading public ("unless writing is made profitable, very few will continue to write"); a "common cultural language" ("a community of cultural heritage between readers and writers, a common fund of cultural experience, and common terms of reference"); and a "theological dimension" in the writer's vision (794–798). In effect, by putting such stringent conditions on writing in English, Bernad was subconsciously, if not consciously, predicting the disappearance of English as a literary language.

Bernad's changing views about English in literature are otherwise well-known. In *Bamboo and the Greenwood Tree* (1961), he was more comfortable with the level of English of Filipino writers:

There is nothing incongruous in the fact that when Filipinos write, they write, for the most part, in English. This is no more strange than that

Philippine Literature in English 213

South Americans, whose ancestry may be Aztec or Inca or some other non-European race, should speak and write Spanish as their own native tongue.

(5)

In the often-anthologized "Philippine Literature: Perpetually Inchoate" (1962), however, he became less triumphalistic about English, deploring instead the "linguistic difficulty" facing Filipino writers:

> It is possible to produce great literature only in a language that has been mastered. By "mastered" is meant more than mere grammatical or idiomatic mastery. It must be the type of mastery which assimilates the thought processes, the verbal nuances and the characteristic rhythms peculiar to an idiom. Every language has its peculiar genius: he is master of the language who has caught that genius. Unfortunately the Philippines has not had a thorough chance to assimilate the genius of any particular language.

(377)

In *Philippine Literature: A Twofold Renaissance* (1963), Bernad changed his mind again, placing his trust in Philippine literature in English:

> It is, then, in this vigorous and sophisticated literature in English that the hope of the Philippine literature chiefly lies. It is a self-conscious literature, and this may be one of its weaknesses; but it is also a daring literature, unafraid to experiment.

(27)

If the 1940s saw English as a great addition to both Tagalog and Spanish, already well-established literary languages for Filipino writers, and if the 1960s doubted the ability of Filipino writers to use English well enough in order to maintain it as a literary language, how *could* we possibly see the future of Philippine literature in English?

In *World Englishes: Journal of English as an International and Intranational Language*, I argued in a paper entitled "English and Tagalog in Philippine Literature: A Study of Literary Bilingualism" (1986) that Filipinos use the two languages for different purposes. Bilingual writers, particularly poets such as Cirilo F. Bautista, Edgar B. Maranan, and Epifanio San Juan Jr., use English to capture certain realities not within the lexical capabilities of Tagalog and to exploit the musical qualities of the foreign language: they use Tagalog to capture nationalist realities. In broad terms, English is used primarily to enhance form and Tagalog to enhance content. The linguistic implications of this literary thesis were spelled out by James E. Alatis in his "Afterword: Conference and Beyond," originally the "Synthesis of Conference Papers/Directions for [the] Future" of the *East-West Center Conference*

214   *Isagani R. Cruz*

on Language as Power: Cross-Cultural Dimensions of English in Media and Literature (6–13 August 1986). Alatis says of my paper:

> Isagani Cruz claims that English currently lacks the power to develop a nationalist literature in the Philippines, at least in poetry. From this stimulating paper developed a controversy that we encountered several times in the conference: Are there certain inherent linguistic character- istics in the English language, regardless where it is used, which equip it for certain sociolinguistic domains and literary genres, such as lyrical poetry in the Philippines? Or are the uses for which English is consid- ered appropriate more a function of users' attitudes toward English and other languages in their total linguistic repertoires, including, for exam- ple, Tagalog in the Philippines? The conventional axiom in linguistics has long been that any language can undergo structural modification and the allocation of new functions to existing structures in order to express any values, belief or speech act in any setting. ... Given the fre- quency of claims at the conference regarding "inherent features of Eng- lish at all linguistic levels, further empirical research may be called for."
>
> (277)

I do not claim that my view of English as an inherently limited language for literary purposes in the Philippines is mainstream linguistic theory, but its acknowledged challenge to linguistic research clearly shows, at least, that it is a serious view that has to be disproven empirically before it is dismissed. I cannot even claim that my view is mainstream literary theory. The *First National Consultative Conference on Literary Theories* (13–15 November 1987), for example, failed to address the question of literary language; that failure, in the light of more than a half-century-old controversy on literary language, is itself significant: perhaps the question of literary language has finally lost its emotional appeal.

What I do claim is that the question of English as a literary language for Filipino writers must be viewed not only a priori, as a linguistic or theoret- ical question, but empirically, as a historical or critical question. Those of our writers who have the facility to write in both English and a vernacular language appear, after my initial investigation as I reported to the Honolulu conference, to prefer English to experiment with form and the vernacular language to communicate. From the point of view of literary history, then, English will remain as a literary language in order to enable our writers to interact with the formal tradition (in T.S. Eliot's sense of the term) of Western literature. The nationalist view of a national language as symbolic of anti-colonial aspirations, on the other hand, has led to an elitization (not equivalent to intellectualization) of Tagalog writing.

From the point of view of literary criticism, English can be seen as eas- ier to manipulate because of its "inherent" musical superiority to Tagalog (English, for instance, has a greater variety of end sounds available to the

Philippine Literature in English 215

poet who uses rhyme). Tagalog, on the other hand, is easier to use for directly political purposes, not only because of the colloquial familiarity of its words, but also because many of the exact nuances of Filipino attitudes and feelings are unavailable in English. These two functions of literature are not equivalent to "domains" in linguistics, but they point to the kind of dichotomy or binary opposition that structuralists such as Tzvetan Todorov love to construct.

From the point of view of literary theory, particularly the theory of translation, a literary target language is not capable of capturing all the literary meanings in a source language. If the New Critics and the early poststructuralists were right about the allusive or intertextual quality of words (i.e. if any word in any text alludes to every other use of the word in earlier texts), then the very change of word or even the change of sound (contrary to early Saussurean Structuralist thought) theoretically diminishes the meaning of the literary work. It cannot be said, then, that English can "express" any meaning, because some meanings are available only in other languages.

I cannot claim to represent the 1980s, despite my belonging to the correct chronological generation. There are some even today who still raise the question of language in literary conferences such as those sponsored by the Philippine Center of International PEN or the Writers Union of the Philippines. Many of the points raised by those in my generation or by those who belong to an even later generation are identical to those raised by Romulo, Rotor, Litiatco, and company. In many ways, the early essay of Romulo, though later disavowed by him, is the last word on the subject. What I can claim is that my generation can look at literary questions such as the question of language from the point of view of literary theory, surely something not available to those in the 1940s and even to those in the 1960s.

As a literary theorist, what do I see as the future if any of Philippine literature in English?

First, the English that Philippine writers use is not the English language that language planners talk about. Recent theorizing about literary reading (such as that by Hirsch) shows that the reading of a literary work demands much more than just linguistic competence. Even if theorists today have already dismissed Jonathan Culler's term "literary competence" together with the rest of naïve Structuralism, the term still has practical use. The difficulty that a reader encounters in reading Philippine poetry in English has less to do with understanding the words, for the words may be perfectly understandable, as in many of Jose Garcia Villa's or of Ma. Fatima Lim's poems, than in comprehending what Bernad calls the "common cultural language" (what Hirsch calls "cultural literacy"). Even in an inner-circle culture in which the English language is the native or even the only language, such as Midwest America, for example, a poem by Villa or Lim may be completely opaque, not for linguistic reasons at all.

If this is true, then no amount of linguistic competence, brought about by increased hours of study of the language or even by the use of English

216   *Isagani R. Cruz*

as a medium of instruction or even by massive exposure to mass media in English, can guarantee literary literacy. Only cultural competence can do that, and information about culture is not language-specific. Americans can understand the *Iliad* without knowing a word of Greek, as long as they are provided with the historical, cultural, and artistic backgrounds of the work. In terms of understanding Philippine writing in English, the issue of which language to use in school is a non-issue. I am, in other words, supporting Quezon's stand, but contradicting that of Lopez, as well as that of Leopoldo Yabes in the latter's professorial chair lecture on "English in the Next Twenty Years" (1977).

Second, the use or non-use of English need not be seen as a political issue anymore. During the first Philippine revolution, Tagalog was seen as an affirmation of nationhood, a kind of symbol, like a flag, of separating from the colonial power. Quezon's advocacy of Tagalog was more pragmatic: as he said in his speech to the writers, he could not be an effective president of a people who could not understand his words (Arguilla 9). The subsequent fortunes of Tagalog, ably documented by Andrew Gonzalez in his *Language and Nationalism* (1980), show how the non-literary criterion of nationalism combined with pragmatism to produce an image of vernacular languages as superior in some way to borrowed languages. Fortunately, the pressure to use vernacular languages is no longer as overbearing. Today, the choice of language is more often dictated by practical (what print space and what fees are available to writers in Tagalog, in Waray, in English, in Spanish, and so on) rather than ideological considerations. In an atmosphere where the use of a language no longer invites strong political repercussions, writers are free to choose a language on aesthetic grounds. Left to themselves, writers will choose English if the language is suited to what they are trying to do. There is, in other words, one less obstacle to the progress of English as a literary language.

Third, a literature in a language will flourish only if a community of readers exists intertextually in that language. In non-critical jargon, this means that Philippine literature in English will survive if and only if there are readers who are educated enough to have read a lot of English poems, plays, short stories, and novels written by Filipinos. In addition, these readers must have read works written by Filipinos in other languages, particularly Tagalog and Spanish. Moreover, these readers must have read works written by non-Filipinos in English, as well as in other languages (the last arguably through translations). In short, in the taxonomy of readers in Reader-Response Criticism, Filipinos have to be educated to become ideal readers of Philippine texts in English.

Finally, will there be a Philippine literature in English 'after Throry' (after Theory)? At the end of the 19th century, physicists loudly proclaimed that everything to be discovered by the 20th century was going to be a footnote to their research. Then came Albert Einstein and relativity: the paradigm shift in physics occurred right after the paradigms of the 19th century

Philippine Literature in English 217

had just been canonized. Similarly, at the end of the 19th century, Spanish seemed unshakable from its perch as the foremost literary language for Filipinos. After all, had we not produced Jose Rizal, acclaimed even then as one of the world's master writers? Then came English. (I am deliberately ignoring, in order not to mix my metaphors or complicate my tropes, our vernacular literatures.) If we now proclaim loudly that literature in English is here to stay forever, we run the risk of being footnotes to Einstein's theories or of being translators of Rizal's novels.

My stand is that we cannot tell what the future will bring. Whatever it brings, it will not be something we expect. I suspect that, 20 years from now, some young writer is going to take this chapter and laugh at how I could have missed such an obvious thing as—what? That Chinese has become the main literary language? That a major novel in Bahasa Melayu has been written by a Filipino? That Filipino has become a world language and, like Esperanto, is used in international conventions? That the United States has finally become bilingual and, Filipinos being colonially minded, Filipino writers have started to write in Spanish again in imitation of their American masters? That the Philippines has finally joined the emergent communist nations and Filipino writers are learning to write in Vietnamese? That the Americans have regained colonial control of the country through Hawaii, and Filipino writers are writing poems in the ethnic language of the Hawaiians, the way we followed Mexican ways in the days of the galleons?

Who can predict the future? Romulo tried to do it, and he had to change his mind 20 years after. If he were alive today, if he saw the enormous number and relatively high quality of Philippine writing in English today, he would doubtless change his mind again. Before him, Rizal tried to do it by writing, in Spanish, that Filipinos should write in Tagalog. Balagtas tried to do it, only to have his language repudiated by a generation of writers who wanted a fresh, modernistic Tagalog. I am sure our ancestral writers, long before Magellan lost his way among our islands, were predicting that the literary language of the future would be Maranao or Mangyan or any of the ethnic languages which boasted even then of a rich epic literature. I am clearly not the first, nor will I be the last, to boldly see the future that no one has seen or can even imagine. My prediction is simple: Philippine literature in English will survive, but it will not be in English.

Note

1 An earlier version of this paper was presented at the *Solidarity Seminar on Language and Development*. Solidarity. Solidaridad Bookshop, Manila. 12 December 1987, and was published in *The Role of English and its Maintenance in the Philippines: The Transcript, Consensus, and Papers of the Solidarity Seminar on Language and Development*. Ed. Andrew B. Gonzalez. Manila: Solidaridad Publishing House, 1988, 125–133.

218   *Isagani R. Cruz*

References

Arguilla, Manuel E., et al. (eds). 1940, 1973. *Literature under the Commonwealth*. Manila: Philippine Writers League. Reprinted in Manila by Alberto S. Florentino.

Bernad, Miguel A., S.J. 1961. *Bamboo and the Greenwood Tree*. Manila: Bookmark.

Bernad, Miguel A., S.J. 1971. *Philippine Literature, a Twofold Renaissance*. Manila: Bookmark.

Florentino, Alberto S. (ed.). 1965. Literature at the Crossroads: 3 Symposia on the Filipino Novel, Filipino Poetry, the Filipino Theater, Sponsored by the Congress for Cultural Freedom. Manila: Alberto S. Florentino.

Lopez, Salvador P. 1940. *Literature and Society: Essays on Life and Letters*. Manila: University Book Supply.

Manuud, Antonio G. (ed.). 1967. *Brown Heritage: Essays on Philippine Cultural Tradition and Literature*. Quezon City: Ateneo de Manila University Press.

Part 5

Psychosociolinguistic Dimensions

17 Intelligibility

Shirley N. Dita and Kristine D. de Leon

17.1 Introduction

The global spread of English has led to a valid concern: that speakers of different varieties of English will soon become unintelligible to one another. Intelligibility has long been the subject of investigations from various scholars dating back more than half a century ago (see Bansal, 1969; Catford, 1950; Irvine, 1977; Smith & Rafiqzad, 1979). Over the years, there have been varying definitions of intelligibility. In fact, there is no universally agreed upon definition of what constitutes this construct, nor is there an agreed upon way of measuring it (Derwing & Munro, 2005; Jenkins, 2000). Intelligibility is the cover term to refer to the degree of success in communication. Catford (1950) opines that intelligibility can be detected and gauged by the effectiveness of communication in purpose. Simply said, it refers to the appropriate response to purpose in speaking. Kenworthy (1987) has a similar take on it, explaining that intelligibility means that the listener has understood the utterances in a given situation and time. Munro and Derwing (1995), on the other hand, redefine the concept of intelligibility by adapting three constructs—intelligibility, comprehensibility, and accentedness. Intelligibility as "extent to which speaker' utterance is understood" (p. 112), comprehensibility as "to the listener's estimation of difficulty in understanding an utterance" (p. 112), and accentedness as "the degree to which the pronunciation of an utterance sounds different from an expected production pattern" (p. 112). Although the common ground of all these definitions is 'understanding', Smith (1992) argues that understanding should be divided into three categories: intelligibility, comprehensibility, and interpretability. These three concepts constitute the Smith paradigm, also known as the tripartite definition: intelligibility refers to the listener's ability to recognize words and utterances of a speech; comprehensibility refers to the ability of the listener to understand the meaning of words in a given context; and interpretability refers to the ability of the listener to understand the intended meaning or the implicature behind the words of the speaker (Smith & Nelson, 1985, 2006). To illustrate the difference between

DOI: 10.4324/9780429427824-23

222 *Shirley N. Dita and Kristine D. de Leon*

intelligibility and comprehensibility, Dita (2018) shares a personal narrative of her experience in South Africa while looking for a Catholic church:

D: (to a police officer): Hey, I'm looking for the Catholic church on this street, as the map says.

POLICE OFFICER: Walk further down and when you see a robot, turn right.

D: (missed the robot so she asked another PO the same question): Hey, was looking for the church and the guy over there pointed me to this direction.

PO: Yeah, turn left after the robot!

D: But I didn't see any robot at all!

The conversation above shows that 'robot' is intelligible, as evident in the last line when D claimed that she didn't see any robot at all. However, 'robot' seems totally incomprehensible to D since she missed the 'robots', or the 'traffic lights' in South Africa.

This notion of intelligibility, as one aspect of intelligibility as a whole, has also been the working definition of studies on intelligibility of Philippine English (PhE). Thus, this chapter probes on PhE intelligibility to other speakers of English, factors affecting PhE intelligibility, issues and significance of PhE intelligibility.

17.2 Philippine English Intelligibility to Speakers of Other Englishes

Various studies have investigated how one variety is intelligible to another (cf. Smith, 1992; Smith &Rafiqzad, 1979). In the Philippines context, this line of pursuit started way before the emergence of indigenized varieties of English. Bautista (2000) sums up into three strands the studies on PhE in the 60s to 90s: status of PhE as a variety of English, linguistic features of PhE, intelligibility and acceptability of PhE. It should be noted that during this time, the notion of American English (AmE) as 'standard' was the norm. The study of Aquino, Duque, Pimentel, and Rojas (1966) compared AmE against PhE with and without phonemic distinction. Findings show that PhE is less intelligible than AmE and that PhE without phonemic distinction is less intelligible than PhE with phonemic distinction. Following the study of Aquino et al. (1966), Tucker (1968) investigated whether PhE is favorable compared to AmE and vice versa. Findings reveal that American group reading English was the most favorable, Filipino group reading English less favorable, and Filipino group reading Tagalog least favorable. Put simply, the study showed highly positive ratings of AmE compared to PhE. Luzares and Bautista (1972), likewise, replicated Tucker (1968) and added another group—American group reading Tagalog passage, which resulted in being less favorable than Filipino reading Tagalog group. The study concludes that AmE was undeniably more prestigious than PhE.

Intelligibility 223

PhE is among the included varieties in Smith and Rafiqzad's (1979) very extensive study on the intelligibility. Although PhE did not land on the top four most intelligible varieties, it is still considered moderately intelligible. For several decades, no investigation has been made regarding the intelligibility of PhE until Dayag (2007) explored the intelligibility of Philippine English by employing mesolectal speaker of PhE and listeners from the three circles of Kachru's concentric circles—inner, outer, and expanding circles. It was then revealed that PhE is highly intelligible, more or less 80% intelligible, to inner and outer circles, but it is only moderately intelligible (50%) to the expanding circle. Dita (2013), on the other hand, investigated the intelligibility and comprehensibility of PhE to Asian international students using proficient and less proficient speakers of PhE. The less proficient speaker, as results show, is more intelligible than the proficient speaker. In addition, Dita also argued that pronunciation did not play a crucial role in facilitating intelligibility, as manifested by the less proficient speaker being more intelligible than the more proficient speaker. Following Dayag (2007) and Dita (2013), de Leon (2016) conducted another study on intelligibility of PhE in the Association of Southeast Asian Nations (ASEAN), employing speakers from three lectal varieties due to ASEAN integration. The study shows that the mesolectal speaker of PhE is the most intelligible speaker of PhE compared to the acrolectal speaker and basilectal speaker of PhE. Also, the study presents that PhE is highly intelligible to Filipinos and moderately intelligible to most of the neighboring countries of Philippines, except for Singapore and Brunei which were excluded from the study. Dita and de Leon's (2017) study tweaked the reading passage to include semantically anomalous words to further test the claim of Dita (2013) that linguistic environment aids intelligibility more than 'correct' pronunciation. Additionally, it was found that PhE is less than 60% intelligible to the English as a Foreign Language (EFL) speakers, therefore supporting Dayag's (2007) and de Leon's (2016) claim on the intelligibility of PhE to the listeners from the expanding circles.

Based on the studies on the intelligibility of PhE, it can be deduced that PhE is highly intelligible to listeners from the inner and outer circles, and moderately intelligible to listeners from the expanding circle. And as PhE is claimed to be in endonormative stage (Borlongan, 2016) going to differentiation stage (Gonzales, 2017) of Schneider's Dynamic Model, then having PhE as moderately to highly intelligible to other speakers of English can therefore be significantly valuable in the standardization of PhE. So far, only a number of studies have explored PhE's intelligibility; thus, there is a need to further investigate the intelligibleness of PhE given that there are several factors that come to play and that PhE is becoming one of the recognized Englishes in the world specifically in Asia.

17.3 Factors Affecting PhE Intelligibility

Knowing if a particular variety of English has high, moderate, or low intelligibility does not end there because there are several factors that affect

224 *Shirley N. Dita and Kristine D. de Leon*

intelligibleness. In the case of PhE, based on the studies mentioned, speaker factors and listener factors can positively or negatively contribute to the intelligibility of PhE.

17.3.1 Speaker

For the speaker factors, syllable-timed rhythm and rate of speech are the main factors affecting the intelligibleness of PhE (Dayag, 2007; de Leon, 2016; Dita, 2013; Dita & de Leon, 2017). In PhE, most speakers enunciate every syllable in a given word which consequently slows down the pacing of the speaker since the speaker exerts some effort in enunciating every syllable in a word, unlike AmE where reduced vowels seems to be the norm. Additionally, the rate of speech is a contributory factor in the (un)intelligibleness of PhE, which is the fastness and slowness of the speakers' utterances. In Dita and de Leon (2017), the listeners specifically pointed out that the speakers' slower pace in speaking has contributed largely in the understanding of the utterances. Thus, the slower the speech, the more intelligible it is for the listener.

17.3.2 Listener

For the listener factors, familiarity with the words' pronunciation facilitates the intelligibility of PhE (Dayag, 2007; Dita, 2013; Dita & de Leon, 2016). Although the pronunciation of some words (e.g., margarine pronounced as 'mar-Ga-rin', and not mär-jə-rən) does not conform with the supposed standard AmE, this is the familiar pronunciation for most Filipinos. As evident in Dita's (2013) study where the LP speaker pronounced 'demand' as 'di-man'—the listeners still found this intelligible. Furthermore, the syllable-timed rhythm of PhE speakers, as remarked by participants in Dita and de Leon's (2017) study, is interpreted by the listeners as the speaker's way of enunciating the words more clearly. Compare to AmE, PhE shows very little, if not totally no evident of reduced vowels when speaking. Various studies have espoused that phonology is not particularly a significant factor in intelligibility (Bansal, 1969; Tiffen, 1974). As Hung (2002) argues, intelligibility is not a matter of pronunciation alone. He even suggested various considerations (usefulness, frequency, difficulty, and appropriateness) in teaching pronunciation for enhancing intelligibility. Aside from pronunciation, listening strategies like context clues and linguistic environment (Dita, 2013; Dita & de Leon, 2016) considerably assist the listeners in understanding the utterances of the PhE speaker. This further demonstrates that pronunciation cannot be considered as highly important in intelligibility as the listeners can still identify the words due to support from the context and the linguistic environment of the text. Another factor that can hinder or enhance intelligibility is proficiency (Smith, 1992), but the listener's proficiency was not given much attention in the studies of intelligibility of PhE.

de Leon (2016), however, mentioned that proficiency is not a significant factor in intelligibility, but then it has to be noted that the listeners' proficiency in her study was self-assessed. Therefore, this is one of the factors that has to be looked into. Attitude of the listeners toward PhE is another factor that is considered in the study of the intelligibility given that PhE is not seen as always favorable to other speakers of English (de Leon, 2016; Dita & de Leon, 2017), but then this does not affect the intelligibleness of PhE. One can deduce that even if the listeners did not find a particular variety suiting their taste, they understood the words or the utterances, which led them to overlook the attitude toward PhE. Tan and Castelli (2013) found in their study on the intelligibility of Singapore English (SgE) that attitude does not guarantee intelligibility; although native speakers' English is still emulated and preferred by most Asians.

17.3.3 Linguistic Environment

Dita (2013) argues that the intelligibility of PhE is influenced by linguistic context more than pronunciation. Findings of the study reveal that the low proficient speaker is more intelligible than the moderately proficient speaker. As expected, there were many words that were pronounced differently from the supposed AmE standard (e.g., 'surviving' pronounced as 'ser-vai-ving'). Since the word appears with the phrase 'the storm' in the passage, the listener automatically understands the 'surviving' word, no matter how it is pronounced. Because of this, Dita and de Leon (2017) extended the study by including a passage where the words that need to be filled in the blanks do not make sense at all. For instance, in the phrase 'fire coming from utensil', the listeners still wrote down 'building' or 'house' even if the speaker clearly uttered 'utensil'. This goes to show that linguistic environment facilitates intelligibility more than correct pronunciation. Dita and de Leon did not just experiment on 'differently' pronounced (not mispronounced) words but tried using semantically anomalous words, too, to further test earlier claims of Dita (2013). As Hung (2002) argues, intelligibility is not a matter of pronunciation alone.

17.4 Issues on Philippine English Intelligibility

There are a few issues surrounding the intelligibility of PhE. First, the attitude of, not just the teachers, but the stakeholders of learning institutions toward General American English (GAE) as the only standard English is still upheld up to this time. Since the educational system in the Philippines is greatly influenced by the Americans, the notion of GAE being the absolute standard variety is still very strong in schools. With this, teachers are keen to subscribe to GAE when it comes to English, and this perspective is passed on to their students. And this applies not only to grammar but to all aspects of the language, especially in terms of phonology. Hence, teachers still impose GAE as the target language in classrooms. The teaching of 'correct' pronunciation is the ultimate objective in speech classes or early grade English classes. In short, students are trained to produce near-native English, even if literature supports the fact that native speaker phonology does not appear to be more intelligible than non-native phonology (Smith & Bisazza, 1982; Smith & Rafiqzad, 1979). As a matter of fact, students who do not conform to the GAE are ridiculed, if not punished. Students are not trained to produce what is intelligible or comprehensible, but what is accurate in terms of pronunciation. Second, the question that Rajagopalan (2010) posed, "intelligible for who?" still holds true up to this day. Who decides whether a certain variety is intelligible or not? The truth is, what is intelligible for one may not be intelligible for the other, so how do we assess intelligibility then? In most studies conducted where PhE is included as one of the varieties being measured (cf. Smith, 1992 Smith & Rafiqzad, 1979), the 'listeners' or those assigned as 'judge' whether PhE is intelligible or not may not be the best choice. There are various studies (e.g., Gass & Varonis, 1984; Munro & Derwing, 1995 among others) that espouse that familiarity with the variety could lead to intelligibility. It is therefore not logical to choose as judge of intelligibility those that are not exposed to the variety they are judging. Otherwise, the result of the judging is something predictable already. Third, the prevailing methodology in measuring intelligibility which is the use of the cloze test poses some issues, as well. In cloze test method, the nth word of the transcript is left blank and listeners are to write down what they heard from the speaker (to test the intelligibility of the speaker). However, Dita (2013) noticed that listeners can still figure out the missing word even if they missed what the speaker said because of context clues. For instance, in the phrase "... close the ___", the missing word is quite predictable. The speaker could mispronounce the word and utter 'dur' or 'dowr' but the listeners will still write the word 'door' as the linguistic environment highly suggests so. Due to this potential problem, Dita and de Leon (2017) modified the methodology a bit and used semantically anomalous words for the blanks so that listeners had to gauge the intelligibility of the words. Surprisingly, there were still a number of listeners who insisted on writing the logical answer over the semantically anomalous word since, as they commented, "'the uttered word does not make any sense at all". This now leaves the question "what could be the most reliable method to gauge the one's intelligibility". Some studies (Kirkpatrick) looked into mutual intelligibility instead.

Lastly, in all studies on the intelligibility of PhE, only the 'educated' English has so far been investigated, following Smith and Rafiqzad's (1979) lead. As is well established in literature, 'educated' English refers to formal education, usually up to and including the tertiary level. This prevailing approach assumes that communication in English is between and among 'educated' speakers only. As is well known, one's English Language Proficiency (ELP) impacts intelligibility, in that a speaker with high ELP is expected to be more intelligible than one with a lower ELP. The same holds true for the listener. But given the fact that most, if not all, studies focus on 'educated' English, it is assumed that there could be issues in the intelligibleness of their Englishes even if both parties are educated or both have considerably high ELPs. The question now lies on the Englishes of those who are not considered 'educated' enough since they have not gone through formal education or, if they did not or have not finished at least high school. Given that communications in English are also carried between and among 'not-so-educated' English (based on the current literature), there is a more pressing need to measure how intelligible their Englishes could be. Better yet, if there are instances of communication breakdown in these situations, is it due to the unintelligibleness of their Englishes? Since studies show that communication between and among 'educated' speakers still pose issues in intelligibility, it is more likely that the 'less educated' English communication poses considerable issues, as well.

17.5 Significance of Philippine English Intelligibility

With the rise of various Englishes, the next big question is, can these Englishes be understandable to other speakers of the English language. Thus, knowing whether PhE is intelligible to other speakers of English or not is imperative because of the following:

1   ASEAN integration—The integration of the countries in South East Asia calls for a working language, English, since none of the countries in this region has a common language. English, like Jenkins (2007) reiterated, is the lingua franca. With this, English occupies a vital role in the economic development of the region, and speakers of PhE, therefore, have to strive hard to be intelligible by being conscious of and considerate to the listeners of PhE by using different speaking strategies. Furthermore, listeners of PhE can also adjust to this variety if they are aware with the features of PhE.
2   PhE Education—Philippines has been a mecca of English Education (Robertson, 2008), and it cannot be denied that those foreigners who study English in the Philippines have learned not the native speakers' English but PhE. Even if others still prefer the native speakers' English, but Filipinos should be proud that a new English has been developed, and is now in the nativization (Schneider, 2003, 2007; Martin, 2014) or endonormative stabilization (Borlongan, 2016) or in the differentiation stage (Gonzales, 2017) of Schneider's dynamic model. Whatever stage PhE is in, what is more imperative is the wide acceptance of PhE in the education system and its intelligibleness to other speakers of English. As opined by Bautista (2000), "Philippine English is not English that falls short of the norms of Standard American English, it is not badly learned English..." (p. 20). Consequently, the educators, especially gatekeepers of the English language, here in the Philippines

228 *Shirley N. Dita and Kristine D. de Leon*

have to recognize that there is PhE and there is a necessity to teach practical linguistic features and strategies to Filipinos, not only due to integration but also because of globalization, in which many Filipinos are becoming citizens of the world. To add, these features have to be seen as beneficial in communication given that these features have to augment the intelligibleness of PhE. However, previous studies (e.g., Matsuura, 2007; Smith, 1992; Smith & Rafiqzad, 1979; Wang & Van Heuven, 2003) have claimed that the native speakers' English does not guarantee intelligibleness.

17.6 Conclusion

With the commencement of ASEAN integration, intelligibility of Asian Englishes is deemed to be more important, politically and economically. This chapter has discussed the intelligibility of PhE, especially for non-Filipinos or for other speakers of English, the many factors contributing to its intelligibility, the issues surrounding the topic, and the significance of its study. Likewise, it has been established that PhE is indeed intelligible to other speakers of English, even if it does not conform to the native speaker model. PhE, just like other Englishes in the Asian context, exhibits syllable-timed rhythm, as opposed to stress-based rhythm of the native speakers of English. The tendency of speakers of PhE toward spelling pronunciation actually aids its intelligibility. Given all these insights from various studies, why do most English Language Teaching (ELT) classes still insist that the performance target is that of a native speaker.

References

Aquino, Milagraos R., Duque, Luzviminda A., Pimentel, Salaverga B. and Rojas, Jose T. (1966). *A study to determine the most intelligible variety of English pronunciation for use in the Philippines* (Unpublished master's thesis). Philippine Normal College, Manila, Philippines.

Bansal, Ram Krishna. (1969). *The intelligibility of Indian English.* Hyderabad: CIEFL.

Bautista, Maria Lourdes. (2000). *Defining standard Philippine English: Its status and grammatical features.* Manila: De La Salle University Press, Inc.

Borlongan, Ariane Macalinga. (2016). Relocating Philippine English in Schneider's dynamic model. *Asian Englishes, 18*(3), 1–10.

Catford, John C. (1950). Intelligibility. *English Language Teaching, 1,* 7–15.

Dayag, Danilo T. (2007). Exploring the intelligibility of Philippine English. *Asian Englishes, 10*(1), 4–23.

De Leon, Kristine D. (2016). *The intelligibility of Philippine English to selected ASEAN countries* (Unpublished doctoral dissertation). De La Salle University, Manila, Philippines.

Derwing, Tracy M., & Munro, Murray J. (2005). Second language accent and pronunciation teaching: A research-based approach. *TESOL Quarterly, 39*(3), 379–397.

Intelligibility 229

Dita, Shirley N. (2013). *Intelligibility and comprehensibility of Philippine English to international students.* A paper presented at the 23rd conference of the International Association for World Englishes (IAWE23), Arizona State University, Tempe, Arizona, USA.

Dita, Shirley N. (2018) *Intelligibility of Englishes: What does it have to do with ASEAN integration.* A Keynote Lecture at the World Englishes Forum, 28th Southeast Asian Linguisitic Society (SEALS28) Annual Meeting, Wenzao Ursuline University of Languages, Kaohsiung, Taiwan.

Dita, Shirley N., & de Leon, Kristine D. (2017). The intelligibility and comprehensibility of Philippine English to EFL speakers. *The Philippine ESL Journal, 19,* 100–116.

Gass, Susan, & Varonis, Evangeline Marlos. (1984). The effect of familiarity on the comprehensibility of nonnative speech. *Language Learning, 34*(1), 65–87.

Gonzales, Wilkinson Daniel Wong. (2017). Philippine Englishes. *Asian Englishes, 19,* 79–95.

Hung, Tony T.N. (2002). English as a global language and the issue of international intelligibility. *Asian Englishes, 5*(1), 4–17.

Irvine, D.H. (1977). The Intelligibility of English speech to non-native English speakers. Language and Speech, *20*(4), 308–316.

Jenkins, Jennifer. (2000). *The phonology of English as an international language.* Oxford, England: Oxford University Press.

Jenkins, Jennifer. (2007). *English as a lingua franca: Attitude and identity.* Oxford, England: Oxford University Press.

Kenworthy, Joanne. (1987). *Teaching English pronunciation.* London: Longman.

Luzares, Casilda E., & Bautista, Ma. Lourdes S. (1972). Judging personality from language usage: 1971 sample. *Philippine Journal of Linguistics, 3*(1), 59–65.

Martin, Isabel Pefianco. (2014). Beyond nativization? Philippine English in Schneider's Dynamic Model. In Sarah Buschfeld, Thomas Hoffmann, Magnus Huber and Alexander Kautzsch (Eds.), *The Evolution of Englishes. The Dynamic Model and beyond* (pp. 70–85). Amsterdam: John Benjamins.

Matsuura, Hiroko. (2007). Intelligibility and individual learner differences in the EIL context. *System, 35,* 293–304.

Munro, Murray J., & Derwing, Tracy M. (1995). Foreign accent, comprehensibility and intelligibility in the speech of second language learners. *Language Learning, 45,* 73–97.

Rajagopalan, Kanavallil. (2010). The soft ideological underbelly of the notion of intelligibility in discussions about 'World Englishes'. *Applied Linguistics, 31*(3), 465–470.

Robertson, Paul. (2008). Foreword. *Philippine ESL Journal, 1,* i.

Schneider, Edgar W. (2003). The dynamics of new Englishes: From identity construction to dialect birth. *Language, 79*(2), 233–281.

Schneider, Edgar W. (2007). How to trace structural nativization: Particle verbs in world Englishes. *World Englishes, 23,* 227–249.

Smith, Larry E. (1992). Spread of English and Issues of Intelligibility. In B. B. Kachru (Ed.), *The other tongue: English across cultures.* Urbana: University of Illinois Press.

Smith, Larry, & Bisazza, John A. (1982). The comprehensibility of three varieties of English for college students in seven countries. *Language Learning, 32*(2), 259–269.

Smith, Larry E., & Nelson, Cecil L. (1985). International intellibility of English: Directions and resources. *World Englishes, 4*(3), 333–342.

Smith, Larry E., & Nelson, Cecil L. (2006). World Englishes and Issues of Intelligibility. In B. B. Kachru, Y. Kachru, & C. L. Nelson (Eds.), *The handbook of World Englishes* (pp. 428–445). Malden, MA: Blackwell Publishing Ltd.

Smith, Larry E., & Rafiqzad, Khalilullah. (1979). English for cross-cultural communication: The question of intelligibility. *TESOL Quarterly, 13*(3), 318–380.

Tan, Ying Ying, & Castelli, Christina. (2013). Intelligibility and attitudes: How American English and American English are perceived around the world. *English World Wide, 34*(2), 177–201.

Tiffen, Brian Witney. (1974). *The intelligibility of Nigerian English*. London: University of London, Compiler.

Tucker, Richard G. (1968). Judging personality from language usage: A Filipino example. *Philippine Sociological Review, 16*, 30–39.

Wang, Hongyan, & van Heuven, Vincent J. (2003). Mutual intelligibility of Chinese, Dutch and American speakers of English. In P. Fikkert, & L. Cornips (Eds.), *Linguistics in the Netherlands* (pp. 213–224). Amsterdam: John Benjamins.

18 Attitudes

Philip Rentillo

18.1 Overview

Studies on attitudes toward Philippine English (PhE) could be considered as one of the earliest endeavors at least in the Outer Circle (Kachru, 1985) if not the whole extra-Inner Circle (cf. McKenzie, 2010). Research on this area was motivated with the conception of the world Englishes paradigm, the pioneering work of Kachru (1976) on the identity of English in postcolonial contexts. While it has been claimed that PhE has become an 'indispensable' and 'legitimate' vehicle of the Filipino thought and identity (Manarpaac, 2003) beyond functional affairs, a look across literature reveals a diverse picture of how PhE as a variety is viewed across domains of Philippine life.

There are enduring questions both on attitudes and on scholarly attention toward PhE. Indeed, it is crucial to understand the true sentiment among Filipinos toward not only English in general but also the local variety which has arisen in the Philippines to also understand its place in Philippine society. To expound on the issue, this chapter will discuss attitudes toward English in the Philippines and the local variety, PhE.

18.2 Attitudes toward English in the Philippines

As a historical byproduct, English in the Philippines is a complicated subject. On one end, it is seen as a symbol of capital and prestige, and, on the other, a colonial consequence furthering class divide (Martin, 2014b). Like in many parts of the postcolonial world, English rose to greater prominence with the advent of globalization bolstered by and resulting in the economic, cultural, and geopolitical dominance of Anglophonic countries (Pennycook, 1994; Phillipson, 1992, 2001). High pragmatic regard for English in the Philippines is facilitated by widespread poverty and stunted national development. English language proficiency became a conduit for socioeconomic mobility as many look toward Inner Circle countries for employment (Gonzalez, 1988). The prestige of English today built by the American colonial regime is amplified by the Overseas Filipino Worker (OFW) phenomenon (Lorente, 2012). To prevent a gravely mismanaged Philippine economy from

DOI: 10.4324/9780429427824-24

232 *Philip Rentillo*

collapsing, the Marcos administration in the 1960s institutionalized overseas employment as a national enterprise. From that period, the sacrosanct position of English as a medium of instruction was justified to help produce a 'world-class' workforce prepared for global labor export—an exploitation and a salvation that it still is today.

Early survey-based studies on Filipinos' attitudes toward English was compiled by Gonzalez and Bautista in 1986. All findings point to English as the premier language of prestige and economy throughout the Philippines. While the vernaculars were extensively used at home and the community, English has been the preferred language in the school (Otanes & Sibayan, 1969) and the workplace (Sibayan, 1978; Sibayan & Segovia, 1982). Later studies have also looked into the impact of proficiency (Casil-Batang & Malenab-Temporal, 2018) and socioeconomic status (Sicam & Lucas, 2016) toward positive attitudes in learning English among Filipino students. Meanwhile, in a qualitative analysis, Gaerlan (2009 in Bernardo & Gaerlan, 2012) also found family language attitudes to be crucial to success in language learning.

18.3 Attitudes toward Philippine English

The earliest mentions of attitudes toward PhE are found in Bautista (2000) and Gonzalez (1985). These would be succeeded by more comprehensive discussions on attitudes toward PhE in Bautista and Bolton's (2008) volume on PhE. Another is a book by Thompson (2003), which specifically covered the sociolinguistic and political attitudes toward English and English-based code-switching (CS) in the Philippines. He also elaborates on the historical development of English in the country, its part in the educational and national language policies, and the position of English and CS across different layers of Philippine society.

18.3.1 Speaker Accent

Quantitative work on attitudes toward PhE speaker accent has been conducted with both Eglish as a second language (Zhang, 2013) and English as a foreign language respondents (Almegren, 2018; Castro & Roh, 2013; Siregar, 2010). One qualitative research to date has been completed by Kobayashi (2008) with EFL learners.

Indirect experimental methods on accent and pronunciation have also been done through verbal (VGT) and matched (MGT) guise techniques/tests—methods common to test accent perception and language attitudes (Garrett, 2010). Studies in this area using PhE as stimulus have used VGT on both ESL (Zhang, 2013, 2010, 2009) and EFL respondents (Ahn & Kang, 2016; Jindapitak, 2010; Kim, 2007). In one VGT study with Thai EFL learners (Jindapitak & Teo, 2012), speakers of PhE were judged to speak in an 'unnatural', 'incorrect' accent. Beyond familiarity and a sense of 'correctness',

Attitudes 233

a strong factor is indeed prestige. Decades-long scholarship on English language attitudes has shown how standardized 'native' English varieties are likelier to be received positively (Bishop et al., 2005; Giles, 1970). Certainly, within the world Englishes paradigm, the so-called Inner Circle remains to be preferred over any other variety. Through more specific descriptions, Inner Circle speakers of English or those whose accent sound closer to those of the Inner Circle are perceived to be more intelligent, educated, or successful (cf. Coupland & Bishop, 2007; Garrett, 2010; Garrett et al., 1999).

Meanwhile Dimaculangan and Pasion (2017) found that among Filipino student-teachers, PhE speakers received the highest rating in terms of prestige above those of American English (AmE). Social attractiveness could be a factor according to McKenzie (2008), who found high preference for heavily accented Japanese speakers of English compared to moderately accented peers among Japanese EFL learners. While Inner Circle Englishes generally remain desired, speakers from other circles may tend to express solidarity with those able to maintain or exhibit an in-group identity. Social attractiveness is likewise a desired quality within Inner Circle groups as attested by Garrett et al. (2003) among Welsh English informants, who rated 'Welshness' more favorably in terms of perceived warmth above other varieties.

In the desire to fully understand attitudes toward PhE, there is a need to consider the complexities of both language attitudes and speaker evaluations (Cargile & Bradac, 2001). For example, asking how much a person likes 'standard international English' versus 'English spoken by Filipinos' is different from asking how much someone likes a speaker based on how competent and engaging they are in the language. This mirrors the importance of measuring attitudes based on general qualities and prestige on the one side and measuring evaluations based on stereotypes and speaker status on the other (Grondelaers & van Hout, 2010; Schoel et al., 2012). Nonetheless, there is yet to be a comprehensive picture of cross-strata attitudes of Filipinos toward PhE. Most studies for the past two decades have been confined to self-report surveys. MGT and VGT studies, aside from being scarce, focus on rigid criteria and separate language attitudes from speaker evaluations. Rarely integrated are mixed-method approaches, which according to Garrett (2010) provide the richest quality of attitudinal data.

18.3.2 Ideology and Pedagogy

PhE is caught in a tug between ideological flanks characterized by linguistic resistance (Tupas, 2011). One side contends the imposition of English in Philippine life as they rally for Tagalog as a language of resistance against colonial hegemony. The masses, for instance, prefer Filipino or any autochthonous language due to either discomfort or shame out of cultural and linguistic dispossession in using English (e.g. Osborne, 2018). The other end decries institutional injustice and argues that English is the key to neutrality and to stymy policies which privilege Tagalog, a language of a single

234   *Philip Rentillo*

non-majority ethnic group over the rest of an ethnolinguistically diverse population (Tupas & Martin, 2016). This conflict, an elephant in the room as they say, remains contentious up to this day.

Amidst these ongoing ideological tensions, years of scholarly work have revealed growing recognition and acceptance of PhE. Bautista (2001a) notes that many Filipino academics possess favorable perceptions toward PhE despite reservations toward features such as neologisms, which continue to be seen as informal. Other studies echo the same positive view expressed among Filipino students (Borlongan, 2009a, 2009b), English language teachers (Bautista, 2001b; Hernandez, 2020), and scholars (Tupas, 2004). Some teachers in fact reject the imposition of 'American standards' (Bolton, 2006). Borlongan (2009b) also found that, while Filipino students strongly value Filipino as the national language, they also consider PhE as a legitimate variety and a part of their national identity. Dimaculangan and Gustilo (2018) meanwhile looked into Filipino English teachers' attitudes toward PhE lexical items. Using a corpus-based questionnaire eliciting each word's acceptability in written and spoken use, they found positive overall attitudes toward PhE as a variety. However, many respondents were either unaware or unaccepting of identified PhE neologisms with merely less than half of the tokens rated as acceptable.

Many Filipinos still put a premium on AmE (Martin, 2014a) and see the 'standard English' used in the Philippines within the mold of AmE (Bautista, 2000a). Even the most educated and proficient have not embraced let alone recognized the existence of a distinct Philippine variety (cf. Martin, 2010; Tupas, 2006, 2010). Bolton and Butler (2004) for one found poor reception toward PhE dictionaries among Filipino academics and high school teachers despite positive attitudes toward localized vocabulary.

Awareness indeed does not instantly reflect acceptance. In one study by Bernardo (2011) preference for AmE over PhE remains prevalent as the former is seen as more economically and culturally powerful. McKenzie (2013) convincingly explains that "attitudes towards languages and language varieties are better viewed as a reflection of the level of prestige associated with particular speech communities" (p. 223). Judgment is derived from sociocultural norms, and such norms are established by groups in power (Crystal, 2003; Garrett, 2010). So long as the United States maintains its influence over the Philippines and the rest of the world, the dominance of AmE may remain as *a* if not *the* basis of standard English among Filipinos (Tinio, 1990).

18.4 Attitudes in Relation to the Dynamic Model

The goal to understand speaker attitudes toward PhE is also important in building a consensus on the position of the variety within Schneider's (2003, 2007) dynamic model of the evolution of postcolonial Englishes.[1] Borlongan (2016), for instance, argues for the movement of PhE from nativization (phase 3) to endonormative stabilization (phase 4), yet it remains arguable. Among many conditions, sociolinguistically speaking, PhE should reach the fourth phase through widespread speaker acceptance. This is characterized by psychological independence, and linguistic self-confidence in support of a local variety with indigenous standards and resources conducive for development (Schneider, 2003, 2007). Unfortunately, the linguistic ecology of the Philippines is mired by relative powerlessness (Tupas, 2006; Tupas & Salonga, 2016), and both standardization and propagation efforts are largely confined within the elite and educated classes.

Contextualizing this Philippine reality to the Kachruvian model, Martin (2014b) expands with additional three circles. The Philippine Inner Circle (PIC) refers to the minority educated elite who embrace standard American and/or PhE. The Philippine Outer Circle (POC) refers to a subset of the educated class who are aware of the Philippine variety but do not fully support its legitimacy and propagation. Lastly, the Philippine Expanding Circle (PEC) describes the underprivileged and less educated class, who see English as a requisite to upward mobility but in many cases lack power to access it. This stratification is parallel to her observation on how literature has typically depicted Outer Circle societies (e.g. Kamwangamalu, 2006; Michieka, 2009) as monolithic ESL environments amidst the co-existence of indigenous ESL and EFL spheres within (Schneider, 2011).

With these in mind, it can instead be claimed that PIC is the only subset of PhE which is headed to endonormative stabilization. This is established by evidence on linguistic behaviors of urban educated classes toward English (Dumdum et al., 2004; Villanueva, 2014). There has been a rise in upper middle to upper class families, mostly in urban areas, who prefer to expose their children to English media and instruction. Meanwhile, a portion of POC and the PEC might remain within nativization. This is evident among lower (and middle) class Filipinos who access and learn English while exhibiting distance from PhE in terms of either acceptance or support. Although an EFL context can be drawn from many communities, existing resources—warranting people have access to such—are produced and maintained by local institutions un/consciously adhering to notions of a local variety of English.

The position and the fate of PhE within Philippine society indeed was never free from trepidations and dissent. English, according to Tupas (2008, 2004), has failed in its role as an equalizing agent especially in diverse postcolonial societies with significant socioeconomic disparities such as the Philippines. As a colonial language, it has transformed into an imperialistic tool to preserve the status quo in favor of the bourgeoise and elites (Tupas & Salonga, 2016). Tupas (2008) contemplates that, while English can be an ideological weapon of subjugation, it can be "an instrument of resistance, empowerment and freedom claim" (p. 17). The colonized seized the language to become their weapon of counter-consciousness and counter-discourse. However, this should not gloss over enduring social inequalities in the access and use of English. The privileged class, who are the gatekeepers of

236 *Philip Rentillo*

English scholarship and education in the Philippines, should remain aware of their role in these pervading structural imbalances. Bolton et al. (2011) and Bernardo (2008), for instance, stress upon the need to constantly accommodate perspectives of the marginalized to foster a truly equalizing English for all Filipinos.

18.5 Summary and Conclusion

PhE resembles the sociopolitical and cultural contours of other postcolonial Englishes; however, it also has its markedly distinct identity and history. The Philippines, within just a generation or two, experienced one of the most phenomenal spreads of English in any postcolonial history (Gonzalez, 1997; Schneider, 2007). Once a foreign language brought by a few thousand Americans more than a hundred years ago, English is now the prime economic and social currency of millions of 21st-century Filipinos. This rapid linguistic transformation carries many insights on the impact of individual and collective human behaviors toward the use, maintenance, and access of language.

PhE indeed is in a crucial position, and while it is widely acknowledged that English in the Philippines persists as a linguistic force to be reckoned with, issues facing its exact locus must likewise be acknowledged. Englishes, just like any other speech variety, are bound across complex layers of human agencies and conditions. It is therefore worthy to note that the Philippine variety is not a monolithic phenomenon but a reflection of a Philippines: a tapestry of cultures, histories, politics, and polarized social classes. And while scholars constantly ask themselves whether PhE is an English *of, by,* or *for Filipinos*, perhaps Filipinos should rather keep asking once again a much more crucial question: English in the Philippines—to what end?

Note

1 Schneider's Dynamic Model, alongside the likes of Kachru's Three Circle Model, has long been challenged (Bolton, 2006, 2012; Deshors, 2018) due to its inadequacy to accommodate the plurality of experiences and nuanced histories of non-postcolonial Englishes, but it stands as one of the most known frameworks on contemporary English ecology.

References

Ahn, So-Yeon, & Kang, Hyun-Sook. (2016). South Korean university students' perceptions of different English varieties and their contribution to the learning of English as a foreign language. *Journal of Multilingual and Multicultural Development, 37*(8), 712–725. https://doi.org/10.1080/01434632.2016.1242595

Almegren, Afnan. (2018). Saudi students' attitude towards World Englishes. *International Journal of Applied Linguistics and English Literature, 7*(4), 238–247. https://doi.org/10.7575/aiac.ijalel.v.7n.4p.238

Bautista, Maria Lourdes S. (2001a). Attitudes of English language faculty in three leading Philippine universities toward Philippine English. *Asian Englishes*, *4*(1), 4–32. https://doi.org/10.1080/13488678.2001.10801062

Bautista, Maria Lourdes S. (2001b). Attitudes of selected Luzon university students and faculty towards Philippine English. In Maria Lourdes G. Tayao, T. P. Ignacio & G. S. Zafra (Eds.), *Rosario E. Maminta in focus: Selected writings in applied linguistics* (pp. 263–273). Philippine Association for Language Teaching.

Bautista, Maria Lourdes S. (2000). *Defining standard Philippine English: Its status and grammatical features.* De La Salle University Press.

Bautista, Maria Lourdes S., & Bolton, Kingsley (Eds.). (2008). *Philippine English: Linguistic and literary perspectives.* Hong Kong University Press.

Bernardo, Alejandro S. (2011). De-hegemonizing the hegemonized: An exploratory study on the dominion of American English in the oldest university in Asia. *i-manager's Journal on English Language Teaching*, *1*(3), 7–22.

Bernardo, Allan B. I. (2008). English in Philippine education: Solution or problem? In Maria Lourdes S. Bautista, & Kingsley Bolton (Eds.), *Philippine English: Linguistic and literary perspectives* (pp. 29–48). Hong Kong University Press.

Bernardo, Allan B. I., & Gaerlan, Marianne Jennifer. M. (2012). Non-native English students learning in English: Reviewing and reflecting on the research. In Radhika Jaidev, Maria Luisa C. Sadorra, Wong Jock Onn, Lee Ming Cherk, & Beatriz Paredes Lorente (Eds.), *Global perspectives, local initiatives: Reflections and practices in ELT.* National University of Singapore.

Bishop, Hywel, Coupland, Nikolas, & Garrett, Peter. (2005). Conceptual accent evaluation: Thirty years of accent prejudice in the UK. *International Journal of Linguistics*, *37*(1), 131–154. https://doi.org/10.1080/03740463.2005.10416087

Bolton, Kingsley. (2012). World Englishes and Asian Englishes: A survey of the field. In Andy Kirkpatrick, & Roland Sussex (Eds.), *English as an international language in Asia: Implications for language education multilingual education* (vol. 1) (pp. 13–26). Springer.

Bolton, Kingsley. (2006). World Englishes today. In Braj B. Kachru, Yamuna Kachru, & Cecil. L. Nelson (Eds.), *The handbook of World Englishes* (pp. 240–270). Wiley-Blackwell.

Bolton, Kingsley, & Butler, Susan. (2004). Dictionaries and the stratification of vocabulary: Towards a new lexicography for Philippine English. *World Englishes*, *23*(1), 91–112. https://doi.org/10.1111/j.1467-971X.2004.00337.x

Bolton, Kingsley, Graddol, David, & Meierkord, Chrisitiane. (2011). Towards developmental world Englishes. *World Englishes*, *30*(4), 459–480. https://doi.org/10.1111/j.1467-971X.2011.01735.x

Borlongan, Ariane M. (2016). Relocating Philippine English in Schneider's dynamic model. *Asian Englishes*, *18*(3), 232–241. https://doi.org/10.1080/13488678.2016.1223067

Borlongan, Ariane M. (2009a). Tagalog-English code-switching in English language classes: Forms and junctions. *TESOL Journal*, *1*, 28–42.

Borlongan, Ariane M. (2009b). A survey on language use, attitudes, and identity in relation to Philippine English among young generation Filipinos: An initial sample from a private university. *Philippine ESL Journal*, *3*, 74–107.

Cargile, Aaron C., & Bradac, James J. (2001). Attitudes towards language: A review of speaker-evaluation research and a general process model. In William B. Gudykunst (Ed.), *Communication Yearbook 25* (pp. 347–382). Lawrence Erlbaum.

238 *Philip Rentillo*

Casil-Batang, Pauline Grace, & Malenab-Temporal, Conchita. (2018). Language attitude and English proficiency of ESL learners. *Asian EFL Journal, 20*(2), 186–205.

Castro, Maria Corazon A., & Roh, Teri Rose Dominica G. (2013). The effect of language attitudes on learner preference: A study on South Koreans' perceptions of the Philippine English accent. *English Language Teaching World Online, 5*, 1–22.

Coupland, Nilokas, & Bishop, Hywel. (2007). Ideologised values for British accents. *Journal of Sociolinguistics, 11*(1), 74–93. https://doi.org/10.1111/j.1467-9841. 2007.00311.x

Crystal, David. (2003). *English as a global language* (2nd ed.). Cambridge University Press.

Deshors, Sandra C. (2018). Modeling World Englishes in the 21st century: A thematic introduction. In Sandra C. Deshors (Ed.), *Modeling World Englishes: Assessing the interplay of emancipation and globalization of ESL varieties* (pp. 1–14). John Benjamins.

Dimaculangan, Nimfa, & Leah, Gustilo. (2018). Attitudes of Filipino English teachers toward 21st century Philippine English writing. *Advanced Science Letters, 24*(11), 8349–8352. https://doi.org/10.1166/asl.2018.12560

Dimaculangan, Nimfa G., & Pasion, Mario C. (2017). Would be teachers' attitude towards the Philippines' official languages. *International Journal of Social Science and Humanities Research, 5*(4), 712–720.

Dumdum, Simeon, Mo, Timothy, & Mojares, Resil. (2004). In conversation: Cebuano writers on Philippine literature and English. *World Englishes, 23*(1), 191–198. https://doi.org/10.1111/j.1467-971X.2004.00344.x

Garrett, Peter. (2010). *Attitudes to language*. Cambridge University Press.

Garrett, Peter, Coupland, Nikolas, & Williams, Angie. (2003). *Investigating language attitudes: Social meanings of dialect, ethnicity and performance*. University of Wales Press.

Garrett, Peter, Coupland, Nikolas, & Williams, Angie. (1999). Evaluating dialect in discourse: Teachers' and teenagers' responses to young English speakers in Wales. *Language in Society, 28*(3), 321–354. https://doi.org/10.1017/S0047404599003012

Giles, Howard. (1970). Evaluative reactions to accents. *Educational Review, 22*(3), 211–227. https://doi.org/10.1080/0013191700220301

Gonzalez, Andrew. (1997). Philippine English: A variety in search of legitimation. In Edgar Schneider (Ed.), *Englishes around the world: Caribbean, Africa, Asia, Australasia* (pp. 205–212). John Benjamins.

Gonzalez, Andrew. (1988). English and economics in the Philippines. In Andrew Gonzalez (Ed.), *The role of English and its maintenance in the Philippines: The transcript, consensus and papers of the solidarity seminar on language and development* (pp. 105–113). Solidarity Publishing House.

Gonzalez, Andrew. (1985). *Studies on Philippine English*. SEAMEO Regional Language Centre.

Gonzalez, Andrew, & Bautista, Maria Lourdes S. (1986). *Language surveys in the Philippines (1966–1984)*. Linguistic Society of the Philippines.

Grondelaers, Stefan, & van Hout, Roeland. (2010). Do speech evaluation scales in a speaker evaluation experiment trigger conscious or unconscious attitudes? *University of Pennsylvania Working Papers in Linguistics, 16*(2), 93–102.

Hernandez, Hjalmar P. (2020). Filipino graduate students' attitudes toward teaching educated Philippine English: A sample from a premier teacher education institution. *Asia-Pacific Social Science Review, 20*(1), 31–42.

Attitudes 239

Jindapitak, Naratip. (2010). *An attitudinal study of varieties of English: Voices from Thai University English learners* (Unpublished master's thesis). Prince of Songkla University.

Jindapitak, Naratip, & Teo, Adisa. (2012). Thai tertiary English majors' attitudes towards and awareness of world Englishes. *Journal of English Studies, 7,* 74–116.

Kachru, Braj B. (1985). Standard, codification and sociolinguistic realism: The English language in the Outer Circle. In Randolph Quirk, & Henry Widdowson (Eds.), *English in the world: Teaching and learning the language and literatures* (pp. 11–30). Cambridge University Press.

Kachru, Braj B. (1976). Models of English for the third world: White man's linguistic burden or language pragmatics? *TESOL Quarterly, 10*(2), 221–239.

Kamwangamalu, Nkonko M. (2006). South African Englishes. In Braj B. Kachru, Yamuna Kachru, & Cecil L. Nelson (Eds.), *The handbook of World Englishes* (pp. 158–187). Wiley-Blackwell.

Kim, Young Soo. (2007). *Korean adults' attitudes towards varieties of English* (Unpublished master's thesis). University of Edinburgh.

Kobayashi, Iori. (2008). "They speak 'incorrect' English": Understanding Taiwanese learners' views on L2 varieties of English. *Philippine Journal of Linguistics, 39,* 81–98.

Lorente, Beatriz P. (2012). The making of "Workers of the World": Language and the labor brokerage state. In Alexandre Duchêne, & Monica Heller (Eds.), *Language in late capitalism: Pride and profit* (pp. 183–206). Routledge.

Manarpaac, Danilo. (2003). 'When I was a child I spake as a child': Reflecting on the limits of a national language policy. In Christian Mair (Ed.), *The politics of English as a world language* (pp. 479–492). Rodopi.

Martin, Isabel P. (2014a). Beyond nativization? Philippine English in Schneider's Dynamic Model. In Sarah Buschfeld, Thomas Hoffmann, Magnus Huber, & Alexander Kautzsch (Eds.), *The evolution of Englishes: The dynamic model and beyond* (pp. 70–85). John Benjamins.

Martin, Isabel P. (2014b). Philippine English revisited. *World Englishes, 33*(1), 50–59. https://doi.org/10.1111/weng.12054

Martin, Isabel P. (2010). Periphery ELT: The politics and practice of teaching English in the Philippines. In Andy Kirkpatrick (Ed.), *The Routledge handbook of World Englishes* (pp. 247–264). Routledge.

McKenzie, Robert M. (2013). Changing perceptions? A variationist sociolinguistic perspective on native speaker ideologies and standard English in Japan. In Stephanie Ann Houghton, & Damian J. Rivers (Eds.), *Native speakerism in Japan: Intergroup dynamics in foreign language education* (pp. 219–230). Multilingual Matters.

McKenzie, Robert M. (2010). *The social psychology of English as a global language: Attitudes, awareness and identity in the Japanese context.* Springer.

McKenzie, Robert M. (2008). Social factors and non-native attitudes towards varieties of spoken English: A Japanese case study. *International Journal of Applied Linguistics, 18*(1), 63–88. https://doi.org/10.1111/j.1473-4192.2008.00179.x

Michieka, Martha M. (2009). Expanding Circles within the Outer Circle: The rural Kisii in Kenya. *World Englishes, 28*(3), 352–364. https://doi.org/10.1111/j.1467-971X.2009.01597.x

Osborne, Dana. (2018). "Ay nosebleed!": Negotiating the place of English in contemporary Philippine linguistic life. *Language and Communication, 58,* 118–133.

240   *Philip Rentillo*

Otanes, Fe T., & Sibayan, Bonifacio P. (1969). *Language policy survey*. Language Study Center, Philippine Normal College.

Pennycook, Alastair. (1994). *The cultural politics of English as an international language*. Longman.

Phillipson, Robert. (2001). English for globalisation or for the world's people? *International Review of Education*, *47*, 185–200. https://doi.org/10.1023/A:1017937322957

Phillipson, Robert. (1992). *Linguistic imperialism*. Oxford University Press.

Schneider, Edgar W. (2011). *Englishes around the world: An introduction*. Cambridge University Press.

Schneider, Edgar W. (2007). *Postcolonial English: Varieties around the world*. Cambridge University Press.

Schneider, Edgar W. (2003). The dynamics of new Englishes: From identity construction to dialect birth. *Language*, *79*(2), 233–281. https://doi.org/10.1353/lan.2003.0136

Schoel, Christiane, Roessel, Janin, Eck, Jennifer, Janssen, Jana, Petrovic, Branislava, Rothe, Astrid, Rudert, Selma Carolin, & Stahlberg, Dagmar. (2012). Attitudes towards languages (AToL) scale: A global instrument. *Journal of Language and Social Psychology*, *32*(1), 21–45. https://doi.org/10.1177/0261927X12457922

Sibayan, Bonifacio P. (1978). Views on language and identity: Limited Metro Manila sample. In Arthur Yap (Ed.), *Language education in multilingual societies* (pp. 3–53). Singapore University Press.

Sibayan, Bonifacio P., & Segovia, Lorna Z. (1982). Language and socioeconomic development: Perceptions of a Metro Manila sample: Implications for third world countries. *Philippine Journal of Linguistics*, *13*(2), 63–103.

Sicam, Faith Patricia M., & Lucas, Rochelle Irene G. (2016). Language attitudes of adolescent Filipino bilingual learners towards English and Filipino. *Asian Englishes*, *18*(2), 109–128. https://doi.org/10.1080/13488678.2016.1179474

Siregar, Fenty L. (2010). The language attitudes of students of English literature and D3 English at Maranatha Christian University toward American English, British English and Englishes in Southeast Asia, and their various contexts of use in Indonesia. *Philippine ESL Journal*, *4*, 66–92.

Thompson, Roger M. (2003). *Filipino English and Taglish: Language switching from multiple perspectives*. John Benjamins.

Tinio, Rolando S. (1990). *A matter of language: Where English fails*. University of the Philippines Press.

Tupas, T. Ruanni F. (2011). The new challenge of the mother tongues: The future of Philippine postcolonial language politics. *Kritika Kultura*, *16*, 108–121.

Tupas, T. Ruanni F. (2010). Which norms in everyday practice: And why? In Andy Kirkpatrick (Ed.), *The Routledge handbook of World Englishes* (pp. 567–579). Continuum Press.

Tupas, T. Ruanni F. (2008). Postcolonial English language politics today: Reading Ramanathan's The English-Vernacular Divide. *Kritika Kultura*, *11*, 5–21.

Tupas, T. Ruanni F. (2006). Standard Englishes, pedagogical paradigms and their conditions of (im)possibility. In Rani Rubdy, & Mario Saraceni (Eds.), *English in the world: Global rules, global roles* (pp. 169–185). Continuum Press.

Tupas, T. Ruanni F. (2004). The politics of Philippine English: Neocolonialism, global politics, and the problem of postcolonialism. *World Englishes*, *23*(1), 47–58. https://doi.org/10.1111/j.1467-971X.2004.00334.x

Tupas, Ruanni, & Martin, Isabel P. (2016). Bilingual and mother tongue-based multilingual education in the Philippines. In Ofelia García, Angel Lin, & Stephen May (Eds.), *Bilingual and Multilingual Education* (3rd ed.) (pp. 1–13). Cham, Switzerland: Springer.

Tupas, Ruanni, & Salonga, Aileen. (2016). Unequal Englishes in the Philippines. *Journal of Sociolinguistics, 20*(3), 367–381. https://doi.org/10.1111/josl.12185

Villanueva, Rey John C. (2014). *The features of Philippine English across regions* (Unpublished doctoral dissertation). De La Salle University.

Zhang, Qi. (2013). The attitudes of Hong Kong students towards Hong Kong English and Mandarin-accented English. *English Today, 29*(2), 9–16. https://doi.org/10.1017/S0266078413000096

Zhang, Qi. (2010). *Attitudes beyond the Inner Circle: Investigating Hong Kong students' attitudes towards English accents* (Unpublished doctoral dissertation). Newcastle University.

Zhang, Qi. (2009). Hong Kong people's attitudes towards varieties of English. *Newcastle Working Papers in Linguistics, 15*, 151–173.

19 Multilingualism

Loy Lising

19.1 The Phenomenon of Multilingualism

Multilingualism is a global phenomenon. Roughly two-thirds of the world's population are multilinguals in varying numbers of languages (Myers-Scotton, 2006). As Maher (2017) argues, linguistic diversity is the norm in society, and functioning in a multilingual repertoire is an "everyday social fact everywhere" (p. 6) despite the sobering reality that some institutions and governments continue to adhere to language policies that render these linguistic diversities silent. Multilingualism is a highly complex phenomenon and is studied as such within the discipline of sociolinguistics. Sociolinguistics, as a field within linguistics, has both language and society at its core of inquiry, investigating the structural features of language relative to social factors of race, age, gender, class, place, time period, among others, as well as the role language plays in social processes. It is therefore imperative that multilingualism is understood:

- in terms of language – This means critically interrogating definitions of languages and dialects; our understanding of the phenomenon of code-switching; and perhaps 'translanguaging' – a more recent postulation of the use of multiple languages (Garcia & Wei, 2014).
- in terms of society – This means paying attention to the causes of multilingualism; its perceived benefits and deficits; and the ideologies that underpin our view of and attitudes toward multilingualism.

These are by no means the only necessary aspects in the understanding and appreciation of the phenomenon of multilingualism, but given the constraints of space here, these have been selected as paramount.

Looking at multilingualism from both the language and the social angles provides a basis for critically evaluating and differentiating the existing typologies of multilingualism in the literature. This section reviews these typologies and the different conceptualizations of multilingualism with which they are associated. The chapter then progresses toward its second section, which discusses the multilingual ecology of the Philippines and the research

DOI: 10.4324/9780429427824-25

work done thus far on multilingual practices, particularly on the nexus between Philippine English (PhE) and the local languages in the country. The third section will provide a critical discussion on how the intersection of multilingualism and PhE has been addressed in current research. The final section will then sketch out future research directions necessary in further mining and understanding variable multilingual practices and beliefs across the archipelago.

19.2 The Varied Meanings of Multilingualism

Fundamental to the sociolinguistic study of multilingualism is an appreciation of the challenges in defining and identifying separate languages. In sociolinguistics, it is recognized that the criterion of mutual intelligibility, as a measure for disambiguating between languages and dialects, remains contentious (cf. Martin-Jones, Blackledge & Creese, 2012; Maher, 2017; Myers-Scotton, 2006; Piller, 2016). The literature has illuminated the fact that the use of apparently clear parameters for distinguishing between languages and dialects, such as the use of certain linguistic features, is often overshadowed by socio-political factors such as distinctions between social identities, government policies, and religious motivations, which become the bases for defining certain varieties of language as A Language and others as A Dialect (or as other languages). The sociolinguistic understanding of multilingualism sees firm boundaries between languages, and between languages and dialects, as social constructs rather than natural facts. Nonetheless, what remains obvious is the variation that exists and that language variation is made socially meaningful. Moreover, beyond this varietal distinction is yet another layer of diversity: The difference in the way language is used by its speaker subject to the register demanded by the context of conversation. Piller (2016) argues that diversity within a language exists relative to a number of factors, in particular, vis-à-vis the speakers' other languages, which can easily influence their production of the new language. It is also important to remember that, especially in multilingual ecologies, language use in "conversations in various situations are acts of identity" (Maher, 2017, p. 97). In other words, the way individuals vary in their language choice as well as in their style of speaking, i.e. their idiolect, is often as much an index of their identity (sometimes even consciously performed) as it is their response to the communicative requirements of the situation at hand or a response to their constraints/proficiencies in each language.

One analytic construct that is useful in studying people's language choices and stylistic shifts is codeswitching. Codeswitching, as is commonly defined in the literature, is the use of two or more languages in a given written or spoken text or discourse (cf. Gumperz, 1982; Poplack, 2004). In this chapter, 'codeswitching' is used in this way. It is a "widely recognised phenomenon in interactions between bilingual and multilingual speakers" (Lising, Peters, & Smith, in press, p. 1). In a linguistic environment where two or more languages

244   *Loy Lising*

could be used for various functions, switching languages – both within and between sentences – can be strategic in achieving the desired communicative goal including creating affinity between interlocutors. While this phenomenon was largely viewed historically from a deficit perspective (e.g. Weinreich, 1953) – seen as evidence for limited proficiency causing a speaker to substitute a term or phrase from another code – contemporary scholarship now recognizes codeswitching as a speaker's strategic use of linguistic resources to serve various functions, one of which may be to index their multilingual identity. Especially for the purposes of learning, the combined use of all the users' languages in their repertoire is hailed as having pedagogically sound motivations and functions (Garcia & Li Wei, 2014).

The paragraph above identifies two quite different approaches, in scholarship, to multilingual speech: as an abnormal, language learner workaround or as a normal and proficient use of language. Different analyses and conclusions will therefore arise depending on which approach to multilingualism a study takes. There are other approaches to multilingualism in the literature, too. This nomenclature describes but also evaluates multilingualism in diverse ways; guiding a reader to identify and critically consider each is the purpose of the following brief literature review. Many of the labels assigned to the phenomenon of multilingualism emanate from a way of thinking that imagines languages as discrete items which develop for learners/speakers in linear ways in parallel to each other. Some of these labels include, among others, 'ideal equilingualism' and 'balanced and (a) symmetrical bilingualism' (Maher, 2017); 'fractional and wholistic view' of bilingualism (Grosjean, 1982); and 'balanced or incipient' bilingualism (Diebold, 1964). These concepts have been criticized for their undergirding monolingual conceptualization of how individuals navigate their multiple languages. Such a view is reminiscent of Jespersen's (1922) postulation that more than one linguistic system taxes the mind, a reasoning which treats multilingualism as an abnormal and problematic interference. By contrast, the approach to multilingualism in this chapter recognizes that languages in one's repertoire do variable social work, and that functioning mostly in uneven ways, they therefore naturally develop in an asymmetrical fashion.

Expanding the discussion now to the constructs pertinent to the role language plays in social processes, it is important to understand how the following have been constructed in society: causes of multilingualism, its perceived benefits and deficits, and the ideologies that underpin our attitudes toward the phenomenon, which consequently impact on relevant language policies.

Multilingualism as a phenomenon is largely seen as engendered by language contact and the transplantation of features of outside languages into the local one(s). This is enabled by factors which are often beyond the individual's control, including, inter alia, political, economic, social, religious, and educational power of the incoming language. Colonization, for instance, has enabled the introduction and spread of English, French, Spanish,

Portuguese, and Japanese to language ecologies throughout the world. Migration, especially with the growth of globalization, has consequently increased language contact, and has the potential both to increase multilingualism and to reduce it, depending on the power of migrating languages to supplant those already in place. There are multiple causes for migration: economic – as in the case of skilled migrations (Lising, 2017; Piller & Lising, 2014, 2016), educational – as in the case of its internationalization (Lising, 2017), social – as in a number of cases particularly intercultural marriages, and socio-political – as in the case of people fleeing from conflict zones. The cause, as well as the scale, of migration can affect how it is received socially and whether immigrants' language practices are actively adopted, actively resisted, overwhelmed, or overwhelming.

Globalization has in fact made multilingual practices not only commonplace but necessary and crucial for people's cross-cultural and transnational communication, for their upward social and economic mobility, and for their sense of belonging. Multilingualism therefore affords economic and social benefits. Maher (2017) emphasizes these benefits and adds that multilingual practices are an expression of our linguistic and minority rights, have aesthetic benefits, improve our cognitive skills (cf. Bialystok, Craik & Ryan, 2006), and – given that the world is increasingly becoming diverse – multilingual practices increase our understanding of diasporas which enriches our existence.

While the benefits of multilingualism abound, biased beliefs about language (particularly about language diversity) engender negative attitudes toward multilingualism. It is important to understand these preconceptions in order to dispel some of the negative views toward multilingual practice. The 'standard language ideology' (Piller, 2015) is one of these beliefs. It is the belief that the language spoken by native speakers is the only acceptable version of that language. The acceptance of this belief fails to appreciate that multiple languages in a person's repertoire reflect (more often than not) knowledge and possession of different phonological features, and the expression of these phonological features is sometimes audible across these languages, and that is very much an intrinsic part of multilingualism. In addition, they may also have lexical and grammatical choices consistent with the rules of an emerging contact variety (or consistent with their other languages). Another ideology that Piller (2015) identifies as common is the 'one nation, one language' ideology, which was popularized in the USA, for example, by the proclamation of then President Theodore Roosevelt (1919, cited in Maher 2017, p. 77): "We have room for but one language in this country, and that is the English language, for we intend to see that the crucible turns our people out as Americans, of American nationality, and not as dwellers in a polyglot boarding house". Both the 'standard language ideology' and the 'one nation, one language ideology' are some of the beliefs that have engendered prejudicial ideas and attitudes about language and language use that are detrimental to and critical of multilingual practices.

246 *Loy Lising*

In this chapter, it will be argued that despite a top-down, one nation, two official languages policy on language use especially in the domains of education, business, and law in the Philippines, and despite its impact on the acceptability of multilingual practices, multilingualism continues to thrive, and it is therefore imperative to understand how multilinguals deploy their languages in their repertoire. As Piller (2016, p. 12) argues, "The unique ways in which each and every one of us uses the linguistic resources at our disposal to communicate in context constitute the basic fact of 'linguistic diversity' irrespective of whether that linguistic diversity involves Afrikaans and Wu, a mixture of the two, or internal variation within each".

19.3 The Multilingual Ecology of the Philippines

In the Philippines, linguistic diversity abounds – in the sense of a presence of varieties of languages and dialects and also lectal variations within a variety – which makes multilingualism a norm in the country. *Ethnologue* (2018) reports 182 living languages in the archipelago, and the majority of the 100 million or so Filipinos (Philippine Statistics Authority [PSA], 2016) can be trilingual, at the very least, in Tagalog, English, and their regional language. As Martin (2018) points out, the Philippines was a multilingual society long before English arrived. In fact, of the 182 living languages, 175 are indigenous languages and only 8 are non-indigenous (*Ethnologue*, 2018). These 175 languages were doing social work for Filipinos in various regions of the country not only long before the arrival of American English through the American colonization in 1898 (Gonzalez, 1996) but long before even the arrival of Chinese Hokkien, around 1570 (Gonzales, 2017), and Spanish during the colonization in the same century. The acquisition, maintenance, and use of the Philippine languages, however, given the perpetually challenging socioeconomic state of the nation, have been fraught. Foremost among the pressures are economic ones: 'Which language best facilitates employment and upward socio-economic mobility?', people ask themselves. And while the previous section explained that multilingualism brings with it many benefits other than economic, in a country where 10% of GDP relies on remittances by Filipino overseas workers (Le Borgne, 2009) whose employment has largely been made possible by their command of English (Lorente, 2017), the economics of language acquisition raises its head above the rest. So, from a sociolinguistic perspective, it is of utmost importance to understand the interplay between English and other languages in the Philippines, and the research that has been done so far to describe, understand, and problematize it. A comprehensive review of recent (2010–2018) publications reveals research that focuses on multilingual practices in conversations; multilingual practices in linguistic landscapes; multilingual practices in education; and multilingual practices in communities. (This review excludes earlier studies as they have already been reviewed by Bautista [1984], Gonzalez and Bautista [1986], Bautista [2000] and Dayag and Dita [2012].)

The first theme – multilingual practices in conversations – emerges from studies which investigate the interplay between English and any of the Philippine indigenous languages. The studies following this theme have largely focused on codeswitching, including borrowings and insertions of specific Tagalog enclitic particles in sentences.

The recent studies in this area by Gonzales (2016), Osborne (2015), and Bugayong (2011) suggest that codeswitching continues to be used productively and is generally seen as an important linguistic tool to navigate multilingual realities. Osborne (2015), for instance, in her investigation of the negotiation of the hierarchy of languages in the Ilocandia, in the northern part of the Philippines, finds that although Filipino and English are the official media of instruction and communication in schools, codeswitching in English, Filipino, and Ilocano is present and serves a phatic role of establishing and reinforcing solidarity. Gonzales (2016), who investigates Hokaglish, "a trilingual code-switching phenomenon involving Hokkien, Tagalog, and English in a Filipino-Chinese enclave" (p. 106), finds that the productive use of codeswitching is particularly pervasive in religious contexts. These switches are predominantly intra-sentential and are generally at the lexical level. Bugayong (2011) similarly finds productive use of codeswitching and has emphasized that

> while there is no emerging grammaticalization of Taglish [fused Tagalog and English], it is neither a matter of incomplete command of either language nor of idiosyncratic choices. Rather, Taglish is a discursive strategy within a social norm, very much similar to low-varieties in diglossic language situations.
>
> (p. 1)

Two more recent studies by Bautista (2011) and Lim and Borlongan (2011) both examine the interplay between English and Tagalog in the International Corpus of English-Philippine (ICE-PHI) component. They are especially relevant to this chapter's focus in that both studies problematize the presence of Tagalog enclitic particles in PhE texts and examine the principles undergirding this interplay. In particular, Lim and Borlongan (2011), following Bautista's (2011) study, investigate the use of enclitic particles *ba, na, pa,* and *'no.* Their corpus-based case analysis shows that the use of these enclitic particles in English texts serves specific discourse purposes such as expressing 'tentativeness' and 'urgency', which are otherwise achieved differently and perhaps in an inefficient way in English. This kind of investigation is pivotal in understanding how the local language, in this case Tagalog, influences the development of the emerging English variety. Similarly, Bautista (2011) investigates the use of the particle *'no* in ICE-PHI. She finds that the 788 tokens of *'no* serve various functions, but, more importantly, its usage seems to point to the fact that it "simplifies tag questions [...] and serves the functions of [...] a hesitation filler, as a means of getting assent and/or holding the person's attention" (p. 87). This, according to Bautista, testifies to the hypothesis that Schneider (2003) puts forward: "Colonial varieties tend to reduce grammatical complexity if it is not functionally required" (p. 130).

What these recent research studies show is that codeswitching remains a necessary linguistic tool in the multilingual speakers' repertoire and serves a unique purpose in a multilingual ecology.

Studies under the second theme – multilingual practices in linguistic landscapes – have as their core of inquiry an understanding of the semiotic displays and their meaning in various identified locations. Three recent studies by Jazul and Bernardo (2017), Magno (2017), and De Los Reyes (2000) focus on this theme and all three studies lament the dominance of displays of written English in an otherwise multilingual ecology. Jazul and Bernardo (2017) analyze the signage in Binondo, Manila's Chinatown. They found that English dominates this particular landscape, and that the use of Chinese is limited to commercial purposes, namely, for ascribing authenticity to transactional goods and services, a strategy which aims at making Binondo a distinct cultural destination. Magno (2017) investigates the language distribution and functions of signage on bulletin boards of various universities' Communication Departments in Cebu. His study indicates that although students themselves prefer signage that utilizes Filipino, English, and Cebuano, the majority of the signage is predominantly in English. De Los Reyes (2000) analyzes the languages used in 76 signage tokens found in two train stations in Metro Manila. The findings in his analysis show that despite the citywide acceptance and use of both Filipino and English, English predominates in these signage, similar to the signage of Cebu's campuses or Manila's Chinatown.

The literature concerning the third theme, which is multilingual practices in education, falls into two clear sub-themes: language preferences in the media of instruction and communication in schools (Cunanan, 2013; Jamora, 2014; Turano and Malimas, 2013) and the emerging consequences of the installation of the Mother-Tongue-Based-Multilingual-Education (MTB-MLE) policy (Amarles, 2016; Barrios, 2016; Mahboob & Cruz, 2013; Tupas, 2015; Walter and Decker, 2011) by the Philippine government in 2013 as part of the Enhanced Education Act (Martin, 2018).

On the first sub-theme, Jamora (2014) investigates the languages acquired and used by Maranao school children in their school and in their community. Jamora's findings indicate a highly productive use of English and Filipino in the schools, Sorsoganon in the community, and Maranao in the home, and also Maranao as a medium of instruction for teaching Arabic. Turano and Malimas (2013) studied private schools in the second largest city in the Philippines – Cebu – to investigate the students' and parents' preferred medium of instruction. Their investigation reveals that both stakeholders prefer English, despite the Bilingual Education Policy of Filipino and English, owing to the globalized status of English. Finally, Cunanan

(2013) explores the issues brought about by the coexistence of Filipino, English, Philippine regional languages, and foreign languages in a university in northern Philippines and identifies the challenge this multilingual context poses in making a decision on the university-wide language policy.

Within the literature pertaining to the recently enshrined Mother-Tongue-Based Multilingual Education policy, Mahboob and Cruz (2013) problematize the proposed use of the policy, and argue that although the initiatives are laudable, the stakeholders' (i.e. parents, teachers, and students) attitudes toward their mother tongues need to be considered. They propose that a "principles-based approach to language policy" (p. 2) can be utilized to change an otherwise negative language attitude toward the successful implementation of the MTB-MLE. This is echoed by Tupas (2015), who maintains a similar argument: for the MTB-MLE to succeed, the teachers' linguistic ideological stance of "internalised hatred" (p. 121) with regard to the use of the regional language as the transition language in the initial years of learning needs to be addressed to align the teachers' ideology with the language education policy. Contrary to the findings in Tupas (2015) and Mahboob and Cruz (2013), Amarles (2016) finds favorable results for MTB-MLE in her study. Through focus group discussions, she examines the opinion of school teachers in seven regional centers on the use of English amidst the multilingual ecology of the Philippines and the implementation of the MTB-MLE. Her findings show that teachers, in general, hold positive views regarding the implementation of MTB-MLE as a policy, and express sincere hope for pre- and in-service training programs that will better equip them in the implementation of the policy. Walter and Decker (2011) also indicate some positive findings in their study where they investigate whether the use of the children's first language as a medium of instruction negatively impacts their "proficiency development in maths, science and reading" (p. 675). Their findings show that children taught in their first language consistently outperform others who did not have their first language as the medium of instruction, certainly a positive nod toward the MTB-MLE policy. Barrios (2016), on the other hand, takes a different tack in her analysis of Chabacano and Filipino and proposes a model of "grammatical consciousness-raising" (citing Rutherford, 1987) as a strategy to be used in mother-tongue-based multilingual instruction.

Finally, the macro theme of multilingual practices in the community includes research studies that have investigated the various ways in which Filipinos in various speech communities deploy the languages in their repertoire for a tapestry of functions and purposes (Asuncion & Madrunio, 2017; Rosario, 2010; Tajolosa, 2011). These three studies focus mainly on communities in the northern part of the Philippines. Rosario (2010) investigates parents in the northern province of Pangasinan to find their language preferences, perceptions, and exposure. He finds that Filipino is the most preferred language at home and in various domains and finds the use of Pangasinan as a medium of instruction impractical. This study shows a very

250 *Loy Lising*

interesting case of internal hegemony where the national language has in essence become a threat to the other indigenous languages in the region. Similarly, Tajolosa (2011) investigates the ethnolinguistic vitality of three Batak communities in the province of Palawan to predict whether language maintenance or shift will prevail. The findings show that the participants reported use of Batak in most domains of communication. She concludes that speakers' language attitude is a better predictor of language use than their beliefs in ethnolinguistic vitality. Finally, Asuncion and Madrunio (2017) investigate the domains of language use for Gaddang, Tagalog, Ilocano, and English among Gaddang speakers, a multilingual ethnic group in the northern part of the Philippines. Despite the acceptability of a multilingual practice in the area, the authors find a preference for Tagalog use among Gaddang speakers in both public and private domains. Like Tajolosa's, this study seems to indicate, that, yet again, the privileged status of Tagalog threatens the local languages Gaddang and Ilocano.

While all the studies discussed in this section present interesting glimpses of how multilingual repertoires are deployed and negotiated on the ground, only a few have directly investigated how the local languages interacted with English, and how this possible dialectic relationship has impacted the development of the Philippine variety of English. As Schneider (2007) argues, the emerging variety of English has become "indigenized and grown local roots" (p. 2). It is therefore crucial to document these processes of indigenization. Especially for a highly multilingual ecology like the Philippines, it is of sociolinguistic interest to investigate how the local languages help shape this indigenized English variety. In the above studies, only Bautista (2011) and Lim and Borlongan (2011) address this concern at a linguistic level. More research is needed to uncover the relevant multilingual practices at the level of domain use, in general, and this can be done through ethnography. At the same time, more research is needed to show indigenization in progress in particular, and one way to do this is by means of corpora.

19.4 Giving Voice to Multilingual Practice in Corpora

Research into multilingual practices, especially in a highly variable multilingual ecology like the Philippines, can take on many forms. This chapter has set out to investigate how the intersection between multilingualism and PhE has been researched.

As shown in the literature reviewed, despite the fact that PhE has evolved and grown alongside the local languages, very few studies have investigated precisely this (potentially dialectic) relationship between these languages. In a preliminary analysis of instances of interaction between Tagalog and English in ICE-PHI of one million words (Bautista, Lising, & Dayag, 2004), 6,628 instances of codeswitching are found in the overall data, with 5,383 and 1,245 tokens in the spoken and written texts, respectively. While Sidney Greenbaum's proposal in 1988 to build the *International Corpus of English*

Multilingualism 251

(including spoken and written data) was undergirded by the motivation to "facilitate comparative studies across national varieties of English" (p. 2), understanding of turn-taking principles (Sachs, Schegloff, & Jefferson, 1974) tells of the roles various parts of a conversation play in co-constructing meaning. At the same time, Schneider (2007) suggests an investigation of the way emerging Englishes have undergone the process of indigenization.

The data in the corpus has been processed to facilitate an investigation of indigenization. In particular, the instruction to the corpus compilers was to code lexical items or short phrases in the local language (spoken or written) as indigenous, like <indig>...</indig> (Nelson, 1996a, 1996b). Longer uninterrupted sections in the local languages are omitted from the transcripts much like in other ICE components (e.g. Vine, 1999 for ICE-NZ).

Here are some examples from the ICE-PHI data.

1   <ICE-PHI:S1A-059#336:1:A>
    Maybe because they're not that young anymore <{> <[> <, > </[> like you don't have to cuddle them <indig> di ba </indig>
2   <ICE-PHI:S1A-097#105:1:B>
    And you never bring me <indig> pasalubong </indig> you know that
3   <ICE-PHI:S1B-046#80:1:A>
    I don't know if you've felt this already <indig> kasi baka <.> mana </.> maraming mga Filipino doon sa Cambridge na kilala ka </indig> but are you enjoying the relative anonymity <indig> na <{> <[> naranasan mo </indig> </[>

This coding of the data was originally intended to simply exclude lengthy indigenous expressions which were not originally seen as part of the emerging English variety.

However, as some of the studies in this chapter have shown, this coding enables the sorts of analysis that reveal the ways in which the local language, in the case of the ICE-PHI examples as above – Tagalog – influences the way PhE evolves. For example, Bautista (2011) studied it and found that the kinds of switches into Tagalog present in ICE-PHI are quite varied, and these variations are further discussed in Lising (in preparation). The main utility, for this chapter's purposes, is that the marking-up of switches into indigenous languages in the corpus signals the way these local languages intersect with English. However, while this coding calls attention to the interplay between languages in ICE-PHI, it can equally be seen as silencing what is otherwise a clear body of evidence for bi-/multilingual practice. This is because the coding elides the differences between indigenous languages, lumping them into <indig>. The range of non-Tagalog, non-English language practices and nuanced data on when they are deployed and by whom are obscured. So far, the studies of ICE-PHI therefore do not illuminate how local languages shape the emerging indigenized variety of English (Schneider, 2007).

252 *Loy Lising*

Furthermore, in failing to consider the role the codeswitched text plays in the co-construction of meaning and structure, the opportunity to understand the principles underlying the organization of turn-taking becomes lost in transcription.

19.5 Moving Forward in Researching Multilingual Practices

As has been established in this chapter, the Philippines has highly vibrant and highly variable micro multilingual ecologies across its archipelago. Together, these make up its diverse macro multilingual ecology. The research that has been done thus far in uncovering its multilingual practices on local and national scales is laudable, but more needs to be done.

This chapter began by noting that multilingualism is a highly complex phenomenon and its study is situated within the discipline of sociolinguistics with a focus on both language and society. What seems to have predominated in the research on the Philippines' multilingual practice is inquiry into societal practices.

Thus, the chapter identifies the need for further language-focused research, particularly on the way indigenous languages contribute to the structural and pragmatic features of PhE. Doing such research would allow for an understanding of the processes that take place in a language contact situation, particularly in uniquely complex contexts where various local languages, e.g. Tagalog, Cebuano, Chabacano, and others, intersect with English. How do these local languages influence the way PhE develops? In addition, it is also crucial to understand the cognitive benefits (and perhaps deficits) that multilingual practices bring, in particular the metalinguistic skills that bi-/multilingualism engenders (Bialystok, Peets, & Moreno, 2014).

On a societal level, more systematic investigations into multilingual practices across different domains (schools, workplaces, religious settings, and so on); across different modalities (spoken, written, in sign language, and online); and across different regions where different local languages operate will be crucial in our understanding of the tapestry of the Philippine multilingual practices.

Both the language- and the society-focused avenues of multilingualism research in the Philippines could benefit from a diversification of methodologies. The studies reviewed in this chapter have utilized an interview, questionnaire, observation, or corpus approach to documenting multilingual practices. It has been noted above the possibility of further 'mining' ICE-PHI for nuanced analysis of indigenous languages' interactions with, and effects on, English. In addition, one of the most comprehensive and systematic ways of documenting the complexity of multilingual practices is through ethnography (Heller, 2009), which allows for the collection of multiple sets of data about multilingual speakers that can enable us to triangulate their attitudes toward the languages in their repertoire, the actual languages they use in various domains of interaction, with the way these are influenced by institutional policies. As Heller postulates, ethnography allows "us to tell a story; not someone else's story exactly, but our own story of some slice of experience, a story which illuminates social processes and generates explanations for why people do and think the things they do" (p. 250). Further research studies which immerse the researcher in the context of micro multilingual ecologies and enable the collection of multiple data can only enrich the way multilingual practices are understood.

Acknowledgment

I would like to acknowledge the invaluable assistance of Pia Tenedero, a Ph.D. student supervised by Prof. Ingrid Piller and me, in locating relevant studies done on multilingual practices in the Philippines.

References

Amarles, Arceli M. (2016). Multilingualism, multilingual education, and the English language: Voices of public school teachers. *Philippine Journal of Linguistics, 47*, 90–105.

Asuncion, Zayda S., & Madrunio, Marilu R. (2017). Domains of language use among Gaddang Speakers in Nueva Viscaya, Philippines. *Philippine Journal of Linguistics, 48*, 1–29.

Barrios, Aireen L. (2016). Cross-linguistic influence in bilingual learners: Implications for mother tongue-based multilingual education in the Philippines. *Philippine Journal of Linguistics, 47*, 46–58.

Bautista, Maria Lourdes S. (2000). Studies of Philippine English in the Philippines. *Philippine Journal of Linguistics, 31*(1), 39–65.

Bautista, Ma. Lourdes S. (2011). Some notes on 'no' in Philippine English. In Ma. Lourdes S. Bautista (Ed.), *Studies of Philippine English: Exploring the Philippine component of the International Corpus of English* (pp. 75–90). Manila: Anvil Publishing, Inc.

Bautista, Maria Lourdes S., Lising, J. Loy V., & Dayag, Danilo T. (Comps.) (2004). *International Corpus of English-Philippines lexical Corpus.* CD-ROM. London: International Corpus of English.

Bialystok, Ellen, Craik, Fergus I.M., & Ryan, Jennifer (2006). Executive control in a modified antisaccade task: Effects of aging and bilingualism. *Journal of Experimental Psychology: Learning, Memory, and Cognition, 32*(6), 1341–1354.

Bialystok, Ellen, Peets, Kathleen F., & Moreno, Sylvain (2014). Producing bilinguals through immersion education: Development of metalinguistic awareness. *Applied Psycholinguistics, 35*, 177–191.

Bugayong, Lenny Kaye (2011). Taglish and the social role of code switching in the Philippines. *Philippine Journal of Linguistics, 42*, 1–19.

Cunanan, Bonifacio T. (2013). The language profile and the language attitudes of the administrators, faculty members, personnel, and students of a Philippine state university: Implications for language policy formulation. *Asian Journal of English Language Studies, 1*, 136.

254 *Loy Lising*

Dayag, Danilo T., & Dita, Shirley N. (2012). The state of linguistic research in the Philippines: Trends, prospects, and challenges. In V.A. Miralao & J.B. Agbisit (Eds.), *Philippine social sciences: Capacities, directions, and challenges* (pp. 110–126). Quezon City: Philippine Social Science Council.

De Los Reyes, Robert A. (2000). Language of "order": English in the linguistic landscape of two major train stations in the Philippines. *Asian Journal of English Language Studies, 2*, 24–49.

Diebold Jr., A. Richard (1964). Incipient bilingualism. In D. Hymes (Ed.), *Language in culture and society* (pp. 495–511). New York: Harper & Row.

Ethnologue: Languages of the World. (2018). *Philippines.* Retrieved February 15, 2018, from https://www.ethnologue.com/country/PH

Garcia, Ofelia, & Li Wei. (2014). *Translanguaging: Language, bilingualism, and education.* New York: Palgrave MacMillan.

Gonzales, Wilkinson Daniel Wong. (2016). Trilingual code-switching using quantitative lenses: An exploratory study on Hokanglish. *Philippine Journal of Linguistics, 47*, 106–128.

Gonzales, Wilkinson Daniel Wong. (2017). Language contact in the Philippines: The history and ecology from a Chinese Filipino perspective. *Language Ecology, 1*(2), 185–212. https://doi.org/10.1075/le.1.2.04gon

Gonzalez, Andrew FSC. (1996). Philippine English. In Ma. Lourdes S. Bautista (Ed.), *Readings in Philippine sociolinguistics* (pp. 88–92). Manila: De La Salle University Press.

Gonzalez, Andrew FSC, & Bautista, Maria Lourdes S. (1986). *Language surveys in the Philippines, 1966–1984.* Manila: De La Salle University Press.

Grosjean, Francois. (1982). Life with two languages: An introduction to bilingualism. Cambridge, MA: Harvard University Press.

Gumperz, John J. (1982). *Discourse strategies.* Cambridge: Cambridge University Press.

Heller, Monica. (2009). Doing ethnography. In L. Wei & M. Moyer (Eds.), *The Blackwell Guide to research methods in bilingualism and multilingualism* (pp. 249–262). Oxford: Blackwell Publishing.

Jamora, Michael John A. (2014). Multilingualism: An ethnographic study on Maranao school children in Sorsogon City, Philippines. *CNU Journal of Higher Education, 9*, 1–14.

Jazul, Maria Eina Maxine A., & Bernardo, Alejandro S. (2017). A look into Manila Chinatown's Linguistic Landscape: The role of language and language ideologies. *Philippine Journal of Linguistics, 48*, 75–98.

Jespersen, Otto. (1922). *Language: its nature, development and origin.* London: G. Allen & Unwin.

Le Borgne, Eric. (2009, July 4). Remittances and the Philippines' economy: The elephant in the room. *The World Bank.* Retrieved from http://blogs.worldbank. org/eastasiapacific/remittances-and-the-philippines-economy-the-elephant-in-the-room

Lim, Joo Hyuk, & Borlongan, Ariane M. (2011). Tagalog particles in Philippine English: The case of Ba, Na, No and Pa. *Philippine Journal of Linguistics, 42*, 58–73.

Lising, Loy. (2017). Language in skilled migration. In Suresh Canagarajah (Ed.), *The Routledge Handbook of Migration and Language* (pp. 296–311). Abingdon: Routledge, Taylor & Francis Group.

Lising, Loy, Peters, Pam, & Smith, Adam. (in press). Code-switching in online academic discourse: Resources for Philippine English. *English World-Wide, 41*(2), 131–161.

Lorente, Beatriz. (2017). *Scripts of Servitude: Language, labor migration and transnational domestic work*. Bristol: Multilingual Matters.

Magno, Joseleanor M. (2017). Linguistic landscape in Cebu city higher education offering communication programs. *Asia Pacific Journal of Multidisciplinary Research, 5*(1), 94–103.

Mahboob, Ahmar, & Cruz, Priscilla. (2013). English and mother-tongue-based multilingual education: Language attitudes in the Philippines. *Asian Journal of English Language Studies, 1*, 2.

Maher, John C. (2017). *Multilingualism: A very short introduction*. Oxford: Oxford University Press.

Martin, Isabel Pefianco (Ed.). (2018). *Reconceptualizing English education in a multilingual society: English in the Philippines*. Singapore: Springer. https://doi.org/10.1007/978-981-10-7528-5_1

Martin-Jones, Marilyn, Blackledge, Adrian, & Creese, Angela. (2012). *The Routledge handbook of multilingualism*. London: Routledge.

Myers-Scotton, Carol. (2006). *Multiple voices: An introduction to bilingualism*. Malden, MA: Blackwell.

Nelson, Gerald. (1996a). Markup systems. In Sidney Greenbaum (Ed.), *Comparing English Worldwide: The International Corpus of English* (pp. 36–53). Oxford: Clarendon Press.

Nelson, Gerald. (1996b). The design of the Corpus. In Sidney Greenbaum (Ed.), *Comparing English Worldwide: The International Corpus of English* (pp. 27–35). Oxford: Clarendon Press.

Osborne, Dana M. (2015). *Negotiating the hierarchy of languages in Ilocandia: The social and cognitive implications of massive multilingualism in the Philippines* (Doctoral thesis, The University of Arizona, USA.). Retrieved from https://repository.arizona.edu/handle/10150/556859?show=full

Philippine Statistics Authority. (2016). *Highlights of the Philippine population 2015 Census of Population*. Republic of the Philippines: Author.

Piller, Ingrid. (2015). Language ideologies. *The International encyclopedia of language and social interaction*. doi:10.1002/9781118611463.wbielsi140

Piller, Ingrid. (2016). *Linguistic diversity and social justice: An introduction to applied linguistics*. Oxford: Oxford University Press.

Piller, Ingrid, & Lising, Loy. (2014). Language, employment, and settlement: Temporary meat workers in Australia. *Multilingua, 33*(1–2), 35–59.

Piller, Ingrid, & Lising, Loy. (2016). Language, employment, and settlement: Temporary meat workers in Australia. In Ingrid Piller (Ed.), *Language and migration: Critical concepts in linguistics* (pp. 112–132). London: Routledge, Taylor & Francis Group.

Poplack, Shana. (2004). Code-switching. In U. Ammon, N. Dittmar, K.J. Mattheier, & P. Trudgill (Eds.), *Soziolinguistik: An international handbook of the science of language* (2nd ed., pp. 589–596). Berlin: Walter de Gruyter.

Rosario, Jr, Francisco C. (2010). Languages at Home: The case of bi/multilingualism in Pangasinan. *International Conference on Language, Society, and Culture in Asian Contexts* (pp. 246–256). Mahasarakham Province: Faculty of Humanities and Social Sciences, Mahasarakham University.

256 *Loy Lising*

Sacks, Harvey, Schegloff, Emanuel A., & Jefferson, G. (1974). A simplest systematics for the organization of turn-taking for conversation. *Language, 50*(4), 696–735. Published by: Linguistic Society of America Stable URL: http://www.jstor.org/stable/412243. Accessed: 15–06–2018 05:22 UTC.

Schneider, Edgar. (2003). The dynamics of new Englishes: From identity construction to dialect birth. *Language, 79*(2), 233–281.

Schneider, Edgar. (2007). *Post-colonial English*. Cambridge: Cambridge University Press.

Tajolosa, Teresita D. (2011). The objective and subjective assessments of the ethnolinguistic vitality of Batak Communities in Palawan, Philippines. *Philippine Journal of Linguistics, 42*, 74–103.

Tupas, Ruanni. (2015). Inequalities of multilingualism: Challenges to mother-tongue-based multilingual education. *Language and Education, 29*(2), 112–124.

Turano, Charity T., & Malimas, Mary Ann P. (2013). The medium of instruction for K1-Grade3 in the private schools in Cebu City: Revelations of language preference, usage, exposure and views of students, school administrators, and parents in relation to L1. *Philippine Journal of Linguistics, 44*, 61–82.

Vine, Bernadette. (1999). *Guide to the New Zealand component of the International Corpus of English (ICE-NZ)*. Wellington: School of Linguistics and Applied Language Studies.

Walter, Stephen L., & Decker, Diane E. (2011). Mother tongue instruction in Lubuagan: A case study from the Philippines. *International Review of Education, 57*(5–6), 667–683.

Weinreich, Uriel. (1953). *Languages in contact: Findings and problems*. New York; The Hague: Mouton.

20 Language Policy

Ruanni Tupas

20.1 Introduction: The Role of Language Policy in the Making of Unequal Englishes

This chapter is an introduction to language policy, which includes language-in-education policy, in the Philippines, focusing on features of the policy and the social mechanisms which produced it which have helped construct the shape of Philippine English (PhE), or, better yet, unequal Englishes in the country. In the same way that "English doesn't exist but *Englishes* do" (Reagan, 2004, p. 56), PhE also does not exist but Philippine Englishes do (Gonzales, 2017; Martin, 2014b; Tupas, 2004). However, the notion 'Englishes' does not end with the argument about the plurality of the language. Englishes may be linguistically equal but are nevertheless still unequally valued socially. Among Filipinos, there is a hierarchy of Philippine Englishes and they are not only associated with different meanings and ideologies. In fact, they are imbricated in individual Filipino lives, creating different worlds of opportunities for the speakers (Tupas & Salonga, 2016). Much of what has been done to account for diversities of English has focused on the structures and functions of the different Englishes, but more work should also be done to probe into the social conditions and mechanisms which engender(ed) unequal Englishes in the first place (cf. Ha, 2015; Lee & Jenks, 2018; Pan, 2015; Park, 2015; Ramanathan, 2015; Sabaté-Dalmau, 2018; Salonga, 2015; Tupas, 2015b).

This chapter looks at how language policy has helped construct unequal Englishes in the Philippines. Language policy was one of the cornerstones of American colonial rule in the country, having imposed English as the sole language of instruction, but even after nominal independence in 1946, postcolonial language policy-making has continued to be a party to the legitimization of the dominant role of English in Philippine society. However, even in the context of language policy research, very little has been done to account for the role of language policy in the unequal distribution of Englishes in the Philippines, understandably because the focus has been more on how English vis-à-vis Philippine languages has contributed to social stratification among Filipinos along their abilities to use particular

DOI: 10.4324/9780429427824-26

258   *Ruanni Tupas*

languages. Aside from the unequal distribution of languages, to what extent has language policy become instrumental in the making of unequal Englishes in the Philippines?

20.2 Unequal Englishes as *Lived* Experience

In 2008, something terrible happened to Janina San Miguel, one of the contestants during the nationwide search for Miss Philippines. In the question and answer portion, she failed to answer the question because of her inability to express herself in English. She spoke in halting English, undifferentiated /p/'s and /f/'s, mixed with Tagalog pragmatic particles and discomfiting laughter:

> Well, my family's role for me is so important, because there was the wa—they're they was the one who's...very...haha...Oh I'm so sorry. Umm, my *pamily*...my family...Oh my God. I'm...O.K. I'm so sorry. I...I told that I'm so confident. *Eto*, umm, wait...Hahahaha! Ummm, sorry guys because this was really my *pirst* pageant ever, because I'm only seventeen years old and...haha...I, I did not expect that I came from one of the *tof* ten. Hmmm...So...But I said *dat* my *pamily* is the most important persons in my life. Thank you.

Janina San Miguel eventually won the Miss Philippines-World title most likely because of her strong performance in other parts of the competition, but this did not stop her from being made the scapegoat for everything that was (and is) wrong with Philippine education. In fact, she eventually relinquished her crown and thus failed to represent the country in the international competition. Everyday Filipinos and political leaders had much to say about this unfortunate enactment of Philippine language politics. "How to answer stupidly and still win a beauty pageant" (Sept 23, 2017), says one random online blog; a major news website describes Janina's answer in English as "ear-splitting English" (*Miss World*, 2008, n.p.); and a senior legislator who was at the time of the controversy a proponent of an English as medium of instruction policy in the Philippine Congress describes it as a "sensational failure" and "tormenting to watch" (*Miss World*, 2008, n.d.). In other words, much of the discourse on this issue has put the blame squarely on Janina herself, instead of locating the controversy within broader historical and socioeconomic contexts of language use. Janina San Miguel, after all, was the daughter of a jeepney driver and a laundrywoman who sent their daughter to school presumably with the hope that she would break the cycle of poverty in the family. Unfortunately, while Janina San Miguel would have attended English-medium classes – officially, at least – her proficiency in English would have been formed by a collusion of many factors, foremost of which are her socioeconomic background, her social network both inside and outside of school, and the type of school she attended. Thus:

Language Policy 259

Speaking in English...is a choice and a nonchoice at the same time. English is a symbolic language of privilege, and thus almost everyone chooses to speak it; however, the stratified nature of Philippine society assures that some Englishes are more powerful than others. Yes, they are all 'English', but some are good and some are bad, some educated and some uneducated; spoken by the rich, the poor, and the middle class; some make money, some make 'servants of globalization'[1] and some make Janina.

(Tupas, 2014, p. 45)

Some two decades ago, Tollefson (1991) also made references to similar structural conditions which shaped (and continue to do so) the contours of English language use in the Philippines. He would also refer to how poor Filipino families' choices in life, especially choices of which jobs to take or which schools to attend, were severely hampered by their socioeconomic position in Philippine society. He described and analyzed the case of Hector and Maja Adolpho and their children who aspired for upward socioeconomic mobility, but found out that most 'good' jobs available to them were out of reach because they required proficiencies in English none in the family could produce or perform. In the specific case of Hector Adolpho, the father, his limited English helped him secure a job as a taxi driver for a company which catered to the growing number of foreigners coming to Manila after President Ferdinand Marcos declared martial law in 1972. However, Hector Adolpho could not go further than being a taxi driver, a money changer, or a hustler for goods on the streets of Manila: "His education prepared him for limited contact with foreigners in his taxi, but not for extended interactions requiring fluency and stylistic variation, reading and writing, and a broad range of vocabulary" (Tollefson, 1991, pp. 137–138).

Despite a high degree of commitment to sending their children to good schools, Hector and Maja Adolpho realized that they could not do so because of poverty. The good jobs were available to not only those who spoke English but, more importantly, those who spoke 'good' English. Thus, "despite the family's best efforts" (Tollefson, 1991, p. 138), they feared that their children would be "doomed to a life in the slums of Tondo" (p. 138).

There is much to say about the way the life conditions of Janina San Miguel and the Adolpho family have been framed, for example, in terms of structural determinism (see Harvey, 2003; Mazrui, 1997), which does not allow some form of agency among speakers of (limited) English who can also creatively navigate spaces of unfreedom in society. However, the purpose of deploying these two examples is not to lay down theoretical debates on the usefulness of structure (Phillipson, 1992; Tollefson, 1991) or agency (Canagarajah, 1999; Jenkins, 2006) or even the dichotomous use of the two terms (Hays, 1994) as explanatory lenses in discussions concerning the politics of language in the Philippines. Rather, the examples are mobilized to alert us to the fact that use of English is *conditioned* use of the language, in

260 *Ruanni Tupas*

the sense that there are broad historical conditions which shape the different ways Filipinos use English. Janina San Miguel and the Adolpho family is a reminder that the Englishes they speak are not only repositories of systematic linguistic, functional, or pragmatic pluralities but also *lived* everyday experiences which impact their life conditions and (im)possibilities of social mobility. Thus, this chapter's focus on the role of language policy in the making of unequal Englishes in the Philippines is precisely to account for such lived experiences of speakers of different Englishes. In his preface to the 2017 edition of his classic book, *Cultural politics of English as an International Language*, Pennycook (1994/2017) states that it "is essential to focus not just on a diversity of Englishes but also on the effects of *unequal Englishes*" (p. ix, italics as original).

20.3 Language Policy and Unequal Englishes in the Philippines

In essence, language policy in the Philippines today continues to bear significant traces of American colonialism (Hsu, 2015; Tupas & Tabiola, 2017). The Philippine Constitution, written in both English and Tagalog, clearly stipulates that in cases of confusion or lack of clarity, the English version prevails. Prior to the Philippine-American War of 1899–1902 which eventually paved the way for the forcible rule of American colonialism, the Philippines was under direct rule of Spain for around 350 years. However, despite repeated instructions from the Spanish crown to help spread the learning of Spanish among local Philippine natives, the Spanish missionaries used the local languages instead as they generally believed that it was through these languages that evangelization could be successfully undertaken. Thus, even after more than three centuries of rule, only 2.6% of the native population were fluent in Spanish in 1898 (Gonzalez, 1998). In contrast, the spread of English was far more successful since the number of Filipino speakers of English based on the 1939 census hovered around 26.6%, certainly a huge jump from almost zero speakers in 1898.

20.3.1 English, Educational Policy, and American Colonialism

The key difference between Spanish and American colonial rules in terms of their use of language and education as tools for subjugation was that universal education and, more specifically, the use of English as the sole medium of instruction in the local schools became the cornerstone policy of American colonial rule in the Philippines: "The first and perhaps the master stroke in the plan to use education as an instrument of colonial policy was the decision to use English as the medium of instruction" (Constantino, 1970/2000, p. 432). The purpose of such a policy, of course, was not the mere teaching of English for communication; rather, it was "to 'civilize' the Filipinos" (Martin, 2014a, p. 70). Thus, from the very start of American colonialism in the Philippines,

Language Policy 261

English was not simply to provide the local population a common language but, more importantly, to change the ways Filipinos would speak, behave, and think about themselves and the rest of the world.

It is for this reason that language policy for most of the 20th century and until today has become one of the key battlegrounds of politics and power in society as the country embarked on its endlessly restive nation-building project. Attempts at revising the policy would always take the role and position of English – essentially what to do with it – as the chief talking point in language debates (Gonzalez, 1980). In the 1935 Philippine Constitution, English and Spanish were the official languages of the country, but, when the new 1973 constitution was promulgated, Spanish was removed, but English remained an official language alongside Pilipino (Gonzalez, 1976, pp. 446–447). Thus, "the place of English, Philippine English, is assured, side by side with Pilipino" (Gonzalez, 1976, p. 447). However, it was only in 1974 when the bilingual education policy was implemented that the position of English in Philippine society, and, more particularly in schools, was seriously challenged (Gonzalez, 1980; Tupas, 2015a), but even this did not make much of a dent on its symbolic power because Filipinos, mainly through the initiatives of the government as well, continued to see English as the language of social mobility and global aspirations (more discussion on this point below). Constantino (1970/2000) sums up the two-pronged impact of American colonial language policy which imposed English as the sole medium of instruction during the whole period of direct colonial rule (1903–1946) and the first two decades of political 'independence' (1950s–1960s) on the structure of Philippine society. First:

> English has created a barrier between the monopolists of power and the people. English has become a status symbol, while the native tongues are looked down upon. English has given rise to a bifurcated society of fairly educated men and the masses who are easily swayed by them.
>
> (p. 439)

What this means is that the use of English as medium of instruction has created a hierarchy of languages—referred to as *inequalities of multilingualism* (Tupas, 2015a)—with the colonial language at the top of such a hierarchy and access to which has been essentially the privilege of a small group of Filipino elite. Thus, the social class-divided Philippine society was partly characterized by proficient or non-proficient use of the English language. However, Constantino (1970/2000) also foreshadowed the making of unequal Englishes through language policy as a tool of colonization:

> Now we have a small group of men [sic] who can articulate their thoughts in English, a wider group who can read and speak in fairly comprehensible English and a great mass that hardly expresses itself in any language.
>
> (p. 439)

262   *Ruanni Tupas*

In this quote, Constantino is no longer referring to competing languages per se but is, in fact, making references to the reality of multiple but unequally distributed proficiencies in English. Such a policy, in other words, generated a hierarchy of English language proficiencies distributed along social class lines as well, with a small Filipino elite comfortable and fluent in the use of English, with a larger group of speakers able to carry on conversations in the language, and the majority of Filipino speakers unable to express themselves in the language with relative ease or comfort. The intensified restructuring of the Philippine economy during the period of the Marcos dictatorship, as well as the successive governments' instrumentalist and economic view of English, would collude to legitimize the unequal distribution of Englishes in the country.

20.3.2 *Bilingual Education Policy and the Marketization of Philippine Labor*

The well-entrenched position of English in Philippine society during the time of direct colonization and early postcolonial years did not go unchallenged. The word 'well-entrenched' refers to the enduring power of English in Philippine society where highly valued material and social goods would be accessible largely through competence in the English language. As mentioned earlier, it was in 1974 that the bilingual education policy was implemented, mainly as a response to nation-building debates concerning pragmatism and globalization (English) and nationalism (Tagalog-based Filipino as national language) (Gonzalez, 1974). In effect, the 'bilingual solution' – use English as medium of instruction in the teaching of mathematics and science, and the national language in all other subjects – was a political compromise (Gonzalez, 1980), especially at a time when anti-colonial street protests had been going on since the 1960s calling for, among other major issues, the nationalization of education and the economy. Ironically, however, the sociopolitical and economic context of the implementation of bilingual education was the dictatorial regime of former Philippine President Ferdinand Marcos where the privileged status of English became even more pronounced, but this time with clearly more economistic reasons.

The Philippine economy under President Ferdinand Marcos was restructured toward a more export-oriented economy with the displacement of an import-substitution policy of the 1950s and 1960s to a "more outward-looking market-oriented labour-intensive policy" (Remedio, 1996, p. 3) of the 1970s. Thus, two of the major engines of such a restructuring were the establishment of export processing zones which were meant to entice multinational investors to put up industries in the country and which would then produce products primarily for export, and the supposedly temporary deployment of Filipino overseas workers which resulted in the "massive exodus of millions of contract workers to overseas destinations over the years" (p. 1). The remittances sent back by Filipino overseas workers helped keep

Language Policy 263

the economy afloat while lack of jobs in the country and the mounting rest-lessness of many Filipinos because of the excesses of martial law were bring-ing the economy down. Thus, while labor migration in the Philippines could be traced back centuries earlier during the galleon trade between Manila and Acapulco from the second half of the 16th century to the early 19th century, it was in the 1970s that labor migration began to be "characterized by the deliberate intervention of the state in the structures and processes of migration" (Lorente, 2012, p. 186). It is in this context that English became crucial in facilitating the deliberate structuring of the Philippine economy because of the need for technical skills for local multinational industries and deployment in the global market. The entire educational system was configured in such a way that it would prepare young Filipinos for *particular* jobs both in the local and in the global markets, and English was definitely crucial in making this possible. Below is part of an advertisement in the *New York Times* paid for by the Philippine government in 1974, barely two years after martial law was imposed:

> We like multinationals...Local staff? Clerks with a college education start at $35. Accountants come for $67, executive secretaries for $148...
>
> Our labor force speaks your language. Whether you're talking elec-tronic components, garments or car-manufacturing. National literacy was placed at 83.4% in 1973 (English is the medium of instruction)...
>
> (cited in Tollefson, 1991, p. 140)

20.3.3 Unequal Englishes

It can be seen here how the bilingual policy served as the educational plat-form through which the symbolic power of English would continue to be perpetuated, with the use of English in the schools reconfigured toward the making of Filipinos as, to borrow the words of Parreñas (2001), "servants of globalization" or, in Lorente's (2012) terms, "workers of the world". In fact, what was initially conceived of as a temporary solution to economic and political problems at the time – Filipino labor export – became a 'per-manent' fixture in successive governments' economic policies (Lorente, 2012; Sanders & Brown, 2012), thus cementing further not only the dom-inant presence of English in Philippine society but also its manifest role as a socially stratifying language. According to Tyner (2004), "[o]ne key to the Philippines' economic strategy was the discursive marketing of an 'internationally attractive labor force'" (p. 30) – as can be seen in the ad-vertisement above as an early exemplar of such discursive marketing – but what is especially important to point out is that this labor force is "a cheap and docile workforce prevented from unionizing and striking" (p. 30). The implications of such a deliberate use of English to train or shape Filipino bodies for particular kinds of work in the local and global markets would be massive as Filipinos with differential access to educational and other social

264 *Ruanni Tupas*

resources (e.g., types of schools, quality of English language teaching, family language repertoires) would eventually generate a plurality of Philippine Englishes. Unequal Englishes, foreshadowed in the quote from Constantino (1970/2000) above, would take greater form within "Philippine education system's pattern of producing a hierarchy of labor *with corresponding levels of English skills*" (Lorente, 2012, p. 193, italics supplied).

Filipino language scholars would aptly describe and examine this phenomenon of the pluralization of PhE. They may vary in their critical accounting of the pluralization but they all provide evidence and/or solid argument for the splintering of English used by Filipinos according to class-driven groups of people (Gonzales, 2017; Martin, 2014b). Bautista's (1982, 1996) three-layered class-driven Philippine Englishes have gender dimensions as well, reflecting the socioeconomic and geopolitical context within which English in the country was examined: Yaya ('nanny') English; bar girl English (spoken near American bases in the country); and colegiala English (spoken by convent-educated female students). According to Tinio (2013), with the changing socioeconomic landscapes, Yaya English has 'globalized' into the English of Filipino domestic helpers around the world, bar girl English into the English of Filipina entertainers, especially in Japan, and colegiala English into call-center English. Sibayan and Gonzalez's (1996) account of the hierarchized pluralization of PhE has a wider range, namely, the Englishes of (1) minimally functionally literate Filipinos; (2) Filipino overseas contract workers; (3) white-collar workers; (4) the middle and upper-middle class; and (5) intellectuals. It seems that, while varied in their accounting of the differences, the scholars' different categories of Filipino speakers fall into Martin's (2014b) concentric circles of PhE – the inner circle, the outer circle, and the expanding circle Englishes, precisely alluding to the reality that Filipinos' Englishes are shaped by their class positions in society. Speakers of inner circle PhE would be those who use English as their mother tongue or at least as their dominant language, and which also approximates the 'standard' variety of international English. The expanding circle PhE speakers belong to the opposite side of the spectrum as they have very limited command of the English language and thus are most likely not formally educated, who come from socioeconomically marginalized sectors of the society, and live in home environments which do not use English.

Although not totally framed within class-driven understandings of PhE pluralities, Gonzales (2017) proposes an even wider range of categorization of Philippine Englishes, namely, substrate-influenced Englishes (e.g., Philippine Chinese English), social Englishes (e.g., occupation-based Englishes), and hybrid Englishes (e.g., Hokaglish [mix of Hokkien, Tagalog and English]). Nevertheless, he also sees the role of unequal Englishes in the context of Philippine Englishes:

> For example, speakers of Iloilo English may perceive their English to be superior compared with Manila English possibly due to the no-'dialect' language policies enforced in some schools or due to other factors. At

Language Policy   265

the same time, they may feel inferior to the seemingly superior Manila English or other 'standard' Englishes.

(Gonzales, 2017, p. 13)

20.4 Conclusion

This chapter is but a sketch of language policy issues in the Philippines, and thus is intended to raise awareness of some pertinent issues related mainly to the impact of language policy on the pluralization of Philippine Englishes. In recent years, Mother Tongue-Based Multilingual Education (MTB-MLE) has replaced bilingual education in kindergarten and the first three years of primary education, and this recent change in Philippine language policy animates discussions on pedagogy (i.e., in which language do students learn most efficiently?), practice (i.e., how is MTB-MLE implemented by individual teachers?), and ideology (i.e., how can the mother tongues serve as vehicles of national identity and unity? (Nolasco, 2009; Tupas, 2015a). Yet, the questions remain centered on stakes for different languages in the country – English, Filipino, and (some) mother tongues – and how their use or lack of it has shaped the lives of Filipinos in different, unequal ways.

This chapter, in turn, frames the language policy discussions within the phenomenon of unequal Englishes in the Philippines. It argues that language policy has been intricately involved in the politics of pluralization of English in the country as well, such that Filipinos do not only speak different Philippine Englishes but they do, in fact, speak unequally valued Englishes. In a sense, the chapter makes a case for the need to bring together language policy research and World Englishes research because, as has perhaps been demonstrated in this chapter, language policy does not only shape or determine the use or non-use of languages. It also does have a huge impact on the contours of linguistic pluralization. Thus, making the link clearer between language policy and PhE through the lens of unequal Englishes, one is able to uncover and examine "often-masked social inequities" (Salonga, 2015, p. 131).

Note

1 Parreñas (2001).

References

Bautista, M. L. S. (1982). Yaya English. *Philippine Studies*, 30, 377–394.

Bautista, Maria Lourdes S. (1996). Notes on three sub-varieties of Philippine English. In M. L. S. Bautista (ed.), *Readings in Philippine sociolinguistics* (pp. 93–101). Manila: De La Salle University.

Canagarajah, A. S. (1999). *Resisting linguistic imperialism in English teaching.* Oxford, the United Kingdom: Oxford University Press.

Constantino, R. (1970/2000). The mis-education of the Filipino. *Journal of Contemporary Asia*, 30(3), 428–444.

266   *Ruanni Tupas*

Gonzales, W. D. W. (2017). Philippine Englishes. *Asian Englishes*, 19(1), 79–95.

Gonzalez, A. B. (1974). The 1973 Constitution and the bilingual education policy of the Department of Education and Culture. *Philippine Studies*, 22, 325–337.

Gonzalez, A. B. (1976). Content in English language materials in the Philippines: A case study of cultural and linguistic emancipation. *Philippine Studies*, 24(4), 443–454.

Gonzalez, A. B. (1980). *Language and nationalism: The Philippine experience thus far*. Quezon, the Philippines: Ateneo de Manila University Press.

Gonzalez, A. B. (1998). The language planning situation in the Philippines. *Journal of Multilingual and Multicultural Development*, 19(5), 487–525.

Ha, P. L. (2015). Unequal Englishes in imagined intercultural interactions. In R. Tupas (ed.), *Unequal Englishes: The politics of Englishes today* (pp. 223–243). Basingstoke: Palgrave.

Harvey, S. (2003). Critical perspectives on language (s). *Journal of Sociolinguistics*, 7(2), 246–259.

Hays, S. (1994). Structure and agency and the sticky problem of culture. *Sociological Theory*, *12*(1), 57–72.

How to answer stupidly and still win a beauty pageant (2017). Accessed on September 27, 2018, from https://www.pinoymoneytalk.com/binibining-pilipinas-funny-video/.

Hsu, F. (2015). The coloniality of neoliberal English: The enduring structures of American colonial English instruction in the Philippines and Puerto Rico. *L2 Journal*, 7(3), 123–145.

Jenkins, J. (2006). Current perspectives on teaching world Englishes and English as a lingua franca. *TESOL Quarterly*, 40(1), 157–181.

Lee, J. W. & Jenks, C. J. (2018). Aestheticizing language: Metapragmatic distance and unequal Englishes in Hong Kong. *Asian Englishes*, http://www.tandfonline.com/action/showCitFormats?doi=10.1080/13488678.2018.14489 62

Lorente, B. P. (2012). The making of 'Workers of the World': Language and the labor brokerage state. In A. Duchene & M. Heller (eds.), *Language in late capitalism: Pride and profit* (pp. 183–206). New York & London: Routledge.

Martin, I. P. (2014a). Beyond nativization? Philippine English in Schneider's Dynamic Model. In S. Buschfield, T. Hoffman, M. Huber, & A. Kautzsch (eds.), *The evolution of Englishes: The dynamic model and beyond* (pp. 70–95). Amsterdam: John Benjamins.

Martin, I. P. (2014b). Philippine English revisited. *World Englishes*, 33(1), 50–59.

Mazrui, A. (1997). The World Bank, the language question and the future of African education. *Race & Class*, 38(3), 35–48.

Miss Philippines World's ear-splitting English an 'eye-opener' for RP – solon (March 15, 2008). *GMA News Online*, from http://www.gmanetwork.com/news/showbiz/content/84929/miss-philippines-world-s-ear- splitting-english-an-eye-opener-for-rp-solon/story/, accessed on September 24, 2018.

Nolasco, R. (2009). *Twenty-one reasons why Filipino children learn better while using their mother tongue: A primer on mother tongue-based multilingual education (MLE) and other issues on language and learning in the Philippines*, Guro Formation Forum, University of the Philippines, Quezon City.

Pan, L. (2015). Globalization and the spread of unequal Englishes: Vernacular signs in the Center of Beijing. In R. Tupas (ed.), *Unequal Englishes: The politics of Englishes today* (pp. 163–184). Basingstoke: Palgrave.

Park, J. S.-Y. (2015). Structures of feeling in unequal Englishes. In R. Tupas (ed.), *Unequal Englishes: The politics of Englishes today* (pp. 59–73). Basingstoke: Palgrave.

Language Policy 267

Parreñas, R. S. (2001). *Servants of globalization: Women, migration and domestic work*. Redwood City, CA: Stanford University Press.

Pennycook, A. (1994/2017). Preface. *The cultural politics of English as an International language*. London, the United Kingdom: Routledge.

Phillipson, R. (1992). *Linguistic imperialism*. Oxford & New York: Oxford University Press, 1992.

Ramanathan, V. (2015). Contesting the Raj's 'divide and Rule' policies: Linguistic apartheid, unequal Englishes, and the postcolonial framework. In R. Tupas (ed.), *Unequal Englishes: The politics of Englishes today* (pp. 203–222). Basingstoke: Palgrave.

Reagan, T. (2004). Objectification, positivism and language studies: A reconsideration. *Critical Inquiry in Language Studies*, 1(1), 41–60.

Remedio, E. M. (1996). *Export processing zones in the Philippines: A review of employment, working conditions and labour relations. Working Paper No. 77*. Geneva: International Labour Office.

Sabaté-Dalmau, M. (2018). 'I speak small': Unequal Englishes and transnational identities among Ghanaian migrants. *International Journal of Multilingualism*. http://www.tandfonline.com/action/showCitFormats?doi=10.1080/14790718.2018.1428329.

Salonga, A. (2015). Performing gayness and English in an offshore call center industry. In R. Tupas (ed.), *Unequal Englishes: The politics of Englishes today* (pp. 130–142). Basingstoke: Palgrave.

Sanders, R. S. & Brown, D. L. (2012). The migratory response of labor to Special Economic Zones in the Philippines, 1995–2005. *Population Research Policy Review*, 31, 141–164.

Sibayan, B. P. & Gonzalez, A. (1996). Post-imperial English in the Philippines. In J. A. Fishman, A. W. Conrad & A. Rubal-Lopez (eds.), *Post-Imperial English: Status change in former British and American colonies, 1940–1990* (pp. 139–172). Berlin /New York: Mouton de Gruyter.

Tinio, M. T. (2013). Nimble tongues: Philippine English and the feminization of labour. In L. Wee, R. B. H. Goh & L. Lim (eds.), *The politics of English: Southeast Asia, Southeast Asia and the Asia Pacific* (pp. 205–224). Amsterdam: John Benjamins.

Tollefson, J. W. (1991). *Planning language, planning inequity*. London: Longman.

Tupas, R. (2004). The politics of Philippine English: Neocolonialism, global politics, and the problem of postcolonialism. *World Englishes*, 23(1), 47–58.

Tupas, R. (2014). Beauty contestant. In J. Barker, E. Harms & J. Lindquist (eds.), *Figures of Southeast Asian modernity* (pp. 43–45). Honolulu: University of Hawai'i Press.

Tupas, R. (2015a). Inequalities of multilingualism: Challenges to mother tongue-based multilingual education. *Language and Education*, 29(2), 112–124.

Tupas, R. (ed.) (2015b). *Unequal Englishes: The politics of Englishes today*. Basingstoke: Palgrave.

Tupas, R. & Salonga, A. (2016). Unequal Englishes in the Philippines. *Journal of Sociolinguistics*, 20(3), 367–381.

Tupas, R. & Tabiola, H. (2017). Language policy and development aid: A critical analysis of an ELT project, *Current Issues in Language Planning* (early online publication), http://www.tandfonline.com/action/showCitFormats?doi=10.1080/14664208.2017.1351329.

Tyner, J. A. (2004). *Made in the Philippines: Gendered discourses and the making of migrants*. London, the United Kingdom: Routledge.

Part 6
Learning and Teaching

21 Acquisition and Learning

Aireen Barrios

21.1 Purpose of This Chapter

Putting children in bilingual (or multilingual) environments serves two important aims: One is to understand mental processes involved in bilingual development; the other is to understand what skills bilinguals need to aid in learning in later years (Hoff, 2014). The multilingual landscape of the Philippines provides for the dynamic interaction of various languages as the child begins to acquire them and to develop competency in these languages. This chapter provides a review of literature on language development studies involving Filipino children. It will also feature a case study describing child language acquisition of a one-year-old's communicative intents in a multilingual household and expressive vocabulary development as he progresses in his early years as a toddler. The chapter concludes by theorizing on how English is acquired, particularly in the Philippine multilingual context.

21.2 Child Language Acquisition Research Post-1986

It has been 30 years since Gonzalez wrote in 1986 the state of the art then on child language studies in the Philippines about which he made several arguments as to what direction child language studies in the Philippines should take. First, he contended that, while Tagalog could further be studied for grammatical and semantic features, there is enough attention given to its early acquisition from the pre-linguistic stage through the first ten years of childhood. The highly multilingual landscape of the country offers greater context of study of the 'wider ecology' for language acquisition. Besides caregiver input and conscious use of English in households, for example, it remains to be figured what exactly are the external factors such as school and community support which would account for early learners' second language success in English? The studies reviewed pre-1986 are found wanting in this dimension of language studies among children.

Gonzalez (1986) also noted that much of the literature examines cross-sectional data, which is limited in sufficiently describing facets of language development. Longitudinal investigations of child linguistic output against

DOI: 10.4324/9780429427824-28

272   *Aireen Barrios*

a range of sociolinguistic variables and interactants would also enrich literature on the development of grammar, semantic, and pragmatic competence, and the child's social construction of reality through speech. Crucial, too, is the systematic description of simultaneous bilingual (or multilingual) children and theorizing about bilingual competence among them. Related to bilingual competence is the question of interrelation of skills among children, specifically of transfer effects between a first language (L1) and a second language (L2) or languages.

Adapting Gonzalez's (1986) review structure, Table 21.1 shows a survey of child language studies in the Philippines since 1986, mapped onto Gonzalez's recommendations for research.

It is interesting to note that hardly any study in the area was done in the decade before the 2000s. While this chapter tried to be exhaustive in its review, it is highly possible that some studies, particularly unpublished master' theses and doctoral dissertations, have been missed. Nevertheless, what is noteworthy is that this research area gathered renewed interest beginning in the 2000s, mostly taking a psycholinguistic perspective. Almost all researchers in this review share a common association with their mentor Professor Allan Bernardo, who himself is a well-respected cognitive psychologist at De La Salle University. Together either with their mentor or with their own advisees or co-authors, or as individual researchers, this group of 2000-era scholars produced a set of studies examining features of child discourse, literacy, and acquisition of grammatical categories and properties.

Lucas and Bernardo (2008) investigate the phenomenon of noun bias among Filipino-English bilingual pre-school children, in relation to adult input variables, particularly frequency of noun and verb productions, utterance positioning of nouns and verbs, and context. Sixty Filipino-English bilingual children aged around three years and their caregivers were audio-recorded at their homes as they interacted with each other in their usual activities. Analysis of data revealed a noun bias in bilingual children's English vocabulary, which is accounted for by the frequency of nouns caregivers provide in their input. Noun bias could not be determined in the Filipino vocabularies of children because it appears that caregivers provide lower number of nouns as opposed to verbs. This finding supports the notion that the noun bias phenomenon is language-specific rather than a universal occurrence.

Syntactic differences between English and Filipino also explained the different associations between salient positions of nouns and verbs in adult input and in children's vocabularies in both languages. Pursuing the same question as the earlier Lucas and Bernardo (2008) study, this time, among a small group of Mandarin-English bilinguals of a Chinese community in Manila, the Philippines, Xin and Lucas (2010) revealed a noun bias in English among 15 pre-schoolers. This bias is associated with the frequency of nouns in the final position of caregivers' input, a variable that predicted noun bias in early lexicon.

Table 21.1 Survey of Child Language Studies from 1986 to Present

Methodology	Researcher	Year	Focus	Specific Gonzalez Recommendation Addressed
Elicitation/task-based	Lalunio	2001	Emergent reading in English of pre-school children	Home and school as important agencies in influencing emergent reading
Case study	Reyes-Wandless	2002	Conceptual associations in English among pre-school children	Home, community, and SES variables in second language acquisition
Experimental	Concepcion	2005	Inflectional awareness on syntactic bootstrapping and fast mapping in Filipino, English, and Chabacano by 4–6-year-olds	Involvement of Filipino-English-Chabacano multilinguals
Mother-child dyads of spontaneous speech	Maxilom	2008	Linguistic cues as input to number word acquisition among toddlers	Involvement of Cebuano-English-Filipino multilinguals
Naturalistic data from child-caregiver interactions	Lucas	2008	Discourse types by Filipino-English bilingual pre-schoolers	Involvement of Filipino-English bilinguals
Naturalistic data from child-caregiver interactions	Lucas and Bernardo	2008	Noun bias in Filipino-English bilingual pre-schoolers	Involvement of Filipino-English bilinguals
Naturalistic data from child-caregiver interactions	Xin and Lucas	2010	Noun bias among Mandarin-English pre-school children	Involvement of Mandarin-English bilinguals
Elicitation/task-based	Barrios and Bernardo	2012	Cross-linguistic transfer in case marking from L1 to L2 among grade 2 children in non-L1-Filipino-speaking areas	Focus on Chabacano and Cebuano as L1 to L2 Filipino
Children's storytelling	Tao and Lucas	2012	Referential adequacy in oral narratives among toddler to school-aged children	Involvement of Mandarin-English bilinguals
Experimental	Miraflores and Lucas	2015	Pragmatic principles in word learning	Involvement of Filipino-English bilinguals

274   *Aireen Barrios*

Examining a subset of the child-caregiver dyads, Lucas (2008) finds that three-year-old pre-school children from middle class families in Manila produce more response-type utterances because of their limited vocabulary and communicative repertoire. Notably, children exhibit a preference for English over their home language, which could be explained by their accessibility to sources of input in English, particularly media and learning materials.

How children learn new words is explained by principles of whole object assumption, mutual exclusivity, and joint reference. Using a slideshow of pictures in audio-visual format and presented in Filipino and in English, Miraflores and Lucas (2015) investigated whether three-year-old pre-school children would use any of the word learning constraints in learning a new word or a label. Results reveal that the 40 children tested assign a new word or label to the whole object and not to any of its parts unless the object is familiar to them. Children do not apparently rely on social cues like looking or gazing when learning a new word or label as they become more perceptually receptive to new objects and more independent in exploring their environment.

Focusing on another set of Mandarin-English bilinguals in the Philippines, Tao and Lucas (2012) investigated referential adequacy in young L1 Mandarin and L2 English children's oral narratives in Mandarin, age, and discourse position. Eighty children aged three, five, seven, and nine were asked to tell stories using wordless picture books that were designed based on three referential functions: introducing, maintaining, and reintroducing a character. Comprehensible stories are produced when the narrator introduces a character, maintains reference to that character, and shows a switch in character. Results reveal that the ability to produce comprehensible stories progresses as age increases. The oldest set of participants performed all referential functions exceedingly well, using different linguistic forms for each type of referential function, whereas the youngest ones could maintain reference to only major characters. Children also demonstrate development of presupposing addressee's knowledge of the referent and his attention toward it.

Literacy develops prior to formal schooling, including affective aspects of the reading and writing experience. The home and the school play an integral role in providing meaningful opportunities for emergent reading. Lalunio (2001) finds these conclusions relevant as she explores literacy among 21 bilingual pre-schoolers from middle class families that speak Filipino and English. Varied age-appropriate reading tasks were used to examine children's awareness of and responses to print, in addition to attitudes and concepts about reading and writing.

Reyes-Wandless (2002) argues that language activities that allowed children to express conceptual associations in L1 could simultaneously develop competence in L2. A case study of six four- and five-year-old typically developing children from financially disadvantaged families residing in an urban

Acquisition and Learning 275

community in Metro Manila, the Philippines, were asked to verbalize their thoughts as they listened to stories in English read aloud by their pre-school teacher. Transcript analyses of the videotaped data reveal that children were capable of making meaningful conceptual associations of the stories and of communicating these effectively in Tagalog, their L1. Despite limited exposure to English which children accessed through media and occasional reading materials, experiences in the home and in the community allowed the children to form images or to create events as they learned a second language.

As Gonzalez (1986) points out, the topic which has received the most attention is bilingual competence. Concepcion (2005) examines the Filipino-English- and Chabacano-English-speaking children's ability to fast map, their morphological awareness, and their ability to use syntactic bootstrapping to identify the referents of novel verbs. In fast mapping tasks designed in two inflection conditions, 60 children aged 4–6 years were taught novel words. Results revealed that both bilingual groups generally showed ability to fast map verbs in both their languages and awareness of inflectional morphemes attached to novel verbs to identify their referents. More important, the results reveal significant difference between bilingual groups, suggesting that exposure to languages with richer morphologies such as Tagalog can facilitate learners' ability to break down a verb into its stem and its inflection because they experience more instances of varying verbal inflection in their vocabulary.

Maxilom (2008) examines the role of linguistic cues in multilingual children's acquisition of number words and in possible variations of these linguistic cues across three languages: Cebuano, English, and Filipino. Twelve Cebuano-English-Filipino multilingual toddlers aged 1.5–3 years old and their mothers shared spontaneous interactions, which were recorded non-continuously for five hours during everyday activities such as bathing, dressing, feeding, playing, and reading. Hypotheses of possible variations of linguistic cues across languages which combine (or not) with specific grammatical units such as count nouns, intensifiers, adjectives, and partitive constructions are posed. Analyses support these hypotheses, particularly that the languages in question combine these linguistic codes differently from one another. Interestingly, too, mothers and their children preferred to use the English code in using number words more frequently than the other languages.

While these studies provide insightful data on language processing and the role the variables play in the process within the realistic contexts of different bilingual situations in the Philippines, the question of what accounts for specific observed linguistic manifestations resulting from acquiring a L2 is thinly explored. Acquisition of Filipino as a L2 is an important area for study because L2 Filipino is widespread in many areas across the archipelago where the regional language is the home language and/or the lingua franca. Liao (2006) emphasizes that few studies on the acquisition of Philippine languages have been done since the 1980s.

Barrios and Bernardo (2012) set out to investigate L1-L2 cross-linguistic transfer effects among young school-aged children whose languages differ in specific grammatical properties. Developments in theoretical linguistics in the Philippines characterize Philippine-type languages as ergative. From this perspective, the study tested whether an accusative language background would influence case marking acquisition of ergative Filipino. A focus on Chabacano is especially given because it appears to exhibit an accusative actancy structure owing to its unique linguistic history as a Spanish-based creole (Nolasco, 2005). The language also operates within a dominantly ergative linguistic environment. It is hypothesized that young L1 Chabacano would experience some difficulty learning Filipino as a L2. Psycholinguistic tasks on picture naming, picture description, and grammaticality judgment performed by 100 children in different parts in the Visayas and in Mindanao do show a contrast in performance between these two bilingual groups with two contrasting L1 typologies. One-way analysis of variance (ANOVA) results show significant overgeneralization errors of the nominative *ang* among the Chabacano L1 learners of L2 Filipino. A typical example is *binasag ang bata ang bote* 'the boy broke the bottle' where both the transitive subject *bata* 'boy' and the transitive object *bote* 'bottle' are case-marked nominative. The comparison group composed of L1 Cebuano-L2 Filipino learners did not exhibit marked difficulty. The study offers theoretical evidence for cross-linguistic transfer accounting for language errors, and it provides empirical support to instructional design in L2 learning for learners from different L1 backgrounds. This is especially relevant to the current mother tongue-based instruction in the first three grades in the elementary.

The last decade has seen child studies in the country as beginning to involve the regional languages, particularly Chabacano and Cebuano, altering the course of inquiry from a heavy attention to children acquiring or learning Tagalog and English. Still, a comprehensive description of bilingual (or multilingual) competence of the Filipino child from differing L1 backgrounds is absent. All studies in the present review involve specific language groups with varied sample sizes, and they are all cross-sectional in design. Since Gonzalez's pioneering longitudinal studies on first language acquisition (Pascasio, 2000), there has been little attempt to do systematic studies over longer periods of time. Such a design is necessary if one is to theorize about what internal and external factors influence bilingual competence, what strategies bilingual learners from differing L1 backgrounds use, and what skills they need to support them in school in later years (Hoff, 2014). Developmental patterns of acquisition of specific aspects of language could be related, for example, to external factors such as increasing age and language proficiency levels. Comparative examination of production data using naturalistic methods and structured elicitations would also yield insightful conclusions from the nexus of these two methodologies. A truly interdisciplinary program of research involving the rich lode of language codes, as Gonzalez (1986) describes it, is still necessary.

21.3 A Case Study

In the study of typical language development, one of the significant turning points in children's early development is the production of their first words. Because infants are just beginning to acquire words, it is understandable that most research examining infant speech involves receptive vocabulary. By the time they enter toddlerhood, measuring productive speech becomes possible and relevant.

At the same time, the range of available assessment tools and approaches varies as the subjects vary in age. Parental report is often useful in reporting children's speech at the onset of their receptive and productive vocabulary development because they are the most natural interlocutors with their children. Recording and reporting data becomes free of the usual complications brought about by children's behavioral or attentional states, degree of familiarity with the assessor, degree of familiarity with articulation patterns, distraction from recording equipment, and effects of topic choice and interlocutor presence.

Spontaneous speech samples also provide valuable data on children's vocabulary particularly on questions such as how caregiver input could influence the degree of variety in children's emerging speech. Spontaneous speech samples are usually video- or audio-recorded in the child's home or in a laboratory, which provides a natural and 'ecologically valid' context, reducing or eliminating practice effects and restrictions on data collection. Transcripts generated from the child's own talk and gestures and the parents' or caregivers' interaction with their child provide a wealth of information which could be analyzed for lexical, phonological, syntactic, and pragmatic domains of speech production (Pan, 2012). In the following section, a case study is reported, the case of child language acquisition of a one-year-old's communicative intents in a multilingual household and expressive vocabulary development as he progresses in his early years as a toddler. In the case study, both these data types (i.e., parental reports and spontaneous speech samples) are considered.

Pragmatic development is "the development of the use of language to serve communicative functions" (Hoff, 2014, p. 209). Babies are not born with the intent to communicate immediately. Newborns cry, make vegetative sounds, smile, and laugh, and caregivers interpret these behaviors as sending a message across, such as being hungry or thirsty, or happy or sad. Bates, Camaioni, and Volterra (1975) propose that infants begin to communicate intents through a perlocutionary phase; that is, infants' behavior has consequences on the hearer but is not produced with a communicative intent.

The subject in the present case study, Mario, belongs to a multilingual household which speaks a number of regional languages, in addition to English and Filipino. Mario started to produce vocalizations at around one month when a cooing exchange was noted between him and his nanny.

278   *Aireen Barrios*

He would produce long vowel-like sounds, mostly /u/ whenever he was contented and happy. In many cases, he would turn to look at the interlocutor, smiling, or gazing up, or fixing his eyes on him or her. Soon after this pre-lexical stage, he produced his first true syllable *ma* at two months when he hit his head hard on the doorjamb. Canonical babbling became more discernible at eight months whenever he was playful, happy, or hungry, producing reduplications as *mama, baba,* and *dede*.

By the time he was 17 months, his repertoire had expanded into at least 13 recorded words in English—*mama, papa, baba* (referring to his nanny named Love-Love), *dada, daddy, mom, yeah, yes, no, coo-coo, ba-bye, hello,* and *oh,* in addition to some honorific terms, expressions, and particles frequently used in the other home languages such as *ate, nay, dede* (referring to his milk bottle), *hala ka,* and *nah.*

Along with the increase in vocabulary size was a development in expressing want for food, a toy, or a book using gaze, communicative pointing, and body movements. In one instance recorded, Mario looked at food, then at his mother, then back at the food, and then pointed at it to express want. In another example, while being carried by his mother, he swayed his body forward to ask to be carried to the chest drawers where his toys were kept. At bedtime once, he picked up a book and showed it to his mother who understood it as a request for her to read it aloud to him. He had also begun by this stage to express negation by shaking his head or stomping his feet, and flailing his arms when he was upset or when he wanted something but could not have it. He demonstrated affection by smiling and embracing and kissing people, waving goodbye, or blowing a kiss.

The use of non-forms of the target language which however successfully conveys communication through behavior is what Bates calls the illocutionary phase of the speech act development. By this stage, the elements of perlocution and illocution are present, in that the behavior as communicated by the child has an effect on the hearer, only that conventional language is absent. In the foregoing examples, Mario's behavior to communicate an imperative is effectively understood by the hearer even without the use of language.

The final stage, locution, starts when the child begins to use language along with behavior to communicate intentions. First words may be used idiosyncratically at first, and gradually children learn to use language forms referentially. Mario's locution phase is characterized by the use of gestures and single words at 18 months. His early use of the word *ba* referred to at least two objects of interest—milk bottle and toys. After gazing at his nanny for some time as she sipped from a cup, Mario uttered *ba* as he pointed at his bottle. In another instance, upon waking up, he pulled at his mom's hair and uttered *ba* in a high pitch, pointing at the crib where some of his toys were kept. In most instances, if the caregiver missed his request, he would turn his interlocutor's face to the direction of his interest. His expression of *ba* appears to mean a request for something he wants. Because children's words

Acquisition and Learning 279

are limited, the use of extralinguistic means such as intonation and gestures helps indicate illocutionary force to the hearer.

In a later instance, while his mother was preparing things for a family trip to the mall, Mario took a pack of biscuits and gave it to his nanny. As he did this, he uttered /ki/ in a rising intonation and raised his hands palm faced up toward his chest. His nanny understood it to mean that he wanted to eat the biscuits. His utterance of /ki/ appears to be a process of segment substitution where the velar /g/ is substituted by /k/, and the final consonant /v/ is deleted. Other referential words containing phonological processes (Vihman, as cited in Hoff, 2014) demonstrate weak syllable deletion and substitution (e.g., /banaɪ/ for *banana*, his favorite fruit), and consonant reduction (e.g., maɪ for *smile* as he held up the cellphone to 'take' a selfie; /do/ for *dog* whom he recognized on the label of a rolled tissue paper; /ba/ for *bus* referring to his favorite character on a cartoon series, *TAYO The Little Bus*; and /ka/ for *car*, his favorite toy.

By the time Mario turned 24 months, his vocabulary had expanded to include verbs, and he had started producing two-word utterances, notably noun and verb combinations, such as *mama cry*, *epeɪn* (airplane) *gone*, *ba-bye nanay*, *ba-bye jabi* (Jollibee), *ba-bye car*, *epen do* (open door), and *call papa* as he held the cellphone to his mother.

21.4 Toward Theorizing on Children's Acquisition of English

Mario's first words within his first two years appear to be categorized into three: nouns, verbs, and social terms. There, clearly, is evidence for a noun bias in his early productive speech. Although literature maintains that universals in early development do not necessarily suggest a noun bias and that clear cross-linguistic and cross-cultural variations are observed in children's early word learning, the present case reveals that nouns do dominate the child's first words regardless of language spoken (the household is multilingual) or context. Whether this phenomenon could be attributed to caregiver input factors, specifically frequency in noun use (Tardif, Gelman, & Xu, 1999), can be explained upon closer examination of interlocutor data.

Nevertheless, Mario's use of more nouns than other lexical categories lends support to the idea that nouns enjoy a 'conceptual advantage' over verbs because they map onto perceptual concepts. Words that involve relational naming systems, spatial relations, and actions are more difficult to learn and are thus acquired later. The case is true with Mario as nouns formed an integral part of his early language acquisition from infancy until he turned one. By the time he turned two years, his sophistication in language use had developed to include categories with more complex meaning relations. Tardif, Liang, Zhang, Fletcher, and Kaciroti (2008) reveal similar findings in an examination of cross-cultural corpora of children aged 8–16 months who were residing in the United States, in Beijing, and in Hong Kong. Frequency counts reveal that common nouns are the most frequently

280   *Aireen Barrios*

occurring words in children's speech in English, Putonghua (Mandarin), and Cantonese. Nouns such as *mommy, daddy,* and the equivalents of these terms were present in all these three language groups.

Second, Mario's vocabulary is clearly replete with terms in English even if input in the household is a combination of four languages—the nanny speaks a mix of Filipino, Bisaya, Chabacano, and infrequently in English; the mother code-switches between Chabacano and English; and the father speaks frequently in Chabacano and at other times in English. It was observed that the child would respond in English even if he was spoken to in any of the other home languages, a finding that is consistent with Lucas (2008).

In the child's everyday activities at home, the television serves as the fourth 'interlocutor'. On average, the child spends at least six hours on television viewing a day in between meals and naps, in addition to occasional playtime with gadgets such as cellphones and tablets. Because both parents go to work every day of the week, the child is left in the nanny's care for at least ten hours a day. As mentioned earlier, the nanny speaks very little English, yet the child demonstrates enough lexical and syntactic proficiency in English that would put him 'on track' with other typically developing children of his age. The television serves as a convenient nanny and tutor to Mario. He delights in watching his favorite shows on cable television. He particularly likes, too, children's shows on a popular American entertainment company that provides streaming video-on-demand service. Mario's favorite show is an animated and interactive series for pre-school-aged children through which he acquired many new words and expressions in English that were not explicitly taught by his nanny or his parents.

In addition to technology, social feedback supports early language ability in children. The child's mother, being a language teacher, is herself key in developing the child's pre-linguistic and linguistic stages of language acquisition through maternal responsivity (Hoff, 2014). Her constant conversation exchanges early on with the pre-speech child drew out from him the intention to speak.

Finally, the community outside the child's home also offers adequate encouragement for acquisition in English. The mother notes that anyone who comes in contact with the child—taxi driver, store clerk, guards, adults at play gym—almost always greets and responds to the child in English. Although not completely sustained in English, interactions with the child by strangers around him offer enough environmental support for acquisition in English. Such conclusion resonates with Lucas (2008) and Maxilom (2008), and it reflects the generally positive language attitude toward English that helps sustain its status in the country as a second language.

The finding that Filipino children appear to favor English over other languages presents possibilities for PhE to develop into a lingua franca in the country. Already, English is acquired as a L1 in Metro Manila by a "small but stable [...] minority of households where English was learned as a first language" (Gonzalez, 1989, pp. 368–369). These households belong to the

Acquisition and Learning 281

middle and upper socioeconomic classes, a small percentage in the National Capital Region. Nonetheless, as Gonzalez surmises, the use of English in these households is increasing.

Whether this phenomenon has indeed strengthened over the course of nearly 30 years would require looking into surveys investigating home language/s. Anecdotal data from the present case study does indicate that among toddlers at the play school where Mario goes to on weekends, children are observed to be interacting with new 'classmates' using words, phrases, and clauses or full sentences in English. Caregivers also interact mostly in English with their own children or wards and other children. Instruction is also delivered mostly in English. English appears to be the default language used involving children at least in the context of the case study.

The use of English in the country is also described to be stable as it is used in various domains of language use—the school, the boardroom, in international business situations, and in homes of high socioeconomic status and highly educated Filipinos. Other domains where English is also used, although not exclusively, include entertainment, music, drama, newspapers, law, science and technology in education, religion, and the government (Gonzalez, 1989). English proficiency is also popularly regarded as a necessary skill in securing jobs, especially abroad (Gonzalez, 1998). Perhaps a shift from the status of English as L2 to an L1 is, by this time, under way.

References

Barrios, A. L. and Bernardo, A. B. I. (2012). The acquisition of case marking by L1 Chabacano and L1 Cebuano learners of L2 Filipino: Influence of actancy structure on transfer. *Language and Linguistics 13*.3, 499–521.

Bates, E., Camaioni, L., and Volterra, V. (1975). The acquisition of performatives prior to speech. *Merill-Palmer Quarterly 21*, 205–226.

Concepcion, C. C. (2005). The impact of inflectional awareness on syntactic bootstrapping and fast mapping of novel verbs in English, Filipino, and Chabacano. *Philippine Journal of Linguistics 36*.1&2, 42–100.

Gonzalez, A. (1986). Child language studies in the Philippines. In B. Narr and H. Wittje (Eds.), *Language Acquisition and Multilingualism: Festchrift for Els Oksaar on her 60th Birthday*, pp. 129–150. Tübingen: Gunter Narr Verlag.

Gonzalez, A. (1989). The creolization of Philippine English: Evidence for English as a first language among Metro Manila children. In Wilfrido V. Villacorta, Isagani R. Cruz, and Ma. Lourdes Brillantes (Eds.), *Manila: History People and Culture (Proceedings of the Manila Studies Conference)*, pp. 359–373. Manila: De La Salle University Press.

Gonzalez, A. 1998. The language planning situation in the Philippines. *Journal of Multilingual and Multicultural Development 19*.5, 487–525.

Hoff, E. (2014). *Language development* (5th ed.). Belmont, CA: Wadsworth Cengage Learning.

Lalunio, L. (2001). Emergent literacy of Filipino preschool children. *Philippine Journal of Linguistics 32*.2, 89–101.

Liao, H. (2006). Philippine linguistics: The state of the art (1981–2005). Paper presented at the Annual Lecture of the Bonifacio P. Sibayan Distinguished Professorial Chair in Applied Linguistics, and the Andrew Gonzalez, FSC Distinguished Professorial Chair in Linguistics and Language Education on March 4, 2006, De La Salle University, Manila.

Lucas, R. I. G. (2008). An examination of the early discourse of Filipino preschool children's direct speech. *Jurnal Sastra Inggris 8*.2, 76–89.

Lucas, R. I. G. and Bernardo, A. B. I. (2008). Exploring noun bias in Filipino-English bilingual children. *The Journal of Genetic Psychology 169*.2, 149–163.

Maxilom, R. M. (2008). Linguistic cues and the number word acquisition in a multilingual context. *Philippine Journal of Linguistics 43*.1, 65–84.

Miraflores, E. and Lucas, R. I. G. (2015). The effects of joint reference and mutual exclusivity on the application of whole-object assumption in 3-year olds Filipino-English bilingual preschool students. *Asia-Pacific Journal of Research in Early Childhood Education 9*.1, 91–109.

Nolasco, R. (2005). The Chabacano challenge to Philippine ergativity. In D. T. Dayag and J. S. Quakenbush (Eds.), *Linguistics and language education in the Philippines and beyond: A Festschrift in honor of Ma. Lourdes S. Bautista*, pp. 401–433, Manila: De La Salle University Press.

Pan, B. A. (2012). Assessing vocabulary skills. In E. Hoff (Ed.), *Research methods in child language: A practical guide*, pp. 100–112. Oxford: Blackwell Publishing Ltd.

Pascasio, E. (2000). The linguistic society of the Philippines at 30. *Philippine Journal of Linguistics 31*.2, 9–25.

Reyes-Wandless, M. (2002). An exploration of the conceptual associations in second language learning among financially disadvantaged preschool learners. *Philippine Journal of Linguistics 33*.1, 17–31.

Tao, L. and Lucas, R. I. (2012). The effect of age and discourse position on referential adequacy in Filipino bilingual children's oral narratives in Mandarin. *TESOL Journal 7*, 43–57.

Tardif, T., Gelman, S., and Xu, F. (1999). Putting the "noun bias" in context: A comparison of English and Mandarin. *Child Development 70*.3, 620–635.

Tardif, T., Liang, W., Zhang, Z., Fletcher, P., and Kaciroti, N. (2008). Baby's first 10 words. *Developmental Psychology 44*.4, 929–938.

Xin, J. and Lucas, R. I. G. (2010). Noun versus verb bias in Mandarin-English bilingual pre-school children. *TESOL Journal 3*, 29–48.

22 Language Teaching

Alejandro S. Bernardo

22.1 Introduction

The spread of the world Englishes (WE) paradigm and its birth in the 1980s is a testament of its resilience as a way of thinking, but borrowing the words of Jenkins (2006, p. 158): "[M]uch work remains to be done, even at the level of theorizing, let alone in practice". This echoes that while many empirical studies on Englishes have been initiated and more and more papers which delve into the aftershock the WE paradigm has caused have been published, what is still needed to date is a well-defined pedagogic approach which language teachers—whether English as a Second Language (ESL) or English as a Foreign Language (EFL) practitioners—may allude to when they teach English in the elementary, secondary, or collegiate level. More effort based on a principled design will have to be directed to designing and developing instructional approaches, methods, and techniques which are not only in congruence with one another but likewise considerate and reflective of the various local sociolinguistic realities which surround both language teachers and language learners who are non-Inner Circle members in the concentric circle model popularized by Kachru (1985).

It is important to note at this point that the WE paradigm has started and continues to permeate classroom teaching in different parts of the globe (cf. Kubota, 2001; Shim, 2002; Matsuda, 2003; McLean, 2004; Song & Drummond, 2009; Mack, 2010; Matsuda & Matsuda, 2010; Jindapitak & Teo, 2012; Lee, 2012; Belibi, 2013; Galloway, 2013; Chang, 2014; Floris, 2014; Bhowmik, 2015; Vettorel, 2015, 2017; Vettorel & Corrizzato, 2016; Dimoski, 2016; Kato, 2016). A survey of these studies which attempted at making English language instruction WE-aligned would show that WE has indeed caught the attention of ESL and EFL practitioners in different postcolonial English-using environments. However, while it is impressive that there have been efforts in making English language teaching (ELT) WE-informed as shown above, several important questions need to be raised: *Are these projects, activities, lesson prototypes, instructional materials, modules, and the like based on clear and definite pedagogical, methodological, and procedural lenses or underpinnings in the first place? What made the teaching-and-learning*

DOI: 10.4324/9780429427824-29

284   *Alejandro S. Bernardo*

approach, method, and techniques in sync? How was the WE, an extremely huge paradigm, fit into a narrower domain such as an English course and its syllabus? Was the process of cascading and fitting seamless and undoubtedly effective? How was the WE paradigm (re)contextualized and operationalized in the teachers' approach, methods, and teaching procedures? It is also important to note that, while the pursuits featured in the papers above adhere to the WE paradigm, they still seem abstract to be applicable to practical classroom instruction, and how they are cascaded to daily classroom pedagogies is still to be articulated. How the WE paradigm actually and observably works in the ESL classrooms remains to be seen.

In teaching English, a necessity is a pedagogic model that is *WE-inspired, WE-based,* and *WE-adherent.* Jenkins (2006) echoed that "[t]eachers and their learners [...] need to learn not (a variety of) English, but about Englishes [...]" (p. 178). Holliday (1994, as cited in Jenkins 2006) earlier underscored that there is a need for an "appropriate methodology for learners in different (and very often, non-Western) contexts of language learning and use". All these point to one thing: what is needed is an instructional backbone that is *WE-moved.* Because WE promotes inclusivity, a pedagogic model that highlights the homegrown varieties of English, that is localized, indigenized, and contextualized, and is realizable and implementable is indubitably fundamental.

In the Philippines, the local variety of English, Philippine English (PhE), has been a center of scientific sociolinguistic inquiry since it was first empirically described in a groundbreaking study of Llamzon in 1969. In fact, it is said that among all South East Asian (SEA) Englishes that have been documented, PhE is the most extensively studied (Tay, 1991) not only by Filipino linguists but also by foreign scholars. Gonzalez (1983, 1985), Bautista (2000, 2004, 2008), Borlongan (2008, 2011), Dita (2011), Tayao (2004), and many others have forwarded a comprehensive linguistic description of PhE, i.e., phonological properties, semantic and syntactic behaviors, pragmatic and discourse qualities. Many have intuited their standpoints as regards its status and prospects (cf. Borlongan, 2016; Martin, 2014) and have defended that PhE is the English propagated by the educated Filipinos and is not deviant, erroneous, and substandard (Bautista, 2000). And now that PhE is at the dawn of endonormative stabilization (Borlongan, 2016) and that it has come of age (Bernardo, 2017), it may be formally nominated as a pedagogic norm in the Philippine ESL classrooms (Bernardo & Madrunio, 2015). In doing so, the call for the improvement of the quality of ELT in the Philippines through more effective methodologies and better training programs for both pre-service and in-service teachers and the fervent call for teaching (in) PhE (Llamzon, 1969, 1972, 1997; Hidalgo, 1970; Gonzalez, 1983, McKaughan, 1993; Bautista, 2001), which has been reverberating for the last four centuries, may finally be responded to. The unpunctuated discussion on the pedagogical implication of WE initiated by the group of distinguished language specialists who represented the Philippines in the convention *Varieties of English and Their Implications for Language Teaching in Southeast Asia* convened in 1981 will continue if PhE is popularized as a pedagogic model for teaching English phonology, lexicon, syntax, and discourse.

This chapter, therefore, proposes a pedagogic model for teaching English in the local ESL classrooms and a guidepost for making ELT approaches, methods, and procedures in sync, with PhE taking the spotlight in the process of making these three instructional domains in congruence with one another. This chapter argues that PhE is more than ready and ripe to be studied, taught, and used in the classrooms and offers Filipino teachers of English with a pedagogical tool or armory which they can employ in their respective ESL classes and incorporate within the framework of changing patterns of language education brought about by the WE paradigm. It should be noted, though, that the model presented here is not meant to be prescriptive, nor does it claim to be all-inclusive. It is necessary to stress that this chapter hardly suggests the replacement or striking out of the established approaches to ELT for that would sound unrealistic and would require much empirical support, which is beyond the scope of this chapter.

Following would be a brief survey of the different approaches, methods, and techniques in ELT. Constructively aligning these three and the present state of the ELT curriculum in the Philippines will be concisely tackled to situate the development of the pedagogic approach forwarded in this chapter.

22.2 Approaches, Methods, and Techniques: A Differentiation and Constructive Alignment

Richards and Rodgers (1986) alluded to Anthony's (1963) definitions of these three levels of conceptualization and organization: *approaches, methods, and techniques*. Until now, this differentiation is the most referred to in ELT. Anthony says:

> The arrangement is hierarchical. The organizational key is that techniques carry out a method which is consistent with an approach....
>
> ...An approach is a set of correlative assumptions dealing with the nature of language teaching and learning. An approach is axiomatic. It describes the nature of the subject matter to be taught....
>
> ... Method is an overall plan for the orderly presentation of language material, no part of which contradicts, and all of which is based upon, the selected approach. An approach is axiomatic; a method is procedural.
>
> Within one approach, there can be many methods....
>
> ...A technique is implementational—that which actually takes place in a classroom. It is a particular trick, stratagem, or contrivance to accomplish an immediate objective. Techniques must be consistent with a method, and therefore in harmony with an approach as well.
>
> (pp. 63–67)

286 *Alejandro S. Bernardo*

The foregoing suggests that approach is a set of assumptions, theories, or philosophies about the nature of language and how it is learned; approach dictates 'what it is' in a language that should be taught and how that 'what it is' should be taught in the classroom. Approach escorts teachers to a definite destination as far as language teaching is concerned, by providing them with a framework, a model, or an overall teaching blueprint. Without one, everything that happens in the classroom is hollow.

Richards and Rodgers (1986) posit that "at least three different theoretical views of language and the nature of language proficiency explicitly or implicitly inform current approaches and methods in language teaching" (pp. 16–7). These are the *structural, functional*, and *interactional* view of the language. The structural view considers language as "a system of structurally related elements for the coding of meaning" (p. 17). The functional view looks at language as a tool for the communication of functional meaning while the interactional view "sees language as a vehicle for the realization of interpersonal relations and for the performance of social transactions between individuals" (p. 17). Each of these, however, Richards and Rodgers argue, is complemented by theories of language learning.

Methods, on the one hand, are procedures informed by a specific view of language and language learning. Richards and Rodgers (1986) enumerated the most common of the ELT methodologies then and now: the audio-lingual method, total physical response, the silent way, community language teaching, and suggestopedia. In addition are the direct method, the grammar translation method, and the situational method (Mwanza, 2017). Techniques, on the other hand, are the most specific and observable among the three levels of conceptualization. Techniques may refer to the classroom tasks which students engage in, e.g., language games, simulations, role plays, written or oral exercises, collaborative activities, and dyadic conversations. The choice of techniques is an offshoot of the theoretical assumptions about language and language learning.

As far as the relational aspect of these three levels of instructional conceptualization is concerned, one important notion may be deduced: approach informs a method, and a method informs a technique. The selection of a technique is based on the method to be employed and the choice of the method is grounded on the approach. Approach is on top of the hierarchy for it serves as the overarching teaching philosophy. It is made evident and at work in the classroom through the methods and techniques implemented. It is also to be stressed that these three should always be in congruence with one another; otherwise, theoretical, methodological, and technical incongruity will occur.

The foregoing discussion about the nature of approach, method, and technique, noticeably, is devoid of the WE paradigm. How the WE framework serves as a paradigmatic inspiration in aligning ELT approach, method, and technique will have to be the subject of today's discourse. As McLean (2004) puts it: "[t]his increased attention and research regarding

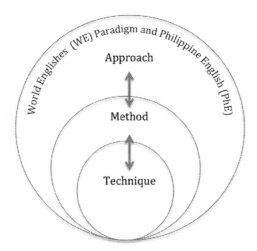

Figure 22.1 The Concentric Circles of the Three Levels of Instructional Conceptualization.

World Englishes subsequently pressures English language teachers to not only familiarize themselves with the issues, but also to incorporate World Englishes into their courses..." (p. 1). How it may be incorporated in ELT is therefore the next route of exploration. The WE paradigm as a whole and the empirical studies on PhE in particular call for making pedagogical choices that are locally and contextually tailored. One way of doing this is to concoct a way of thinking where the "constructive alignment" (Biggs & Tang, 2011) of approach, method, and technique positions WE and PhE as the fulcrum or the point where the alignment rests. This may be schematically represented through the concentric circles of instructional conceptualization shown in Figure 22.1.

Figure 22.1 shows that the WE paradigm and the PhE moorings provide a theoretical foundation for a principled approach to language teaching. WE and PhE are both situated as an overarching platform in bringing into line ELT approach, method, and technique. Under this framework, there is a conscious effort for the language teacher to select a WE- and PhE-inspired pedagogic guidepost, a well-sequenced teaching procedure and activities constructively aligned with one another.

22.3 The Endocentric Pedagogic Approach for Teaching English

The approach forwarded here is the *endocentric pedagogic approach* to ELT. This approach draws inspiration from the concentric circle of the three levels of instructional conceptualization in Figure 22.1. 'Endocentric' literally means focused or centered within itself or inside, and not on something external or outside. This approach promotes the deliberate teaching of acceptable phonological, lexical, syntactic, and even discourse features of PhE proven to have been thriving within and outside the classroom. As an illustrative case, *based from, result to, cope up with* are established and pedagogically acceptable features of PhE (cf. Bernardo & Madrunio, 2015); hence, there is no reason for language teachers to be afraid of teaching them formally in the classroom and to be scared of persuading the learners to use these in various forms of communication. The endocentric pedagogic approach urges language teachers to welcome PhE as a pedagogic norm thus prompting them to 'look within or to look inside', i.e., to rely on the local norms that PhE has to offer. There might not be a reason at all for formally teaching the inner circle structures such as *a majority, pieces of advice,* and *pieces of furniture* because in (and for) intranational communication; these AmE syntactic items are rarely used by the majority of Filipino ESL speakers and are pedagogically unacceptable to both language teachers and learners (cf. Bernardo & Madrunio, 2015). The endocentric pedagogic approach, put more succinctly, draws inspiration primarily from the homegrown variety making itself PhE-centric and PhE-philic.

However, because it seems rather impractical and unrealizable to completely veer away from PhE's parent variety, AmE, its other pedagogically acceptable features may likewise be taught under the endocentric pedagogic approach, e.g., *unless* instead of *not unless, for example* instead of *like for example, 'I' and my siblings* instead of *'me' and my siblings* (cf. Bernardo & Madrunio, 2015). This implies that, in a way, in learning English, both Englishes are taught, both varieties are accorded equal treatment, and both Englishes receive the same amount of pedagogical respect and attention. The endocentric pedagogic approach looks at English as a plural language and thus its attribute as a multifaceted language is emphasized in the classroom. The formal teaching of an Outer Circle English alongside an Inner Circle English is therefore legitimized, making the learners cognizant that these two Englishes co-exist and that there is nothing strange in learning both. If the endocentric pedagogic model is adhered to, PhE will then be celebrated, formalized, and institutionalized.

Kirkpatrick (2013) posits that it is only through the efforts of local educators that WE can thrive because only they can legitimize their own English. Corollary to this, it is only through the efforts of teachers that PhE can be institutionalized because only they can endorse PhE in the educational space where they serve as leads or frontrunners. As an instructional backbone, the endocentric pedagogic approach affords them with lenses, which allow them to see English as a language with localized norms and idiosyncratic structures that may be used for both functional and interactional purposes.

22.4 A Philippine English-Aware Method for Teaching English

In a paper by Bernardo (2017, p. 138), a PhE-aware five-stage teaching procedure was presented. The steps under the procedure accord the language

Language Teaching   289

teachers the opportunity to gradually raise the learners' level of awareness of the WE paradigm in general and of PhE in particular.

Stage 1: Notice—Students are made to notice the distinctive features of PhE. Teachers direct students' attention to grammatical, lexical, or phonological items that significantly differ from American English or British English.

Stage 2: Compare—Teachers lead the students to compare and contrast idiosyncratic PhE phonological, syntactic, or lexical features with American English or British English highlighting that the differences are acceptable and not strange.

Stage 3: Comment—The teacher comments that the distinctive features are not errors and abnormalities; rather, they are innovations that are allowed and permissible in formal and informal discourses.

Stage 4: Encourage—Teachers encourage learners to use the local variety both in formal and in informal discourses without uncertainties or hesitations or fear of being penalized or laughed or frowned at.

Stage 5: Familiarize—Teachers encourage students to be familiar with other established varieties of English and train them to shuttle from one variety to another to effect more successful communication.

How this five-stage teaching procedure may be inserted anywhere in the instructional period or instructional blueprint will now be explored. This method may be employed every time teachable episodes in the class surface. In fact, this method hardly interferes with or distracts the pre-instruction, during instruction, and post-instruction phases in the teaching process. However, the prototypical stages, if they are to be used in ESL classes, may need to be modified. The method may be used even at the motivation part of the lesson, lesson proper, generalization segment, and task time as long as the goal is to raise core issues of WE and PhE. The method aims for consciousness-raising and eventually acceptance of PhE. Making such explicit reference to WE and PhE through this method is a welcome step toward formalizing an awareness of the important role they play in ELT.

As an illustration, the teacher may find a teachable moment in class after certain texts that contain PhE have been presented to the class. These texts may be newspaper articles, blogs, social media posts, and other text types that contain PhE lexico-syntactic features. For instance, if phrasal verbs such as *based from, fill out,* and *cope up with* occur in the text presented to the students, the classroom scene would appear like this: The teacher leads the learners to notice that *based from, fill out,* and *cope up with* are idiosyncratic features as far as local English is concerned. The teacher provides input about the local English and the WE paradigm if the learners are hardly cognizant about these. The teacher raises questions like *Do you also use these phrasal verbs in speaking and*

290   *Alejandro S. Bernardo*

in writing? Do you find them different or strange? Where else could you hear about or read these? Do you hear educated Filipinos say these, too?

The teacher presents the AmE variants *based on, fill out,* and *cope with* to the students and positions them vis-à-vis their PhE counterparts. The students realize that there exists a different pattern of use in PhE. The teacher asks: *How does the pattern of use differ in AmE and in PhE? Would you consider 'based from', 'fill up', and 'cope up with' erroneous?* The teacher, after processing the students' responses, comments that these are not errors or abnormalities but features of PhE. The teacher convinces the learners that PhE is not a bastardized form of English and encourages the students to use these phrasal verbs in both formal and informal communications without reservations. Finally, the teacher asks the students to spot other features of PhE and advises them to be familiar with these.

22.5 'Noticing a Variety' Technique

One technique employable in class is the noticing task. 'Noticing language', which was first popularized by Schmidt in 1990, has recently gained recognition in language learning. Research into noticing, Batstone (1996) says, "is still in its infancy, but given its importance as a gateway to language learning, it should be a subject of vital interest for all those involved in language teaching" (p. 273). This task is based on the premise that students learn the language items they pay attention to and thus learning language structures is driven by attention and awareness. Contextualizing the noticing theory in the teaching of PhE, the student will learn about PhE phonology, grammar, lexicon, and discourse if they are deliberately led to pay attention to PhE structures that are central and typical.

A facet of noticing a variety in the classroom is its explicitness (Batstone, 1996). Features of PhE may be explicitly presented to the learners by engaging them with various input sources and by providing metalinguistic explanations afterward. The input could be texts teeming with PhE features, e.g., newspaper headlines, memoranda, acknowledgments, legal texts such as bills and acts, press releases, transcribed telephone conversations, magazine articles, advertisements, poetry, and other literary pieces written in PhE. The texts may also be oral productions of proficient Filipino speakers of English or any attentional resources available—whether authentic materials or teacher-developed. In doing so, Cook's (2001) suggestion remains convincing: that "the model for language teaching should be the fluent L2 user, not the native speaker" (p. 179) When the learners manifest familiarity with PhE, these PhE-rich inputs may be collected by the learners themselves. They may be asked to accumulate texts that they feel contain distinctive features of PhE and use these as subjects of classroom discussion.

When learners have achieved a much higher level of noticing ability, the teacher may also provide situations that would require students to shuttle from one variety to another. For example, in writing for publication, the students may be made to realize that in the realm of local and international

Language Teaching 291

publications, they may shift from PhE to AmE. They may use *based from, fill up,* and *cope up with,* when they communicate intranationally but they will have to use *based on, fill out,* and *cope with* when they communicate internationally. Truly, the reality is that not all English speakers would tolerate such idiosyncratic features in formal and academic communications. The ability to shuttle from one variety to another, however, gives the learners a competitive advantage. They will be able to "...adjust their speech in order to be intelligible to interlocutors from a wide range of L1 backgrounds, most of whom are not inner-circle native speakers" (Jenkins, 2006, p. 174).

Following the five-stage teaching procedure outlined above, the teacher will be able to create classroom conditions where learners can notice aspects and features of PhE. However, because a singular noticing task would not suffice, the language teacher should endeavor to re-expose the learners to PhE inputs and make covert efforts to make them re-notice PhE idiosyncratic structures. Flooding students with central and typical PhE features to notice and re-notice will be of value, not to mention that constantly exposing the learners to PhE will heighten its noticeability. When this happens, the teacher may later spur the learners to talk about issues material to the WE paradigm and PhE and the contentious issue that have to do with the use of English in a much higher level of discourse.

A PHE-INSPIRED PEDAGOGICAL PROCEDURE

Note: This lesson is only a chunk of a larger content taken up in class. It should be noted that ELT in the Philippines follows the integrative approach, that is, a lesson covers all the macro-skills. The procedure below may be followed if and when the 'PhE teachable moment' surfaces in class.

A. Intended Learning Outcome:

The students should be able to discuss what phrasal verbs are and use them in compositions appropriately and to be able to demonstrate favorable attitude toward the local variety of English.

B. Content:

Phrasal verbs.

C. Procedure:

1   Present a text that bears PhE phrasal verbs. Ask the students to identify the phrasal verbs in the text.
2   Ask the students to describe what phrasal verbs are and to give more examples.

292 *Alejandro S. Bernardo*

3 Direct the students to 'notice' the phrasal verbs *based from, result in,* and *cope up with*. These may be written on the board or highlighted on the screen. Ask: *Do you also use these phrasal verbs in speaking and in writing? Do you find them different or strange? Where else could you hear about or read these? Do you hear educated Filipinos say these, too?*

4 Provide a two-column table similar to what is shown below. The first column presents the PhE phrasal verbs while the second column indicates their Standard English counterparts. Ask: *Which between the two groups would you consider 'more' correct? How does the pattern of use differ? Would you consider 'based from', 'fill up', and 'cope up with' erroneous?* Welcome as many answers or opinions as possible. Remark that both are acceptable and underscore that these are only variations. Emphasize that one is PhE while the other is AmE. Give comments that these are not errors or abnormalities but features of PhE. Elicit more opinions from the students. Convince them that PhE is not a bastardized form of English and encourage the students to use these phrasal verbs in both formal and informal communications without reservations.

  based from based on
  result to result in
  cope up with cope with

5 Give sentence drills to the students. Sentences may be similar to the following. Ask them to supply the phrasal verbs needed in the sentences. If students use the PhE *based from, result to,* and *cope up with*, or their AmE counterparts, appreciate students' answers by saying that their answers are correct.

  1 *The findings show that 99% of the students favor K-12. _____ the data, it could be seen that they do appreciate this educational reform.*

  2 *Failure in the examination would _____ in debarment and cancellation of candidacy.*

  3 *The students had difficulty in the course. They could hardly _____ the demands of the program.*

6 Ask the students to give more examples of phrasal verbs they use. Make them list these down and lead them to decide whether these may be regarded as PhE phrasal verbs. Ask them to look for texts produced by Filipinos where these phrasal verbs occur. Make them realize that when these structures are used most especially by educated Filipinos, there is nothing wrong if they will use these as well either in written or in spoken communication.

22.6 The English Teacher and the ELT Curriculum

Dorgu (2015) argues that "[t]eaching is a deliberate activity done in a professional manner to bring a positive change on the learner..." (p. 77). As such, there is also a need for a deliberate effort to resort to other WE-inspired pedagogical alternatives or, in the words of Matsuda (2003, p. 727), to "... put on a new pair of eyeglasses" so that teaching becomes attuned to the demands of the times and the learners themselves. Changes in pedagogical approaches, however, hardly take place if there is no institutional mandate. In an earlier analysis of the English curriculum, Bernardo (2017) concludes that "...the WE paradigm in general and PhE in particular are hardly regarded as a serious pedagogical agendum in the present-day English language teaching-and-learning curriculum implemented in the Philippines" (p. 121). This implies that language teachers are not in any way obligated either to use PhE as a pedagogic norm or to introduce PhE and WE to the learners. Throughout this chapter, it has been argued that it is only when the imparting of WE is made a curricular requirement or a permanent fixture in the ELS classroom can it be taught and only then can PhE become the "taught variety" (Kirkpatrick, 2002, p. 222).

For the English curriculum to be regarded both innovative and liberating, reference to it should allow teachers to depict that the "...complexity of the sociolinguistic reality of English is needed to prepare learners for their future use of English that may involve both NNSs and NSs and that may take place in any part of the world" (Matsuda, 2003, p. 726). The curriculum should also embolden language teachers in making sound and brave pedagogical decisions. Crystal (2001, p. 59) exclaims that "It is a brave new world, indeed; and those who have to be bravest of all are the teachers" (p. 59). Teachers should be fearless to untie themselves from the native-speaker-centric model for language teaching for it is not robust enough to meet the changing communication needs of the learners. It should be remembered, nevertheless, that "[i]t is up to each teacher, working with real students, and subject to a variety of administrative and pedagogical requirements and constraints, to decide how to respond to the reality of English as a world language" (Gupta, 2001, p. 18).

Language teachers themselves, for the endocentric pedagogic approach to work, are expected to project favorable attitudes toward the WE paradigm. Otherwise, the teaching of WE and PhE will hardly flourish. As an inevitable reality, WE is seen to become a pedagogical backbone and they are encouraged to find ways by which it can be infused as an overarching pedagogic principle.

22.7 Concluding Remarks

This chapter advances an endocentric pedagogic approach for teaching English. Through this approach, language teachers 'look within' the local

294 *Alejandro S. Bernardo*

variety of English and entice the learners to do the same. It is hoped that when English teachers teach the target language, they are guaranteed that they are armed with a pedagogical implement that is compliant with a paradigm expected to gain further prominence in the years to come. As it is, WE "...encompasses many different approaches to the study of English worldwide" (Low & Pakir, 2017, p. 5). It is hoped that through the endocentric pedagogic approach for teaching English presented here, when English teachers face their students in their everyday instruction, they would be confident to challenge the notion of adopting a 'monomodel' (Kachru, 1992) and would be bold enough to exclaim: "Today I am going to teach (in) PhE".

References

Anthony, E.M. (1963). Approach, method and technique. *English Language Teaching, 17*, 63–67.

Batstone, R. (1996). Key concepts in ELT. *ELT Journal, 50*(3), 273.

Bautista, M.L.S. (2000). *Defining standard Philippine English: Its status and grammatical features.* Manila: De la Salle University Press.

Bautista, M.L.S. (2001). Studies of Philippine English: Implications for language teaching in the Philippines. *Journal of Southeast Asian Education, 2*(2), 271–295.

Bautista, M.L.S. (2004). The verb in Philippine English: A preliminary analysis of the modal *would. World Englishes, 23*(1), 113–128.

Bautista, M.L.S. (2008). Investigating the grammatical features of Philippine English. In M.L.S. Bautista & K. Bolton (Eds.), *Philippine English: Linguistic and literary perspectives* (pp. 201–218). Hong Kong: Hong Kong University Press.

Belibi, P. (2013). Teaching a standard variety of English or a local standard: The case of Cameroon. *International Journal of English Language Education, 1*(3), 172–185.

Bernardo, A.S. (2017). Philippine English in the classroom: A much closer look. *Philippine ESL Journal 19*, 117–144.

Bernardo, A.S. & Madrunio, M.R. (2015). A framework for designing a Philippine-English- based pedagogic model for teaching English grammar. *Asian Journal of English Language Studies, 3*, 67–98.

Bhowmik, S.K. (2015). World Englishes and English language teaching: A pragmatic and humanistic approach. *Colombian Applied Linguistics Journal, 17*(1), 142–157.

Biggs, J.B. & Tang, C. (2011). *Teaching for quality learning at university* (4th ed.). Maidenhead: McGraw Hill Education & Open University Press.

Borlongan, A.M. (2008). Tag questions in Philippine English. *Philippine Journal of Linguistics, 39*(1–2), 109–34.

Borlongan, A.M. (2011). *A grammar of the verb in Philippine English.* (Unpublished doctoral dissertation). De La Salle University, Manila.

Borlongan, A.M. (2016). Relocating Philippine English in Schneider's dynamic model. *Asian Englishes*, DOI: 10.1080/13488678.2016.1223067

Chang, Y. (2014). Learning English today: What can World Englishes teach college students in Taiwan? *English Today 117, 30*(1), 21–27.

Cook, V. (2001). *Second language learning and language teaching* (3rd ed.). London: Arnold.

Language Teaching 295

Crystal, D. (2001). The future of Englishes. In A. Burns and C. Coffin (Eds.), *Analysing English in a global context: A reader.* London/New York: Routledge, pp. 53–64.

Dimoski, B. (2016). A proactive ELF-aware approach to listening comprehension. *The Center for ELF Journal, 2*(2), 24–38.

Dita, S.N. (2011). The grammar and semantics of adverbial disjuncts in Philippine English. In M.L.S. Bautista (Ed.), *Studies on Philippine* English: Exploring the Philippine component of the International Corpus of English (pp. 33–50). Manila: Anvil Publishing, Inc.

Dorgu, E.T. (2015). Different teaching methods: A panacea for effective curriculum implementation in the classroom. *International Journal of Secondary Education, 3*(6-1), 77–87.

Floris, F.D. (2014). Idea sharing: Introducing English as an international language (EIL) to pre-service teachers in a World Englishes course. *PASAA, 47*, 215–231.

Galloway, N. (2013). Global Englishes and English language teaching (ELT): Bridging the gap between theory and practice in a Japanese context. *System, 41*, 786–803.

Gonzalez, A. (1983). When does an error become a feature of Philippine English? In R. Noss (Ed.), *Varieties of English in Southeast Asia. Anthology Series No. 11.* Singapore: SEAMEO Regional Language Centre, 150–72.

Gonzalez, A. (1985). *Studies on Philippine English.* Singapore: SEAMEO Regional Language Centre.

Gupta, A.F. (2001) Teaching World English. *Mextesol, 25*(2), 1–17.

Hidalgo, C. (1970). Review of Teodoro A. Llamzon, SJ's Standard Filipino English. *Philippine Journal of Linguistics, 1*(1), 129–132.

Holliday, A. (1994). *Appropriate methodology and social context.* Cambridge: Cambridge University Press.

Jenkins, J. (2006). Current perspectives on teaching World Englishes and English as a lingua franca. *TESOL Quarterly, 40*(1), 157–181.

Jindapitak, N. & Teo, A. (2012). Thai tertiary English majors attitudes towards and awareness of World Englishes. *Journal of English Studies, 7*, 74–116.

Kachru, B.B. (1985). Standards, codification and sociolinguistics realism: The English language in the outer circle. In R. Quirk and H.G. Widdowson (Eds.), *English in the world: Teaching and learning the language and literatures* (pp. 11–30). Cambridge: Cambridge University Press.

Kachru, B.B. (1992). Models for non-native Englishes. In B.B. Kachru (Ed.), *The other tongue: English across cultures* (2nd ed., pp. 48–74). Urbana: University of Illinois Press.

Kato, C.T. (2016). *Promoting English as a lingua franca: ELF awareness in a university. World Englishes course* (Unpublished doctoral dissertation). Rikkyo University, Tokyo, Japan.

Kirkpatrick, A. (2002). ASEAN and Asian culture and models: Implications for the ELT curriculum and for teacher selection. In A. Kirkpatrick (Ed.), *Englishes in Asia* (pp. 213–224). Melbourne: Language Australia Ltd.

Kirkpatrick, A. (2013). *World Englishes: Implications for international communication and English language teaching.* Cambridge: Cambridge University Press.

Kubota, R. (2001). Teaching world Englishes to native speakers of English in the USA. *World English, 2*(1), 47–64.

296　*Alejandro S. Bernardo*

Lee, K. (2012). Teaching intercultural English learning/teaching in world Englishes: Some classroom activities in South Korea. *English Teaching: Practice and Critique, 11*(4), 190–205.

Llamzon, T. (1969). *Standard Filipino English.* Quezon City: Ateneo de Manila University Press.

Llamzon, T. (1972). A new approach to the Teaching of English in the Philippines. *RELC Journal, 3*(1–2), 30–39.

Llamzon, T. (1997). H.L. Mencken and English language teaching in the Philippines today. *Philippine Journal of Linguistics, 28*(1–2), 69–74.

Low, E. & Pakir, A. (2017). *World Englishes. Rethinking paradigms.* New York: Routledge.

Mack, L. (2010). Teaching global English to EFL classes. *Intercultural Communication Studies, 19*(3), 202–220.

Martin, I.P. (2014). Beyond nativization?: Philippine English in Schneider's dynamic model. In S. Buschfeld, T. Homann, M. Huber, & A. Kautzsch (Eds.), *The evolution of Englishes: The dynamic model and beyond* (pp. 70–85). Amsterdam: John Benjamins Publishing Co.

Matsuda, A. (2003). Incorporating World Englishes in teaching English as an international language. *TESOL Quarterly, 37*(4), 719–729.

Matsuda, A. & Matsuda, P.K. (2010). World Englishes and the teaching of writing. *TESOL Quarterly, 44*(2), 369–374.

McKaughan, H.P. (1993). Toward a Standard Philippine English. *Philippine Journal of Linguistics, 24*(2), 41–55.

McLean, T. (2004) A world Englishes mini-unit for teachers to use in the EFL context. *Asian Englishes, 7*(1), 92–96.

Mwanza, S.D. (2017). *International Journal of Humanities Social Sciences and Education (IJHSSE), 4*(2), 53–67.

Richards, C. & Rodgers, T. (1986). *Approaches and methods in language teaching.* Cambridge: Cambridge University Press.

Shim, R.J. (2002). Changing attitudes toward teaching English as a world language (TEWOL) in Korea. *Journal of Asian Pacific Communication, 12*(1), 143–158.

Song, K. & Drummond, H. (2009) Helping students recognize and appreciate English language variations. *Foreign Language Research and Education, Hiroshima University, 12*, 201–215.

Tay, M.W.J. (1991). Southeast Asia and Hong Kong. In J. Cheshire (Ed.), *English around the world: Sociolinguistic perspectives* (pp. 319–332). Cambridge: Cambridge University Press.

Tayao, M.L.G. (2004). The evolving study of Philippine English phonology. *World Englishes (Special Issue on Philippine English: Tensions and Transitions), 23*(1), 77–90.

Vettorel P. (2015). World Englishes and English as a lingua franca: Implications for teacher education and ELT. *Istoria, 6*, 229–244.

Vettorel, P. (2017). The plurality of English and ELF in teacher education: Raising awareness of the 'feasibility' of a WE- and ELF-aware approach in classroom practices. *Lingue Linguaggi, 24*, 239–257.

Vettorel, P. & Corrizzato S. (2016). Fostering awareness of the pedagogical implications of World Englishes and ELF in teacher education in Italy. *Studies in Second Language Learning and Teaching, 6*(3), 487–511.

23 Language Testing

Dave Kenneth Tayao Cayado and
James F. D'Angelo

23.1 Introduction

The emergence of world Englishes (WE) has revolutionized the way scholars and linguists view the English language. Before Kachru (1985, 1986) introduced the concentric circles model of WE, there were only two varieties of English that were widely accepted in the world, namely, American English (AmE) and British English (BrE)—both of which fall in the category of Inner Circle Englishes. The existence of WE has impacted different fields of linguistics such as sociolinguistics, diachronic linguistics, and even applied linguistics. And, more specifically, language pedagogy and language assessment. The investigations and documentation efforts which were conducted to further expand the body of knowledge about WE came at a very timely juncture as this research can be used in changing how people perceive English. To this day, one of the most documented and studied Asian Englishes is Philippine English (PhE). PhE has now been investigated at various linguistic levels, and there is even some evidence that its features have diverged from its parent AmE (Collins & Borlongan, 2017). As such, Borlongan (2016) has suggested that PhE has already reached endonormative stabilization (phase 4) in Schneider's dynamic model (2003, 2007). This indicates that local linguistic norms have now emerged in the variety and native-speakers of PhE have developed a positive attitude toward its existence. This advancement of PhE is of importance as it can now be used in changing language assessment in the Philippines.

Despite having its own linguistic norms, PhE is yet to be recognized and accepted in the discipline of language assessment. It is a commonly known fact that classroom-based assessments and high-stakes exams such as International English Language Testing System (IELTS), Test of English as a Foreign Language (TOEFL), or even the local examinations like the National Achievement Test (NAT) are based on 'native-speaker' linguistic norms, e.g. AmE. This occurrence can be considered as a form of 'monopoly' of the language in favor of the Inner Circle Englishes. AmE and BrE take control of the language norms, even in places where they are not being spoken, and in disciplines like language assessment where validity is one of

DOI: 10.4324/9780429427824-30

298 *Dave Kenneth Tayao Cayado and James F. D'Angelo*

the main concerns. The apparent misalignment of the speakers and the variety of English raises various issues: The learners are being assessed using a set of standards that are completely irrelevant to them and the way they are being tested does not match the linguistic needs that their context requires (Tomlinson, 2010). While the ideas promulgated by Tomlinson make sense from a sociolinguistic perspective, it is argued that the challenge goes far beyond contextual use of language when talking about language assessment. Rather, the misalignment between the speakers and the linguistic norms is a form of Differential Item Functioning (DIF) or item bias.

This chapter argues that language assessment in the Philippines must be WE paradigm-informed, due to the following reasons, which will be further discussed in the next section: First, the view that native-speaker norms need to be utilized because they are superior shows monopoly and linguicism. Second, the inclusion of the standards of PhE will ensure the validity of the language assessment. And, lastly, the resistance to incorporate the linguistic norms and standards of PhE may result in DIF or item bias in language testing. Since, as Borlongan (2016) has suggested, PhE has already reached the endonormative stabilization in Schneider's (2003, 2007) dynamic model, it is high time for language experts and scholars to be more accepting of the PhE standards, to make language assessment appropriate and valid for Filipino users of English.

23.2 Issues in Testing Philippine English with Focus on Appropriate Norms

The resistance to include appropriate linguistic norms is one of the issues in testing WE. Most of the high-stake language exams such as IELTS and TOEFL still use 'native-speaker' linguistic norms even when the exam takers use a different variety of educated English. This could be attributed to the perception of people that certain Englishes are superior than others. In this case, the Inner Circle Englishes are perceived to be superior to Outer and Expanding Circle Englishes, for most would believe that the latter lack legitimacy (Shohamy, 2006). This is the traditional belief that speakers are only considered 'proficient and communicatively competent when they adhere to native-speaker ways of using the language. As a result, this is where the aforementioned 'monopoly' of language emanates. Inner Circle Englishes still monopolize language testing because of the perception that being 'native-like' is the only way to be proficient and communicatively competent. This has to be addressed because this traditional belief proliferates linguicism, for the different varieties are not being viewed equally. Linguists, language teachers, and language professionals have to be progressive and give consideration to different varieties' linguistic norms when assessing someone's proficiency and make such assessment appropriate, or at least not inaccessible vis-à-vis the variety of English they speak, and the cultural milieu from which they originate.

The general validity of language assessment will also be at risk when appropriate linguistic norms are not utilized to assess language proficiency. For instance, despite PhE having its own norms and standards, AmE is still being used as a basis to determine Filipinos' language proficiency, even though the variety of English we speak is different from that of AmE. This is problematic because Filipinos' language proficiency is being assessed using a variety that has little relevance to them. (A possible exception would be the case where a Philippine student was planning to attend graduate school in the USA, in which case American norms can have validity.) As Davidson (2006) posited, when a language test that uses a particular variety of English as a basis of scoring is administered in a context where different norms exist, the calibration of items in that language test will be locally invalid since it does not measure what it intends to measure. Therefore, to ensure the validity of the language exams, it is imperative to incorporate and consider the distinct norms of the English being used in the particular setting where the exam will be administered. Although AmE is oftentimes viewed as the model of English for second language learners, it is argued here that this still dominantly held belief is irrelevant in today's context of language assessment, now that there are more English speakers in Outer and Expanding Circle contexts that need to be given consideration.

As argued earlier, the failure to incorporate the linguistic norms of PhE results in DIF or item bias because it favors a particular variety of English, while ignoring the global sociolinguistic reality. DIF transpires when the same set of items behaves differently or varies in difficulty when administered to different groups of learners (Ellis & Raju, 2003). More particularly, DIF happens in language assessment when a specific language exam made for a variety of English is used in another variety. When the native-speakers of English take high-stakes language exams like IELTS, they find the items easier to answer as compared to Filipinos because the linguistic norms used in the exam favors them to begin with although further research needs to be conducted into whether even among native varieties, a UK-based test such as IELTS may contain usages unfamiliar to American test-takers. To eradicate the presence of DIF in language exams and ensure fairness, the distinctive norms which emerged from PhE have to be incorporated in the construction of the assessment or given consideration when the norms suddenly emerge from the students while doing classroom-based assessments. Therefore, each variety of English must have language exams specifically constructed and contextualized for their own variety to ensure that speakers are being assessed appropriately and accurately.

23.3 Local Classroom-Based Assessment

Despite the fact that the variety of English being used in Philippine classrooms is PhE, the assessment tasks and standards taught are still those of AmE. When doing any type of classroom-based assessments such as

300   *Dave Kenneth Tayao Cayado and James F. D'Angelo*

diagnostic assessment, formative assessment, or summative assessment, learners will be considered incorrect if the way they use English does not conform to 'standard' English, e.g. AmE. This has become a serious issue in assessment because it makes the misalignment between the variety being spoken and the standards being instilled more apparent. To address this, language teachers need to be well-informed about the existence of acrolectal PhE. They need to be educated that English is no longer being viewed as a monolithic entity as Lim and Borlongan (2012) noted. Rather, the emergence of other Englishes and their norms has made English pluricentric. Language teachers need to start incorporating the standards of educated PhE whenever they make different tests and performance tasks. This will not only ensure the validity of the assessment but, more importantly, it will raise the awareness of Filipino learners about a new legitimate English that they are already using.

Another problem that we see is the kind of textbook being used in English classes in the Philippines. AmE monopolizes not only assessment but also the textbooks used by English teachers. In the Philippines, PhE is not the basis of the English textbooks even though it is very well-spoken in the classroom. AmE is favored because of the perennial perception that Inner Circle Englishes are the only legitimate Englishes and being native-like equates to high language proficiency. There needs to be an authoritative reference work for PhE that can be used by both language teachers and learners. This will be beneficial in a sense that once there is a reference grammar book, learners will more readily recognize the sense of its legitimacy. This volume on PhE is one fine example of a reference work on the local variety of English in the Philippines. More importantly, the PhE-informed textbook can be used by teachers as a basis of their assessments and pedagogy.

For the issue of classroom-based assessments and PhE to be solved, language teachers and English textbook writers need to work collaboratively to teach an educated form of PhE in the classroom. Now that the endonormative stabilization is proven, it is high time for English writers to incorporate PhE when writing textbooks. This will make the teachers more informed and educated about the variety; hence they will be more prepared to teach it to their students. When norms of PhE are used by students, their commonly accepted features will not be seen as learner errors but rather a distinctive acceptable feature of the variety they speak. The outcome is not necessarily about making PhE the target variety; it just needs to be integrated in the classroom so that language learners will be aware of its existence. In this way, we are targeting not only the linguistic competence of the learners, but also their sociolinguistic competence, which is one of the facets of communicative competence.

23.4 Standardized Tests

The issue of globally used standardized tests is even more complicated to change than locally used tests. In this context, we are not only dealing

Language Testing 301

with assessments in the classroom but, rather, we are facing high-stakes standardized exams that are being used on a large scale. The perfect examples are IELTS and TOEFL. Even though these high-stakes language exams are being taken by language learners/users from a broad range of varieties, IELTS and TOEFL still remain highly Anglo-American-based. In local contexts, standardized exams like the NAT that is being taken by secondary students also opt to remain AmE-based when it comes to their standards. The emergence of this problem can be attributed to the fact that the International Testing Commission (ITC) is yet to acknowledge other varieties of English in language testing. If a big agency such as ITC or Educational Testing Service (ETS) supports the use of PhE in language testing, it would help in instigating the needed institutional change and paradigm shift in language assessment. However, as pointed out earlier, the resources that we have for PhE are still not sufficient. The existing corpus-based descriptions of PhE need to be used to create a reference work. This will be beneficial in concretizing the standards of PhE and including them in standardized tests. It must be realized that, practically speaking, the large well-entrenched organizations which write the dominantly used internationally tests will be almost impossible to supplant. Thus, the academia should go beyond the ivory tower, to work with them to raise their awareness level of the rich variation and pluralistic ownership of educated English around the world. Just as the *Oxford English Dictionary* has hired scholars from Outer Circle contexts such as the Philippines to add new words to their official lexicon (Salazar, 2014), scholars from non-Inner Circle contexts should be brought on board to work in the large testing agencies. Not so much to add interesting new terms such as *comfort room* or *dirty kitchen* to their tests, but in the opposite sense, to make sure that the terminology, syntax, and cultural content used on the tests is not so uniquely derived from Inner Circle Englishes that it is mainly intelligible only to American test-takers. In this sense, from the point of view of international tests, an effective way to take into account the diversity of English around the globe is not so much to introduce items from the Philippines, Singapore, and Nigerian Englishes, but to make sure the items do not disadvantage test-takers from those contexts. From a listening point of view, however, it would make sense to slowly introduce acrolectal speakers from outside the Inner Circle, since in a globalized world, multicultural faculty membership will be part of higher academe in every country, perhaps especially in the Inner Circle.

Unfortunately, standardized language tests still favor 'standard' AmE and the majority of the standardized tests in English available in the market are developed by American authors who use an Inner Circle English. In light of WE, ELF, and English as an International Language (EIL) paradigms, as stated above, scholars of Philippine and other Englishes need to be included in the group that makes the standardized exams. This shall be done in the hope of balancing out the perspective of different circles of

Englishes. Linguists who documented and described the localized English will be able to provide insights as to how the norms of PhE can be accounted for in high-stake standardized tests.

Despite being complicated and difficult, unrelenting effort must be exerted in revolutionizing the way we view standardized tests and language assessment in general. Since the main goal of standardized language tests is to measure learners' language proficiency and competence, it is necessary that we measure it accurately by ensuring fairness of the items and their validity. This can only be done by being sensitive to the sociolinguistic reality of PhE and taking it into consideration in standardized tests. The number of people eager to learn English is increasing day by day due to inexorable globalization. Because of this, it has become necessary for linguists and assessment experts to meet halfway and promote a more inclusive and WE-informed language assessment.

23.5 Directions for the Future of Language Assessment in Philippine English

The traditional view of language testing has affected two of assessment's most important concepts: reliability and validity. The goal of producing a reliable and valid language assessment for Filipino learners can be achieved by considering the norms of localized English. This is where corpus-based descriptions and a reference grammar of PhE became necessary and important. As articulated earlier, having a reference work will not only raise awareness but it will also demonstrate to learners that PhE is a legitimate variety that should not be seen as lesser or lower than AmE and BrE.

It may seem impossible in the present reality we are in; however, this should not hinder the reconceptualization of language assessment that must be done to ensure valid and appropriate language tests and examinations for speakers of PhE. This is even more important now that the latest developments of PhE demonstrate that it has reached endonormative stabilization. This development and a production of a reference work may warrant an entire paradigm shift and institutional change that Borlongan (2012) suggested. In this paradigm shift, the existence of a quite stable form of PhE needs to be incorporated in all areas of language education such as curriculum, teaching, and assessment. It must be stated in the curriculum that the framework for teaching language is that of educated PhE. Moreover, the content of the curriculum must include the norms and descriptions of said variety. This idea will make it easier for language teachers to confidently include the norms of the local acrolectal English in their classes, since it is already guided by the curriculum. Once the two areas become successful in their implementation, the process of revolutionizing language assessment will go much more smoothly, since it can be made clear that an educated form of PhE is the underlying framework of language classes.

23.6 Concluding Remarks

This chapter focuses on the issues of testing PhE with respect to linguistic norms. The issues of using the native-speaker's linguistic norms in assessing other varieties can be encapsulated into four ideas: monopoly of the language, linguicism, validity, and DIF/item bias. It has been suggested that for these problems to be eradicated, a reliable and comprehensive reference book for PhE needs to be produced to establish its image as a legitimate English. This reference work must be available for local language teachers for they will be the ones to implement this in the classroom context. The production of this may be quite realistic and achievable today, given the recent developments of PhE and, as was mentioned earlier, this volume is considered one such reference work. Lastly, the chapter highlights the much needed paradigm shift in language education in the country, for this is the only way that PhE will be successfully given consideration in language assessment. Making all this possible is by no means an easy task; however, this should not stop us from exerting the effort and sacrifices that will ensure a language assessment that is reliable, valid, fair, and sensitive to the sociolinguistic realities of our own legitimate English.

References

Borlongan, A. M. (2016). Relocating Philippine English in Schneider's Dynamic Model. *Asian Englishes,* DOI: 10.1080/13488678.2016.1223067

Collins, P., & Borlongan, Ariane Macalinga. (2017). Has Philippine English attained linguistic independence?: The grammatical evidence. *The Philippine ESL Journal, 19*, 10–24.

Collins, P., Yao, X., & Borlongan, A. M. (2012). *Relative clauses in Philippine English: A diachronic perspective.* Paper presented at the 31st International Computer Archive of Modern and Medieval English (ICAME) Conference, May 30-June 3, Louvain, Belgium.

Davidson, F. (2006). World Englishes and test construction. In B. B. Kachru, Y. Kachru, & C. L. Nelson (Eds.), *The handbook of World Englishes* (pp. 709–717). Malden, MA: Blackwell.

Ellis, B. & Raju, N. (2003). *Test and item bias: What are they, what they aren't, and how to detect them.* Washington, DC: US Department of Education.

Kachru, B. B. (1985). Standards, codification and sociolinguistic realism: the English language in the Outer Circle. In R. Quirk & H. Widdowson (Eds.),. *English in the World: Teaching and Learning the language and literatures.* Cambridge: CUP Press for the British Council.

Kachru, B. B. (1986). *The alchemy of English: The spread, functions, and models of non-native Englishes.* Oxford & New York: Pergamon Institute of English.

Lim, J. & Borlongan, A. M. (2012). Corpus-based grammatical studies of Philippine English and language assessment: issues and perspective. *The Assessment Handbook, 8,* 51–62,

Salazar, D. (2014). Toward improved coverage of Southeast Asian Englishes in the *Oxford English Dictionary. Lexicography, 1*(1), 95–108.

Schneider, E. W. (2003). The dynamics of new Englishes: From identity construction to dialect birth. *Language, 79*, 233–281.

Schneider, E. W. (2007). *Postcolonial English: Varieties of English around the world.* New York: Cambridge University Press.

Shohamy, E. (2006). *Language policy: Hidden agendas and new approaches.* New York: Routledge.

Tomlinson, B. (2010). Which test of which English and why. In A. Kirkpatrick (Ed.), *The Routledge handbook of world Englishes* (pp. 599–616). London: Routledge.

24 Teacher Education

Edward Jay M. Quinto and
Sterling M. Plata

24.1 Introduction

Teacher education plays a crucial role in preparing language teachers to teach Englishes away from Anglo-American standards and close to the realities put forward by the world Englishes paradigm. No less than Professor Braj Kachru, the father of the study of world Englishes, "has sounded the call for a reformed teacher education in the teaching of English" (Velasco, 2019, p. 295), in response to the pluricentricity of English and the need to teach English language learners the reality of Englishes – their features, contexts, and use (Kachru, 1992).

In the context of the Philippines, scholars have long encouraged English language teaching (ELT) practitioners to incorporate Philippine English (PhE) realities in their practices (Bernardo & Madrunio, 2015) and even endorsed models for teaching English based on PhE (Bernardo, 2018). However, different forces continue to hinder language teachers in fully embracing an endocentric model for ELT. Teacher education policy is one such force. Although numerous strategies in applying a PhE paradigm in teaching English among Filipino students have been recommended, teacher education policies mediate between language teacher preparation and their capacity to transcend from mere awareness of PhE to an integration of the local variety in their ELT strategies and practices.

In this chapter, studies conducted in the area of teacher education and PhE are first reviewed. Then, three major educational reforms, namely, the adoption of the Philippine Professional Standards for Teachers (PPST) through DepEd Order 42 s. 2017, the implementation of the K-12 Classroom Assessment Policy (DepEd Order 8 s.2015), and the mandate to use Philippine Commission on Higher Education's (CHED's) new teacher education curriculum (CMO 75 s.2017), are examined as well as their implications for the responsiveness of teacher education curricula to PhE. Finally, by closely looking at the connections between teacher education and PhE, it is argued that the disregard of PhE in teacher education reforms continues to complicate the English language teachers' task of setting their sights on teaching English from the lens of world Englishes and using the standards of PhE.

DOI: 10.4324/9780429427824-31

24.2 Realizing Philippine English in the Classroom

Teacher research in relation to PhE has received significant attention in the two decades following Bautista's (2001a, 2001b) landmark studies which reported awareness and acceptance of PhE among university teachers. Thereafter, teacher research focused on documenting endonormative practices and proposing frameworks for teaching PhE in the classroom ensued. A clear progression from surveying attitudes and awareness, teacher research concretized into investigations of how PhE can be taught and which norms and standards can be targeted in the classroom.

Reflecting on his work on the preparation and writing a grammar of the verb in PhE, Borlongan (2011) pointed out a "challenge waiting to be overcome" (p. 121) in putting PhE at the level of other established Englishes. This includes retraining teachers, developing teaching materials, and re-envisioning educational leadership, which succeeding scholars would second (e.g. Bernardo, 2014, 2017). While Borlongan reiterates that the purpose of teaching PhE is toward an increased awareness, acceptance, and admiration toward the variety, the development of teacher research in relation to PhE in the last ten years has exceeded the probable outcome of integrating endonormative standards in ELT. Today, teachers who wish to teach using PhE standards enjoy a myriad of strategies and frameworks to do so.

Bernardo and Madrunio (2015) were one of the first to heed the call for the production of what they termed as a "general blueprint for designing a Philippine-English-based pedagogic model for teaching grammar" (p. 42). The model they proposed was based on the results of a pedagogical acceptability test of American English (AmE) and PhE grammatical structures. Acceptability was judged by teachers and students from leading Philippine universities. The outcome was a hybrid model for the teaching of grammar based on the speakers' actual use of the grammatical structures and their judgment of the same. In the case of Bernardo and Madrunio (2015), evidence points to the acceptability of certain PhE structures, which, together with AmE structures, provides teachers to teach English endonormatively.

Besides acceptability judgment, teaching materials, such as textbooks, may also be a gateway to examine the presence of PhE in educational texts. Bernardo's (2013) content analysis of English textbooks used in leading Philippine universities revealed that textbook authors use distinctive PhE grammatical structures, although adherence to AmE was observed. Bernardo (2013) argues that this phenomenon makes the authors, who themselves were English teachers, propagators of the pluricentric model. In closer analysis, while Bernardo (2013) hints that these standards are rarely extensively reflected in textbooks, his findings also suggest that textbooks can become a rich resource for the teaching of endonormative standards, which have to be more abundant in frequency – the textbook author's role – and more explicit in classroom use – than the English teacher's role.

Drawing from his earlier works (Bernardo, 2013; Bernardo & Madrunio, 2015), Bernardo (2018) discusses an endocentric approach, which language teachers can adopt as a pedagogical philosophy and where they "adhere to General American English (GAE) and educated Philippine English in teaching grammar" (p. 101). While ideal, Bernardo's (2018) approach presents a daunting task for the teacher who will have to engage in more instructional tasks than Borlongan's (2011) general proposals. Bernardo (2018) maintains that adopting this endocentric approach to teaching English grammar requires corpus-driven instruction, hybrid syllabi design, production of instruction materials where the world Englishes paradigm is explicitly incorporated, and testing language learners on the Englishes. This challenge is further constrained by language policy in relation to the adoption of PhE, or the lack thereof, which contrasts language teachers' effort, if any, to teach English endonormatively.

Velasco (2019) provides evidence that language teachers did not know of any policy which endorses a particular standard in the teaching of English. She further reported that teachers often mix standards being taught. One teacher was reported to be teaching some British words because of economic reasons, while another teaches American and British standards for a future instrumental purpose of travel. Based on the prevailing sentiment that the American and the British standards remain the standards of choice, Velasco argues that English language teachers in the Philippines "have yet to fully come to terms to a shift in the teaching paradigm of English that necessitates a change in the way non-standard features of the language are perceived and how teaching methods should be modified to match the current reality of English as an international language" (p. 294). Despite this discouraging reality on the ground, Quinto (2018) reports an encouraging study of identity construction among practicum and first-year language teachers. In his study of new language teacher identities, this new breed of language teachers expressed confidence in being good models of the target language and providing quality language instruction at par or even beyond that of native language teachers of English. The study argues for the need to integrate teacher education strategies and policies which allow language teacher candidates to imagine a future where they are empowered, capable, and free in making pedagogical and professional development choices, such as ones away from the notion of "nativeness" in ELT.

Clearly, while language teachers are at the receiving end of the constraints between policy and practice in adopting endonormative standards of ELT, hope also rests on them. As practitioners of ELT, teachers shall continue to carry the vision of putting PhE at the pedestal of other standardized Englishes, as Borlongan (2011) quips. On the other hand, teacher education policies and reforms have a strong influence on the direction that teacher education shall take if it is to champion the preparation of language teachers who will be ready, equipped, and free to teach English using PhE standards.

24.3 The (Mis)place of Philippine English in Recent Educational Policies and Reforms

In the previous section, it was made clear that inputs for the adoption of PhE standards in the language classroom are at the teachers' and administrators' disposal. In an endonormative-supportive context, strategies and framework would ideally be a primary consideration in designing curricula of language teacher training and education. However, the hoped-for endonormative approach to ELT and the corresponding modification in the curriculum remain elusive. This can be seen in the way PhE has been misplaced in recent educational reforms and policies. Four educational reforms which would have had a collective impact on the preparation of language teachers who will be ready, equipped, and free to teach the language using endonormative standards are thus looked at more closely in this section. These are the Philippine Department of Education's (DepEd) K-12 English curriculum and the K-12 Classroom Assessment Guidelines (DepEd Order 8 s. 2015), the PPST, and the CHED's Bachelor of Science in Education Curricula.

24.4 K-12 English Curriculum

According to the Department of Education (2016), the two goals of the English language component of the K-12 curriculum are communicative competence and multiliteracies. The K-12 English curriculum is anchored on the assumption that successful language learning is one where students are able to recognize, accept, value, and build on their existing language competence. Strikingly, the curriculum stipulates that the conditions for success include the use of non-standard forms of the language and expanding the linguistic range of students. Elsewhere, the description of the English curriculum of the country's most recent reform in the basic education is silent on PhE – whether it is a target standard or if it is, in fact, considered to be part of the "non-standard form" mentioned in the curriculum. This condition set by the K-12 English curriculum is likely to exacerbate the difficulties of teachers in teaching English based on a policy which endorses PhE standards (Velasco, 2019).

When it comes to assessment in language learning, it also seems that PhE as a standard is likely to be left out as seen in the way that the DepEd Order 8 series of 2015 titled Policy Guidelines on Classroom Assessment (CA) for the K-12 Basic Education Program exhibits a disconnect between the grading system and the complex K-12 English curriculum with targets referred to as content standards, performance standards, domains, and learning competencies (Plata, 2017). Plata (2017) argued that, although the gaps in assessment of the expected assessment literacy of teachers presently exist, it is also a viable condition where teacher education can prepare future language teachers for assessment literacy. In preparing language teachers for PhE pedagogy, assessment literacy can then be expanded to include competencies

Teacher Education 309

where English language teachers are able to assess data-driven, endonormative features and usage of language. For this purpose, Bernardo and Madrunio's (2015) general blueprint for teaching grammar will be of particular use in PhE-based assessment literacy among prospective language teachers.

24.5 Philippine Professional Standards for Teachers

DepEd Order 42 series of 2017 finalizes the adoption of the PPST. The objectives of the PPST are to: (a) set out clear expectations of teachers along well-defined career stages of professional development from beginning to distinguished practice; (b) engage teachers to actively embrace a continuing effort in attaining proficiency; and (c) apply a uniform measure to assess teacher performance, identify needs, and provide support for professional development (DepEd, 2017, p. 1). In sum, the PPST is a public statement of what teachers need to know, value, and be able to do in the teaching profession and practice. Built on the National Competency-based Teacher Standards (NCBTS), the PPST identifies four career stages: beginning, proficient, highly proficient, and distinguished.

PPST has seven domains comprising various strands of teacher practice. The seven domains are: (1) content knowledge and pedagogy, (2) learning environment, (3) diversity of learners, (4) curriculum and planning, (5) assessment and reporting, (6) community linkages and professional engagement, and (7) personal growth and professional development.

While the policy sets general standards for the professional development of teachers, the implications for the professional development of English language teachers in particular could mesh well with the expectations of PhE pedagogy at various career stages. For example, for Domain 1 – Content Knowledge and Pedagogy, teacher education institutions must begin reforms in BS Education, Major in English curricula, which shall embody the learning of PhE, its features and characteristics, and the teaching of the standard (Bernardo, 2017, 2018; Bernardo & Madrunio, 2015). Language teachers must also be prepared to encourage a PhE-supportive learning environment where teachers and students understand the endonormative standard, have positive attitudes even admiration toward it, and encourage its use (Bautista, 2001a, 2001b; Borlongan, 2009). This is in conjunction with PPST's Domain 2 – Learning Environment. Resources and frameworks are readily available in meeting the demands of the connect between PPST and PhE-based language teacher preparation.

24.6 Revised Bachelor of Science in Education, Major in English Curriculum

The most recent reform on the policy mandating the preparation of English language teachers in the Philippines is encapsulated in the CHED's

310   *Edward Jay M. Quinto and Sterling M. Plata*

new teacher education curriculum (CMO 75 s.2017). Under this reform, the Bachelor of Science in Education, Major in English program, aims to train future elementary and high school teachers in teaching English. While Plata (2017) reported that the CHED was responsive to the PPST and to the K-12 curriculum, a quick survey of required core and professional courses in the curriculum sidelines PhE in teacher preparation. The absence of a required PhE course and the silence of the other critical courses in encouraging endonormative standards both point to the misplacing of the local standard in this reform. Also, Arnuco, Lintao, Plata, and Madrunio (n.d.) uncovered some misalignments between PPST and courses in the revised BS Education curricula, namely, Assessment of Learning 1, Teaching and Assessment of Macro Skills, and Teaching and Assessment of Grammar.

At the backdrop of the misplacements and misalignments, opportunities for the integration of PhE-based pedagogy are available. As a primer, teacher education institutions, if they are to indeed endorse an endonormative framework in teaching English, may start with revisions on the descriptions of critical courses that cover a great deal of teaching English based on a standard. Table 24.1 makes such suggestions as it compares original and proposed revisions on descriptions of BS Education, Major in English course.

Table 24.1 Proposed Revisions on the Descriptions of BS Education, Major in English Courses

Course	Original Description (Based on CHED CMO 75 s.2017)	Proposed Revision
Teaching and assessment of macro skills	Explores the nature of reading and theoretical bases, principles and methods and strategies in teaching and assessing reading. It aims to familiarize students with various strategies for pre-reading, during reading, and post-reading	The course explores the nature, theoretical bases, and principles of reading, writing, listening, speaking, and viewing anchored on the K-12 English curriculum and research. Also, it introduces endonormative standards for the assessment of the productive skills, particularly conventions of writing and speaking that research supports are based on the acceptable features of written and spoken PhE. Students therefore demonstrate assessment literacy by developing assessment tools for each of the macro skills

Course	Original Description (Based on CHED CMO 75 s.2017)	Proposed Revision
Teaching and assessment of grammar	The course engages learners in understanding the distinctions between and among the four types of grammar: functional, descriptive, prescriptive, and pedagogic. Aside from the emphasis on how teaching and assessment vary considering the four types, the course also provides opportunities to discover the role of grammar in achieving communicative competence	The course engages learners in understanding the distinctions between and among the four types of grammar: functional, descriptive, prescriptive, and pedagogic. The course is anchored on the Dynamic Approach to Language Proficiency. Also, it introduces endonormative standards for the teaching and assessment of grammar, particularly that which is based on PhE. Students will be able to teach and assess grammar using an endonormative approach
Structures of English	Develops the ability to use the phonological, lexical, syntactic, and semantic structures of English with ease and explain the form, meaning, and use of their elements	The course develops in students an ability to describe and analyze the phonological, lexical, syntactic, and semantic structures of English. Furthermore, the course also enables students to distinguish PhE from other Englishes, but particularly AmE, and be able to determine variation and change of English(es) with reference to structure

24.7 Concluding Remarks

Resources and pedagogical frameworks to enact the teaching of PhE in schools are at teachers' disposal. That the teaching of PhE is a proposition lacking practical moorings against long-held exonormative views on ELT is today a claim which shuts its eyes to the rich resource resulting from teacher research in relation to PhE. The work of Filipino scholars led to the production of materials, strategies, and pedagogical designs for the teaching of PhE in schools. Yet, teacher education policy continues to stand in the way of preparing language teachers who are ready, equipped, and free to teach English using PhE standards. Thus, decision and policy makers, including teacher education institutions, must be bold and creative in giving PhE due consideration in the policies and reforms ahead. In this chapter, it was made clear that, while language teachers are not ill-equipped and resources are not scarce, teacher education is a strong force which can influence the (mis) direction of teacher preparation toward or away from a revered local variety of English. Borlongan (2016) argued that PhE has reached endonormative

312   *Edward Jay M. Quinto and Sterling M. Plata*

stabilization and "that this phase may be dawning in the development of Philippine English" (p. 232). As such, this chapter conjectures that teacher education has to be a very important feature of policy and reforms, if PhE is indeed endonormatively stable and has furthered in Schneider's (2007) dynamic model. Truly, while sociolinguistic engineering done through language and language-in-education policies are overarching and nationwide, the classroom remains the mouth from which English is heard by millions and millions of Filipino children and the kind of English used and explicitly or implicitly taught in the classroom is the kind of English which they will learn and acquire and use and pass on to the next generation of English users in the country for better or for worse.

References

Arnuco, A., Lintao, R., Plata, S. M., & Madrunio, M. R. (2018).

Assessment education of pre-service English teachers in the Philippines: Prospects and challenges. In S. Zein & R. Stroupe (Eds.), English Language Teacher Preparation in Asia: Policy, Research and Practice (pp. 157–177). London: Routledge..

Bautista, M. L. S. (2001a). Attitudes of English Language Faculty in three leading Philippine Universities toward Philippine English. *Asian Englishes, 4*(1), 4–32. https://doi.org/10.1080/13488678.2001.10801062

Bautista, M. L. S. (2001b). Attitudes of selected Luzon University students and faculty towards Philippine English. In R. E. Maminta (Ed.), *Focus: Selected Writings in Applied Linguistics* (pp. 235–273). Quezon City: Philippine Association for Language Teaching.

Bernardo, A. S. (2013). English(es) in College English textbooks in the Philippines. *US-China Foreign Language, 11*(5), 355–380. https://doi.org/10.17265/1539-8080/2013.05.003

Bernardo, A. S. (2014). Changing and changed stance toward norm selection in Philippine Universities: Its pedagogical implications. *I-Manager's Journal on English Language Teaching, 4*(3), 26–37. https://doi.org/10.26634/jelt.4.3.2859

Bernardo, A. S. (2017). Philippine English in the ESL classroom: A much closer look. *Philippine ESL Journal, 19*(July), 117–144.

Bernardo, A. S. (2018). An endocentric approach to English grammar teaching. In I. P. Martin (Ed.), *Reconceptualizing English Education in a Multilingual Society* (pp. 101–117). Singapore: Springer. https://doi.org/10.1007/978-981-10-7528-5_7

Bernardo, A. S., & Madrunio, M. R. (2015). A framework for designing a Philippine-English-based pedagogic model for teaching English grammar. *Asian Journal of English Language Studies, 3*, 42–71.

Borlongan, A. M. (2011). The preparation and writing of a Grammar of the Verb in Philippine English and the teaching of the English Verb system in Philippine Schools. *Philippine ESL Journal, 7*, 120–123.

Borlongan, A. M. (2016). Relocating Philippine English in Schneider's dynamic model. *Asian Englishes, 18*(3), 232–241. https://doi.org/10.1080/13488678.2016.1223067

Borlongan, A. M. (2009). A survey on language use, attitudes, and identity in relation to Philippine English among young generation Filipinos: An initial sample from a private university. *Philippine ESL Journal, 3*, 74–106. https://doi.org/10.1007/s13398-014-0173-7.2

Department of Education. (2016, May). *K to 12 Curriculum Guide English (Grade 1 to Grade 10)*. Accessible from https://www.deped.gov.ph/k-to-12/about/k-to-12-basic-education-curriculum/

Kachru, B. B. (1992). Teaching world Englishes. In B. B. Kachru (Ed.), *The Other Tongue: English across Cultures* (pp. 355–365). Urbana, IL: University of Illinois Press.

Plata, S. M. (2017). Identifying gaps between DepEd's Assessment Reform and CHED's Teacher preparation Program. In *Proceedings of DLSU Research Congress 2012*. Manila, the Philippines: De La Salle University.

Quinto, E. J. M. (2018). *Towards a Possible Selves-Based Model of Language Teacher Identity among New Teachers: An Exploratory Sequential Analysis*. (Unpublished doctoral dissertation). De La Salle University, Manila, the Philippines.

Schneider, E. W. (2007). *Postcolonial English: Varieties Around the World*. New York, NY: Cambridge University Press.

Velasco, Y. P. (2019). The Kachruvian connection and English language teaching in the Philippines. *World Englishes*, *38*(1–2), 294–302. https://doi.org/10.1111/weng.12374

Part 7

Contemporary Issues

25 Internet

Leah E. Gustilo and Chenee M. Dino

25.1 Introduction

In today's digital age, most of the world's population access the internet to argue, express, do business, educate, influence, and much more (Naughton, 1999). Concomitant to these verbal activities is the use of language shaped by and shapes the different agents and processes involved in the wide gamut of human interaction. As a result, the conventions of speech and writing everyone used decades ago may no longer be the same due to technology-conditioned processes (Bodomo, 2010; Hassan & Hashim, 2009). With all its subsumed terms, such as online communication and computer-mediated communication (CMC), internet communication has seen and aided the development and changes in the use of language. It paved the way for language evolution that allowed a new communication medium that digresses from the perceived standard form of speech and writing, introducing new lexicon features, grammar, and spelling (Crystal, 2004; Li Lan, 2000). Because of these features, Crystal (2001, 2004) claimed that a new natural language variety had arrived, and he called this Netspeak. He based such a claim on the "lexico-graphological distinctiveness" (p. 92) and other characteristics of the new medium, which he outlined in his book *Language and the Internet.* The present chapter draws on Crystal's description of internet language and aims to describe the features of Philippine English (PhE) as used on the internet. It hypothesized that technology shapes this particular English variety by engendering neologisms, new constructions, and new ways of communication (Hassan & Hashim, 2009). This electronic discourse in Philippine English is referred to in this chapter as Internet Philippine English (IPhE) or Filipino Digitalk in English.

25.2 Internet Language

The linguistic revolution on the internet engendered new conventions spreading in the online community and spilling over into non-internet situations, causing linguists to document the characteristics of internet language. Investigations on the language of the internet started as early as the

DOI: 10.4324/9780429427824-33

mid-80s, delving into the question of categorization of internet language: whether it complies with the conventions of writing or speech tradition (Ferrara, Brunner, & Whittemore, 1991). To answer this question, Crystal (2001) first differentiated the characteristics of written and spoken language conventions. Then he claimed that internet language, which he termed Netspeak, possesses characteristics belonging to both sides of the spoken and writing dichotomy but displays conventions unique only to internet communication; hence, he concluded that Netspeak is something different – an authentic "third medium" (p. 52). His analysis of web sources, blogs, chat groups, virtual worlds, emails, and instant messaging proved that internet language varieties have unique graphic, orthographic, lexico-grammatical, and discourse features different from written and spoken language.

Several other investigations from different parts of the world have been carried out on an increasing scale. Hassan and Hashim (2009) documented the local forms and structures that have been used to expand the lexicon of Malaysian English, utilizing a two-million-word corpus of electronic discourse by Malaysian multilinguals. They found that code-mixing (CM), code-switching (CS), affixed words, coinages, borrowings, abbreviations, discourse particles, acronyms, compounds, and blends which fulfill discourse functions enable the users to communicate in the online community using the new forms in the Malaysian electronic variety of English. Turner, Abrams, Katic, and Donovan (2014) focused on the digital language of American adolescents and found that while four of the analyzed features were considered standard, the rest were deemed non-standard. These are missing end periods, non-standard capitalization, abbreviations, acronyms, missing apostrophes, non-capitalization, multiple vowels, multiple consonants, run-ons, logograms, and rebus forms. American adolescents used these features to be efficient and to meet the readers' expectations.

The language of the African youth in relation to social media has been investigated by Hollington and Nassenstein (2018). They claimed that African youth linguistic practices, which center on identity construction, creative use of language, and resistance to existing hegemonies through their posts on Facebook, WhatsApp groups, Twitter, and forums, abound. Also, in Netherlands, the language of the Dutch youth was documented by Verheijen (2018). Verheijen utilized a 400,000-word Dutch youth's digital writing from MSN chats, SMS text messages, Twitter posts, and WhatsApp messages. He claimed that the orthographic deviations produced in CMC contexts are not random violations but products of orthographic principles producing specific forms with intended functions. This finding was unearthed through a systematic analysis of textism types, edit operations, and functions. The functions of Dutch textisms, which are also found in other studies, include casualness and colloquialism, clarity and comprehension, creativity and coolness, compensation and cues, and conciseness and curtailment. Verheijen (2018) concluded that it is not the standard form but the 'incorrect' language that has been the preferred communication style among Dutch youths.

In the Philippines, the role of the internet as a tool for communication for religion, government, education, health, and business has been documented in the study by Minges, Magpantay, Firth, and Kelly (2002). However, despite the thoroughness of Minges et al.'s study, the language of Pinoy internet or e-language was not part of its focus. Still, their study can be praised for its view that Filipino internet users are e-citizens who are not bound by societal involvement alone but by the language they use. Minges et al. (2002) claimed that Filipinos use the short messaging system, which originated from text messaging through mobile phones, and such messaging systems are prevalent in the present-day IPhE.

Curiosity about the language used by Filipinos on the internet perhaps began when the use of Facebook became prevalent in 2015 (Dino & Gustilo, 2015). The then population of 100,981,437 Filipinos (Philippine Statistics Authority, 2017) was given access to the World Wide Web. In 2018, Rappler reported that 60 to 70 million Filipinos became active Facebook users (Mendoza & Maglunog, 2018). Since then, various developers and service providers have introduced more applications and promotions in the country. The launch of Facebook, its partnership with Internet service providers, and its free access have invited more Filipino netizens to join the (global) online community; thus, more Filipinos had access and exposure to the language of internet-aided communication.

Since the beginning of the 21st century, internet language has been well documented in many studies abroad. Still, it was not until 2015 that the first publication about Filipino Digitalk was documented (Dino & Gustilo, 2015). Dino and Gustilo (2015) published their pilot analysis on nearly 2,000 Facebook statuses, revealing that Filipinos created creative expressions in the internet-mediated environment. Of the nine types of linguistic features used by Filipino Facebookers, CS and acronyms were the most frequently used features for efficient communication in digital writing. They also found that discourse particles (DPs) play a central role in the understanding and transmission of a message in digital writing. This finding was confirmed in the study of Palacio and Gustilo (2016), who focused on the discourse-pragmatic functions of DPs using Facebook posts of college students from Metro Manila. DPs in Filipino electronic discourse enable the Filipino youth to decode the received message, express clarity of message, and establish speaker-receiver attitudes and perceptions on Facebook. Seeing that previous investigations have demonstrated the ubiquitous presence of CS in CMC, Caparas and Gustilo (2017) investigated the frequency, forms, and functions of multi-lingual CS in Filipino electronic discourse and concluded that CS in electronic discourse enables the users to "express their ideas spontaneously, to retain native terminology, to express disappointment, and to promote relationship," providing evidence for the "viability of regional languages to co-exist with English and other languages in the gamut of human interactions on the internet" (349). These previous investigations provide empirical findings that describe the features of IPhE.

320   *Leah E. Gustilo and Chenee M. Dino*

25.3 Linguistic Features of Internet Philippine English

Data used in the characterization of IPhE or Digitalk presented in this chapter are composed of roughly 500,000 words from the online interactions of Filipino Digitalkers on Instagram, Facebook, Edmodo, Twitter, Online Gaming, and Blogs. Most of the features in previous investigations describing electronic discourse, such as CS, compounds and blends, acronyms and abbreviations, discourse particles, non-sentence structures, and the like, also emerged in the data analyzed for this chapter.

25.3.1 Acronyms

Acronym, shortening, initialism, and abbreviations are among the words connected to acronymy. In IPhE, acronymy was used in a combination of patterns. Although previous literature (Yule, 2010) discussed that abbreviation is not entirely similar to acronyms because the former is marked by shortening a word while the latter is shortened by taking some letters of the word and putting them together, the present chapter considered them under one category (i.e. acronymy). Acronymy is based on Bodomo's (2010) approaches to shortening and is more applicable to computer-mediated-discourse analysis. Several utterances were found with this feature using Bodomo's framework for analyzing shortened expressions. Acronymy may be any of the following: a word represented by only one letter [*s* for student], initial letters of a proper noun [*LP* for Liberal Party], initial letters of a phrase [*idk* for I do not know], and last syllable of a word [*cher* for teacher].

Shortened expressions have long been used in writing to save time and space. In electronic discourse, they abound not only because of the physical limitations of the medium but because of the social motivation which indicates in-group membership (Hassan & Hashim, 2009).

25.3.2 Affixation

Affixation is a lexical feature marked by the attachment of prefixes or suffixes to a word (Hassan & Hashim, 2009). Both Filipino and English affixes were attached to the English base to form new words, as exemplified in the following:

1   *Filipino Affix Attached to English Base.* It is customary for Filipinos, being bilinguals, to combine these two languages in creating words or expressions such as *pag-download, i-install, nag-report,* and *mag-conduct.*
2   *English Affix Attached to English Base.* Attaching these morphemes results in a change in the part of speech of the base as in the case of *year-ender* and *pigging.* The suffix *-er* was added to the noun *year-end* deriving an adjective (e.g., *year-ender photo*). After the affixation process, the noun becomes an adjective for the word *photo.* The suffix *-ing*

Internet 321

was added to the noun *pig* deriving a verb (e.g., I am *pigging* out). The new word in the post, *pigging out,* is similar to the usual Filipino phrase *dining in* or *dining out* terms of Filipinos.

Aside from the widely known Filipino and English affixes used in IPhE, corpus evidence also showed the presence of internet-engendered prefix e-, producing a long list of e-affixed IPhE words such as *e-load, e-conference, e-business, e-machine, e-certificate, e-games, e-gift, e-dictionary, e-shopping, e-purse, e-copy,* and *e-cigarette.*

25.3.3 Contractions

Contracted words are often discouraged in formal writing, and they are usually evident in conversations that are not structured formally. Filipino Digitalkers did not consider this rule in IPhE, as their interactions were replete with the informal use of contractions or contracted expressions. The most frequent contracted words in the data are *it's, he's, we'll,* and *she's.*

25.3.4 Blending

Blending or combining parts of two words or more to form a new one is prevalent in IPhE. Examples include *netizen* (internet+citizen), *digitalk (*digital+talk), *lotsa* (lots+of), *sorta* (sort+of), *kinda* (kind+of), *autodesk* (automatic + desktop), *homies* (home + buddies), *playning* (playing+learning), *shoefie* (shoe + selfie), and *mema (merong + masabi).* The last example is a borrowed blend from Filipino.

25.3.5 Compounds

Aside from combining parts of words (blending), new expressions were also formed by combining words in IPhE. When two or more words are combined to form new expressions, the feature is called compounding. Some compound words in IPhE are *sharepost, screenshare, overthink, fangirl, cheatday, realtalk (real + talk), trashtalk (trash + talk), skyporn (sky+ porn, addiction to the sky of getting photos of the sky), foodporn (food + porn, addiction to eating), furmom (fur + mom, a female owner of a pet dog/cat), furbaby (fur+baby, a pet dog or cat), pasaload, and pasabuy.* The last two examples are Filipino and English compounds. *Pasa* is a Filipino word which means to pass or transfer. Hence, *pasaload* means 'to transfer a load credit from one's account to another.' *Pasabuy* means 'the task of buying is passed onto somebody and that person will hand over or pass the items to the requesting party.'

An interesting set of compounds in IPhE is a compound attached to the word mode. Corpus evidence includes *beast mode* 'to be in extreme anger,' *teacher mode* 'to be doing tasks of a teacher,' *shopping mode* 'to be on the activity of purchasing goods,' *badass* mode 'to be ready to cause trouble,' and *gym mode* 'to be working out in a gym.'

322   Leah E. Gustilo and Chenee M. Dino

25.3.6 Coinage

The invention of totally new words was categorized by Yule (2010) as coinage. A good example in IPhE is the expression *chuchu* (i.e. a term used to point to a topic being talked about in context) and the term *keme,* which is used interchangeably with *chuchu.* These two terms are evident both in mediated and in face-to-face communication, and their prevalence in the Philippines is attributed to the gay language.

25.3.7 Pun

Creative language is also manifested in the puns or wordplay in IPhE which involves addition of sounds (e.g., *nope* in no), deletion of sounds and addition of morphemes (e.g., *keri* from *okay*; *o* and *y* sounds were deleted and *-ri* was added to *ke-*), changing the spelling of a word which means one thing (e.g., delicious) to mean another thing (e.g., *dealicious,* the root word is *deal,* which means 'an offer' in restaurants, and *-licious* from the word *delicious*), addition of a creative suffix to an English root (*momshie,* from *mom* + *shie*), changing *-y* to *i* and addition of English suffix *-er* to adjectives to mean more (*cheezier* from *cheezy* + *er, meatier* from *meaty* + *er, beefier* from *beefy* + *er*), parallelism of meaning (*monthsary, month* + *sary* from *anniversary*; *juicylicious, juicy* + *licious, licious* from the word *delicious*), and the like.

25.3.8 Transcription of Sigh, Laughter, and Other Physical Actions

Filipino netizens try to be as expressive as they can while exchanging messages with other netizens. Their being expressive was evident in transcribing their emotions or physical gestures. They transcribed their expression of awe or surprise (e.g., *ala*), laughter (e.g., *ahahah)*, sadness (e.g., *huhuhu*), and hugging (e.g., *hugsss*). These speech-like features compensate for the lack of paralinguistic cues absent in writing (Verheijen, 2018).

25.3.9 Rebus Forms

IPhE's word formation processes include using existing sounds or letters to form words, which is referred to as rebus writing. For example, later can be written *l8er;* forever, *4ever;* sexy, *6c;* see you, *cu;* you and me, *unme;* celebrate, *celebr8;* total, *2tal;* and Duterte, *Du30.*

25.3.10 Capped Expressions and Non-Capitalization

While Filipinos use capped expressions in IPhE (e.g., FOREVER) to emphasize or intensify their utterance, they also tend to use lower case letters for the personal pronoun I and initial letters of proper nouns (e.g. *i, leah*). Automatic capitalization is done when the Caps Lock key is on. However, whether

Filipino netizens use capped expressions or switch back to non-capitalized letters still involves language choice, which shows their writing in IPhE.

25.3.11 Reduplication of Letters and Words

Doubling (e.g., *Eww*) or tripling of letters in a word (e.g., *whyyy*) or repeating words (*yes yes; no no no*) abound in IPhE.

25.3.12 Emoticons and Other Symbols

Representations of facial expressions by combining punctuations and letters referred to as emoticons are represented in IPhE data. The most common ones represent happiness:), sadness =(, and love < 3. These ideograms and other symbols are used to visually enrich the post and convey emotions (Verheijen, 2018).

The @ sign used in email addresses is used in place of the preposition *at* (e.g., *Meeting @ our place*). Another symbol that abounds in IPhE is the pound key which netizens term as hashtag. The hashtag (#) is used to indicate a title or update or cluster words, phrases, and even sentences in the posts on social networking sites.

25.3.13 Non-Standard Use/New Usage of Punctuation

In IPhE, one type of punctuation that acquired a new usage is the asterisk (*). Conventionally, asterisk is used as a footnote sign or an indication that something is emphasized or has additional information. In the IPhE data analyzed, an asterisk is used after an error in utterance, indicating that a typographical error was committed in the previous utterance; it is meant to replace or suggest the expression 'correction.'

IPhE also showed evidence of a combination of two punctuations such as question mark (?) and exclamation point (!) or multiple uses of the same punctuation in utterances that show emphasis or heightened emotion (e.g. *really?!, absurd!!!!!*). This feature shows a deviation in the accepted usage of punctuation because it is unusual to find both punctuations or multiple punctuations at the same utterance in a formally written text. In addition, it is customary for some Pinoy netizens to overuse punctuations and combine them with other symbols (*Im okay!!!?@#$%^@*). The absence of punctuations also abounds in IPhE. Filipino netizens write their sentences without putting commas or periods (e.g., *I do not care if he is hurting he deserves it*).

In addition, in the conventional usage of ellipsis, it indicates that something has been omitted from the sentence either in the middle or at the end. In IPhE, ellipses can introduce complete sentences (e.g,.....my journey is longer than the future), and the dots can be more than three. In addition, sentences can be interrupted in the middle of a sentence by ellipses not to show omitted words but a long pause (e.g., *I know..... it is not enough*).

324 *Leah E. Gustilo and Chenee M. Dino*

Similar to using symbols and emoticons/emojis, non-standard usage of punctuation helps replace the lacking paralinguistic cues in writing.

25.3.14 Reduced or Non-Sentence Structures

Filipino netizens employ *grammatical reductions*. IPhE seems to follow the *"The shorter the better* or *less is more"* principle since they tend to reduce the characters or length of their utterances. They tend to remove some grammatical items such as nouns/pronouns and linking verbs (e.g., *happy for you*) and retain only the key parts of their utterances which were deemed to be the core of their messages (e.g., *will send you* in *I will send you the file*). One-word utterances punctuated as one sentence (e.g., *Fun. Food. Fellowship*) also abound. Previous studies have also documented that netizens preferred informal conventions in digital writing and often used fragment structures instead of complete sentences (Crystal, 2004; Danet 2001).

25.3.15 Code Alteration

Code alteration or CS is common in IPhE. Nearly half of the data were a combination of intra-sentential CS and inter-sentential CS using English and Tagalog languages, with intra-sentential CS as more frequent than inter-sentential CS. CS has pragmatic functions in IPhE. They provide ease in posting the netizens' statuses in SNS platforms, show in-group solidarity, and maintain interpersonal relationships with fellow netizens. Their findings confirmed that CS is prevalent and functional in PhE, formerly documented in previous PhE studies (Bautista, 2000; Go & Gustilo, 2013).

25.4 Conclusion

Since the introduction of English in the Philippines, PhE vocabulary has dramatically expanded and developed (Dimaculangan & Gustilo, 2017). This growth in the vocabulary, which is regarded as the foremost indication of language change (Crystal, 2004), has been documented in previous lexicon studies in PhE (Bautista, 2000; Borlongan, 2007; Dimaculangan and Gustilo, 2018). Gustilo and Dimaculangan (2018) have already established the expansion of PhE vocabulary through existing and newly developed word-formation processes in their 400,000-word corpus of 21st-century written PhE. They claimed that PhE is already transitioning to Stage 4 of Schneider's (2007) dynamic model and that PhE variety has surpassed the nativization stage and is slowly developing its linguistic forms.

The present chapter claims a PhE variety on the internet that helps confirm the stabilization of PhE, as suggested by Borlongan (2016). The present chapter has exemplified that PhE on the internet has developed local forms and uses that may have been extended in offline communication. Like Crystal's (2001) claim, the lexicon and the graphological features of IPhE, most

Internet   325

of which lack dictionary evidence, are the most significant and prevalent features supporting IPhE variety. It seems that some features of IPhE are distinct only to Filipinos; some tend to be universal because they have already been documented in other English varieties. This finding about internet English as being exclusive or universal could be verified by conducting contrastive/comparative studies of corpora across online Englishes.

It is difficult to predict whether the description of IPhE will become part of the features of standard PhE or it will remain an online phenomenon. As Crystal (2001) predicted, Netspeak features may become part of "Netspeak's identity in fifty years; others may not last another year" (p. 92). However, whether the IPhE would live or die, it is worth documenting that at the time this chapter was being written, the ultimate achievement of IPhE was the expansion of PhE with a number of lexico-graphological features that originated from internet language.

References

Bautista, M. L. S. (2000). *Defining standard Philippine English: Its status and grammatical features.* Manila: De La Salle University Press.

Bodomo, A. B. (2010). *Computer-mediated communication for linguistics and literacy: Technology and natural language education.* Hershey, PA: IGI Global.

Borlongan, A. M. (2007). Innovations in Standard Philippine English. In C. C. Mann (Ed.), *Current research on English and applied linguistics: A De La Salle University special issue* (pp. 1–36). Manila, the Philippines: De La Salle University-Manila, College of Education, Department of English and Applied Linguistics.

Borlongan, A. M. (2016). Relocating Philippine English in Schneider's dynamic model. *Asian Englishes, 18*(3), 1–10.

Caparas, P., & Gustilo, L. (2017). Communicative aspects of multi-lingual code-switching in computer-mediated communication. *Indonesian Journal of Applied Linguistics, 7*(2), 349–359.

Crystal, D. (2001). *Language and the internet.* Cambridge: Cambridge University Press.

Crystal, D. (2004). *Language and the internet* (2nd Ed.). Cambridge: Cambridge University Press.

Danet, B. (2001). *Cyberpl@y: Communicating online.* Oxford, United Kingdom: Berg.

Dimaculangan, N., & Gustilo, L. E. (2017). Lexical patterns in the early 21st century Philippine English writing. *Advanced Science Letters, 23*(2), 1094–1098.

Dimaculangan, D., & Gustilo, L. E. (2018). A closer look at Philippine English word-formation frameworks. *Advanced Science Letters, 24*, 8384–8388.

Dino, C. M., & Gustilo, L. E. (2015). Digitalk: An exploration of the linguistic features of CMC. *International Journal of Languages, Literature and Linguistics, 1*(1), 51–55.

Ferrara, K., Brunner, H., & Whittemore, G. (1991). Interactive written discourse as an emergent register. *Written Communication, 8*(1), 8–34.

Go, M., & Gustilo, L. E. (2013). Tagalog or Taglish: The lingua franca of Filipino urban factory workers. *Philippine ESL Journal, 10*, 57–87.

326 *Leah E. Gustilo and Chenee M. Dino*

Gustilo, L., & Dimaculangan, N. (2018). Attitudes of Filipino English teachers towards 21st century Philippine English writing. *Advanced Science Letters, 24*, 8349–8352.

Hassan, N., & Hashim, A. (2009). Electronic English in Malaysia: Features and language in use. *English Today, 25*(4), 39–46.

Hollington, A., & Nassenstein, N. (2018). African youth language practices and social media. In A. Ziegler (Ed.), *Jugendsprachen/Youth Languages: Aktuelle Perspektiven internationaler Forschung/Current Perspectives of International Research* (pp. 807–828). Berlin, Boston: De Gruyter. https://doi.org/10.1515/9783110472226-036

Lan, L. (2000). Email: A challenge to standard English? *English Today, 64*, 23–29, 55.

Mendoza, G, & Maglunog, CJ. (2018, October 26). Did you know that some PH cities have more Facebook users than actual population? *Rappler.* https://www.rappler.com/

Minges, M., Magpantay, E., Firth, L., & Kelly, T. (2002). Pinoy internet: Philippine case study. Retrieved from www.itu.int/ITD/ict/cs/philippines/material/phl%20cs.pdf

Naughton, J. (1999). *A brief history of the future: The origins of the internet.* London: Weidenfeld and Nicolson.

Palacio, M., & Gustilo, L. (2016). A pragmatic analysis of discourse particles in Filipino computer-meditated communication. *Gema Online Journal of Language Studies, 16*(3), 1–19.

Philippine Statistics Authority (2017). 2015 Census of population, Report No. 2-Demographic and Socioeconomic Characteristics Philippines. ISSN 0117-1453.

Schneider, E. (2007). *Postcolonial English: Varieties around the world.* Cambridge: Cambridge University Press.

Turner, K. H., Abrams, S. S., Katic, E., & Donovan, M. J. (2014). Demystifying digitalk: The what and why of the language teens use in digital writing. *Journal of Literary Research, 46*(2), 157–193.

Yule, G. (2010). *A study of language* (4th ed.). Cambridge: Cambridge University Press.

Verheijen, L. (2018). Orthographic principles in computer-mediated communication: The SUPER-functions of textisms and their interaction with age and medium. *Written Language & Literacy, 21*(1), 111–145.

26 Migration

Beatriz P. Lorente

26.1 Introduction

Migration to and from the Philippines is crucial to understanding the continuing 'grip of English' (Lorente, 2013), and the persistence of unequal Englishes (Tupas, 2015a) and unequal multilingualisms (Tupas, 2015b) in the country. The Philippines is both a sending and a receiving country and English looms large in how these flows were and are constructed. As a sending country, the Philippines is considered to have a 'culture of migration' (Asis, 2006), with around 11% of the country's population working and living overseas. It is the world's largest exporter of government-sponsored temporary contract workers in terms of both magnitude and geographic scope (Tyner, 2004). Overseas Filipino Workers (OFWs) are represented as ideal transnational workers who are highly skilled and whose English skills provide them with a competitive edge (Gonzalez, 1998; Lorente, 2012, 2018; Martin, 2012; Valdez & Tan, 2018). The Philippines is also one of the largest source countries of immigrants to the United States, Canada, Australia and New Zealand (Bedford, 2018; Darvin, 2017; Zong & Batalova, 2018), all of which are traditional countries of immigration where English is the dominant language. In these countries, Filipinos seem to assimilate easily, in part because of their English skills, with second-generation Filipino migrants often acquiring English at the expense of knowledge of their parents' mother tongues (cf. Axel, 2011; Nical, 2000). The Philippines is also a receiving country (see, for example, Gonzales 2017). In relation to English, the Philippines is emerging as 'budget English' destination (Choe, 2016; Choe & Son, 2018; Imperial, 2017; Jang, 2018; Lorente & Tupas, 2014; McGeown, 2012), with increasing numbers of students from South Korea and neighboring countries heading to Baguio City, Cebu, Metro Manila and other major Philippine cities to intensively study English for a short period of time. The number of foreign students who head to Philippine universities for what is perceived to be an affordable English-medium tertiary education is also on the rise.

This chapter focuses on the Philippines as a sending country and in particular on the outflows of Filipinos to other countries. A discussion of

DOI: 10.4324/9780429427824-34

328   *Beatriz P. Lorente*

English in relation to the Philippines as a receiving country and as a country of return (for *balikbayans* or returnees) is beyond the scope of this chapter. This chapter first considers the relationship between migration and the history of English in the Philippines. It then looks at how English has been positioned and valued in the flows of migration from the country. Specifically, it will discuss permanent migration, especially to the United States, which has been largely shaped by American colonialism. It will then examine temporary labor migration where there seems to be a shift from English being considered as the competitive edge of OFWs to English being a minimum requirement. For the purpose of this chapter, migration is defined as the movement of people between national boundaries.

26.2 Migration and the History of English in the Philippines

The current position of the Philippines in global migration circuits and the role that English plays in this position needs to be understood historically. The Philippines has long been part of global migration circuits. Long before the Spanish colonial period, the archipelago was "the easternmost edge of a vast network of Chinese, Southeast Asian, Indian and Arab traders that circulated porcelains, silks, glass beads, and other luxury goods throughout the South China Sea and through the Malacca Straits into the Indian Ocean" (Junker, 1999, p. 3). It was during the Spanish colonial era that the country became integrated into global migration circuits as a source of labor. As such,"... the Philippine workforce was, in the first instance, global before it became national" (Aguilar, 2014, p. 58). In the 16th and 17th century, the Spanish instituted a transpacific slave trade with Manila as the colonial outpost where slaves (including indigenous Filipinos, Muslim war prisoners, Chinese and the like) were purchased and the Manila galleons served as the means for transporting slaves to Mexico (Seijias, 2014). It was also during the Spanish colonial period that men from the Luzon and Visayas islands became part of seafaring crews led by Spaniards and other Europeans (Aguilar, 2014). They were first part of Spanish-led explorations of the New World that departed from the Philippines in the mid to late 1500s. By the 1600s, they formed the majority of galleon crews in the Spanish galleon trade between Acapulco and Manila, recognized for their seafaring prowess but, like now, paid less than Spaniards and other Europeans for working in the same positions. Some native sailors abandoned ship and settled in parts of the Americas. Even before the galleon trade ended in 1815, 'Manilamen', as they became known and as they called themselves, had spread beyond the Spanish realm, becoming part of multiethnic crews on international merchant ships trading between Alaska and China, or in sandalwood in various parts of Oceania (Aguilar, 2014).

The Philippines was not just integrated in global migration circuits as a source of labor. In the last two decades of the 19th century, it was part of what one would call 'early globalization' and of the global exchanges of revolutionary, anti-colonial and anti-imperial ideas during that time

Migration 329

(cf. Anderson, 2005). It was in this context and in view of the rise of the British Empire that Filipino intellectuals came to know and learn English. Jose Rizal passed through the United States and spent time at the British Museum during his second stint abroad, and, in his letters to his sister Saturnina from Dapitan, he encouraged her to learn English and to write back to him in English (Gonzalez, 2004). It is also striking that, in the education program proposed by Apolinario Mabini under the Malolos government,

> the plan for secondary school, based on a European pattern of six years, put more stress on English than Spanish, not only because of the negative feelings against Spain at the time but perhaps the realization that English would be an important world language in the future as the British Empire was then at its height.
>
> (Gonzalez, 2004, pp. 7–8)

The Philippine independence movement, however, was crushed by the Americans during the Philippine-American War. Thus, instead of being introduced as a language in the education system of an independent republic, English was introduced to the Philippines during the American colonial period where it was invested with transformative and liberating power (Kramer, 2006; Martin, 2004; Tupas, 2003, 2008). This investment was rooted in the ideology of benevolent assimilation (Kramer, 2006) and facilitated by migration flows to and from the country that were part of American colonialism. These flows centered around the most important component of America's 'civilizing' mission in the Philippines: the public education system where the medium of instruction was English, it being "the language that would provide the Filipinos access to civilization [...] the life of reason and prudence" (Martin, 1999, p. 134). It was also marked by a power differential: "The Americans' voyage to the Philippines was one of conquest to a colonized territory, while the Filipinos' journey to the United States was a 'return' of subjugated nationals to the center of empire" (Espiritu, 2003, p. 57). American soldiers were the first English teachers in the Philippines; they began teaching (presumably, in English) in Corregidor as early as August 1898 (Martin, 2012). They were soon followed by the Thomasites, i.e. American teachers from all over the United States who were recruited to teach in the Philippines; 2,000 of them arrived between 1901 and 1921 (Gonzalez, 2004). Because of this public education system and the use of English as the sole medium of instruction, English was disseminated more widely and entrenched more effectively in state policies and in the national imagination (Hau & Tinio, 2003). In terms of migration flows from the country, "(t)here was no better condensation of the projects of tutelage and assimilation than the *pensionado* program, inaugurated in 1903, which would eventually send 300 Filipino students to the United States for government-funded higher education" (Kramer, 2006, p. 204). The program selected sons and daughters of the elite, as well as ambitious and bright students to study at American

330   *Beatriz P. Lorente*

universities as "disciples of democracy" (Mabalon, 2013). The program not only oriented an emerging English-speaking elite class toward American customs and loyalties, it also served as a showcase of successful assimilation to the American public (Kramer, 2006).

Since the American colonial period, English has remained entrenched and dominant in the Philippine education system (Bernardo, 2004), despite challenges to it, first by the introduction Bilingual Education Program (BEP) in 1974, then by the implementation of Mother Tongue-Based Multilingual Education in 2009 (Tupas & Lorente, 2014). This entrenchment is due, in part, to the structural insertion of the Philippines at the margins of the world system, first as an export-oriented economy catering to foreign capital and then as a labor-sending country catering to particular niches in the global labor market (Gonzalez, 1998; Lorente, 2018, 2013, 2012). In the same year that the BEP was instituted in 1974, the first batch of government-sponsored OFWs was deployed to the Middle East, an early indication of how the search for a national linguistic symbol of unity would soon be overtaken, or had already been overtaken, by the insertion of the Philippines into the world system as a labor-sending country. For the groups whose rallying cry for English had been that Tagalog or Filipino would not represent them in the national arena, their almost indisputable argument now was that English was necessary if the country was to participate and fully benefit from the global economy. Arguably, in this light, the BEP's biggest winners were English which remained preeminent in the country's linguistic economy and the elite groups whose interests were now legitimized. The biggest losers were the Filipinos whose wages had been eroded by their incorporation into the global labor market and whose varying levels of English competence facilitated their entry either as (mainly) low-waged workers in an export-oriented, labor-intensive light industry financed by foreign capital (Tollefson, 1991) or as OFWs. The Philippine education system continues to produce this hierarchy of labor with corresponding levels of English skills meant for an externally defined labor market (cf. Ortiga, 2017; Toh & Floresca-Cawagas, 2003). This has resulted in a deteriorating education system that is unable to respond realistically and relevantly to the social and economic needs of the country. This is most evident in the disparity between the degrees of most college graduates and the demand for such skills or expertise in the domestic labor market (along with the failure to create such demand), leading to a rise in the number of educated underemployed and unemployed who, in turn, may be funneled into overseas labor migration.

26.3 English and Permanent Migration from the Philippines

The United States, Canada, Australia and, increasingly, New Zealand are the home countries of most of the permanent migrants from the Philippines. All of these countries are traditional countries of immigration which have historically encouraged immigration for permanent settlement on a large

Migration 331

scale. English is also the dominant language in all of these countries. Relative to other immigrant groups, it appears that Filipinos blend in quickly, in part because of their English skills (cf. Cave, 2018; Darvin, 2017; Espiritu & Wolf, 2001). However, Filipino permanent migrants are also and continue to be constructed as cultural and linguistic Others who occupy subordinate positions in the host country's social hierarchy (cf. Labrador, 2009).

By far, the United States is home to the largest number of Filipinos abroad, and the Philippines is the fourth-largest origin country for immigrants since 2010, after Mexico, India and China (Zong & Batalova, 2018). As of 2013, there were around 3.1 million Filipinos in the United States (Commission on Filipinos Overseas, 2014). The migration of Filipinos to the United States was structured by colonial relations (Takaki, 1998). Mabalon (2013) describes how, during the American colonial period, "the economic shifts that resulted from the changing economy created conditions that, along with colonial education pushed thousands of Filipinas/os to look for better opportunities and wages overseas" (p. 40). The first wave of Philippine migration to the United States began in 1906, soon after the creation of the *pensionado* program. The ones who left were mainly Filipino men, many of whom were from northern Luzon. They filled temporary labor needs in agriculture in Hawaii and the West Coast. This first wave of Filipino migrants experienced brutal racial discrimination. As nonwhite people, they were limited to agricultural labor and barred from citizenship, meeting outside of their ethnic neighborhoods, marrying whites and owning property (Mabalon, 2013). English did not seem to play a role in how these workers were recruited. Mabalon notes that migrants at that time had widely varying English proficiencies, a reflection of the 'inequalities of English' (Tupas, 2015a) produced by the American colonial system of public education. Those with a high school education could use English fluently while those who did not go beyond an elementary education had more limited English fluency. The second wave of Philippine migration to the United States started in the 1960s and was made up mostly of Filipino professionals, many of whom were nurses. They went to the United States after major reforms in US immigration law opened the door to a steady and significant flow of Asian permanent migration to the country (Choy, 2003). According to Choy, the important preconditions that enabled the *mass* migration of Filipino nurses to the United States were established under the American colonial regime and included: (1) Americanized professional nursing training, (2) English-language fluency, (3) Americanized nursing work culture and (4) gendered notions of nursing as women's work. These preconditions laid the foundations for a "gendered, racialized and professional labor force prepared for export to the United States in the tens of thousands by the 1950s through the present" (Choy, 2003, p. 42).

Currently,

> Filipinos are more likely than other immigrants to have strong English
> skills, and have much higher college education rates than the overall

332   *Beatriz P. Lorente*

foreign-and U.S.-born populations. They are also more likely to be naturalized U.S. citizens than other immigrant groups, have higher incomes and lower poverty rates, and are less likely to be uninsured.

(Zong & Batalova, 2018)

This picture though is incomplete. Filipino migrants are considered to be the most linguistically assimilated with rapid transition to monolingual English in the second generation (Espiritu & Wolf, 2001). In a review of literature on Filipino language maintenance, Umali (2016) notes that Filipino migrant parents tend to abandon their own ethnic practices in favor of full assimilation to the cultural and linguistic practices of the host country. The variety of English that Filipinos speak in the United States appears to be different from American English (cf. Jubilado, 2016 on Philippine English in Hawaii). More importantly, Filipinos bring their unequal Englishes (Tupas, 2015a) with them when they migrate to English-dominant countries. In his study of immigrant Filipino adolescents in Vancouver, Darvin (2017) highlights how class differences back in the Philippines influence adolescents' sense of linguistic confidence and security and their general dispositions toward using English in Canada. Darvin's (2017) study may have focused on Canada but what he found is probably relevant and applicable to Filipino immigrants in English-dominant countries as well.

26.4 English and Temporary Labor Migration from the Philippines

The Philippines is a labor brokerage state (Rodriguez, 2010), that is, it is a state that "negotiates with labor-receiving states to formalize outflows of migrant workers and thereby enables employers around the globe to avail themselves of temporary workers [...]" (Rodriguez, 2010, p. x). State-sponsored temporary labor migration from the Philippines began in the 1970s as an attempt to resolve deteriorating social and economic conditions in the country brought about by the restructuring of the economy toward commercial agriculture and export-led industrialization under Ferdinand Marcos' 'New Society' (Tyner, 2004). What was supposed to be a temporary measure has become a permanent feature of the Philippines. As of 2013, 4.2 million Filipinos were working as temporary migrants (Commission on Filipinos Overseas, 2014), with contracts ranging from six months to two years. Seventy-five percent of OFWs are in five countries: Saudi Arabia, the United Arab Emirates, Singapore, Hong Kong and Qatar (International Organization of Migration, 2013, p. 65). The Philippines is highly dependent on remittances. They are the country's premier foreign exchange earner, dwarfing foreign direct investments and exports. Remittances from overseas Filipinos amounted to USD 28.1 billion in 2017.

Migration 333

Language has always played an important role in the Philippine labor migration enterprise (Lorente, 2018). The importance of language in Philippine migration is such that the position of the Philippines as a labor-sending state has been considered to have influenced Philippine language policy significantly (Gonzalez, 1998), in particular with regard to the maintenance of English as a medium of instruction. This is because, by and large, English is considered to be a 'competitive edge' of OFWs (Lorente, 2010, 2012, 2018), with the Philippines positioned as the 'obvious' choice for recruiting English-speaking labor (Polanco & Zell, 2016) and with OFWs maneuvering their linguistic capital to enhance their status (cf. Lan, 2003). While the continued maintenance of the grip of English in the Philippines due to the country's dependency on the continued 'competitiveness' of its workers may be the most visible impact of labor migration on the language policies of the country, it is not the only one. There seems to be a shift in how English is positioned as the 'competitive advantage' of OFWs. While English proficiency is still portrayed as the linguistic capital of OFWs, it is also starting to be depicted as the *minimum* linguistic capital of OFWs (see, for example, Otomo, 2017). This will be discussed in relation to the requirements for Filipino domestic workers (FDWs) who currently represent the largest flow of migrant workers from the country.

On February 5, 2007, the Philippine Overseas Employment Administration (POEA) issued the guidelines for the 'Reform Package affecting Household Service Workers (HSWs)'. Under the new guidelines, HSWs with visas issued after December 16, 2006, would have to meet the following requirements: a minimum age of 23, a minimum entry salary of USD 400, a Technical Education and Skills Development Authority (TESDA) NC2 certificate for Household Services and attendance at an Overseas Workers Welfare Administration (OWWA) country-specific language and culture orientation. With regard to the new language and communication requirements set by the POEA, there are three interesting points to note: (1) the ability to communicate in English is considered to be a 'minimum requirement'; (2) 'workplace communication skills' (presumably in English, and on top of the basic ability to communicate in English) is one of the basic modules in the TESDA training program and (3) some knowledge of a 'foreign' language other than English is considered to be necessary as seen in the requirement that prospective domestic workers undergo a country-specific language and culture training with the OWWA.

The discourse of English being the 'competitive edge' of Filipino migrant workers is translated into English being a 'minimum requirement' at the local scale where would-be housemaids, housekeepers and cleaners are trained for deployment. As Tollefson (1991) has already pointed out, that English competence can be made a 'minimum requirement' and that there is no lack of Filipinos lining up to leave the country are the results of a large labor surplus in the country. As a minimum requirement, it would seem that

334 *Beatriz P. Lorente*

the ability to communicate in English is no longer sufficient to sustain the 'competitiveness' of FDWs.

On top of being able to communicate in English, it appears that FDWs are also supposed to have the ability to 'participate in workplace communication'. The introduction of a communication skills element in the curriculum for HSWs points to how the new work order with its linguistic demands has, at least discursively, come to be inserted in the economy of labor migration from the Philippines. It is indicative of how global developments (or the new work order) linguistic and communication 'skills' have come to dominate forms of work, and in the case of the Philippines, forms of migrant labor. For domestic workers, the 'Competency-Based Curriculum Exemplar' for the TESDA Household Services National Certificate 2 (NC2) is generic when it comes to the kind of communication skills which are considered to be valuable for service workers. The module 'Participating in Workplace Communication' is supposed to cover parts of speech; sentence construction; effective communication; communicating with the employer; communicating with other members of the household; familiarizing with common places and terminologies; basic mathematics; technical writing; types of forms; recording information. The assessment criteria include the following: specific relevant information is accessed from appropriate resources; effective questioning, active listening and speaking skills are used to gather and convey information; appropriate medium is used to transfer information and ideas; appropriate non-verbal communication is used; appropriate lines of communication with superiors and colleagues are identified and followed; defined workplace procedures for the location and storage of information are used; personal interaction is carried out clearly and concisely. These assessment criteria place an emphasis on the transfer of information, on 'obtaining and conveying workplace information' according to what is 'appropriate' and/or according to 'defined workplace procedures'. There is also a literacy component where the emphasis is on completing relevant work-related documents, i.e. filling up forms and recording information. The final component is participation in workplace meetings and discussions where 'own opinions are clearly expressed and those of others are listened to without interruption', 'workplace interaction are conducted in a courteous manner appropriate to cultural background and authority', 'questions about simple routine workplace procedures and matters concerning conditions of employment are asked and responded'. These suggest that the communication skills that are considered to be valuable are 'passive'; they are not about constructing or questioning knowledge or procedures. It is not just FDWs who are required to undergo training in communication skills; programs for maritime professionals, for example, include a course in Business English and communication skills (see Sioson & Valdez, 2016; Valdez & Tan, 2018).

Apart from knowing English and having workplace communication skills, FDWs are also constructed as being knowledgeable in the language and culture of the destination country. This means being able to understand

Migration 335

Cantonese if they are heading to Hong Kong, Arabic if they are going to any of the countries in the Middle East and possibly Mandarin Chinese if they are going to Singapore. Six language and culture familiarization courses are currently being offered: Arabic, Hebrew, Italian, Cantonese, Mandarin and English. The 20-hour courses (Arabic, Hebrew, Italian, Cantonese and English) last three days. Of these 20 hours, 16 go to training in language and culture, and 4 hours are allotted to a stress management workshop. In 2007, 129,159 OFWs ready for deployment underwent the country-specific language and culture training. This number has remained quite steady through the years with 156,452 OFWs attending the training in 2012. In the booklets used for the language and culture familiarization training, the following topics are covered: introduction to the destination country and culture, introduction to the destination country's alphabet and numbers, greetings, vocabulary lists for vegetables, fruits, tastes, kinds of meat and parts of the body, parts of the home, household chores and family members. Expressions and words used for caring for the sick and describing common illnesses are also given, as is a list of specific cultural dos and don'ts in the destination country. The expressions in the booklets constitute a limited register explicitly meant to facilitate trans-actional communication; many of the expressions were one-way directives meant to be understood by the domestic worker. More importantly, the book-lets modeled a 'script of servitude' (Lorente, 2018) for the domestic worker, one where the domestic worker is mostly a passive participant on whom the burden of understanding the employer is placed.

Obviously, the OWWA orientation and the TESDA communication skills training will not be sufficient to make would-be HSWs proficient in the language of their destination countries and 'fluent' in workplace commu-nication skills, but these developments point to a shift away from English being considered to be the competitive advantage of OFWs. This shift is the state's response to increasing competition and faster and more unpre-dictable changes to global labor markets. This shift also reinforces the im-age of migrant Filipino workers as being 'flexible' (see Piller & Lising, 2014; Polanco & Zell, 2016) and able to work with anyone, because of their lan-guage skills, in addition to their English proficiency.

26.5 Summary

In tracing how migration to and from the Philippines is crucial to under-standing the continuing 'grip of English' (Lorente, 2013) in the country, this chapter has shown how English is embedded in the history of migration from the Philippines. It has traced how the image of the English-speaking Filipino migrant—from the pensionado of the American colonial era to the OFW in the current period—came to be historically constructed. It seems that English will continue to be entrenched in the country for as long as the Philippines remains at the margins of the world system as a labor-sending country catering to particular niches in the global labor market.

336 *Beatriz P. Lorente*

References

Aguilar, Filomeno V. (2014). *Migration revolution: Philippine nationhood and class relations in a globalized age*. Singapore and Kyoto: NUS Press and Kyoto University Press.

Anderson, Benedict (2005). *The age of globalization: anarchists and anticolonial imagination*. London: Verso.

Asis, Maruja M.B. (2006). The Philippines' culture of migration. See https://www.migrationpolicy.org/article/philippines-culture-migration. Accessed on 30 July 2018.

Axel, Joseph (2011). *Language in Filipino America*. Unpublished PhD dissertation. Arizona State University.

Bernardo, Allan B.I. (2004). McKinley's questionable bequest: over 100 years of English in Philippine education. *World Englishes, 23*(1), 17–31.

Bedford, Richard, & Didham, Robert (2018). Immigration: an election issue that has yet to be addressed? *Kotuitui: New Zealand Journal of Social Sciences Online*, DOI: 10.1080/1177083X.2018.1503606.

Cave, Damien (2018). Australia's immigration solution: small town living. *New York Times*, May 21. https://www.nytimes.com/2018/05/21/world/australia/immigration-philippines.html

Choe, Hohsung (2016). Identity formation of Filipino ESL teachers teaching Korean students in the Philippines: how negative and positive identities shape ELT in the Outer Circle. *English Today, 32*(1), 5–11.

Choe, Hohsung, & Son, Eunmi (2018). Southeast Asian ESL countries as study abroad destinations: a Korean perspective. *English Today, 134*(34), 46–52.

Choy, Catherine C. (2003). *Empire and migration: nursing and migration in Filipino American history*. Quezon City: Ateneo de Manila University.

Commission on Filipinos Overseas. (2014). *2013 CFO Compendium of Statistics on National Migration*. Manila: Commission on Filipinos Overseas.

Darvin, Ron (2017). Social class and inequality of English speakers in a globalized world. *Journal of English as Lingua Franca, 6*(2), 287–311.

Espiritu, Yen Le (2003). *Home bound: Filipino American lives across cultures, communities and countries*. Berkeley: University of California Press.

Espiritu, Yen Le, & Wolf, Diane L. (2001). The paradox of assimilation: children of Filipino immigrants in San Diego. In Ruben G. Rumbaut & Alejandro Portes (Eds.), *Ethnicities: children of immigrants in America* (pp. 157–186). Berkeley: University of California Press.

Gonzales, Wilkinson Daniel W. (2017). Language contact in the Philippines: the history and ecology from a Chinese Filipino perspective. *Language Ecology, 1*(2), 185–212.

Gonzalez, Andrew (1998). The language planning situation in the Philippines. *Journal of Multilingual and Multicultural Development, 19*(5/6), 487–525.

Gonzalez, Andrew (2004). The social dimensions of Philippine English. *World Englishes, 23*(1), 7–16.

Hau, Caroline S., & Tinio, Victoria L. (2003). Language policy and ethnic relations in the Philippines. In Michael Edward Brown & Sumit Ganguly (Eds.), *Fighting words: language policy and ethnic relations in Asia* (pp. 319–349). Cambridge, MA: The MIT Press.

Imperial, Rowland Anthony (2017). *Speech production and sociolinguistic perception in a 'non-native' second language context: a sociophonetic study of Korean learners of English in the Philippines.* Unpublished MA thesis, National University of Singapore.

International Organization for Migration. (2013). *Country Migration Report: The Philippines 2013.* Makati City/Quezon City: International Organization for Migration and Scalabrini Migration Center.

Jang, In-Cheol. (2018). Legitimating the Philippines as a language learning space: transnational Korean youth's experiences and evaluations. *Journal of Sociolinguistics, 22*(2), 216–232.

Jubilado, Rodney C. (2016). Where is the CR? A description of Philippine English in Hawaii. *Philippine ESL Journal, 17*, 86–101.

Junker, Laura Lee (1999). *Raiding, trading and feasting: the political economy of Philippine chiefdoms.* Honolulu: University of Hawai'i Press.

Kramer, Paul A. (2006). *The blood of government: race, empire, the United States, and the Philippines.* Quezon City: Ateneo de Manila University.

Labrador, Roderick N. (2009). "We can laugh at ourselves": Hawai'i ethnic humor, local identity and the myth of multiculturalism. In Angela Reyes & Adrienne Lo (Eds.), *Beyond yellow English: toward a linguistic anthropology of Asian Pacific America* (pp. 288–308). Oxford: Oxford University Press.

Lan, Pei Chia. (2003). "They have more money but I speak better English": transnational encounters between Filipina domestics and Taiwanese employers. *Identities 10*, 133–161.

Lorente, Beatriz P. (2010). Packaging English-speaking products: maid agencies in Singapore. In Helen Kelly-Holmes & Gerlinde Mautner (Eds.), *Language and the Market* (pp. 44–55). Basingstoke and New York: Palgrave-MacMillan.

Lorente, Beatriz P. (2012). The making of workers of the world: language and the labor brokerage state. In Alexandre Duchene & Monica Heller (Eds.), *Pride and profit: language in late capitalism* (pp. 183–206). London and New York: Routledge.

Lorente, Beatriz P. (2013). The grip of English and Philippine language policy. In Lionel Wee, Robbie B.H. Goh & Lisa Lim (Eds.), *The politics of English: South Asia, Southeast Asia and the Asia Pacific* (pp. 187–204). Amsterdam/Philadelphia: John Benjamins Publishing Company.

Lorente, Beatriz P. (2018). *Scripts of servitude: language, labor migration and transnational domestic work.* Bristol: Multilingual Matters.

Lorente, Beatriz P., & Tupas, T. Ruanni F. (2014). (Un)Emancipatory hybridity: selling English in an unequal world. In Rani Rubdy & Lubna Alsagoff (Eds.), *The global-local interface and hybridity: exploring language and identity* (pp. 66–82). Bristol: Multilingual Matters.

Mabalon, Dawn B. (2013). *Little Manila is in the heart: the making of the Filipina/o American community in Stockton, California.* Durham: Duke University Press.

Martin, Isabel P. (1999). Language and institution: roots of bilingualism in the Philippines. In Ma. Lourdes S. Bautista & Grace O. Tan (Eds.), *The Filipino bilingual: a multidisciplinary perspective* (pp. 132–136). Manila: Linguistic Society of the Philippines

Martin, Isabel P. (2004). Longfellow's legacy: education and the shaping of Philippine writing. *World Englishes, 23*(1), 129–140.

Martin, Isabel P. (2012). Diffusion and directions: English language policy in the Philippines. In Ee Ling Low & Azirah Hashim (Eds.), *English in Southeast Asia: features, policy and language use* (pp. 189–205). Amsterdam: John Benjamins.

338 *Beatriz P. Lorente*

McGeown, Kate (2012). The Philippines: the world's budget English teacher. *BBC News* (12 November). https://www.bbc.co.uk/news/business-20066890. Accessed 22 March 2013.

Nical, Iluminado C. (2000). *Language usage and language attitudes among education consumers: the experience of Filipinos in Australia and in three linguistic communities in the Philippines.* Unpublished PhD dissertation. University of Adelaide.

Ortiga, Yasmin Y. (2017). The flexible university: higher education and the global production of migrant labor. *British Journal of Sociology of Education, 38*(4): 485–499.

Otomo, Ruriko (2017). *Japan's economic partnership agreement as language policy: creation, interpretation, appropriation.* Unpublished PhD Dissertation. The University of Hong Kong.

Piller, Ingrid, & Lising, Loy (2014). Language, employment and settlement: temporary meat workers in Australia. *Multilingua, 33*(1–2), 35–59.

Polanco, Geraldina, & Zell, Sarah (2016). English as a border-drawing matter: language and the regulation of migrant service worker mobility in international labor markets. *International Migration and Integration, 18*, 267–289.

Rodriguez, Robyn Magalit (2010). *Migrants for export: how the Philippine state brokers labor to the world.* Minneapolis: University of Minnesota Press.

Seijias, Tatiana. (2014). *Asian slaves in Colonial Mexico: From Chinos to Indians.* Cambridge, the United Kingdom: Cambridge University Press.

Sioson, Irish, & Valdez, Paolo Nino (2016). Exploring the sociolinguistics of investment: mapping tensions between institutional discourse vis-a-vis narratives of Filipino maritime professionals. *Language, literature and society: Paper proceedings of third international conference.* Malabe: International Center for Research and Development.

Takaki, R.T. (1998). *Strangers from a different shore: a history of Asian Americans* (Updated and revised edition). Boston: Little Brown.

Toh, Swee-Hin, & Floresca-Cawagas, Virginia (2003). Globalization and the Philippines' education system. In Ka-ho Mok & Anthony Welch (Eds.), *Globalization and educational restructuring in the Asia Pacific region* (pp. 189–231). Houndmills: Palgrave Macmillan.

Tollefson, James W. (1991). *Planning language, planning inequality: Language policy in the community.* London: Longman.

Tupas, Ruanni (2003). History, language planners, and strategies of forgetting: the problem of consciousness in the Philippines. *Language Problems and Language Planning, 27*(1), 1–25.

Tupas, Ruanni (2008). Bourdieu, historical forgetting, and the problem of English in the Philippines. *Philippine Studies, 56*(1), 47–67.

Tupas, Ruanni. (Ed.) (2015a). *Unequal Englishes: the politics of Englishes today.* Houndmills: Palgrave Macmillan.

Tupas, Ruanni (2015b). Inequalities of multilingualism: challenges to mother tongue-based multilingual education. *Language and Education, 29*(2): 112–124.

Tupas, T. Ruanni F., & Lorente, Beatriz P. (2014). A 'new' politics of language in the Philippines: bilingual education and the challenge of the mother tongues. In Peter Sercombe & T. Ruanni F. Tupas (Eds.), *Language, education and nation-building: assimilation and shift in Southeast Asia* (pp. 165–180). Basingstoke and New York: Palgrave-MacMillan.

Tyner, James A. (2004). *Made in the Philippines: gendered discourses and the making of migrants*. London: Routledge Curzon.

Umali, Ronalyn M. (2016). *Tagalog language maintenance and shift among the Filipino community in New Zealand*. Unpublished MA Thesis, Auckland University of Technology.

Valdez, Paolo N., & Tan, Nestle C. (2018). Migrant workers, language learning and spaces of globalization: the case of Filipino maritime professionals. In Isabel P. Martin (Ed.), *Reconceptualizing English education in a multilingual society* (pp. 177–190). Singapore: Springer.

Zong, Jie, & Batalova, Jeanne (2018). *Filipino immigrants in the United States (March 14)*. Migration Information Source. Migration Policy Institute. https://www.migrationpolicy.org/article/filipino-immigrants-united-states. Accessed 22 September 2018.

27 Outsourced Call Centers

Eric Friginal and Rachelle Friginal

27.1 Introduction

Customer call center services in the US and other English-speaking countries have been *outsourced* to strategic nations such as the Philippines and India since the early 1990s, essentially to lower operational costs in how these call centers are maintained (Friginal, 2007). The World Bank defines outsourcing as "the contracting of a service provider to completely manage, deliver and operate one or more of a client's functions such as data centers, networks, desktop computing and software applications" ("World Bank E-Commerce Development Report," 2003). Advancements in global telecommunication and satellite and fiber-optic technologies have allowed many multi-national corporations to easily move their customer service operations overseas, and take advantage of available, college-educated human resources (Friedman, 2005; Friginal, 2007; Vashistha & Vashistha, 2006).

From the first call center company established by US-owned Accenture Group in 1992, the call center industry in the Philippines has become one of the major drivers of the country's once sluggish economy, now making it one of the fastest-growing economies in the Asian region. In 2016, the country's call center and Business Process Outsourcing (BPO) revenues reached $23 billion, a 160% increase from 2010, when the Philippines was declared as the world's BPO Capital (Deloitte, 2016; Lee, 2015; PSA, 2018). This growth also translated into 1.3 million total BPO jobs for Filipinos during that period. Despite recent political events in the US and various global economic shifts, the BPO industry in the Philippines remains stable and relatively positive, projected to maintain growth in the next ten years. The US continues to be the biggest market for call center operations, comprising 66.8% of all transactions and infusing Php80.5 billion in revenues annually since 2013. The UK follows at 14.7% or Php14.7 billion and then Canada at 4.5% or Php5.5 billion in revenues (Deloitte, 2016; Natividad, 2015).

Primarily due to its tradition of bilingual education (in English and Tagalog or Filipino), language and cultural affiliation with the West, and relatively cheap labor market, the Philippines has become the leading global hub for US-based customer service outsourcing, over-taking India in the

DOI: 10.4324/9780429427824-35

Outsourced Call Centers 341

total number of personnel for 'voiced support' or service transactions facilitated in English over the telephone (Dizon, 2015; Friginal, 2013b). The Philippines produces over 400,000 English-speaking college graduates every year. Of these, 80,000 are in the fields of information technology, computers, and engineering. Another 110,000 graduates are in business-related fields, such as commerce, finance, and accounting (BPAP, 2010, 2018). The general global perception of Filipinos' English language competency and trainability is positive due to the high number of professionals in the workforce, compared to other developing countries.

This chapter highlights emerging patterns of language (i.e., English) as used by Filipino call center representatives (henceforth, 'agents') as they support their customers/callers from the US. An exploratory comparison of linguistic distributions from call transcripts collected in the Philippines, India, the US, and four Central American countries (grouped together) serves to show the unique characteristics of English in customer service emanating from the Philippines.

27.2 Philippine English and Cross-Cultural Communication in Call Centers

Industry insiders and marketers supporting Philippine call centers claim that Filipinos are better than Indians because of their more *neutral accent,* which is arguably easier to understand for Americans, as compared to Indian agents who speak British English as an exo-normative model. Unfamiliar idioms and expressions for most Americans such as *"We will do the needful and I will revert on the same"* (instead of *"We will work on that and I will follow up on that"*) are said to have been reported by callers (Dizon, 2015). It also helps that as early as the first grade, most Filipinos are taught English in schools, are typically familiar with American fast food and other products, and follow the NBA and American TV shows and movies. The Philippines, even according to some of its Indian counterparts, has a unique combination of Eastern, attentive hospitality and attitude of care and compassion mixed with *Americanization* (Natividad, 2015). For this reason, even Indian-based call center companies have started to shift or expand their operations in the Philippines. Aegis Global, an outsourcing firm based in Mumbai, India, for example, acquired Manila-based People Support in 2008 and now employs nearly 13,000 Filipinos (Bajaj, 2011; Dizon, 2015).

Cross-cultural communication in customer service has become an everyday phenomenon in the US, as callers come into direct contact with agents who do not share some of their basic assumptions and perspectives. Before the advent of outsourcing, Americans had a different view of customer service facilitated on the telephone. Calling helpdesks or the customer service departments of many businesses mostly involved call-takers who were able to provide a more localized service (Friedman, 2005; Friginal, 2008). Interactants typically shared the same 'space and time' and awareness of

342 Eric Friginal and Rachelle Friginal

current issues inside and outside of the interactions. These transactions, therefore, have produced a relatively new register of cross-communication involving a range of variables not present in other globalized business or international and interpersonal communication settings. In addition, the political and economic implications related to the outsourcing of American jobs have also saturated the media and the realm of popular opinion in the US, affecting callers' attitudes and prompting calls from some sectors for policy changes and possible restrictions in business outsourcing practices (Friginal, 2013b). Philippine English (PhE) is at the forefront here as customers typically demand to be given the quality of service they expect or can ask to be transferred to an agent who will provide them the service (and the level of language/English) they prefer. Filipino agents' "performance" in language and explicit manifestations of pragmatic skills naturally are examined closely when defining "quality" during these outsourced call center interactions (Bajaj, 2011; Friginal, 2009a, 2009b, 2013b; Hayman, 2010).

27.3 Method and the Focus of This Chapter

This chapter utilizes corpus analysis to describe some of the prominent linguistic characteristics of Filipino call center agents' discourse in English as they serve their customers from the US Specifically, an exploratory comparison is presented here from a corpus of call center transactions collected in the Philippines, India, the US, four countries located in Central America, and other calls not particularly marked for location. Previous related comparison based only on data from the Philippines, India, and the US were reported in Friginal (2011, 2013a, 2018). The recorded transactions were provided by three US-owned call centers outsourced to various overseas locations for research purposes. These transactions were retrieved following the list of audio files cued in a database of recorded calls for a particular work shift. The calls that qualified in the corpus used in this chapter ranged from 5 to 18 minutes in duration. The composition of this current collection is provided in Table 27.1.

Table 27.1 Composition of a Test Call Center Corpus[a] Analyzed for This Chapter

Location	No. of Recorded Calls	Average Length (min)	Total Number of Words	Average Words per Call
Philippines	2,233	8.45	2,456,773	1,100.21
India	1,433	7.56	1,333,231	930.38
US	1,233	6.33	997,667	809.14
Central America (four locations combined)	877	8.55	334,233	381.11
Others	544	4.44	221,004	406.26

a The corpus was compiled by the author from an ongoing corpus collection of call center transactions from three US-owned call centers in various outsourced locations outside the mainland US. The corpus is not publicly available.

Outsourced Call Centers 343

The corpus was transcribed into machine readable text files and annotated (i.e., tagged) electronically using a part-of-speech tagging program developed by Biber (2006). Personal information about the callers, if any (e.g., names, addresses, phone numbers, credit card or social security numbers, etc.), was consistently replaced by generic proper nouns or a series of numbers in the transcripts. No attempt was made to transcribe phonetically and the transcribed texts were manually checked for format consistency and accuracy.

The focal comparisons in this chapter rely first on a multi-feature, multi-dimensional (MD) analytical framework developed by Biber (1988) in establishing the statistical co-occurrence of linguistic features from corpora. From this, the comparative distribution and subsequent analysis of selected grammatical politeness features are provided, suggesting interesting patterns of use across agent groups. The concept of linguistic co-occurrence, which is the foundation of MD analysis, highlights common differences in the linguistic composition of various types of registers. For example, spoken registers are different from written registers because of factors such as dysfluencies and the co-occurrence of numerous linguistic features that show immediate interactivity (e.g., overlaps and backchannels, questions and responses, speech-act formulae, or inserts). With computational tools such as grammatical tagging programs, it is possible to statistically identify and establish these sets of co-occurring linguistic features and compare how they are used by different groups of speakers (Friginal, 2013c). In this case, in a call center corpus, it is possible to compare how Filipino, Indian, and American agents, across two types of tasks they perform (troubleshooting and responding to product inquiry), make use of these co-occurring features and to describe their unique functions derived from agents' distinctive demographic characteristics. An extensive discussion of the statistical procedure and interpretation of corpus-based, MD analysis can be found in Biber (1988, 1995, 2006), Conrad and Biber (2001), Friginal (2008, 2013c), and Berber-Sardinha and Veirano-Pinto (2014).

27.4 Linguistic Dimensions of Outsourced Call Center Discourse

Friginal (2008, 2009b) first identified the linguistic dimensions of outsourced call center discourse using the MD approach from a pilot corpus of call center texts collected in the Philippines (N of texts=364, approximately 453,630 words). Three linguistic dimensions are extracted and interpreted microanalytically: (1) addressee-focused, polite, and elaborated speech vs. involved and simplified narrative; (2) planned, procedural talk; and (3) managed information flow. The first dimension statistically represented more than 50% of variance in the transactions and is used in this present analysis and comparison. The linguistic composition of this dimension is shown below.

344 *Eric Friginal and Rachelle Friginal*

Table 27.2 Addressee-Focused, Polite, and Elaborated Speech vs. Involved and Simplified Narrative in Call Center Interactions (Friginal, 2008, 2009b)

Dimension	Features
Dim 1: Addressee-focused, polite, and elaborated speech vs. involved and simplified narrative	Positive: Second person pronouns, average world length, *please*, nouns, possibility modals, nominalizations, average length of turns, *thanks, ma'am/sir*
	Negative: Pronoun *it*, first person pronouns, past tense verbs, *that* deletion, private verbs, WH clauses, perfect aspect verbs, *I mean/you know*, verb *do*

To summarize, the merging of positive and negative features above describes a linguistic dimension that differentiates addressee-focused (e.g., use of second person pronouns *you/your*), polite, and expanded discourse (e.g., longer average length of turns, nouns, and nominalizations) from an involved and simplified narrative. These features collectively portray how informational content is produced and transferred by agents in customer service transactions. As shown in Table 27.1, a total of 18 linguistic features comprise Dimension 1, with 9 features on each of the positive and negative sides of scale. Positive features include politeness and respect markers (e.g., *thanks, please, ma'am, and sir*), markers of elaboration and information density (e.g., long words and turns, nominalizations, and more nouns), and second person pronouns (e.g., *you, your*), which indicate 'other-directed' focus of talk (White, 1994). Possibility modals (*can, could, may, might*) also loaded positively on this dimension. The features on the negative side, especially the pronoun *it*, first person pronouns, *that* deletion, private verbs (e.g., *think, believe*), WH clauses, and verb *do*, resemble the grouping in the dimension "Involved Production" identified by Biber (1988) and White (1994).

The co-occurrence of positive features in this dimension also appears to represent the dominant objectives of agents' turns. Agents who use more positive features are likely intending to give details or instructions. In the process, these speakers use more nouns, nominalizations, and longer utterances to provide such information. Most turns are elaborated and also hint at giving explanations, expression of likelihood, or risks though the use of a significant frequency of possibility modals (e.g., "...*reinstalling the network **can** help at it **can** automatically restart the daemon, Sir*."). The grouping of features on the negative side of the factor appears to illustrate personal narrative and experiences or also share highly simplified information. The combination of past tense verbs, private verbs, pronoun *it*, and discourse markers *I mean* and *you know* demonstrates the specific goal of the utterances to provide a personal account of how a situation happened (Friginal, 2013a.)

Outsourced Call Centers   345

27.5 Findings

27.5.1 Comparison 1: Addressee-Focused, Polite, and Elaborated Speech vs. Involved and Simplified Narrative

Figure 27.1 shows the average dimension scores of Filipino, Indian, American, and Central American agents along a positive and negative scale for Dimension 1. These dimension scores reveal differences in the way these agent

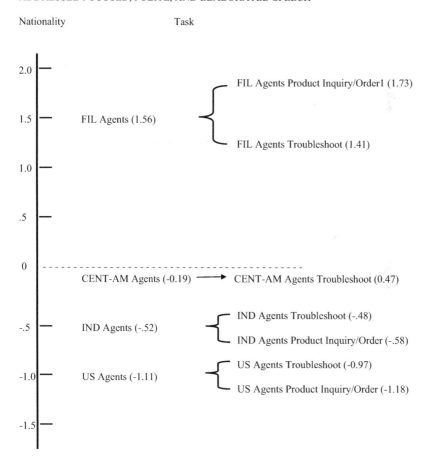

Figure 27.1 Comparison of Agents' Average Dimension Scores for Dimension 1: Addressee-Focused, Polite, and Elaborated Speech vs. Involved and Simplified Narrative. Note: Only troubleshoot tasks were available from Central American agents.

346   *Eric Friginal and Rachelle Friginal*

groups (from two task groups: troubleshooting and product inquiry) make use of these co-occurring linguistic features. Filipino agents plot on the positive side of the scale, while the other three groups are on the opposite, with US agents receiving the lowest negative average dimension score.

The consistent use of addressee-focused, involved production features, and politeness and respect markers establishes the linguistic preferences of Filipino agents compared to the three other agent groups. In general, service encounters commonly allocate for courteous language and the recognition of roles (e.g., server/servee), and call center agents are expected to show respect and courtesy when assisting customers (D'Ausilio, 1998; Friginal, 2007). However, of interest here is the variation between these groups of agents who are, in fact, dealing with similar contexts or tasks. Filipinos overwhelmingly prefer a collective use of these features in responding to their US customers. Filipinos also differ dramatically from their American (predominantly native English speakers) counterparts, which poses a series of relevant research questions for future detailed investigation.

The range of explanation and details Filipino agents provide their callers is shown by higher frequencies of longer turns, longer average word length, and more nouns and nominalizations than the other agent groups. Transcripts from the sub-corpus of Filipino transactions show more elucidation and repeated confirmation of callers' understanding from Filipino agents (e.g., "... *is that correct, Sir? Are you referring to your BT contact provided by* [the company]?"). Call center agents are typically tasked to include reminders to callers about products for sale or issues with legal or monetary implications with the company. Whenever additional selling and explanation occur, the features of elaboration in the texts increase. A quick scan of the texts in the corpus indicates that Filipino agents had more repeated attempts at selling related products than other agent groups, which may have been locally stressed and emphasized often in Philippine call centers by their account managers and trainers more than the groups of agents from India or the US.

27.5.2 Comparison 2: Politeness Markers in Call Center Interactions

Politeness in spoken interaction, covering a range of contexts and speaker demographics, has been enthusiastically explored by linguists over the past several years (e.g., Beeching, 2002; Lakoff, 1976; Locher, 2004; Mills, 2003; Tannen, 1990, to name only a few). Politeness and respect markers are highly expected in call center service transactions, with the nature of business defining the social roles of customers and agents and, in turn, perceptions and impositions related to the use of polite terms in maintaining transactions (Cameron, 2008; Economidou-Kogetsidis, 2005). The typical training practice in the Philippines is that Filipino agents are constantly coached about the value of maintaining customer loyalty by providing efficient service and establishing rapport during service interactions. In the process, these agents employ linguistic strategies that they perceive will satisfy their callers, especially during difficult or complicated transactions (Friginal, 2009a).

As agents in outsourced call centers, Filipinos also bring with them their cultural background, including the use of their repertoire of polite and respect markers in communicating with their American callers. Filipinos have traditionally maintained a warm and hospitable behavior in service encounters, especially those involving foreign customers or guests in hotels and restaurants and other tourist areas in the Philippines (Friginal, 2009b). Most Filipinos in the service industry are genuinely engaging and willing to help and serve. As mentioned earlier in this chapter, this trait has been regarded as one of the advantages of outsourced call centers in the Philippines (but, ironically, it may also have the potential for adverse effects in cross-cultural transactions). It is apparent, as shown in Figure 27.2, that Filipinos value respecting their customers and making the necessary accommodations to maintain customer loyalty.

For this chapter, politeness and respect markers are grouped into four sub-categories: (1) polite speech-act formulae (*thank you, thanks, appreciate*), (2) polite requests (*please*), (3) apologies (*sorry, apologize, pardon*), and (4) respect markers (*ma'am, sir. Mr., Ms.,* titles). As shown in Figure 27.2, Filipino agents use more of these types of polite markers than do the other agents (based on normalized frequency counts per 1,000 words in the corpus). Respect markers *sir/ma'am* are used very frequently by Filipinos, especially when compared to US-based agents (8.0123 vs. 2.112 per 1,000 words,

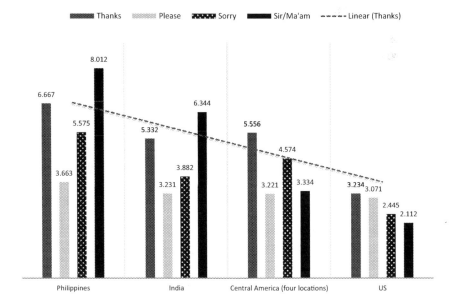

Figure 27.2 Politeness and Respect Markers across Agent Groups. Note: Frequency of features reported here is normalized per 1,000 words.

348   *Eric Friginal and Rachelle Friginal*

respectively). Polite speech-act formulae (*thanks/appreciate*) are very common across groups of agents in the transactions, as these markers characterize the discourse of customer service relative to other registers or genres of speech. Filipinos also use more of these features repeatedly than the other groups, with agents from Central America following next (Filipinos = 6.667; Central Americans = 5.556, per 1,000 words).

A closer scrutiny of data from Figure 27.2 and transcripts from the corpus suggests that Filipino politeness and cultural norms may be playing a major role in the overall frequency distribution and patterning of these markers from Philippine agents. Aside from satisfying the common purposes of these politeness and respect markers, it appears that many Filipino agents have developed speech mannerisms that often almost automatically include the use of *thanks* or *thank you* whenever they receive a response from their callers. In addition, most of the calls in the corpus begin with *"Thank you for calling..."* as agents' initial greeting sequence. The repetitive use of *thanks* or *thank you* as agents' acknowledgment of callers' response to questions or requests is common in all groups, but noticeably increased in transcripts from the Philippines. Aside from a possible mannerism acquired through months or years of work in the industry, Filipinos potentially use these repetitive speech-act formulae to ensure a continuous flow of response in the transactions to avoid pauses or dead air (Friginal, 2009a). In some instances, *thanks* or *thank you* appears to act as discourse markers to introduce the agents' next question or main response to the callers. Text Sample 1 below shows the constant use (perhaps overuse) of *thank you* by the Filipino agent as part of her response after the caller's turns:

AGENT: **Thank you** for calling [company name] my name is [agent name] how can I help you please?
CALLER: Hello have I reached the right uhm person to speak with about service or help on uhm my my postage meter?
AGENT: Uhm yes ma'am, **thank you**, I could provide help for you, can I have your name?
CALLER: Great, thank you [caller name]
AGENT: **Thank you**, and your model and serial number [caller name]?
CALLER: Yes the model number is F as in Frank 9m0 actually, oh I'm not sure if it's an o or 0
AGENT: OK, **thank you**, serial number?
CALLER: 8-8-8–9-9-0-0-0-0
AGENT: **Thanks**, please just give me a moment while I pull up your account OK? [long pause] I have your account right now could you please verify your account name company address city state and zip?
CALLER: Yes, [company name] our administrative offices are located at [address]
AGENT: **Thank you**. Can I have your phone number plus extension?
CALLER: My phone number here is area code [...] my extension is 5454

Outsourced Call Centers 349

AGENT: **Thank you**. Please let me repeat [545-454-545] extension [5454] right?
CALLER: Yes
AGENT: **Thank you.**

Most of the uses of *thank you* in the excerpt above clearly indicate a polite recognition of response or turn from the caller. The Filipino agent maintained a respectful tone/intonation throughout the transaction with clear pronunciation and good command of English. There was no indication in the transaction that the caller did not like the agent's use of politeness markers or was not satisfied with the agent's overall level of engagement and service. However, it is obvious that the agent overused some of the instances of *thank you* in the excerpt with no specific communicative purpose aside from the recognition of the caller's response, and that many such usages could probably have been eliminated with no significant adverse effect on the transaction.

27.6 Discussion and Concluding Remarks

With these resulting comparisons, a relevant question to ask here is: <u>So what?</u> It appears then that Philippine communicative norms in English can be identified and measured using corpus analysis and compared with distributions from other groups of agents. From a related previous study (Friginal, 2009b), it was reported that the high frequency of politeness and respect markers are indicators of quality of service in Philippine-based call centers. This means that Filipino agents with high performance evaluation scores have more counts for *thanks*, *please*, and *sir/ma'am* than agents in lower performance evaluation groups. In addition, agents in the high-performance group have lower frequency of apologies (*sorry/apologize*) than the agents in the mid and low-performance groups. The limited occurrences of apologies for agents in the high-performance group suggest that these agents have better understanding of the procedural aspects of the transactions and higher-level mastery of information given to the customers (Friginal, 2013a). When compared to Indians and Americans, on the other hand, Filipinos consistently preferred a repeated usage of these markers—those on the positive features of Dimension 1 and politeness/respect markers overall. This result suggests the existence of unique register and discourse-specific quality in PhE by Filipino agents worthy of continuing investigation and analyses.

The first 20 years of outsourced call centers in the Philippines brought investment money and provided jobs for many English-speaking professionals in the country. The Philippine government and the nation's call center industry have provided consistent support in addressing the training needs of Filipinos in cross-cultural customer service with Americans and the use of the English language. So far, it continues to be sustainable. It may be difficult to confidently predict the continuing growth of outsourced call centers outside of the US, given the many economic and political challenges

350   *Eric Friginal and Rachelle Friginal*

(Friginal, 2013b), but monetary realities and basic business intangibles still indicate that outsourcing, especially in the Philippines, is a very viable option for most US corporations.

Still, public sentiment in the US about the quality of outsourced call center communications and the "English of offshore agents" continues to shift to the negative, as revealed by national surveys and qualitative interviews with customers (e.g., Brockman, 2010; Casiraya, 2008; Deloitte, 2016). Starting from the early 2000s, for example, Anton and Setting (2004) reported that most American consumers base their perception of companies directly on their call center experience; these consumers claim that communication issues with offshore call center agents have negatively impacted their customer service satisfaction levels and their future purchasing behavior. Based on a 2010 survey by the CFI Group, customer satisfaction with calls perceived to be handled in the US was more than one-fifth higher than with calls perceived to be handled outside the country. Furthermore, callers said that one of the biggest differences between "foreign and American call centers" was the ease of understanding the customer service agent (Brockman, 2010; Friginal, 2018).

It will be interesting, given the results presented in this study, to see what best English training programs can be provided to Filipinos in the industry. These training programs will have to be developed and redefined further to incorporate strategies and skills that address callers' linguistic attitudes and perceptions (i.e., sociolinguistic attitudes). High-level English competence in this context is necessary, but this alone does not determine success in transaction handling and accuracy. Other factors that will ensure effective delivery of service such as establishing rapport, personalization of support, comprehension, and correctness of information in transactions given to callers are all equally important. Additional research of the kind described in this study can contribute to the measurable successes of this training and staffing endeavors.

References

Anton, J., & Setting, T. (2004). The American consumer reacts to the call center experience and the offshoring of service calls. Retrieved March 15, 2006 from http://www.kellyconnect.com/eprise/main/web/us/kcnt/en/kc_offshoring.pdf

Bajaj, V. (2011, May 12). A new capital of call centers. Retrieved January 5, 2018 from https://www.nytimes.com/2011/11/26/business/philippines-overtakes-india-as-hub-of- call-centers.html

Beeching, K. (2002). *Gender, politeness and pragmatic particles in French.* Amsterdam: John Benjamins Publishing Company.

Berber-Sardinha, T., & Veirano-Pinto, M. (Eds.) (2014). *Multidimensional analysis 25 years on: A tribute to Douglas Biber.* Amsterdam, the Netherlands: John Benjamins Publishing Company.

Biber, D. (1988). *Variation across speech and writing.* Cambridge: Cambridge University Press.

Biber, D. (1995). *Dimensions of register variation: A cross-linguistic perspective.* Cambridge: Cambridge University Press.

Biber, D. (2006). *University language: A corpus-based study of spoken and written registers.* Philadelphia, PA: John Benjamins Publishing Company.

[BPAP] Business Processing Association Philippines (2010). Back office outsourcing in the Philippines. Retrieved January 12, 2010 from http://www.bpap.org

[BPAP] Business Processing Association Philippines (2018). Philippine call center industry updates. Retrieved January 12, 2018 from http://www.bpap.org

Brockman, J. (2010, August 27). Who's taking your call? CFI Group's 2010 Contact Center Satisfaction Index. Retrieved August 30, 2010 from http://www.cfigroup. com/resources/whitepapers_register.asp?wp=46

Cameron, D. (2008). Talk from the top down. *Language and Communication, 28,* 143–155.

Casiraya, L. (2008, October 20). Customer help in RP call centers suffers. *Philippine Daily Inquirer Online.* Retrieved August 19, 2009 from http://newsinfo. inquirer.net/breakingnews/infotech/view/20081020-167463/Customer-help-in-RP-call-centers-suffers

Conrad, S., & Biber, D. (Eds.) (2001). *Variation in English: Multi-dimensional studies.* Harlow: Longman.

D'Ausilio, R. (1998). *Wake up your call center: How to be a better call center agent.* West Lafayette, IN: Purdue University Press.

Deloitte (2016). [Company Report: Online]. Deloitte's 2016 global outsourcing survey-May 2016. Retrieved January 5, 2018 from https://www2.deloitte. com/content/dam/ Deloitte/nl/Documents/operations/deloitte-nl-s&o-global-outsourcing-survey.pdf

Dizon, D. (2015, June 5). Why Philippines has overtaken India as world's call center capital. Retrieved February 15, 2018, from http://news.abs-cbn.com/ nation/12/02/10/why-philippines-has-overtaken-india-worlds-call-center-capital

Economidou-Kogetsidis, M. (2005). "Yes, tell me please, what time is the midday flight from Athens arriving?": Telephone service encounters and politeness. *Intercultural Pragmatics, 2–3,* 253–273.

Friedman, T.L. (2005). *The world is flat.* New York: Picador.

Friginal, E. (2007). Outsourced call centers and English in the Philippines. *World Englishes, 26*(3), 331–345.

Friginal, E. (2008). Linguistic variation in the discourse of outsourced call centers. *Discourse Studies, 10*(6), 715–736.

Friginal, E. (2009a). Threats to the sustainability of the outsourced call center industry in the Philippines: Implications to language policy. *Language Policy, 5*(1), 341–366.

Friginal, E. (2009b). *The language of outsourced call centers: A corpus-based study of cross- cultural interaction.* Philadelphia: John Benjamins Publishing Company.

Friginal, E. (2011). Interactional and cross-cultural features of outsourced call center discourse. *International Journal of Communication, 21*(1), 53–76.

Friginal, E. (2013a). Linguistic characteristics of intercultural call center interactions. In G. Nelson & D. Belcher (Eds.), Critical and corpus-based approaches to intercultural rhetoric (pp. 127–153). Ann Arbor: University of Michigan Press.

Friginal, E. (2013b). Assessment of oral performance in outsourced call centers. *English for Specific Purposes, 32,* 25–35.

Friginal, E. (2013c). 25 years of Biber's MDA: Introduction to the special issue and an interview with Douglas Biber. *Corpora, 8*(2), 137–152.

Friginal, E. (2018). Quantifying cross-cultural communication. Paper presented at the American Association for Applied Linguistics (AAAL) Conference 2018, March 24–27, 2018, Chicago, IL.

Hayman J. (2010). Talking about talking: Comparing the approaches of intercultural trainers and language teachers. In G. Forey & J. Lockwood (Eds.), *Globalization, communication and the workplace* (pp. 147–158). London: Continuum.

Lakoff, R.T. (1976). *Language and women's place.* New York: Harper Colophon Books.

Lee, D. (2015, April 17). The Philippines has become the call-center capital of the world. Retrieved March 20, 2018 from http://www.latimes.com/business/la-fi-philippines- economy-20150202-story.html

Locher, M. (2004). *Power and politeness in action.* New York: Mouton de Gruyter.

Mills, S. (2003). *Gender and politeness.* Cambridge: Cambridge University Press.

Natividad, N. (2015, July 12). A history of the BPO industry in numbers. Retrieved March 20, 2018 from https://www.rappler.com/brandrap/stories/98207-bpo-philippines-timeline

[PSA] Philippine Statistics Authority (2018). Business process outsourcing (BPO) activities preliminary results. Retrieved March 20, 2018 from https://psa.gov.ph/article/business-process-outsourcing-bpo-activities-preliminary-results

Tannen, D. (1990). Gender differences in topical coherence: Creating involvement in best friends' talk. *Discourse Processes, 13,* 73–90.

Vashistha, A. & Vashistha, A. (2006). *The offshore nation: Strategies for success in global outsourcing and offshoring.* New York: McGraw-Hill.

White, M. (1994). *Language in job interviews: Differences relating to success and socioeconomic variables.* Unpublished Ph.D. Dissertation, Northern Arizona University.

"World Bank E-Commerce Development Report" (2003). World Bank Publications, Retrieved March 5, 2008 from http://publications.worldbank.org/

28 Teaching English as a Foreign Language in the Philippines

Aiden Yeh

28.1 Introduction

Claiming to be the world's third largest English-speaking country after the United States and the United Kingdom, the Philippines has tapped into the English language teaching (ELT) market and carved a niche as the place-to-go for English as a Foreign/Second Language (EFL/ESL) learning. As shown in the 2017 press release promoting Philippine ESL and the country's fine beaches, the Philippine Department of Tourism (DOT) proudly claims that learning English "is more fun in the PHL" (DOT, 2017). But why learn English in the Philippines? Well, aside from the fact that English is an official language of the country, it is widely spoken by the majority, and it is used in business, education, media, and government communications (Bernardo, 2004; Friginal, 2007). According to the ICEF Monitor (2016a), with roughly 100 million speakers (more than the United Kingdom) 93.5% of Filipinos can speak and understand English. Capitalizing on the large number of English speakers and the use of English as a medium of instruction in various courses and programs, the Philippines positions itself as "a reputable education centre for English language learners" (para. 2) at a fraction of the cost of their competitors. This chapter presents some of the issues regarding EFL in the Philippines, i.e., low-cost factors, quality of teaching, the Philippine English (PhE) accent and Tagalog-English code-switching and their ramifications on pedagogy, and the need to re-package the whole Philippine EFL label.

28.2 Low Cost

Aiming to be competitive in the global EFL industry, the Philippines adopted the low-price strategy approach, which has undoubtedly enhanced the demand among its target market – mainly Koreans, Japanese, Taiwanese, and many others who come from the Expanding Circle (cf. Kachru, 1992) countries. The ICEF Monitor (2015) adds that Asian students are drawn to study in the Philippines due to the "geographical proximity and exceptional value relative to traditional ELT destinations" (para. 2), thus

DOI: 10.4324/9780429427824-36

354 *Aiden Yeh*

making it a popular destination for English language learning (UNESCO, 2013). But how affordable are these EFL programs? In 2012, tuition fee rates were approximately US$500 per course – based on about 60 hours class contact (McGeown, 2012). By 2016, a similar course cost between US$800 and US$1,600 inclusive of accommodation and meals (ICEF, 2016b). Ozaki (2011) posits that "the average cost for an hour one-to-one lesson [...] was only US$7.25" compared with the US$87.93 demanded in Sydney, Australia (Ozaki, 2011). As Kobayashi's (2008) paper aptly puts it, Philippines is "a cheap substitute for such study destinations" (p. 86), and their teachers are disappointingly labeled as "the world's low-cost English language teacher" (McGeown, 2012, para. 1). Despite the increase in fees, these courses are still relatively economical in comparison to what they would cost for a similar course in North America. In addition to lower course fees, the modest cost of living in the Philippines is also a significant factor that lures foreign students (Johnson, 2009). The affordable travel costs are also important considerations (McGeown, 2012; Satake, 2015; WENR, 2018). A direct flight from Japan or Korea to the Philippines is less than four hours, and Taiwan is even nearer taking only two hours with return flights costing approximately US$250 to US$400. For price-conscious students, the ability to stretch a dollar can be a deal breaker when choosing their study destination.

28.3 Pedagogical Factors

English language providers in the country claim that they offer top quality learning facilities and small group instruction which lasts from 8 to 12 hours per week (Cabrera, 2012; Taipei Times, 2017). The use of English as the medium of instruction (EMI) and an English-only learning environment are also used as part of their marketing pitch. The findings of Ozaki's (2017) small-scale ($n = 19$) pilot study using a survey questionnaire on Korean learners' views of Filipino EFL teachers' expertise (i.e., language abilities, instructional skills, and knowledge of English), reveals a favorable response which suggests that the Filipino teachers from a private university were perceived to be exceptionally competent EFL teachers. Ozaki (2017) noted that the Filipino teachers' language skills were evaluated "highly", and he surmised that the Philippines being in the Outer Circle (cf. Kachru, 1992), where English is an official language and is used as the primary language in education and business on a daily basis, explains why they have a good grasp of English language skills. However, merely possessing good grammatical skills does not often equate to excellent pronunciation skills. Ozaki posits that students' low ratings on Filipino teachers' pronunciation and speaking skills can be attributed to their view that good pronunciation is having a native-like (sic.) pronunciation akin to American-accented English. The Filipino teachers' heavy Philippine English (PhE) accent and their use of local idiomatic expressions were both given a low evaluation. This can also be attributed to the Korean learners' familiarity (or the lack thereof) with native English teachers' use of colloquialisms and their lack of exposure to PhE linguistic features and phrasal expressions (Dita & De Leon, 2017; Ozaki, 2017).

Kobayashi's (2008) research participants also voiced the same concerns that "Filipino teachers are good, but not their accent" (p. 90) and that they "would have preferred that teachers had an L1 accent" (p. 90). The learners also viewed the disparity in accent negatively and commented on the differences in pronunciation, for example, rolled "r" sounds and the unaspirated /p/ which sounded like a /b/ to them sometimes caused communication breakdown and misunderstanding. In spite of the learners' criticisms about PhE, Filipino teachers still received positive evaluation on their "pedagogical qualities such as willingness to adjust the pace to the learners' level" (p. 93) and they fared well when compared with native teachers from the "inner circle".

The Philippines' EFL pitch boasts of its near-native English accent while the results of studies presented in this chapter reveal a discontent in the Filipino teachers' quasi-American English accent. Others have criticized PhE and pointed out a few of its linguistic features, i.e., pronunciation and accent, which caused communication breakdown and led to learning difficulties. These issues concerning the comprehensibility of PhE to foreign students are similar to the findings of Dita and De Leon's (2017) research which suggest that PhE is 60% less intelligible to speakers of English from the Expanding Circle (cf. Dayag, 2007). They attribute the lack of intelligibility (recognition of individual words or utterances) to the students' inadequate exposure to PhE. Dita and De Leon believe this can be remedied by raising the students' awareness of the different varieties of English and their phonological features (p. 111). They also argue that English teachers in the Philippines should resist from using the native speaker model as the "performance target in the classrooms" (p. 111), citing Smith and Rafiqzad's (1979) view that the phonology of native speakers are not more intelligible than for non-native speakers. The teaching of pronunciation is often a challenge for Filipino teachers, but as English language teachers, it is one of the skills that they need to practice and be good at.

The qualitative study of de Guzman, Albela, Nieto, Ferrer, and Santos (2006) using semi-structured interviews on the English language learning difficulties of Korean students found a number of pedagogical factors that made class discussions difficult. For example, they pointed out that Filipino teachers use difficult words and vocabulary, have inaccurate pronunciation, lack fluency in English, and use topics Koreans cannot relate to (cf. Rosario & Narag-Maguddayao, 2017). They also noted some of the Filipino teachers' teaching style that the Koreans found problematic: No hand-outs, no group activities, and the emphasis on lecture-based learning (p. 155). De Guzman et al. (2006) posit that these pedagogical flaws in the classroom "complicate the subjects' understanding of the lessons" (p. 155). Another issue noted in the studies cited above was that of foreign students' complaints about Filipino teachers' constant code-switching – the shifting or switching from one language to another (cf. Auer, 1988; Bullock & Toribio, 2009) or the use of Tagalog English (Taglish) in class. However, code-switching is particularly common among bilingual speakers, and is predominant in bilingual societies such as the Philippines (Viduya, 2018). de Guzman et al. (2006) also noted that Filipino students also converse in their vernacular and generally switch from English to Tagalog in front of the Korean students. Nonetheless, Filipino teachers have a professional duty not to code-switch with their students. Foreign students choose to learn English in the Philippines; they want to learn how to speak English properly, and they want to learn it in an ESL context. Students do not have external control outside the classroom but in the classroom; it is the teachers' responsibility to provide the kind of language these students have paid for.

28.4 Taglish

According to Bautista (2004), the code-switching between Tagalog and English is a kind of informal discourse among college-educated, middle-/upper-class Filipinos living in urban areas. Sibayan (1985) argues, "No discussion on the language situation in the Philippines today is complete without a note on the mixing (mix-mix), or code-switching [...] popularly known as Taglish" (p. 49), which has largely become fossilized in the Philippine conversational language. Some linguists view Taglish code-switching as a form of additive bilingualism since it is regarded as a positive linguistic resource (Bautista, 2004), while others criticize it as a kind of subtractive bilingualism (cf. Lambert, 1975, cited in Landry & Allard, 1993) whereby learning English has negative consequences on the first language, i.e., interference in successful learning of the Filipino language and culture (cf. Gonzalez & Sibayan, 1988). Sibayan (1985) speculated that Taglish will be modernized and intellectualized while lamenting the fact that "the development of Taglish is irreversible" (p. 50). More than 35 years later, this mix-mix (Taglish) used by bilingual Filipinos is still "deemed a *sine qua non* for effective communication" (Marasigan, 1986, pp. 340–341), and is considered the language of the youth (Nolasco, 2008). For foreigners, however, Taglish is hard to comprehend, and for students learning English in the Philippines, the constant alternation can be overwhelmingly/seriously problematic (McGeown, 2012).

28.5 Immersion in Philippine English

Foreign students are lured to the Philippines by the low costs of education and costs of living, which includes a total immersion in language education and culture where they get to speak the language they are learning. The ICEF Monitor (2016b) reports that the Philippines appears "particularly well-placed to attract beginner ELT students" (p. 7). Perhaps if it is immersion in the target language students are after and the chance to use

Teaching English as a Foreign Language 357

the language in real-life contexts, then the Philippines is good enough as it can genuinely deliver what this particular ELT market wants and needs.

The findings of Cruz and Pariña (2017) where they examined the implicit and explicit knowledge of Korean learners in the Philippines found that being immersed in an ESL learning environment has a positive effect on the learning experiences of foreign students. Their findings share comparative results with the studies conducted by Cruz (2013) and Mamhot, Martin, and Masangya (2013). Cruz and Pariña also claim that the country's English-speaking context is one that "the Philippines can offer" (p. 83), and that "apart from its English speaking culture, it is equipped with mechanisms that help develop the language skills of foreign students" (p. 83).

However, the subjects in Kobayashi's (2008) study noted the constant use of Filipino by the locals which made them feel that the learning environment was not entirely an English-speaking one. Nonetheless, they still found the Philippines a good place to learn and use English because that is the only means of communicating with others, thus enhancing their sociolinguistic competence, i.e., their ability to communicate using the target language (cf. Bayley & Regan, 2004; Holmes & Brown, 1976; Regan, Howard, & Lemée, 2009). The study of de Guzman et al. (2006) also suggests that the Korean students used English "almost everywhere in the Philippines" (p. 154). One student was quoted as saying that there were more opportunities to speak English in the Philippines compared to Korea, while another student commented on the possibility to use all the four language skills – a far cry from the grammar-based style of learning in Korea. The participants in this study also remarked that the pronunciation and accent of the Filipino teachers and classmates also caused some learning difficulties.

28.6 Teachers' Qualifications

Choe's (2016) qualitative study on the identity formation of Filipino ESL teachers teaching Korean students in the Philippines examined their perceived image and status as non-native teachers. These teachers, who had not received any Teaching of English to Speakers of Other Languages TESOL teaching certificate or bachelor's/ master's degrees in TESOL and related fields, were all affiliated with two different language academies in Manila. All 12 described themselves as non-native teachers because of their Filipino English accent. They openly discussed the discrimination they had experienced because of their accented English; some had previously not been accepted for teaching posts because they did not sound American enough, while others were strongly recommended to hone their American English. A few had undertaken a pronunciation and "accent-reduction" training sponsored by the hiring institution. In comparison to native speakers of English, they perceived themselves as "deficient" or even inferior. Some felt that they would never be as good as native speakers in spite of the number of years in service as English teachers. The lack of knowledge of the target culture

358 *Aiden Yeh*

(American culture) and historical facts about US history also made them feel less competent. Nonetheless, they considered themselves to be qualified ELT professionals despite the lack of ESL teaching training qualifications and regardless of their perceived inferiority issues brought about by their non-nativeness. It is through this lack of ESL teaching qualifications on the part of Filipino teachers that TESOL and/or ESL teacher training organizations found a marketing niche (Lorente & Tupas, 2002). They capitalize on the Foreign Teachers FTs' insecurities as non-native speakers with strong PhE accent vis-à-vis the desired American native speaker accent. The native-speakerism ideology is still prevalent throughout the world and sends out a clear message that American English is something to be desired, and that having a PhE accent is simply unsatisfactory and will not help them get the highly coveted ESL teaching jobs.

Choe's (2016) study has touched on valid issues relating to the lack of regulations on teaching standards. Teachers' qualifications are not regulated by the government; thus, Filipino ESL teachers are vulnerable to becoming victims of fraudulent organizations. Hicap (2009) points out that there are numerous online job and classified ads aimed at recruiting ESL teachers that do not require qualifications. The key to getting these jobs, he adds, is having an American accent. He posits, "Some online English teachers have noted that ESL centers in the Philippines offer below-standard wages despite the fact that they charge hefty fees for Korean students" (par. 33). Unfortunately, there has been little research done on this issue, particularly on the plight of Filipino ESL teachers in private language academies.

28.7 The EFL Industry: What Needs to Be Done

The issues of teacher training, qualifications, and professional development need to be underscored. Filipino teachers ought to get recognized qualifications such as Certificate in Teaching English to Speakers of Other Languages (CELTA), Diploma in Teaching English to Speakers of Other Languages (DELTA), TESOL Core-Certificate Program, and other teaching qualifications and courses endorsed by the British Council, International Association of Teachers of English as a Foreign Language IATEFL, and TESOL International Association. The country needs to recognize the training and qualification needs of Filipino ESL teachers and managers, particularly those directly involved in delivering language courses to foreign students, and to ensure strict quality guidelines in improving the teaching and learning of English. The government needs to partner with established academic schools, top universities in the country, and acclaimed and renowned local scholars who can establish regular training programs and workshops for continuous professional development in major cities and areas.

The Philippines needs to establish a governing body solely for the EFL industry to ensure the quality of ESL institutions and teacher training centers that will raise teacher quality, which in turn will raise student outcomes and

Teaching English as a Foreign Language 359

success in ESL learning. The accreditation process must be transparent, less bureaucratic, and efficient. This body shall guarantee an effective way to standardize and improve ESL education being provided by individual schools and ensure that they are effectively managed and deliver world-class ESL curriculum standards, provide continuous teacher professional development for ESL teachers and staff, and ensure that the language schools/centers in the Philippines meet the demands and quality standards of the ESL industry.

It has been established in this chapter that the teaching of English as a foreign or second language in the Philippines is a booming industry, and the future prospects are indeed promising. Even the DOT and other government agencies and foreign representatives have shown support in promoting the country as an EFL destination. The DOT (2015) has also showcased the programs and facilities of Philippine ESL schools in international education exhibitions and ESL fairs. While these international promotional efforts are significant, the government has to pull all these resources together and place them under one ESL umbrella agency, and organize an ESL education trade exhibition where all ESL stakeholders in the Philippines can participate. The aim is to bring together all registered ESL schools in the Philippines for them to showcase their wares, i.e., facilities and programs, ESL teachers and managers can share ideas, practices, and technologies via workshops and symposiums. In this way, there is transparency as to who's who in the industry. There is a dire need for the government to release an ESL directory for information on school services, training, and accreditation accessible to anyone and anytime. In this way, teachers, learners, and suppliers are assured of standardized quality of services and accountability of the stakeholders.

28.8 Rebranding EFL in the Philippines

A search about learning EFL/ESL in the Philippines on Google reveals a long list of media coverage-related results that seem to suggest a common sales pitch used to describe the country as an increasingly popular destination for English language learning, especially for people in/from South East Asia. Yet, however you dress up popularity, one has to look beyond the headlines to see what kind of narrative is being constructed. These are examples of the labels used to frame EFL/ESL/ELT in the Philippines as a 'cheap' alternative: the world's budget English teacher; bargain for high-quality and affordable education; less expensive, low-cost English teacher to the world? The connotations suggest that the Philippines is offering something that is poorly made, second-best, perhaps even an imitation of the real thing, something better. Focusing on the benefits without any reference to (the low) financial costs, the Philippines can and does provide high quality education/learning, albeit with an "American accent"; indeed, the country offers a place/context where English is spoken almost everywhere, in a variety of surroundings where EFL learners are widely exposed to the target language, and where they can use it in meaningful, real-world situations. This

360   *Aiden Yeh*

means that they are able to converse with genuine "native" speakers, watch films and televisions shows, read authentic English materials, learn English through art, music, and other cultural forms, thereby enhancing their proficiency as they are provided with an array of opportunities to both learn and practice English in a 'natural' setting (cf. Krashen & Terrell, 1983).

The problematization of the commodification of EFL/ESL in the Philippines is bounded by cultural and linguistic hybrid identities as perpetuated by media exposure and representations. In the (re)construction of the national identity as an ESL provider, and in attempting to make sense of what it is about plus what it stands for, the Philippines needs to look at and reflect upon the media discourse as an identity mirror – bouncing back reflections of external interpretations as images of the country (Strauss, 2017). It further needs to understand how it projects/promotes itself as a (re)source for ESL learning. In the end, the government, together with EFL/ESL providers, still needs to decide on how best it can deliver and satisfy the learning needs of the overseas EFL students.

The notion of low-cost and quality ESL is a classic business marketing strategy that changes the nature of competition (Porter, 1989; Teece, 2010). However, the industry's growth also suggests that language institutions are making a profit, and this is something made possible by keeping the labor costs low with a ready supply of cheap labor and the ability to recruit teaching staff on a lower salary scheme. The economic strategy of the country as the supplier of a "large pool of cheap, English-speaking workers (McKay, 2004, p. 27)" is marked in its history (cf. Tupas & Salonga, 2016). While the Philippines can claim the legitimacy of "low cost", she has to justify "quality ESL" and match the top quality standards that foreign students are clamoring for.

References

Auer, P. (1988). A conversation analytic approach to code-switching and transfer. *Codeswitching: Anthropological and Sociolinguistic Perspectives*, *48*, 187–213.

Bautista, M. L. S. (2004). Tagalog-English code- switching as a mode of discourse. *Asia Pacific Education Review*, *5*, 226–233.

Bayley, R., & Regan, V. (2004). Introduction: The acquisition of sociolinguistic competence. *Journal of Sociolinguistics*, *8*(3), 323–338.

Bernardo, A. B. (2004). McKinley's questionable bequest: Over 100 years of English in Philippine education. *World Englishes*, *23*(1), 17–31.

Bullock, B. E., & Toribio, A. J. (2009). *Themes in the study of code-switching*. Cambridge: Cambridge University Press.

Cabrera, M. (2012). *Textbooks in the tropics as the Philippines lures students*. Retrieved September 20, 2018, from https://www.reuters.com/article/us-philippines-english/textbooks-in-the-tropics-as-the-philippines-lures-students-idUSBRE-86G06A20120717

Choe, H. (2016). Identity formation of Filipino ESL teachers teaching Korean students in the Philippines: How negative and positive identities shape ELT in the Outer Circle. *English Today*, *32*(1), 5–11.

Cruz, S. A. (2013). Rule or feel? The application of implicit and explicit knowledge of Filipino and Korean college students in responding to English tests. *AJELS*, 62, 61–85.

Teaching English as a Foreign Language 361

Cruz, S. A., & Pariña, J. C. M. (2017). Implicit and Explicit Knowledge of Korean Learners in the Philippines across Contextual Shift. *Online Submission, 18*, 73–85.

Dayag, D. T. (2007). Exploring the intelligibility of Philippine English. *Asian Englishes, 10*(1), 4–23.

de Guzman, A. B., Albela, E. J. A., Nieto, D. R. D., Ferrer, J. B. F., & Santos, R. N. (2006). English language learning difficulty of Korean students in a Philippine multidisciplinary university. *Asia Pacific Education Review, 7*(2), 152–161.

Department of Tourism (DOT). (2015). *Philippine Tourism 2015.* Retrieved September 20, 2018, from http://www.tourism.gov.ph/files/2015%20DOT%20YEAR%20END%20as%20of%20%2011%20August%202016.pdf

Department of Tourism (DOT). (2017). *DOT to Koreans: 'ESL training is more fun in PHL'.* Retrieved September 11, 2018, from http://web.tourism.gov.ph/news_features/dot_koreans.aspx

Dita, S. N., & De Leon, K. D. (2017). The intelligibility and comprehensibility of Philippine English to EFL speakers. *The Philippine ESL Journal, 19*, 100–116.

Friginal, E. (2007). Outsourced call centers and English in the Philippines. *World Englishes, 26*(3), 331–345.

Gonzalez, A., FSC, & Sibayan, B. P. (Eds.) (1988). *Evaluating bilingual education in the Philippines* (1974–1985). Manila: Linguistic Society of the Philippines.

Hicap, J. (2009). Koreans flock to the Philippines to learn English. *Korea Times.* Retrieved September 15, 2018, from https://www.koreatimes.co.kr/www/news/nation/2009/09/117_51729.html

ICEF Monitor. (2015). *UK losing share in global ELT market.* Retrieved September 15, 2018 from http://monitor.icef.com/2015/08/uk-losing-share-in-global-elt-market/

ICEF Monitor. (2016a). *Australia's ELICOS enrolment grew in 2015 but source markets are shifting.* Retrieved September 15, 2018, from http://sb-monitor-1.icef.com/2016/08/australias-elicos-enrolment-grew-2015-source-markets-shifting/

ICEF Monitor. (2016b). *ELT enrolment in the Philippines on the rise.* Retrieved September 15, 2018, from http://monitor.icef.com/2016/03/elt-enrolment-in-the-philippines-on-the-rise/

Johnson, A. (2009). The Rise of English: The language of globalization in China and the European Union, *Macalester International*: Vol. 22, Article 12. Retrieved September 20, 2018 from https://digitalcommons.macalester.edu/cgi/viewcontent.cgi?referer=https://www.google.com.tw/&httpsredir=1&article=1447&context=macintl

Kachru, B. B. (1992). World Englishes: Approaches, issues and resources. *Language Teaching, 25*(1), 1–14.

Kobayashi, I. (2008). They speak 'incorrect' English understanding Taiwanese learners' views on L2 varieties of English. *Philippine Journal of Linguistics, 39*, 81–98.

Krashen, S. D., & Terrell, T. D. (1983). *The natural approach: Language acquisition in the classroom.* Hayward: Alemany Press.

Lambert, W. (1975). Culture and language as factors in learning and education. In A. Wolfgang (Ed.), *Education of Immigrant Students* (pp. 55–83). Toronto: Ontario Institute for Studies in Education.

Landry, R., & Allard, R. (1993). 'Beyond socially naive bilingual education: The effects of schooling and ethnolinguistic vitality of the community on additive and subtractive bilingualism', *Annual Conference Journal* (NABE '90–'91): 1–30.

Lorente, B. P., & Tupas, T. R. F. (2002). Demythologizing English as an economic asset: The case of Filipina domestic workers in Singapore. *ACELT Journal, 6*(2), 20–32.

Mamhot, A. M., Martin, M. H., & Masangya, E. M. (2013). A comparative study on the language anxiety of ESL and EFL learners. *Philippine ESL Journal, 10*, 200–231.

362　*Aiden Yeh*

McGeown, K. (2012). The Philippines: Low-cost English teacher to the world. *BBC News Business.* Retrieved September 10, 2018, from https://www.bbc.com/news/business-20221155

McKay, S. C. (2004). Zones of regulation: Restructuring labor control in privatized export zones. *Politics & Society, 32*(2), 171–202.

Nolasco, R. M. (2008, July). The prospects of multilingual education and literacy in the Philippines. In The 2nd International Conference on Language Development, Language Revitalization, and Multilingual Education in Ethnolinguistic Communities, Bangkok. Retrieved July 14, 2022 from https://www.seameo.org/_ld2008/doucments/Presentation_document/NolascoTHE_PROSPECTS_OF_MULTILINGUAL_EDUCATION.pdf.

Ozaki, S. (2011). Learning English as an international lingua franca in a semi-English-speaking country: The Philippines. *Asian EFL Journal, 53*(3), 51–60.

Ozaki, S. (2017). Learners' perceptions of Filipino EFL Teacher Expertise. *Journal of Education and Social Sciences, 7*(1), 123–128.

Porter, M. E. (1989). How competitive forces shape strategy. In: D. Asch, & C. Bowman (Eds.), *Readings in Strategic Management* (pp. 133–143). London: Palgrave.

Rosario, O., & Narag-Maguddayao, R. (2017). Code-switching of English language teachers and students in an ESL classroom. *The Asian EFL Journal's International Conference on Research & Publication*, August 24–26, 2018, Clark, Philippines. Retrieved September 20, 2018, from https://www.asian-efl-journal.com/pubcon2018/breakout-sessions-schedule/code-switching-of-english-language-teachers-and-students-in-an-esl-classroom/

Satake, M. (2015). English students flock to Philippines for low cost, sunshine. In *Nikkei Asian Review.* Retrieved September 15, 2018 from https://asia.nikkei.com/Business/English-students-flock-to-Philippines-for-low-cost-sunshine

Sibayan, B. P. (1985). Reflections, assertions and speculations on the growth of Pilipino. *Southeast Asian Journal of Social Science, 13*(1), 40–51.

Smith, L. E., & Rafiqzad, K. (1979). English for cross-cultural communication: The question of intelligibility. *TESOL Quarterly, 13*(3), 371–380.

Strauss, A. L. (2017). *Mirrors and masks: The search for identity.* London: Routledge.

Taipei Times. (2017). More Taiwanese flock to Philippines to study English. *Taipei Times.* Retrieved September 22, 2018, from http://www.taipeitimes.com/News/taiwan/archives/2017/12/16/2003684071

Teece, D. J. (2010). Business models, business strategy and innovation. *Long Range Planning, 43*(2–3), 172–194.

Tupas, R., & Salonga, A. (2016). Unequal Englishes in the Philippines. *Journal of Sociolinguistics, 20*(3), 367–381.

United Nations Educational, Scientific and Cultural Organization (UNESCO). (2013). *The international mobility of students in Asia and the Pacific.* Retrieved September 22, 2018, from http://unesdoc.unesco.org/images/0022/002262/226219E.pdf

Viduya, M. (2018). Strands of tongue: Code-switching in ESL classes. *The Asian EFL Journal.* 20(12.4), ch12. Retrieved May 18, 2022, from https://www.asian-efl-journal.com/main-editions-new/2018-quarterly/index.htm

World Education News Reviews (WENR). (2018). *Education in the Philippines.* Retrieved September 15, 2018 from https://wenr.wes.org/2018/03/education-in-the-philippines

Special Feature
World Englishes and Social Change

Ahmar Mahboob and Ruanni Tupas

Introduction

Research on World Englishes, including that on Philippine English, looks at how the English language is indigenized by local populations to suit their needs and purposes. This work typically looks at the changes and variations in the English language as it is adopted and used by people who speak other languages at home and in their communities. In doing so, research on World Englishes often focuses on specific linguistic features, e.g., grapho-phonology (Dayag, 2012; Tayao, 2004), morpho-syntax (Borlongan, 2011), lexico-grammar (Bolton and Butler, 2004), semantics (Dita, 2011), and discourse semantics (Cruz, 2015). It also looks at the historical and political dimensions of the use of English in these contexts (Gonzalez, 2004; Martin, 2014; Tupas, 2004). What is often missing in the literature is a study of the impact of English or other colonial languages on the local communities, including on their languages and on social and cultural practices and beliefs. In this chapter, we will examine how English (and Spanish, in the context of the Philippines) influence(d) local languages, with a focus on local varieties of Englishes. We will do this by drawing on the Sapir-Whorf hypothesis (SWH) which highlights the relationship between language, thought, and culture. Specifically, we will share examples of the impact of the introduction of colonial languages on local languages and examine their potential socio-political implications. In doing so, the chapter will discuss both the implications of SWH on WE and the potential contributions of WE on understanding SWH.

SWH, as presented in most textbooks today, focuses on whether and how language impacts cognition and thought. This work is often interpreted and taught in terms of two versions: the strong version and the weak version. The strong version, also known as linguistic determinism, is posited as the view that language determines our thought patterns, whereas the weak version, also known as linguistic relativity, is posited as the view that differences in language can lead to differences in thought. However, recent re-evaluation of this work, based on a close reading of Whorf's writings, challenges such a reduced interpretation of Whorf. For example, Lee (1996) notes that there is

DOI: 10.4324/9780429427824-37

364 *Ahmar Mahboob and Ruanni Tupas*

"no evidence that Whorf intended to make either of the assertions" (p. 85). Extending this critique, Pavlenko (2016) notes that this misinterpretation of SWH can be traced back to work by psychologists Brown and Lenneberg (1954) who interpreted Whorf (1940) in ways that fit into their disciplinary goals and research procedures, and, in doing so, ignored a number of aspects of Whorf's work. She argues that it is this reduced interpretation of SWH that became popular – even if it does not capture the goals and intentions of Whorf's work – and fails to serve the goals of linguists in general and those interested in questions of second language acquisition and multilingualism in particular.

Pavlenko, drawing on work by Fishman (1960), Lakoff (1987), Lucy (1992), amongst others, argues that one goal of Whorf's work was to question the Western beliefs about the world as norm-defining. She refers to Whorf (1941):

> Western culture has made, through language, a provisional analysis of reality and, without correctives, holds resolutely to that analysis as final. The only correctives lie in all those other tongues which by aeons of independent evolution have arrived at different, but equally logical, provisional analyses.
>
> (p. 313).

By reducing Whorf's work to a debate between determinists and relativists and investigating these interpretations through controlled experiments using mostly monolingual speakers, as is common in psychology, Pavlenko argues that we have ignored how SWH is relevant to research in the fields of second language acquisition and multilingualism.

Pavlenko's paper is relevant here because it also explains a lack of research in World Englishes that draws on or contributes to discussions of SWH. To date, as far as we are aware, there are no studies on WE that draw on or discuss SWH. This gap in research is also noted by McWhorter (2008) who points out that SWH literature has yet to explore "what its implications would be for how a language has changed over time" (pp. 148–149). One possible reason for this lack of interest in SWH in World Englishes literature lies in the development of World Englishes descriptions. Descriptions of World Englishes, mirroring those of other dialects/varieties of languages, primarily focus on phonological, morphological, and syntactic variations and features of the language. In doing so, these descriptions, as pointed out in Lavandera (1978), "suffer from the lack of an articulated theory of meanings" (p. 171). World Englishes research, while it describes localized features, often fails to discuss what these variations mean or how they relate to the social beliefs and practices of a community – and, even more importantly, how these changes may reflect and, to some extent, perhaps constitute social change. In this chapter, we will attempt to look at this relationship by focusing on how Spanish and then American English influenced Philippine English and Filipino, as well as the social values and meanings associated

World Englishes and Social Change   365

with particular aspects of these languages. In addition, to further substantiate our arguments, we will also look at examples of how British English influenced Pakistani English and Urdu.

Philippine English

One example that reveals how language change can potentially impact social practices and attitudes is the shift in the status of women in the Philippines. This can be studied in terms of both lexical semantics and discourse semantics.

According to historical sources, there was a single kinship term, 'asawa', that referred to both husband and wife in precolonial Tagalog (Stoodley, 1957). This term, which can perhaps be considered similar to the modern English term 'partner', reflected equality between the asawa. Women and men both had equal rights, including that to divorce (Abalos, 2017). With the Spanish conquest of the Philippines in 1521, the Spaniards introduced both their language and their religion to the colony. Spanish, like English – which was later introduced to the Philippines by the Americans at the turn of the 20th century and served as the source variety for the development of Philippine English – marked a differentiation between 'esposo' (husband) and 'esposa' (wife), with different roles and responsibilities for each. The Spaniards gave a lower status to women as compared to men. This differentiation was encoded within the lexical semantics of the terms 'wife' and 'husband' as can be seen in the following extract from a Spanish translation of the Bible:

Efesios 5:22–24 (Nueva Version Internacional)
[22]Esposa, sométanse a sus propios esposos como al Señor.[23]Porque el esposo es cabeza de su espoa, así como Cristo es cabeza y Salvador de la iglesia, la cual es su cuerpo.[24]Así como la iglesia se somete a Cristo, también las esposas deben someterse a sus esposos em todo.
[Translation: *Wives, submit yourself to your own husbands as you do to the Lord. For the husband is the head of the wife as the Christ is the head of the Church, his body of which he is savior. Now as the church submits to Christ, so also wives should submit to their husbands in everything.*]

The extract above gives a differential status to husbands and wives, where wives are asked to submit to their husbands 'in everything'. The terms 'esposa' and 'esposo' were introduced to the Philippines along with this differentiation of status. This marked a shift from the local cultural attitudes where husbands and wives had a more equal, albeit complementary, set of responsibilities. Scholars of gendered relations in precolonial Philippines note how women and men then were indeed operating within a bilateral kinship system where women, among many examples, participated actively in economic activities and exercised more control over their own economic

366   *Ahmar Mahboob and Ruanni Tupas*

resources, as well as took on roles of community leaders – or 'chieftains' (Alcantara, 1994; Brewer, 1999; Mananzan, 2003; Reid, 1988). The introduction of the differentiation between 'esposa' and 'esposo' to the Philippines – part of the cultural importation of a European discourse on sex and gender which essentialized and compartmentalized 'women' within the realm of nature and nurture (Brewer, 1999) – impacted the lexical meaning of the word 'asawa'. While the term 'asawa' continues to be used in modern Filipino for both husband and wives, the roles of the wife and husbands have changed – wives are now seen as subservient to their husbands and have lost many of the rights that they had in precolonial Philippines which was characterized by an "otherwise sexually egalitarian" social structure (Alcantara, 1994, p. 95).

The influence of Spanish colonization can be seen in early Philippine literature. For example, consider the following passage from Jose Rizal's *Noli Me Tangere* (Touch me not) (cited in Mamac, 2018) where he describes Sisa, a wife excessively abused by her husband as:

> Weak in character, with more heart than intellect, she knew only how to love and to weep. Her husband was a god and her sons were her angels, so he, knowing to what point he was loved and feared, conducted himself like all false gods: daily he became more cruel, more inhuman, more willful.

The extract from Rizal's book reflects a shift from precolonial notion of asawa to the gendered roles of husband and wife, where a wife was seen as less than a husband. This shift also marked a shift in the status of women in society and loss of equality. Of course, such an essentialized view of women cannot simply be reduced to Rizal's passive understanding of gendered relations in colonial (Spanish) Philippines. It can be argued, in fact, that he drew on colonially induced constructions of 'men' and 'women' in order to critically intervene in the violent oppression of the local population through material and symbolic means. Rizal's characterization of Sisa and other women in his novels from all social classes was his way of highlighting "repressive laws and institutions [which] were put in place in the guise of protecting women, but proved to be the exact opposite" (Jopson, 2014, p. 124). Our interest here is in Rizal's realistic characterization of women during Spanish colonial times which has survived colonization and, thus, can still be observed in contemporary Philippine life. For example, although divorce was practiced in precolonial Philippines among many ancestral tribes (Abalos, 2017), this was "prohibited" (p. 1523) during the Spanish colonial period, an enduring practice today because it is, in general, still not a viable option and women are expected to tolerate and accept their husbands' infidelities or other abuse.

The shift in the social status of women – influenced by the colonizing power and language of the Spanish and the Americans – came along with changes in local languages that repositioned the status of women in society and their position vis-à-vis men. This influence of Spanish and American English on Philippine English and the formation of social values associated with it can be observed in the discourse semantics of texts written in Philippine English, including those used in school textbooks. For example, the following extract taken from the text 'Mothers' used in a third year high school textbook reiterates the belief, first introduced during the Spanish era, that a wife needs to accept her husband, even if they are not honest or are abusive.

> I gave her wisdom to know that a good husband never hurts his wife, but sometimes tests her strength and her resolve to stand beside him unfalteringly.
> And finally, I gave her a tear to shed. This is hers exclusively to use whenever it is needed.
>
> (Gorgon, Bermudez, & Nery, 2012)

This extract reinforces the husbands' status in society while absolving them of any wrongdoing: husbands only test their wives' resolve and commitment. The only recourse permitted to the women in this text is for women to weep. The shifts from old Tagalog to modern Filipino and Philippine English, influenced first by Spanish and then sustained through English, reflects a shift in the lexical semantics of 'asawa' along with social changes, which, in this case, show a weaker positioning of women and wives in the society.

The introduction of Spanish and English, in other words, cannot be naively viewed simply as the imposition of colonial languages which had immense impact on the local linguistic ecologies of the Philippines through these varying periods of colonial subjugation. Such linguistic imposition, rather, must be viewed within a general ideological and material gendering of the Philippines: "With Western colonization came the restructuring of the Philippine household, especially along patriarchal lines" (Alcantara, 1994, p. 95). We can then see how colonial gender relations and practices were transmitted and enforced through Spanish and English as colonial technologies of control on both the social and individual levels, now traceable semantically and discursively through Philippine English.

Mahboob (2015) refers to the use of language to influence social and individual changes as a form of identity management. Mahboob defines identity management as "any institutionalized or localized effort to shape or direct individual or group identities" (p. 156). Cruz (2015) provides detailed analysis of Philippine English texts used in English language textbooks for public schools in the Philippines to demonstrate how the texts use appraisal to encourage particular beliefs and attitudes. For example, in analyzing the text "Art: A lovely and dangerous mistress", Cruz notes:

> The text, thus, only positions women as one of two types, one to love, help, and possibly, protect, and another who is powerful, seductive,

368   *Ahmar Mahboob and Ruanni Tupas*

maybe evil, but can be 'used' to claim a goal... In this way, the text also attempts to manage the behavior of women. To be loved and rewarded, they must retain a weakened, weeping persona. The powerful woman exists outside the confines of the happiness brought about by the comfort of social institutions so she can always just exist in the fringes, someone who is meant to come in only as necessary... Art, though, can be controlled by a masculine spirit that the text judges as virile. This realization of + judgement: capacity particularly appraises men. A virile spirit is a macho one. This judgement carries meanings of the 'power' of the masculine sex drive over a woman who can be mastered by this power. The virility of a man, which is revisited through vitality, a judgement in the macroNew, is one that exists in the real world as opposed to the power of a woman which is relegated to an unreal 'cloud-cuckooland'. The comparison between Mariang Makling and art is not unproblematic. Instead, it carries interpersonally charged meanings that position men as individuals who can 'tame' powerful women. Of course, what is also suggested here is that art is only the province of men.

(pp. 161–162)

The text, and its analysis as presented in Cruz's work, once again shows how Philippine English creates and sustains a weakened position of women (and wives) in the community. If historical descriptions of Tagalog are to be trusted, this analysis shows how the position of women in society changed after colonization and how Philippine English today continues to project women as lesser than men, through both changes in the lexical semantics of key terms and the positioning of women/wives as weaker through discourse semantics. The reflection of social changes in and through language can perhaps be considered one way in which language variation can be used to study shifts in thoughts, beliefs, and attitudes.

Pakistani English

Similar to the influence of the Spaniards and Americans on Filipino and Philippine English, the British colonization of South Asia also brought about significant social changes in the region, including Pakistan. These social shifts can also be studied in terms of how semantics were influenced by the British and British English, the source variety for Pakistani English.

There were three recognized genders in pre-British South Asia: males, females, and third gender. People who belonged to the third gender were traditionally known as 'khwaja sira', where 'khwaja' (a word borrowed from Persian) was a honorific. Khwaja sira included transvestites, transsexuals, and transgender people and were both recognized and respected in the community. Some khwaja sira held important roles in the royal courts (Lal, 1994).

English does/did not have three genders and the British Raj did not recognize a third gender when it became the colonial rulers of India. This lack of recognition of the third gender in English led to the persecution of the khwaja sira. When the British took over India, khwaja sira lost their legal and official entitlements and recognition and were categorized as a 'criminal tribe' according to the British 1871 Criminal Tribe Act. This persecution of khwaja sira had and continues to have implications for this community. Many khwaja sira were forced into begging and prostitution. Khan (2014) provides a short and pointed analysis of the impact of the British colonization on people of the third gender:

> The colonial state declared 'obscene acts and songs' a crime and, in 1860, they inserted section 377 into the new Indian Penal Code, which criminalized sodomy and punished those who have carnal intercourse that the state considered against 'the order of nature'. Further, in 1871, laws to regulate these folk were included in the Criminal Tribes Act by the British Governor General of India. Through this act, 'persons of the male sex who admit themselves, or on medical inspection clearly appear to be impotent' were subjected to mandatory registration, surveillance, and control. Changes in inheritance laws meant that khwaja sara and hijra could not pass on sanads and hereditary stipends to their disciples. The British hoped to diminish their chances of survival by curtailing the various policies that ensured the economic viability of these individuals from being passed on to the next generation.
>
> (p. 1287)

The change in the social and economic position of khwaja sira also resulted in a shift in the lexical terms used to refer to them. Over time, khwaja sira were called hijra, chukkas, and khusras. All these terms are considered derogatory and project a negative stereotype of khwaja sira. Hijra was borrowed into English and continues to be used in Pakistani English, including in popular media. The use of the term hijra has a negative connotation, as opposed to the term khwaja sira, which includes a respected honorific.

In recent times, Pakistan has recognized people of the third gender and their legal rights have been restored. Activists today are advocating the use of the term khwaja sira over hijras, chukkas, and khusras. However, this campaign has only recently started and its impact on attitudes toward and status of this community cannot yet be studied. While there is some effort being put into changing the lexical item used to refer to the people of the third gender, there is little positive (public) discourse to support the community – for example, as far as we are aware, there is no mention of the third gender in Pakistani English textbooks or other teaching-learning material.

Conclusions

What our chapter has hopefully done is to highlight one dimension in the study of pluralities of English which has so far been sidelined in the

370 *Ahmar Mahboob and Ruanni Tupas*

research literature – the study of Englishes as reflective and constitutive of historically mediated changes in society. In the case of our examples of semantic-discursive changes in Philippine English above, with supporting views drawn from Pakistani English, we have located such changes within the coloniality of the localizing processes of Philippine English, arguing that such a localized variety of English has taken on semantic and discursive configurations traceable back to how colonial rule imposed different categories of 'men' and 'women'.

Here we see how the SWH may help push forward the study of Englishes in the realm of history and semantic-discursive change. Localization in this sense is not a straightforward (socio)linguistic phenomenon where speakers make cultural imprints on the language. If we go by Bakhtin's (1986) theoretical take on language – or *utterance* to be precise – as always generative of past and new personal and social histories in every sound and word being produced by any speaker, Philippine English too expresses multiple historical and ideological trajectories, reaffirmed but also transformed by its users. With precise linguistic tools of description, coupled with critical and broad historicization of language change in Philippine society, we may have a broader view of Philippine English as language change – a dynamic, historically situated phenomenon, but always ripe for linguistic – and semantic and ideological – intervention by modern-day Filipino speakers.

References

Abalos, J. B. (2017). Divorce and separation in the Philippines: Trends and correlates. *Demographic Research*, 36(5), 1515–1548.

Alcantara, A. N. (1994). Gender roles, fertility, and the status of married Filipino men and women. *Philippine Sociological Review*, 42(1/4), 94–109.

Bakhtin, M. M. (1986). *Speech genres and other late essays*. Austin: University of Texas Press.

Bolton, K., & Butler, S. (2004). Dictionaries and the stratification of vocabulary: Towards a new lexicography for Philippine English. *World Englishes*, 23, 91–112.

Borlongan, A. M. (2011). *A grammar of the verb in Philippine English* (Unpublished doctoral dissertation). De La Salle University, Manila, the Philippines.

Brewer, C. (1999). Baylan, Asog, transvestism, and sodomy: Gender, sexuality and the sacred in early colonial Philippines. *Intersections: Gender, history and culture in the Asia context*, 2, 1–5.

Brown, R., & Lenneberg, E. (1954). A study in language and cognition. *Journal of Abnormal and Social Psychology*, 49, 454–462.

Cruz, P. (2015). *Construing axiology: A study of identity management in Philippine English language teaching* (Unpublished doctoral dissertation). Ateneo de Manila University, Manila, the Philippines.

Dayag, D. (2012). Philippine English. In E.-L. Low & A. Hashim (Eds.), *English in Southeast Asia: Features, policy, and language in use* (pp. 91–100). Amsterdam: John Benjamins.

World Englishes and Social Change   371

Dita, S. N. (2011). The semantics and grammar of disjuncts in Philippine English. In M. L. S. Bautista (Ed.), *Studies in Philippine English: Exploring the ICE-Philippines* (pp. 33–50). Manila: Vibal Publishing.

Fishman, J. (1960). A systematization of the Whorfian hypothesis. *Behavioral Sciences*, 5, 323–329.

Gonzalez, A. (2004). The social dimensions of Philippine English. *World Englishes*, 23, 7–16.

Gorgon, E.G., Bermudez, V.F., & Nery, R. (2012) English Expressways III. Quezon City: National Program Support for Basic Education, Department of Education, Republic of the Philippines.

Jopson, T. L. (2014). A radical Rizal – A review of Sisa's Vengeance: A radical interpretation of Jose Rizal by E. San Juan Jr. Humanities Diliman. *A Philippine Journal Humanities*, 11(2), 124–129.

Khan, F. A. (2014). Khwaja Sira: Culture, Identity Politics, and "Transgender" Activism in Pakistan. (Unpublished doctoral dissertation). Syracuse University, Syracuse, NY.

Lakoff, G. (1987). *Women, fire, and dangerous things: What categories reveal about the mind*. Chicago, IL: University of Chicago Press.

Lal, K. S. (1994). *Muslim slave system in medieval India*. New Delhi: Aditiya Prakashan.

Lavandera, B. R. (1978). 'Where does the sociolinguistic variable stop?' *Language in Society*, 7(2), 171–182.

Lee, P. (1996). *The Whorf theory complex: A critical reconstruction*. Amsterdam: John Benjamins.

Lucy, J. (1992). *Language diversity and thought: A reformulation of the linguistic relativity hypothesis*. Cambridge: Cambridge University Press.

Mahboob, A. (2015) Identity management, language variation, and English language textbooks. In: D. Djenar, A. Mahboob, and K. Cruickshank (Eds.), *Language and identity across modes of communication*. Boston, MA: Walter de Gruyter.

Mamac, M. (2018). Tracking Women Marginalization through the Philippine Colonial History: A Linguistic Relativity Perspective. (Unpublished term paper). Department of Linguistics, University of Sydney, Sydney, Australia.

Mananzan, M. J. (2003). The Filipino women: Before and after the Spanish conquest of the Philippines. Institute of Women's Studies, St. Scholastica's College.

Martin, I. P. (2014). Philippine English revisited. *World Englishes*, 33(1), 50–59.

McWhorter, J. (2008). *Our magnificent bastard tongue: The untold history of English*. New York: Gotham Books.

Pavlenko, A. (2016). Whorf's lost argument: Multilingual awareness: Whorf's lost argument. *Language Learning*, 66(3), 581–607. doi:10.1111/lang.12185

Reid, A. (1988). Female roles in pre-colonial Southeast Asia. *Modern Asian Studies*, 22(3), 629–645.

Stoodley, B. H. (1957). Some aspects of Tagalog family structure. *American Anthropologist*, 59, 236–249.

Tayao, Ma Lourdes. (2004). The evolving study of Philippine English phonology. *World Englishes*, 23(1), 77–90.

Tupas, R. (2004). The politics of Philippine English: Neocolonialism, global politics, and the problem of postcolonialism. *World Englishes*, 23(1), 47–58.

Whorf, B. (1940). Science and linguistics. *Technology Review, 42*, 229, 247–248. Reprinted in B. Whorf (2012), *Language, thought, and reality: Selected writings of Benjamin Lee Whorf* (2nd ed., pp. 265–280). Cambridge: MIT Press.

Whorf, B. (1941). Languages and logic. *Technology Review, 43*, 250–252, 266, 268, 272. Reprinted in B. Whorf (2012), *Language, thought, and reality: Selected writings of Benjamin Lee Whorf* (2nd ed., pp. 299–314). Cambridge: MIT Press.

Epilogue
Philippine English: Past, Present, and Future

Kingsley Bolton

Introduction

My initial encounter with Philippine English (PhE) came in the early 1980s, when I first started to visit the Philippines as the guest of a Filipino-American family living in the Paranaque, a city south of Manila, quite close to Roxas Boulevard. As my hosts explained, the patriarch of the family had arrived with the US forces in 1898, and had stayed on as a businessman in the US colonial period, and had fathered seven children with his wife who was an Ilocano, a major ethnolinguistic of northern Philippines. During the Japanese occupation of the country during World War Two, he was imprisoned and died in the notorious internment camp in the grounds of the University of Santo Tomas in Manila. One of his children had sons who had served as a medical officer during the Vietnam War, and, on several occasions, he kindly invited me to stay at his house in a fishing barrio in Ilocos Sur, a province near the northern tip of the Philippines. At that time, I was a rather young and very inexperienced lecturer at the University of Hong Kong (HKU), but during those early visits in the 1980s, I had little contact with the Philippine academia, but was very moved by the hospitality and kindness of the Filipino people.

At that time, my interest in Filipiniana, PhE, and Philippine languages was largely autodidactic and self-directed. I scoured branches of the National Bookstore, a large bookstore chain in the Philippines, and collected Philippine literature in English, including, as I recall now, books by Nick Joaquin, Bienvenido Santos, and, especially, the work of F. Sionil Jose, whose Solidaridad Bookstore in Manila's Padre Faura Street I later discovered and visited. I was also bemused and fascinated by the English-language newspapers I read, not least by the inventive quality of PhE vocabulary, with its expressive and innovative neologisms, juxtaposed with the lexicon of archaic legal terms from bygone days, with their references to *blotter reports, coddling criminals, corrupt solons, hoosegow,* and *mulcting cops.* I was also fascinated by the quality of spoken English I encountered, and the fluency of many speakers of the language in all walks of life, which was particularly noticeable coming from 1980s Hong Kong, where the language was far less widely spoken. Some 20 years later, I commented on my initial impressions of PhE thus:

DOI: 10.4324/9780429427824-38

374   *Kingsley Bolton*

In the capital Manila (population twelve million), the street signs are in English; the disc jockey on the radio woos the station's listeners in dulcet American; the bookstores are full of English books (many penned by local writers); [... and] the presence of an American-influenced variety of English permeates public and private life in an unusual and surprising fashion. The taxi driver may give you a nuanced account of local politics, the coffee shop waitress may discuss Tess of the D'Urbervilles, and the salesperson in a store may crack a joke in colloquial Philippine English (*Joke only!*), interactions unlikely to be repeated in other Asian cities. Our foreign visitors may take this somehow for granted as they head to their business meeting, or in the case of tourists, head for their beach vacation. Or they may find time to consider and to ponder how it is that this predominantly Malay society, with its diaspora of overseas emigres and workers, happened to become one of the largest English-speaking societies in the world.

(Bautista & Bolton, 2008, p. 1)

Throughout the 1980s and early 1990s, I taught a course on 'Varieties of English' in Hong Kong, and in time this became a course in 'World Englishes' (WE), which proved to be a rather popular elective for HKU students. At that time, the WE perspective was something very new, and, although I became an advocate for the Kachruvian perspective in English studies, I had very little contact with WE scholars until 1996, when I attended a conference at De La Salle University. For me, that was something of a turning point, as, for the first time, I met not only Professors Braj and Yamuna Kachru, Susan Butler of the Macquarie Dictionary, but also Br. Andrew Gonzalez and Professor Ma. Lourdes Bautista. Following the 1996 Manila conference, my interest in WE intensified, and during the following years, I made a number of trips to the Philippines in order to learn more about the sociolinguistics of this fascinating country. In 2001, Professor Ma. Lourdes Bautista helped organize a symposium at De La Salle University on the topic of 'Philippine English: Language and Literature'. Largely inspired by this event, in 2004 we were able to publish a special issue in the journal *World Englishes* with 15 substantive articles on this topic. This later became the basis for a 2008 volume on *Philippine English: Linguistic and Literary Perspectives* published by the Hong Kong University Press. Throughout this period, I was very fortunate and privileged to work with Professor Ma. Lourdes Bautista on these projects, which for me were immensely educative and productive experiences.

Philippine English Lessons

It is encouraging today to see how many younger scholars, particularly from the Philippines, but also from Europe and elsewhere, have recently been attracted to WE as a field of research. Many of these younger academics have

Epilogue 375

rarely had the opportunity to meet such WE pioneers as Michael Halliday, Braj Kachru, Yamuna Kachru, Larry Smith, and Peter Strevens, and might therefore be forgiven for believing that WE studies are of very recent origin. Indeed, many newcomers to the field apparently assume that WE studies date mainly from the first decade of the 21st century. In the case of PhE, one is also uncertain of how many younger scholars are aware of the foundational work of such pioneers as Teodoro Llamzon, Andrew Gonzalez, and even Professor Ma. Lourdes Bautista herself, or the range of previous research in this area. Nevertheless, once one delves into the literature, it becomes apparent that studies of PhE have a long and interesting history.

One of the very earliest studies of the variety, however, set out to decry its use rather than to valorize its existence. This was a report named *Language Teaching in the Philippines*, authored by Clifford Prator in 1950, which provides an instructive snapshot of English-language education in the postwar period, at a time when American educational experts were still highly influential in the Philippines. Prator was nothing less than scathing about the merits of 'Philippine English'. Starting with a discussion of falling standards of pronunciation, he suggested that "[m]ore than any other element of the language, then, pronunciation was affected by the nearly complete disappearance of native models" (p. 53), that "a partial break-down of communication between Americans and all but the best-educated Filipinos has already occurred" (p. 53), and warning that "[t]he point is not far distant when English will no longer serve as a means of oral communication with outsiders for a majority of those who speak it in the Islands" (p. 53). Prator then went on to link a perceived failure in the teaching of spoken English to a discussion of PhE, in somewhat alarmist tones concerning the 'defeatism' of educators whose excuses for low standards of pronunciation were rationalized by 'championing Philippine English'. He then went on to write in dire terms about the multiple effects of a permissive attitude to a localized variety of English:

> There is actually no basis for supposing that a single 'Philippine English' would develop. More probably there would be many different regional versions: a 'Tagalog English' a 'Bisayan English', even an 'Igorot English'. These might well all be quite different in the absence of any single accepted standard. Even now Manila teachers state that the English of a pupil who transfers, for example, from the Ilocano region sounds very strange to them. [...] The language is likely to be more and more the medium whereby the educated elite of the country maintain communication with the outside world, and to be progressively less essential as the Filipinos' means of communicating among themselves. Needless to say, only an English which at least approached accepted international standards would serve to maintain liaison with the outside world of culture, science, and commerce.
>
> (pp. 54–55)

376   *Kingsley Bolton*

Throughout the report, the assertion is repeated constantly that English would never become fully accepted in the Philippines and that it would always remain 'distinctly a second language' and never a language of 'everyday life'. However conservative and dated Prator's views might appear now, there can be little doubt that, at the time, he was expressing opinions shared not only by other US educators in the Philippines, but by many Filipino teachers at that time, and echoes of such attitudes are still heard today.

The British Heresy and World Englishes

Clifford Prator's significance in the WE story lies not only in his engagement in the Philippines, but in his subsequent debates with a number of the very earliest pioneers of the WE approach. The figures in question are none other than the trio of Michael Halliday, Angus MacIntosh, and Peter Strevens, as well as Professor Braj Kachru, the founding editor of the *World Englishes* journal. In 1964, Halliday, McIntosh, and Strevens famously asserted:

> English is no longer the possession of the British, or even the British and the Americans, but an international language which increasing numbers of people adopt for at least some of their purposes [...] In West Africa, in the West Indies, and in Pakistan and India [...] it is no longer accepted by the majority that the English of England, with RP as its accent, are the only possible models of English to be set before the young.
> (Halliday, MacIntosh, & Strevens, 1964, p. 293)

Some four years later, Prator (1968) labelled such linguistic liberalism as a form of educational 'heresy' that he associated with British linguists worldwide, in a paper entitled *The British Heresy in TESL*. In this article, he identified seven fallacies associated with the British heresy, namely, (i) that second-language varieties of English can legitimately be equated with mother-tongue varieties; (ii) that second-language varieties of English really exist as coherent, homogeneous linguistic systems; (iii) that a few minor concessions in the type of English taught in schools would tend to or suffice to stabilize the language; (iv) that one level of a language, its phonology, can be allowed to change without entailing corresponding changes at other levels; (v) that it would a simple matter to establish a second-language variety of English as an effective instructional model once it had been clearly identified and described; (vi) that students would be content to study English in a situation where they were denied access to a mother-tongue model; and that (vii) granting a second-language variety of English official status in a country's schools would lead to its widespread adoption as a mother tongue. According to Prator, these attitudes were definitely a British heresy, as the Americans were of like mind in asserting that the only possible model of pronunciation was a "mother tongue" one, and that "in the eyes of both the French and the Americans, [...] if teachers in many different parts of

Epilogue 377

the world aim at the same stable, well documented model, the general effect of their instruction will be convergent", and that, just as there is increasing homogenization in mother-tongue societies, the forces of "greater mobility, new media of communication, urbanization, mass education" will also influence second-language varieties. Prator suggested that the reasons for the British view included (a) the élitist model of Received Pronunciation (in contrast to the more democratic General American); (b) the 'British' distrust of the foreigner who speaks English too well (unlike the French who were willing to assimilate their colonial subjects into French culture and language); and (c) a British-promoted 'instrumental motivation' toward English (as opposed to an American and French 'integrative' motivation). Finally, Prator concluded:

> The limitation of objectives implied in the doctrine of establishing local models for TESL seems to lead inevitably in practice to a deliberate lowering of instructional standards. [...] The total British effort on behalf of the teaching of English as a second language is too intelligently planned, too well executed, too crucial to the successful development of the emerging countries to allow for an indefinite prolongation of this flirtation with a pernicious heresy.
>
> (Prator, 1968, p. 474)

The Kachruvian Challenge to Prator

The next episode in this debate came some eight years later when Professor Braj Kachru (1976) by then active at the University of Illinois at Urbana-Champaign published an article on "Models of English for the Third World: White Man's Linguistic Burden or Language Pragmatics?" In a counter-blast against the seven 'fallacies' identified by Prator (1950), Kachru charged that Prator's arguments were themselves damned by seven 'attitudinal sins'. These were specified as: (1) the sin of ethnocentricism, (2) the sin of wrong perception (about the language attitudes of Britain versus those of the US), (3) the sin of not recognizing the non-native varieties of English as culture-bound codes of communication, (4) the sin of ignoring the systemicness of the non-native varieties of English, (5) the sin of ignoring linguistic interference and language dynamics, (6) the sin of overlooking the 'cline of Englishness' in language intelligibility, and (7) the sin of exhibiting language colonialism. For Kachru, it was important to recognize that, internationally, the choice of functions, uses, and models of English had to be determined on a pragmatic basis, in tune with local conditions and needs, suggesting that Prator needed to jettison 'linguistic chauvinism' in favor of 'linguistic tolerance', and recognize that international varieties of English contribute to "the linguistic mosaic which the speakers of the English language have created in the English-speaking world" (Kachru, 1976, p. 236).

378   *Kingsley Bolton*

Two years after publishing this response to Prator (1950), Braj Kachru collaborated with Larry Smith in arranging two key conferences devoted to WE and English as an international language. In 1985, Braj Kachru and Larry Smith began editing the *World Englishes* journal, and, in doing so, facilitated a major paradigm shift in English-language studies. Around the same time, Braj Kachru started to propose a model of WE that distinguished between the 'Three Circles' of Englishes, namely, the Inner Circle (countries where English is the 'first language' of a majority of the population, for example, the UK, US, Canada, Australia, and New Zealand), the Outer Circle (where English was regarded as a 'second language', for example, India and the Philippines), and the Expanding Circle (where English has typically had the status of a 'foreign language', for example, China and Japan). The Three Circles model was explicitly formulated by Kachru as a challenge to the previously dominant tripartite distinction between 'English as a native language' (ENL), 'English as a second language' (ESL), and 'English as a foreign language' (EFL). Braj Kachru's Three Circles model has proved resilient for a number of reasons, but not least because it set out to replace the somewhat discriminatory and misleading dichotomy between 'native' and 'non-native' Englishes (Kachru, 1985, 1992; Webster, 2015).

The genealogy of these distinctions is unclear, although references to the teaching of 'English as a second language' can be traced back to various initiatives by the British colonial government in 1870s (India Department of Education of India, 1872). A more recent and more plausible explanation for spread of this terminology, however, was the emergence of applied linguistics as a discipline in the American context during and after World War Two. Key figures here were Charles Carpenter Fries (1887–1967) and Clifford Prator (1911–1993). Charles Fries was responsible for founding the English Language Institute of the University of Michigan, and was also active in establishing the Linguistic Society of America (Marckwardt, 1968). Clifford Prator, for his part, joined UCLA in 1949, where he set up various programs in ESL and applied linguistics (Campbell & Celce-Murcia, 1993). Braj Kachru's turn in proposing the Three Circles model thus challenged the applied linguistics orthodoxy of the day, which previously had been strongly invested in a 'native' versus 'non-native' (first versus second) discourse on language acquisition and language teaching. The Kachruvian model provides a way out of these conceptual blinkers, allowing for an escape from what was (and remains) the trap of a monolingual mindset. It is therefore ironic that many recently published scholars, typically but not always from Europe, seem very keen on retaining such terms as 'native' and 'non-native', and discussing 'first-language' (L1) versus 'second-language' (L2) varieties of English rather than utilizing the Three Circles terminology. Such scholars appear not to realize that such discourse suggests the bias of a viewpoint shaped by a Western European 'monolingual' environment, unaware that many people elsewhere in the world grow up in complex linguistic contexts where multilingual acquisition is the norm rather than the exception.

Philippine English Studies Past, Present, and Future

PhE studies might, in some senses, be traced back to the Prator report of 1950, or even to much earlier reports of the American colonial period, including the so-called Monroe report of 1925 (Board of Educational Survey, 1925). However, modern PhE studies are generally thought to begin with the publication of Llamzon's (1969) *Standard Filipino English*, which has been justly founding text in this area. Later in the 1980s and 1990s, various other scholars joined Llamzon in exploring this topic, including such linguists as Br. Andrew Gonzalez, Emy Pascasio, and Bonifacio Sibayan. Professor Bautista was a leading light within this group of researchers and her work at this time included studies of sub-varieties of PhE, Philippine English lexis, standard PhE, as well as English corpus linguistics (Bautista, 1982, 1996a, 1997a, 1997b, 2000a, 2000b, 2000c, 2001a, 2001b, 2001c). Her research interests were not narrowly confined to English, but also included many aspects of Philippine sociolinguistics (Bautista, 1996b; Bautista & Tan, 1999; Gonzalez & Bautista, 1981, 1986). She also published a ground-breaking body of work on code-switching and code-mixing (Bautista, 1975, 1980, 1986, 1991, 1995, 1998a, 1998b, 1999).

One strong similarity between Professor Bautista's approach to WE and PhE and that of Professor Braj B. Kachru was that they both aimed to shift attitudes to Asian Englishes, away from complaint, as exemplified by Prator (1950), toward tolerance, description, and analysis. To some extent, at least, a number of the linguistic battles of the 1980s and 1990s have been won, in the sense that, today, there is a far greater acceptance of a pluralistic approach to Asian Englishes and WE than there ever was in the past. PhE studies have also continued to develop, and it is encouraging to see the diversity of approaches included in this present volume. These include chapters on aspects of globalization, language attitudes, language policy, learning and teaching, lexicography, linguistic structure, multilingualism, and sociolinguistic variation. A number of these chapters may point the way to future research in the field, although personally I would hazard that one of the most important areas for future research will be multilingualism. Across the Asian region, it now seems very clear that the status and functions of English in all societies in the region is everywhere influenced and shaped by their multilingual ecologies, which is certainly the case in the Philippines, where linguists have identified more than 180 different languages (Bolton, Botha, & Kirkpatrick, 2020). In recent years, Filipino educators have set out to promote 'mother-tongue based multilingual education' (MTB-MLE), but, although some educational work has been done in this area, it seems that much more needs to be done in the field of linguistic description and language documentation. In conversation some 20 years ago, Br. Andrew Gonzalez related regretfully how difficult it was to find and fund students interested in carrying out research on Philippine languages and linguistics. Today, judging by the relative scarcity of studies in this area, it is obvious that the situation has changed for the better.

380 *Kingsley Bolton*

Conclusion

As I noted at the beginning of this chapter, my interest in Philippine linguistics was kindled as a lone traveler during the era of the Marcos dictatorship. Since then I have spent time in the Philippines on many occasions, and I have also had the opportunity of working with a number of Philippine scholars. It was therefore very gratifying to receive an invitation from Ariane Borlongan for me to write an epilogue for a volume honoring Professor Bautista's contribution to Philippine language and linguistics. Professor Bautista's knowledge of these fields is exemplary, and her work from the 1980s to the present has been crucially influential for many scholars, including me. Ariane Borlongan should be commended for bringing together an impressive resource on PhE. It is especially heartening that many of the chapters explicitly acknowledge Professor Bautista's contribution to the Philippine studies and to the international academic community, both as an outstanding scholar and, at a personal level, as a generous and warm-hearted lady, known to most of her colleagues and friends simply as 'Tish'.

References

Bautista, Ma. L. S. (1975). A model of bilingual competence based on an analysis of Tagalog-English code-switching. *Philippine Journal of Linguistics, 8*, 51–89.

Bautista, Ma. L. S. (1980). *The Filipino bilingual's competence: A model based on an analysis of Tagalog-English code-switching.* Canberra: The Australian National University.

Bautista, Ma. L. S. (1982). *Yaya* English. *Philippine Studies, 30*, 377–394.

Bautista, Ma. L. S. (1986). English-Pilipino contact: A case study of reciprocal borrowing. In W. Viereck & W-D. Bald (Eds.), *English in contact with other languages: Studies in honour of Broder Carstensen on the occasion of his 60th birthday* (pp. 491–510). Budapest: Akademiai Kiado.

Bautista, Ma. L. S. (1991). Code-switching studies in the Philippines. *International Journal of the Sociology of Language, 88*, 19–32.

Bautista, Ma. L. S. (1995). Tagalog-English code-switching revisited. *Philippine Journal of Linguistics, 21*(2), 15–29.

Bautista, Ma. L. S. (1996a). Notes on three sub-varieties of Philippine English. In Ma. L. S. Bautista (Ed.), *Readings in Philippine sociolinguistics* (pp. 93–101). Manila: De La Salle University.

Bautista, Ma. L. S. (Ed.). (1996b). *Readings in Philippine sociolinguistics* (2nd ed.). Manila: De La Salle University Press.

Bautista, Ma. L. S. (1997a). The lexicon of Philippine English. In Ma. L. S. Bautista (Ed.), *English is an Asian language: The Philippine context* (pp. 49–72). Sydney: The Macquarie Library Pty., Ltd.

Bautista, Ma. L. S. (Ed.). (1997b). *English is an Asian language: The Philippine context.* Sydney: The Macquarie Library Pty., Ltd.

Bautista, Ma. L. S. (1998a). Another look at Tagalog-English code-switching. In Ma. L. S. Bautista (Ed.), *Pagtanaw: Essays on language in honor of Teodoro A. Llamzon* (pp. 128–146). Manila: Linguistic Society of the Philippines.

Bautista, Ma. L. S. (1998b). Tagalog-English code-switching and the lexicon of Philippine English. *Asian Englishes, 1*(1), 51–67.

Bautista, Ma. L. S. (1999). An analysis of the functions of Tagalog-English code-switching: Data from one case. In Ma. L. S. Bautista & G. O. Tan (Eds.), *The Filipino bilingual: A multidisciplinary perspective (Festschrift in honor of Emy M. Pascasio)* (pp. 19–31). Manila: Linguistic Society of the Philippines.

Bautista, Ma. L. S. (2000a). *Defining standard Philippine English: Its status and grammatical features*. Manila: De La Salle University Press.

Bautista, Ma. L. S. (2000b). Studies of Philippine English in the Philippines. *Philippine Journal of Linguistics, 31*, 39–65.

Bautista, Ma. L. S. (2000c). The grammatical features of educated Philippine English. In Ma. L. S. Bautista, T. A. Llamzon, & B. P. Sibayan (Eds.), *Parangal cang Brother Andrew: Festschrift for Andrew Gonzalez on his sixtieth birthday* (pp. 146–158). Manila: Linguistic Society of the Philippines.

Bautista, Ma. L. S. (2001a). Attitudes of English language faculty in three leading Philippine universities towards Philippine English. *Asian Englishes, 4*(1), 4–32.

Bautista, Ma. L. S. (2001b). Attitudes of selected Luzon University students and faculty towards Philippine English. In Ma. L. G. Tayao et al. (Eds.), *Rosario E. Maminta in focus: Selected writings in applied linguistics* (pp. 236–273). Quezon City: Philippine Association for Language Teaching.

Bautista, Ma. L. S. (2001c). Introducing the Philippine component of the International Corpus of English. In E. C. Bala et al. (Eds.), *Parangal sa Philippine Normal University: Festschrift for Philippine Normal University on its 100th foundation anniversary* (pp. 341–351). Manila: Philippine Normal University.

Bautista, Ma. L. S. (2004). Researching English in the Philippines: Bibliographical resources. *World Englishes, 23*, 199–210.

Bautista, Ma. L. S., & Bolton, K. (2008). *Philippine English: Linguistic and literary*. Hong Kong: Hong Kong University Press.

Bautista, Ma. L. S., & Tan, G. O. (Eds.). (1999). *The Filipino bilingual: A multidisciplinary perspective – Festschrift in honor of Emy M. Pascasio*. Manila: Linguistic Society of the Philippines.

Board of Educational Survey. (1925). *A survey of the educational system of the Philippine Islands by the Board of Educational Surveys*. Manila: Bureau of Printing.

Bolton, K., Botha, W., & Kirkpatrick, A. (2020). *The handbook of Asian Englishes*. Oxford: Wiley-Blackwell.

Campbell, R. N., & Celce-Murcia, M. (1993). Clifford H. Prator, English: Los Angeles. *Calisphere*. Retrieved from http://texts.cdlib.org/view?docId=hb0h4n99rb;-NAAN= 13030&doc.view=frames&chunk.id=div00064&toc.depth=1&toc.id=&brand=calisphere

Department of Education of India. (1872). *Translation of the report of the members of the select committee for the better diffusion and advancement of learning among the Muhammadans of India*. Benares: Medical Hall Press.

Gonzalez, A., FSC, & Bautista, Ma. L. S. (Eds.). (1981). *Aspects of language planning and development in the Philippines*. Manila: Linguistic Society of the Philippines.

Gonzalez, A., FSC, & Bautista, Ma. L. S. (1986). *Language surveys in the Philippines (1966–1984)*. Manila: De La Salle University Press.

Halliday, M., MacIntosh, A., & Strevens, P. (1964). *The linguistic sciences and language teaching*. London: Longmans, Green and Co.

382 *Kingsley Bolton*

Kachru, B. B. (1976). Models of English for the Third World: White man's linguistic burden or language pragmatics? *TESOL Quarterly, 10*(2), 21–39.

Kachru, B. B. (1985). Standards, codification and sociolinguistic realism: The English language in the Outer Circle. In R. Quirk & H. G. Widdowson (Eds.), *English in the world: Teaching and learning the language and literature* (pp. 11–30). Cambridge: Cambridge University Press.

Kachru, B. B. (1992). World Englishes: Approaches, issues and resources. *Language Teaching, 25*, 1–14.

Llamzon, T. A. (1969). *Standard Filipino English*. Quezon City: Ateneo de Manila University Press.

Marckwardt, A. H. (1968). Charles C. Fries. *Language, 44*(1), 205–210.

Prator, C. H. (1950). *Language teaching in the Philippines*. Manila: US Educational Foundation in the Philippines. Report.

Prator, C. H. (1968). The British heresy in TESL. In J. A. Fishman, C. A. Ferguson, & J. Das Gupta (Eds.), *Language problems in developing nations* (pp. 459–476). New York: John Wiley & Sons.

Webster, J. J. (Ed.). (2015). *Collected works of Braj B. Kachru* (Vols I–III). London: Bloomsbury.

Index

Note: **Bold** page numbers refer to tables; *italic* page numbers refer to figures.

Abad, Gemino 3, 201
Abrams, S. S. 318
Accenture Group 340
acoustic analyses: of consonants 63–66; of vowels 51–61
acquisition and learning 271–281; case study 277–279; child language acquisition research 271–276; children's acquisition of English 279–281
acrolectal PhE 130
acronyms: and digital writing 318; Internet Philippine English 320
adjectival suffixes *-y* and *-ish* 81–82, **82**
adjectives 93
adverbs 93
Aegis Global 341
/æ/ vowel 50, **50**
affect indicating phrases (AIPs) 105
affixation: and encoding of meaning 189; Internet Philippine English 320–321
Alatis, James E. 213
Albela, E. J. A. 355–357
Alberca, Wilfredo L. 14–15
Algeo, John 143, 150
Amarles, Arceli M. 249
American colonization 260; American military 12; and educational policy 260–262; and English 260–262; expansion 11–12; and Philippines English language use 10–11
American English (AmE) 126–127, 135, 297, 299; adherence to 306; beginning of differentiation in 13; choices per categories, corpora, and varieties **148**; endonormative stabilization 12; *get*-passives 91; pedagogical acceptability

test of 306; and Philippine English (PhE) 16, 143–152; PVI of *68*; structural similarities with PhE 145–152; *t*-test results between PhE **68**
American English 2006 Corpus (AE06) 139
American-plus-Filipino identities 13–14
American spelling 114, 117–119
Ansary, Hasan 102
Anthony, E. M. 285
Anton, J. 350
Anvil-Macquarie Dictionary of Philippine English for High School (Bautista and Butler) 28, 190, 192, 202
Aquino, Benigno, Jr. 20
Aquino, Corazon 21
Aquino, Milagraos R. 222
Arguilla, Manuel E. 210
Asian Englishes 106
Asian permanent migration 331
aspect 88–91
Association of Southeast Asian Nations (ASEAN) 223, 227, 228
Asuncion, Zayda S. 250
Ateneo de Manila University 27
attitudes: in relation to dynamic model 234–236; toward English in Philippines 231–232; toward Philippine English 231–236
Australian Corpus of English (ACE) 137
Australian English (AusE) 127, 136
Ayala, Jose V. 212

Babaii, Esmat 102
back-clipping 83
Bakhtin, M. M. 370
Balgos, Anne Richie G. 103

384   *Index*

Bamboo and the Greenwood Tree
   (Bernad) 212
Bamgbose, Ayo 42
Bargirl English 129
Barrios, A. L. 276
Bates, E. 277
BATH vowel 50–51; in American
   English (AmE) 51; in British English
   (BrE) 51; for male and female
   speakers 59, *60*
Batstone, R. 290
Bautista, Cirilo F. 213
Bautista, Ma. Lourdes S. 4, 5–7, 27–28,
   94, 143, 165, 190, 200, 202, 203, 232,
   246; ICE-PH 161; modality in PhE
   92; and Philippine English 41–43; on
   subject-verb concord 95
B-Brown corpus (B-Brown) 138–139
Before-LOB Corpus (B-LOB) 138–139
Bell Trade Relations Act 18
Bernad, Miguel A. 212–213, 215
Bernardo, A. B. I. 204, 234, 272, 276,
   288, 293
Bernardo, Alejandro S. 28, 248, 306
Bernardo, Allan 272
bibliography, PhE 29
Bickerton, Derek 157
Bienvenido Santos 373
Biermeier, Thomas 74–75
Bilingual education policy: implemented
   in 262; and marketization of
   Philippine labor 262–263
blending, and Internet Philippine
   English 321
Bodomo, A. B. 320
Bolton, Kingsley 41, 190, 193, 234
Borlongan, Ariane M. 4–5, 10, 16, 23,
   27, 41, 87, 109, 128, 200, 203, 234,
   247, 250, 297, 300, 380; conyo English
   129; Phil-Brown corpus 145; on post-
   Event X incidents 18; on tag questions
   in PhE 95; on tense and aspect (PhE
   grammar) 89–90
borrowing 170; defined 163; hybrids with
   171–173; in PhE 163–165
British Council 358
British English (BrE) 126–127, 135, 204,
   297, 302; *get*-passives 91; Inner Circle
   Englishes 73
British English 2006 Corpus (BE06) 139
The British Heresy in TESL 376
British National Corpus (BNC) 75,
   95, 115

British Raj 368
British spelling 114, 117–119
Brown, R. 364
Brown corpus 116, 136–138
Brown Heritage 212
Brown University Standard Corpus of
   Present-Day American English 136
Brylko, Arina 105
Bugayong, Lenny Kaye 247
Bush, George W. 19
Business Process Outsourcing (BPO) 340
business writing 110
Butler, Susan 190, 193, 202, 234

call centers: Philippine English and
   cross-cultural communication in
   341–342; test call center corpusa **342**;
   US-owned 342
Camaioni, L. 277
Canadian English (CanE) 73
Caparas, P. 319
capped expressions, and non-
   capitalization 322–323
Catford, John C. 221
Cebuano 175–176
Certificate in Teaching English to
   Speakers of Other Languages
   (CELTA) 358
CFI Group 350
Chabacano 176
child language acquisition research post-
   1986 271–276
Choe, H. 357–358
Choy, Catherine C. 331
classroom: -based assessments 297,
   299–300; 'noticing language' 290–291;
   realizing Philippine English in
   306–307
clippings 83; back-clipping 83; fore-
   clipping 83; mid-clipping 83
code alteration (CS) 324
code-switching 165–166, 170; hybrids
   with 173–176
codification: covert 203–204; efforts
   toward 202–204; as element of
   endonormative stabilization 206; overt
   203–204
coinage 322
Collins, Peter 92, 96, 128, 140
compounding 75–77
compound nouns **75**, 75–76
compounds, and Internet Philippine
   English 321

Index   385

computer-mediated communication 110
Concepcion, C. C. 275
consonants 61–66; acoustic analyses of
  63–66; cluster simplification 62, **63**;
  perceptual analyses of 61–63
Constantino, R. 261–262, 264
contractions, and Internet Philippine
  English 321
conversion 82–83
Conyo English/Englog 22, 129, 171–172
Cooper, Henry 13
corpora: and multilingual practice
  250–252; PhE 28–29
Corpus Linguistics 146
Corpus of Contemporary American
  English (COCA) 75, 115
Corpus of Global Web-Based English
  (GloWbE) 73, 75, 77, 113, 140,
  146–147
covert codification 203–204
cross-cultural communication: in call
  centers 341–342; in customer service 341
Cruz, Isagani R. 190, 202
Cruz, P. 249, 367–368
Cruz, S. A. 357
Crystal, D. 293, 317–318, 324–325
Culler, Jonathan 215
cultural borrowed forms 164
cultural diversity 21
cultural literacy 215
*Cultural politics of English as
  an International Language*
  (Pennycook) 260

/ɒ/–/ɔː/ vowel pair *56, 57,* 59
Davidson, F. 299
Davies, Mark 146
Dayag, Danilo 28, 41, 94, 100, 223, 246;
  on Asian Englishes 106; on written
  discourse in PhE 101–102
de Guzman, A. B. 355–357
De La Salle University 27
De Leon, K. D. 224–226, 355
De Los Reyes, Robert A. 248
de Nebrija, Antonio 188
Derwing, Tracy M. 221
*Diachronic Approaches to Modality in
  World Englishes* 135
diachronic change, PhE 116–119;
  findings 139–140; overview 135–136
dictionaries: Philippine English 190–192;
  in the Philippines 187–190; *see also
  specific dictionaries*

A Dictionary of Philippine English (Cruz
  and Bautista) 28, 190, 202
Differential Item Functioning (DIF) 298
Diksyunaryo ng Wikang Filipino 189
Dimaculangan, Nimfa G. 75, 233, 234
Dino, C. M. 319
Diploma in Teaching English to
  Speakers of Other Languages
  (DELTA) 358
Discourse Completion Test (DCT) 103
discourse studies: culture in Philippine
  English discourse 104–107; overview
  100; PhE in mass media 100–101;
  Philippine English (PhE) 100–110;
  Philippine English discourse *vs.*
  Filipino discourse 107; spoken
  discourse 103–104; written discourse
  101–103
Dita, S. N. 28, 41, 93, 222–223,
  224–226, 355
diversity: cultural 21; social 21
Donelan, James F., S.J. 211
Donovan, M. J. 318
Dorgu, E. T. 293
D'Souza, Jean 203
Duque, Luzviminda A. 222
Duterte, Rodrigo 18
dynamic model: attitudes in relation
  to 234–236; of the evolution of
  postcolonial Englishes 9–10, 22, 73

/ɛ/–/æ/ vowel pair 58
*East-West Center Conference on
  Language as Power: Cross-Cultural
  Dimensions of English in Media and
  Literature* 213–214
Educational Decree of 1868 11
educational policies and reforms: and
  American colonialism 260–262;
  and English 260–262; (mis)place of
  Philippine English in 308
Educational Testing Service (ETS) 301
Einstein, Albert 216
*Electronic World Atlas of Varieties of
  English* (Borlongan and Lim) 28
Electronic World Atlas of Varieties of
  English (eWAVE) 203
Eliot, T. S. 214
emoticons and symbols 323
enclitic particles 94
endocentric pedagogic approach
  287–288
endonormative model 199, 204–205

386 *Index*

English as a Foreign Language (EFL)
283; industry 358–359; rebranding, in
the Philippines 359–360
English as an International Language
(EIL) 301
English as a Second Language (ESL) 283
English as a World Language (EWL) 156
Englishes 42; Asian 106; Philippine 145;
World 42, 146
English language: and American
colonialism 260–262; children's
acquisition of 279–281;
colloquialization of 128; educational
policy 260–262; endocentric pedagogic
approach for teaching 287–288;
hybrid varieties of 171–179; as
important language in Philippines
13, 17; migration and history of
328–330; and permanent migration
330–332; Philippine English in general
dictionaries of 192–195; in Philippines
3; and temporary labor migration
332–335; use in Philippines before
American colonization 10–11
English Language Institute of the
University of Michigan 378
English language teaching (ELT):
curriculum, and English teacher 293;
EFL industry 358–359; immersion in
Philippine English 356–357; low cost
353–354; pedagogical factors 354–356;
rebranding EFL 359–360; Taglish 356;
teachers' qualifications 357–358
English teacher: and ELT curriculum
293; world's budget 359; *see also*
teachers
Enriquez, Ma. Althea 161
Escalante, Rene R. 12
ethno-geographic Englishes 179
Ethnologue 246
Event X 18

Facebook 194
Ferrer, J. B. F. 355–357
Filipino Digitalk 317, 319
Filipino English Mini-Dictionary 190
Filipino language 172
Filipino nationalism 19
Filipino-plus-American identities 13–14
Filipinos: understanding and speaking
English 3; use of enclitic particles 94
First Filipino Writers' Conference on
Modern Literary Objectives 210

*First National Consultative Conference
on Literary Theories* 214
First Philippine Commission 11
Firth, L. 319
Fletcher, P. 279
Florentino, Alberto S. 210
fore-clipping 83
Francis, W. Nelson 136
Freer, William B. 190
Freiburg Brown Corpus (Frown) 136
Freiburg Lancaster-Oslo/Bergen Corpus
(F-LOB) 136
Fries, Charles Carpenter 378
Friginal, E. 343
Fuchs, Robert 115–116
full and reduced vowels (F/RV) 67
full vowels (FV) 67

Garvida, Mignette Marcos 129–130
General American English (GAE) 13,
204, 206, 225
Genuino, Cecilia. F. 104
globalization 228, 231, 245, 262,
379; advent of 231; early 328;
inexorable 302
Gonçalves, B. 114–115
Gonzales, Sydney D. 104
Gonzales, Wilkinson Daniel Wong 10,
22, 145
Gonzalez, Andrew 4, 28, 41, 101, 126,
165, 200, 201, 203, 216, 232, 246, 247,
271, 275, 276, 374, 375, 379
Google Books Corpus of Davies 115
grammar of PhE 87–97; adjectives and
adverbs 93; morphology 88; negation
95; noun phrase 92–93; particles
94–95; prepositions 94; relativizers
96; subject-verb concord 95–96; tag
questions 95; tense and aspect 88–91;
verbs 88–96; voice 91–92
*Grammatical Change in English World-
Wide* (Nöel) 135
Graphic 211
Greenbaum, Sidney 93, 146
Gustilo, L. E. 75, 105, 106, 234, 319

Halliday, Michael 102, 375–376
hard-to-reach groups 131
Hasan, Ruqaiya 102
Hashim, A. 318
Hassan, N. 318
Haugen, Einar 163, 202, 206–207
Heller, Monica 253

Hickey, Raymond 201, 203
Hidalgo, Cesar A. 4, 188, 201
Hiligaynon 179, 188
Hoffmann, Sebastian 95
Hokkien-Lánnang-uè-Tagalog-Filipino-
    English code-switching 174–175
Hollington, A. 318
Hong Kong English (HKE) 76, 92
Honna, Nobuyuki 42
Hundt, Marianne 96, 127, 200
Hung, Tony T.N. 224–225
Hunston, Susan 4
hybridization: defined 170; hybrid
    varieties of English and Philippine
    languages 171–179; and indigenous
    vocabulary 77–78; linguistic 170–181
Hyland, Ken 102

/iː/–/ɪ/ vowel pair 52–55, 52–58
IATEFL 358
Ibero-Romance language 13
ICEF Monitor 353, 356
ideology, and Philippine English 233–234
Iliad 216
illocutionary force indicating devices
    (IFIDs) 105
Ilocano 11, 188, 247, 250, 373, 375
immersion, in Philippine English 356–357
Indian English (IndE) 92, 126, 136, 149
indigenous vocabulary 77–78
inequalities of multilingualism 261
Inner Circle Englishes 73; Canadian
    English (CanE) 73
Institute of National Language 17
intelligibility *see* PhE intelligibility
internal variation: postcolonial Englishes
    125–132; regional variation 128–129;
    sociolectal variation 129–130; stylistic
    variation 126–128
International Corpus of English 250
International Corpus of English (ICE)
    28, 42, 146
International Corpus of English
    (ICE-PH) 6, 135, 161, 200
International English Language Testing
    System (IELTS) 297, 298
International Phonetic Association
    (IPA) 50
International Testing Commission
    (ITC) 301
Internet 317–325; Internet language
    317–319; linguistic features of Internet
    Philippine English 320–324

Internet Philippine English (IPhE) 323;
    acronyms 320; affixation 320–321;
    blending 321; capped expressions
    and non-capitalization 322–323; code
    alteration (CS) 324; coinage 322;
    compounds 321; contractions 321;
    emoticons and symbols 323; linguistic
    features of 320–324; non-standard
    use/new usage of punctuation
    323–324; puns or wordplay 322; rebus
    forms 322; reduced or non-sentence
    structures 324; reduplication of letters
    and words 323; transcription of sigh,
    laughter, and other actions 322
Isabella II, Queen of Spain 11

Jambalos, Thelma V. 200
Jamora, Michael John A. 248
Jazul, Maria Eina Maxine A. 248
Jenkins, J. 227, 284
Jespersen, Otto 244
Joaquin, Nick 212, 373
Jose, F. Sionil 373
Journal of English Linguistics 135

K-12 English curriculum 308–309
Kachru, Braj B. 21, 42, 158, 201, 231,
    305, 375, 377–378
Kachru, Yamuna 375
Kaciroti, N. 279
Katic, E. 318
Kaufman, Terrence 156, 159
Kelly, T. 319
Kenworthy, Joanne 221
Khan, F. A. 369
Kirkpatrick, A. 41, 288
Kobayashi, I. 354, 355, 357
koinéization 13
Kolhapur Corpus of Indian English
    136–137
Komisyon ng Wikang Filipino
    (Commission on the Filipino
    Language) 189
Kortmann, Bernd 203
Kučera, Henry 136

Lalunio, L. 274
Lancaster-Oslo/Bergen Corpus (LOB)
    116, 136
Language and Nationalism (Gonzalez) 216
Language and the Internet (Crystal) 317
Language Bioprogram Hypothesis
    (LBH) 157

388 *Index*

language contact 170; and language creation 157–159; language maintenance 163–166; and language shift 159–163; overview 156; types of contact situation 156–157
language creation 157–159; approaches to 157–158; New Englishes 158–159; Substrate approach 157; Superstratist approach 157; Taglish explored as 159; Universalist approach 157–158
language maintenance 163–166
language policy 257–265; bilingual, and marketization of labor 262–263; English, educational policy, and American colonialism 260–262; and making of unequal Englishes 257–258; and unequal Englishes 260–265; unequal Englishes as *lived* experience 258–260
language shift 159–163
language teaching 283–294; approaches 285–287; differentiation and constructive alignment 285–287; endocentric pedagogic approach for 287–288; English teacher and ELT curriculum 293; methods and techniques 285–287; 'noticing a variety' technique 290–291; Philippine English-Aware Method for Teaching English 288–290
Language Teaching in the Philippines (Prator) 375
language testing 297–303; directions for assessment in PhE 302; local classroom-based assessment 299–300; standardized tests 300–302; testing with focus on norms 298–299
Lánnang-uè 172–173
Lee, Aldrin P. 189
Lee, P. 363
Leech, Geoffrey 200
Lenneberg, E. 364
letters, reduplication of 323
lexical properties/lexicon: clippings 83; compounding 75–77; conversion 82–83; hybridization and indigenous vocabulary 77–78; of Lánnang-uè 172; PhE and AmE 149–150; of Philippine English (PhE) 73–84; suffixation 78–82
lexical stress 66, **66**
lexicography 187–196; dictionaries in Philippines 187–190; ideal dictionary

of PhE 195–196; Philippine English dictionaries 190–192; Philippine English in General Dictionaries of English 192–195
Liang, W. 279
Lim, Joo Hyuk 203, 247, 250, 300
Linangan ng Wika sa Pilipinas (Institute of Philippine Languages) 189
linguistic environment/features: of Internet Philippine English 320–324; PhE intelligibility 225
Linguistics and Language Education in the Philippines and Beyond: A Festschrift in Honour of Ma. Lourdes S. Bautista 41
linguistic sketches and descriptions 199–200
Linguistic Society of America 378
Linguistics Society of the Philippines (LSP) 27, 41
Lising, Jenifer Loy 28
listener, and PhE intelligibility 224–225
"literary competence" 215
Literature and Society: A Symposium on the Relation of Literature to Society (Lopez) 210–211
Literature under the Commonwealth 210
Litiatco, Alfredo E. 211
lived experience and unequal Englishes 258–260
Llamzon, Teodoro A. 4, 27, 39, 100–101, 128–129, 199–200, 375, 379
local classroom-based assessment 299–300
Longman Spoken American Corpus (LSAC) 95
Lopez, Salvador P. 211
LOT vowels 51
Loureiro-Porto, L. 114–115
Lucas, R. I. G. 272, 274, 280
Lunkenheimer, Kerstin 203

Mabini, Apolinario 329
MacIntosh, Angus 376
Macmillan Dictionary 195
Macquarie Asian corpus 74
The Macquarie Dictionary: Australia's National Dictionary (Delbridge) 28, 164, 202
Madrunio, Marilu R. 28, 41, 250, 306
Magellan, Ferdinand 187
Magno, Joseleanor M. 248
Magpantay, E. 319

Index   389

Mahboob, Ahmar 249, 367
Maher, John C. 242, 245
Mair, Christian 200, 202
Malimas, Mary Ann P. 248
Manila Lannang English (MLE) 178
Maranan, Edgar B. 213
Marasigan, Elizabeth 159
Marcos, Ferdinand 20–21, 262, 332
marketization of Philippine labor
   262–263
Martin, Isabel P. 10, 21, 28, 131, 144,
   235, 246
mass media, and PhE 100–101
Matsuda, A. 293
Maxilom, R. M. 275, 280
McKaughan, Howard P. 129, 201
McKenzie, Robert M. 233, 234
McKinley, William 12, 13; on English as
   common medium of communication 14
McLean, T. 286
McWhorter, J. 364
Merriam-Webster's 74, 75, 187
mid-clipping 83
migration 327–335; Asian permanent
   331; and history of English in
   Philippines 328–330; permanent
   330–332; temporary labor 332–335
Military Bases Agreement 18
Minges, M. 319
Miraflores, E. 274
Morales, Miren M. 203
morphology 88
Mother Tongue-Based Multilingual
   Education (MTB-MLE) 248–249,
   265, 379
Mufwene, Salikoko 157, 158
multilingual ecology of the Philippines
   246–250
multilingualism 242–253; examples from
   ICE-PHI data 251–252; multilingual
   ecology of the Philippines 246–250;
   multilingual practice in corpora
   250–252; phenomenon of 242–243;
   researching multilingual practices
   252–253; varied meanings of 243–246
multilingual practices: acceptability of
   250; in corpora 250–252; negative
   views toward 245; researching 252–253
Munro, Murray J. 221
Myers-Scotton, Carol 164, 166

naïve structuralism 215
Nassenstein, N. 318

National Achievement Test (NAT) 297
National Competency-based Teacher
   Standards (NCBTS) 309
National Institute of Education
   Spoken Corpus of English in Asia
   (NIESCEA) corpus 49
nationalism 21; Filipino 19
negation 95
Nelson, Cecil 42
Nelson, Gerald 93
Netspeak 317–318
New Englishes 157, 158–159; varieties
   160–161
New York Times 263
New Zealand English (NZE) 127, 136
Nieto, D. R. D. 355–357
Noli Me Tangere (Rizal) 366
Nolledo, Wilfrido 212
nominal suffix: *-ee* 80–81; *-ism* **79**, 79–80;
   -ness 80; *-ship* and *-hood* 78–79, **79**
nonce borrowings, in PhE 165
non-standard use/new usage of
   punctuation 323–324
'noticing a variety' technique 290–291
noun phrase 92–93

Older Englishes 160
online news galleries 110
orderly heterogeneity 130
Osborne, Dana M. 247
Osmeña, Sergio 18
"Our Literary Heritage" 211
Outer Circle English 288
outsourced call centers 340–350;
   linguistic dimensions of 343–344;
   method and focus 342–343; PhE and
   cross-cultural communication 341–
   342; politeness markers in interactions
   346–349; speech *vs.* narrative 345–346
outsourcing: customer service 340–341;
   defined 340; economic implications
   related to 342; political implications
   related to 342
Overseas Filipino Workers (OFWs) 231,
   327–328, 330, 332–333, 335
Overseas Workers Welfare
   Administration (OWWA) 333, 335
overt codification 203–204
Oxford English Dictionary (OED) 20,
   73–74, 75, 193, 203, 301; recently
   added PhE words to 194; "Webster
   Words" in 193
Ozaki, S. 354

390 *Index*

Pairwise Variability Index (PVI) 67, **67, 68**
Pakistani English 365, 368–369, 370
Pariña, J. C. M. 357
Parreñas, R. S. 263
particles 94–95
Pascasio, Emy 379
Pasion, Mario C. 233
Pavlenko, A. 364
pedagogy, and Philippine English 233–234
'Pencionados' 14
People Power Revolution 21
perceptual analyses: of consonants 61–63; of vowels 49–51
permanent migration: Asian 331; English and 330–332
PhE intelligibility 221–228; factors affecting 223–225; issues on 225–227; linguistic environment 225; listener factors 224–225; significance of 227–228; speaker factors 224; to speakers of other Englishes 222–223
phenomenon of multilingualism 242–243
Phil-Brown corpus 28, 136–137, 145; comparison of PhE Using **138**; composition of **138**
Philippine-American War of 1899–1902 260, 329
Philippine Center of International PEN 215
Philippine Commission on Higher Education (CHED) 305, **310–311**
Philippine component of the International Corpus of English (ICE-PHI) 87, 115, 135, 161
Philippine Constitution 260
Philippine Department of Tourism (DOT) 353, 359
Philippine English (PhE) 3, 187, 231–236; and AmE 16, 143–152; attitudes in relation to dynamic model 234–236; attitudes toward 232–234; attitudes toward English in the Philippines 231–232; British Heresy and World Englishes 376–377; circles of 21; conceptual model of standardization of *205,* 205–207; and cross-cultural communication in call centers 341–342; definition of 5; diachronic change 116–119; diachronic studies of 139–140; directions for language assessment in 302; discourses on 4;

discourse studies 100–110; education 227; endonormative stabilization (1946?–present?/1986?) 18–22; exonormative stabilization (1901–1935) 13–16; foundation (1898–1901) 11–13; in General Dictionaries of English 192–195; h lessons 374–376; ideal dictionary of 195–196; ideology and pedagogy 233–234; immersion in 356–357; -inspired pedagogical procedure 291–292; Kachruvian challenge to Prator 377–378; lexical development of early 16; lexical properties of 73–84; linguistic independence of 20; and Ma. Lourdes Bautista 41–43; morphological and syntactic restructuring 16; nativization (1935–1946?) 16–17; overview 231; past, present, and future 373–380; phonology 49–69; PVI of *68*; social change 365–368; speaker accent 232–233; standardization and codification 4–5; structural similarities with AmE 145–152; studies of 4–5, 379; testing with focus on appropriate norms 298–299; toward an ideal dictionary of 195–196; *t*-test results between AmE **68**; vowel inventory of **61**
Philippine English-Aware Method for Teaching English 288–290
Philippine English dictionaries 190–192
Philippine English discourse: culture in 104–107; *vs.* Filipino discourse 107
Philippine English: Linguistic and Literary Perspectives 374
Philippine Expanding Circle (PEC) 235
The Philippine Experiences of an American Teacher 190
Philippine Hybrid Hokkien 172–173
Philippine Independence Act 16
Philippine Inner Circle (PIC) 235
Philippine Journal of Linguistics (PJL) 104
Philippine Korean Learner English (PKLE) 177–178
Philippine labor, marketization of 262–263
Philippine Literature: A Twofold Renaissance (Bernad) 213
Philippine literature in English 210–217
"Philippine Literature: Perpetually Inchoate" 213
Philippine Normal University 27
Philippine Organic Act 13

Philippine Outer Circle (POC) 235
Philippine Overseas Employment
Administration (POEA) 333
Philippine Professional Standards for
Teachers (PPST) 305, 309
Philippines: American colonization
11–12, 260–262; attitudes toward
English in 231–232; bilingual
education policy 262–263;
development of national language 17;
dictionaries in 187–190; English and
educational policy 260–262; English
and permanent migration from
330–332; English and temporary labor
migration from 332–335; English
established as important language
13, 17; English in 3; independence
16–17; language policy and unequal
Englishes in 260–265; marketization
of labor 262–263; migration and
history of English in 328–330;
multilingual ecology of 246–250; post-
independence 18; rebranding EFL
in 359–360; self-independence 18;
unequal Englishes 263–265
Philippine Writers League 211
phonology: consonants 61–66;
Philippine English (PhE) 49–69;
vowels 49–61
Pigafetta, Antonio 187
Pilipino loan words in English 192
Piller, Ingrid 243–246
Pimentel, Salaverga B. 222
Plata, S. M. 308, 310
politeness markers, in call center
interactions 346–349
Poplack, Shana 166
postcolonial Englishes 9, 87, 119, 125
pragmatic development 277
Prator, Clifford 375, 376–378
prepositions 94
progressive passives 91
Pulido, Dennis H. 102
punctuation: non-standard use/new
usage of 323–324; in Philippine
English, empirical evidence on
114–116; variations in 116
puns/wordplay 322

Quezon, Manuel L. 16, 210–211
Quinto, E. J. M. 307

Rafiqzad, Khalilullah 223, 226, 355
Rajagopalan, Kanavallil 226

Ramasco, J. J. 114–115
Rañosa-Madrunio, M. 105, 106
rebranding, EFL in Philippines 359–360
rebus forms 322
rebus writing 322
Recto, Claro 18
reduced/non-sentence structures 324
reduced vowels 49–50, **50**
reduplication: of letters 323; of
words 323
reference Englishes 135
reference works 29–39; *Anvil-Macquarie
Philippine English dictionary* (Bautista
and Butler) 28; *A Dictionary of
Philippine English* (Cruz and Bautista)
28; *Electronic World Atlas of Varieties
of English* (Borlongan and Lim) 28;
*The Macquarie Dictionary: Australia's
National Dictionary* (Delbridge) 28; on
PhE 28
regional variation 128–129
relativizers 96
residual linguistic conservatism 206
Revised Bachelor of Science in
Education, Major in English
Curriculum program 309–310,
310–311
Reyes-Wandless, M. 274
rhoticity 63, **65,** 65–66
rhythmic patterning **67,** 67–68, **68**
Richards, C. 285, 286
Rizal, Jose 11, 217, 329
Rodgers, T. 285, 286
Rojas, Jose T. 222
Rojo-Laurilla, Mildred A. 107
Romero, Ma. Corona S. 200
Romulo, Carlos P. 211
Roosevelt, Theodore 245
Rosario, Jr, Francisco C. 249
Rotor, Arturo B. 211

Sánchez, D. 114–115
San Juan, Epifanio, Jr. 213
San Miguel, Janina 258–260
Santos, R. N. 355–357
Sapir-Whorf hypothesis (SWH)
363–364, 370
Schneider, Edgar W. 9, 13, 42, 87,
202, 234, 248, 250; dynamic model
of the evolution of postcolonial
Englishes 9–10, 22, 73, 109, 144;
on endonormative stabilization 18;
internal variation 125; modality in
PhE 92; on PhE and AmE 145; on

392 Index

PhE in nativization phase 10; on PhE phases 13
Schurman, Jacob 11
Second Language Acquisition (SLA) 156, 158
Second World War 189
semantic concepts 76
"servants of globalization" 259, 263
Setting, T. 350
Sibayan, Bonifacio 27, 379
Singapore English (SgE) 50, 92, 126–127, 149; formation of 158; PVI of 68
Smith, Larry E. 42, 221, 223, 226, 355, 375, 378
Smith, Nicholas 200
Sobolewski, Frank Andrew 165
social change: Pakistani English 368–369; Philippine English 365–368; World Englishes and 363–370
social diversity 21
sociolect, defined 130
sociolectal variation 129–130
Southeast Asian Ministers of Education Organization (SEAMEO) 204
Spanish-American war 12
Spanish language: *vs.* English language in Philippines 14–15; use in Philippines 11
speaker: accent, and Philippine English 232–233; of other Englishes 222–223; PhE intelligibility 224
spelling: American 114; British 114; *indigenes* 113; *indigenous* 113; in Philippine English, empirical evidence on 114–116; standards used in Englishes 113
standard American English (AmE) 4
standard Filipino English 17
Standard Filipino English (Llamzon) 4, 379
standardization of Philippine English *205,* 205–207
standardized tests 300–302
Standard PhE 4, 27
Standard Philippine English (SPhE) 199–207; aim and outline 199; conceptual model *205,* 205–207; defined 205; efforts toward codification 202–204; endonormative model for language teaching 204–205; existence of standardized variety 200–202; linguistic sketches and descriptions 199–200
Strevens, Peter 375, 376

stylistic variation 126–128
Suárez-Gómez, Cristina 96, 128
subject-verb concord 95–96
Substrate approach, to language creation 157
substrate-influenced hybridized Englishes 176–179
substratum influence 171
suffixation 78–82; adjectival suffixes *-y* and *-ish* 81–82, **82**; nominal suffix *-ee* 80–81; nominal suffixes *-ship* and *-hood* 78–79, **79**; nominal suffix *–ism* **79,** 79–80; nominal suffix *-ness* 80
Superstratist approach, to language creation 157
suprasegmental features in PhE: lexical stress 66, **66**; rhythmic patterning **67,** 67–68, **68**
Survey of Child Language Studies from 1986 to Present **273**
synthetic compounds 76

Taft, William 13
Tagalog 188, 200, 211–217, 222, 233, 246–247, 250–252, 260, 264, 271, 275, 276, 324, 330
Tagalog English *see* Taglish
Tagalog-English code-switching 165
Tagalog-Filipino-English code-switching 173–174
Taglish 159, 356; in stable bilingualism 165–166
tag questions 95
Taishanese 175
Tajolosa, Teresita D. 250
Tao, L. 274
Tardif, T. 279
teacher education 305–312; K-12 English curriculum 308–309; PhE and educational policies and reforms 308; Philippine English in classroom 306–307; Philippine Professional Standards for Teachers (PPST) 309; Revised Bachelor of Science in Education, Major in English Curriculum program 309–310, **310–311**
teachers: English language teaching (ELT) 357–358; qualifications 357–358
Technical Education and Skills Development Authority (TESDA) 333–335
temporary labor migration 332–335; English and 332–335

Index 393

tense 88–91
TESOL Core-Certificate Program 358
TESOL International Association 358
Test of English as a Foreign Language
    (TOEFL) 297, 298
Thomasites 14–15, 143–144
Thomason, Sarah Grey 156, 157,
    159, 160
Thompson, Roger M. 232
THOUGHT vowels 51
Thumboo, Edwin 42
Tokyo University of Foreign Studies 27
Tollefson, James W. 259, 333
Tomlinson, B. 298
Tottie, Gunnel 95, 150
Toulmin, S. E. 101
transcription: of laughter 322; of other
    physical actions 322; of sigh 322
TRAP vowel: for male and female
    speakers 59, *60*
Treaty of Paris 12
Tse, Polly 102
Tucker, Richard G. 222
Turano, Charity T. 248
Turner, K. H. 318
Twitter 115, 194, 318, 320
Tydings-McDuffie Act 16; *see also*
    Philippine Independence Act
Tydings Rehabilitation Act 18
Tyner, J. A. 263

unequal Englishes 263–265; as *lived*
    experience 258–260; role of language
    policy in making of 257–258
Universalist approach, to language
    creation 157–158
University of Santo Tomas 27
UP Diksiyonaryong Filipino (UPDF) 189
/ʊ/–/uː/ vowel pair *57, 58, 59*

*Varieties of English and Their
    Implications for Language Teaching in
    Southeast Asia* 204, 284–285
Velasco, Y. P. 307
verbs 88–96
Verheijen, L. 318

Villanueva, Rey John Castro 22
Visayan languages 11, 188
voice 91–92; modality 92
voiceless stops 63
Voice Onset Time (VOT) 63, 64, **65**
Volterra, V. 277
vowels 49–61; acoustic analyses of
    51–61; perceptual analyses of 49–51
/ʌ/–/ɑː/ vowel pair *55, 56, 58*–59

*Webster's New International Dictionary
    of the English Language* 193; "Webster
    Words" in 193
*Webster's Third New International
    Dictionary of the English
    Language* 193
Webster's Third Unabridged 193
Wellington Corpus of Written New
    Zealand English (WCWNZE) 137
Wells, J. C. 50–51
White, M. 344
Whorf, B. 363–364
"Will Filipino Literature in English
    Endure?" 211
Wolf Passage 49–50, **51**, 61–63, **62**
Wong, May L.-Y. 95
words, reduplication of 323
World Bank 340
World Englishes 42, 146; British Heresy
    and 376–377; descriptions of 364;
    research 265, 286–287; and social
    change 363–370
*World Englishes: Journal of English as
    an International and Intra-national
    Language* 213, 374, 376, 378
Writers Union of the Philippines 215

Xin, J. 272

Yabes, Leopoldo 216
Yao, Xinyue 128, 140
yaya English 22, 129
Yule, G. 322

Zhang, Jin-Pei 103
Zhang, Z. 279

Printed in the United States
by Baker & Taylor Publisher Services